The Letters and Diaries
of
John Henry Newman

The Letters and Diaries
of
John Henry Newman

Edited at the Birmingham Oratory

by

Charles Stephen Dessain

of the same Oratory

and

Vincent Ferrer Blehl, S.J.

Volume XIV

Papal Aggression

July 1850 to December 1851

Thomas Nelson and Sons Ltd

London Edinburgh Paris Melbourne Johannesburg
Toronto and New York

THOMAS NELSON AND SONS LTD
Parkside Works Edinburgh 9
36 Park Street London W1
117 Latrobe Street Melbourne C1

THOMAS NELSON AND SONS (AFRICA) (Pty) LTD
P.O. Box 9881 Johannesburg

THOMAS NELSON AND SONS (CANADA) LTD
91–93 Wellington Street West Toronto 1

THOMAS NELSON AND SONS
18 East 41st Street New York 17, N.Y.

SOCIÉTÉ FRANÇAISE D'ÉDITIONS NELSON
97 rue Monge Paris 5

Nihil obstat:

JOANNES C. BARRY
Censor Deputatus

Imprimatur:

GORDONIUS JOSEPH
Archiepiscopus Sancti Andreae et Edimburgensis
Edimburgi, die 17 junii, 1963

Printed in Great Britain by
Thomas Nelson (Printers) Ltd, London and Edinburgh

Preface

WITHOUT the gradual building up at the Birmingham Oratory of a very full collection of Cardinal Newman's correspondence (an account of which will be found in the Introduction to Volume XI), the present work could not have been undertaken. Its aim is to provide an exhaustive edition of Newman's letters; with explanatory notes, which are often summaries of or quotations from the other side of the correspondence. Some of these letters *to* Newman, when they appear to have particular importance, or to be necessary for following a controversy, are inserted in the text. Every one of the letters written *by* Newman is included there, in chronological sequence. Should there eventually be any of his letters, whose existence is known to the editor, but of which he has failed to obtain a copy, this will be noted in its place. On the other hand, no attempt has been made to include a list of letters written by Newman and now lost, nor the brief précis he occasionally made of his reply, on the back of a correspondent's letter, although these are utilised for the annotation.

In order that the text of each letter may be as accurate as possible, the original autograph, when it still exists, or at least a photographic copy of it, has been used by the editor as his source. (The very few cases in which he has been content with an authenticated copy will be noted as they occur.) Always the text of the autograph is reproduced, or, when the autograph has disappeared, that of the copy that appears most reliable. When only Newman's draft exists, that is printed. The source used in each case is to be found in the list of letters by correspondents.

Such alterations as are made in transcribing the letters aim, without sacrifice of accuracy, at enabling them to be read with ease. Newman writes simply and has none of those idiosyncrasies which sometimes need to be reproduced for the sake of the evidence of one kind or another which they provide.

The following are the only alterations made in transcription:

ADDRESS AND DATE are always printed on the same line, and at the head of the letter, even when Newman puts them at the end. When he omits or gives an incomplete date, the omission is supplied in square brackets, and justified in a note unless the reason for it is obvious. The addresses, to which letters were sent, are included in the list of letters by correspondents. The information derived from postmarks is matter for annotation.

THE CONCLUSION of the letter is made to run on, irrespective of Newman's separate lines, and all postscripts are placed at the end.

NEWMAN'S CORRECTIONS AND ADDITIONS are inserted in their intended place. His interlinear explanations are printed in the text in angle brackets ⟨ ⟩, after the word or phrase they explain. His erasures are given in footnotes when they appear to be of sufficient interest to warrant it. Square brackets being reserved for editorial additions; all Newman's brackets are printed as rounded ones (the kind most usual with him).

NEWMAN'S PARAGRAPHS AND PUNCTUATION are preserved, except that single quotation marks are printed throughout, and double ones for quotations within them. (Newman generally used the latter in both cases.) Further, a parenthesis or quotation that he began with the proper mark but failed to complete, or completed but did not begin, is supplied. All other punctuation marks supplied by the editor are enclosed in square brackets. Newman's dashes, which frequently do duty either for a full stop, a semicolon or a comma (especially when he is tired or writing hurriedly), are represented by a ' — ' with a space before and after. His spelling and use of capitals are left unchanged, but 'raised' letters are lowered in every case.

NEWMAN'S ABBREVIATIONS are retained in the case of proper names, and in the address and conclusion of each letter, since these are sometimes useful indications of his attitude at the time. In all other cases, abbreviations are printed out in full, where Newman employs them.

When he uses the initials of proper names, the full name is normally inserted in square brackets after the initials, at the first occurrence in each letter, and more often if it seems advisable in order to avoid confusion. No addition of the full name is made in the case of Newman's correspondent, whether his initials occur at the beginning of the letter or in the course of it.

When Newman uses only a Christian name, the surname is sometimes added in square brackets for the reader's convenience. The Christian names of members of the Oratory, since they are of frequent occurrence, are listed in the index of proper names and the reader is referred to surnames.

When transcription is made from a PRINTED SOURCE, typographical alterations clearly due to editor or printer are disregarded.

Sometimes Newman made HOLOGRAPH copies of his letters or of portions of them, when they were returned to him long after they had been written. In order that the reader may be able to see how much he copied and what changes he introduced, the copied passages are placed in quarter brackets ⌈ ⌉, and all additions of any importance included in the text in double square brackets, or, where this is impracticable, in the annotation.

Newman's letters are printed in CHRONOLOGICAL ORDER, with the name of his correspondent at the head (except that those of each day are arranged alphabetically), and, when more than one is written to the same person on the same day, numbered I, II. In the headings the name of the correspondent is given in its most convenient form, sometimes with Christian names in full, sometimes only with initials.

THE LIST OF LETTERS BY CORRESPONDENT, at the end of each volume, shows whether the source used was an autograph, draft, printed source or copy, and in the last case, whether a holograph made by Newman later; and gives the present location of the source, as well as of any additional holograph copies or drafts. When a letter, or a considerable portion of it, has been printed in a standard work, references are given; but mistakes or omissions in these previous publications are noticed, if at all, in the annotation.

THE LETTERS WRITTEN TO NEWMAN, when inserted in the text, are printed in type smaller than that used for Newman's own letters, and headed by the name of the correspondent. These letters are not arranged in chronological order, but are placed either just before or just after the letter of Newman to which they are related. A list of them is given at the end of each volume in which they occur. These and the quotations from letters in the annotation are always, unless otherwise stated, printed from autographs at the Birmingham Oratory, and are transcribed in the same way as Newman's letters.

NEWMAN'S DIARIES cover the years 1824 to 1879 (with a gap from July 1826 to March 1828). They are written in a series of mottled copy books, 12 × 18½ centimetres, printed for a year each, and entitled *The Private Diary: arranged, printed, and ruled, for receiving an account of every day's employment* . . ., with the exception of the four periods July 1847–May 1850, January 1854–January 1861, January 1861–March 1871, March 1871–October 1879, each of which is contained in a somewhat thicker copy book.

These diaries are printed complete for each day in which Newman has made an entry, except that the lists of people to whom he has written or from whom he has received letters are omitted, as not being of sufficient general interest. The original diaries are, of course, available for consultation. At the end of each diary book are various notes, lists of addresses, of people to be prayed for, accounts, etc. These, also, are omitted, except for occasional dated notes of events, which are inserted in their proper place. Of the rest of the notes, some are theological and will be reserved for a volume of Newman's theological papers, and others will perhaps have room found for them in any fuller edition of *Autobiographical Writings*.

Newman compiled with his own hand, on quarto sheets sewn together, a book of *Chronological Notes*, drawn largely from the diaries. Any new matter in these *Notes* is printed in italics with the appropriate diary entry. (It should be noted that the diary entries themselves were sometimes written up considerably later than the events they record.)

Each volume is preceded by a brief summary of the period of Newman's life that it covers. Summary, diaries and annotation give a roughly biographical form to the whole, and will, it is hoped, enable the ordinary reader to treat it as a continuous narrative.

THE BIOGRAPHIES OF PERSONS are collected in the index of proper names at the end of each volume, in order to simplify the annotation of the letters. Occasionally, when a person is mentioned only once or twice, and a note is required in any case, biographical details have been given in the notes, and a reference in the index. Volume XI, being the first of a new period in Newman's life, contains an account of every person mentioned, with the exception of a few for whom a notice seemed unnecessary, and of still fewer who have not yet been identified. The indexes of Volume XII and of subsequent volumes contain notices of persons who appear in them for the first time, and references back, in the case of those who have been noticed in an earlier volume. (The editor will be grateful for information as to persons not identified.)

These notices have been compiled from such various sources—books of reference, letters at the Oratory, information supplied by the families or religious communities of the persons concerned, and by librarians and archivists—that the giving of authorities would be a very complicated and lengthy process. Like others faced with the same problem, the editor has decided usually to omit them. References are given, however, to *The Dictionary of National Biography*, or *The Dictionary of American Biography*, in all cases where there is an article there, and failing them, to Boase's *Modern English Biography* or Gillow's *Bibliographical Dictionary of the English Catholics*. When all the volumes of letters have been issued, a final index volume will be compiled for the whole work.

Acknowledgements

It should be noted, first of all, that the editing of the letters written during the very complicated last six months of this present volume, July–December 1851, has been done chiefly by Fr Vincent Ferrer Blehl, S.J. He too is responsible for the greater part of the work in the subsequent volume, which covers the years 1852–3.

Many of those whose help was gratefully acknowledged at the beginning of Volume XI have continued to assist the editor in various ways. Although not mentioned again by name, renewed thanks are due to them for their continuing kindness. In addition the editor is indebted for information to the following: Mr R. K. Browne, Mr Charles Crawford, Mr J. J. Dessain, Fr Raymund Devas, O.P., Mgr John Dinn of Sheffield, Fr Karel Kasteel, Fr Edward Kelly, S.J., of St Mary's College, Kansas, Mr Frank V. Laferrière, Mr Edward MacDermot, Fr Justin McLoughlin, O.F.M., Sister Mary Paton, R.S.M., Miss Jean Smith, Miss Dorothy Scott Stokes, and Miss Meriol Trevor.

Among those who have provided further Newman letters, or allowed them to be copied, are: Mr John Alden, Keeper of Rare Books, Boston Public Library, Fr A. M. Allchin of Pusey House, Oxford, Fr John Allen, Archivist of the English College, Rome, Mr Harold Boag of Newcastle upon Tyne, Mr William C. Bruce of Wauwatosa, Wisconsin, Dr Paul Cassar of Malta, Sister Catherine Anita, Librarian of the Charles Willard Coe Memorial Library, Los Angeles, Sir George Clutton, K.C.M.G., Mr John Creasey, assistant librarian Dr. Williams's Library, Fr Geoffrey Curtis, C.R., of Mirfield, Fr Aidan Duggan, O.S.B., of Fort Augustus, Fr Eugene Fitzpatrick, O.C.S.O., of Mount Melleray, Mr J. H. Gilchrist, the late Cardinal Godfrey, Mr R. J. Hayes, Director of the National Library of Ireland, Miss E. M. Haynes, Fr Edward Leicester of the London Oratory, Sir Shane Leslie, Fr Peadar Mac Suibhne, Mr David Newsome of Emmanuel College, Cambridge, who kindly obtained photostats of many letters to Robert and Samuel Wilberforce, Mr F. G. Roberts, Archivist of Cotton College, the Earl of Selborne, Mgr Daniel Shanahan, Mr P. A. Spalding, Miss Angela V. Tighe, Mrs Todhunter of Gillingham Hall, who lent copies of the letters to Lord and Lady Henry Kerr, Mr Thomas Wall, Librarian of the Irish Folklore Commission, Mr David R. Watkins, Chief Reference Librarian at Yale, the Rev. R. H. Isaac Williams and Miss K. Mary Williams.

To these and to all who have assisted him, the editor wishes to express his sincere gratitude.

Contents

Abbreviations in Volume XIV

THE abbreviations used for Newman's works are those listed in Joseph Rickaby, S.J., *Index to the Works of John Henry Cardinal Newman*, London 1914, with a few additions.

References to works included by Newman in his uniform edition are always, unless otherwise stated, to that edition, which was begun in 1868 with *Parochial and Plain Sermons*, and concluded in 1881 with *Select Treatises of St Athanasius*. From 1886, until the stock was destroyed in the 1939–45 war, all the volumes were published by Longmans, Green and Co. They are distinguished from other, usually posthumous, publications by having their date of inclusion in the uniform edition in brackets after the title, in the list of abbreviations below. The unbracketed date is, in every case, the date of the edition (or impression) used for giving references. (Once volumes were included in the uniform edition the pagination usually remained unchanged, but there are exceptions and minor alterations.)

Add.	*Addresses to Cardinal Newman with His Replies etc. 1879–82*, ed. W. P. Neville, 1905.
Apo.	*Apologia pro Vita Sua*, (1873) 1905.
Ari.	*The Arians of the Fourth Century*, (1871) 1908.
Ath. I, II	*Select Treatises of St Athanasius*, two volumes, (1881) 1920.
A.W.	*John Henry Newman: Autobiographical Writings*, ed. Henry Tristram, 1956.
Call.	*Callista, a Tale of the Third Century*, (1876) 1923.
Campaign	*My Campaign in Ireland, Part I* (printed for private circulation only), 1896.
D.A.	*Discussions and Arguments on Various Subjects*, (1872) 1911.
Dev.	*An Essay on the Development of Christian Doctrine*, (1878) 1908.
Diff. I, II	*Certain Difficulties felt by Anglicans in Catholic Teaching*, two volumes, (1879, 1876) 1908.
Ess. I, II	*Essays Critical and Historical*, two volumes, (1871) 1919.
G.A.	*An Essay in aid of a Grammar of Assent*, (1870) 1913.
H.S. I, II, III	*Historical Sketches*, three volumes, (1872) 1908, 1912, 1909.
Idea	*The Idea of a University defined and illustrated*, (1873) 1902.
Jfc.	*Lectures on the Doctrine of Justification*, (1874) 1908.
K.C.	*Correspondence of John Henry Newman with John Keble and Others, 1839–45*, ed. at the Birmingham Oratory, 1917.
L.G.	*Loss and Gain: the Story of a Convert*, (1874) 1911.
M.D.	*Meditations and Devotions of the late Cardinal Newman*, 1893.
Mir.	*Two Essays on Biblical and on Ecclesiastical Miracles*, (1870) 1907.

Mix.	*Discourses addressed to Mixed Congregations,* (1871) 1909.
Moz. I, II	*Letters and Correspondence of John Henry Newman,* ed. Anne Mozley, two volumes, 1891.
O.S.	*Sermons preached on Various Occasions,* (1870) 1927.
P.S. I-VIII	*Parochial and Plain Sermons,* (1868) 1907–10.
Prepos.	*Present Position of Catholics,* (n.d. 1872) 1913.
S.D.	*Sermons bearing on Subjects of the Day,* (1869) 1902.
S.E.	*Stray Essays on Controversial Points,* (private) 1890.
S.N.	*Sermon Notes of John Henry Cardinal Newman, 1849–1879,* ed. Fathers of the Birmingham Oratory, 1913.
T.T.	*Tracts Theological and Ecclesiastical,* (1874) 1908.
U.S.	*Fifteen Sermons preached before the University of Oxford,* (1872) 1909.
V.M. I, II	*The Via Media,* (1877) 1908, 1911.
V.V.	*Verses on Various Occasions,* (1874) 1910.

*   *   *

Boase	Frederick Boase, *Modern English Biography*, six volumes, Truro 1892–1921.
Culler	A. Dwight Culler, *The Imperial Intellect, a Study of Newman's Educational Ideal*, New Haven 1955.
D A B	*Dictionary of American Biography*, London 1928–36.
D N B	*Dictionary of National Biography*, to 1900, London, reprinted in 1937–8 in twenty-two volumes, the last being a Supplement, *D N B*, Suppl.
D N B, 1901–11	*Dictionary of National Biography*, 1901–11, three volumes in one.
D R	*Dublin Review.*
D T C	*Dictionnaire de Théologie Catholique*, Paris 1903–50.
Finlason	*Report of the Trial and Preliminary Proceedings in the case of the Queen on the Prosecution of G. Achilli v. Dr. Newman*, with an Introduction by W. F. Finlason, London 1852.
Gillow	Joseph Gillow, *Bibliographical Dictionary of the English Catholics*, five volumes, London 1885 and later.
Harper	Gordon Huntington Harper, *Cardinal Newman and William Froude, F.R.S. A Correspondence*, Baltimore 1933.
Liddon's *Pusey* I-IV	H. P. Liddon, *Life of Edward Bouverie Pusey*, four volumes, London 1893–7.
de Lisle	E. S. Purcell, *Life and Letters of Ambrose Phillipps de Lisle*, two volumes, London 1900.
McGrath	Fergal McGrath, S.J., *Newman's University Idea and Reality*, London 1951.
Newman and Bloxam	R. D. Middleton, *Newman and Bloxam*, London 1947.
Trevor I	Meriol Trevor, *Newman the Pillar of the Cloud*, London 1962.
Ward I, II	Wilfrid Ward, *The Life of John Henry Cardinal Newman*, two volumes, London 1912.

Introductory Note

EARLY in July 1850, having delivered in the Oratory at King William Street, Strand, the last of his *Lectures on Difficulties felt by Anglicans in submitting to the Catholic Church*, Newman returned to Birmingham, where he wrote the preface for their publication in book form. In August it was agreed to set up the London Oratory as an independent house, by virtue of the powers conferred on Newman as founder of the English Oratory. It was also agreed to abandon the house and church at St Wilfrid's, in which the London Oratorians declined to interest themselves, Newman meanwhile working to secure for them a return on the money they had sunk in it. It was transferred to the Passionists at the end of the year. R. A. Coffin thus received a summons from St Wilfrid's to London early in October, where, on the 12th, Faber was elected the first independent superior. The decision to become a Redemptorist which Coffin took soon afterwards, drew from Newman letters that illustrate his view of the religious life and vocation.

In the autumn the 'papal aggression' storm consequent on the appointment of a Catholic territorial hierarchy burst forth, and during the weeks before Cardinal Wiseman's return to England, Newman was continually consulted by those in London who were acting for the Catholics. At Birmingham he preached at Ullathorne's installation as bishop on 27 October, and was one of the chief targets for attack in the newspapers, and in both the letterpress and the pictures of *Punch*. His correspondence reveals his reaction to the appointment of a hierarchy, and then to the storm thus aroused. He felt that this was supremely the moment for the laity, and especially the gifted lay converts, to come forward, and his letters in February and March 1851 encouraged J. M. Capes to organise lectures by laymen in the large cities. At Birmingham, where Ullathorne was distrustful of lay effort, Newman decided himself to lend a hand, and at the end of June began a weekly series, later known as *Lectures on the Present Position of Catholics in England*. With humour and satire the prejudices and false principles at the basis of the Protestant view of the Catholic Church were laid bare. The final lecture on 1 September outlined the duties of the Catholic laity, who were to bring out the real meaning of their religion each in his own circle, without arrogance and without party combination.

In the fifth lecture, on 28 July, after taking advice of his legal friends David Lewis and James Hope, and after much prayer, Newman denounced the ex-Dominican Giacinto Achilli, who, brought to England by the Evangelical Alliance, enthralled audiences with his accounts of the Roman Inquisition, into whose hands he had fallen for a series of crimes against morality. In enumerating these, to offset the influence of Achilli, who had lectured in Birmingham, Newman relied on Wiseman's documented account in the *Dublin Review* of July 1850, reprinted as a pamphlet and never seriously challenged.

Realising at the end of August 1851 that Achilli, backed by the Evangelical Alliance, intended to bring an action for libel, Newman wrote at once to Wiseman for his documents, and to Talbot for evidence from the Inquisition and elsewhere. Neither realised the urgency. On 4 November, when Achilli swore that all the charges against him were false, and brought a criminal action, Newman pleaded for time to collect evidence. Because he had no substantial proof of the charges, and because the judges claimed that he did not himself believe them, the plea was rejected on 21 November. Six hours too late Wiseman's documents were found, and two days later those which Talbot had kept by him at Rome for twelve days arrived. The imputation of the judges Newman indignantly denied in a letter to the newspapers.

The trial, which eventually took place in June, was fixed for February 1852. Only witnesses and direct evidence would now suffice, and unless all Newman's accusations were proved, he was liable to, and expected, a sentence of imprisonment. He sent off at once for the witnesses, but these were women, now settled in life, who had to be persuaded to come to England and to testify to Achilli's behaviour years previously. Newman kept saying that prayer alone could save the situation, and procure, if not a legal, at least a moral victory. His own account will be found in Appendix 5, p. 508. Catholics rallied to his support, but the first encouraging news as to securing witnesses did not reach him until 1 January 1852.

Amid this harassing suspense, Newman still had his ordinary cares. At Birmingham the cellars being built for his new house had been denounced in Parliament as cells in which murders might be committed, and odium was aroused locally. The London Oratory remained an anxiety. Not only was recourse had to him constantly for advice, but at the separation in October 1850, certain powers of control had been conferred on him. In the autumn of 1851, the London Oratorians found Faber's rule irksome, and the latter's health was so impaired that he was ordered abroad for six months. His restlessness brought him back at the end of December, and Newman had to calm the community and to insist that Faber should continue his cure.

Meanwhile in July 1851 Archbishop Cullen invited Newman to be the Rector of the proposed Catholic University of Ireland. Early in October Newman paid his first visit to that country, in order to discuss plans, and Cullen invited him to deliver the lectures 'On the scope and nature of University Education.' Newman began work on them at once, expecting to deliver them early in the new year. On 12 November he was appointed the first Rector of the University.

Summary of Events covered by this volume

* * *

1850

4 July	Last of the 'Lectures on Certain Difficulties felt by Anglicans in submitting to the Catholic Church.'
22 Aug.	Newman receives from Bishop Ullathorne the doctorate of divinity conferred by Pius IX.
26 Sept.	After a final visit, Newman leaves St Wilfrid's for good.
29 Sept.	The new Catholic hierarchy is set up by Pius IX.
9 Oct.	The London Oratory is separated from that of Birmingham, and becomes an independent house.
27 Oct.	Newman preaches the sermon 'Christ upon the Waters' at the installation, in St Chad's Cathedral, of Ullathorne as first Bishop of Birmingham.
19 Nov.	Cardinal Wiseman, having returned to England, issues his 'Appeal to the English People.'
27 Nov.	R. A. Coffin is released from the London Oratory, and joins the Redemptorists.

1851

1 Feb.	W. G. Penny leaves the Birmingham Oratory.
7 Feb.	The Ecclesiastical Titles Bill is introduced into Parliament. It becomes law in July.
2–5 April	Newman receives the converts from St Saviour's, Leeds.
6 April	Manning and Hope are received in London.
25–26 May	Döllinger and Sir John Acton visit Newman in Birmingham.
30 June	Newman delivers at the Corn Exchange, Birmingham, the first of the 'Lectures on Catholicism in England.'
18 July	Archbishop Cullen visits Birmingham and invites Newman to become the first Rector of the Catholic University of Ireland.
28 July	Fifth lecture on Catholicism in England. Newman denounces Dr Achilli.
22 Sept.	Joseph Gordon and Nicholas Darnell go to Italy to collect evidence against Achilli.

30 Sept.–8 Oct.	Newman visits Ireland, and with the Sub-committee of the University, draws up plans for its organisation.
4 Nov.	Achilli denies on oath all the charges against himself, and brings against Newman a criminal information for libel.
12 Nov.	Newman is appointed Rector of the Catholic University of Ireland.
21 Nov.	The rule, bringing Newman to trial, is made absolute. After a short attempt at a compromise, Newman's lawyer goes, early in December, to Italy, to collect direct evidence, followed by Miss Giberne, who is to bring back the women witnesses.

The Letters and Diaries
of
John Henry Newman

Oy. Bm. July 7 [5]/50[1]

My dear Capes,

Your proofs came too late for me to look them over — i.e. I could not do so at once i.e. so as to *finish* them — so it was no good writing to you, considering I was very much pressed for time. This is the first day I have begun to answer my letters, which form a basket full of arrears.[2]

As far as I got in your article, I liked it very much, and did not see any fancifulness in it.[3] I still am annoyed, there is not a quarterly going — considering the additional talent coming in to us. Consider what a work might be supported by you, Ward, Thompson, Maskell, H Wilberforce, and Allies, not to mention others. It seems hard too that an *Irish Review* should block up English ground.[4]

My lectures are not yet off my hands, as I must put a preface.[5] How are you?

Ever Yours affectly in Xt   John H Newman   Congr. Orat.

TO ARCHBISHOP CULLEN

Oratory Birmingham. July 7 [5].[6] 1850

My dear Lord,

I feel exceedingly your Grace's kindness in the letter I received from you the other day, and should have answered it at once, but that I could not do without receiving a letter from Sussex which has this instant arrived.[7]

---

[1] Newman misdated all the letters he wrote on Friday 5 July, as his diary list of them for that day confirms.

[2] Newman delivered the last lectures on Anglican Difficulties on 4 July, and returned to Birmingham at once.

[3] 'The Miraculous Life of the Saints,' the *Rambler* (July 1850), pp. 22–57. Capes began by arguing how the marvel was that men were not habitually conscious of the Divine Presence, rather than that God should occasionally communicate with them through the senses.   [4] Wiseman's quarterly *Dublin Review* is meant.

[5] The preface, pp. v–xiv, of *Lectures on Certain Difficulties felt by Anglicans* is dated 'In fest. S. Bonaventurae, [14 July] 1850.'

[6] Newman again wrote '7' by mistake. See his explanation on 9 July.

[7] 'I first knew Dr Cullen at Rome in 1847, when he was very civil to me. . . . After he came to Ireland, as Archbishop of Armagh, he showed his recollection of me by asking me to preach in the summer of 1850, at the dedication of a Church in his diocese.' 'Memorandum about my connection with the Catholic University.' *A.W.* p. 280. The church was that at Killiany, Co. Armagh.

It would have given me the greatest gratification, to have been able to avail myself of your Grace's invitation myself — but I do not see how it is possible. The Fathers of the Oratory do not commonly preach out of their own Church, and the F. Superior in particular does not quit the Town where he is situated (at least it is so in Rome) during the period that he holds office. Accordingly I have begged permission of Dr Wiseman, Dr Ullathorne, Dr Hendren, and various religious bodies, to decline requests which they have made me most kindly and condescendingly to preach on different occasions.

I trust this representation will plead my excuse with your Grace if I beg a like permission from you. As I found you would allow me to substitute Father Dalgairns for myself, I at once wrote to him — and I now beg to say, that, should you kindly accept his services, he would be much gratified to offer them.

Begging your Grace's blessing upon us here and in London, I am, My dear Lord, Your Grace's most obedient Servant,

John H Newman   Congr. Orat.

TO F. W. FABER

Oy. Bm. Friday July 7 [5]/50

My dear F W

I did not mean my talk with F Richard to be a formal one — but, considering Barnabo's 'exactissimum', and F. Caesarini's words, and Dr Grant's suspicions I think that we cannot go on without leave.[1]

I think it would be better for you, if you *do* ask, as you propose, to mention some definite time, e.g. three years, or five years; — which might be continued on a second application.[2]

---

[1] Newman had told Stanton in conversation that the Oratory at London must be separated from that in Birmingham, since the Rule required each house to be independent, and Barnabò, the Secretary of Propaganda, had said that the Rule must be observed 'exactissime.' See Newman's letter to him of 2 Dec. 1849. For the words of Fr Cesarini, the Superior of the Roman Oratory, in the same sense, and Dr Grant's suspicions that Newman wanted power, see letters of 24 and 25 Nov. 1849 to Faber.

[2] Newman is replying to Faber's letter of 3 July: 'But you, as Padre, are bound to help us all you can. We are quite unanimous in our desire to exhaust all means to prevent our being separated from you. . . . Of course the superiorship is a bore and responsibility for you; but it is necessary to the success of the institute. We cannot do without you. I could show you this in a dozen ways, which are constantly before me; but you must see it yourself . . .' Faber then proposed that the London Oratorians should petition Rome to have Newman as superior for life, notwithstanding his residence in another house, 'We could set forth how that we are who we are—how we came into

At the same time, I really do think *practically* that, even if you got the leave, you must act *as* a house — i.e. must choose a Superior, even if you call him Rector, and be in all respects complete — so that (e.g.) were I to die suddenly, you would be a formed body.

I hope you have got well   Ever Yrs affly J H N.

Send me all the misprints in my Lectures you know of.

TO MRS LOCKHART

Oratory Birmingham July 7. [5] 1850

My dear Sister Mary Monica,[1]

You cannot suppose it is from want of interest in your very joyful news that I have not answered your kind announcement of it.[2] It has simply been from my present load of work, which has been too much for mind or body. I trust it will soon be over, but this is the first day which I have been able to give to answering letters.

It is indeed a great instance, for which we cannot be too thankful, how God answers persevering prayer. You have your reward in His mercy — How blest you are — few indeed are those, who, like you, have their immediate relatives gathered into the fold. And who can say who is not to follow? I suppose your daughter has good hopes of Archdeacon Manning. I see H. Wilberforce has resigned his living.

Give to William,[3] and receive yourself, our warmest congratulations. May God, and His Blessed Mother, do for you abundantly more than they have done already — for the more you ask, the more you will obtain

Ever Yours affectionately in Xt   John H Newman   Congr. Orat.

the Church with you, and chose to live under you—that you . . . sent us to London . . . case of *Founder* . . . wish of Mgr W [Wiseman], who forwards the petition . . .'

[1] Martha Lockhart was at this time with the religious community at Greenwich, formed from the converts, the 'Sisters of Charity of the Precious Blood.'

[2] Her stepdaughter, Elizabeth Lockhart (1812–70), had just become a Catholic. She had previously worked under Manning at Chichester, and had been, since 1847, the first superior of the Anglican Sisters of St Mary the Virgin at Wantage. In 1852 she joined the community at Greenwich.

[3] Mrs Lockhart's only son, who had left Newman at Littlemore in 1843, and had then become a Catholic and a Rosminian.

TO WILLIAM MASKELL

Oratory, Birmingham. July 7 [5]/50

My dear Maskell,

This is the first day I have begun to answer my letters, and a pretty lot I have got to discharge — else, it would have been unkind not to send you my congratulations sooner.[1] You will not suppose you have not really had them. I have been saying Mass for you and others several times.

You must let me know how you go on, and what your plans are. It is premature to talk to *you* about it, but considering the great accession of literary force now showing itself among us, I hardly [heartily] wish we could set up a Quarterly Review, but there are difficulties in the way.

I find you are selling your Library. Had I known you had quite decided on it, I should have talked with you about the schoolmen you offered me. I suppose it is too late now.

I have been saying Mass, as you wished, for Mr Bastard. Already they had been praying for him at St Wilfrid's and [Joseph] Simpson, who is a friend of his, had been corresponding with him. I had a glimpse of him two years since, when he came to reclaim Simpson — and was much struck with his appearance[2]

Ever Yours affectionately in Xt   John H Newman   Congr. Orat.

P.S.   I wish you would spur Allies on — I see that H Wilberforce has resigned his living.[3]

TO GEORGE RYDER

Oratory Birmingham July 7. [5] 1850

My dear George,

I have nothing to say, but wish to write you a line on the first day I have begun to answer my letters, after a great spell of literary work. I sent up my last bit of MS yesterday, but have a Preface to write still.

I saw Sophy on Tuesday — she told me that F Cobb told her, that F Brownbill had received Mary Wilberforce (not Wm's wife) within the

---

[1] Maskell had been received into the Church at Spanish Place, London, on 22 June.

[2] See the diary for 24 June 1848. Newman received Edmund Bastard on 1 Dec. 1850.

[3] Both were received in Sept. 1850.

last few days. This is a distinct account from the report about 3 weeks ago.[1]

Ever Yours affly in Xt   John H Newman   Congr. Orat.

TO ARCHBISHOP CULLEN

Oratory Birmingham July 6. 1850

My dear Lord,

I have just received your Grace's second letter, and am very sorry you should have had the trouble of writing it.[2]

I trust by this time you will have received mine of yesterday, thanking your Grace for your condescending request, and stating that Father Dalgairns would avail himself of it.

I wrote to him by the first post after receiving your Grace's letter, and wrote to you yesterday in answer, the next minute after his letter, (written from the sea side whither he has gone for a few days for his health,) was brought me

Begging your Grace's blessing, I am, My dear Lord, Your obedient Servant in Xt

John H Newman   Congr. Orat.

TO AMBROSE ST JOHN

Oratory Bm July 8/50

Charissime

Poor Jones, who goes today, did not take the letters to the Post on Saturday — so you will receive this with a letter I wanted an answer to, *to-morrow*.

⌜Do not cry, dear boy — but cheer up — I *do* think you act on

---

[1] Newman saw Sophy Ryder at the Good Shepherd Convent, Hammersmith, on 2 July. In spite of his letter of 24 June, Newman seems not to have been certain about the reception of Mary, the wife of Henry Wilberforce. Mary Frances Wilberforce (1800–80) was the wife of William Wilberforce, Henry's brother. Newman had dissuaded her from becoming a Catholic in 1834. She was received in 1852, and her husband nine years later.

[2] Cullen in his second letter, dated 5 July, urged, 'Your presence in this part of the black north would do good.'

7

impulse frequently, but all will be well. F. Joseph is in the best dispositions — and I would have you try to be *very frank* with him.[1]

I know he thinks you go into the same fault with him,[2] which you impute to F Wm [[William Penny]] viz [[you]] are not confidential. It is true, charissime — it is your conduct to me also — not in your intention, but you act on impulse — forget what you have said a minute before — don't say what you are doing etc.[3] I could mention a number of little things [[in evidence]] — And you often, from eagerness, thinking no one else will act, go [[and act]] *out of your place* and office. But, charissime, they [[these things]] are nothing — don't annoy yourself. I think it would be well to be [[very]] frank with F Joseph. He tells me that Mrs Wootten and Miss Woolley have taken no notice whatever of him, since they left the House. I don't know what notice they *could* have taken — but you will see how things lie. Don't make too much of things — all will be well directly. I shall say Mass for you and him together on Wednesday morning.⌐

Don't go by George R's letter — Henry will not open to him[4]

Ever Yrs affly J H N

PS. You were wrong in *saying without authority* that Br Bernard was coming *directly* and that for a *day or two* — I said just the reverse. Such things do harm.

⌐No news of your Houses. Mr Newton promised me faithfully that I should hear on Saturday.⌐[5]

TO RICHARD STANTON

July 8/50

My dear F R

Yes — we agree to your propositions about the office of St Ph [Philip] etc.

[1] St John had decided on the spur of the moment that he must go for a rest to St Wilfrid's, and wrote from there on 6 or 7 July, 'I cannot get up spirit at all at all . . . and I don't know what to do for I am bad company, but I must try. I am afraid I am out with F. Joseph, and I can't get in—He did not seem kind in his manner when I spoke to him on Friday and altogether these things have sadly blue-devilled me. . . .' He concluded, 'I don't know whether I am biggest fool or hypocrite, but I am always your affectionate though not obedient Fool.'
[2] [[in his case]]   [3] [[what you are about to do now.]]
[4] Henry Wilberforce, who had resigned his living, was not likely to confide in his brother-in-law, George Ryder, about his further intentions.
[5] St John was buying two houses next to the site acquired for the Oratory at Edgbaston, and wrote, 'I am bent on having H W [Wilberforce] as a tenant.'

Talbot *won't come back from Rome*.[1] It is an awkwardness. If we don't take for our Patron a person close on the Pope's person, it may be a slight to him — yet is he clever enough? If so, it might be a good hit. If, I don't say it is likely, you all had a *view*, it would be a compliment to him to secure him before he went. And there is another difficulty — will he seem a great person enough to cut out Dr Grant? is he great enough for a Patron? Depend on it, if the Pope lives he will rise — but will he be a Shrewsbury man?

Ever Yrs affly J H N.

TUESDAY 9 July 1850   F Joseph went to St Wilfrid's (*one chief reason of these visits was to keep from solitariness Coffin, Penny and Darnell, who, I think, were mostly there*)

TO ARCHBISHOP CULLEN

Oratory. Birmingham July 9. 1850

My dear Lord,

I am truly distressed to find that your Grace has had the trouble to write a third letter. Unless these new postal regulations are in fault, you should have received a second letter from me before now. My first was sent on the 5th, though by mistake I dated it the 7th, being led wrong by its being the 7th day of the Octave of the Holy Apostles.

I will not repeat what I have said in my former letters, making no doubt your Grace has received them by this time — and begging your Grace's blessing on me and mine I am, My dear Lord, Your Grace's obedient Servt in Xt

John H Newman   Congr. Orat.

TO F. W. FABER

O. B. July 9/50

My dear F W

Will you kindly send to Burns at once any erratums you have in my Lectures 1. 2. 3. 4 which are going to be reprinted. And please send to *me* erratums in the subsequent numbers.

[1] Faber wrote on 6 July that George Talbot, attached to St George's, Southwark, had been to take leave, having been summoned to Rome, under obedience, by Pius IX. '. . . he is to be high up—attached to the pope's person—he begs to be our friend at Court.' As Newman foretold, Talbot remained at Rome, and only left in 1869, to enter an asylum at Paris.

Each Father pays his *full* pension at St Wilfrid's — when F Rector says 10/ he meant (I suppose) that the *Brothers* went *gratis*. As to the place, the difficulty is how to *support* it — If we don't support it in Pensions, we shall have to give hard cash for nothing.[1] Pigott is going.

I am most concerned to hear what you say about Rivington — what can it mean?[2]

Ever Yours affly J H N

P.S.   Your list of subjects is admirable.[3]

TO F. W. FABER

Oy. Bm. July 11/50

My dear F W

I shall say Mass for you and your Brother tomorrow morning. I can of course *say* nothing which will be in point in your present affliction. Your best and great consolation is your brother's good faith.[4]

Thanks for your volume, which is of a very decent size.[5] My Preface is not yet out of my hands. I *cannot* write it, do what I will.

As to St W's [Wilfrid's] I will say nothing now, except that everything you now urge, might have been urged at the beginning of the year — and if you speak now you should have spoken then. It does not answer to undo. However, you shall have my judgment, in few words, in about a week's time.[6]

Ever Yrs affly J H N

[1] In Jan. 1850 the two Oratories had agreed to set up jointly a college at St Wilfrid's, and meanwhile, in order to support the place, each to supply two Oratorians, one resident, and another who would change every month or so. See letters of 3 and 10 Jan. to Faber. Faber now complained of the pension which had thus to be paid for each Oratorian, and especially of the cost of the railway fare from London. See next letter.

[2] Faber had received from Rivington a bill for £110, with a summary demand for payment.   [3] For Sunday afternoon sermons.

[4] Faber had asked his sister-in-law if he might visit his brother, who was dying, but had received no reply. See letter of 21 April 1850.

[5] F. W. Faber's *The Spirit and Genius of St. Philip Neri*, London 1850. See letter of 2 Aug. to Dalgairns, for the explanation of Newman's 'faint praise.'

[6] Faber wrote on 10 July from London, 'Must the house pay full pensions for FF. Bernard and myself at St Wilfrid's, receiving none from us here? . . . It seems hard on the house here, and not nice to us nonpaying members . . .' He also complained that pensions were not being paid for lay brothers sent to St Wilfrid's, 'if the B [Birmingham] Brothers go for nothing, and ours are precluded by distance from going, we, nearly bankrupt, are compelled at once to board our own brothers at Lancing [in

TO MISS HOLMES

Oratory Birmingham. July 12/50

My dear Miss Holmes

I have been wishing to write to you a long while, and now your letter comes on the very day I hoped to do so. I have been most portentously busy — but it is almost over, my lectures being nearly all out. I would give you them, if they were worth a parcel. I could not give them from London so well as from here. I suppose they will bring me into controversy, and that my labours are only beginning — but it will be a respite. Let no one suppose that my books do not cost me labour — they are as severe a trial as hedging and ditching, though it is not one's back that aches or one's muscles that are worked . . . .

MONDAY 15 JULY 1850   F Austin went to St W's *Wilfrid's*

TO WILLIAM MASKELL

Oratory. Birmingham July 15. 1850

My dear Maskell,

I am glad you have got to Clifton — for moving it [sic] a sad work. Do let me hear from time to time how you are going on. As to the Dublin, you will be certainly useful in writing in it — but it is losing its chief support, for I suppose it is hardly a secret (but do not mention it from me, but *wait* till you hear it from other quarters) that Dr Wiseman is going for good to Rome — and the report in this district is that our Bishop is going to London in his place.[1] This will affect the prosperity of the Dublin most seriously.

Sussex, rented with money given by W. G. Ward] or at home, and to contribute to the support of the Birmingham brothers. . . . The 2 houses do not stand on an equal footing about S. Wilfrid's, either in respect of expense because of distance, or of facilities for preventing our work being greatly interfered with. . . .' Faber also said, 'All you have to do is to give us orders: and . . . we have nothing more to say.' He admitted 'There is no denying that we are committed to St W's, and we must bear the burden; still to injure this house . . . will be penance enough, without our having as we might fancy, to complain of the way in which our share was apportioned.' Newman's decision is in his letter of 18 July.

[1] Wiseman was summoned to Rome, with a view to being made a Cardinal in curia. Instead, he returned to London in November as Cardinal Archbishop of Westminster. Bishop Ullathorne remained in Birmingham.

As to yourself, you don't seem to me the man to act hastily, still it will be no harm saying, pledge yourself to nothing in a hurry. A hundred plans of usefulness will be laid before you — but your inexperience in the Church will be a sufficient apology for your doing nothing just now. Look about, and get a clear view of the *lie* of things, before you commit yourself.

Perhaps you have made Neve's acquaintance before now — I have never known him intimately, though I have known him almost a ¼ of a century. His whole course, according to my knowledge of him, has been that of an earnest straightforward man.[1]

Remember us in your prayers and believe me, Yours affectly in Xt

John H Newman   Congr. Orat.

P.S.   Will you kindly direct the inclosed to Miss Moore, who has not given me her address?[2]

WEDNESDAY 17 JULY 1850   F Ambrose returned.
THURSDAY 18 JULY   Lady O Acheson came.

TO F. W. FABER

Oy Bm July 18/50

My dear F Wilfrid,

Thanks for your corrections — the nominative pendens was but apparent, but I dissipated the delusion by putting nevertheless for yet.

Take the Ballards by all means, i.e. if you think there is no objection in *brothers* — which I am not at all sure.[3]

Though only 6 o'clock, it is so dark with a thunder storm, I can hardly see to write.

I have thought over your wishes in London — and I hereby, in accordance with the leave given me in the Decree of the beginning of

---

[1] F. R. Neve lived at Clifton as secretary to the Vicar Apostolic of the Western District.

[2] Mary Moore came under Maskell's influence when he was Vicar of St Mary-church, Torquay. She was received at Tiverton on 3 July 1850.

[3] Two sons of Rear-Admiral Volant Vashon Ballard had recently become Catholics, Edward Humphrey, matriculated at Wadham in 1837 at the age of 17, and George Frederick, matriculated at Worcester in 1847 at the age of 24. They joined the London Oratory, but left in 1864 and worked in the diocese of Southwark.

the year, dispense the whole London House for good, from the month's residence at St Wilfrid's[1]

Yours affly J H N

You may set up the Confraternity[2] if you think best.

FRIDAY 19 JULY 1850   F Antony came over from St W's *Wilfrid's* and returned *there* with F Frederic.

CIRCULAR LETTER

Oratory, Birmingham, July 19, 1850.

Oratory of St. Philip Neri, Birmingham.

The Fathers of the Oratory of St. Philip Neri, established by Apostolic Brief in Birmingham, have come to the resolution of appealing to the pious liberality of Catholics and others, in the erection of the Church of their Congregation in that town.[3]

They consider that they have a claim so far on the attention of the faithful, in the initial and necessary work of establishing themselves in the place which the holy Father has assigned to them, that, according to the Rule of the Oratory, they take no money from the people for their own maintenance, but live solely on their own resources. This then is the first and last time, did the Congregation remain in Birmingham for a thousand years, of its asking pecuniary assistance, or making collections, in its own behalf.[4] Once located in a neighbourhood, it is no burden on the Catholic body, its ministrations being strictly gratuitous to all comers.

These ministrations are especially suited to the wants of the present time, consisting principally of uninterrupted attendance in the

[1] See letter of 11 July, and cf. those of 10 Jan. and 22 July.

[2] That in honour of the Precious Blood.

[3] As soon as the present site of the Oratory had been acquired, it was decided, on 22 May 1850, to build a house for the community, and to collect funds for the erection of a church.

[4] At the beginning of the twentieth century a widespread appeal was made, under the presidency of the Duke of Norfolk, for the building of the present church of the Birmingham Oratory, with a view to providing a memorial to Newman.

Confessional all through the day, the superintendence of young men, popular services, preaching, lecturing, and the inculcation of sacred and profane knowledge.

The Fathers have secured the Freehold of a large plot of ground at Edgbaston, sufficient for the erection of both Church and House. Moreover, as they propose erecting their House simply at their own cost, the contributions which they are soliciting will go entirely towards the expences of the Church itself and the Ground it stands upon.

The sum they contemplate raising for this purpose in the first instance, is £6000 or £7000; which may be collected some such way as the following:—

Five persons	at £50	...	...	...	£250
Ten	at £25	...	...	...	250
Twenty	at £10	...	...	...	200
Twenty	at £5	...	...	...	100
Fifty	at £1	...	...	...	50
Hundred	at 12s. (1s. a Month)		...		60
Five Hundred at	6s. (6d. a Month)		...		150
					£1060

This continued for four years ...			...	4240
Ten £100 on starting	...	...	...	1000
Existing Subscriptions ...		...	...	800
Collection Boxes, etc. ...		...	...	500
				£6540

However formidable an aspect their undertaking naturally presents to persons like themselves, who have so few friends among the rich, yet the Fathers cannot, and do not doubt, that the mercy of their God and Saviour, and the intercession of His Virgin Mother, and the blessing of their dear and tender Father and Master St. Philip, will ultimately prosper what they are beginning for God's glory and the salvation of His elect, even though the work be slow. And they would remind all those who have at heart the cause of the Catholic Church, that, if St. Philip's Congregation is intended, in the decrees of Providence, to be an instrument of good to the people of England, blessed will they be, who are allowed to have any share in so excellent a work.

John H. Newman,   Congr. Orat.

Contributions may be paid to Father Newman's account at the Birmingham Banking Company, Bennett's Hill.

The Fathers are gratified to state, that the Right Rev. Dr. Ulla-thorne, Vicar Apostolic of the District, has given the undertaking the sanction of his approval by a donation of £30.

TO THE EARL OF SHREWSBURY

Oratory, Birmingham July 19. 1850.

My dear Lord,

I was very sorry to hear from F. Hutchison, that, owing to some mistake of mine, I have left your Lordship under a false impression of the state in which I conceived our correspondence of January last to terminate. Pray accept my apology for any apparent want of attention or respect to your Lordship, which has been the consequence.

I took the liberty of sending your Lordship a statement of the view taken by Fr Hutchison of the grant of the property at St Wilfrid's to him and his companions, and your Lordship was kind enough to say that you would at your leisure favor me with your remarks upon it. I waited to write more, till those remarks came: since I did not hear from you on the subject, I certainly have been tempted to hope that Fr Hutchison's explanation was in the event satisfactory to you.[1]

It is with great concern I hear that this is not the case. May I not still hope that you will have the great kindness to show us where you differ from it? As Fr Hutchison is at present stopping at St Wilfrid's, I avail myself of this circumstance to make him the bearer of this note to you — and am, My dear Lord, with great respect, Your Lordship's faithful servt.

John H Newman   Congr. Orat.

TO BISHOP ULLATHORNE

Alcester Street July 19. 1850

My dear Lord,

I called yesterday, and should have called today if possible, to find your Lordship's feelings on a request I wished to urge, which I hardly could do, as I should wish, in conversation, and still less by letter.

I am quite aware how very occasional and incomplete a work the

---

[1] See letter of 17 Jan. 1850 to Lord Shrewsbury. He replied on 25 July, that he had kept silent 'in the hope that your ultimate determination would be favourable to my views.'

Lectures will make which I have lately been delivering, and you may think it quite thoughtless in me to wish to connect them, in any way, with your Lordship. And yet I venture to ask you whether you will allow me to put your Lordship's name at the head of them.

Pray let not this bold request be any embarrassment to you — and should you think it would be better that a series of discussions, which consist of a perpetual skirmish rather than a grave and regular engagement, should not be dedicated to any one in authority, I shall acquiesce, I was going to say, concur in your Lordship's decision. Only be so good as to take the offer as the sincere wish on my part to show that I am, My dear Lord, Your Lordship's faithful & grateful Servt

John H Newman   Congr. Orat.[1]

SATURDAY 20 JULY 1850   F Austin returned from St Wilfrid's   Mr Molloy came

TO ANTONY HUTCHISON

Sunday July 21/50

My dear F Antony

Perhaps you have heard that poor Dr Morgan has had a coach accident in Scotland — broken his collar bone and received a concussion of the brain. So he will not be Bishop or arbiter either. This is very sad.[2]

I have heard much of Mr Lambert as a sound judging man, and I should suppose impartial. I approve your idea of a Protestant lawyer — should not the Catholic lawyer *name* him? else how will you get strangers to each other to meet together to do us a favor? Unless you think some great man, as R. Palmer, would undertake it for F Wilfrid's sake.[3] What would you say to a lawyer friend of Coffin's named Buller? I know nothing of him. The Bishop might be the third.

You have mentioned other names who, I dare say, would do very well — only I do not know them to judge of, as Mr Barnewall.[4]

Ever Yrs affly J H N

[1] Newman's letter of 14 July dedicating *Certain Difficulties Felt by Anglicans* to Ullathorne is printed at the beginning of *Diff.* 1.

[2] Hutchison and Lord Shrewsbury had agreed to try to settle the question of St Wilfrid's by arbitration. George Morgan, D.D., was at various times a professor at Oscott, and eventually President there.

[3] Roundell Palmer (1812–95), created Baron Selborne in 1872, was made a Queen's Counsel in 1849. For his friendship with Faber see R. D. Middleton, *Magdalen Studies*, London 1936, pp. 129–30.

[4] Henry Barnewall, of an Irish Catholic family, a merchant in London.

MONDAY 22 JULY 1850 Br Bernard went to St Wilfrid's. Neve called. Mr Molloy went

TO F. W. FABER

Oratory. Bm. July 22/50

My dear F Wilfrid,

As to J. Morris, I suppose he has destroyed my letter to him of 1846.[1] If not, you might ask him for it, and be yourself the judge. Of course I should like him to be at St W's [Wilfrid's]; but it is equally of course that I should like him there, as a member of a College, not of a community. The only addition I should make, κατ' εὐχῆν,[2] would be, that he had a room on the ground floor — I mean, I think he would put in disorder all the adits to his room — at least he did at Maryvale. On the whole, if you ask what I *wish*, it certainly would be his coming — on the footing of a member of a college, with a room all his own, common meals, and no duties. I wish this for our sake, as tending to maintain St W's, by his pension and by his giving us a priest there — and from the eclat of his name; — and for his sake, for I don't think he would be so comfortable any where else, and I wish him to be doing something with his books.

2. Thank you for the sight of Dr Wiseman's very pleasing and taking letter.[3]

3. Unluckily that 11th Lecture never got to F Bernard, and I am much fidgetted about it, and ready to make a cancel, if there is any thing imprudent in it.[4] As to your Brother H. [Henry Faber], should you not have clearly before you the cui bono of your going? I have some painful perplexity about an old relation of mine, now at least half way between

[1] It was suggested that J. B. Morris, who was without employment, should live at St Wilfrid's. Morris, when asked by Faber to take counsel with Newman on the subject, referred to the latter's long letter of 8 May 1846, about the faults he, Morris, must correct, if he was to live successfully in a community. Morris had kept this letter, which will be found in vol. XI. Newman wrote to Morris, who also thought of settling at Prior Park, on 29 July 1850.

[2] 'as a wish.'

[3] This was a note, marked 'private,'—almost certainly the letter printed in W. Ward, *The Life and Times of Cardinal Wiseman*, I, 2nd ed. London 1897, pp. 522–3, in which Wiseman expressed his disappointment at having to leave England for Rome. 'My only consolation has been, and is, that, according to S. Filippo's maxims, one cannot go wrong by obedience. . . .'

[4] This was the lecture 'Heretical and Schismatical Bodies no prejudice to the Catholicity of the Church,' in which Newman took a hopeful view of the salvation of non-Catholics. Faber, who was wondering whether he ought to visit his dying brother, and speak to him about religion, wrote on 20 July, 'your lax view (not in a bad sense) in your lectures soothes me.'

80 and 90;[1] — I have told her strongly, (tho' after anxious deliberation) that I expected she would be a Catholic before she died, for God's grace would bring her forward. This I did thinking, that, even on her death-bed, it might lead her to make an act of contrition cum voto etc. But humanly speaking, she cannot be a Catholic — and I should be quite afraid to attempt dissipating prejudices, at present held in good faith. And I thought certainly *not* to go and see her, if I heard she was dying, though she has been most intimate with us all from children. Whether all this is consistent, I cannot tell.

4. I hardly like your signing the petition about Dr W. [Wiseman] If everyone else did, you might have a second deliberation.[2]

5. And now I am brought much against my will to the subject of the conduct of the London House concerning St W's — which has hurt me very much.[3] But I say in starting, that it is a thing done — it cannot be undone — matters can only be corrected in future. It has hurt me tot nominibus, that to say justly what I mean, would require a skeleton and rough plan like a Sermon. It is idle, and worse than idle, to talk of the expedient, for it is nothing else, of having me for a Superior a while, when the root of the matter is left untouched. A common Superior no more makes united houses, than England and Ireland would be one, with one queen, after the repeal of the Union. From the first moment I thought of the Oratory, the natural difficulty that occurred was to secure unity. It is very well in Italy, where even neighbouring dioceses are cut off from each other by mountains, to let Oratories take this course — Naples may differ from Rome, and Rome from Florence — without harm. They cannot come into collision — but bodies, — which have a common name, yet no common government, must either be good friends or 'better strangers.' The latter alternative is the Italian solution of the difficulty, which they adhere to so strictly that (I suppose this is its meaning) they do not even take in the members of sister-Oratories respectively. *Here* such strangeness is impossible — Birmm. is a three hours journey from London; and Oxford would be just half way between them. Difference of spirit and opinion would be as clearly seen and felt as between members of the same house, yet without any arbitrating power. Jealousy, rivalry, and distance would be sure to follow. All this would be a great scandal — there would be continual gossipping, tale-

---

[1] Newman's aunt, Elizabeth Newman (1765–1852).

[2] A protest by the clergy was being organised against Wiseman's removal to Rome. Faber objected to 'this English democratic way of letting' the Holy See 'know our mind.'

[3] Newman's letters of 5, 11, and 18 July, with their notes, give the immediate background to this letter which is an important one for the history of the relations between the two Oratories.

bearing etc etc — At this very moment I hear of two stories of 'what I have said — ' one that 'I wish to make three houses out of us' — the other that 'St W's is to become a boys school.' At present such things are as harmless as they are unavoidable. If Ch Ch [Christ Church] and Oriel used to have continual sparring, and Lloyd and Whately perpetual tiffs,[1] so will it be with Oratorians — they will quarrel with each other, while they will be opponents of the whole world too. Accordingly, feeling this, I mentioned to Mgr. Brunelli, that Mary vale might be the Panionium, which should *morally* cement us. When Mary vale was given up, still I felt St Wilfrid's was to take its place — a place of joint retirement from work — and at length a place of burial, I wished much more with the same object a common school for boys who might turn out Oratorians — a common seminary — a common semi-novitiate. Meanwhile a counter spirit arose, with which I could not sympathise, to the effect, that we could love none, we ought to love none, but those with whom we were always to live — and therefore separation was the sine qua non, the first step, in beginning to live an Oratorian life.[2] Else, still with a view of keeping us together as long as possible, I should have wished nearly every one to have had his turn at Birmingham. Well, the London House was to be formed, and was formed — but what was to become of St W's? Here then again I felt the same selfish spirit showing itself in the London Community. They seemed to think Father Robert (Coffin) would *do* there; ⟨or Father William, or F Austin —⟩ they would get it off their hands; they did not care for him or for it.[3] And so it went on till Christmas — and the expence forced us again to take matters up. Then I said to myself, these London fellows *shan't* thus throw off the *charge* of St W's. They shall put their shoulder to the work. It is not fair to throw two or three fathers into Coventry there. For three chief reasons then did I determine that all the Fathers of both houses should go to St W's. 1. by way of *forcing* the London fathers to take a *practical share* in the responsibilities of the place. 2. by way of providing the Fathers stationed there with companions — as a compensation of their solitariness. 3 as fulfilling my original wish to keep up a moral union between the two Houses. And I was resolved that I would not be for *keeping* St W's unless I forced the London Fathers to wake out of their

[1] During the second decade of the century Richard Whately was a Fellow of Oriel, and the High Churchman Charles Lloyd a tutor and then Censor at Christ Church. In 1825, Whately became Principal of St Alban Hall, and in 1822, Lloyd Regius Professor of Divinity and a canon of Christ Church. Both men had a considerable influence on Newman's development. Cf. *A.W.* p. 69.

[2] See the correspondence in Feb. and early March 1849, and especially Newman's letter of 10 May 1849 to Faber.

[3] See the correspondence during the second half of June 1849.

slumbers and to share the trouble of the place. Consequently I showed no eagerness for keeping the place — on this the London House came round, and we all turned together to the *surprise* of the two Fathers at St W's — *I* gladly turning, as soon as I had raised some practical interest for the place in your breasts.[1] (It is nothing to the purpose that you did not know my *reasons* — what I speak of is a *spirit*, and a breach of engagement.)

Now the time has come for your fulfilling your engagement — and to my disgust, you break it, and that on no grounds but what you must have been able to urge at the time you made it. Either you should have urged your objection then, or not now. And so far from putting your shoulder to the wheel, when Ward would readily have given you money to pay your expences of travelling there, you let him give you money for a house at Lancing instead, and that merely for the convenience (something certainly) of being able to run up and down for a day, as if you were to suffer no inconvenience of any kind as the price of keeping St W's. For myself, I had not a dream that you were not likely to keep your engagement, till the day I came to town, (when you were on the point of starting for St Edmund's) and found that next week you were going to Lancing, not for a night or a day, but for three weeks consecutive.[2]

And now, my dearest F. Wilfrid, I have unburdened myself. The whole plan of St W's is overset. I do not see how I can ask any of our Fathers to go there next year. I shall not suggest difficulties — but I cannot *persuade* — and if we really do want F Nicholas I shall have no delicacy in recalling him. As to the Fathers from the London House, the London House must send them, not I, as I think the decree intended.

You must not suppose that I am at once putting an end to College scheme, or boys scheme, or any thing else; — but since the London Fathers have broken the engagement, (I say broken, for it is impossible that I should bind them to it unwillingly; it is not like any act of firmness on the Superior's part towards this or that individual Father) you must put your heads together and suggest some plan. If you would reinstate yourselves in my good opinion, you must *put your shoulders to the wheel*; this will be fulfilling my *first* object of January last. 2 You must devise some plan to render the residence of Fathers in banishment *endurable* — which would be a second of my three objects. 3. As to the third, our union, 'you may bring a horse to the water, but can't make him drink.' I *can't* make you all wish to keep up intimacy with us all, if you won't, so I must give this up.

---

[1] See the letters of the first half of Jan. 1850.
[2] This was in June 1850.

In saying this, I know quite well that you love *me*. I know quite well that some of you love some of us; but I know too that the continuance of that love depends on intercourse, which you are now breaking off.

Ever Yours affly J H N[1]

TUESDAY 23 JULY 1850   F Joseph and Aloysius from St W's [Wilfrid's]   Capes came

WEDNESDAY 24 JULY   Capes went   went to St Wilfrid's

THURSDAY 25 JULY   rain   Mr Philpot and Mr Fenn came over *to St Wilfrid's* from Derby

FRIDAY 26 JULY   rain   the two men went[2]

SATURDAY 27 JULY   rain   returned to Birmingham   Capes, W Clifford, and Maskell came.

TO MRS JOHN MOZLEY

Oratory Birmingham July 27/50

My dear Jemima

I have just returned from St Wilfrid's, and find your kind letter on my table. The report of my indisposition was quite unfounded — I am glad to say — at least the only foundation was the circumstance that I had had a good deal of toothache — (for which I have had two teeth out) and from press of work had had to sit up good part of several nights running, and to break an engagement — some two months ago.

I am very anxious about Aunt[3] — what you say, of course, cannot surprise me, though it grieves me much.

I have been since Wednesday at St Wilfrid's for fresh air — and it

---

[1] Faber replied on 27 July: 'My dearest Padre

After having written and rejected two letters, and made sundry other attempts, to convey to you what your startling letter has caused me to feel, I have relinquished the task as hopeless, and in the fear of leading to still further misunderstanding and displeasure: and now I must not keep you waiting any longer for an acknowledgment of your letter. As to what we are to do now, I cannot at all see; and as superior we must look to you to propose something. You say we must devise some plan for carrying out objects 1 and 2: I can devise none, except our non use of the dispensation unwittingly extorted from you: then on the other hand you say that that is not to be undone, and that we are to look at it as done and over. We do not see how to move either way.

Yrs affly and obedly F. W. F.'

[2] Newman appears to have gone specially to St Wilfrid's to enable these two men to consult him privately. They were perhaps David Fenn and George Philpot, who after being at Cambridge together, where they took their degrees in 1849, were now Anglican curates at Covent Garden and Saffron Walden respectively. Fenn became later a missionary in India.   [3] Elizabeth Newman.

has rained incessantly. The only thing I know of out of doors, is to have got very wet, by attempting to accompany a stranger on his way to the rail.

I do not like to delay a post to answer your kind anxiety — though I have not many minutes

Ever Yours affectly John H Newman

MONDAY 29 JULY 1850   Capes, W Clifford, and Maskell went

TO MRS J. W. BOWDEN

Oratory Bm. July 29/50

My dear Mrs Bowden,

I hear a report that you have given up the idea of Ushaw — is it so?[1] if so, I doubt not it has been for good reasons. I sent you a message by John, when last I saw him, to the effect that I thought Ushaw seemed to promise better than any thing else — but if you ask me whether I have any *view* on the subject, I certainly have none. Tell Charlie I shall say Mass for him tomorrow, with my love.

I have only just got my Lectures off my hands — and am attacking the arrears of work which has accumulated these two months. They tell us we shall roof in our new house by winter — but as the first stone is not laid yet, I am slow to believe it. We are having some circulars printed — I shall send you one for form sake, but you won't suppose I expect a single penny from you. By the bye, one thing you *can* do. When I make up entirely the Mary vale account between the boys and the house, which I am ashamed to say is not done, though I suppose it will be in a few days, there will, I suspect, be a sum over in your favor. Might it go towards green vestments for us?

We are still in the greatest difficulties about St W's [Wilfrid's] — though I trust they are clearing, by coming to a crisis, but I can't tell. We are hoping to have an arbitration between the Earl and us, which will simplify matters.

You see how bright our prospects are getting at Rome,[2] — but every thing is uncertain in this life.

---

[1] It had been proposed to send Charles Bowden aged 14, who had been living at the London Oratory, to Ushaw College, as a cure for laziness. Instead, his mother took him for the winter to Malta.

[2] i.e. the prospect of Wiseman there as a Cardinal.

I have nothing to say except that St Philip continues to prosper us
Ever Yours affectly in Xt   John H Newman   Congr. Orat.

P.S.   Love to the girls — I don't know where you all are.

TO J. D. DALGAIRNS

Oy Bm. July 29 1850

My dear F Bernard,

Thank you for your useful letter — I ought rather to talk of boring
you. I have stopped for a week. I hope my alterations will satisfy you.
Though the Church punishes as a matter of justice, yet surely the *reason*
why she has been *given* this power, may have been (among others) what
Aristotle calls a κάθαρσις, a heading of a movement, *viz* that there may
be a power in the world to *satisfy* this feeling of justice — so I have
altered to 'It *is plain, if only* to *prevent* the occurrence of persecution
(i.e. persecution as distinct from punishment) she must head a movement
etc.' Also I have altered 'violence' as applied to her into 'severity —'
and 'Doubtless in 1800 years there are events . . . which the *world*
would wish otherwise.'[1]

You can't conceive what trouble that end took me — I *must* mention
our principle — yet *how* to do without *either* creating a prejudice, *or*
getting into a *new argument*.[2]

Ever Yrs affly J H N

TO J. B. MORRIS

Oratory Bm. July 29. 1850.

My dear Morris,

I will throw all the light I can upon your question, but I feel with
you the difficulty of deciding.[3] First, I think you should, if you can in
this world, decide for good. If you will let me say it, though I don't
mean it has been your fault, I have been sorry that you have been so
long on the world. It seems to me you should have your books about
you, and be shedding your light on one place. I shall not be happy 'in

[1] Newman is correcting lectures by Dalgairns on the Sacred Heart, later incor-
porated in his *The Devotion to the Heart of Jesus*, London 1853.
[2] Newman is referring to the twelfth and last of the *Lectures on Certain Difficulties
felt by Anglicans*, in which he explained the principle of development in the Church.
[3] Urged by Faber, Morris wrote on 26 July for Newman's advice, as to whether to
go to Prior Park or St Wilfrid's. See first note to letter of 22 July to Faber.

your regard' (as Catholics say) till I see you fairly seated in some solid Cathedra, mortared into the wall, or rather built out of the wall of some massive home, which may be shown in after ages as the place where the Doctor Orientalissimus lived and died.

The main question then is, *where* are you most likely to be settled, at Prior Park or St Wilfrid's — and really I can't tell. For us, we are in a very uncertain state, as not inhabiting St W's. Till we in some way incorporate it into the Oratory, it may pass out of our hands; and then, where are you? on the other hand it might be said, that such as *you* might be the beginning of a superior College there, which *we* could not ultimately take part in. Therefore your coming might be looked on as a means of others coming. It is a great idea, and would be of great service to the Catholic Cause in time to come. You would know people at St W's more than at Prior Park, and I think would be happier with them much *on the long run*, than at Prior Park. I very much doubt whether you should make emolument part of your *scheme* at Prior Park more than at St W's. If it comes, well; but I should very much fear your anticipating and reckoning on it.

For myself I have two grounds for wishing you at St W's, over and above personal ones — 1. that your name would give us a certain reputation in the eyes of the world — 2. that you would be a *priest* there — but were I you, I should somewhat incline on the side of Prior Park. Would it not be safest of all to pay them a visit at Prior Park? — of *sufficient* length as to enable you to determine whether you should like the place for good.

Ever Yours affectly in Xt, John H Newman   Cong. Orat.

P.S.   My *kindest remembrances* to my old acquaintance Biddulph Phillipps.[1] He does me wrong to say he never met me in Bowden's rooms — for, I suspect, we have met frequently, wined, and supped at each others! Not [And] that he was a great Whig and a great herald, and a great musician. He had to come late on Sunday into Hall and lose his dinner for the sake of Vicary and New College Chapel.[2] And then he would have sharp arguments with Bowden against the Manchester Massacre and perhaps in favour of Queen Caroline.[3]

[1] Morris was staying at Robert Biddulph Phillipps's house, Longworth, Ledbury, Herefordshire. Phillipps was matriculated at Trinity College six months before Newman, whose recollection that they wined and supped together is confirmed by the 'Early Journals,' *A.W.* p. 155. See also note to letter of 12 Jan. 1851 to Morris.

[2] Walter Vicary was the organist at New College, 1797–1845.

[3] The Tory government incurred great unpopularity in 1819 on account of the intervention of soldiers at the meeting in St Peter's Field, Manchester, when eleven people were killed, and again in 1820, over the affair of George IV's Queen.

TUESDAY 30 JULY 1850   F William went, for St W's [Wilfrid's] and retreat at Hanley

TO ANTONY HUTCHISON

Oratory. Bm. July 30/50

My Dear F Antony,

As we ought to have as full light thrown on our position as regards Lord S [Shrewsbury] as possible, I have been looking over the correspondence of Lent 1848, and though I can't say that much satisfactory comes of it I will quote the passages.[1]

I was led to do this, I must tell you candidly by a strong impression on my memory that F Wilfrid, before he joined the Oratory, and I suppose as I was on the point of going abroad in September 1846, said to me, either by letter or as I think at St W's [Wilfrid's], 'The Church will run here, shutting out the Protestant building etc etc. Lord S is giving us the whole place, and house, and as we could not afford to sacrifice our capital, he has promised, if *we* build, he will guarantee us the interest.' And I think some thousand pounds, say 2 or 3 were mentioned.

This *admits* perhaps your explanation of the matter — but it makes you build and (virtually) borrow, not him — and it disjoins the capital from the interest, allowing of a plausible change of it into a *bargain* such as this, '*You* lay out, and *I* will endow.'

Now on looking through the correspondence, I cannot find any thing on your part to bear out this impression — *On the contrary*, as you will see from the extracts below. But *the Earl* seems *then* to have had the view he has *now* — and he *asserts it* to F. Wilfrid and you, and you do not deny it; you have not protested against it; and you have not asserted in like manner *your* view to *him* — (*valeat quantum*) — however, the extracts shall speak for themselves.

Lord S. to F. Newman.

Febr 23/48. 'We hear that it is decided not to keep up St W's as a *community*. Now, I made it over to the Wilfridians *because* they were a community. I have *guaranteed* them in a sum of £2300 of which I pay the interest, etc. This has all been done for a *community* etc, so that I consider it a *complete breach of contract* to abandon it as a *monastery* etc.'[2]

---

[1] Newman writes in view of the proposed arbitration. See also his letter of 17 Jan. 1850, to Lord Shrewsbury.

[2] See Newman's reply on 25 Feb. 1848, and further correspondence in the following month.

Lord S. to F. Faber.

March 10. 1848 'To make up the store of a *community*, I would *increase* the bond to the amount specified,' (from 2300 to 3000) 'and pay you the interest on it in the same manner as I do now. This of course is beyond the £50 a year that I allow for the *mission*.' (As if he was to pay the interest on £3000 for a community, and £50 a year for a mission.)

Lord S. to F. Newman.

March 12/48

$$
\begin{array}{lll}
& & £ \\
\text{Dividend on £3000} & \text{say} - & 125 \\
\text{etc etc} & & \ldots\ldots \\
& & \overline{} \\
& & 200
\end{array}
$$

To this I would agree. . . . I had no idea whatever of doing more at first than to give them the land and £50 a year for the mission; but I found them so liberal that I thought it necessary to assist etc etc.

March 19./48. 'I agreed to give them £50 a year for the mission, and something for the school. It was also clear that a church of some sort was requisite; and though I had at first expected them to have built it, yet, seeing they were pressed, I agreed to be *answerable* for £2300 for the purpose.' — (F. Newman having written to Lord S. for an *endowment*, and saying that Lord S. had only offered £5 additional.) 'You observe that £5 is the *sole* increase which I offer. Now this is clearly an error. I offer to *make* the £2300 into £3000. This alone would I presume, be an increase of about £30 a year etc etc.'

Lord S. to F. Faber.

March 20. 'Seeing the necessity for a Church, I agreed to *indemnify* you for *your loss* of income through the *cost of construction* to the amount of £2300. I have consented to *extend my* assistance thus, to make the £2300 into £3000 etc etc.' (Here, as in the foregoing the £2300 is put on the same ground as the additional £700, viz as implying a stipulation on our part.). 'Thus, insuring you £200 a year in hard cash, which is full as much as I *now* receive for the whole Cotton Estate. Surely this is more than could have been *reasonably expected* in *such times* as these with *every one begging* right and left — etc' (here the interest on the 2300 which is included in the £200 is spoken of as a *gift*.)

March 24. 'When I reply' (to F. Newman) 'that beyond this £5, I take on myself the payment of the dividend on an extra £700,' he observes, 'What signifies it to the community whether they get their dividend from you or from the Government?' (I do not quote his very words.) 'Now, as I understand Father John' (Newman) 'The case is thus. He says "The Community have wasted too much of their principal and have thus sacrificed their income." I reply, "I am willing to take this into consideration and to supply the income which they have sacrificed by restoring the principal to the extent of £700 over and above the 2300." Is it not then a clear case that, if I had not come forward, you would neither have had your dividend from government or from any one else?'

In these letters there is no hint that Lord S. distinctly gave £2300 for building the Church — but he implies that he eased the halter to those who did build it. There may be something more definite in a letter of F Wilfrid's to me, describing a conversation which took place at the same date between him and Lord S — which I put into F. Wilfrid's hands in November 1848 and which was not returned to me.

Now for your and F. Wilfrid's letters.

F. Hutchison to F. Newman.

(middle of March) He has given them a large House together with several acres of land in the centre of his estate — He has *sunk* £2300 in assisting them to build their church . . . sunk at least £500 on the new part of the House. *All this* (including £2300) he has done on the tacit *understanding* that the Wilfridians were to do *their best to catholicize* his people; he could have no other intention. With regard to what has been said about the *endowment* of the Church, this cannot justly be expected from him. For it should be remembered that *he gave us* in the first instance the £2300 to *enable us* to build a little chapel, . . . It was we who built the church, and *we*, or at any rate Br Austin and myself and, I believe, Br Alban, *endowed* it, or intended to do so.

F. Faber to F. Newman.

(about same date). 'Lord S.'s £2300 *was advanced* by us. He pays the dividend with the right to *pay us back* in building, if he likes.'

F. Hutchison to F. Newman.

(about same date) 'We determined to anticipate the reversions of Br Austin and myself by borrowing some of our own principal to be repaid when those reversions fell, and thus we brought to the *Oratory* a greater number of persons than our *actual income* was able of itself to support, so that, when I have transferred the required amount of stock to Brs Alban and Austin, my income will be reduced to £350 about.' Does not this imply that the interest of the £2300, (the capital) advanced by the Wilfridians, belonged *not to the Oratory*, ⟨or to any member of the O.⟩

by [but] to *St Wilfrid's?* the £350 *not including* the interest on £2300.
March 26. 'At first he certainly offered to *borrow* an *additional* £700 of
us and to expend it in building at St W's, paying us interest for it. . . .
It seems his offer is much more liberal. In addition to the £2300 already
advanced, he offers to take on himself to *pay interest* for £700 of the
money which we have already sunk.'

F. Faber to F. Newman.

March 30. 'The Patron gave a sum which he considered adequate to
build a chapel for the people; £2300 towards our Church — the property
is thus intrinsically burdened with a *mission*; the possessors of it pro
temp. must *keep up* the mission etc. Whether you would retain S.
Wilfrid's was always an uncertainty to us; that you would keep up the
mission while you retained it, we never doubted.' (Here £2300 seems
connected with the mission.)

I do not say that all this throws much light on the whole matter —
but I thought you might like to see it

Ever Yours affly J H N

TO MISS HOLMES

Oratory Birmingham July 31/50

My dear Miss Holmes

I have been from home which will account for my silence. Else I
should certainly have answered you sooner. . . .

Never be afraid, my dear child, of telling any weakness to me,
because we all have our faults, and those who take confessions of course
hear many. . . .

Do not be disheartened by these inconsistencies, whatever they may
be, for your dear Lord will give you grace to overcome them.

As time goes on you will know yourself better and better. Time
does that for us, not only by the increase of experience, but by the
withdrawal of those natural assistances to devotion and selfsurrender
which youth furnishes. When the spirits are high and the mind fervent,
though we may have waywardnesses and perversenesses which we have
not afterwards, yet we have something to battle against them. But when
men get old, as I do, then they see how little grace is in them, and how
much what seemed grace was but nature. Then the soul is left to lassi-
tude, torpor, dejection, and coldness which is its real state, with no
natural impulses affections or imaginations to rouse it, and things which
in youth seemed easy then become difficult. Then it finds how little

self command it has, and how little it can throw off the tempter when he comes behind and places it in a certain direction or position, or throws it down, or places his foot upon it. Then it understands at length its own nothingness, and that it has less grace than it had but it has nothing but grace to aid it. It is the sign of a saint to *grow*; common minds, even though they are in the grace of God, dwindle, (i.e. seem to do so) as time goes on. The energy of grace alone can make a soul strong in age.

Do not then be cast down, if you though not *very* aged feel less fervent than you did ten years since — only let it be a call on you to seek grace to supply nature, as well as to overcome it. Put yourself ever fully and utterly into Mary's hands, and she will nurse you and bring you forward. She will watch over you as a mother over a sick child. . . .

TO F. S. BOWLES

Oy. Bm. August 2. 1850

Charissime,

I feel for you in your great loss[1] — yet all is well. It is better that it has been so far sudden, that you had not to go — and better that you should be quietly at St W's [Wilfrid's] than in this bustling house — I shall say a Mass for your Mother, that is, for your intention, as soon as I can next week.

As to your going to the Funeral, the only ground I see for going is the *rest wishing it*. It is important to keep on good terms with them.

Tell your sister I shall say a Mass for her and you, as soon as I can.

There is no great news here — Some one who won't be known, has sent me £100 for the church.

We will not forget you — With my best love Ever Yours affectionately

John H Newman   Congr. Orat.

TO J. D. DALGAIRNS

Oratory. Birmingham August 2. 1850

My dear F Bernard,

I write a line, to make assurance double sure, for you are not likely to want it, to caution you against anything like puffing St Philip or the Oratory in Ireland.

[1] The death of his mother.

F Wilfrid's Lectures are making somewhat of a commotion — as if he had taught that St Ph. was not only the representative Saint, but the instrumental Saint of modern times — as if he alone was the go, and all here ought to be Oratorians.[1] Beware of any word or laugh which would savor of what may be called the 'House' spirit.[2]

And don't say a word disparaging of Gothic — praise every thing, and show a great devotion to St Patrick

Ever Yrs affly J H N

PS   Your lectures came safe.

TO F. W. FABER

Oy. Bm. Aug. 2/50

My dear F Wilfrid,

What were the rules we determined on about novices being in each other's rooms — and going to other's rooms — and letting others come to their rooms?

I am sorry to hear you have been ill again

Ever Yrs affly J H N

P.S.   Richardson called here the other day. He said that the 6 numbers a year plan caused a failure and wished it to be reduced to 4.[3] What do you say to this? He consented to give a sum to the revisors, and wished to know what it should be. What do you think it should be for a volume of 300 pages? How much per 96 pages or six sheets?

[1] Faber had delivered in May three lectures, published as '*The Spirit and Genius of St. Philip Neri Founder of the Oratory.*' The second was entitled 'St. Philip the Representative Saint of Modern Times,' and the third 'St. Philip in England,' as to which Faber said, p. 100, 'If the land had been measured for him and for his Oratory, the fit could not have been completer.' His exaggerated ultramontanism and depreciation of the Middle Ages led to an outcry among many besides the 'Gothic' party. Faber expected trouble, but did not make this clear to Newman beforehand. (See Newman's letters of 21 May 1851 to Dalgairns, and 23 May 1851 to Faber.) Newman disliked the book. (See letter of 11 July 1850 to Faber, and 23 Dec. 1850 to Hutchison.) It also helped to upset Coffin. (See letter of 24 Nov. 1850 to Faber.)

[2] An allusion to Christ Church, Oxford—'the House.'

[3] This refers to the *Lives of the Modern Saints*. Faber replied suggesting that revisors should receive £5 for a volume.

TO ANTONY HUTCHISON

Oy. Bm. August 2/50

My dear F Antony

If I possibly can, I will be with you at the Ordination on the Assumption, for I wish to see Dr W [Wiseman] before he goes.

Please, look over the extracts[1] a *second* time before you decide any thing. I suppose what we all wish is to get at *facts*. It is not a question of opinion or liking. For myself, I am hardly able to say *how far* the passages go. Some go one way, some another

Ever Yours affly J H N

F Frederic has lost his mother.

SATURDAY 3 AUGUST 1850   Garside came

TO MRS T. W. ALLIES

Oratory, Birmingham Aug. 3. 1850.

My dear Mrs Allies,

I have been thinking very anxiously of you, and am glad to hear from you. We have a house for you, where there are one or two ladies. Inquire for Warwick Street, or rather come *here*, (40. Alcester Street) and we will direct you. Friday will suit me quite well.

Ever yours most sincerely in Xt.

John H. Newman   Congr. Orat.

TO MISS M. R. GIBERNE

Oratory Birmingham August 3. 1850

My dear Miss Giberne,

I have been expecting to hear of your arrival with great impatience. We have at present a house here, where we can receive you. It is extremely pleasant to hear that you have settled to come to take up your abode here for good at no *distant* day — for so I understand your letter.

May our Blessed Lady and all Saints who have brought you

---

[1] i.e. Newman's letter of 30 July about St Wilfrid's.

here, bless your coming and settling. I shall have many things to say to you[1]

TO WILLIAM MASKELL

Oy Bm Aug. 4/50

My dear Maskell,

Thank you for Baron Alderson's pamphlet.[2] It is sensible and clear, as might be expected from a Lawyer — but it *assumes* of course, with most of the pamphlets on his side, the Catholicity of the Anglican Church — and does not consider that what is now happening in it, though not sufficient to unchurch it, if a church, may be sufficient to prove it never was a church.

I am much pleased at what you kindly say about your visit here — and wishing you all grace and blessing from the Giver of good I am
Yours very truly in Xt

John H Newman   Congr. Orat.

MONDAY 5 AUGUST 1850   Lady O. Acheson went?

TO BISHOP ULLATHORNE

Oratory Birmingham Aug. 6 1850

My dear Lord,

I write a hasty line to thank your Lordship for your most kind letter, and to express my extreme gratification at the Holy Father's condescending notice of me.[3] I will write to Mgr Barnabo by Dr Wiseman next

[1] The conclusion and signature have been cut off. Miss Giberne expected to come to Birmingham to the house for Ladies, who were to assist the Oratorians. Cf. letter of 30 Oct. 1849.

[2] Sir Edward Hall Alderson (1787–1857), a distinguished judge and baron of the Court of Exchequer from 1830, published in 1850, during the Gorham controversy, *A Letter* and *A Second Letter to the Bishop of Exeter*, by 'A Layman.'

[3] Ullathorne wrote on 5 Aug., enclosing the Rescripts by which Pius IX conferred on Newman a Doctorate of Divinity. Already on 22 July Stanton had quoted to Newman extracts of a letter just received from Dr Grant in Rome: 'The Rescript making F. Newman D D will be ready in a day or two—I beg my congratulations.' 'F. Newman's discourses are causing great interest here from the accounts we have of them, but we have not seen them—I sent him a paper (the one which the Pope reads) about his sermons, and I will send another by this Post, to shew him what kind things are written about him with reference to the Gorham case from England—You cannot imagine in what kind and hearty terms Bishop Ullathorne writes respecting F. Newman, begging the Pope to be informed of his admiration and regard for F. Newman.'

week. I have no claims on so great an honor, except what would be sufficient to make every sincere Catholic a doctor, an earnest desire to serve my mother the Church, of which I am the latest and most unformed son

Pray give me your blessing, my dear Lord, and believe me,

Ever Yours most sincerely in Xt

John H Newman   Congr. Orat.

TO CHARLES WATERTON

Aug 7/50

Sir[1]

I have no sort of claim upon your attention, except that I am the son of a great Saint, who seems set upon doing a good turn to this unhappy country. St Philip lived when it fell away from the faith; he ever took an interest in the remnant of Catholic martyrs, and confessors who alone [?] remained to it, — and now, when God seems to have purposes of mercy towards it again, he at once comes to it by means of that institution which he founded and which has spread almost throughout the Catholic world. Every order or Congregation in the Church has its own work; and ours especially lies among the population of great towns, and still more directly with the educated or half educated or professedly educated portion of it.

Here in Birmingham our object will be to influence the tone of thought and opinion prevalent in the various circles of society high and low, to recommend Catholicism, to expose Protestantism, and especially to take care of young men. We have been here about a year and a half and have been sufficiently blessed to feel sanguine that St Philip will make us of use here, if once we get established. We are collecting subscriptions for a Church, as the inclosed paper explains,[2] and knowing your zeal for the Catholic faith, we are sure that you will not be offended at least at our applying to you to help us, being sure also that, if you do not, you will have the best reasons for declining, and if you do, that St Philip will not forget it.

Praying that all blessings may be poured on you in this world and the next from the Giver of grace

I am &c. J H N

Charles Waterton Esqr

---

[1] Newman kept the draft of this appeal to Charles Waterton (1782–1865), the naturalist, an old Catholic, who lived an ascetic life at Walton Hall, in Yorkshire, and gave away large sums in charity.   [2] The circular of 19 July.

TO JOHN HARDMAN

Oratory Birmingham August 8. 1850

My dear Mr Hardman,

I inclose you one of our circulars. You are so full of good works, that I can't quite say it is fair to send you a begging letter. But such is the way of the world, the more a person gives, the more is expected of him — And besides that, we really should not like to build a church, without your co-operation.

Whatever you can give us, St Philip will pay you back in some way or other — though *we* shall not be able

Yours, My dear Mr Hardman, Very sincerely in Xt

John H Newman   Congr. Orat.

TO ANTONY HUTCHISON

Oratory. Bm Aug. 8/50

My dear F. A.

The Bishop had rather not be an arbitrator in the *first* instance — and proposes, or assents to, the notion of two, one to be chosen by each party. He, as well as Lord S. [Shrewsbury] is afraid of Protestants. Should we have Mr Lambert? or whom? I suspect our man would have *less* weight if he were either Protestant or convert; and *more* still, if he is a man of business. Make up your mind as soon as you can. If all is well, I will come to you in the 14th to return on the 15th.

Ever Yours affly J H N

FRIDAY 9 AUGUST 1850   Mrs Allies came

TO GEORGE TALBOT

Oratory. Birmingham. August 11. 1850

My dear Talbot,

Dr Wiseman will kindly be the bearer of this. It is a most interesting and important measure of the Holy Father's, this moving him and you to Rome — and the more painful to you, *which I fully believe and understand*, the greater blessing will go with it to you.[1] I shall say a Mass for

[1] Talbot wrote on 16 July from Pisa that he had been summoned to Rome by Pius IX. 'My name was suggested to him as that of an Englishman knowing Italian

you and him every first day of the Month, and shall not be the only one, I am sure, who, even from a sense of the importance and anxiety of your position, will continually bear you in mind.

Thank you for the great kindness of your letter from Pisa. As to my Lectures, I very much doubt if they will do to translate.[1] They are addressed solely to Puseyites, about whom the good Monsignori and Padri of Rome are about as ignorant as Protestants are of them. They are based upon principles and arguments, of which *they* never heard — and will not feel interest in — or may misunderstand. This is what I feel myself — which makes me say, Think twice, before you decide on translating. It is your kind zeal for me which makes you wish it.

As to your question,[2] I think you can be of the greatest use to the Catholic cause in England by bringing before the Holy Father our real wants — but I should be diffident in suggesting any thing without knowing I had the countenance of Dr Wiseman. I suppose our most crying want is the want of theology. The Pope of the day sent over St Theodore, St Adrian etc. into England. How he could do any thing now without interfering with the existing Colleges, I don't know — but I am sure it is a point which deserves considering. At Ushaw they have theologians — whether they have at St Edmund's, Oscott, and Prior Park, I don't know, though Dr Weathers at St E's is a most excellent and useful man. Could he call English to *Rome* for the purpose? *then*, I suppose he would be interfering with the English College there — so there is difficulty every way. Could Dr Grant suggest any thing? But any how, if you ask me, *this* is one of the first wants, i.e. of those, in which the Holy See is *able* to do any thing. For myself, nothing would be a greater comfort to me than to know there was in England some theologian who had the express sanction of the Holy See, and whom I might consult on various difficult questions in *controversy*, not simply in *theology*. I could name several in England who are quite sufficient

and of a noble family which is indispensable . . .' Talbot added that he tried to refuse, representing 'what I was doing at St George's, hearing hundreds of Confessions receiving persons into the Church, catechising numbers of children. . . . I would infinitely rather be teaching the Catechism in my poor school in the borough than pass about the Vatican in purple—'

[1] Talbot wrote of the *Lectures on Difficulties of Anglicans*, 'I find they have made a sensation all over Europe . . . they are very well calculated to give an idea to the Italian Divines of what Puseyism really was and is.'

[2] Talbot explained in his letter, 'I do not wish to remain idle in Rome . . . but I wish to make myself as useful as I can to England and the Catholic Church in general. I wish therefore that you would kindly suggest to me any way by which I may do good, as your advice will be of the greatest weight, and I have no doubt the Pope will equally value it.

I shall be in immediate attendance on the Pope so that I shall constantly have his ear, and will be able to tell him any thing that it may be useful for him to know.'

authority in dogmatic theology, but who cannot from the *nature* of the case be such in *polemical*, as not having the distinct *sanction* of the Holy See — e.g. in such questions as the inspiration of Scripture, how far may be conceded as to it; — again minute points about faith and reason; about the origin of ideas etc etc. As you well know, our controversies in England are running to these questions; and for myself, I am frequently perplexed what I may grant and what I must not — and others write to me for information, and I do not know what to say. No theological writer, as Suarez or De Lugo, will exactly do, of course — for controversy changes its shape and bearings, century by century. But perhaps I am wishing what the Holy See *never does*.[1]

What the Pope will like most, I should think, would be being made *au courant* with the state of things in England. If you would like me to do it, I would try to send you letters now and then on matters of the day.

Pray convey my respects to young Prince Hohenlohe, if he recollects seeing me — and ask his prayers — [2] Do not forget us at some of the great Shrines of the City; — I kiss the Holy Father's foot and am, My dear Talbot, Most sincerely Yours in Xt

John H Newman   Congr. Orat

PS   Must not I say *Monsignore* Talbot? It is safer.

TO ALEXANDER BARNABÒ

Dabam Birminghamiae. Die 12. August. 1850

Utinam, Domine Reverendissime, possim justo verborum ambitu exprimere, ea, et quae intus sentio, et quae jure sentienda intelligo, propter summum illum honorem, quo per Te nuper me cumulavit Sanctissimus Dominus noster;[3] — quo quidem ideo solum modo non indignus mihi videor, quod ex ipso veridico honorum et praemiorum sacrorum Fonte ad me indignissimum profluxerit.

Accedat hoc, precor, Domine Reverendissime, Tuae erga me benevolentiae, ut Sanctitatem Suam certiorem facias quām grato et laeto et

---

[1] Talbot wrote on 24 Sept., 'Regarding Theology, I told the Pope who takes a great interest in you what you said, likewise about S. Theodore and S. Adrian. Alas! he said I have no Saints to send to England. And, really, as you know yourself there are but few, if any, *profound* Theologians in Rome itself. . . .'

[2] Newman had met Gustav Adolf Prince von Hohenlohe in 1847. Ordained in 1849, he was now a Papal Chamberlain.

[3] i.e. the degree of Doctor of Divinity.

tenero animi affectu indicia haec nova amplexus sim pristinae illius curae et dilectionis Suae paternae, quâ fretus et recreatus, gloriosissimo Patrono meo, Sancto Philippo, me et mea principio commendare ausus sum.

Faxit idem sapientissimus et amantissimus Magister meus, ut, in militiâ adversus subtilissimas harum regionum haereses, cui mancipatum est quod reliquum est vitae meae, indies magis valeam et dicendo et agendo ostendere, quantâ et quâm simplici et devotione et amore tum Sanctitatem Suam tum ipsam Petri Sedem colam et venerer.

Tui, Domine Reverendissime, Observantissimus Servus

Joannes H. M. Newman   Congr. Orat.

Revmo et Colmo Dno
Domino Al. Barnabò
à Secretis Sacr. Congr. Prop. Fid.

TO F. W. FABER

Oratory Bm. August 12/50

My dear F Wilfrid,

It has just struck me whether it is not *necessary*, in prudence, to erect the London Oratory on the Assumption.

If Dr Briggs, with Dr Cox co-adjutor come to London, (and I hear there are strong influences at work for this) it will *never* be set up.

If Dr Wiseman goes, the new appointment, may come down upon us any moment, plump.

Ever Yours affectly John H Newman   Congr. Orat.

TO WILLIAM GOWAN TODD

Oratory Birmingham August 12. 1850

Dear Sir,[1]

No apology was necessary for your letter just received. I answer it at once, lest, if I delayed, I should be obliged to delay it longer than I

---

[1] The autograph of this letter, written to an Anglican in doubt as to his position, has been preserved, but it has no name on it. As the first paragraph shows, it was the reply to a letter received the same day. Both in the list of letters received and in that of those sent, in the diary for 12 Aug., occurs the name 'Mr Todd.' (The only other men listed among the correspondents of this day are Catholic priests.) William Gowan Todd, a curate at St James's, Bristol, became a Catholic at the end of the year.

wished. So you must excuse me, if what I say might be better put together. I shall burn your letter as soon as I have written this.

As to the sentiments which you speak of as your own, it is scarcely necessary for me to say how much I concur in them. I have felt it as an axiom for years, that there is no medium between scepticism and Catholicism; if I did not act upon it at once, and become a Catholic, it was, because, though my reason told me it was an axiom, I did not like to trust my own private judgment against others; but when it had steadily continued with me without interruption, or rather with greater distinctness and sense of certainty, and under various circumstances and in many states of mind, for a certain period, and [I] reflected that all men agreed with me except pretty nearly those who could not, consistently with their existing religious position, I felt I had a right to trust myself to the force and results of my conviction.

It will grow upon you too — and it will grow on others also — the only wonder is that there should be any who at least have not *begun* to recognize it. It is indeed too clear to argue about, and it is an exercise of patience to argue, though it is often one's duty to do so.

1. I think you would find that the Greeks have practically given up the principle of dogmatism — not that they do not use it *against* the Church of Rome — but they allow all sorts of opinion to exist among themselves. It is so, I believe, in Russia — and the greater favor, compared with Catholics, in which the Greek priests are held by Protestant Missionaries, seems to show that it is the same in Greece proper.

2. Your companions, friends etc. thinking your views wrong is no presumption they are so, if others, their equals in age, information, piety etc, think the contrary — unless a man has reason to suppose it intended for those around him to have a quasi infallibility with respect to him.

3. If no one may judge his own Church, no member of the Kirk can join the Church of England, no Methodist — no Nestorian may become a Catholic, no Jew may become a Christian. It is right to 'pause and reflect,' but if there is responsibility in speaking against Anglicanism, there is also responsibility in quenching grace. What I dislike most in Anglicans just now, is their most unfair way of *frightening* men, without a basis of *reason*.

As to your objections

1. As to the duty of her sons standing by the Anglican Church, and the harm she has got by secessions to Rome, all depends on the *previous question*, *Is* she a Church? If she is, then, secessions *would* tend to diminish the prospect of her continuing a Church — But, if she is not, her members stopping with her cannot make her one. Those who left

her felt most intensely, when they left her, that grace was not to be got in her — and that, if they continued in her, they were supporting a *lie* — and making themselves answerable for the souls of their brethren.

2. As for fighting for freedom from the State, the State is the bond which keeps you in *one*. Your victory would be your death. You would break up into a score of bodies, were it not for the force of law and the inducements of property.

3. Whether you would be disappointed in the Catholic Church, when joined, must to you be a matter of conjecture. If you will judge by *those who have already joined* it, you will decide negatively. They will with one voice cry out that they have only *gained* and lost nothing. Of course the argument can as well be urged by Jews against a Jew wishing to become a Christian.

4. 'It is a matter of fact that the moral and religious tone of many of the converts is deteriorated.' This, among others, means *me*. It is marvellous. — When I began the movement in 1833, I was accused of two things — 'fanaticism' — (the *word* was used) and 'levity — ' *Then*, since the objects of them were the Evangelicals, my friends felt them not — now, when they are directed against Anglicanism, they are shocked. But, besides this, *of course* to those who hold Anglicanism to be divine, to deny it *will* seem profane. It is the *thing itself* which is the profaneness, not any particular *manner*. The deterioration lies *in* becoming a Catholic (which is of course a begging of the question) — if a man is a Catholic, he *must* seem profane to an Anglican. Have those who call us profane, read our Catholic works? or do they not commonly religiously refuse to do so, and found their charges on half sentences of them, passed about from mouth to mouth? Thus judged the Evangelicals, the Record, of us, years back.

5. As to *authorities*, I confess I always thought Jeremy Taylor most unsatisfactory and shuffling. Laud died confessing himself (honestly) a *Protestant* — Leslie has nothing spiritual about him — Hammond, Wilson, Ken, I revere; nor would I willingly pull them to pieces — yet I suppose there have been as good men as they in the world, who have thought just the opposite. Nor did they, in their day, see the *consequences* of Anglicanism, and its internal nothingness, developed, as we do now. Exitus acta probat.

Excuse these abrupt answers — I shall be glad to give others of the same rough character, if you wish for them.

With my earnest prayers, and my belief, that you will by God's grace be led on into the Truth

I am, My dear Sir, Very faithfully Yours,

John H Newman   Congr. Orat.

39

P.S.   Should you be inclined to come here (Alcester Street Number 40) you will learn more about Catholicism in a few hours, than by many letters.[1]

TO RICHARD STANTON

Oratory Bm Aug 13/50

My dear F Richard,

I do not like to lose even a day, so I put down the following thoughts — though not worth much.

1. Would you not all be sadly unsettled, if Dr Briggs said, 'I would rather not establish you for a year?' *unless* he promised he would do so at the end of the time. Or if Dr Ullathorne said 'I will establish you on condition you take a mission.'

2 Since, *any how*, I should be obliged to let you be established in the course of few months (say anniversary of the Brief, November 25 (?))[2] this is only anticipating by a short time what is inevitable.

3 You could make any by law you pleased, putting yourselves under me in such respects as seemed expedient — should you wish it.

4. If you determined on it, some *act* should be done on Thursday coram Episcopo, which would serve for his recognition of it — E.g. if you elected a Superior, and I sat as his guest, before the Bishop. But I throw this out[3]

Ever Yours affectly John H Newman   Congr. Orat.

P.S.   I go round by Wasperton to see poor Dayman, who is simply given over and left by the medical men — so I shall not get to Town early.[4]

[1] Todd came to Alcester Street on 28 Nov. 1850.

[2] The Brief empowering Newman to found the English Oratory was dated 26 Nov. 1847.

[3] Newman drew up a letter addressed to the London Oratorians, from Wiseman, which he was to be asked to sign. In it he gave his sanction to the house the Birmingham Congregation had opened in London, which would be set up as a separate Oratory in virtue of Newman's Brief of 1847. Wiseman signed the letter on 16 Aug. 1850 (see *Appendix* 1, p. 499), and the same day Stanton wrote to Newman, 'We are all much pleased that you drew it up in such a form, as not to make it the final act, and thank you for this consideration.' The separation was made on 9 Oct. 1850.

[4] Alfred Jeken Dayman was the former curate at Wasperton, Warwickshire, whom Newman had received into the Church on 4 Jan. 1850.

WEDNESDAY 14 AUGUST 1850 went to Dayman at Wasperton and so on to
London Garside left

TO W. G. WARD

Oratory, Birmingham Aug. 14/50

My dear Ward,

Thank you very much, in the name of St Philip and his congregation,
for your munificent intention of assisting us — but I assure you, we
shall not reckon on it, or consider you pledged. I understand quite
your feelings, for they are my own; so, if the money comes, we shall be
thankful — if not, we shall be thankful too.[1]

You make me anxious, as you have before, in saying that my
doctrines are not to be found in any theologian.[2] I am not conscious of
it myself, and not at all desirous of it, or willing to believe it. Nor can I
make out what you mean. Is it that theologians have not spoken so
tenderly of heretics (Protestants) as I? If it is any thing else, I have not
ascertained it. And then my notions of faith — I don't at all twig them.[3]
But really you make me anxious. Old Brownson will be coming down
upon me — and finding a thousand and one heresies in my Discourses
and Lectures. Some one showed me that in his last or almost last
number, he had *three* several attacks on my Developments in it.[4] How

[1] W. G. Ward, who had just inherited his family estates, but had heavy expenses
to meet, wrote on 12 Aug., in answer to Newman's appeal for his church in Birmingham, 'I can promise you £50 next year for certain; and most fully intend to give the
same sum for the three following years.'

[2] In the same letter Ward wrote 'I was delighted to hear the news of your doctorate.
How very remarkable altogether the position you are allowed to take up! A number of
things in your lectures are (as far as I know) perfectly unprecedented on the Catholic
side of the controversy, and in spirit are directly *opposed* to the whole old line of
polemics: but I cannot hear of a single Catholic, old or new, who does not unite with
the very loud chorus of praise which has greeted it on every side: a sort of tacit election
of you into the position of controversial leader. And so your "development": after all
the attempts at a row, and the many unguarded expressions in the work etc, no sort,
even of *explanation* called for, and the doctor's degree quietly following. But indeed,
as far as I can see, all the young priests are actually taking up the "development"
theory, and almost as a matter of course.'

[3] Ward added, 'I want, inter alia, to have a talk with you upon what I spoke to you
about once before, various statements of yours on the subject of *faith*: quae mihi
quidem maximè arrident, but for which I can find no sort of precedent or warrant in
treatises. Perhaps ascetic treatises, which I know nothing about, may contain much
more to the point than dogmatic.'

[4] *Brownson's Quarterly Review*, IV (new series), (July 1850). On p. 306 Brownson
wrote, 'We have never pretended that our conversion to Catholicity was a progress or
the result of a progress in our Protestant life. It was a change, and consisted not in
being clothed upon, as Mr. Newman would say, with Catholic truth, but in throwing
off Protestant heresy, and accepting Catholic truth in its place. The only progress we

it would set him up, if I have gone beyond and against the Schools in my Catholic works! He seems to think he has a mission of opposing me; why, I know not.

You must not come in three weeks time — for I suspect we shall be rusticating at St Wilfrid's. Six weeks, which is your alternative, will be better. We shall be very glad to see you; you have long promised to come.

What you say of my material and formal faith, and the Irish, is like the good lady who set down all her acquaintances on the margin of the chapter on vices in the Whole Duty of man. Don't let us quarrel with our neighbours.[1]

What makes me more anxious about my theology is, that I have had such a run of luck — and St Philip may be preparing a rod for me. Kindest remembrances to Mrs Ward.

Ever Yours affectionately in Xt

John H Newman   Congr. Orat.

THURSDAY 15 AUGUST 1850   Philip [Gordon] ordained priest   James [Rowe] and Edward [Bagshawe] subdeacons   John [Bowden] and Raphael [Balston] ministers   Bowyer, just converted, at breakfast

TO AUGUSTINE THEINER

[15 August 1850][2]

Accipias precor, Pater charissime, per manus Reverendissimi Dni Wiseman, Vicarii Apostolici Londinensis, literas hasce, ut signa quibus

lay claim to is a progress, by the grace of God, not *in* Protestantism, but out of it.' Then, in a review of J. M. Capes's *Four Years' Experience of the Catholic Religion*, Brownson, on p. 342, accused Capes of holding as to the act of faith 'that probability is sufficient in this case. So Mr. Newman, in his *Essay on Development*, conceded that the infallibility of the Church can be only probably established, and yet contends that we may be infallibly certain of the doctrines we believe on her authority.' Finally, on p. 350, Brownson said of Capes, 'His errors arise from his retaining his Oxford philosophy, from his partiality for Mr. Newman's theory of development, his wish to write in a popular style, and from the low state of Catholic theology in Great Britain. From the latter proceeds his twaddle about conscientious Protestants, and wishy-washiness on the subject of exclusive salvation . . .'

[1] Ward said of the *Lectures on Difficulties of Anglicans*, 'Nothing delighted me so much in your lectures as the distinction (in re schismatical Greeks) between *faith* and *habit*: which put me in mind directly of the poor Irish; who seem to have hardly any idea of a living Church with claims on their allegiance.' On the misuse of the chapter in *The Whole Duty of Man*, see Addison, *The Spectator*, No. 568.

[2] The date is fixed by the letter having been given to Wiseman to deliver in Rome. He left London on 16 Aug.

gratias agere velim, paternitati tuae, propter eruditissima illa et apprimè opportuna opuscula tua quae ad me iampridem misisti.[1] Felix qui tempus habes ad amoenissimum et fructuosissimum historiae ecclesiasticae campum et colendum et peragrandum! Nos in medio populorum tumultu actuosissimorum in summâ missionariorum apostolicorum paucitate terga solummodo et latera contemplamus tacite librorum nostrorum, non aperimus. Felix homo et amplius, qui in ipso civium pravi violentorum furore confugere possis ad propitia templa sanctorum, ad sepulchros et relliquias eorum pontificum qui suo ipsorum sanguine olim locupletam ecclesiam nascentem irrigarunt, etiam nunc non deserunt!

Tu ergo, Pater optime, quando ad sanctissima illa quibus Urbs repleta est, adeas loca praecipue autem cum coram charissimi Patris et Patroni tum tui tum mei, S. Philippi altari astas, nostri aliquando ne sis immemor

FRIDAY 16 AUGUST 1850   returned to Birmingham   called on Dr Wiseman who left England for good in the evening (*at this time I set up the London Oratory, acting with Dr Wiseman*)

TO J. M. CAPES

Oy. Bm. Aug. 17/50

My dear Capes,

Simpson's article is very much improved.[2] I have no fault to find with it, except that in places his sense ought to have been drawn out in some places at greater length — so that, as composition, it is at certain places crude or raw. By the bye, p 199 'to show no *great respect* to the Scriptures,' is a bold expression.[3]

I think you had better *omit* the Oratorium Parvum this month. Faber's 3 Lectures[4] are making a disturbance, and people may say they have heard enough of St Philip

[1] In May Fr Theiner, the Roman Oratorian, sent to Newman his *Lettere storico-critiche intorno alle Cinque Piaghe della Santa Chiesa del chiarissimo sacerdote D. Antonio Rosmini-Serbati*, Napoli 1849, his *Storia del ritorno alla Chiesa Cattolica di varie case regnante e principesche della Germania nel secolo XVII e XVIII*, Napoli 1850 and his *Der Cardinal Johann Heinrich, Graf von Frankenberg*, Freiburg im Breisgau 1850. Theiner wrote Newman's name in each volume.

[2] 'Religion and Modern Philosophy,' in the *Rambler* (Sept. 1850), pp. 185–204. Simpson discussed the Mosaic account of creation in relation to scientific discovery. A letter from Capes of 16 July shows that Newman had made criticisms of the draft of this article a few days earlier.   [3] This was altered before publication.

[4] *The Spirit and Genius of St. Philip Neri*. See letter of 2 Aug. to Dalgairns.

By good luck, having a long time fancied I had lost Palmer's pamphlet I have lately found it — and will send it you with any thing I have to say on the *other* articles, if any thing.[1]

Thank you much for your Bible history — I had not heard of it

Ever Yours affectly John H Newman   Congr. Orat.

SUNDAY 18 AUGUST 1850   preached in morning at St Peter's on the re-opening of the Church[2]

MONDAY 19 AUGUST   Mrs Allies went

TO WILLIAM GOWAN TODD

Oratory. Birmingham August 20. 1850

My dear Sir,[3]

Your letter dated the 16th came to me yesterday. — As to your further questions,

1. Certainly, 'such Roman practices as the worship of the BVM [Blessed Virgin Mary] are *not* contained in the letter of Holy Scripture.' Your objection which follows, goes on the assumption that Scripture is the whole Rule of faith — you say 'it is more probable that your intellectual conviction should be mistaken, than that such practices are in accordance with the letter *and spirit* of Holy Scripture.' Also, on the assumption that you, or the Protestant *body*, are judges of the letter and *spirit* — It is an act of private judgment, not an admitted *fact*. You say, 'Since *all* admit such practices are not in the *letter, therefore* we may safely affirm that they are not in letter *or spirit*.' I suppose you admit the notion of a *Sacrifice* (continual) under the Gospel. Now is not such an ordinance as much opposed to both letter and spirit of new Testament, as the doctrines concerning our Lady? Might not a common Protestant re-echo your words, and say 'It is much more probable that the early church should have gone wrong, than such a rite as the Eucharistic Sacrifice be really in accordance with the letter and spirit of Holy Scripture.' I doubt whether the Divinity of the Holy Ghost is not

[1] Capes wanted materials for his review of *Lectures on Certain Difficulties felt by Anglicans*, 'Rise, Progress, and Results of Puseyism,' the first part of which appeared in the *Rambler* (Dec. 1850), pp. 506–44. Palmer's pamphlet was evidently *Letters to N. Wiseman, D.D., calling himself Bishop of Melipotamus*, Oxford 1841, mentioned p. 514. It was reprinted the following year as *Letters to N. Wiseman, D.D., on the Errors of Romanism*.

[2] 'On External Religion,' *S.N.* pp. 47–9 (wrongly dated there 18 Oct.).

[3] The diary again confirms that this letter was addressed to 'Mr Todd.'

in *the same sense* opposed to the letter and spirit of Scripture. And the 'spirit' as well as 'letter' of such passages as 'Why callest thou Me good?' 'not the Son, but the Father,'[1] are against the divinity of the Son, in the same sense.

2. Nothing is clearer than that a *habit* of critical inquiry is wrong. I suspect it leads to infidelity, not to Catholicism; but what has this to do with the process by which a soul is led from falsehood to truth? Is *every* one born in a true system? is it not undeniable that, if there *be* a truth, the majority of men *have* to change? *Can* they change without doubt and inquiry? Do you think that those who have become Catholics, have done so to their own *gratification*? Was truth forced on them, or a change passionately and greedily sought for? When I say that 'never to be troubled with a doubt about the truth of what has been taught us is the happiest state of mind,' I mean *of course* happiest *in itself* — *but those who are in error* CANNOT *have it.* If I said that to be surrounded by every sort of good for soul and body is the happiness of man, I should not therefore mean, that it was at once possible — or that it was not ultimately attainable by *certain means*, or in a *certain way.* Dr Pusey's state of mind is not necessarily the happiest *in him*, because it is happiest *in itself.* No one can deny that doubt is an imperfect state of mind — yet no one can deny that it is often a duty. Pain is a duty — we get to heaven by suffering. It would not do for a soldier, when the enemy is on his lines, to go to bed, and say 'I say then that never to have any sorrow, or distress, or annoyance, never to have had a wound, never to have inflicted one, is the happiness of men;' yet he would be enunciating a great truth.

3. I agree with you that grace is received in schismatical portions of the Church (I am not allowing here that the English Establishment *is* a portion of the Church, i.e. *has* the Sacraments,) by those who are in involuntary ignorance; but directly a person begins to doubt, he is bound to pursue his doubt. *An Anglican has no excuse for not pursuing his doubt.* His Church *bids* him inquire. I wish you to bring passages from the formularies or the divines of your Church bidding you exercise that absolute submission of reason which the Catholic Church injoins. On the contrary the article expressly says that every particular Church has erred, (I forget the wording.) —[2] In trying the truth of your Church, you are but obeying her invitation. And the one idea of religious dutifulness in the Anglican Church, *is inquiry*, and rules are continually given

---

[1] St Mark 10 : 18, 14 : 32.

[2] Article XIX: 'As the Church of *Jerusalem, Alexandria*, and *Antioch*, have erred; so also the Church of *Rome* hath erred, not only in their living and manner of Ceremonies, but also in matters of Faith.'

in religious books *how* we ought to conduct it. What *warrant* then have you to quench doubt? nature does not teach it — nor your Church — *who?* the private decision of this man or that, whom you have taken for your guide.

As to the injury you will do by changing to the souls of others, there is responsibility on *every side* of you — you cannot speak or move without responsibility. *Supposing* you are out of the Catholic Church, and God is calling you by means of doubts *into* it; will your responsibility be small that you have kept yourself and others from it?

4. The tests of certainty, and that we are not in a delusion, form a larger subject than I can enter upon here. One test is the *continuance* of the idea upon the mind as true — another is its growth — a third is its being received by others — and by others in the same, or again in different circumstances — or in both — your own state of mind, whether excited or not, etc. Again, the consequences of *denying* its certainty — e.g. to my mind religion and catholicism have long been so bound together, that to deny catholicism is *logically* to deny religion — the same arguments, position, etc etc being common to both.

Certainly, I think that those who have witnessed the conversions of the last 5 years, and who now stand *where they* stood, need in *God's sight* very little for this conviction. I mean, I should feel a great anxiety, were they to die unconverted.

With my best prayers that you will soon find your way out of your present position, I am, My dear Sir, Very truly Yours

John H Newman

WEDNESDAY 21 AUGUST 1850   Miss Monro came

TO MRS J. W. BOWDEN

Oratory. Bm. August 21/50

My dear Mrs Bowden,

I fancied you would stop over the 15th in London, and so did not write to thank you for your most munificent and unexpected aid to our Church. The working plans of our House are in progress, but, alas, the season is in progress too. Thank you too very much for the vestment which you expect from Naples.

Poor Charles's eye was a great disappointment. It got bad *for* the day — for the very next day it got better. What a big boy he grows. In his cassock he almost looks a man.

I am thankful for the Pope's late favor, for I think it may tend to dissipate expectations and suspicions about me which people *will* cling to. Do you know I find that *still*, i.e. as late as last Christmas, my dear sister solemnly assured a lady who told me, that I should return to the Anglican Church. She said she knew me well, better than any one else — and she got quite agitated when my informant did not at once acquiesce. I sometimes fancy that she has made her husband promise not to speak to me for seven years (or a fixed term) and that she was sure, and is bent on my return before that time. But the whole matter is incomprehensible to me.

My books, I am glad to say, continue selling. We are expecting two or three clerical conversions, but it does not do to talk before hand

Ever Yours affectionately John H Newman   Congr. Orat.

TO F. W. FABER

Oratory. August 21/50

My dear F Wilfrid,

The three thin paper (Tracts) you can get in London.[1] If you cannot, I can give you copies, (i.e. with Printer's note in writing upon them). I can give you Number 90, Jelf, and Bagot.[2] Whether I can give Suffragan Bishops,[3] I can't tell till I get to St W's [Wilfrid's]; but I doubt whether it is out of print. Plain sermons volume 5, I *think* is the Number.[4] I have no copy here. But it is at St W's, and by looking into it you will see; e.g., there is a Sermon on 'Calls' — another on Fame and Glory, St Simon and St Jude — another on the Sundays in Epiphany etc.

As to poor Jack [Morris], I don't think he is different.[5] Four years ago at Mary vale he wished everyone to wait on him, and they did. I doubt not Lady H's people have been put to it on the same account. And now he can find no one such at Prior Park — but he will settle down.

I can give you several volumes of Sermons — and perhaps Prophetical Office and Justification, if you have not paid Stewart — but any how I suppose he would give you what you gave him for them.

I think you had better be setting down *what* you wish to propose to me, as connecting me with you after the separation. Then I, as having

[1] Faber was collecting Newman's pamphlets, in order to present them to Wiseman. Cf. letter of 13 Oct. to Stanton. The three tracts were *Introduction of Rationalistic Principles into Religion (Ess. 1), The Patristical Idea of Antichrist (D.A.)* and *Holy Scripture in its Relation to the Catholic Creed (D.A.).*

[2] i.e. *Letter to Dr Jelf,* and *Letter to the Bishop of Oxford (V.M. 11).*

[3] *The Restoration of Suffragan Bishops (V.M. 11).*

[4] *Plain Sermons,* volume v was by Newman, now *P.S.* VII and VIII.

[5] Faber enclosed a letter from J. B. Morris, who had gone to Prior Park.

no bond of obedience to you, shall be *able* without delicacy to speak out and say what I like in it and what I don't — and if I want any thing added

Ever Yours affectionately, John H Newman   Congr. Orat.

PS   F. Bernard brings a very poor account of you.
The Revd F. Wilfrid.

THURSDAY 22 AUGUST 1850 Dr Ullathorne admitted me into the doctorate, *which had been sent me from Rome*, and supped with us

TO T. W. ALLIES

Oratory, Birmingham Aug. 22. 1850.

My dear Allies,

I write a line to acknowledge your kind letter. It is a great joy to me that your time of waiting is drawing to a close.

Will you give the enclosed to your wife. It is from Fr St John, and she will be clever if she makes it out. Also, please tell her, that I consider I may sanction her in continuing to use Cosin's Prayer Book, supposing she finds it specially suits her.[1] However, she must put in the Hail Mary, the *Fidelium Animae*, and any other Catholic form that is wanting, and must look sharp that there is no Anglicanism in the prayers. And I do not give her permission for good and all, but *durante beneplacito*.

Say every thing kind and Catholic from me to her and believe me

Yours affectionately John H. Newman   Congr. Orat.

FRIDAY 23 AUGUST 1850 W Clifford called in his way thro to Bristol to be ordained.   French Jesuit to dinner[2]

TO J. M. CAPES

Oy Bm Aug 23/50

My dear Capes,

F Vincent[3] has not made his appearance — so your letter to him lies on my mantlepiece.

---

[1] John Cosin's *Collection of Private Devotions*, 1627, was compiled for the English maids of honour of Queen Henrietta Maria. Mrs Allies had been a Catholic for three months and her husband was about to follow her.

[2] Fortunat de Montézon, S.J. See letter of 10 March 1851 to him.

[3] Vincent Grotti the Passionist.

You cannot of course do any thing in the way of an account of the Oxford movement without going to Froude's Remains — We cannot lend you (by our Rule) the Library copy — but I suspect I should find another copy in the house.

The verses you speak of 'Lead thou etc' were written on Sunday June 16. 1833 on the deck of a Sicilian sailing vessel, when I was becalmed in the sun off Sardinia for a week, on my way from Palermo to Marseilles.[1]

The British Critic became the organ of the movement in the middle of 1838 — the number has (I think) articles on Ingram's Oxford and Exeter Hall.

Don't return the Palmer till you have done with it. You do not bore me with any questions you want answered[2]

Ever Yours affectly J H N

TO F. W. FABER

Aug 23/50

My dear F Wilfrid,

I am very much concerned at your ailments — it is my comfort to think they are only your trial, and not our loss — for you do as much as if you were well.[3]

As to the Pamphlets, I can't tell till I rummage about at St W's [Wilfrid's], what I can give you. But I should like you to try to get them in London — If the price asked is above the original price (and I don't suggest it would be for Suffragans and Catholicus *if* they can be got *at all*) I won't offer them you, supposing I have them — but if the price is raised, then I will.[4] Or what comes to the same thing, if you find you have the refusal of them through Stewart, I will take the opportunity of buying them for myself, and you shall have my (cleaner) copies. I ought to have more copies of my books. Any how I can give you Number 90, which I *know* is dear — so you need not inquire of Stewart for it

Ever Yrs affly J H N

[1] Cf. *Apo.* p. 35.

[2] See note to letter of 17 Aug. to Capes. *The British Critic* (July 1838), pp. 133–46, contained Newman's review of James Ingram's *Memorials of Oxford*, H.S. III, pp. 315–35, and a review of *Random Recollections of Exeter Hall*, pp. 190–211, also by Newman.

[3] Faber wrote this same morning from St Wilfrid's, 'I have been more off work this summer than I ever was. In London I could get no air—at St Edmund's the damp brought on rheumatism—at Lancing my leg was bad—here my bowels . . .'

[4] See letter of 21 Aug. Catholicus is *The Tamworth Reading Room*, now in *D.A.*

TO WILLIAM MASKELL

Oy. Bm Aug 23/50

My dear Maskell,

Mr Bagshaw is a (I think) Barrister in London, and editor of the Dublin. You can easily guard yourself from being supposed to be engaged to write for good.

As to a new review, it depends on so many conditions, that I fear the idea is not likely to be fulfilled speedily. You must get your staff of writers, and an Editor who is at any time able to write half a Number at a sitting, and funds sufficient to stand the necessary loss of the concern for a dozen years.

I am not saying this to discourage the notion far from it — but that we may see the difficulties fairly and consider how to meet them. In addition, we must take care not to be disrespectful to the Dublin, or to diminish the prospects of the Rambler, which has done much good and is likely to do more. There is nothing like agitating a matter, and turning men's thoughts to it — so the sooner it is talked about, the better.

You are right in supposing the Pope has made me a doctor in divinity.

All grace and blessing be with you, and[1]

SATURDAY 24 AUGUST 1850   Miss Monro went   MRG [Giberne] came.
MONDAY 26 AUGUST   Weld called

TO ANTONY HUTCHISON

Oratory Bm August 26/50

My dear F Antony,

You or some one has told me that Lord S. [Shrewsbury] is going abroad next month for two years.[2] No time is to be lost, if he is to come to some decision about St W's [Wilfrid's]. *How* shall I write to him? Actually *proposing* Lambert as our man? You had better get ready your statement.

I asked F Alban for the statement of our debt to him, which we have never had — when it dates from etc. By the bye, I suppose it is but one of various charges you or he or others has upon us; will you let us have them all? On the other hand, Dr Grant has been sending in his

---

[1] The rest of the letter is missing.   [2] Faber wrote this news on 23 Aug.

account — and I find that F Ambrose advanced him for congregation letters etc £10 some two years ago — which the said Father claims — and which I suppose the two houses must share between them. Also some of you had better get from Stewart or Burns the remains of the £20 for St W's advertisements etc which I sent and which I will restore to the St W's fund.

Mrs Cosham, whose name you may know, called here to-day, begging me to get F Wilfrid to get her a housekeeper's place at Lord Arundel's place in the North or elsewhere. I said I would write, but that I had no interest whatever. I believe her case is a very pitiable one — her husband has *beaten* her for being converted — and beat the children too.

Ever Yours affectly John H Newman Congr. Orat.

TUESDAY 27 AUGUST 1850 F Ignatius [Spencer] came

WEDNESDAY 28 AUGUST F Ignatius went Burns and Lambert here for several days. Bathurst came Ryder came

TO J. M. CAPES

Oratory. Bm August 28/50

My dear Capes,

1. Were I at St Wilfrid's, I could give you the exact date of the day — but I must go by memory here. I was inducted then to St Mary's in the beginning or middle of March 1828.[1]

2. Ditto, if I were at St W's. Here I must answer from memory. The following is *tolerably* correct.

Vol. 1 Sermon 1. 1825   9. 1833   18. 1831
           2. 1833   10. 1831⎫   19. 1830.?
           3. 1830? 11. 1831⎪   20. 1830.?
           4. 1824   12. 1831⎬ or   21. 1831 or 32?
           5. 1832? 13. 1831⎪1830 22 1830–32?
           6. 1831, 2 14. 1831⎭   23 1830–32?
           7. 1831, 2 15. 1830?   24. 1832
           8 1833   16. 1830?   25. 1831
                     17. 1831   26. 1832?

I should add that a few of my *earliest* sermons are among the Plain Sermons.[2]

[1] Actually 20 March.
[2] The dates when the sermons were first preached are to be found in *S.D.* pp. 411–24.

3. The Surplice Row was in 1844 towards the end. It was the occasion old Walter took of ratting round in the Times.[1]

4. Catholicus appeared in the Times in February 1841. Old Walter called on me at Oriel, and pressed me several times to write against Peel's Address, before I consented. It was just when the Times took us up, and just as the publication of Number 90 (the *same month*) took us down. It was a false step in the Times — had it waited a month, it would not have made it.

5. I took no interest in the Guardian, and can't recollect. It was when I was steadily looking towards Rome. I should say in 1844.[2]

6. I took the place at Littlemore in July 1841, put it to rights in the autumn — it made a talk all thro' the October Term. I went up there the following Lent. I had already been two Lents (1840, 41) there. I think I heard of little Jenks and big Ben, going to see the progress of the Building.[3]

7. Hampden, I believe, was made Bishop in the Winter of 1847–8, just as I returned from Rome.

8. The contest for the Poetry Professorship, I think, was the winter of 1841–2, the year after Number 90.

Ever Yrs affly J H N.

TO RICHARD STANTON

Oratory Bm August 28/50

My dear F Richard,

I will take time to think over F Wilfrid's points.[4]

My mind sadly misgives me, I have never paid you for the carriage of pictures etc. I have your letters, and will try to make out what it is. Also, I owe you for the inkstand which went to the good Padre Preposito at Naples. Tell me what it came to.[5] Is there any thing else, I owe you, or any other of you?

---

[1] In Jan. 1841, John Walter II of *The Times*, 'old Walter,' urged on by his son, John Walter III, persuaded Newman to write for him the letters by 'Catholicus,' *The Tamworth Reading Room*, attacking Peel's utilitarianism. Until then suspicious of the Tractarians, John Walter II began to look on them more favourably. He seized the opportunity of the Surplice Riots at Exeter in 1844 to revert to his attitude of opposition. [2] The *Guardian* was founded in 1846.

[3] i.e. Richard Jenkyns, Master of Balliol, and Benjamin Symons, Warden of Wadham College. Cf. *Apo.* p. 172.

[4] These were suggestions, drawn up by Faber, as to the powers over itself which the London Oratory should confer on Newman, to take effect when that house was separated from Birmingham. See letter of 19 Sept. to Faber, and note there.

[5] See letter of 23 Nov. 1849 to Faber.

Also, I do not forget about the Rescripts etc Give me time, and I will give you all.[1]

How is F Wilfrid? he is at Lancing, is he not?

Will you ask Rowe, i.e. Father James (I beg his pardon, and he a subdeacon) to take the inclosed to Dolman, and pay for me the sum 4/6 *on his delivering* the Bonetty?[2]

Ever Yrs affly J H N

P.S.   I am getting ready the Rescripts etc. Please, send me the one you have — I think it is about St Wilfrid's.

THURSDAY 29 AUGUST 1850   Bathurst received   F Sebastian [Hanmer] came
FRIDAY 30 AUGUST   Ryder went

TO F. W. FABER

Aug 30 [1850]

My dear F Wilfrid,

My reason for sending you this is this:— have we ever refused a Bishop?[3] *I* have — but he does not ask for me. I can easily (I am sorry to say) assign your health, should you think it better to negative it on principle — or else I could suggest to him F Bernard

You will see by the date that I must be as quick as possible in my answer

Ever Yrs affly J H N

SATURDAY 31 AUGUST 1850   F. Sebastian went (*Hanmer*)

TO F. W. FABER

Sept 1/50

My dear F Wilfrid,

I think there are several reasons for your accepting Dr Brigg's invitation.

[1] Stanton was collecting the Roman Rescripts, giving various spiritual privileges to the English Oratory.

[2] The only work connected with Augustin Bonnetty still to be found among Newman's books is *Annales de philosophie chrétienne* for 1844 and 1845.

[3] Dr Briggs, the Yorkshire Vicar Apostolic, asked that Faber should preach on the occasion of the opening of the church of St Marie at Sheffield, on 15 Sept.

1. He *may* be your Bishop, and it would be well for you to have an opportunity of getting on with him.

2. You may rub off some of the misconceptions to which your Triduo has given rise.[1]

You had better write a line to the good Bishop — homageful, asking particulars etc, I have already written to him to say you *will* go, and told him about your health, and asked for money for expences.

Ever Yrs affectly J H N.

P.S. This is the anniversary of my putting on Dr Morris' mitre at Cheadle.[2]

P.S. I see two Bishops are advertised for the Sermons — but write to Dr Briggs nevertheless.[3]

MONDAY 2 SEPTEMBER 1850 Bishop *Allemani* of California called[4]

TO THE EARL OF SHREWSBURY

Oratory Birmingham Sept. 2. 1850

My dear Lord,

As the Bishop prefers not to take part in the arbitration in the first instance, I suppose it will be best to name the two arbitrators as soon as possible. If they agree together, there will be no need of going to the Bishop at all.

We wish then to propose Mr Lambert of Salisbury as one of them; but, before writing to him, I mention his name to your Lordship. Perhaps you will kindly name the other at once.

I am, My dear Lord, Your Lordship's faithful Servant,

John H Newman Congr. Orat.

---

[1] See letter of 2 Aug. to Dalgairns.

[2] This seems to be the only reference to an incident at the consecration of Cheadle church in 1846. Dr Morris was the retired Vicar Apostolic of Mauritius.

[3] Faber was to preach on the Sunday following the opening of the church at Sheffield.

[4] Joseph Alemany had just been consecrated in Rome as Bishop of Monterey, and was collecting priests for his missionary diocese.

TUESDAY 3 SEPTEMBER 1850   paid into Bank Mr Murphy's £50   Mrs Gordon and daughter 12.   Countess de la Pasture 5.

TO F. W. FABER

Oy Bm Sept 3/50

My dear F W

I heard of your Sunday from the Bishop of California who described the rush.

F. Ambrose wishes some notice like the following sent to 'The Lady's Magazine and Family Herald.'[1] 'F St John acknowledges the polite permission of the Editor to reply to his criticisms on his Sermon, but he regrets he is unable to avail himself of it, as he is engaged to exhibit of [on] the tight rope at Vauxhall for every evening in the ensuing week.'

I prefer an ante-Christmas Day,[2] 1. because it is the anniversary of the Brief. 2 because it is well to begin the year *with* the year, as we have already found, as regards the accounts, which we have been obliged to put back a month. 3. Because *then* the Immaculate Conception inaugurates it.

I congratulate you on your new house.[3] Can't you get a few feet of promenade between them

Ever Yrs affly J H N

Goodbye   we are all going to California.

TO R. A. COFFIN

Oy. Bm Sept 4/50

My dear Father Rector,

I have had a letter from Lord S. [Shrewsbury] this morning, fixing the arbitration for some day before the 16th. Mr A Phillipps is his arbitrator, and Mr Lambert (I believe) ours. They will meet at the

---

[1] Faber, on 2 Sept., enclosed from this periodical an attack on a sermon St John had preached in London the previous May. The Editor said he was ready to insert St John's reply in his columns.

[2] For electing the officers of the London Oratory.

[3] Faber had rented a house with ten rooms, adjoining the chapel in King William Street.

Towers for the purpose. Thus the matter will be speedily brought to a conclusion, *if* they agree. Else, it goes to the Bishop. Should they decide that we must keep a community there, (tho' I am not sure that point will come into discussion) we *can't do it* — even keeping a mission there will be a great difficulty. I wish to bring every thing to a speedy arrangement. It is now finally proved that St W's [Wilfrid's] is no use to the Oratory as such — which was the only ground for keeping it.

Whether the Passionists will take it, is doubtful. The new Church at Aston Hall, that tumble-down place, is the difficulty.

I took it for granted that the day of the Solemn Black Mass was the dies obitûs, which this year is the 16th.[1] We think of sending over a lot of persons for that day; though I don't see how we can without sacrificing our Sunday. If so, we shall put it off to the 17th Tuesday. I thought she died on the 15th. If it is on the 14th, we may have the Mass then, and our people might get back in time to Birmingham for the Sunday.

I come on Saturday and will gladly talk about Mr Scholefield.[2]

You know they have succeeded in London in getting an additional house — which gives plenty of room for all.

Mr Kenny[3] of course will be an acceptable guest.

Poor Mrs Wootten has a bad face — Miss Giberne has been here, and is gone on some visits.

Caswall wishes the inscription to lie over till the fate of St W's is settled.

If the weather were settled, I should bring F Thomas [Scratton] with me on Saturday *and perhaps Bathurst*; but the poor old man fears the climate of St W's.

There is talk of F Stanislas going to Liverpool, to see on what terms the Bishop of California will ordain him.[4]

Au revoir — it seems a long time since I saw you.

Ever Yours affectly John H Newman   Congr. Orat.

P.S.   Will you give the Baron the inclosed note, and (as I believe) *bill*.

---

[1] This refers to the annual Requiem Mass for Mrs Caswall.

[2] Schofield wanted to discuss plans, being unwilling to spend the winter at St Wilfrid's.

[3] It was he who had just let the house to the London Oratory, where he was choir-master.

[4] Bishop Alemany came from Vich in Spain, where there was an Oratory. He proposed that it should make a foundation in California. Newman had thoughts of sending English Oratorians to help temporarily, and Stanislas Flanagan might have been ordained with that in view. See note to diary for 6 Sept.

TO F. W. FABER

Oy. Bm. Sept 4/50

My dear F Wilfrid,

I suppose there is no *need* of you being so long as from Wednesday to Sunday at York, unless you think it is a good thing as regards Dr Briggs. It may be so — there is of course a considerable *chance* of his being your Bishop — and yet I can't think he will either. You would easily get him to like you, but I don't know him enough, to know if it would last.

As to Sebastian, your letter has of course superseded longer deliberation on my part. I dare say I should have come to the same conclusion, as you — indeed I do not doubt it — but I had resolved, before entering into the consideration, to have advised him to lay the matter before you frankly; and it is only an accident the letter to him has not gone.[1]

As to Thomas, I am very sorry that Sebastian chattered to him, ⟨(*Sebastian began.*)⟩ and he to Sebastian.[2] The whole affair shows, what I have long felt keenly, that the two houses should see a great deal of each other, or nothing at all.

Whether we should feel it possible to take Sebastian, since you all feel you had better be without him, I really cannot say. I don't like the thought of a man putting off the habit, if it can be avoided. I will have a consultation with others here, and see whether we can go so far as this, viz to ask him on a visit here.

As to what you say about Edward, I don't understand your account of it — why should your novices be disturbed because we recreate in the evening with the Brothers? I mean, it is nothing to *them*.[3]

---

[1] Sebastian, A. J. Hanmer, a novice at London, was behaving oddly and was worried about his health. The London Oratorians wanted him to go, as Faber wrote on 3 Sept. Faber wondered if he could join the Birmingham house, wishing the matter decided soon, before other novices were unsettled by him.

[2] Faber also wrote that Hanmer 'spoke rather bitterly of the want of cheerfulness and of the strict rule here, on which it appeared Scratton [Thomas Scratton, a novice at Birmingham] had commented to him in a way I should not have thought right; but Sebastian may have understood him in his own sense . . . he frets because he thinks the work you give your novices in catechising etc, and the absence of all "rule or system", as Scratton tells him, would enable him to be happy even in an Oratorian vocation. . . .'

[3] Scratton had praised to Hanmer the Birmingham custom of priests and lay brothers taking recreation together. Hanmer had recounted this fact to his fellow novice Edward Bagshawe, and others. 'Here is already a mischief come,' wrote Faber, 'some of the novices here have been a little disturbed.' To what Newman here says Faber replied on 5 Sept., 'How slow you are, my dear Padre! When ever do novices attend to nothing but their own business? Don't you see you and yours are the models; what *you* HAVE and *we* HAVEN'T is a mark against *us*. . . .'

We are thinking whether the Bishop of California would not ordain Stanislas for a year's service in the diggings.

Ever Yours affectly John H Newman   Cong. Orat.

P.S.   Bathurst is very glad of your congratulations[1]

TO ANTONY HUTCHISON

[4 September 1850]

My dear F. Antony,

You see by Lord S's [Shrewsbury] choice, that an arbitration by means of two arbitrators is impossible[2] And it will go the Bishop.

We must promise Mr Lambert really to be our *counsel*. I thought of writing to him by this post, but on second thoughts, since Lord S's choice seems extraordinary, I will not do so without your opinion. If you think nothing better can be done, write to Mr Lambert in my name by the first post. His going to the Towers, is it dangerous? it is so hard to resist that sort of influence; I think he had better be our guest at St W's and *I* shall be there. I suppose from what the Earl says, you or F Wilfrid ought to be on the spot.

Ever Yours affectly John H Newman   Congr. Orat.

P.S.   Would it be well to get the Bishop to *name* a third arbitrator instead of himself — to join the two arbitrators at the Towers; else nothing will be done. If you think so, write to me at once.

F Caswall says that, if *any one* could get over A. Phillipps, it would be Mr Lambert. He speaks of him as a most shrewd man.

TO F. W. FABER

Oy. Bm. Sept 5/50

My dear F Wilfrid,

Sebastian, in the theory, is a member of the Bm [Birmingham] Congregation. If the London does not suit him, he falls back here. Whether he will suit us, or we him is another question.

---

[1] On his becoming a Catholic.

[2] After Newman had proposed John Lambert as one arbitrator, Lord Shrewsbury on 3 Sept. named his close friend, Ambrose Lisle Phillipps, as the other. Hutchison shared Newman's view that the arbitrators should be more or less independent lawyers, and wrote on 5 Sept., 'As the Earl . . . does not stick at having a personal friend no more need we and I dont see why we may not withdraw Lambert and put in *Lewis*. . . . Phillipps adores the Earl and anything but adores us.'

Let him come here then, or to me at St W's [Wilfrid's] (whither I go on Saturday) as soon as he will — except that he must not take F. Rector of St W's by surprise, I suppose.[1]

The Passionists and Mr L [Leigh] are not at one, but that does not hinder our treating with the Redemptorists. I will write to F Ignatius before anything comes of it.[2]

I will write soon about the propositions you sent to FF B [Bernard Dalgairns] and R. [Richard Stanton][3]

Ever Yrs affly J H N

FRIDAY 6 SEPTEMBER 1850 Stanislas went to Liverpool to see Bishop of California[4]

[1] Hanmer was not well enough to come, and his doctor, as Faber wrote on 18 Sept., 'would not hear of his trying Birmingham,' saying 'the climate at B would do for him.'

[2] The Passionists were in disagreement with Mr Leigh, who had built them a church at Woodchester, and were to leave the place in a month. It was thus worth while approaching them through the Passionist, Ignatius Spencer, to see if they would take over St Wilfrid's. The Redemptorists were also beginning to show interest in the place, but cried off, and at the end of the year the Passionists went there.

[3] See letter of 19 Sept. to Faber.

[4] Flanagan took with him Newman's instructions:

'Memorandum for F Stanislas   Sept 6. 1850.

Our position is this—we are not sufficiently formed to profess to found a foreign Oratory, nor numerous enough to give subjects to one—the utmost we could contemplate would be lending subjects for a fixed time to an existing body, and that with the object of teaching them English, and preaching in their place till they were able. Hence

1. we could not *move* in the matter, but must wait till the Spanish Fathers come to England in their way to America.

2 we could not lend subjects, for more than *two years* from the time they left England.

3. We think there should be at least three Spanish fathers—and, if possible, they should bring with them a lay brother.

4. we ought to do *Oratory work* only, not mere missionary—i.e., we should be stationed in a large town, and not have charge of a mission or Parish.

5. we should wish to send one or two fathers (not necessarily priests), and a lay brother.

6. we suppose the Spanish Fathers would have something of their own.

7. we would meet what they brought with as much as we could give.

8. the passage of our Fathers to be paid there *and back.*

9. we understand that F Flanagan is to receive the priesthood from the Bishop—if so, what will his title be? it must be *patrimonii.*

10. Is Mgr Alemany co-adjutor or independent of higher local authority? if the former, how can he promise for his superior?

11 We are anxious about the climate.

12. Who is to determine the *place* of residence? e.g. the Spanish Fathers might like a

TO J. M. CAPES

Oy Bm Sept 6/50

My dear Capes

I suppose you see old Brownson's criticisms on you. I have found the inclosed in a Newspaper.[1] He will not let any one be right but himself, and till he comes down from his high throne and acknowledges himself, not a Pope who can exhibit Damnatae Theses, but a layman and a sinner, he is not to be acknowledged in any sense by others — So I think.

Suspend the Oratorium Parvum for October *also*   I go to St W's [Wilfrid's] for a fortnight tomorrow

Ever Yrs affly J H N

P.S.   As F Vincent never came, I have taken the liberty to open and inclose your letter to him.

TO ANTONY HUTCHISON

Oy Bm Sept 6/50

My dear F Antony

I have written to Lord S. [Shrewsbury] to propose Lewis — so write to him at once to *prepare* him

Ever Yrs affly J H N

Let me have Lord S's letter back.

small Spanish town like Monterey, while the English felt that they ought to settle in a larger English one.
13. What is the direction of the Spanish Fathers at present, that we may correspond with them?
14. will the Bishop write to me as soon as he can, to tell us his prospects, acting as a pioneer?
15 how can money can [sic] be got to California, and is it safe to send it?'
Nothing came of these plans. See letter of 19 Nov. to the Superior of the Oratory at Vich, from which the Spanish Oratorians were to have come.
   [1] This must have contained extracts from *Brownson's Quarterly Review*, IV (new series), (July 1850), pp. 330–53, concerning Capes's *Four Years' Experience of the Catholic Religion*. Brownson complained that 'Our Oxford converts . . . write on as they were accustomed to write before their conversion, in very good English, it is true, but with a choice of terms which leaves us perpetually in doubt whether their thought is sound or heretical,' and that 'Moderation towards heretics avails nothing to win them, and is usually a wrong to our Catholic friends,' pp. 332, 334. See also letter of 14 Aug. to W. G. Ward.

TO THE EARL OF SHREWSBURY

Oratory, Birmingham, Sept. 6. 1850

My dear Lord,

I have thought over the letter with which you have kindly favoured me;[1] since your Lordship proposes Mr Phillipps for your arbitrator, [I] think it best to offer you Mr Lewis for ours.

I go to St Wilfrid's to-morrow — and will write to Mr Lewis at once, if I do not hear from your Lordship to the contrary.

I am, My dear Lord, Your faithful Servant,

John H. Newman   Congr Orat.

TO RICHARD STANTON

Oy Bm Sept 6/50

My dear F R

Dr Fergusson of Fulham writes me word distinctly that he had never got his Prop. [Propaganda] faculties countersigned — and he thinks it a simple encroachment of the Bishop's.[2]

Dr Nicholson writes me word, 'The Holy See always expressly adds, "de Ordinarii consensu," or words to that effect, when it desires to have the sanction of the Ordinary.'

I have found the inclosed and send it. Say something civil to Mr Mobb

Ever Yrs affly J H N

Tell F Wilfrid I will write to Mgr Briggs that F Wd will make his appearance at Fulford House, York on Saturday the 14th.

Ask F Antony to send me back Lord S's [Shrewsbury] letter

[1] See note to letter of 4 Sept. to Hutchison.
[2] Ullathorne was claiming that as Vicar Apostolic he should countersign privileges granted to the English Oratorians by the Congregation of Propaganda. Thomas Tierney Fergusson had been at Propaganda; Dr Nicholson was coadjutor to the Archbishop of Corfù, and had been long connected with Propaganda.

SATURDAY 7 SEPTEMBER 1850   went to St W's *Wilfrid's*

TO ANTONY HUTCHISON (I)

St W's Sept 8/50

My dear F Antony

I suppose I shall see the Earl this afternoon — but too late for the Post. However I inclose his note. It seems as if he would rather withdraw A. Phillipps than take Lewis.[1]

They say that Fr Buggenoms, the Redemptorist acting man, is a very bad man of business — and we shall certainly get into a scrape with him, if we do not look very sharp. Don't mention this, except to F Wilfrid. Try to get an immediate answer from the Redemptorists — for we must be looking out for our secular priest else, if we are to have one.

Ever Yrs affly J H N

TO ANTONY HUTCHISON (II)

St W's Sunday night Sept 8 [1850]

My dear F A

I have had a long talk with Lord S. [Shrewsbury] No — *he* talked for an hour and a half. At length I charged in column, broke his line, and threw him into confusion, by being obliged to tell him that we *could not*, even if he gained his point about the £2300, continue a community here. I said it ate us out, and we had not the money for it.

All this was unpleasant, though I am glad it came out. However, my reason for writing is this — He will not hear of Lucas, and suggests our taking Mr Langdale if we are at a loss for a man — I did not say we were.

I know nothing of Mr Langdale. Is he a suitable man? I would rather he should be the *sole* arbitrator. In that case he would have the *responsibility*. *With* Mr Phillips it would not do — for *neither* would have the responsibility. He was willing to take Mr Langdale instead of Mr Phillips.

[1] Lord Shrewsbury wrote on 7 Sept., 'I cannot imagine why, because I have proposed Mr Phillipps, you desire to substitute Mr Lewis for your own arbitrator Mr Lambert: whilst I am equally at a loss to conceive how you could think of referring any concern of mine to the late sub-Editor of the Tablet.'

Say what you think best — and send me down word *at once*; as Lord S. is eager to get the matter over.[1]

Ever Yrs affly J H N

MONDAY 9 SEPTEMBER 1850   F Mazio came with Mr Maurice[2]

TO F. S. BOWLES

St Wilfrid's Sept 9/50

My dear F Fred.

Tell F Wm [William] *not* to give any order about a collection for the Archbishop — but it would be good thing to know if Mr O'Neil, etc etc give any thing *themselves*.[3]

F Rector here wants some thinnish yellow lights for the Altar, but I believe he will write himself. He says we must not have the organ in the dead mass — if so, the organist must not go, but some more *singers*.

Tell F Joseph that Mr Schofield is ready to negociate about the Boys' home. I have offered him our hospitality, I suppose directly, in Alcester Street After talking the matter over, he wishes to go to Hanley, to make up his mind. He might sleep in my room, if I am away.

I told Lord S. [Shrewsbury] yesterday we could not longer keep a community here — Nothing settled about the arbitration.

Send me the *Tablet* — and the *Spectator* which Capes has lent me to look at.[4]

Ever Yrs affly J H N

F Mazio comes here today.

The Baron says that he has often heard organ in Requiem Masses. We

[1] Hutchison thought the hon. Charles Langdale, one of the leading old Catholics, not 'much of a hand at business,' and 'a very benevolent old gentleman.' Hutchison suggested W. G. Ward instead, and added, 'I am so sorry that you should be put to all this trouble and exposed to the Earl's impudence on my account.'

[2] Giacomo Mazio, the Jesuit Professor at the Gregorian University, whom Newman had met in Rome in 1846, was now an exile, living at St Beuno's, North Wales. Newman put a '?' above 'Maurice' when copying in *Chronological Notes*. He was presumably another Jesuit.

[3] Mr O'Neil was one of the priests at St Chad's, Birmingham. The Archbishop is perhaps the Syrian Archbishop Nakar, who was on a begging tour at this time.

[4] The *Spectator* (31 Aug. 1850), pp. 832–3, contained a long review of *Lectures on Certain Difficulties felt by Anglicans*, which thought the reasoning poor but literary merit high, and admired the delicate controversial skill directed against those Tractarians who were still Anglicans.

want a subdeacon and ceremoniere, if possible, to let loose F Rector's voice for the choir — but I dont know how you can afford them.

F Rector tells me to order thro' you 6 high altar brown candles, not too thick. 6 for the bier, thinner.

Let me know how many beds are wanted.

TUESDAY 10 SEPTEMBER 1850 F Mazio went and Mr M. [Maurice] Allies came and M. L'abbé [Labbé]

TO ANTONY HUTCHISON

[10 September 1850][1]

My dear F A

This is the *third*, beginning with Roundell Palmer, that Lord S. [Shrewsbury] has rejected.

I did not in any sense and way object to A. Phillipps I only said 'If you take a friend, we must take one too.'

The arbitration will come to nothing — and we must act in our own way.

Can you think of any secular priest to put in here — one will be enough.

Ever Yours affectly J H N

P.S.   If you *can* think of anyone else, do.

TO THE EARL OF SHREWSBURY

St Wilfrid's Sept 10/50

My dear Lord,

I have received letters this morning, and I now have to inform your Lordship that we gladly accept *Mr Langdale* as your arbitrator, as you have proposed.

---

[1] Newman named W. G. Ward as the Oratorian representative in the arbitration about St Wilfrid's. See next letter. To this Lord Shrewsbury replied at once, 'I am sorry you have named Mr Ward, for he is equally out of Court in any concern of mine as Mr Lewis.' Newman sent this note of 10 Sept., on the same day, to Hutchison, with the covering letter that follows, whose date is confirmed by the diary.

On our part we beg to name *Mr Ward* of the Isle of Wight. Should your Lordship assent, he will come down at once.

I am, My dear Lord, Your Lordship's Faithful Servt

John H Newman Congr. Orat.

WEDNESDAY 11 SEPTEMBER 1850 Allies received.[1]

TO F. W. FABER

St W's Sept 11/50

My dear F Wilfrid,

I have told Dr Briggs to pay your expences; so I hope you will hold out your hand at the proper moment. He ought to pay you double, considering your state of indisposition.

I wrote some time since to Dr Newsham, asking what would be a fair remuneration for revision of the Lives — but he did not answer me.[2] I wish you would write to someone on the subject. Also I think the leaves at the beginning of the Volumes, containing the account of the cessation and the recommencement of the Lives with your and my Letters may now be omitted. F. John [Cooke] spoke as if he were well enough to do something in the revising line now.

At first sight I do not like omitting any passages in the life of S Camillus, but I must see them if I am to give an opinion.[3]

Revision will not be 'worth a farthing,' unless it is paid for.

Ever Yrs affly J H N

[1] 'On September 8, Feast of the Nativity of our Blessed Lady, I announced publicly from the pulpit of my church that I was about to resign my living, and cease to belong to the Anglican communion. On the following Wednesday, September 11, after general confession and absolution, I was received by conditional baptism into the Catholic Church, by Father Newman, at St. Wilfrid's, and the same morning made my public profession in the church adjoining, of the Creed of Pope Pius, when a *Te Deum* was sung. On Friday, September 13, I received my first communion from the hands of P. L. Labbé, who had so kindly accompanied me from Launton, and watched over me as a parent over a child.' T. W. Allies, *A Life's Decision*, London 1880, p. 328.

[2] Cf. letter of 1 Dec. 1848, about the *Modern Saints' Lives*.

[3] Two passages in the *Life of St Camillus* had been omitted, following an objection by Richard Simpson, which Fr de Buggenoms passed on. Faber wrote on 10 Sept. that one omission was about St Camillus 'turning a Jew out of a diligence because he wouldn't uncover to a Crucifix, the other I forget.' Cf. letter of 29 May 1851 to Faber.

TO MRS MARSH

⌐September 11. 1850

I cannot resist sending you a line, in consequence of the mournful news I heard yesterday from my sister Jemima.[1] It took me quite by surprise. In a certain sense your loss is like the loss of my own dear Mother over again — so bound up together are they both in the recollection of my boyhood.

And so are you, my dear Cousin, though it is so long since I have seen you — and so are all of you. I made an effort to see my aunt and cousins in 1844, when I knew that events were likely to take place, which would perhaps hinder me from seeing them again, and, when I left England for Rome, just this time four years, I made another attempt. Only yesterday I happened to turn up Annie's letter, in which she said that the time I named for calling would not suit.[2]

Be sure, that you, Annie, and Eliza, are much in my thoughts and will be. I remembered your dear Mother with my own in the Holy Sacrifice this morning. *You* are, except my Aunt Newman, my *oldest* friend now — for I knew you before several of my brothers and sisters were even born. Give my love to Henry.⌐

THURSDAY 12 SEPTEMBER 1850 dined at the Towers with M L'abbé and Allies FRIDAY 13 SEPTEMBER Stanislas came — and Edward and F Fred. Austin, Br Frederic and others *lay brothers* for tomorrow's mass.

TO J. M. CAPES

St Wilfrid's Cheadle Sept 13/50

My dear Capes,

I confess I am figetted with your first article.[3] I have no books here, and, though I have no good reason to say that the text should be altered,

---

[1] Mary, the widow of Charles Fourdrinier, Newman's uncle, died on 6 Sept. Mrs Marsh was one of her daughters. See postscript to letter of 25 July 1847 to Mrs John Mozley.

[2] Newman visited the Fourdriniers on 30 July 1844. As to his later attempt see letter of 4 July 1846 to Henry Fourdrinier. Annie and Eliza were the two other daughters of Mrs Charles Fourdrinier. Cf. *Ward* II, p. 484.

[3] In the *Rambler* for Oct. It was the second of Richard Simpson's articles on 'Religion and Modern Philosophy.'

it is dangerous ground for one who is neither priest nor theologian. To say that the *revisor* is one, and ought to be the other, is only to make *him*, against his will, *theorize*, a line of thinking for which I have not any taste at all. What is the use of setting up theories for the sake of knocking them down again? Such writers ought to come to you with their certificate, testamur, etc and not force a revisor to decide what is, what is not, temerarious.

His theory that order is before chaos, is to me *new*.[1] If he has an authority, he should put it in the note. I never saw the notion before — and if it is new, what right has he to originate it?

What authority has he for saying that the 'Spirit of God' certainly is not the Third Person of the Blessed Trinity?[2]

And p 297 makes me suspicious — where he says that man is not *good* on his creation. At first sight I call the doctrine dangerous.

I confess he seems to me going ultra crepidam. I am far from saying that he must be wrong, but it is more than clear that he need not be right.

In the beginning of Northcote's article, does he not imply that the Romans have lost faith in good measure?[3] does not Perrone ⟨Bellarmine?⟩ say that it is the common opinion that the Roman *Church* is indefectible?

Thank you for your incidental puff of the Oratory in your 'Popular Services.'[4]

Ever Yrs affly J H N

TO THE EARL OF SHREWSBURY

St Wilfrid's Sept 13/50

My dear Lord,

I am going to ask your Lordship the favor of suspending your letter to Mr Langdale for a post or two. I wish to be sure of Mr Bethel's coming to meet him, and do not like to name the *day* at once.[5] On Monday, when I am to have the pleasure of dining at the Towers, I will give you an answer

Your Lordship's faithful Servt.

John H Newman   Congr. Orat.

---

[1] *loc. cit.* p. 283.　　[2] In *Genesis* 1 : 2; *loc. cit.* p. 281.

[3] Northcote in his article, 'Celebrated Sanctuaries of the Madonna,' p. 298, quoted Gregory XVI as saying to an ecclesiastic who was about to visit Naples, 'Bring back with you some of the Neapolitan faith.'

[4] This was a review of Faber's *The Spirit and Genius of St. Philip Neri*, pp. 315–51.

[5] Hutchison had secured John Bethell, the recently converted London solicitor, as arbitrator.

SATURDAY 14 SEPTEMBER 1850   black high mass for Mrs Caswall   M L'abbé and Allies went

MONDAY 16 SEPTEMBER   dined at the Towers with Stanislas.   F Ambrose and F de Buggenoms came.

TO J. M. CAPES

St W's Sept 16/50

My dear Capes

I write in great haste. I am quite satisfied. Thank you for F. Pianciani, whom I will return.[1] It relieves me to find that to deny the universality of the deluge is not even temerarious. At the same time, the time is not come for confidence about any theory. The 'Spiritus Dei' may mean electro-magnetism ten years hence, then the vital principle, and at the end of 50 years 'the Spirit of God' as of old

Ever Yrs affly J H N

TO WILLIAM MASKELL

St Wilfrid's Cheadle Sept 16/50

My dear Maskell,

I had hoped to have answered your letter before this, and hope the delay has not inconvenienced you.

A Catholic may go to *any* priest for confession and absolution, who has *faculties*. He may go to a dozen priests at once. He may tell his mortal sins to one priest, and his venial to another. He may tell one venial sin to one, and another to another. He may go to a second to commute the penance of a first. No leave is necessary for him — the *penitent* requires *no faculties*.

But the Priest of course requires faculties and they are local. M. Labbé, who came here with Allies, could not even publicly reconcile him to the Church — I was obliged to do it. He *could* give him communion, for this requires no faculties.[2]

Abroad, I believe, the annual confession and Easter communion must be made in the *Parish* where a person lives — but not even this is of necessity in England, being a missionary country.

---

[1] In defence of Simpson's article in the *Rambler* for Oct., Capes had evidently sent Newman some work of the prolific writer Giambattista Pianciani (1784–1862), Jesuit scientist from the Papal States, who wrote on physics and electro-magnetism, and on problems connected with religion and science. In 1851 he published *In historiam creationis mosaicam commentarius*.   [2] See diary for 11 Sept.

No leave is necessary from a priest, to enable the penitent to go to another Confessor. Of course I am speaking of what is necessary, about validity and invalidity, not about expedience, or propriety.

Cantu[1] is not followed in his exposition of Scripture etc — nevertheless, though bold, he is a great writer[2] — I do not know the work you speak of.

I do not enter into Pusey's argument sufficiently to see the drift of your question. The question seems to me *who* gave Pusey faculties — not who gave his penitent leave.[3]

Ever Yours most sincerely in Xt

John H Newman   Congr. Orat.

TUESDAY 17 SEPTEMBER 1850   F de Buggenoms went.

TO ANTONY HUTCHISON

St. Wilfrid's Sept 17/50

My dear F Antony

F Buggenoms has come and gone; and is (apparently) smitten with the place. He wishes to keep it for ever, i.e. to buy it, with Douglas's money — paying the interest of the purchase till D. comes in to it.[4] He has the offer of St Edward's at Liverpool, *without* a Church, for £4000 — and seemed not unprepared for a larger sum in the case of St W's [Wilfrid's].

1. *Can* it be sold without simony.
2. If we sell the *house* and grounds, and so get back the money, will not the Earl have a specious ground for coming down upon us? And he will have the Bishop with him.[5]

---

[1] Cesare Cantù (1804–95), the Italian romantic historian, whose *Storia universale* began to appear in 1837.

[2] Newman first wrote 'authority' and then erased it.

[3] In May 1850, Allies, Dodsworth, and Maskell had asked Pusey whence clergymen of the Church of England derived their faculties for hearing confessions. Pusey replied in a *Letter to the Rev. W. U. Richards* that the power of the keys remained 'in the hands of her presbyters.' Maskell was preparing his answer to this. See letter of 11 Oct. to Allies.

[4] Edward Douglas (1819–95), after being at Eton and Christ Church, became a Catholic in 1842, and a Redemptorist in 1849. He was to receive a large inheritance on his mother's death.

[5] The house at St Wilfrid's had been a free gift from the Earl of Shrewsbury to the Wilfridians. Newman was trying to recover for Hutchison and others the £3000 spent on the church.

3. Can we sell without going to Propaganda — seeing the property is really the Pope's?

4. Would it be an evasion to put it thus — that the Redemptorists shall give the sum, say £5000 or £6000, (if so much) *to* the building of an Oratorian Church in London?

5 What do *you* all say to the sale of St W's? To *us* it has no use. It is one of the most beautiful places I was ever in, and I always tear myself away from it, but except as a *school*, a *seminary*, or a *noviciate* for Oratorian Houses, I do not see how it can answer any Oratorian purpose — and these uses of it have been negatived. It is then no use whatever to the Birmingham Oratory.

6. I would not sell it for an inadequate sum — but if you really get a good sum for it, which would buy your London ground, it would be worth selling.

We put down to F Buggs. the interest of £3000 among the incomings of the place — saying that we were not quite certain of it. The Earl quite came into the arrangement of a compromise yesterday, we giving up the quasi endowment, he the community — *but* he seemed to think *he* was to choose the new community, and suggested the Lazarists,[1] about whom he had been making some inquiry. He objected to the Redemptorists, and, when I talked of our getting money, he laughed, looked surprised, said that that was giving with one hand and taking with the other, and said, 'if you can get it.'

On F de Held's return next week, if he and we both continue to agree, each party is to choose a lawyer — and they two are to settle the sum. So choose your man — I should be for Lambert, having heard so much of him — but I don't know him, and you might know a better.[2]

They wish to come in before Christmas. I shall write a note to the Earl today to sound him[3]

Ever Yours affly J H N

P.S.   It would be well that you had a talk with F de Buggenoms and (if you think of the *sale*) to put the purchase money at once in the shape of a contribution to the London Oratory *Church*. '*We* will give you St W's if you will help building the London Church.' I can't conceive this would be simony — it is merely securing for God's church £6000 *more*. It never passes even through our hands.

[1] i.e. the Vincentians.

[2] Hutchison accepted Newman's suggestions with alacrity, and maintained that no question of simony could arise. However, the negotiations fell through, and the Passionists eventually took over St Wilfrid's from the London Oratorians, who had become the sole owners, after receiving on 9 Oct. the share of those at Birmingham.

[3] See the two letters of 17 Sept. which follow.

Henry Wilberforce is received. Let me see the Ami de la Religion anent the Oratory.

J H N.[1]

TO THE EARL OF SHREWSBURY

St. Wilfrid's Sept. 17. 1850

My dear Lord,

Father de Buggenoms has been here, and I think I may congratulate your Lordship and ourselves that a prospect opens of our settling our difficulties here. The Redemptorists are very well disposed to take the place, but they can say nothing definite till F. de Held returns from Belgium. Fr de Buggenoms was obliged to return to London early this morning.

The Redemptorists will be a numerous, and (I believe) a wealthy Community, will take great care of the people, and I think will be very good neighbours to your Lordship.[2]

I am, my dear Lord, Your Lordship's faithful Servt.

John H. Newman   Congr. Orat.

P.S.   Father Douglas and Weld and the novices are *English*

TO BISHOP ULLATHORNE

St Wilfrid's, Cheadle. Staffordshire Sept 17. 1850

My dear Lord,

I am sure you will be glad to hear that we are beginning to see our way out of our St Wilfrid's difficulties. We hope the Redemptorists will take the place of us. Thus Lord Shrewsbury will have every thing he has asked. He will have a large and wealthy community to take care of his people, and to extend their labours to the whole population. I have had some talk with him about our intention generally, and he seemed

---

[1] The last two sentences were added in pencil. Wilberforce was received at Brussels on 15 Sept. The *Ami de la Religion* contained an account of the English Oratory.

[2] The Earl replied the same morning 'I am very happy at what you tell me,' and arranged to send his carriage for Newman the next day, so that they could discuss the subject. In sending this note to Hutchison, Newman wrote on it 'This is the Earl's answer just received to my announcement that "the Redemptorists are well disposed . . ." Cheadle will be the crux. J H N. Let F Buggenoms know of this letter.'

very favorable — but I shall write to him again today Begging your Lordship's blessing

I am, my dear Lord, Your faithful Servt in Xt

John H Newman   Congr. Orat.

(Turn over)

P.S.   I open my letter to say that Lord Shrewsbury has written to me a kind note, expressing pleasure at the Redemptorists coming.

WEDNESDAY 18 SEPTEMBER 1850   dined at the Towers
THURSDAY 19 SEPTEMBER   Mr Schofield went?

TO F. W. FABER

St W's. Sept 19. 1850

My dear F Wilfrid,

I have been saying Mass on the subject of the establishment of your house this morning, and had intended to write to you about it. If it is to be set up before the new Bishop is appointed, no time is to be lost — but you all shall be the judge on this point.

I meant to *supersede* your paper by mine[1] — and I did not like to

---

[1] Faber's paper sent out at the end of Aug. (see letters of 28 Aug. to Stanton and 5 Sept. to Faber) contained the powers he thought should be conferred on Newman by the London Oratory when it became a separate house. In it Faber put forward five propositions:

'1. That no book should be published by any member of the London Oratory without the consent of the Padre, who may submit them to what censorship he pleases. This includes articles in reviews, or any thing in papers beyond report of functions, and such like.

2. In all public lectures and other public developments, beyond the ordinary spiritual preaching and novenas etc. such, e.g. as we may make in order to fulfil the Decree [XI of the Oratorian Rule, added by Newman] which refers to the present condition of England, reference shall be made to the Padre, and his consent be necessary, whenever the Superior and Deputies, or a majority of them, shall decide it to be of sufficient importance.

3. In the introduction of all costumi, beyond those which the variable character of our work, hours, local situation, etc introduce, such e.g. as might lead to *an eventual discrepancy between Houses*, reference shall be made to the Padre, and his consent be necessary, the Superior and Deputies, or a majority of them, deciding on the importance of the case, and the necessity of reference.

4. *In all outward transactions with Bishops*, Superiors of Orders, and others, *which seem in any way likely to compromise the Oratory*, or be otherwise serious, the same

send mine to you till I had thought more about it — and had time to say Mass for it. I propose then for the consideration of you all whether, if you are to have a bye-law concerning me, it might not stand under the following heads rather than those which you put—

1. That I should have the right to give advice.
2. That I should have the right of proposing through the F Superior matters to be voted on by the Congregatio Deputata.
3. That a minority of two in the Congregatio Deputata might always refer to me.[1]
   (F. Antony has suggested a change in this 3rd which he will explain to you.)[2]
4. That these resolutions continue only for three years.
5. That they are annulled by the circumstance of my ceasing to be head of the Birmingham House.

I cannot make out just your important word apropros of F Francis — 'mom-power' of the Superior to F Philip. I will send you the Santa Croce paper, but it is nothing out of the way — it is at Birmingham.[3]

Give Sebastian my love, and thank him for his letter.

I trust everything is going well about St W's [Wilfrid's]. Tell F Antony that the Earl was quite agreeable ⟨he makes the £2300 £3000.⟩ yesterday to our parting with the place, and getting money for it. I inclose Dr U's [Ullathorne] letter which has come by this post — let me have it back, and the Earl's which I sent to F Antony on Tuesday.[4]

Mr Schofield's reflections have led him to go to Rome — he left this morning. They tell me he talks of being made a priest there, but I speak from report.

reference shall be made, the Superior and Deputies, or a majority of them, deciding as before.

5. 'In all petitions to Rome for privileges, item, item.'

At the bottom of this paper of Faber's (the text of which here is taken from Newman's letter to Wiseman of 10 June 1856, with underlinings presumably added), Newman wrote, 'I should wish to supersede these by those I now send up. J H N. Sept 19. 1850'

[1] These three propositions were passed for three years, on 12 Oct. See Newman's letter to Faber of 13 Oct.

[2] He suggested that there should always be reference back to Newman, in matters proposed by him, unless a majority of four to one decided to the contrary.

[3] Faber wrote on 18 Sept. that Knox 'has propounded a doctrine of the non-power of the Superior to F. Philip [Gordon]—which seems ruinous. F. Bernard said you drew up a paper at Sta Croce which they accepted under similar circumstances: may we have a copy of it?' Faber needed to know the extent of his powers. The paper, a long one in Newman's hand, on obedience in the Oratory, is preserved at Birmingham. On it Newman later wrote: '(This has no authority beyond what comes of its having been drawn up by the Father and assented to by the rest at Santa Croce in August or September 1847. J H N. Jan 15/52)'

[4] Ullathorne too was satisfied with the arrangement proposed for St Wilfrid's.

You have not said a word of Mgr Briggs and your expedition —
Has he given you any money?[1]

Ever Yours affectionately J H N

TO A. J. HANMER

St W's Sept 19/50

My dear Sebastian

God direct all you do for His greater glory, and bless you wherever
you are

Ever Yrs affly J H N[2]

TO WILLIAM MASKELL

St W's. Sept 19/50

Tourneley de Sacram. Poenit. p 93

Instabis, nihil possunt Episcopi, imo nec S. Pontifex contra Decreta
Conciliorum Generalium, *quale est Decretum* Concilii Lateranensis de
confessione annua proprio Parocho faciendâ — ergo etc,

Resp. distinguendo anteced. — in his quae spectant fidem et mores,
concedo — quae spectant disciplinam, subdistinguo — si Ecclesia potes-
tatem non fecerit Episcopis, disciplinam, prout expedire judicaverint,
immutandi, concedo — secus, nego.

So much on the general question of change.

Next I am not aware that any Council or ecumenical authority has
said anything except about the prescribed ANNUAL confession — not
about *voluntary* confessions through the year.

'S.C. Episc. 1584 declaravit quod si Episcopus juberet, ne quis confessiones audiret *sine licentiâ curati*, talis decreti *nulla* habenda sit ratio.'
Scavini t 3. p 157

'Fideles libere se possunt confiteri cuicumque confessario approbato.
— Et hoc etiam tempore paschali, *et invito parocho*. S Alphonse.
Cependant cette coutume universelle, dont parle ce docteur, n'est pas

---

[1] Faber replied that he had paid 'handsomely.'

[2] It had been agreed that Hanmer should leave the London House (see letters of
4 and 5 Sept. to Faber), and his doctor having warned him against the Birmingham
climate, he wrote to Newman that he must leave the Oratorians. He remained always
one of Newman's faithful supporters.

en vigueur dans toutes les églises de France. Il est un bon nombre de diocèses où les fideles ont besoin d'une permission générale ou particulière de la part du curé, *pour le temps pascal*.' Gousset t 2 p 181.

'Nemo tenetur umquam Parocho confiteri, ne quidem in Paschate.' De Lugo, Diana, Suarez, etc — 'Joannis vii damnavit opinionem Joannis Poliaci dicentis, confessiones factas Regularibus repetendas apud Curatum. Deinde Clemens vii an 1592 et Clem. X decreverunt bene satisfacere Confessioni annuae qui confitentur religiosis simpliciter approbatis.' S Alphons. Theol. Moral. p 387 (art 574 de Sacram. Poenit.) ed. 1837.[1]

My dear Maskell

I cannot find a word about *leave* being necessary for *voluntary* confessions

Ever Yrs J H N

TO GEORGE RYDER

St W's Sept 20/50

My dear George

I write in a great hurry. 1. My Lord *would not let* the Watts Russells come here — because it is a religious house.[2] 2 The *Redemptorists are buying* it of us.

I do hope that Allies will take boys in Bm [Birmingham]. If you give him yours, etc — with the Morgans, he would have 7.

Ever Yrs affly J H N

TO T. W. ALLIES

St. Wilfrid's, Cheadle Sept. 21. 1850.

My dear Allies,[3]

Clifton is a *most eligible* place, and I shall be glad if you go there. But I cannot advise you to move all your goods there or to take a lease of a house. At least all my experience goes against its advisableness. If others have an opposite experience, I have no objection to offer.

We shall be most sorry to lose you from Birmingham. We want a

[1] For the bearing of these quotations see letter of 16 Sept. to Maskell.
[2] Lord Shrewsbury refused to allow the Watts Russells to rent St Wilfrid's. See letter of 6 June 1849 to Ullathorne.
[3] Allies was at his Rectory, Launton, Oxfordshire, packing up to leave.

boy's school there, and at this moment have seven boys from 11 to 16 to offer.

Ever Yrs affectly J. H. N.

P.S. I turned up the bill, and found that in 1836 a room above a Billiard room in High Street Oxford, cost me £3 a year for keeping the furniture of my mother's house at Iffley on her death.

Your book is most satisfactory but I have not yet done justice to it. I shall read it carefully, as I return.[1]

TO GEORGE RYDER

Edgbaston Sept. 21. 1850

My dear George,

I have delayed writing by return of post, wishing to say Mass for your intention, which I have done this morning.

Certainly my view is clear, that, if you can take the step of which you speak with peace of mind, *you should take it*. I shall be glad to hear that you have been able to take it[2]

Ever Yrs affly in Xt   John H Newman of the Oratory

TO F. W. FABER

St W's Sept 22/50

My dear F Wilfrid,

I am stopping here a few days longer to pack up and so leave the place for good. I do not see any objection to defer the separation of the Houses till next February 2nd, if you prefer that time, but I am decided on their separation.

Not only has Barnabo told us to keep the Rule 'exactissime,' and one of the two cardinal points of it is the independence of each Oratorian House, but it is impossible to be a non-resident Superior, or to govern an absent House. Moreover, it is impossible for one Superior to govern two independent, non-communicating bodies, as England and Ireland

---

[1] *The See of St Peter*, London 1850, giving the reasons that induced Allies to leave the Church of England.

[2] It is not clear to what this refers. Ryder, who was now six months a widower, had thoughts of becoming a priest.

were two kingdoms under one king. If the head is one, the body must be one; and since we have no vows, the body cannot be one without the noti vultus; one school, one noviciate, one home, or at least the desire of unity and fellowship, to bring the two communities in contact, and to make them recognise each other. Such an arrangement being incompatible with the proper working of the London House, that House must have a head of it's own.[1]

As to my becoming a Bishop, no one can seriously wish it, who is loyal to St Philip; and there are no lengths to which I would not go to prevent it. I would lose hundreds in embassages to Rome first.

The Earl went, I suppose, yesterday. He is well pleased; and I suppose we shall be able to get about the money laid out on the place. You must see F de Held, and then the two lawyers may come down at once. You must not be impatient for the money, for you could not use it, if you had it, till you have three times as much as you have yet — meanwhile you get the interest.

Ever Yours affectly John H Newman   Cong. Orat.

MONDAY 23 SEPTEMBER 1850   began packing up (*we were leaving St Wilfrid's for good*)

TUESDAY 24 SEPTEMBER   F. Ambrose left St W's [Wilfrid's]?

THURSDAY 26 SEPTEMBER   returned to Birmingham, with Br Francis (*Davis*), leaving St W's for good

  N.B On the sale of St Wilfrid's furniture to the Passionists, and the allocation of the money to the Oratories vid Private Journal [Diary] *1850–1851 p 118.*

FRIDAY 27 SEPTEMBER   Bathurst and his sister in Birmingham[2]

TO LADY OLIVIA ACHESON

Oy Bm Sept 27/50

My dear Lady Olivia,

Come when you will — we shall be most glad to see you. Mrs Wootten has a friend stopping with her — but there is a room in

---

[1] The London Oratorians at first had wished their separation delayed, but Faber wrote on 20 Sept., that they did not want to be set up, but if this had to be, then it should be at once. He added 'Otherwise I would rather go on as we are till you are made bishop yourself.' This was a reference to the new hierarchy, which was established on 29 Sept., and to proposals and rumours that Newman was to fill one of the sees.

[2] Catherine Anne Bathurst, who was henceforth to be one of Newman's close friends, had just followed her brother's example, and become a Catholic, having been received by Fr Brownbill S.J. in London.

Warwick Street, where Miss Bathurst is. She and her brother do not go to St W's [Wilfrid's] — they hope to be confirmed here.

I think you certainly may come here for the winter. F St John is away, but I am writing to him, and will give your message

Ever Yours very sincerely in Xt

John H Newman   Congr. Orat.

SATURDAY 28 SEPTEMBER 1850   French agent of M. Jaricot came and took up with us[1]

TO MRS JOHN MOZLEY

Oratory Birmingham. Sept 28/50

My dear Jemima,

┌Thank you for your affectionate letter. We are leaving St Wilfrid's for good, and I have been bringing all my papers etc here, and am, as far as I can, so arranging them, that they may be no more of a trouble to me than if they did not exist. I am now getting to a great age; and, though I earnestly trust it may not be so, I cannot shut my eyes to the possibility of my being put into situations, in which I should have no leisure whatever for ever again recurring to matters of a private or personal nature, and from which I should only be released by death. Just now there seems a very precious time given me for setting my house in order, and under this feeling I have sent you what it would only be a charge to me, and not a comfort, to keep.

You are quite right in saying that I do not and cannot forget those, who by death have been taken from me. You might have said more; — I think of them with far greater comfort than of the living. Of them I can think without pain. *They* were taken away before the truth was offered to them; *they* were taken away in their ignorance. They had no warnings to look out elsewhere, for the True church of God. They died in good faith. They had not the call, year after year, month after month, sounded in their ears, by means of the successive conversion of their teachers and friends, to put their souls, their faith, their prospects, into God's hands, to do with them what He would. They had not that experience of the heterodoxy and the impotence of their own communion and its authorities, which now grows broader and clearer daily. Of them, alas, it must be said, 'Blessed are your eyes, for they did *not*

───────────

[1] i.e. a promoter of the Association for the Propagation of the Faith, for assisting missionaries, founded at Lyons in 1822, by Pauline Marie Jaricot (1799–1862).

see, and your ears, for they did *not* hear.' They never came to the determination that they would not let the idea of Catholicism being true ever enter into their mind, and turned away from it, (lest they should 'see with their eyes and hear with their ears, and understand with their heart, and be converted,')⌐ and that, from an intimate sense of the misery of that inward unsettlement, and confusion on all sides of them and in all their relations, which would be the first immediate consequence of their admitting the thought. They never cherished their dislike of those doctrines and usages of the Catholic Church, which are difficult to Protestants, instead of making an effort to see if they were not really pious and true, in order that they might have thereby an excuse for remaining where they were. ⌐And so, [[as to them, (in the words of Scripture)]] 'Weep not for the dead, neither bemoan him; but weep sore for him who goeth away,' who turns his back on his true home, and refuses to give ear to the voice which calls him thither.[1]

You say, you are 'only half resigned to an ever new misfortune.' And do you think that I have not a portion of the Apostle's 'great heaviness and continual sorrow, for his brethren, his kinsmen according to the flesh,' who are losing what they might claim, and, instead of being first, are making themselves less than the last. O my dear Jemima, bear with me in thus writing to you; you have led me to do so. I have few opportunities of doing so; you will not be troubled with such words often, but I should have to answer for it, if I did not avail myself of an opening such as you have given, to set you right in a most serious matter, and to remind you how *I* view matters, which, surrounded by influences so fatal to you, you seem to forget *can* be viewed in any other way than your own.

That God may touch your heart is the constant prayer of

Yours ever affectly John H Newman⌐

M R G. [Giberne] I suppose, comes to live here. At present she is on visits, and, I am told, at Brighton.

---

[1] [[I was thinking especially of T. Mozley, when I wrote this.]] Newman's brother-in-law, Thomas Mozley, nearly became a Catholic, as a result of a visit to Normandy with his wife, Harriett, in Sept. 1843. Newman persuaded him not to take the step impulsively, but to wait. Newman quotes Jeremiah 22 : 10.

SUNDAY 29 SEPTEMBER 1850   sang high Mass.   in retreat

TO T. W. ALLIES

Oratory, Birmingham Sept. 30. 1850.

My dear Allies,

I cannot but think you have done right, in suspending the transference of your books. Since I wrote to you, I have been thinking about you at various times — I wish, with more success. Had Mrs Allies's health allowed, much might have been said for Rome — much too for Belgium.

I feel what you say about boys, and it had grown on me before your letter came. You are not specially fitted for a small boy school, and I fear that, unless you had as many as would deserve that name, small boys would not answer. On the other hand, you would not *quickly* get *youths* at a proper sum. I think you would ultimately.

I do not know who has Mr Fullerton's boy now. He was with Church, and I should think they would wish much a person like yourself.[1] Mr Walker, Catholic Priest at Scarborough, takes several pupils at £150 a year, I am told, and Mr Waterworth the same.[2] Such youths then are to be got, but they are Priests. You must be in a Catholic neighbourhood, then, if you are to succeed; Clifton would be very good, being a sea place, a beautiful place, and the residence of a Bishop. Our neighbourhood too would not be a bad one, and we are sure to remain. A body is more permanent than a Bishop's residence, for I have not heard that Bristol is permanently fixed on, but, if it is, it is still some way off Clifton.

It would be a great thing, could you manage to be independent of receipts for a year or two, for you must reckon, I should think, on doing little at first.

I have nothing more to say at the moment.

Ever yours affectly in Xt, John H. Newman   Congr. Orat.

TO MRS J. W. BOWDEN

Oratory. Bm. Sept 30/50

My dear Mrs Bowden,

So you are really going again — you seem hardly returned. It is a great annoyance that you can't go to Malta — every other place is an

---

[1] Lady Georgiana Fullerton's only son, Granville, was now sixteen. Cf. letter of 25 June 1846.   [2] James Waterworth was from 1833 to 1876 the priest at Newark.

experiment. I doubt Rome suiting John. If you go to Rome, it must be as a pilgrimage. People feel so differently, that of course I cannot answer for others — they say there is something in the air of Rome very depressing — this is acknowledged by the faculty — This was not so with me — but the moral effect is such — Such endless ruins, such wastes, dilapidation, decay — Churches once splendid, now faded and dishonored — poverty inducing a general slovenliness in their appointments and services. It is nothing but the unseen world, the haunt of Martyrs, the home of spiritual power, which sustains one there — I should shock many persons by saying so — but I no more like Rome for its own sake, i.e. for what is visible, than I should like a long fast or a sharp discipline. There, so I found it, every one is about his own business — each monastery or College is its own world — so that you must depend simply on yourself, and live either in your own duties or with the Saints who are around you. I suppose I was unfortunate in my weather — but it was about the same when I was there in 1833.

Your most splendid vestments came just in time for the Nativity — we shall not use them again till the Conception We shall be very careful of them here, dreading the atmosphere of gas; at Edgbaston we shall eschew gas, I think. I believe I have not written to thank you for your most acceptable and unexpected gift towards the new Church. I am sanguine we shall raise enough to build the chancel and transepts — which will allow more room for a congregation than our present building. When they are up, they must gain for us subscriptions by their own persuasiveness. Our architect[1] has been so fearfully slow in his preparation of the working plans, that we are losing the season; — but the beginning is so important, that we do not like to hurry him, lest he should be slovenly. He now promises them in 10 days.

I suppose you know that we have all but parted with St Wilfrid's to the Redemptorists — Personally I am sorry to give it up, if it were only from my great reluctance to undo what is once done — but the place was exhausting us

Don't direct to me 'Dr,' please, but Father, which is my proper title — I don't know myself in so strange a dress.

H Wilberforce *talks* of going to Rome for the winter — there are a number of our friends there, which certainly would be pleasant, if you went — and you all would be of use to them

Love to the children

Ever Yours affectly in Xt   John H Newman   Congr. Orat.

[1] i.e. Terence Flanagan. Later Viollet-le-Duc was approached. See letter of 11 Aug. 1851 to William Froude.

TO F. W. FABER

Oy. Bm. Sept 30/50

Charissime,

Will you give me your opinion of the following sort of form, in which I thought of casting the Decree? We have had a meeting on the General Subject but shall not pass it until you fix the time.

Whereas it is the intention of the Holy Father, Pope Pius ix, as expressed in his Brief of foundation under date of November 26, 1847, that we should extend the Congregation of the Oratory of St Ph. N. [Philip Neri] thro' England, and whereas those of our Fathers whom we sent up to the Metropolis in May 1849 for the purpose of preparing the way for an Oratory there, have been blest with increase of numbers, internal consolidation, openings of usefulness, success in their labours, friends and wellwishers, and prospects for the future, which warrant our contemplating their immediate erection into a separate Congregation, we, the Fathers of the Birmingham Oratory, in General Congregation assembled, (after celebrating the solemn Mass of the Holy Ghost,) do hereby set free from their obedience to ⟨connexion with⟩ our House, with a view to their becoming members ⟨being received⟩ into the Oratory of Westminster ⟨?⟩, the following Fathers:— viz ' etc.'[1]

At the same time we shall make over St Wilfrid's to you; else we should come in for half the profits.

Ever Yrs affly J H N

TO RICHARD STANTON

Oratory Bm Sept 30/50

My dear F Richard,

I thought we all had looked forward to the Purification, as the time when the London House would be set up. Certainly after Barnabò's letter of last November, I don't see how it can be delayed.

And the state of things is too anomalous to continue. The only way in which the status quo could be justified would be, if the members of the two Houses had interchanged. To this I think you were all opposed — and a separation of them from each other seemed to me in conse-

[1] For this decree see letter of 9 Oct. to Faber.

quence inevitable. I only thought you would have been pressing it at an earlier date.[1]

It is impossible that two bodies can have one head. Had we even met together at St Wilfrid's, so as to be morally one, this would have been an alteration of the state of things — but considering you have felt you must be so completely distinct and individual in all other things, you must be in your head also.

And I am sure you require a head — then *he* will have the responsibility, and *you* the bond of obedience. You cannot be a real community without a resident head — and you are a real community all but it. At present you are neither one thing nor the other; neither a deputation or mission from Birmingham, nor a London House.

We had a meeting on the mode of doing it on Saturday, and I wish you to consider these previous questions — say, you and F. Wilfrid together. 1. *Who* sets up the House? I, or the Congregatio Deputata? vid the Brief.[2] 2. What has the Congregatio Generalis to do with the matter? to give congé to those who go to London? I mean, having *admitted* them, it may claim to *release* them of their allegiance. This would apply to FF Wilfrid [Faber], Bernard [Dalgairns], Robert [Coffin], Richard [Stanton], Antony [Hutchison], Francis [Knox], Alban [Wells], who went to Town Triennials and Decennials; — but Philip [Gordon] and John [Bowden] who went to Town novices, must have their leave from our Congregatio Deputata? or the Generalis? Then as to James [Rowe], Edward [Bagshawe], Raphael [Balston], Camillus [Ballard], George [Ballard], and id genus omne, we ignore them, and have nothing to say to them, their names not appearing on our books. Is this right?

3. Can we have a Mass of the Holy Ghost, if solemn, on a double, (as we can have a solemn Black Mass)? I mean, is there any way in which we could vote on the subject after a Mass de Sp. S. [Spiritu Sancto]?

4. As this instance would be a precedent for all others turn the whole matter in your mind.

5. Ought you to be formally styled 'the Congregation of the O. [Oratory] of St Ph. N. [Philip Neri] in the City of *Westminster*,' or how?

We are obliged to you for the Oratorian supplement to the Breviary, and will take 100 copies as you propose — I can hardly say, of what sizes; whatever *you* do, I suppose.

Dr Grant took the agency of the Oratory, *on condition* of having an advance of money, which accordingly F. Ambrose advanced for me.

[1] Stanton replied on 1 Oct. agreeing that the separation should be made quickly.

[2] The power to erect Oratories lay either with Newman or with him and the four deputies he had chosen. See letter of 3 Oct. to Stanton. Stanton agreed to Newman's further suggestions.

You may do one of two things, it is the same to us — either pay half, and let it run out — he paying your letters etc as well as ours out of it; — or inquire of him the state of the account *now*, and *halve* with us what he has actually spent — the rest being ours for the future — the latter gives him the trouble of two accounts, but it is no matter to us in Bm. [Birmingham]

Keep Thomas's copies of the Rescripts — they will do for the next House we set up.

Ever Yours, Charissime, Most affectly in Mary & Philip

J H N.

TUESDAY 1 OCTOBER 1850   The French friend of M. Jaricot went.   Mr Schofield returned from Hanley   Lady O. A. [Olivia Acheson] came for the winter   Mrs W Wilberforce called

TO J. D. DALGAIRNS

Oy Bm Oct 1. 1850

My dear F. Bernard,

Directly F Ambrose returns, he shall have old Maher's bill, which I am sorry you are so constantly troubled with. I thought it had been paid an age ago.

Thank you for your hint and the affectionate way in which it is conveyed.[1] I sincerely think you ought to be a separate house, indeed I don't see how I am justified at Rome in not proceeding to make you one. I only had expected you yourselves would have found it out before this — There is the greatest possible disadvantage in your not having a resident head.

It is no use talking, and I wish utterly to bring it to an end, and not say or think ought about it again — but I cannot deny that there has been that in the London House's treatment of St W's [Wilfrid's] which has pained me. Two years since (Lent 1848) we were earnestly pressed to go there, as a duty to Lord S. [Shrewsbury], (unless we *at once* gave

[1] Dalgairns wrote, 'I do feel you are angry with us, and I think we all of us feel it, though no one knows that I am writing to tell you so. You cannot tell what a damper it would be to me individually in all my exertions, if I thought we were set up as a house, with your displeasure upon us. Everything seems to have come to a dead stand-still, and, (though I really believe that you have adequate motives for setting us up quite independent of any conduct of ours) you seem to wish to mark your last acts, as our Superior with coldness and displeasure, as if disgust with us was your reason for separating us from you. . . . The comfort however is that we shall still be connected with you through the bye-law. . . .'

up the property to him) — it was to be a novice-house, a villagiatura etc.[1] For it we gave up Mary vale — then, when we got there, the Congregation was literally shoved out of Church, and the Mission was to be made all in all.[2] But still I have stood by it since we took it — and wished to make it what Mary vale was to have been — either an elementary school, or a seminary, or something of the kind. In nothing has the London House supported me. There has been a wish to be obedient, and to go by my wishes, but when the time of action came, difficulties have been thrown in the way. I have been nearly the only one to take any interest in the place. I got into trouble with Propda [Propaganda] on no interest of mine.[3] Determined to bring it to a point, last Christmas I got you to pass resolutions which *bound* you to take interest in it — and then when the time comes for fulfilling them, you say you are too poor to do so[4] — And it ends in our removing back again, bag and baggage, wardrobe and closet, having lost Mary vale which was our natural place, and to which our boys might have recourse and now have none.

The only gratification I have in the whole matter is, that, having firmly resisted all along the unconditional surrender of St W's to the Earl, I have gained for you its purchase money (as I trust) from the Redemptorists.

To all this is added a still deeper sorrow, arising from the frustration of all my wishes for some sort of moral union between the Houses. But I trust St Philip will guide it all to good; may he ever bless you with his most tender affection.

What more can I say?

Ever Yours affectly.[5]

P.S.   I had been going to write to Langres. The good priest understands English, so I can write in my own way. I am much pleased and gratified by his translation — which, as far as I can judge seems very good and to have very few faults.[6]

---

[1] See letter of 6 March 1848 to Faber, and the letters following it.

[2] See letters of 23 and 25 Oct. 1848 to Coffin, and Memorandum 1 of 14 Jan. 1849 in *Appendix* 4 to Vol. XII.

[3] See the correspondence in June 1849 and letters of 24 and 25 Nov. 1849 to Faber.

[4] See letters of early Jan. 1850 and of 11, 18 and 22 July to Faber.

[5] Newman forgot to put his signature.

[6] Dalgairns had sent to Newman the translation by Abbé Deferrière at Langres of nine of the University Sermons, *Discours sur la théorie de la croyance religieuse prononcés devant l'université d'Oxford*, Paris 1850.

TO F. W. FABER

Oy. Bm Oct 1. 1850

My dear F Wilfrid,

Be sure I wish to leave you most entirely to your own feeling of what is best as to the resolutions — and have done nothing more than suggest.[1] You know, I don't make it the condition of your being set up, so I don't see what voting has to do with it. All voting will be *after* you are set up. You have not to submit your final resolutions to me — the only reason for talking with me previously to your being set up, is, 1. In case I can say anything useful to you — 2 (which is more important) because there might be conditions, to which I on my part did not assent.

As to the other matters of your letter, I love you, and all of you, too tenderly to be able to enter into a discussion with you.[2] And I know you love me. Why will you bring up what is done and over? — I may be wrong in this or that matter of detail — but, on the whole *lie* of the matter, I don't think I can be persuaded that I am wrong.[3]

Ever Yrs affly in Mary and Philip J H N.

WEDNESDAY 2 OCTOBER 1850   Mrs W [W. Wilberforce] to mass and breakfast Austin and Lawrence went severally home, thro' London   Mr Vincent of Oxford called[4]   Stanislas returned

[1] i.e. the resolutions giving Newman certain rights in the London House. See letter of 19 Sept.

[2] Faber wrote on 30 Sept.: 'I feel keenly about St Wilfrid's. I am devotedly attached to the place, and I have felt all along that there was a danger of my sacrificing the interests of the Congregation to it. I think I did fail about it in my correspondence with you in the 1st Lent after I joined the Congregation, and have never ceased to regret it; but I had not confidence in you then, and did not know you. In the deliberations about leaving M Vale, I tried to act indifferently, tho' my heart was in my mouth.' Faber added that later in a discussion between Stanton and Hutchison and some of the Birmingham Oratorians about the College plan, these last had 'said they had voted for what you wished, not according to their judgment, and F. Joseph [Gordon] ending to F. Anty said, "St Wilfrid's is a mill stone round our necks, *and F Wilfrid tied it there.*" I can't tell you what I felt when I heard this . . .

Lastly I think your letter the other day [22 July] was very bitter and harsh, and I don't think I quite acknowledge the justice of it about our indifference to unity and sympathy with the Birm House. . . .'

[3] Faber replied on 2 Oct., 'My dearest Padre, I have been in bed all day, so can only thank you very much for your affectionate letter to me, and also your letter to F. Bernard which I have seen. It gives me plenty to think about, and plenty to wish otherwise, for your sake as well as my own. Ever most affecly and obely F W F.'

[4] Presumably Joseph Vincent the Oxford bookseller at 90 High Street.

TO CHARLES RUSSELL

Oratory Birmingham. Oct 2. 1850

My dear Dr Russell,

Thank you very much for your kind letter, and your most acceptable and valuable present, which I shall esteem very highly for its own sake and for yours.[1]

I cannot tell how a report has risen that I am going to Cork — nothing of any sort has occurred to occasion it, that I know of. Certainly if any thing took me to Ireland, I should not have a greater pleasure than to accept your invitation to visit Maynooth. It would be a true recreation to me — but, as you know, when one is in a place, there are a thousand ties and bonds to keep one in it — and our own institution discourages locomotion in a remarkable manner.

Your approbation at my Lectures[2] is very valuable, and I am very much pleased to have it. At the same time I am conscious that they are a mere ephemeral publication, and I shall be far more than satisfied, if, as you think, they will do good at the moment.

Does not your way to London pass through Birmingham? or have new railroads made a change? — We should be so glad to see you at any time. We are in a poor place just now — but if you could condescend to it, we should not be on our part ashamed of it. In a year or two we hope to move to a better vicinity — but we cannot hope or desire to be prospered any where more than we have been here.

Begging your good prayers, I am, My dear Dr Russell, Very sincerely Yours in Xt

John H Newman   Congr. Orat.

P.S.   I doubt whether you know any of our Birmingham party — FF Faber and Dalgairns are in London, and, I know, would desire their warmest remembrances, did they know I was writing.

[1] Russell sent Newman a copy of his translation of Leibnitz's *A System of Theology*, London 1850. In the preface, dated 15 Aug., Russell explained that he had made the translation in 1841, 'in the hope that the *System of Theology* might contribute to the diffusion of those Catholic views which at that time had begun to make sensible progress in England, and had just received a strong impulse from the publication of the memorable Tract XC . . .'
[2] *On Certain Difficulties felt by Anglicans.*

THURSDAY 3 OCTOBER 1850 F de Held and F Nicholas came (*From St Wilfrid's?*) (*was this the time when he told me Coffin had left us for the Redemptorists?*)

TO R. A. COFFIN

Oy Bm Oct 3/50

observe the paging[1]

My dear F Rector,

F. Nicholas has read me your important and most interesting statement — and be sure I enter into your anxieties and difficulties. I will tell you what strikes me upon the whole matter.[2]

And first I will be very frank with you, as I know you would wish me to be. I distinctly think it would have been a higher course and more truly Philippine, to mortify the razionale, which, in your objections and difficulties as to the state of the Oratory in England, you have not done at all. You simply criticize — and I really think St Philip would have been displeased with you. I think you would have got greater merit by submitting, than by seeking for what you consider in itself better.

Should you find you have a vocation to a religious life, pained indeed as I shall be to part with you out of the Oratory, yet far from regretting it, I shall only rejoice that God has called you to what is more perfect. But in that case you will betake yourself either to the Jesuits or the Redemptorists, for I don't suppose that *what you seek, a tradition of spiritual direction*, is to be found in England any where else — not in the holy Trappists or Passionists — not in the Benedictines or Dominicans. Perhaps the Rosminians or Conceptionists may be added, but they have no *tradition* from any saint.

I tell you what it strikes me as best to propose to you. You feel your want of training and theological reading. You want the Oratorian *tradition*. Well then, go for two or three years to the Oratory at Florence. I think your reception would be easy, and you could not be in a better

---

[1] Newman inverted the second and third pages, and so had to number them. With this letter the story of Coffin's leaving the Oratory begins.

[2] Newman has left a memorandum dated 'Jan 14/52': 'October 3. 1850 F. Nicholas came suddenly from St Wilfrid's to Birmingham, and told me with great emotion that he had got a letter to read to me from Coffin, which (I think) was to go back to him.

As far as I recollect it was to the effect that there was no tradition of spiritual life or spiritual training in the Oratory—and he was determined he would not join the London House. J H N' Faber had written to Coffin on 2 Oct., telling him that the London Oratory was to be separated off on 9 Oct. and would elect its officers on 12 Oct. Coffin was asked to come to the London Oratory, of which he was a member, a few days beforehand. See also letter of 23 Nov. to Faber.

place than the city of St Philip, and in an ancient Oratory, which is fully able to initiate you into the things you desiderate. The Fathers have wished to come to England, and have written to me on the feasibleness of doing so. At the end of your time, perhaps some would return with you and still direct you, and with you found an Oratory in Clifton, or Brighton, or Torquay, or Exeter, or other suitable place. At Clifton there are rich converts; and, if I could talk confidentially to Neve about it, I dare say a fund might be begun, which would accumulate till you return.

Meanwhile, all that would be known to the two Houses, would be that I had recommended you, since you had had so little time for study etc, to go to Florence for a certain time.

Tell me what you think of this — I am going to make one condition, which I hope you will not think ungracious; — that, as I have been bound by F. Nicholas to special secrecy, and do not mention the subject to any one here, so you must not say a word about what I have said in this letter, or take any advice about your position, from any one at St Wilfrid's. As an Oratorian, you must seek advice from Oratorians, not from strangers.

Excuse me, my dear F Rector, if I seem to write abruptly — but I am pressed for time, and have still to write to F Wilfrid, as F Nicholas wishes, under obligation of his secrecy[1]

      Ever Yours very affectly John H Newman   Congr. Orat.

P.S.   I have written to Mr Lambert, to see if he can go next week to St W's for the valuation.

TO F. W. FABER

Oct 3/50

My dear F. Wilfrid

I write in the strictest confidence. Yet it is cruel to say so, considering the astonishment which will come on you at my project, which needs a

---

[1] Coffin replied on 4 Oct., 'I thank you with all my heart for your most kind letter, and especially am I obliged to you for being so open with me. It is useless now to regret what is past, but I am convinced that in this as in all other things I might have acted much better. . . .

I accept most willingly and thankfully your proposal for me to go to the Florence Oratory for as long a period as others shall think necessary. . . .

My dearest Father, I know how much trouble and anxiety I have ever caused you . . . bear with me, I pray you, a little longer . . .'

confidant for relief, tho' you ought to be astonished at nothing after California.

I propose to recommend F Rector of St W's [Wilfrid's] to go to Florence (to the Oratory) for several years — to read his *theology* there — to imbibe the Oratorian traditions — and to return with some Florentine Fathers, who have already wished to come here, to found an Oratory, say in Clifton.

I have reason to think I must write by this very first post — though the idea has only quite now come into my head. At least, whatever comes of it, I think I shall subtract the Rector from the London Oratory — but don't mention this, till you hear again from me on the subject.[1]

Ever Yrs affly J H N

TO RICHARD STANTON

Oy Bm Oct 3/50

My dear F Richard,

I had come to the same conclusion as you that we need not say *who* erected the House — only you must guard in your first entry of seeming to set it up yourselves. I don't like the word 'sent' — it is so *obviously* vague. Would it do to say that you had been released by the Bm [Birmingham] House *in order* to your erection in the Metropolis? This would record the condition of the *will* of the Bm House in doing it. Or you could express that the Bm House had communicated to you the Brief? that you set up your House under the Brief as extended to you by the Bm House?

From what you say, the existing Decennials in London *wish us* to raise Francis, Alban, and Philip to the rank of Decennials? is it so?

Have I told F. Wilfrid that we will take St Denys's day for the day of Institution and our High Mass?

We will use the word Metropolis in our decree, and so avoid London and Westminster.[2] Yet I think you must not refuse to contemplate an East London or a Southwark House, if you are where you are about.

This is an answer to F Wilfrid too.

Talbot writes the word that our friends at the Chiesa Nuova are hurt

---

[1] Faber replied by return, 'Poor old Coffin! all will be sorry when they hear. But perhaps he would have found it hard coming back again, tho' I suppose he would have been F. Minister . . .' Faber went on to suggest Philip Gordon for that post.

[2] Faber and Stanton disliked Newman's suggestion of 'Westminster Oratory,' as tying them to a particular spot. The objection to 'London Oratory' is stated in the next sentence. For the decree see 9 Oct.

at our not writing to them. This must be F Rossi about what I fear you have *not* sent. Why have you not?[1]

Ever Yrs affly J H N

P.S. Tell F Bernard he would be doing me a great kindess if he looked over *one* of the more difficult of my Discourses in M Gondon's translation — e.g. The Infinitude of the Divine Attributes etc — I have to write to him to give him an account of them[2]

F. de Held has just called with Nicholas — he is gone to the Bishop — and is well disposed, but must go to France to consult Superiors — and meanwhile wishes the men of business to repair to St W's [Wilfrid's] next week — so I am writing to Mr Lambert — I shall tell him to call on F Antony in passing, who must show him *all* the bills. The other man is Mr F Capes.[3]

FRIDAY 4 OCTOBER 1850   F Nicholas went

TO R. A. COFFIN

Oct 4. [1850]

My dear F Rector

Last evening I wrote generally to F Wilfrid — now I shall again saying that, considering your time has been so taken up with the duties of the Congregation, I thought you had better go to Florence to read theology — and that, as the Florentines had already expressed a wish to come to England, you might come back as one of a number to found an Oratory (say) at Clifton.

Of course I should not contemplate your coming back as F Superior or in any particular post, but as one of a number of Fathers.

Also, you would go on leave of absence from the London House, but with the understanding that you were to be separated from them on your return to England, or now.

I will write to Florence as soon as I get your and F Wilfrid's answers.

Ever Yours affectly J H N

[1] See letters of 6 and 14 Feb. 1850 to Stanton, about writing to Fr Rossi, which he had failed to do.

[2] i.e. Gondon's translation of *Mix.*, *Conférences adressées aux Protestants et aux Catholiques*, Paris 1850.

[3] The Redemptorists were still negotiating for St Wilfrid's.

Oy Bm Oct 4/50

My dear F Wilfrid,

I am quite aware that the London House must formally give leave
to F Robert to go to Florence — but I had reasons for taking the matter
into my hands.[1]

I suppose the L. [London] House will do one of two things — either
give leave of absence with the understanding of permission to leave for
good on his return — or permission to leave for good now. The former
way is the pleasanter.[2]

He goes to read Theology, and learn the ways of the foreign Oratory
— When he gets persons to return with him, he will not come as F
Superior, or necessarily in *any post*.

I do not see any harm can arise from separate traditions etc, since
we are not to be morally one. The more, the better.[3]

When I get your answer, I shall write to Florence, i.e. to Watts
Russell.

When you hear from F Robert, *tell* it.

Ever Yours affly J H N

TO VISCOUNT FEILDING

Oratory Birmingham Oct 4. 1850.

My dear Lord,

I feel truly glad of the opportunity you have given me of tendering
my heartfelt congratulations to you and Lady Feilding, on your reception into the Catholic Church.[4] You must have many anxieties and pains,
but the consolation and the peace will abide, and abound a hundred fold.
I shall have great pleasure in making your and Lady Feilding's acquaintance, as you are kindly proposing to permit me to do. We live, however,
at present in so out of the way a part of Birmingham, and our house is
so strange a one, that I hardly like the thoughts of obliging you to find
us out — and would propose to call on you, should you prefer it
wherever you are to be found.

[1] In the rough draft of this letter Newman wrote ' I had put it so to avoid invidious-
ness to one or other party.'
[2] Faber wrote by return agreeing to this.
[3] Since it had been settled that each Oratory was to be separate, there could be no
harm in one being founded in England with the traditions of Florence.
[4] They had been received on 28 Aug.

I have no engagements from home except on next Monday the 7th, when I go to a place beyond Worcester, returning home the same day.[1]

Accept my best prayers that your Lordship may receive from the Giver of all grace fresh and fresh rewards of the sacrifices which that grace has enabled you to make, and believe me to be,

My dear Lord with great respect, Your Lordship's faithful Servant
John H. Newman   Congr. Orat.

TO MISS M. R. GIBERNE

Oratory Birmingham Oct 4. 1850 St Francis
My dear Miss Giberne

I gave my Mass this morning to dear Mrs Copeland — and FF St John and Bowles have said Mass for her too, or are going to do so.[2] It was a great surprise and sorrow to me, as it must have been in a very distressing way to you. But you must thank God, that you have gained a soul to Him. She is now *safe* — Your work is carried home, and pleads for you in God's sight. You have by your prayers and exertions turned a soul to justice — and you have gained a double recompense — the salvation of a dear friend, and the reward of a good act.

As to the children, don't trouble yourself. They are in God's hands — and their baptism will show itself in time to come. Even if they have not Catholic education, they will, through His grace and mercy, be drawn to the dear Mother who received them in infancy into her holy arms, from those of their earthly parent.

I was going to write to you on your own matters — You will think me changeable, yet I have a cause. As I wished you to take the Warwick Street House, now I am going to wish you not. My reason is that Lady Olivia A. [Acheson] to whom it was first offered has come here — but not only so, so has Miss Bathurst, and they know each other — and the house will be cheaper for two than one.[3] I should not make this change, if I had the most remotest suspicion that you had in any way set your heart on the house — but I believe you simply took it because I recommended it. If you see no objection then to giving it up, should I look about for lodgings? or will me [you] give me some description of what

---

[1] See diary for 10 Oct.

[2] Miss Giberne's friend, Selina Bacchus, was married in Jan. 1846, and became a Catholic in June 1848. She died on 13 Sept. 1850, leaving two daughters. Her husband, George Copeland, became a Catholic about 1855.

[3] Cf. letter of 27 Sept. to Lady Olivia Acheson.

you would like? Another reason that weighs of course with me is, that the above ladies, having money, will rid us of all expence of the house.

Ever Yours affectly in Xt   John H Newman   Congr. Orat.

P.S.   Where are F St John's medals?

TO F. W. FABER

Oy Bm Oct 6/50

My dear F Wilfrid,

I don't see any reason against Ph's [Philip Gordon] being minister and deputy; but how will you manage it without unkindness to F Fr. [Francis Knox] and causing him great irritation? *You* will see best.

You have put him down as Confessor. If you can trust him, nothing can be better.

I think it would be better not to fill up an office than put a novice — except it was clear he could be. Not to fill up, is not a *precedent*.

I doubt whether F Bernard will make a good Praef. Orat.[1] but perhaps he will have little to do.

I have nothing more to say.

As to the Lives of the Saints, on all accounts, they had better fall to the London Oratory. We shall be very glad to *help* if we can. This would only involve an insertion of the word 'London' or 'Metropolitan' in the notices.

I suppose Montalembert is the writer of the letter. Pray convey to him, if Lord Arundel will kindly take the message, my most respectful thanks for the honor he has done me — assure him how I value his criticism — and how much encouraged I am by its favorable character.[2]

Tell F Bernard I have done without his looking over the Sermon. I have stupidly fancied that I had left a copy of the Translation in London.

Ever Yrs affly J H N

[1] Prefect of Oratory, i.e. of the confraternity for men.

[2] Newman guessed right as to the authorship of a long letter, which was being shown round. Montalembert wrote it to A. L. Phillipps on 30 Sept., and spoke of Newman and the Oratorians as follows: 'Although a great admirer of Father Newman, and particularly of his last *lectures on Anglican difficulties*, I quite agree with you on their absurd system of architecture—and having had lately an opportunity of writing to Lord Arundel, I have told him my mind about the shocking idea of building up in smoky London a counterfeit of the horrible Roman Churches . . . it is now proved throughout Europe that no new Churches can be built *by subscription* except Gothic ones. . . .' E. S. Purcell, *Life and Letters of Ambrose Phillipps de Lisle*, II, London 1900, p. 247. See also Newman's letter of 9 Oct. to Faber, and H. Tristram in *D R*, Spring 1949, p. 122.

Mr Lambert comes to town to see F. Antony on Tuesday afternoon. Will you let Mr F Capes know (through F de Held) that Mr L. wishes Mr Capes to be at St Wilfrid's Wednesday or Thursday next.[1]

TO GEORGE RYDER

Oy Bm Oct 6/50

My dear George

I have not written because I have had nothing to say.

I have done my utmost to keep the boys — but I do fear we can't do it.

As to your moving, you must not think of such a step hastily. Remain quiet till Henry and Mary [Wilberforce] return. See how you *bear* being there.

Ever Yours affectly John H Newman   Congr. Orat.

P.S.   There is *not a chance* of the boys remaining at *St W's* [Wilfrid's]. The London House is set up next Wednesday, and St W's goes from *us* to *it*.

I can't tell *how long* the boys will remain at St W's — I suspect till November 15.

I am trying now to get Harry and Lisle in our house here — but, even if I could do it, you might not like it, nor their health suit it.

Allies is going to Paris.

Be patient about your plan. I can say nothing about it yet. All saints be with you.

J H N.

TO T. W. ALLIES

Oratory Bm, Oct. 8./50

My dear Allies,

I don't know how to answer your question. I was thinking of the effect on my own mind of reading various Catholic divines, e.g. falling back upon Billuart after reading Suarez and Vasquez, or upon Tournelay. You yourself give an instance of it in your quotation from Bossuet, in the early part of your work just published.[2]

---

[1] To arrange about the Redemptorists taking St Wilfrid's.

[2] When he inserted this letter in *A Life's Decision*, pp. 332–3, Allies explained that it was 'in answer to a question I had raised about studies and authors.' The work he had just published was *The See of St. Peter, the Rock of the Church, the Source of*

Nothing can be better than the Treatise on Grace, if you wish a subject. Tournelay is reckoned best — it is certainly exceedingly good, and to me more interesting than Suarez, but Suarez of course is the greater writer. Viva, though short is a writer I like, particularly when taken in connection with the *Damnatae Theses*.[1] St. Thomas himself would be most instructive. But any how go to a real thorough thinker, though a partisan, not to a mere expounder of wealth, or an eschewer of scholastic quarrels, as Perrone, useful and accurate as he is. The fault of Suarez is his great length. I speak diffidently, for tastes differ so, but I should prefer to recommend to you Tournelay.

I am exceedingly pleased with what I have read of your new work, but have not yet finished it. The argument is very well and powerfully put.

So, you are going to Paris; I don't think you can be sorry hereafter for having done so. I heard from Wilberforce yesterday, and was surprised to find he was looking out for employment. I should not wonder if he found he had to turn to small boys. He now is afraid of Rome from the expense.

I want to say three Masses for you. Are there any days you would prefer? I am not engaged on many.

Ever yours affectly in Xt   John H. Newman   Cong. Orat.

P.S.   On looking at your wording again, I find you speak of *development*. I spoke of *quarrel*, but it is true of development, here I should take the good doctrine of the Incarnation.

WEDNESDAY 9 OCTOBER 1850   Mass solemn of the H G *Holy Ghost* (I celebrant) for the setting up of the London House.   London House released from Bm. [Birmingham] this day in General Congregation.   M. Robert called with a friend

TO F. W. FABER

Oct 9/50

My dear F. Wilfrid,

I send you an Extract from our Register Book, recording our proceedings this day —[2]

Jurisdiction and the Centre of Unity, London, with a dedication dated Sept. 1850, to Gladstone. On pp. 26–31 Allies quoted from Bossuet's 'Sermon sur l'unité.'

[1] The first edition of this work of the Jesuit Dominic Viva (1648–1726), dealing with the condemnations of Jansenism, was published 1708. The fourth edition, 1711, included the condemnations of Quietism.   [2] See next letter.

I am amused at Montalembert's attack on our Paganism. In 1844, he attacked us, because, *though* Camdenians (!), we were not Catholics, and now he laments because, *though* Catholics, we are not Camdenians. How can we please him? It is hard to be blamed both ways — we have kicked down our ladder![1]

Ever Yrs affly J H N

DECREE RELEASING THE LONDON ORATORIANS[2]

9 October 1850

Whereas it is the design of the Holy Father, as expressed in his Brief of foundation under date of November 26 1847, that the Congregation of the Oratory of St Philip Neri, established by him in Birmingham ad instar the Mother House of the Vallicella at Rome, should be extended through England, and whereas certain fathers were sent up to the Metropolis from Birmingham according to the decree of General Congregation of May 28. 1849, with the purpose of their ultimate formation into an Oratory there, and whereas in the short time that has since elapsed, they have been there blest with increase of numbers, internal consolidation, openings of usefulness, success in the duties of their vocation, friends, and well-wishers and prospects for the future, sufficient to warrant the carrying into effect at this time of the said purpose, and whereas the Right Reverend the Vicar Apostolic of the London District has, by his letter given to the London Fathers under date of August 16 of this year, signified his cordial cooperation in the same and his Episcopal sanction thereunto,[3] and whereas Father John Henry Newman, at this time Father Preposto of the Congregation, to whom especially was given the aforesaid Brief of foundation of the English Congregation, has expressed his wish that, in order to its due execution the said Fathers should be released from their allegiance to this House,

We therefore, the Fathers of the Oratory of Birmingham, in General

---

[1] Cf. letter of 6 Oct. to Faber. The High Church Camden Society, founded in 1839 for the study of ecclesiastical art, devoted much of its attention to Gothic architecture, the ladder which was supposed to have led Tractarians to become Catholics. In the early forties of the century, Montalembert was elected an honorary member, and responded with a protest 'against the most unwarrantable and unjustifiable assumption of the name Catholic by people and things belonging to the actual Church of England . . . and against the object of this society, and all such efforts in the Anglican Church, as absurd.' Mrs Oliphant, *Memoir of Count de Montalembert*, II, London 1872, pp. 25–8.

[2] Composed by Newman and to be found in the decree book of the Birmingham Oratory.　　　　[3] See letter of 13 Aug. to Stanton, and *Appendix* 1, p. 499.

Congregation assembled, after solemnly celebrating the Mass of the Holy Ghost and invoking His Divine aid upon our proceeding, do hereby on this feast of St Denys, Apostle of France, Bishop and Martyr, for the glory of God and the advantage of Holy Church, His Spouse, yet with much regret and with sorrowful hearts, set free from their connexion with our body, our dear brothers and intimate friends whose names follow, to wit,

Father Bernard Dalgairns, Father Robert Coffin,

Father Richard Stanton, Father Wilfrid Faber,

Father Antony Hutchison, Father Francis Knox,

Father Alban Wells, Father Philip Gordon,

and we commend them to the love of our Blessed Lady our Patron and our Holy Father St Philip and all the Saints, whose tender care and watchful protection have been so manifest over them and us during the years in which they have belonged to our Congregation, begging those heavenly intercessors to gain us this grace from our Divine Lord and Saviour, that we and the aforesaid Fathers and our successors and theirs, may ever be united in mutual love, and in the spirit, mind and judgment of our glorious Founder, as we are united in one faith, and have hitherto been united in one body.[1]

THURSDAY 10 OCTOBER 1850   M Robert went   Mrs Ainsworth called[2]   Mr Lambert came.

TO J. SPENCER NORTHCOTE

Oratory, Birmingham Oct 10. 1850

My dear Northcote,

I am hardly a fair judge of the plan you mention, because I *wish* it so much.[3] It has fretted me, ever since I was a Catholic, that so little

[1] At the same time St Wilfrid's was transferred entirely to the London House.

[2] Sophia Ainsworth (1819–82), a sister of A. J. Hanmer, was married in 1839, and had been received into the Church by Newman at King William Street, on 14 June 1850. She was now living with her family at Hanley, Worc. Her father, greatly distressed at her conversion, died on 4 Oct., and Newman visited her three days later. (See letter of 4 Oct. to Lord Feilding.) After her husband's death, she became in 1875, a Redemptorist nun.

[3] Northcote wrote on 9 Oct. from Clifton, 'Maskell told me yesterday he had an idea that it would be a very good thing if half a dozen or a dozen public lectures on the state of Anglicanism just now were given here by Catholic laymen, who *had been* English clergymen. . . . The fact is, I think, that both he and many other of the converts (especially of course the married ones) feel very much their suddenly being *thrown off work*.'

use was made of married converts, like Anglican clergymen, who, I have said and truly, viewed together have an amount of talent, which the unmarried clergy converted have not.

The only difficulty I have in the plan as proposed to you is in Maskell himself having part in it, who is but just converted. It will increase indeed the interest, but diminish the rhetorical force of his lectures. Besides, there is something out of keeping in a person, one day preaching in a pulpit and in the next lecturing against the pulpit in which he preached. When years have passed, a person has a right to do so — and has a right to be *heard* — but else, people may say, 'It's only a month or two, since you said just the reverse; are you sure you will not contradict your present self some months hence?'. A mere *history* of one's change, indeed, if it can be done without egotism, is not open to this retort — for it is the statement, not of an opinion, but a fact — but I think *M.* would have a difficulty in doing this *persuasively* — On the other hand, he would quite ruin his remaining influence, and the prospect of its revival, if for the moment lost, among his former friends, especially young Anglican parsons. I should certainly think it is best for him to remain quite quiet — and his very eagerness to be doing something shows this. Were I his director, I should bid him simply do nothing, if I thought he would. I am writing very freely, I hope not too much so — but I have that confidence in your judgment, that I have been led to do so. I don't like to talk of anyone to a third person, and yet I don't like to give you a half opinion, when you ask me a question.

I shall be very sorry if what I have said spoils the plan itself. Could M. give lectures on some subject, not directly against the Church of E. [England] but opening the mind of his hearers on the general subject, and preparing the way for others? So learned a man could not be at a loss, if he looked about him. E.g. to bring out *historically* the jurisdiction of the Papacy in England from St Augustine to the 16th century, would be such a point — etc etc. But I am speaking almost at random, merely to suggest ideas.

One most interesting series of lectures would be, if every one of you gave his *own* ground of conversion — for each, I suppose, would be different from the rest. But I have said more than enough. *You* know what is needed at Bristol. Anyhow they ought to be polemical or historical, *not doctrinal.*

Of course you must get the Bishop's sanction — nothing can be done without it. I don't know what Dr Hendren's feeling would be — Dr Ullathorne, I fear, would be against the whole plan.

Whether you do any thing at this moment or not, I earnestly hope you will not let the idea go — many of the early apologists were lay men.

99

I knew Wayte very fairly, and I am truly rejoiced to hear what you say about his father — I wish there was a chance of *him*. We know nothing about Forbes.[1]

With kindest remembrances to Mrs Northcote, I am, My dear N. Very sincerely Yours in Xt

John H Newman   Congr. Orat.

P.S.   I have been the last day or two thinking a good deal, of what some time ago many of us thought to no purpose. The possibility of making the Dublin available for the married converts. There are so many good writers now, who might be had; Maskell, Allies, H Wilberforce, besides you, Thompson, Ward etc. Morris again, perhaps Seager.[2] All depends, I suppose upon the Editor. Writers must take *interest* in the work they write for. I don't know what the Irish contributors would say — Dr Russell is a learned man, and has been from the first most warmly disposed to the converts. I meant to have had some talk with the Cardinal, before he went to Rome, and now I suppose I must wait till his Eminence returns.[3]

J H N

TO RICHARD STANTON

Oy Bm Oct 10/50

My dear F Richard

Not only did I tell you we would raise the three Fathers to the rank of decennials, but I actually transcribed the entry which was to be made, and got you to send me back *the very paper* that *we* might use it. I now transcribe it again —

'C.D.[4] Oct. 9. Resolved that it be proposed to the G.C.[5] that Fathers Francis Knox, Alban Wells, and Philip Gordon, be admitted

[1] Samuel Simon Wayte, a leading Bristol solicitor, was on the point of becoming a Catholic. His son Samuel William (1819–98), was a Scholar at Trinity College 1838–42, and then a Fellow and tutor there until his election as President of his College in 1866. Alexander Penrose Forbes (1817–75), who entered Brasenose College in 1840, was greatly influenced by the Tractarian movement. Pusey nominated him Vicar of St Saviour's, Leeds, in 1847, and in the following year he was appointed Bishop of Brechin.

[2] Maskell was now a widower and J. B. Morris unmarried, but all the rest, in this list of convert clergymen, were married men.

[3] Wiseman was made a Cardinal on 30 Sept.

[4] Congregatio Deputata, or governing council.

[5] Congregatio Generalis, or meeting of the whole community.

to the rank and privileges of Decennial Fathers of the Congregation —
in consequence of the existing necessities of the London House.

C.G. Oct 9. Decreed unanimously that Fathers Francis Knox etc'

Yrs affectly J H N

FRIDAY 11 OCTOBER 1850 M. Robert went.[1] F Joseph went. Mr Molloy
came with the plans of the House.

TO T. W. ALLIES

Oratory, Birmingham Oct. 11. 1850.

My dear Allies,

We shall be glad to see you at any time, but I am sorry to say that I
cannot be *sure* whether we shall have room inside the house. At *present*
three of our party are away, or rather a fourth whose room Bathurst
occupies, but I don't know quite when they return. Even if, however,
by bad luck we were full, we would manage for you in some way.

We set up formally the London House on the anniversary of my
reception (thank you for remembering it). They are now quite separate
from us and me. It is a sorrowful thing and anxious, yet hopeful.

I have just received Maskell's able and settling pamphlet, but I am
very sorry the three letters did not appear, as you intended, immediately
on their being written. Then they would have produced an effect, the
question would have been before the world, and the *doubt* would have
thrown the *onus probandi* on Pusey. Now, it is to be feared, the *onus
probandi* will be upon the 'Why should I read Maskell?' The more I
think of it, the more I regret it.[2]

Dear C. Marriott could make up his mind tomorrow to be a Catholic,

---

[1] This is repeated from 10 Oct.

[2] In May 1850, Allies, Dodsworth and Maskell, while still Anglicans, wrote three
letters jointly to Pusey, in which they asked him 'What authority is there for supposing
that the acts of a priest are *valid* who hears confessions and gives absolution, in mere
virtue of his orders, without ordinary or delegated jurisdiction from his bishop?' The
Anglican bishops of 1850 disapproved almost entirely of the practice of confession.
Pusey's questioners told him they intended eventually to publish the letters that passed
between them. Pusey issued a public reply, a *Letter to the Rev. W. U. Richards*, dated
25 July, and entitled *The Church of England leaves her Children free to whom to open
their Griefs*. Maskell then wrote the pamphlet, dated 8 Oct. 1850, to which Newman
refers, *A Letter to the Rev. Dr. Pusey on his practice of receiving persons in Auricular
Confession*. In it the questioning letters of May were published for the first time. See
letters of 16 Sept. and 20 Oct. to Maskell. This led Pusey to re-issue his pamphlet with
a postscript of over a hundred pages, in Nov. 1850. See also Liddon's *Pusey* III, pp.
265–70.

if he would; at least this is my feeling, though you have seen him so much lately, and I not. I don't think he has any argument, unless arguments have grown on him, except Pusey and sanguineness.

All kind thoughts to Mrs Allies.

Believe me Ever yours affecty John H. Newman Congr. Orat.

TO VISCOUNT FEILDING

Oratory Oct 12/50

My dear Lord,

I find I made a mistake in telling you about our preachers tomorrow — It being St. Edward's Day, one of our principal feasts, I sing the High Mass. Accordingly the Sermons run thus: at 9 F Bowles, at 11 F St John, at 3, catechising, F Flanagan — and at 7 F Penny.

Yours very truly in Xt   John H. Newman   Congr. Orat.

TO BISHOP ULLATHORNE

Oratory Birmingham Oct 12. 1850

My dear Lord,

I feel very much gratified by the honor your Lordship has done me by your wish that I should preach at the Mass of thanksgiving and the Installation at St Chad's, which I am very glad to hear is so soon to take place.[1]

I can do nothing else but accept this mark of your Lordship's favor, though I am conscious how little able I am, duly to fulfil such an office on an occasion so solemn and special.

I am, My dear Lord, begging your Lordship's blessing, Your faithful Servt

John H Newman

TO F. W. FABER

Oratory Bm Oct 13/50

Very Revd and dear Father,

I congratulate your Very-reverence on your establishment as a House of St Philip and on your own elevation in particular.[2] It synchronises

[1] Pius IX established the new hierarchy in England on 29 Sept., and Ullathorne was to be installed as first Bishop of Birmingham on 27 Oct.

[2] Faber was elected first independent Superior of the London Oratory, on 12 Oct.

with the elevation of your diocesan, the Cardinal Archbishop, and the promulgation of the Hierarchy. It is a great era, and Pugin, not to be wanting to himself, has paid us the delicate compliment of turning a plea for plain chant into a plain chant of our virtues. A *profound silence*, I suppose your Very-reverence will agree with me, is the only way of bearing such blushing honors.[1]

Thank you for his Eminence's message about me, which was read out at Recreation.[2]

This House gave its Masses and Communions to yours yesterday.

Love to all of you Ever Yours affectionately

John H Newman   Congr. Orat.

P.S.   I accept your kind offer of the three Propositions, i.e. for such time as they hold in force — and use the 1st and 2nd upon it. As to the 3rd, I suppose *I* do not *rule* ⟨decide⟩ any appeal[3]

I sent Number 90 and Letter to Jelf to St W's [Wilfrid's] for F Robert to bring to London. I can't find letter to Bishop of O. [Oxford] to my surprise.[4]

Will you direct the inclosed to Watts Russell. I will owe you the postage.

[1] *An Earnest Appeal for the Revival of the Ancient Plain Song*, just published, contained violent complaints about the Oratorians. See letter of 18 April 1851 to Ullathorne.

[2] Faber wrote on 9 Oct. to Joseph Gordon, ' I send you an extract from a dispatch I had from the Cardinal this morning: I send it to you, for the same reason he gives for mentioning it to me.

"But you will be more deeply interested to hear, that, beginning with the Holy Father, down to the least prelate, the confidence in your Padre and the esteem for him are *unbounded*. The Pope, every Cardinal, and Mgr Barnabò, speak of Padre *Nevman* or *Neüman* with sincere affection and tenderness, and look forward to his being, even more than he has been, a great instrument in the hands of Divine Providence, for the conversion of many in England. He must not therefore be disheartened by any little domestic, or transatlantic, contradictions, but must do his work confidingly and generously. I write all this to you instead of to him, because I fear if I wrote to him, his modesty would urge him to conceal it all; and the character and estimation of a Superior with the Holy See are the property of the entire Congregation and of a common value to all." Ever dear F. Joseph Yr most aff brother F. W. F.'

[3] See letter of 19 Sept. to Faber. Newman's three propositions were received unanimously by the Congregation of Deputies in London. The third allowed matters to be referred to Newman in certain cases, but, he now settles, only for his advice, not for his decision.

[4] See letter of 21 Aug. to Faber.

TO RICHARD STANTON

Oratory Oct 13/50

My dear F Richard,

I fear that letter to Chiesa Nuova has given you a good deal of trouble, but I thought you would do it better than anyone else. Send it down if we can be of any use. Mrs Bowden sends me word they go on Wednesday. Should you not be ready, I will send a Latin line or two to F. Rossi by them. So let me know about it.[1]

It seems Cardinal W. [Wiseman] left your present to him to go after him — and the good Priests of St George's, who had the management of it, thought it was a present from *me* to the *Pope*. So there is a chance of his Holiness receiving from me my heresy bound in morocco.[2]

I wish you joy on your start.

Ever Yours affectly John H Newman

MONDAY 14 OCTOBER 1850 Lord and Lady Feilding breakfasted here, and went. Mr Molloy went. Frederic went to St W's [Wilfrid's] Charles returned and young Flyn Marshall came

TO J. M. CAPES

Oy Bm Oct 14/50

My dear Capes

Somehow, I suppose by my own fault, I cannot find pp. 401, 402. I don't suppose you need be at the trouble of sending them.

At p. 414 is it right to say that St Paul declares he is 'not always *divinely guided*?' — Counsels of perfection, I suppose, come from God. But I dare say you have authority.[3]

A little before, 'unrecorded *sayings* innumerable?' sayings or *works*?

'St Paul certainly has said that his letters are not in every part inspired;' — where?

[1] See letter of 15 Oct. to Carlo Rossi of the Roman Oratory.
[2] Newman's books, referred to in letter of 21 Aug. 1850 to Faber, were sent to Rome. See letters of 2 July 1851 and 28 April 1854 to Faber.
[3] Cf. 1 Cor. 7: 25. Throughout, Newman is suggesting corrections for Capes's article in the *Rambler*, (Nov. 1850), pp. 409–40, 'The Pope,' which were accepted by him. Pp. 401–2 were part of an article by Northcote, 'Celebrated Sanctuaries of the Madonna.'

Only have a good author with you, and I am satisfied.

I suppose, on thinking, you allude in your 'letter' and writer, to Pugin. Whether *you* will think it necessary to say a word, I know not — but, please, don't say a word in defence of *us* — One must not notice such a madman.[1]

You have not said a word about the Bishop of Avignon's [?] wish, tho' Burns said you could give me some hints

Ever Yours affly J H N

P.S. My 'Prophetical Office' was a development of a controversial paper I wrote against the Abbé Jager in 1834, with additions or systematizings from Lectures I read in Adam de Brome's Chapel in 1836.[2]

TUESDAY 15 OCTOBER 1850 F Austin returned? Marshall went

TO CARLO ROSSI

Dabam ex aedibus nostris, Birmingham Oct. 15. 1850.
En paucula verba, Pater reverendissime et charissime, per manus juvenis mihi et in saeculo et in S. Philippi dilectione conjunctissimi, Joannis Edwardi Bowden, Congregationis Oratorii Londinensis novitii, hoc autem tempore valetudinis causa peregrinantis.

Ille paternitatem tuam certiorem faciet de rebus et negotiis nostris, et apud Birmingham et apud Londinum; quae quidem ut plenius intelligas, Patri Riccardo Stanton, quem nosti, pater, id muneris detuli, ut narrationem litteris mandatam a te mitteret, eorum omnium, quae nobis contingerent ex illo tempore, quo, urbe relicta, Sanctissimi Patris et Fundatoris nostri instituta et traditiones in patriam nostram introduximus.[3]

Tu autem memineris nostri, cum in conspectu S. Philippi astas, sacrificium augustissimum oblaturus, et praesertim mei,

Pater colendissime, Tui observandissimi Joann. M. Newman.

[1] On pp. 425–7 Capes spoke of the violent differences that could exist between Catholics. Cf. letter of 13 Oct. to Faber.
[2] See *Apo.* p. 64, and *John Henry Newman Centenary Essays*, ed. H. Tristram, London 1945, pp. 201–22.
[3] Stanton's letter is printed immediately after this one, in G. Bondini, *Della fondazione dell' Oratorio in Inghilterra*, Rome 1852, pp. 139–43.

WEDNESDAY 16 OCTOBER 1850   F Thomas (*Scratton*) returned
THURSDAY 17 OCTOBER   F. Austin in retreat

TO THE EDITOR OF THE TABLET

Oratory, Birmingham, Oct. 20, 1850.

Dear Sir,

Will you allow me to correct a misapprehension concerning the Fathers of the Oratory, contained in the letter of your correspondent 'S.M.' in last week's *Tablet*?[1]

He says 'If they are not exclusively bound to popular services, *I cannot help thinking it is a pity that they do not*, along with these, *cultivate the Ritual branch.*'

On the contrary, *we are bound by our rule* to the solemn Ritual services of the Church, *and we keep it*. Both our own House here, and the Oratory in London, sings High Mass and Vespers *every* Sunday, and other principal festivals, besides observing the services prescribed for All-Souls, Candlemas, Ash-Wednesday, Holy Week and other sacred seasons. The Congregations of the Oratory have ever been remarkable for their exact attention to the rubrics of the Ritual; and a great judge of these matters, the Prelate who has just been raised to a place among the Princes of the Church, has before now been pleased to say that nowhere did he find them more carefully fulfilled than in the London Oratory.

It is only because we have *daily* sermons and prayers, and have thence been led to adopt vernacular and familiar services *also*, that we are supposed to neglect what in fact we scrupulously observe. People fancy we *substitute*, because we *add*. They assume we hold what we do not dream of holding, and then proceed to refute their own assumptions. Of course in saying this, I am not alluding to the temperate and judicious writer who has given occasion to this note.

I am, dear Sir, yours very truly,

John H. Newman, Congr. Orat.

[1] The *Tablet* (5 Oct. 1850), p. 635, in an account of the *Rambler* for Oct., criticised the review of Faber's *Spirit and Genius of St Philip Neri*, the article entitled 'Popular Services,' for disparaging Vespers. The *Tablet's* criticism was supported, 12 Oct., p. 658, by a correspondent who referred to the Oratorians, and to whom Newman now replies. His letter was published in the *Tablet*, 26 Oct., pp. 676–7.

TO WILLIAM MASKELL

Oratory Birmingham Oct 20. 1850

My dear Maskell,

I meant before now to have thanked you for your new Pamphlet, which I read with great interest. It is quite conclusive. I only regret that the Three Letters were not published at the time without note or comment. I shall be curious to see if the Anglican Periodicals take any notice of it.[1]

How curious the state of the party is now. The Anti-Catholics of them seem increasing in power — and likely to throw the Romanizers either into the church, into inaction, or into a sect. Monro's pamphlet of which I have only seen an extract, is a remarkable sign of the times.[2] Then, I suppose, they will gradually eschew doctrine, fraternize with liberals and such Evangelicals as will trust them, and consent to the relaxation of tests; though this must be a work of time with such zealots as Palmer. It is strange to see how *consistent* men are. Palmer is just what he was 17 years ago — and advocating precisely the same measures.

Yours very sincerely in Xt   John H Newman   Congr. Orat.

TUESDAY 22 OCTOBER 1850   James Pitts went   Capuchin monk here

TO F. W. FABER

Oy Bm Oct 23/50

My dear F Supr

Don't be surprised if you see two lines from me in the Tablet in answer to a letter therein last week. It is merely to say that we *do* have high Mass and Vespers.[3]

[1] See letter of 11 Oct. to Allies.

[2] Edward Monro, *A Few Words on the Spirit in which Men are Meeting the Present Crisis in the Church. A Letter to Roundell Palmer, Esq. Q.C., M.P.*, London 1850. Monro urged that the Anglican clergy, instead of struggling against subjection to the State, and instead of trying to work out an intellectual basis for their position, should devote themselves to pastoral work. He complained that Maskell had made the question of membership of Christ's Church too much 'a mathematical or philosophical' one, p. 34. Edward Monro (1815–66), brought up an Evangelical, came under Tractarian influence while at Oriel College, 1832–36. He was Perpetual Curate of Harrow Weald, Middlesex, 1842–60, and then Vicar of St John's, Leeds.

[3] Letter of 20 Oct.

I have just heard from Watts Russell ⟨(not in answer to mine)⟩ —
He is at Leghorn in his way to Rome — and complains of your not
writing to him.

I thought you told me F Robert was coming to see you. As to the
Cardinalate, it gives me the stomach-ache. We ought to give all our
spare Masses to its success

Love to all, Ever yours affectly J H N

TO CHARLES RUSSELL

Oy. Bm Oct 23/50

My dear Dr Russell,

I write in strict confidence, and that will enable me to take a great
liberty, which I shall trust to you to excuse.

Friends of mine are willing to spend money on the Dublin, which
they fancy would be an object to it — (whether this is true or not, I
know not) and to bring to it a considerable addition of contributors.
Now so far as this, I am only taking the liberty of *meddling* in matters
which don't concern me — but then, these friends continue, that it is
natural that, should they throw themselves into it in the way I have
mentioned, they should wish to be able to take a greater *interest* in the
Review than they can do under its present management.

I have turned the whole matter over in my mind, and think it worth
while mentioning it to you. I see in the distance the almost certainty of
a new Catholic Quarterly being set up, unless the Dublin can contrive
to divert into itself the new powers and influences which would have
this issue. On the other hand the Dublin has so flourished under its
present Editorship, and the Editor is so excellent a man, and deserves
so well of Catholics, that the first question to ask is, Does *he* like the
responsible task, or does he undertake it out of consideration for Dr
Wiseman and others, because there is no one else to do the work?[1]

What my friends say is, English Catholics *must* have a Quarterly —
but I don't see why, as the Edinburgh represents a *British* political
party, so the Dublin should not represent a United-Kingdom religious
one — so that both Irish and English Catholics might have a joint
interest in it.

Will you kindly give me your opinion on this proposition, if you

[1] Henry Bagshawe was the editor of *D R*, and many of the articles were contributed
by Wiseman and Russell, who chiefly supported it. See also the letters of 28 Oct.

think it worth talking about — else, pray put this note into the fire, and think no more of the subject

I am, My dear Dr Russell, Ever Yours very sincerely in Xt

John H Newman   Congr. Orat.

TO RICHARD STANTON

Oratory. Bm Oct 23. 1850

My dear F Richard

I meant to have written before now, could I have answered your questions.

Thank you for the Supplement and Office — they are beautifully got up. We think what you have sent will do, and I have put down the cost in the account, which I hope to send you, as lying between us.

It perplexes me why F Robert has not been to you. You told me he was going soon, and I gave him Number 90 etc to take to you. (Don't bind up the volume at once; I *may* find the Letter to the Bishop of Oxford[1] — *I* should like the 'Suffragans' which Stewart found, if the price was not very high (I have neither Plain Sermons or 2nd of St Athanasius) I can't tell what is come to Coffin, *entre nous*. I fear nothing will content him. Today comes a letter from Watts Russell from *Leghorn* in his way to Rome — but I hope he will get my letter there, and so write to Florence for me — but it is unlucky.[2]

I get more and more fidgetted about the Cardinal-Archbishoprick, which good Talbot should never have urged. It seems to me we are at a most critical moment. A Cardinal is a station of *this world*; now *who is there* who knows any thing of the world to put about the Cardinal? I wish he could be kept from England for a while, and the hierarchy set on foot sub silentio. We have not Canonists, theologians, or men of the world — but since Sanctissimus Dominus has done it, I suppose it is all right. You should give any spare Masses you have to the happy issue of the existing difficulties.

Your letter to F Rossi seemed to me to do very well — but I had no particular criticism to make.

Many thanks indeed for the books you propose to send us — put your name in them, as presented to the Brummagem Oratory.[3]

[1] See letter of 21 Aug. to Faber.
[2] Newman had asked Watts Russell to arrange about Coffin's stay at the Florence Oratory.
[3] Stanton replied, 'Most of them being Anglicans, I feel ashamed to put my name in them, as you suggest.'

We are not *bound*, but only are *allowed*, to say the office of St Philip on the 30th?

Ever Yours affectionately J H N

PS.   The inclosed is F Bernard's

TO GEORGE TALBOT

Oratory Birmingham Oct 23/50

My dear Talbot,

This is to say how I had hoped soon to write to you and to thank you for your interesting letter — but I am led to take up my pen at once, and to put before you some anxious matters connected with the coming of the Cardinal.[1] The whole public is up against him, and the press, I believe, without the exception of any Paper.[2] The first question that arises is, Should his Eminence wait awhile at Florence, till the first ferment is over? I have asked a friend to write to him, and put him in possession of the whole state of the case,[3] yet still I think it best to write to you also. Next, ought he not to have about him, not only good Canonists, but some good *English Constitutional* lawyers? a false step would be most damaging and disastrous — We might find ourselves in

---

[1] Talbot wrote on 24 Sept. of the importance of his position as a chamberlain to Pius IX, 'It is to us that he opens his heart, and even seeks for advice, specially regarding the countries with which we are connected. . . . I tell you in confidence that I have done all I could to induce the Pope to allow Dr Wiseman to return to England as Cardinal Archbishop of Westminster—'

[2] The first leading article in *The Times* of 14 Oct. was a violent attack on 'the new-fangled Archbishop of Westminster,' and was followed by another on 19 Oct. On Sunday 20 Oct. Wiseman's pastoral 'from out the Flaminian Gate' was read in the Catholic churches. Whitty, who was acting as his Vicar General, considered he had no mandate to withhold it, although he realised how it would fan the flames of the agitation that was beginning. On 22 Oct. *The Times* returned to the attack, and the rest of the newspapers followed its lead.

[3] This was George Bowyer, who had become a Catholic in Aug. Badeley, Bellasis, and Hope being still Anglicans, Bowyer, an authority on the Constitutional Law of England, was the Catholic lawyer most qualified to advise. Whitty asked him to consult Newman about the situation, and he wrote on 22 Oct. about its seriousness, and Wiseman's need of worldly-wise advisers. Whitty himself wrote to Newman the same day. 'It seems that the Cardinal and Hierarchy have become awfully notorious. Cardinal W. has of course no idea of this and accordingly he was to have left Rome for England on the 12th of Oct. Do you think we ought to write and try to stop him. By remaining quietly in Italy for two or three months until this fever subsides we may have peace—whereas one really begins to fear that his speedy return may keep up and increase the ferment. . . .'

a Praemunire[1] and I don't know what. Then, ought he not to have some persons who know the English world well? It seems most impertinent in me thus to write to you about the Cardinal, treating him as a third person — but I do it to save time, and to put you au courant. I dare say all I have said or have to say, has occurred to him, and that he has provided against it, but, depend upon it, we shall have a hard game to play, and it does not do to leave it to chance. As you know well, besides the Cardinal himself, there is no one, I may say, in England, who knows how to deal with the world, no one has lived in society so as to be a match for politicians and lawyers. Our enemies would like nothing so much as to get his Eminence into some technical difficulties, and then to ridicule us. The *status* of the Cardinal is perfectly [new][2] every thing has to be determined — and so of the Hierarchy. It seems very presumptuous in me to say all this, but, if you can extract any one good suggestion from it, it may be worth the saying — and you must pardon what is absurd, and put my letter behind the fire.[3]

One great advantage of the erection of the Hierarchy and the coming of the Cardinal is that it *will force us* to have Canonists, theologians, men of business, and men of savoir faire; but at present every thing has to be organized. My only fear is, that in the process of gaining experience and the necessary defences of our new position, we shall have reverses and mishaps.

I shall have a talk with Dr Ullathorne, or, as I ought to say, the Bishop of Birmingham on this matter tomorrow, and perhaps I shall have something to add to this before closing it.

I have spoken above of the Cardinal delaying his coming — at the same time I cannot help thinking the whole matter of the hierarchy should be settled before Parliament meets, i.e. before the end of January next.

Don't interpret me to be an advocate of *fears*. Fear is the worst of counsellors. We must not retreat a foot. The Holy See has decided — but we must be very cautious.

I want you to get me a good opinion on another question. I have lately had good advice from Rome that one may act as if the rule about prohibited books had not been promulgated in England.[4] Now about

---

[1] i.e. the statutory offence, dating from the fourteenth century, of promoting papal encroachments on rights claimed by the Crown.　　　　[2] Paper torn.

[3] Newman is reproducing advice received from Bowyer in his confidential letter of 22 Oct.

[4] Stanton copied out part of a letter written from Rome, by Grant, in July: 'I have consulted a learned Theologian about the Index in England and about the *mala fides*, in which some are: and he says that as no one in England amongst the Ecclesiastical Superiors has pressed the censures and the special laws of the Index upon the people, and as the general impression is that each one may read any book *not* injurious to his

my own parochial sermons. They do good and advance people to Catholicism, I do not doubt. I have *personally* no difficulty on the *moral* question. Now, I have attempted a new edition *corrected*, i.e. leaving out whatever sounds uncatholic — , *and people wont buy it*.[1] Might I publish it, (leaving out indeed any *distinctly* heterodox sermon, but) leaving uncorrected what is incidentally heterodox, and *putting a notice at the beginning* that I submit it to the Church and wish unsaid whatever is inconsistent with faith and morals?[2]

Ever Yours most sincerely in Xt   John H Newman

P.S.   Will you thank Case very much for his letter which I hope to answer soon.[3]

conscience, that is to say not forbidden *jure naturali*, it is quite lawful for you to act as if the laws of the Index did not apply to England, except as furnishing information as to what books are dangerous. Hence those penitents who have even in *mala fides* read books in England or in any country where the same *non-observance* of the Index prevails on account of the same quality of literature and the same cast of society existing there (e.g. United States) do not incur the censures, simply because they cannot impose a penalty by their *mala fides* from which every one else is practically exempt, although they sin, of course, more grievously in consequence of the more violent disobedience implied in such *mala fides*.

This Theologian strongly dissuades you from applying to the Holy See on this subject, as then the Sacred Congregations would of course try to enforce the strict law, which in the temper of English people would or might cause great trouble, whereas the present non-usage is sufficient to set consciences at ease about the censures, and the natural law will or ought to check people from reading books dangerous to them individually.'

[1] The fourth edition of Vol. IV of *P.S.* appeared in 1849, with this *Advertisement*, 'The following Sermons, written when the Author belonged to the Anglican Communion, are so far altered in the present Edition, as they contained any thing contrary to Faith and Morals. More than this has not been attempted.

The Dedication [to Hugh James Rose] is retained as an historical record of his feelings towards a friend, who, from the time of his death, has had a place in his daily thoughts. Oratory, Birmingham, Feb. 21, 1849.' Besides altering anything 'contrary to Faith and Morals,' Newman changed phrases that 'sounded uncatholic.'

[2] Talbot replied in a letter of which Newman copied an extract at the back of his diary on 13 Dec., the day after he received it, '. . . your question . . . "whether you can continue to publish the Sermons which you wrote before you were a Catholic, and which have the effect of leading persons into the Church. . . ." I accordingly consulted Perrone, who is the oracle here upon it. His reply was, "Newman cannot publish them in his own name; but he can allow any bookseller to sell them who chooses." So that you can allow Burns or any one else even to reprint your old Sermons and sell them.' Cf. letter of 21 Dec. 1867 to Copeland, where Newman explains that the altered edition of *P.S.* Vol. IV, in 1849, was against his own wish, and due to the insistence of Dr Newsham (letters of 27 Oct., 5 and 9 Nov. 1848), and that he took an early opportunity to get a more authoritative opinion.

[3] George Case (1823–78) entered Brasenose College in 1841, and after being a curate at All Saints, Margaret Street, became a Catholic in 1850. He then went out to Rome and was ordained. In 1857 he entered the Jesuit novitiate, but left to work as a priest in the Clifton diocese, where he was made a Canon.

Oct 24. I have seen Dr Ullathorne today, and he advises some of the Cardinal's immediate friends meeting together and some one going out to him. I have written to Dr Whitty on the subject — but *he* says he does not know where he is. I hope all will go well, still we can't be too cautious

Do you think you could get me an answer I could safely go on, to this question?

A person of landed property has been recommended to put into a mission on his property, the Rosminian Fathers. *Should he be advised to do so?* Of course I will keep most profoundly secret your answer as coming from you or from Rome.[1]

THURSDAY 24 OCTOBER 1850   Lord and Lady Feilding here   Allies came with his son

FRIDAY 25 OCTOBER   Lord and Lady Feilding here   conditionally baptized Edwd Allies

TO F. W. FABER

Oy Bm. Oct 25/50

My dear F Wilfrid,

I can only conjecture that Dr G. [Grant] wrote in a bad humour, or has perpetrated a very clumsy joke. Can it be that, having done his utmost to separate you from me, now he begins to be afraid of his own work, and wishes to take my place in keeping you in order?[2]

[1] Two of Rosmini's books had been placed on the Index in 1849, and in the autumn of 1850 he was under attack in Italy, and threatened with further condemnations. Wiseman would not allow the Rosminians to preach in his diocese.

[2] Faber copied for Newman, on 22 Oct., an extract from a letter that had just arrived from Grant in Rome: 'Our poor catholic body is very much divided, and I do not like to take any side in its innumerable quarrels. Now, many questions are connected with the Oratorians, and their sayings and doings, and as I cannot persuade myself that they are free from the ordinary defects of our nature and composition, I try to forget these, and abstaining from any side, I am content to love you and your confrères, and suspend my judgment until we meet here or in England, when you may bully me as much as you like—I have tried to befriend and defend you where praise or blame is most important in your eyes,—in this Holy City of Rome; and yet I hear things at times which induce pious people to blame you, and as long as I am assured that the S. Padre and Propaganda love and esteem the Oratorians, I try to forget what any one else may say, and go on loving you. Two things I will tell you as I heard them:— 1 that the peculiar views about architecture which are attributed to the Oratorians are *yours personally* (italics are Dr G's) and that you have moved others to attach an importance to them which they have not in themselves, and I think it is said even in the opinion of some of your confrères. 2. It is said that *you* are too positive when you have

What he says I think shows this:— that it is our line to keep simply and entirely on the defensive — even if we do nothing, the fact of violence on the other side will be taken as a *proof we must* have been violent too — and the very shadow of any agression on our part will increase it to a demonstration.

They say the Red Hat is to be proceeded against in court of law on its arrival. The whole matter is an anxious one — a Cardinalate is a thing of *this* world — he must take a worldly post unless he comes incognito — this brings him into the society of the Catholic nobility, such as Lord Camoys[1] etc etc. men of little religion, gallicans etc etc. Now when a country is Catholic, this matters little — but here, it would be choosing his friends and counsellors, from hangers on of the Court etc etc.

I will have a talk with F Thomas about his translation.[2]

I have on Sunday morning to do the penitenza of preaching at St Chad's at the thanksgiving Mass — Can you conceive a greater of its kind?

Thank F Richard for his letter, which I am too tired to think of answering

Ever Yrs affly J H N

SATURDAY 26 OCTOBER 1850   H W [Wilberforce] came

SUNDAY 27 OCTOBER   preached at St Chad's at the thanksgiving Mass for the Hierarchy[3]

taken a side, and that no one may attempt to advise you. *Now*, mind I will have nothing to say to our wretched English disputes, and I will never quarrel with you, so that you must make no attempt to answer this letter, at least on these points. Go on working as hard as you can, and do not *talk* more than you can help about Grecian or Gothic, and examine whether you or your confreres are or are not subject to fits of censoriousness about others who are more Gothic than yourselves. Unfortunately this is ascribed to you, and it is nearly as bad to be accused as it is to be guilty in these days.' Faber added, ' I hope you consider the above an *adequate* wigging even for my impudence.' Grant who had accused Newman of imitating the French Oratory and wishing to be a 'general,' was insistent as to the separation of Oratories. See Newman's letters of 24 Nov. and 25 Dec. 1849 to Faber.

   [1] Thomas Stonor (1797–1881) became fifth Baron Camoys in 1839, when the barony, in abeyance since the reign of Henry VI, was revived by Queen Victoria, who made him in the same year a lord-in-waiting. He refused to sign the Laity's Address of congratulation and gratitude to Wiseman on his return to England as a Cardinal, in Nov. 1850, and made his refusal public.

   [2] Scratton wanted some translation work to eke out his income.

   [3] 'Christ upon the Waters,' *O.S.* pp. 121–62. Ullathorne wrote to Newman, 'All to whom I have spoken agree that your discourse yesterday was a remarkable one— one of your most remarkable ones. . . . you will oblige me and a great many by publishing it.' See letter of 7 Nov. to Ullathorne.

TO J. M. CAPES

Oy Bm Oct 28/50

My dear Capes

I was very sorry to see that the Tablet had headed my letter 'The Rambler etc'[1] It has nothing to do with the Rambler, and it never entered my head that it could so be understood.

The Dublin Review is likely, I think, to come more or less into the hands of our friends. Whatever arrangement is to be made awaits the Cardinal's coming. The notion is, but don't mention it, to have a new Editor

Ever Yours affectly John H Newman   Congr. Orat.

TO WILLIAM MASKELL

Oratory Birmingham Oct 28. 1850

(Private)

My dear Maskell,

I have no right yet to speak on the following subject, and yet it is necessary in order to its further prosecution.

We should be able, I think, to get the Dublin into our hands, if only we had money. I write to ask then, if you would take part, in such a scheme.

There are now various good writers who have nothing particular to do — e.g. Allies, H Wilberforce, yourself — Ward, not to speak of Thompson, Northcote, Bowyer, etc.

Oct 29 — I assume that the Dublin pays at the rate of £5.5 a sheet. This is not enough to make it worth while for a man to write for it. Double the remuneration, i.e. make it 9 or 10 guineas, and it would be possible for writers to make it a source of income. A man writing four times a year an article averaging 2 sheets would make £84 — and one man might well do so, for, the review containing 16 sheets, such a contribution would allow of 8 articles in the number, of two sheets (average) each.

To raise up the remuneration to this sum viz 16 sheets, 4 times a year at an additional £55 would take £336. Now do you see any way to

---

[1] 'The Rambler and Popular Services.' See letter of 20 Oct. to the Editor of the *Tablet*.

forward such a scheme? can you think of any persons who would contribute towards it? could you do any thing towards it yourself? There
are so few rich persons we have to apply to, that I fear the plan is
impracticable, unless, when it is taken up, it is taken up warmly.

I am, My dear Maskell, Very truly Yours in Xt

John H Newman   Congr. Orat.[1]

TO CHARLES RUSSELL

Oratory Birmingham Oct 28. 1850

My dear Dr Russell,

Though I cannot yet reply to your questions, I write to thank you
for your kind and satisfactory answer. The sort of arrangement which I
suppose might suit would be for the persons I allude to to name the
Editor, and you the revisor i.e. a theologian.

While I am writing, I will set right a misapprehension which must
have been unpleasant to you, and which is quite unfounded. I have
nothing to do with the Rambler, except that lately Mr Capes has consulted me on some points of theology and the like. I have [had] no hand
whatever in its setting up — I never wrote a line of prose in it, as far
as I recollect — I never suggested any article. Nor, I believe, has any
Oratorian written in it, but F. Dalgairns, and he not a great deal, some
papers on St Philip and one article besides.

Again the idea *never* came into my head that there was any rivalry
between it and the Dublin — I never saw any difference of opinion, or
at least noticed or was aware of any — and never heard any one speak
of them as antagonists. They have different objects, and occupy different
spheres. They are, I am sure, quite compatible with each other — and
I should be most concerned to think, nor can I fancy, that any support
friends of mine might give the Dublin, would hurt the Rambler.

The Oratory, hitherto, has had nothing to do with Reviews or Maga-
zines — nor do I suppose, we should have time even now for such
literary engagements. As to the Rambler, I think it began when I was
abroad.[2]

Ever Yours very sincerely in Xt

John H Newman   Congr. Orat.

---

[1] Maskell wrote at the top of this letter 'Promised 20£ for the first year.' Nothing
came of Newman's hopes for *D R*.

[2] The first number of the *Rambler* is dated 1 Jan. 1848. Newman returned to
England on 24 Dec. 1847.

TUESDAY 29 OCTOBER 1850   F Joseph returned?

WEDNESDAY 30 OCTOBER   Bathurst went?   H W [Wilberforce] went

TO F. W. FABER

Allhallow's Eve 1850

My dearest F Wilfrid

I am in retreat to-day. I am made exceedingly anxious about Father Richard. *It is the first word I have heard about it. What* says Dr Watson?[1]

By no means take *any* part about the Cardinal. At the same time I earnestly trust high persons won't be frightened. *That* is the game of Times and Company[2]

Ever Yrs affly J H N

SATURDAY 2 NOVEMBER 1850   Allies went

TO F. W. FABER

Oratory Bm Nov 4. 1850

My dear F Wilfrid

I have wished to write to you since your letter came on Saturday, but have been both engaged and knocked up with writing for publication my Hierarchy Sermon. I expect it will be out on Thursday next. Get a number of copies from Burns for your Fathers.

I said Mass for you all this morning in consideration of Times and Punch persecution to which you are exposed.[3] Caswall's brother[4] was followed by the rabble the other day in London, having on a long cloke

[1] Stanton was coughing and spitting blood, and low spirited.

[2] Faber wrote on 29 Oct., 'Oakeley has written to say he is coming to *consult me* about the Cardinal's being stopped! What has he or what have I to do with it? I shall simply say we have nothing to do but *pray*, which will be "pious and good"; but I am sorry to say F. Bernard has committed himself to McMullen who is a vehement anti-cardinalite and antiTalbotite.' Cf. W. Ward, *The Life and Times of Cardinal Wiseman*, I, 2nd ed. London 1897, p. 553.

[3] *The Times* campaign was gathering momentum. Besides leading articles against 'Papal Aggression,' which had begun on 14 Oct., and included, on 30 Oct., an attack on Newman's sermon at St Chad's, there appeared frequent reports of protest meetings, and letters objecting to the new hierarchy. *Punch*, too, had numerous attacks on Catholics and Puseyites, in which the Oratorians figured. More frequent were the attacks on Newman himself, both in articles and cartoons.

[4] Henry Caswall (1810–70), Vicar of Figheldean, Wilts.

which they took for an Oratorian. He faced round, pulled aside the cloke, and showed his trousers — When they saw him all sound below, they gave him a cheer and left him.

Let me hear how you go on[1] — How have you managed about your Series of sermons, and of Lectures? I suppose it will be hardly safe now to undertake persecution; also our Protestant brother will give us a touch of it. All is very quiet here, tho' some apostate Polish priests are going about describing horrors, and saying they doubt not our hands are red with blood. There is a talk of burning the Pope and Bishop in effigy for Guys tomorrow.

My best love to F Richard — I would write a letter, half-rowing, half-comforting to him, were I not so pulled down myself.

We are beginning a Novena for the success of these Hierarchical arrangements.

Let me know all about you, chiefly about F Richard

Ever Yours affectly John H Newman   Congr. Orat.

TUESDAY 5 NOVEMBER 1850   Father John (*Cooke*) taken ill

TO F. W. FABER

Oratory Bm Nov 6/50

My dear F W

I can't make out *how* they will frame a bill to suppress us — viz that no half-dozen priests may live today [together]? how do you define living? is 9 months in the year living? — Then again, what would hinder us, though we should not be able to keep the rule, to divide off into 3s and 4s, in different towns, with a number of lay brothers, and persons, novices and others, not priests. I do trust they cannot hurt us — Vows constitute an idea — and cannot be evaded — but numbers are vague.[2]

[1] Faber had written on 29 Oct., 'Sunday passed over quietly, tho' riots were expected in some of the chapels; so far as we were concerned, a sermon against us at S. Martins [in the Fields] from the vicar was all; but we expect some more serious visitation on the 5th of November, and perhaps the house will be mobbed, and our shutterless windows broken.' On that day a detachment of police stayed at the London Oratory, and the crowd only burned Oratorians in effigy.

[2] Faber wrote on 4 Nov. that the Cabinet was said to be 'divided between a revival of the laws against religious orders, modelled so as to include us,' and an ecclesiastical titles bill.

The unsettled state of things makes me not sorry you have not got rid of St W's [Wilfrid's] — it may be more truly your Cave of Adullam than King Wm [William] Street.[1] Again, how do you know that a year at St W's would not set up F Richard? and you have several ailing subjects. As to F de B. [Buggenoms], I suppose they wished to get it for nothing or not at all — if it be not rash judgment to say so.

Of course the delation of F Bernard is absurd.[2] However, I do think you must all avoid quasi-political subjects — If we are attacked for not praying for the Queen, I suppose we must say we are not a district Church.[3]

It is curious that the Goths should have got us into this trouble — for I suppose the *Hierarchy* movement is simply theirs. I doubt whether the Cardinal was for it a year or two ago. Dr Grant was against it.

If they forbid 'all communities recognised by the Church of Rome,' would not a rescript from Rome allowing us to suspend our titles etc etc. and our abstaining from the name of Oratorian, secure us? We should thus be a community of Priests living in King Wm Street etc. Another plan would be to set up a school, and be masters.

I don't think much of Dr Doyle's sermon. We have only to take things calmly.[4] The Liberals will be exceedingly disgusted at any penal laws — and I trust they will be soon a dead letter, while they give us the advantage of seeming persecuted.

Certainly I think you must keep right with the Bishop of Birmingham — but till I know what exactly you think of, I can't tell whether F Antony need have the trouble of coming[5]

Ever Yours affly J H N

[1] Fr de Buggenoms had just written to Faber that the Redemptorists would not buy St Wilfrid's 'because of its remoteness from any large town.'

[2] Dalgairns had been delated to Whitty, the Vicar General, 'for a sermon on the temporal power of the pope, which was all out of Suarez; this was preached 3 weeks ago; and also for intemperate language on the day of the pastoral. I was at Lancing both these Sundays. . . . As far as I can make out it is a sheer piece of fright on the part of some low Gallican, who in the present panic wishes to victimize an "injudicious convert."' Faber to Newman on 4 Nov.

[3] On this see letter of 18 Dec. 1850 to Faber.

[4] Faber enclosed in his letter what he called 'Dr Doyle's *awful* sermon against the temporal power of the pope etc etc,' preached at St George's, Southwark, on 3 Nov., and widely reported. Doyle said the new bishops were 'what it would have been well for the Church if her Bishops had always been—Bishops of souls, and not of temporalities—spiritual Bishops and not earthly Bishops.' He also explained that now we could 'manage our own spiritual matters here in England without sending over every week to have them managed in Italy.' The Church's 'glorious days were when she was steeped to the mouth in blood . . .' B. Bogan, *The Great Link*, London n.d. [1948], pp. 184–6.

[5] Faber thought it wise to consult Ullathorne about the future of St Wilfrid's.

TO ARCHDEACON ALLEN

Oratory Birmingham Nov 7. 1850

Dear Sir

I am sure you mean nothing but what is kind — and I thank you for the good intention of your Protest.

Protest it is, and nothing else — for I cannot conceive you wish me to argue with you, when you speak of the Church encouraging 'idolatry,' and sanctioning 'lying miracles.'[1]

I am, Dear Sir, Very truly Yours,

John H Newman   Congr. Orat.

TO GEORGE RYDER

Oy Bm Nov 7/50

Charissime

I am occupied *intensely* with the Sermon I am writing and publishing.

Had I *any thing* to say I would have written.

I never said the boys were to come on *any* day at all. Go by what *I* say. They must not come till *I* say so. We *cannot* get Mrs Fuller, our next door neighbour, to say whether she will turn out or not. *We are at her every day*. Do trust us. We are not forgetting, nor ever do.

Don't think me out of humour, because I write this off

Most affectly Yours J H N.

Forgive my rudeness — I will write again.

TO BISHOP ULLATHORNE

Oratory. November 7. 1850

My dear Lord,

I send you my Sermon, as I interpreted your silence to allow me to do — Mr Maher wishes it back as soon as convenient, but I know your Lordship's engagements.

In two places, (in quoting Gamaliel's words and in using the word

---

[1] See letter of 10 Nov.

'effectual' instead of 'evident,' in 1 Cor xvi) I have adopted the Protestant version. I did it, because Protestants are so familiar with it, that the passages would lose their force in any other words.[1]

I hope you will not think me *violent* — but my experience tells me that the more you show a bold face to the world, so cowardly is it, the more you gain. It does not appreciate concession. Also, following your Lordship's hint, I think it not a bad move to draw the world's indignation on myself, who, not being in a place of authority, cannot suffer from it.

It has seemed to me on consideration, prudent, not to introduce your Lordship's name as sanctioning my Sermon, but let it stand on its own merits — so I have merely spoken of the wish of friends as a reason for publishing it.[2]

Begging your Lordship's blessing, I am, My dear Lord Your faithful Servt

John H Newman   Congr. Orat.

The Rt Revd The Bp of Birmingham

TO A. LISLE PHILLIPPS

Oratory. Birmingham Nov 8. 1850

My dear Mr Phillipps

I thank you very much for the present of your noble protest against the outcry.[3] It is just what all who knew you would expect from you.

I should have acknowledged it sooner, but that I have been much engaged in writing and printing a Sermon of my own, which I preached about a fortnight since at St Chad's. Mr Maher has been directed to send you a copy, which I hope you will kindly accept.

---

[1] Acts 5 : 36, 1 Cor. 16 : 9. The A.V. was retained when the sermon was published, but when it was inserted in *O.S.* the Douay text was used, pp. 138 and 160.

[2] Ullathorne replied, the same day, that he thought the discourse prudent, and 'so far from being "violent" . . . a very fair and full answer to the spirit of violence, adding that he saw 'not the least objection to the stating of the fact' that he wished its publication. It was put out by Maher on 9 Nov. with 'Published by desire of the Bishop' on the title-page. Ullathorne also said 'I think you understand my feeling goes with yours as to holding a confident front . . .'

[3] Ambrose Lisle Phillipps's *A Letter to the Earl of Shrewsbury on the Re-establishment of the Hierarchy of the English Catholic Church, and the Present Posture of Catholic Affairs in Great Britain*, London 1850, dated 28 Oct.

All will turn to good, though we have a fight.

With kindest regards to Mrs Phillipps I am, Very sincerely Yrs in Xt
John H Newman   Cong Orat.

SATURDAY 9 NOVEMBER 1850   my Sermon came out   Mr Eyston called

TO F. W. FABER

Oy Bm. Nov 9/50

My Dear F Wilfrid

You must not be cast down, for the battle is just beginning. I suppose you (plural) must now reckon on having spies or rather listeners at your (plural) Sermons, who will report every thing to Lord Burleigh's ear or the ear of Dionysius, i.e. the Newspapers. So be on your guard.

Our position is a fine one — It is not impossible we may be cast at Common Law. If so, our Bishops go to prison — there the Cardinal will change his Cardinalitian Basilica — and for St Pudentiana will take S Niccolò in carcere. If the Government can be kept from laying its paws on our property, it will be most edifying and consolatory, and do much good to religion. Then the Holy Father will write a letter to his venerable Brother Nicholas or William Bernard on his sufferings, and they will be shipped off to join Smith O'Brien.[1]

Don't be saddened

Ever Yours affectly J H N

We have paid and are paying for the Baron, all along.[2]

P.S.   I could not be sorry at your sad news about your Brother.[3]
Could you sell my Sermon at your door? or is it against rule?

TO ANTONY HUTCHISON

Oy Bm Nov 9. 1850

My dear F Antony,

I have copied out for you every thing I can find, and I trust every thing that passed, in my correspondence with the Bishop and Lord Shr.

[1] i.e. Wiseman and Ullathorne would join William Smith O'Brien, one of the leaders of the Young Ireland party, who was transported to Tasmania in 1849.

[2] i.e. von Schroeter at St Wilfrid's.

[3] Henry Faber died of cancer on 26 Oct.

[Shrewsbury] You will find very little to your purpose, except as proving that I committed you to scarcely any thing.[1]

I think I HAVE allowed that, while we keep the place, we provide for the Mission, but I don't see what else I have allowed. This however is your main question.

As to your three questions,[2] I observe first of all, that the question must be first determined which I have heard you moot, whether he who builds endows — and next who built.

If he built ⟨Lord S.⟩, his £50 per annum I suppose is due (provided the canon law so stands about the builder) — If you built, your £70.

I don't see how it is possible for me, or any one, to answer your three questions — for they must be judged of, not in the abstract, but in the particular case and circumstances. *To a looker on*, so great a gift as the Earl's implied a correlative use of it — a large house, increased with reference to the Congregation, implied the fact or condition of a large Congregation. I do not think public opinion would understand your keeping the House yet not taking the Mission — but I say this only to express my view, because you ask what I think. But since I appeal here to the common feeling of the world, it would be best to put it, not as an abstract question, but as a concrete fact, before others: thus — 'what would you say, if we kept St Wilfrid's, and left the Bishop to find the curate?' what is the primâ facie view of the case.

Let me know if I can say any thing else.

Every Yours affly John H Newman   Congr. Orat.

TO RICHARD STANTON

Oy. Bm Nov 9/50

Charissime

Your books have come; they are not yet opened, but I thank you for them. It is a bad compliment not to open them at once, but we think it best to keep them from lying about.

I want you to give me an account of yourself — You must not be cast down about any thing. The battle is just beginning. Tell me how your cough is. And get leave to go to St Leonard's, if you need it.

[1] The Redemptorists having refused St Wilfrid's, Hutchison wrote on behalf of the London Oratorians, now its owners, to ask what obligations were attached to it. Newman copied from letters and memoranda of 1848–9.

[2] As to whether, if the various sums paid as endowment income were withdrawn, the owners of St Wilfrid's would still be bound to maintain a chaplain there.

We are all in a pretty kettle of fish, ain't we? My hope is *you* are all in a Praemunire before us — for you have read the Letter from the Flaminian Gate.[1] By the bye, what does that mean? — I have told F Wilfrid, I think, to get from Burns a lot of my new Sermon for the community

Ever Yrs affly J H N

TO ARCHDEACON ALLEN

Oratory Birmingham Nov 10. 1850

Dear Sir,

You are under a mistake in conjecturing I am not at rest. I have not had a moment either of doubt or anxiety, ever since I became a Catholic.

Allow me to say you are rather likely to 'get helps of the same kind as from my Parochial Sermons,' from my '*Discourses*,' published last year at Longmans, than in my refutation of Anglo catholicism in my Lectures published this year at Burns's.

Do you not think, forgive me for saying it, you have sent me enough Protests? By your making them, I conjecture you are not at ease yourself — nor will you be my dear Sir, take my word for it, till you are a Catholic as I am.

I entreat you, do not neglect to call on God to enlighten you with His grace in this matter

and believe me, Yours truly John H Newman   Congr. Orat.[2]

TO T. W. ALLIES

Oratory Birmingham Nov. 11, 1850.

My dear Allies,

The only difficulty I see in your going to Rome, is your distance from the scene of action, which is not a slight one. In so critical a time

[1] The London Oratorians had read Wiseman's pastoral on 20 Oct. and thus came under the statutes of Praemunire against those who promoted papal claims. The pastoral was 'Given out of the Flaminian Gate,' because etiquette forbad its being issued from Rome itself.

[2] The Evangelical Archdeacon Allen replied on 11 Nov., 'I am sure your courtesy deserves my thanks . . . I will not trouble you with any more protests. . . . Though I have had so little personal intercourse with you I must always regard you with affectionate esteem from your practical books. . . .' [From copy at Birmingham Oratory].

important schemes may turn up any day. Since I saw you, I have heard (*entre nous*) of a plan for a Catholic newspaper. Nothing may come of it, but the contemplating it shows how much all people feel the need of an organ.[1] I doubt the expedience of taking a recent convert for the Editor of a newspaper for this reason; because articles are more impromptu, and (quite over and above matters of doctrine) there are various minutiae of expression, tone and thought, which it is impossible to possess except by being among Catholics for some little time. In saying this, I am speaking of the *superintendence* of a Paper, which is the place of a tip-top Editor.

It is with the greatest satisfaction I hear of the Cardinal's arrival in London.[2] I was so afraid he would not come. We must not show any sort of fear. And the quicker the appointments are got over the better. I have been made anxious by hearing the rumour that the measure is contrary to Common Law, which I should think a very specious ground, were it not so inconvenient in its consequences to present political principles and proceedings, the rights of other religious bodies, and the recent precedents and admissions of lawyers and statesmen. And then, how can they save the Irish Bishops from the operation of an adverse decision? not to do which would almost be to throw Ireland again under disabilities. I should like Lord John, a creature of the people, brought to account for calling the religion of one third of the British Empire a superstition and a mummery.[3] Whether it is prudent at the moment I don't know, but it would be a proper counter-movement to frighten him.

[1] There is preserved, among correspondence about the Hierarchy trouble, a printed circular concerning this projected paper, the *Investigator*. It was to be 'a Weekly Journal of Catholic interest, which will promote the great cause of Free Trade, Parliamentary Reform, and Social Progress, as embodied in the views of the Irish Brigade, the Manchester School, and the Peel party,—the only liberal sections now remaining in the House of Commons. . . .

The great want of a Catholic Journal, written in a high tone and vigorous spirit, has been long acknowledged. . . . Great care shall be taken that no language appear in its articles unworthy of the meek Christianity they defend. . . .' Cf. letters of 1 Jan. 1851 to Allies, and 24 Dec. 1850 to Russell. Wiseman was backing the project, but when Allies went to inquire of him about it, at the end of March 1851, he found it had 'not gone beyond a *design*.' See letter of 10 Feb. 1851.

[2] Wiseman arrived on 11 Nov. George Bowyer, who, with Whitty, was advising him from London, had been acting in concert with Newman. Faber wrote to Newman on 10 Nov., 'The excitement increases here and is laying hold of the lower orders. . . . Things seem pointing more at us—"Beware of the Oratorians," "Down with the Oratorians, Banishment to the Oratorians, Don't go to the Oratory"—are now all over the town. . . . Bowyer's agitation and the meetings in his rooms are exciting unfavorable comment among catholics; but he says everywhere that you sanctioned all he has done. Our excellent Vicar General [Whitty] has quite lost his head. . . .'

[3] This came at the end of the Prime Minister Lord John Russell's *Letter to the Bishop of Durham*, 4 Nov., which fanned the agitation still further.

Of course we shall be glad to give you letters if you go to Rome, but you will not need them.

Ever yours most sincerely in Xt,

John H. Newman   Congr. Orat.

TO F. W. FABER

[11 November 1850?][1]

My dear F Wilfrid

I am sorry I did not answer you at the time — but I have been so busy and fidgetted about my sermon. It is too late now, I suppose.

I can't make out what the F Minister has to do with inside windows etc.

But everyone ⟨officer⟩ should provide his own *furniture*. The cook, i.e. F Minister, cooking implements and therefore kitchen range — the librarian shelves for his books. There seems an analogy with the Fathers providing their own furniture — tho' the Officers come to the *Congregation* for money

Ever Yrs affly J H N

TUESDAY 12 NOVEMBER 1850   Father John [Cooke] died   had sermon as usual but no singing.   matins and lauds for F John   F Nicholas came for good

WEDNESDAY 13 NOVEMBER   I sang high mass for F John — presente cadavere Mr Jefferys, Bond, O Neil, Ilsley, and O'Sullivan etc present[2] — the last to dinner   funeral service, presente cadavere.   crowd[3]

[1] This is the undated reply to a letter of questions from Faber on which Newman wrote 'Nov 7/50.'

[2] The first three were clergy from St Chad's, Ilsley was chaplain to the Dormers at Grove Park, and O'Sullivan from St Peter's, Birmingham.

[3] *The Times* account on 15 Nov. headed 'The Oratorians in Birmingham' was less laconic. 'A tumult of an unusual description occurred at the chapel of the Oratorians (an order of Monks), in Alcester-street, in this town on Wednesday night . . . the body [of Fr Cook] was exhibited in the chapel. . . . In the evening a large number of persons congregated in Alcester-street and the chapel was soon crammed to suffocation by a most miscellaneous assemblage . . . although the congregation within was as far as possible orderly, the mob without was somewhat tumultuous. . . . Many persons in the street, attracted by curiosity, if not by other less worthy motives, attempted to force an entrance into the edifice. . . .' Newman sent for the Police, who restored order, and the service was concluded behind closed doors.

TO J. M. CAPES

Oratory Bm Nov 14. 1850

My dear Capes,

I like your article on the Hierarchy very much.[1]

In the next, there is one obscure sentence, which I can't give a satisfactory sense to. 'Nor does it tend to the exaltation of the earth and of man, to be the physical and moral centres of the universe.' p 480[2] The earth *is* the moral centre, and is *not* the physical.

My criticism on these Scientific articles was not on the *allowableness* of their statements, but the advisableness. We ought not to theorize the teaching of Moses, till philosophers have demonstrated their theories of physics. If 'the Spirit of God' is gas in 1850, it may be electro-magnetism in 1860

Yours affectly John H Newman

TO RICHARD STANTON

Oratory Birmingham November 14. 1850

My dear F Richard,

We all send you our best thanks for the resolution, to which you have come, about our deaths. I shall bring it before the Congregation and doubt not we shall gladly reciprocate your kindness.[3]

I must give you, if time will let me, a short account of F. John's death. He was taken ill last Tuesday week — just a week before his death, almost suddenly. About the 2nd day he was frightfully altered, looking the colour of iron, black and yellow — and, since no one fancied he was *unusually* ill *then*, I think we got used to it. He had no sleep at night, and that nearly to his death. He was very weak — and the apothecary who attended him kept making experiments on him, as we thought — but it was explained to our satisfaction by reflecting that *nothing* agreed with him, and there was no complaint he had not, and no medicine which did him good or harm. One doctor had said his

---

[1] The *Rambler* (Dec. 1850), pp. 467–79. Capes emphasised the private and internal nature of the new arrangements.

[2] This sentence, in the last of Richard Simpson's four articles on the Mosaic account of creation, 'Religion and Modern Philosophy,' was altered before publication.

[3] After Fr Cooke's death, Stanton wrote to Newman that the London Oratorians had 'determined to give the same Masses, Coronas etc for the members of your house, as the rule requires of our own.' The reciprocity still continues.

heart was wrong, another his liver, and a third his lungs. It was plain to me he could not last, but no one fancied his end was near.

On Monday afternoon, Stanislas, who nursed him most assiduously, sitting up all night with him, and one night turning him in bed every half hour, wanted some one else called in. So I went with him to the apothecary's house to tell him our wish. He said he was making a new experiment, and wished us to wait till morning. In the morning ⟨Tuesday⟩ he said that F John was better, and certainly he had had some hours sleep. When I saw him, he was sitting up, but as he was sitting facing the fire, and the room is narrow, I could not see his face. He however declared himself worn. The apothecary said he should like much to wait till one o'clock — and at one o'clock he said there was no cause for alarm, that F John's distress was symptomatic, and he was better — He wished us then to wait till evening. In the afternoon he got decidedly worse, being hardly able to breathe. So without waiting for the evening we sent for Dr Johnson, who was out, and sent word he would come at 9. PM.

Our supper recreation was nearly over, Stanislas having left F John to Lawrence during it, when Lawrence ran in to us to say that F John was very ill. Stanislas rushed to his room, and rushed back to us to say he was dying. F Ambrose at once went in to give him absolution — and we followed. Next minute extreme unction was administered — but I think he was dead before it was ended. When we entered the room he *looked* dead — and I suppose died in a fainting fit, to which he was very subject. He had been talking up to his death — and his last words were to ask Lawrence for his handkerchief. He had no notion he was *near* death, which is the only drawback we have to the comfort of the whole matter. E.g. if he had died at *night* in a fainting fit, how sad it would have been!

FF Joseph and Stanislas washed and laid him out. Next morning, Wednesday, we brought him into chapel in Priest's vestments without shell — and had the solemn requiem mass — and the body lay exposed, till evening — when it was still exposed, but in the shell. The coffin is not yet made, but comes tomorrow — when the body goes with FF Stanislas and Edward to St Wilfrid's to be buried on *Saturday*.

On Tuesday evening I lectured, and at the end (we had no singing) gave out what had happened. It produced an audible sensation, and some poor woman cried immoderately. So they did the next day — All day they were round his corpse in tears. He had as many as 40 women penitents, all very much attached to him, some have got his hair, others (I think) bits of his cassock — and others (I doubt its propriety) have touched their rings with his remains, but I suppose it *is* proper. A great number of people have pressed to see him, today — when we had removed him into the school room and engine House.

We had a great row last night and had to send for the police — and tonight also. The people are making a great row under my window now, while F Joseph is preaching.

Last night we had a sort of funeral service, and no sermon.

Curious, tho' so in the sight of death, he had made no will, — except one 12 years ago

Ever Yrs affectly J H N.

FRIDAY 15 NOVEMBER 1850 the body went to St Wilfrid's, with F William (*Penny*), Stanislas, and Edward.

TO VISCOUNT FEILDING

Oratory, Birmingham. Nov 15. 1850

My dear Lord Feilding,

I should have written to you sooner, but we have had a death in our community, at last sudden, though we had cause to expect it. This has occupied my thoughts

As to Mr Askew's Letter, it is at once angry and pompous, and it would be very easy to demolish his whole structure — but I do not think it is worth while. There is no call on you to answer every one who chooses to make free with you — and I do not suppose it would do any kind of good for any one else to get into controversy with persons who have prejudged the matter, and who think every refutation of their opinions only serves to make those opinions more irrefragable and more engaging.[1]

It was with deep sorrow I read what you told me about your family matters.[2] Time, however, please God, will set all to rights, or at least indefinitely soften the acuteness of feeling which such steps as you tell me of express. Such feeling in course of time may give place to a very different sentiment. For such a change you must pray unceasingly.

[1] Joseph Askew, Vicar of Northleach, Gloucestershire, formerly Fellow of Queen's College, Oxford, wrote *A Letter to the Viscount Feilding, on the Grounds of his Secession to the Church of Rome*, London 1850, a reply to one by Lord Feilding in *St James's Chronicle* of 5 Sept. Lord Feilding was under fire also in *The Times*, which devoted a leading article to him on 16 Nov.

[2] The Earl of Denbigh, Lord Feilding's father, who had been writing him voluminous letters on religion, had just decided that it was his duty to disinherit his heir.

I will not forget your message to our Bishop. He is away just now, but I shall have opportunity in a day or two. Be of good cheer, my dear Lord, the first months of a convert's life, though filled with joy of their own, have a pain and dreariness of their own too. We feel the latter when nature overcomes grace — the former, when grace triumphs over nature. But no one made a sacrifice without effect. God does not forget what we do for Him — and whatever trouble you may have now, it will be repaid to you a hundred fold.

As to this hubbub, I was anxious just at first, when indeed you were here — but I do not see what can come of it, except indeed inconvenience to individuals, and black looks from friends and strangers. We must take it coolly, and leave the British Lion to find he cannot touch us. If he put some of us in prison, we should but gain by it — and I suspect his keepers are too sharp-sighted for that, whatever *he* is.

My kindest remembrances to Lady Feilding — With my kindest wishes and prayers, I am My dear Lord, Your Lordship's faithful Servt in Xt

John H. Newman.

TO HENRY WILBERFORCE

Oratory, Bm. Nov 15/50

My dear Henry

⌜Poor Isaac's [[Williams']] letter is wonderful — yet they complain that we cut them!⌝

I will write to Todd.

⌜As to a House, Ambrose has written to you, I believe. We can get the House and Land, but cannot beat him down. We are willing to go halves with you in the expence.⌝[1]

Was the row going on, when you were here? Our Bishops seem desirous to be put into prison. I should not be sorry. It will be sure to do us good.

Do you recollect Father Cook when you were here? We have just lost him. He was *always* going, but at last we were taken by surprise. He was a friend of the Cardinal's, who recommended him here.

Ever Yours affectly J H N

---

[1] There was a plan that Henry Wilberforce should take a house next to the Oratory soon to be built at Edgbaston, Birmingham.

SATURDAY 16 NOVEMBER 1850   Burial of F John at St Wilfrid's

TO J. M. CAPES

Oy Bm Nov 16/50

My dear Capes

The only criticism I should make on your Hierarchy Article is, that things are moving so quick that it may not perhaps be au courant a fortnight hence. The Cardinal's Address is just making its appearance.[1] The Quarterly always keeps back its political article for the last in the Number.

p 510. Pewter was used at Trinity, Queens, I think Ch Ch [Christ Church] — indeed almost every where — but these things may have changed now.[2]

Please, don't call me Dr but Father p. 530.

It is not surprising that *I* should think your History of Puseyism very interesting. At least, however, I may say it is very well written.

I wish you by all means to keep back the *Verses* at present.

Yrs affly J H N

MONDAY 18 NOVEMBER 1850   meeting at St Chad's about Addresses on subject of the Hierarchy.[3] FF Wm. [William] Stanislas and Edward returned from St Wilfrid's with Br Edward.

TUESDAY 19 NOVEMBER   MRG *Giberne* returned

TO PEDRO BACH, SUPERIOR OF THE VICH ORATORY

The Oratory, Birmingham. Die Novembris 19a 1850.

Ausus eram, Pater Reverendissime, jam duos fere menses spem fovere, litteras a patribus S. Philippi apud Vich, gloriosissimi et tui et nostri Patroni, ad humilitatem meam esse venturas. Ea quippe erat expectatio Reverendissimi Episcopi de Monterey, Joseph Alemany,

---

[1] Wiseman's *Appeal to the English People* was published as a pamphlet on 19 Nov.

[2] Capes's first article on the 'Rise, Progress, and Results of Puseyism' appeared in the *Rambler* (Dec. 1850), pp. 506–44. On p. 510 Froude's Journal was quoted, in which he accused himself of asking for a china plate, directly he had finished his meat, in order to show how little he ate. A note explains 'In college meat is served on pewter.'

[3] Newman was the proposer of an Address of congratulation to Ullathorne.

O.P. qui, Californiam petens, apud Birminghamiam autem nostram in itinere commoratus, multa nobis de te et tuis, magnifica sanè illa et perjucunda Philippinorum auribus locutus est.

Dixit enim sanctissimus Praesul, consilium inire Patres Oratorii Vichensis, se, sacra, altaria, domum, omnia denique sua, ab Hispaniâ in Californiam transferendi; id vero praecipuè habere impedimenti, quominùs conceptum propositum in actum ferant, quod linguam Anglicanam, inter Californiae colonos vernaculam, non calleant. Quae cùm ita sint, hoc postulavit à nobis supradictus Reverendissimus Episcopus, ut ex nostris inveniremus quos vobiscum per aliquod tempus mitteremus in illam regionem, interpretes vestros in quotidiano vitae usu, in fidei vero famulatu et in scientiâ sanctorum servos nimirum atque discipulos.

Jam vero, Pater Reverendissime, quae tua est benevolentia et charitas et fraternus animus erga vel novissimos et humillimos Philippinos, ad nos de his rebus scribas, precor, ut citius ad Venerandum Episcopum Alemany quae opportuna erunt respondere valeamus.

Paternitatis tuae studiosissimus

Joannes H. Newman   Congr. Orat. Pr.[1]

TO ANTONY HUTCHISON

Oratory Birmingham November 19. 1850

My dear Father Antony

I will gladly see the Bishop on the subject of St Wilfrid's. Perhaps I have some fear that he will recollect what Lord S. [Shrewsbury] said about women in the House, but of course I shall not put it into his head.[2]

We will have a meeting after dinner to-day on the subject of your offer of St Wilfrid's — and I will add at the end of this what comes of our deliberations. The first flush in the two or three Fathers who have come into the room, has been against it.

I suppose you had better sign the address to the Queen — we are doing so. It is certainly informal, but it really comes from the Arch-

[1] Pedro Bach replied on 13 Dec. that the Oratorians at Vich being only four in number, and old, could not go to California.

[2] Hutchison, on 18 Nov., asked Newman to negotiate with Ullathorne about the chaplain the London Oratorians had to furnish for St Wilfrid's. A man and wife were to keep house for him. For Lord Shrewsbury's objection see letter of 7 June 1849 to Ullathorne. Hutchison also asked whether the Birmingham Oratorians would accept the place as a gift.

bishop. And it is a very particular case — not one of party politics, but one which may be decisive of our status in England.[1]

You say nothing of the Cardinal's being sent out in 48 hours; it can't be a coming event throwing forward its shadow. I wonder they don't talk of some new *Test* for Catholic priests and chapels, as necessary for a license. It might be such a declaration of the Queen's absolute jurisdiction, as most priests would sign, but not the readers of Suarez.[2] If we had enemies, they would put the ministers up to this

Ever Yours affectionately John H Newman   Congr. Orat.

P.S.   We have had our meeting, and agree in opinion that we could not take St Wilfrid's with any prospect of advantage to the Congregation.

WEDNESDAY 20 NOVEMBER 1850   Cardinal Wiseman's pamphlet came out.[3] Miss Braine here

TO JAMES HOPE[4]

Oratory Birmingham November 20. 1850

My dear Hope,

⌐It is with the greatest pleasure I have just read the letter which you wrote to Bathurst and which he has forwarded to me.[5] Not that I took

---

[1] *The Times* published the text of the Address on 16 Nov., introducing it thus: 'The following address which is understood to be from the pen of Cardinal Wiseman— a fact which gives additional importance to it—will, we understand, lie at the various Catholic churches and chapels on Sunday next, and will be otherwise circulated with the view of obtaining signatures to it, to testify to the loyalty of the Catholics of England to "Her Majesty's Royal person, crown and dignity" . . .' At Bowyer's suggestion, Newman had urged to Ullathorne the advantage of such an address, a few days before Wiseman's return to England. The London Oratorians, Hutchison wrote, feared it would be 'a very strange precedent to have the clergy led by the laity in these matters.'

[2] Suarez taught that the Church had an 'indirect power' over Christian princes, even in their own sphere.

[3] *The Appeal to the English People* was printed in full in *The Times* and four other London daily papers on this day. See letters of 3 Dec. to Talbot and 24 Dec. to Russell, for Newman's testimony to its effect.

[4] In copying this letter Newman headed it 'Personal.'

[5] Hope wrote from Abbotsford, on 4 Nov., 'Dear Bathurst

Your kind letter needed no apologies—and for your prayers and good thoughts for me I thank you much—may they of God be blessed to me in clearer light as well as in a purer conscience. As yet I do not see my way as you have done yours, but I pray that I may not remain in such doubt as I now have.

From your address I conclude that you are with Newman. Tell him with my kind

it to mean more than it said, but it showed me that you still thought and felt kindly of me, and that I have not hurt or annoyed you by any thing I had said to you in the letter which I sent to you from Rome some years since.[1] Indeed it was very far from my intention to do any thing of the sort. I wrote, if I recollect to thank you for your letters of introduction, and the service they had been to me at Milan, and I always have had cause to admire, and have expressed it to others, the justness and sagacity of the general views you have given me of the state of things in Rome and elsewhere. I now fully see, by your letter to Bathurst that your silence has arisen merely from the difficulty of writing to one in another communion, and the irksomness and indolence (if you let me so speak) we all feel in doing what is difficult, what may be misconceived, and what can scarcely have object or use.

I know perfectly well, my dear Hope, your great moral and intellectual qualities, and will not cease to pray that the grace of God may give you the obedience of faith, and use them as His instruments. For myself, I say it from my heart, I have not had a single doubt, or temptation to doubt, ever since I became a Catholic. I believe this to be the case with most men — it certainly is so with those with whom I am in habits of intimacy — My great temptation is to be at *peace*, and let things go on as they will, and not trouble myself about others. This being the case, your recommendation that I should 'take a review of doctrine and of the difficulties which beset it to an Anglican,' is any thing but welcome, and makes me smile. Surely, enough has been written — all the writing in the world would not destroy the necessity of faith — if all were made clear to reason, where would be the exercise of faith? The simple question is whether *enough* has been done to *reduce* the difficulties so far as to hinder them absolutely blocking up the way, or excluding those direct and large arguments on which the reasonableness of faith is built.

Remember me to Badeley, when you see him, for I suppose he is returned from Naples, or Jerusalem, or California, or wherever he has gone this year to brush off the dust of his chambers and the Privy Council. I always love to think of him⌐

Ever Yours affectionately John H Newman[2]

regards that I hope he has not forgotten me—I have often thought of him and have sometimes been near writing to him—but have had nothing definite to say. I have read his last lectures and wish they were extended to a review of doctrine and the difficulties which beset it to an Anglican. . . .'

[1] Letter of 23 Feb. 1847, after which there had been no further correspondence.

[2] For Hope's reply see letter of 29 Nov. The correspondence is printed in Robert Ornsby, *Memoirs of James Robert Hope-Scott*, II, London 1884, pp. 66–8.

THURSDAY 21 NOVEMBER 1850 Miss Braine here all day Bastard here all day
F Ignatius came and went at night

TO R. A. COFFIN

Oratory Birmingham November 22/50
My dear Father Robert,

Thank you for your letter; how could you suppose it would be a distress to me?[1] I never can be distressed at any one being called to what he considers a more religious life than he is leading at present. You may as well apologize for leaving a life of sin, as for leaving a life of tepidity.

And I am sanguine in thinking that the obligation of vows may exert the most beneficial effect upon you.

Thank you too for all you say affectionate about myself. We all send you our love — and can rejoice even more simply than the London House, because in Birmingham we lose nothing in your resolve. But the London House will in the event feel it has lost nothing either, whatever human feeling may say at the moment — for it is only a cause of rejoicing that you have been led on, as I trust you have, to greater seriousness and strictness — and St Philip would never wish to keep any one who did not wish to be kept.

With my kindest thoughts & best prayers for you, Very affectionately Yours in Xt

John H Newman Congr. Orat.

[1] Coffin wrote on 21 Nov. 'With regard to the Florence matter you will be pained perhaps, tho' not surprised after all you heard from me through F. Nicolas, to learn that I have determined to give up the scheme which . . . would have been attended with endless difficulties, without its answering to my expectations. . . But besides all this I seem irresistibly drawn to leave the world and give myself up wholly and entirely to Almighty God, will you then my dear Father, and ever most kind and affectionate friend, while you cannot approve, say Godspeed to my resolution to enter religion, and give me your prayers and ask for those of the community . . . .' After promising his prayers for Newman and the Oratory, Coffin asked for 'one line from you that I may leave the world with the knowledge of your good wishes towards me—always and for ever your most affectionate and most grateful and obliged R. A. Coffin.' He added that he would enter the Redemptorist novitiate as soon as possible, and was writing to tell Faber of his resolution. In a further P.S. he released Newman from the secret which bound him. See letter of 24 Nov. to Faber.

TO F. W. FABER

In fest. S. Caecil. [22 Nov.] 1850

My dear F Wilfrid

I thought you would have got my Sermon from Burns — I have told Maher to send you 50.

Coffin's resolve surprises me. I am very glad, that is, under the idea that a vow may *keep* him — but he will have so much to go through and no one to sfogue to,[1] that it is kill or cure.

I suppose he has been in correspondence with F. Lans. I had forbidden his saying a word to the Baron, and I believe he has kept to it.

F Alban must take care of the cold and damp at St W's [Wilfrid's] — I intend to go to the Bishop about his faculties to-day

Ever Yrs affly J H N

TO CARDINAL WISEMAN

Oratory Birmingham Nov 22. 1850 In fest. S. Caecil.

My dear Lord Cardinal

Though your Eminence is not Cardinal Wolsey's successor, as in other things, so in taking your title from the great Saint and Martyr of this day, yet, considering all the associations which go with her name, also that she is a special saint of the Oratory, this is a good day to offer your Eminence the congratulations of the Birmingham Oratory on your return to us.[2]

I have not written sooner knowing how anxiously you were engaged — but now that your most convincing and triumphant Address is off your hands, I take up your time for a few minutes with these lines, which do not require of course any reply.[3]

I should have sent your Eminence a fourp'orth of letter press I have just been publishing — except it was so small a thing, and next because it was originally meant only for local distribution.

You heard from Dr Whitty of poor Father Cook's death. He had been ailing just a week — and, though certainly in an alarming state,

---

[1] Grumble to, Italian 'sfogare.'

[2] Wolsey's titular church was S. Cecilia in Trastevere, Wiseman's S. Pudenziana.

[3] Wiseman replied affectionately on 24 Nov. that God had given him, 'in spite of outward and occasional anxieties, a calm and peace of mind . . . and a resolution . . . not to act the part of a hireling. . . .'

the medical man thought him better — when he went off in a fainting fit in five minutes time — when we could hardly run to be in time — but luckily we were in recreation, and thus he died in the presence, and amid the prayers of all his brethren. He was hastily anointed, and died upon it. His executor has been here, and is coming again.

We have had a novena in behalf of your Eminence and the state of the Church in England, and, as bound in duty, are ever holding you and the other Bishops in remembrance — Give us then your blessing, My dear Lord Cardinal, and believe me, while I kiss your purple,

Your Eminence's affectionate Servant

John H Newman   Congr. Orat.

SATURDAY 23 NOVEMBER 1850   Mr Flanagan (*architect?*) came

TO F. W. FABER

Oratory Bm Nov 24 [23]/50[1]

My Dear F Wilfrid,

Coffin says in his letter to me, 'I write to F Faber to acquaint him of my resolution to-day; of course what I told you in confidence through F. Darnell is now no longer so, if you wish to mention anything; tho' — I am not going to enter into details to F. Faber.'[2] This permission at once leads me to tell you all that passed between us — and, as I have not yet put it in writing, perhaps you will keep this letter as a record.

On the 3rd of October Nicholas came here, to read me, what he did not put into my hands, a letter of F. Coffin's. It was to this effect:— that the idea had some time since come into his mind that he had not a vocation to the Oratory — that he mentioned it to F. Lans, when in retreat, who told him it was a temptation, and made him give it up. Then he read your Triduo, which perfectly unsettled him. He could not believe it was a fair representation of the Oratory; if it was, he conceived the Oratory was a mere free and easy club, or the like.[3] Then he

---

[1] The context and the second postscript dated 'Sunday,' 24 Nov. show that this letter was written on 23 Nov.

[2] Newman is quoting from Coffin's letter to him of 21 Nov.

[3] Faber had written of St Philip that 'He was emphatically a modern gentleman . . . very neatly dressed . . . in a modern room with modern furniture, plain, it is true, but with no marks of poverty about it; in a word, with all the ease, the gracefulness, the polish, of a modern gentleman of good birth, considerable accomplishments, and a very various information.' *The Spirit and Genius of St. Philip Neri*, p. 52.

considered that none of you in London had any tradition of any kind —
it was all your own — you had hardly any experience, and no training.
Then he found that several of our Fathers (I don't know what this
means) took your view of the Oratory as little as he did. How then
could he submit himself to your rule? To complete it, a regulation had
been passed by your house, to the effect that no one should make a
retreat out of the House — thus he was condemned for life to be shut
up for all his spiritual advantages to the four walls of the London
Oratory. His conclusion was, that he could not be a member of the
London House, and he had to make up his mind in a few hours, for you
had just summoned him to London. F. Nicholas confirmed this in the
most emphatic manner, saying it was utterly out of the question his ever
consenting to go to London. Lastly I was to receive what was told me
(i.e. his *reasons*) as if it had been said in confession.

I answered him as follows:—[1] that I thought St Philip would have
recommended obedience to his house, and would have preferred the
sacrifice of the razionale to any exercise of reason. But, however, if he
would not take the best way, but only a second rate way, he might 1. *not*,
become a secular, for that was going *back*.

2 become a regular, it is true — *but* what regulars had *traditions* of
direction? not the Trappists of Mount St Bernard, or the Dominicans,
or the Benedictines, or the Passionists — He must go either to Redemptorists, Jesuits, Conceptionists, or Rosminians — and the last two
could hardly be said to have a *tradition*. If however, he *did* join a stricter
rule than ours, I could but be glad that he was called to it.

3. If he remained an Oratorian, and yet would not go to London,
let him by all means go to some foreign house, and learn the tradition
there. Then he might return and form one of a third house. The
Florence Fathers had wished to come to England — he might go to
them for a time, and come back in their train. They might set up an
Oratory, say at Clifton, and he would be one of their members.

I thought this was staving off the difficulty — for I could not wish
him to be a mere secular — and, as for being a regular, I agreed with
F. Nicholas that he had no vocation that way. I had a hope that, as time
went on, he would cool down and become more sensible and sober in his
notions; though from what F. Nicholas said, I despaired of his ever
being willing to join the London House. I bargained only that, since
I was to keep silence, *he* too would mention his doubts etc to no one
else. Nor has he, I believe.

From what I have said, you will see I do *not* think him acting
rightly, and have told him so. At the same time, as he has not asked my

---

[1] Letter of 3 Oct. to Coffin.

advice, just the contrary, I have not given it. I think him possessed with a bad spirit; and if I thought he would believe me, or that it would do any good, would tell him so. Whether it will improve matters to bring him to London, I cannot tell — for he is cantankerous.[1]

I earnestly pressed him, I think a year ago, to go into residence in London, and to let another take his place at St Wilfrid's; he declined. I feared that would take place, which has. He broods over imaginary insults, slights, difficulties — he finds things going on in London without him — he feels he shall be (at first) strange there — and he sets himself against it. F. Nicholas is strong in the opinion that he never will acquiesce in London — but of course I have not seen him enough to know.

Someone has told him (I have not a notion who) that he has the air of a religious

Ever Yours affectly John H Newman Congr. Orat.

P.S.   Though he *begins* in a bad spirit, yet it may happen that vows are of the greatest use to him. He then will not be *able* to escape, and must be ground down, willy nilly. I don't think he will ever make a good Philippine. He says to me — 'I propose to offer myself to the Redemptorists, and to beg to be sent to the noviciate as soon as possible — so that directly I have wound up matters here, I suppose I shall be on my road.'[2]

Sunday.   In consequence of your letter this morning, I have written another letter to F Robert, which I inclose.[3] You may read it or not as you like.

[1] On 22 Nov. Faber wrote summoning Coffin to London, the Oratorians there having decided that, although he could leave on his own if he wished, they would not grant him a release on his ground, that they were 'leading a mere secular life like Oxford and Cambridge men.' (Faber to Newman, 22 Nov.) Coffin wrote to Newman on 23 Nov. 'My dearest Father I am very much obliged to you for your kind letter. I am summoned up to London at a moment's notice by virtue of obedience by F. Faber. . . . God alone knows what good will come of an interview which cannot but be full of misery and pain . . .' It was agreed that Coffin should ask the Redemptorist Fr Lans whether he thought he could still settle down as an Oratorian. If the answer was 'no,' his release would be granted.

[2] Letter of 21 Nov. to Newman.

[3] See next letter. Faber complained of the superior attitude Coffin was adopting.

TO R. A. COFFIN

Oratory. Birmingham Nov. 24. 1850

My dear F. Robert,

Thank you for your letter, but from it and other circumstances I am led to conclude that you have not quite understood what I wrote to you.[1]

Do not let it pain you improperly if I add in explanation that you must not take me as *approving* what you are doing.[2] It must indeed be right to put off sloth and lukewarmness, and yet not right to leave St Philip. I told you in my letter of the beginning of October, that I thought you were *not* taking St Philip's way or pleasing him in deciding on not belonging to the London House; and now I distinctly state, (if you have not gathered it from my last letter to you,) that in reality I have no sympathy whatever in what you are doing.

I leave you to God and our Lady, if you will not be commended to St Philip

Yours affecty John H Newman   Congr. Orat.

TO PHILIP HENRY HOWARD, M.P.

Oratory, Birmingham, November 24, 1850.

Dear Sir,

I write at once in answer to your request, and you are quite at liberty to make what use you please of my letter.[3]

[1] On the draft of this present letter Newman noted that it was 'written in consequence of F Richard's letter to me.' Stanton, who was at St Wilfrid's with Coffin, wrote on 23 Nov., '. . . he persuades himself and would persuade others that your congé is a simple approval. . . .' Stanton wrote in the same sense to Faber, who forwarded his letter at once to Newman.

[2] On the draft Newman added in pencil, 'vid F Coffin's own expression in his letter of November 21,' i.e. 'while you cannot approve,' which Newman underlined in Coffin's letter (quoted in note to Newman's of 22 Nov.).

[3] P. H. Howard, Member of Parliament for Carlisle, and a prominent Catholic, sent Newman the *Carlisle Journal's* report of a speech delivered on 19 Nov. by A. C. Tait, Dean of Carlisle (one of the four tutors who had denounced Tract XC, and later Archbishop of Canterbury): '[Dr Ullathorne] had allowed Dr. Newman to preach over his head, he was sorry to say, one of the most blasphemous discourses he had ever read. (Applause.) He had heard Dr. Newman preach often, he knew him in private, and could not but believe him to be a good man, but his language on this occasion appeared very far from what should be expected of a good man. Dr. Newman had said that Dr. Ullathorne, on that occasion, could only be compared in his magnificence, to Christ rising from the dead. (Sensation.)'

To tell the truth I have been now for seventeen years the subject of so much daily misrepresentation, in the public prints and at public meetings, that I never think at all about what ever[1] is said against me in the one or at the other. Did I attempt to answer them all, my life would be spent in the occupation; if I answered only some, the rest would be taken for granted as true. Moreover, time clears up all errors; the untruth of to-day is driven out by the contrary untruth of to-morrow, and the many-coloured impressions of particular minds are all eventually absorbed by the consistent light of truth. In consequence, I have never done anything but smile at the extravagant things which have been said against me, unless a call of duty interfered. Such a call is your letter.

As to the charge, then, urged against me by certain persons, of having preached 'a most blasphemous discourse,' it is, perhaps the not unnatural misconception of respectable but prosaic thinkers. So, at least, I am willing to consider it. What I really said in the sermon in question was this, not that 'Dr. Ullathorne in his magnificence was Christ,' but, as you suppose, that our Lord's resurrection is the archetype, or prophecy, or anticipation, or pledge of what goes on all through the history of the church. He is ever dying and rising again in His church. The revival, then, and growth of Catholicism in the present generation may be likened to His coming out of the tomb.[2]

For such modes of speech we have His own sanction when He told St. Paul, who was breathing vengeance against the Christians of Damascus, that he was persecuting *Him*. And all through that great apostle's epistles the church is represented as the mystical *body* of Christ.

Moreover, even if I used of an individual bishop (*which I did not*) what scripture says of our Lord, this is only what the Church of England does as regards a king, in the service of King Charles's day. If Dr. Tait thinks that service 'blasphemous,' let him say so, or else not cast the first stone.

Pray accept my best thanks for the kind interest in me, which has prompted your letter; and believe me, my dear sir, With much respect, Your faithful servant,

John H. Newman, Congr. Orat.[3]

P. H. Howard Esq., M.P.

---

[1] The newspaper printed 'was or is,' but Newman has corrected it.

[2] *O.S.* pp. 136–7, pamphlet ed. 1850, pp. 15–16. The first leading article in *The Times* of 30 Oct. called this passage, in the sermon which it had printed on 29 Oct., 'a mixture of blasphemy and absurdity,' and added 'We are not aware that the misuse of language ever reached a more frightful perversion.'

[3] See Newman's letter of 2 Dec. for Tait's reply.

TO RICHARD STANTON

Oy Bm Nov 24/50

My dearest R

I have nothing to say, yet do not like not to acknowledge your letters. In consequence I have written to F Coffin to say I have no sympathy in what he is doing.

Love to Alban — I went on Friday to the Bishop about him — he was out, and I have (to my surprise) had no answer

Keep from cold both of you. Coffin *promised me* he would not speak to the Baron. As to the B. the 29th of September was to be his last day. I could not refuse him when he wanted to stay, but I said distinctly *he must not stay to* FINISH *our picture.*

Ever Yrs affly J H N

5 o'clock PM. I have just heard from the Florence Preposto accepting F. Coffin!

TUESDAY 26 NOVEMBER 1850   Bathurst in Birmingham

TO F. W. FABER

Oratory Bm Nov 26. 1850

My Dear F Wilfrid,

As being bound to love St Philip and the Oratory, more than to consult for individuals, I do earnestly hope you will get rid of Coffin.

That he has caught up things from the Baron, I do not doubt, but that is not at the bottom of it. The Baron may have determined the shape the rebellion has taken, but that is all.[1]

Since he is evidently in gross and absurd error and sin, it is no rash judgment to assign it to a particular cause. My own theory then, which rests on facts independent of the actual event, is this:— he seems to have caught up some words which I used in July 1848 about *three* houses, one in the city of London, one at Bayswater, one at Birmingham, when I said he would be naturally head of the Bayswater. This he

[1] Newman is replying to the letter, written 23–25 Nov. by Faber. He reported the London Oratorians as thinking Coffin 'under a delusion.' According to the report of Stanton, who was at St Wilfrid's, Coffin's real director was not Fr Lans, but Baron von Schroeter. Faber entirely agreed, and gave examples of criticisms made by Coffin, and derived from von Schroeter.

142

reminded me of indirectly afterwards, and I think has now forgotten. I think he has shrunk from humbling himself to you and the London House. His position at St W's [Wilfrid's] fortified this feeling. The suspicion made me really desirous that he should *not* be at St W's, but in London a year ago — but nothing would convince him, nor you perhaps, that I was in earnest, because it so happened my expression of it arose out of his saying he was only on obedience to me at St W's.[1] This, I was conscious, was not the case — I was indifferent about his being there in itself — and strongly against it when he saddled the scheme simply on me. I recommended him 'to take his year at St W's.' (i.e. on the assumption that every one in turn would have a year,) *afterwards* — ⟨i.e. a year or two later —⟩ and at once 'to take his place' in the London House, that it might not be strange to him. He deliberately resolved on the former.

What he means by 'diplomacy' in me, I say it in the face of God, I do not understand, nor am at all conscious.[2] I suppose the word means either having some secret end, or using some underhand means. I am quite conscious *always* of not liking to tell people how keenly I feel things, both from tenderness to them, and again from a consciousness that, when I once begin, I am apt to let out and blow them out of the water. But if I have done any thing more towards Coffin, all I can say is, I have quite forgotten it, and have not a dream what he means. Certainly, I have kept him at St W's against my own will.

Well, in addition to this original weakness of his, of not wishing to come down from a station of importance to a secondary place, has been added the opportunity St W's afforded him, to brood over his fancied misfortunes. The solitude etc etc. was the mother of unreal slights, neglects and injuries, and most real irritation and alienation. The Baron has given an imaginary intellectual basis to this moral disease — and his present illusion is the consequence.

I think I gave the Baron notice to quit immediately I began to suspect what was going on, viz at the Assumption. In Michaelmas, when he asked leave to stay to finish our picture, I said quite violently and harshly, that the picture should be left unfinished. Yet I did not know how to say, 'Go,' when his stay was asked for its own sake, considering the Passionists, whom we expected at the Assumption, had not come.

---

[1] See Newman's letter of 20 Oct. 1849 to Coffin.
[2] Faber reported a complaint of Coffin's and its obvious source: '. . . you manoeuvre, and are diplomatic. Now when I was at St Wilfrid's in the autumn, the Baron used that very word diplomatic, and Coffin was full of your diplomacy and the Baron's holy simplicity. . . .'

If in the beginning of October, I was convinced and ruled that Coffin should not belong to you, it is not wonderful, that now I should not only earnestly deprecate it, but utterly wish him dissociated from the Name of St Philip.

Let FF Bernard and Richard see this letter

Ever Yours affectly John H Newman   Congr. Orat.

P.S.   In this letter I have said nothing about my feeling toward Coffin himself because I have been writing about the Congregation. However, I think it is decidedly for his good that he should become a Redemptorist, if he will — and, as men may enter the Church on imperfect motives yet be blest in it, so, I suppose, they may a religious body. When he wrote to me in October, my feeling was, 'If Coffin becomes a secular, he will lose his soul —' therefore, since I did not dream of his becoming a regular, I thought all that could be done, was *to keep him* an Oratorian; to separate him (since he was so bent on it) from you, leaving it to the future whether he got better and could be brought round. But now since he will not be an Oratorian, and wishes to be a Redemptorist, I do earnestly think nothing can be better for him, — if (also) he perseveres.

Any how what has happened is certainly a call on all of us to greater personal exactness and devotedness to God. St Philip means it for this. He means, by means of it, to make us more serious, collected and sober, though not less cheerful and childlike. These indeed are times which impress upon us the necessity of being men, of pruning luxuriances, lest we get thin and shabby about the roots.

J H N.

TO GEORGE RYDER

Oy. Bm. Nov 26/50

My dear George,

Would such a plan suit you? We *trust* at Easter to be able to take the boys. What say you to their going with one of our Fathers (Scratton) to St Leonard's for the winter? Arthur W. [Wilberforce] would join them and perhaps another or two. Scratton's health requires it — he has had boys before this, and is fond of them.

The difficulty is the *expence* — what it will be, we can't say — but before calculating, I want to know what you think of it. The priest there is F Melia, a Jesuit

Ever Yrs most affectly John H Newman   Congr. Orat.

THURSDAY 28 NOVEMBER 1850   Mr Todd came.   Lord Feilding called   Coffin passed thro' (*having left us?*)   Baron brought his picture

TO F. W. FABER

Oy Bm November 28/50

My dear F Wilfrid,

I am exceedingly pleased at having been of any use to you in your deliberations, and I have no doubt at all you have decided rightly.[1] Painful as the matter is, it will do us all good. It will bind us more to each other, both House in itself, and House with House. I mean nothing harsh when I say, that, when I think of Coffin, St Paul's words come into my head 'there must be heresies among you, that they which are approved, may become manifest.'[2] Such things bring out before us more strongly that the Oratory is a vocation — and fill us with zeal and loyalty towards our dear Patron, whom, with God's grace, we at least will not forsake. 'Ye are they who have continued with me etc'[3]

I am made anxious by what F Coffin tells me (who is in Birmingham now for a few hours) of F. Richard. *How* is he? *ought* he to go abroad? And is Alban up to St Wilfrid's in this raw weather?

The Bishop has given Alban faculties and leave to duplicate. And (tell F Antony) he is quite agreeable to the notion of a secular priest. He says that *his* business was only to see the *mission* served, that Lord Shr. [Shrewsbury] must look after the *house*. I have not put before him any definite terms, nor shall I, till you tell me to do so.

Thank F Richard for his letter[4] — there was no idea of the Baron staying here — and we had no notion whatever of sending him to Rome. All we had contemplated was, that, *if* he found himself at Rome, we would employ him. I think him, as F Richard says, under an illusion.

Ever Yrs affly J H N

P.S.   F Lans's letter seems to me a very good one. I shall send him a line of kindness.[5]

You will observe that Coffin in his letter confirms my view so far as this, that he says he leaves because he is not with *me* — or at least that

[1] Faber was delighted with Newman's letter of 26 Nov., 'I cannot tell you the comfort and support your letter has given us. I read it to the deputies today, and they all desire me to thank you for it very much.' The London House decided to grant Coffin the release he asked for, without waiting for the opinion of Fr Lans.

[2] 1 Cor. 11 : 19.   [3] St Luke 22 : 28.

[4] See note three to next letter.   [5] Letter of 25 Dec.

this is a RUDIMENTAL ground of his leaving — *I* say, 'because he is with *you*.'[1]

TO BARON VON SCHROETER

Oratory, Birmingham November 28. 1850

My dear Baron de Schroeter,

I thank you for your letter, and for the picture which you are to bring today.[2]

To my surprise and pleasure, a friend has put into my hands a sum which he wishes conveyed to you; this will account for the cheque which I inclose[3]

All blessings be with you, my dear Baron, wherever you go. I say so the more heartily, because I cannot think of you without sentiments, which it is very painful to me to entertain towards one who has been in the relation towards us which you have held.

The Birmingham Oratory received you a year ago, a stranger coming without letters of introduction, with open arms. It has treated you with the frankness and warmth which it shows towards its own subjects. It has consulted for you with the most anxious delicacy and tenderness, and has honored you for the grace God had given you. It has cherished you in its bosom with the most unsuspicious love.[4]

---

[1] On a collection of the correspondence Newman wrote: '1849–1850 Coffin's case. *His Letters* with some of the *Father's* [i.e. Newman's] of F Wilfrid's etc.

NB. The upshot seems to have been this:— neither Congregation suited him; not London, because he wished to be with the Father; not Birmingham, because he wished not to be with F. Ambrose. The Father from the first took his feelings as serious, and wished him to take up his position in London—but F. Wilfrid persuaded the Father to the contrary, saying it was only Coffin's sfogi.' [letting off steam] Cf. letters of 9 and 23 Nov. 1849, and the postscripts to those of 5 and 8 Jan. (II) 1850, to Faber, and that of 13 Jan. 1850 to Coffin.

[2] Announcing he was bringing his painting, von Schroeter wrote 'It will be a great consolation for me to see you for some moments again.'

[3] In the list of letters sent, in the diary for 25 Nov. is 'send 15/ to Baron Pritchard Bristol.'

[4] Stanton and Faber had already told Newman of their suspicions as to the part von Schroeter was playing at St Wilfrid's, and from London on 27 Nov. Stanton wrote at Faber's advice: 'There can be no want of charity in it, as the Baron himself openly and *voluntarily* told it to F. Alban, and defends it.

He acknowledges fully the part he has had in C's [Coffin's] business—he also says that certain members of your house (I think) A B and C, as he says, are in the habit of coming to him for counsel and that [he] thinks *it his duty* to give it—In short he seems to feel that he is called to live under our roof for the purpose of undermining the Congregation. He predicts the downfall of the Oratory from want of confidence between superiors and subjects! . . . I believe him to be good but under some strange delusion. . . .'

In recompense, you have availed yourself of the opportunities these gave you to do your utmost to ruin the Institution of St Philip, to make its subjects despise it, to fill them with suspicions against it and against each other, to prejudice externals against it. I am not simply speaking of the instance of F. Coffin, but of the general action of your presence among us on all who have come near you. One has heard of seducers getting into families, and ruining their peace. You have breathed out from you a sort of moral infection, which nothing could resist, under God's grace, but the antagonist spirit of loyalty towards our great Saint and his institution.[1]

Etenim homo pacis meae, in quo speravi, qui edebat panes meos, magnificavit super me supplantationem.[2]

And now I have but one request to make to you; that you will not write to any of us, or hold any communication with us. I have sent the Guest Master of the house to give you this letter, and you will see no one else. Not that I fear you; St Philip has guarded this body and will still; but from charity to the souls of any you may have tempted, I am bound to make this request.

And now all good Angels go with you, and God bring you to a truer knowledge of yourself

I am, My dear Baron de Schroeter, Yours sincerely in Xt,

John H Newman   Congr. Orat.[3]

TO JAMES HOPE

Oratory, Birmingham November 29. 1850

My dear Hope,[4]

⌈I write a line to thank you for your letter, and to say how glad I shall be to hear from you, as you half propose, whether or not I am able

---

[1] This last sentence is erased in the draft, and was evidently omitted.

[2] Ps. 40 : 10.

[3] Von Schroeter wrote on 30 Nov. of his actions, '. . . it is impossible for me to subordinate higher duties to human affection or regards, and led by this principle it was my duty to communicate open and free my opinion about your Institute *as it is carried out in England* to those of your Fathers by whom I was urged to do so. . . .'

[4] Referring to Newman's letter of 20 Nov., Hope wrote on 27 Nov. that it 'renews a correspondence which I value very highly and which my own stupidity had interrupted—Offence I had never taken, but causes such as you describe much better than I could have done, were the occasion of my silence. You may now find that you have brought some trouble on yourself, for there are many things on which I should like to ask you questions. . . . However at present my chief object is to assure you how very glad I am again to write to you as the friend whom I almost feared I had thrown away. Whatever occurs do not let us again be estranged. It is not easy as one gets older to form new friendships of any kind and least of all such as I have always considered yours. . . .'

to say any thing to your satisfaction, which would be a greater and different pleasure.

It makes me smile to hear you talk of getting older. What must I feel, whose life is gone ere it is well begun?[1]

Ever Yours affectionately John H Newman   Congr. Orat.

SATURDAY 30 NOVEMBER 1850 Mr Todd went to Ratcliffe College. Bastard came and was received

TO AN UNKNOWN CORRESPONDENT

(for publication)   [December 1850][1]

My dear Sir,

I have received your message, directing my attention to a letter in the Times of November 26 signed 'A Protestant, thank God.'[2] The accusation it insinuates against the Catholic Church, for it does not distinctly state it, is, I suppose this:— that she puts into the hands of young persons, even of the female sex, religious books, which contain, among much other matter of a devotional or practical nature, allusions to various gross sins of impurity.

I do not know the particular work from which the extract is made, which 'a Protestant, thank God' calls 'a breviary or missal' which it certainly is not, but I will suppose it fairly made. I observe then as follows.

[1] This letter, which Joseph Gordon appears to have commissioned, is among the 'Copied Letters' of 1856, together with that to Joseph Gordon, which follows. They can be roughly dated from letter in *The Times* which occasioned them.

[2] *The Times* (26 Nov. 1850), p. 3. This was one of the letters evoked by the 'papal aggression' agitation. Its writer explained that 'Having a wish to peruse a Roman Catholic breviary or missal, I borrowed one from a young lady, a friend of mine. Yesterday (Sunday) I read it. Many parts of it surprised me, but at last I came to "Devotions for Confession," and, to my horror I found the following passages. I must premise that at the commencement the reader is to "consult the 'Table of Sins' to help his memory," and that the owner of this book is a young woman of 20 . . .' The list of the sins of impurity is then reproduced in full, and the writer concludes, 'But I cannot proceed. Every crime for which Sodom and Gomorrah were burnt is here openly alluded to; and this book is a Roman Catholic lady's daily companion! It is entitled "The Daily Companion; with a complete Preparation for the Sacraments, and other useful additions; published at Liverpool, by R. Rockliff, 49 Castle Street, 1845" . . .
I append my name and address, but would not wish it to be published in connexion with such an infamous work.'

148

If an admission of this kind is a fair argument against the Church, it is *à fortiori* an argument against the Protestant community, who, making their watchword 'The Bible, the whole Bible, and nothing but the Bible,' and denouncing Catholics for making selections from it, proceed to place it, with all it contains, in the hands of women and children. I conceive that the inspired volume states certain shocking offences as nakedly as a Catholic manual, or more so, and not in one place but in many, and not merely in order to self-examination and repentance, but in narrative and history.

I conceive that whatever offends 'A Protestant, thank God,' in the Catholic manual, consists of simple *quotations* from this or that part of Scripture.

Moreover, in matter of fact, it is notorious that such passages of Holy Scripture are curiously sought out and dwelt on by young people, who are deficient in correct feeling; and are perverted by them into means of corruption.

Moreover, in the Anglican Church all these very passages of Scripture are read aloud in the course of the Service without the omission of a word, or at most with a few unauthorized omissions; and many of the most distressing of them on Sunday, to good and bad, to young and old, to men and women, looking into each other's faces.

It seems to me then, that it is hypocritical in the correspondent of the Times, thus to strain at a gnat and to swallow a camel.

Again, Jeremy Taylor's Holy Living contains in it passages of the very same character, yet is a book commonly given away to young people.

From such passages any virtuous and delicate mind instinctively turns away; or, if it comes across them, it does not understand them, or wish to do so, and passes them by; whereas they are *necessary* for the guilty. If repentance is necessary, examination of conscience is necessary; and a strange sort of examination of conscience would be that, which passed over all but genteel sins, which caused no pain or shame. Discretion indeed is necessary what particular heads of sin should be put into print, and Christian prudence will limit the catalogue to the end proposed; but I suppose that those who have the cure of souls are better judges on this point than their worldly and superficial critics

Moreover, in such passages there is nothing to excite the passions; many a modern novel is far more dangerous.

I am, My dear Sir, Yours faithfully A Catholic Priest[1]

---

[1] This letter was not published in *The Times*, although some of its arguments and of those in the letter which follows were put forward in letters to *The Times* of 30 Nov. and 11 Dec., signed respectively 'A Catholic Thank God,' and 'A Priest, Once a Protestant.'

TO JOHN JOSEPH GORDON

[December 1850]¹

My dear Fr Joseph,

As to Mr —— 's question, I don't suppose he would take it rude, he is too much a man of the world for it, if I suggest to him that 'a little knowledge is a dangerous thing.' Don't let him go by extracts — let him rather take the testimony of impartial persons, who have examined the whole subject

There is Thirlwall, the Bishop of St David's. I recollect he made a speech a few years back in the House — I think on the Maynooth grant. The objection to which Mr —— alludes, was brought up, and he made a speech against it (the objection). I wish Mr —— could find it. It is, I suppose, *two* years ago — if not *four*; for I was in England. He quoted [a French?]² book in defence of what he said.³

If I must make any remark on the subject it would be this:— that any book on a scientific subject must suppose all possible cases — and that Confessors could not be allowed to ask and settle questions out of their own head, but the more serious the subject, the more necessary it is they should go by rule. I know I have heard good Confessors at Rome say this of some of the most famous works on the subject, viz. that they were books of *reference* — that where a difficulty arose they were to be *consulted*. But it is impossible to answer the objection, if it is really to be answered, in a mere note. All I can say is, that I was aware of all that could be said on this subject against the Catholic Church for years before I was a Catholic, and it never affected me at all, or formed the

¹ See first note to previous letter.
² A space is left blank in the copy.
³ 'With regard to the influence of these [Roman Catholic] doctrines on domestic morality, it has been studiously kept out of sight that there is really no difference whatever between the teaching of any books used at Maynooth on this subject and that of the most approved treatises ever produced by Protestant writers on ethics. . . . I have in my hand an extract from a book of the highest authority, a French work, containing directions to confessors, from which I may be allowed to read one sentence, which will enable you to judge how far the principles there inculcated are dangerous to morality. . . . "It would be impossible to use too much reserve in interrogations relating to the subject of purity . . . especially when there is danger of losing greater benefit than the material completeness of confession. . . ."

But let your Lordships apply a practical test to these doctrines. How do they work in practice? . . . with regard to purity, I apprehend the morals of the Roman Catholics of the lower orders in Ireland will bear a comparison with those of any other part of the United Kingdom.' Connop Thirlwall, Bishop of St David's, in the House of Lords, 4 June 1845. Hansard's *Parliamentary Debates*, third series, LXXXI, 4 June–3 July 1845, columns 88–9.

slightest objection in my mind — nor, as I know, in the minds of others, some of whom are still Protestants.

Ever Yrs affectly J. H. N.

TO F. W. FABER

Oy Bm Dec 2/50

My dear F W

As Bastard leaves here at 9 tomorrow, i.e. before post, I had half hoped that a telegraph would have come from you this evening. I find you got mine at 1.10 PM today.[1] I received him yesterday — he is a particularly nice fellow, going to Madeira for his health. Perhaps you have sent Richard to a medical man to inquire. The vessel proposes to sail from Southampton on Thursday, but it may of course be later. He talks of staying at Madeira till April. The Church is in a bad state there, and it would be a great thing for him to have F Richard — on the other hand it struck me it really might be a good thing for Richard. On his offering to pay expences, I did not absolutely accept, because I did not know F Richard's feeling, but it rests with R. to accept it. Bastard will call at the Oratory. I have nothing more to say about it.

Coffin passed thro' on Thursday, to leave St W's [Wilfrid's] for Hanley on Saturday. I trust it will all turn out well, though I was not overpleased with his manner. It is better than his going back to the world, which he would have gone [sic] otherwise

Ever Yrs affly J H N

TO PHILIP HENRY HOWARD, M.P.

Oratory, Birmingham, Dec. 2, 1850.

My dear Sir,

It gives me great pleasure to find that your kind interposition has succeeded in informing the Dean of Carlisle that the representation of my late sermon in the *Times* newspaper was not a fair one.[2] Yet I could

[1] Newman suggested that the invalid Stanton might accompany Bastard to Madeira, but Stanton declined.

[2] In answer to Newman's letter of 24 Nov. Tait wrote to Howard on 30 Nov. that he had been incorrectly reported, but he still thought Newman 'blasphemous.' He asked Howard to forward his explanation to Newman, 'for I should be concerned if he supposed me capable of joining in that thoughtless abuse to which at times he has not

not doubt that such would be its effect upon a person of so candid and equitable a mind and of such gentleman-like feelings as Dr. Tait. I wish he could have felt it a duty to withdraw the word 'blasphemy;' but I will trust and pray that the day will come at length, when he will be able to do what a conscientious sentiment as yet forbids.

I am, my dear Sir, Most faithfully your's

John H. Newman, Congr. Orat.[1]

To Philip H. Howard Esq, M.P., Corby Castle.

TO ANTONY HUTCHISON

Oratory Birmingham Dec 2. 1850

My dear F Antony,

I saw the Bishop yesterday about St Wilfrid's and he says he is still quite agreeable — but he says he has nothing to do with the money arrangement. He wants you to recommend a Priest to him, and he says he will license him.[2]

Ask F Bernard whether I ought not to take notice of poor John Walter's effusion. He speaks of *kicking out* the Catholics from the country; and corrects himself to the effect that he means, not the Catholics, but the converts. This is after a correspondence with Estcourt. Poor fellow, I have no doubt he did not know what he was saying. It was at the County meeting, he was fidgetted and pressed and in a stew what to say — he must say something strong. He first ran against all Catholics, and then backing out of his shove against the old ones, he ran stern against us. But still I doubt whether he ought to be allowed to go on, especially as he ought to know so much better.[3] What I thought

unnaturally been exposed. No one of us could so join who had an opportunity of witnessing the marvellous influence which his character once exercised over minds of the highest order in Oxford . . .'

[1] For Tait's reply see letter of 6 Dec. to Howard.

[2] Newman was negotiating with Ullathorne at Hutchison's request. See letter of 19 Nov. However, on this same 2 Dec., Hutchison wrote that the Passionists had agreed to take over St Wilfrid's absolutely, the London Oratorians retaining Lord Shrewsbury's annual £70, interest on the money they had lent.

[3] John Walter came under the influence of Newman when he went up to Exeter College in 1836, and in 1841 persuaded his father, the chief proprietor and manager of *The Times*, to take a more favourable view of the Tractarians. See letter of 28 Aug. 1850 to Capes. He took over *The Times* after his father's death in 1847, in which year he was also elected to the House of Commons. He attended a Berkshire County Meeting of protest against 'papal aggression,' held in the town hall at Reading on 28 Nov. 1850,

of doing was to send him back the Madonna he gave me and which I placed over my bed head at St Wilfrid's with a kind note, telling him I sent her to do him good and to plead with him and for him. My laziness will easily catch at any excuse to let things alone.[1]

Ever Yours affectly John H Newman   Congr. Orat.

P.S.   This letter ought to have been written to F Bernard — there is another message you must give him. I am anxious lest the good Langres Priest, my translator, should be quite cut out by M. Gondon, who is now going to translate my Lectures — what can be done?

TO GEORGE RYDER

Oy Bm Dec 2/50

My dear George

I am very glad to find you think you can keep your boys with you this winter. You can't do better, they will get good from being with you, and you will have companions. Give them my love.

I would not have you go to any mortifications. I will tell you what is the greatest — viz to do well the ordinary duties of the day. Determine to rise at a certain hour — to go through certain devotions — to give certain hours to your boys — Don't oppress yourself with them, but *keep to* your rules — and you will find it a sufficient trial.

Our Blessed Lady be with you whose great feast is coming, and all Saints and Angels

Ever Yrs affectly in Xt   John H Newman   Congr. Orat.

P.S.   I received Mr Bastard of Devonshire yesterday.

and found himself unexpectedly called upon to make a speech, which was reported in *The Times* next day. He accused Newman of having spoken in his sermon of 27 Oct. 'as if we were heathens,' and said that if those who were trying to make England Catholic appeared likely to succeed, they would be 'kicked out.' He contrasted them with 'the old-fashioned Roman Catholics, whom I shall always distinguish in my own mind from those who have lately separated from our church, and who, of course, are more envenomed against it.'

[1] John Walter sent a copy of the Madonna del Gran Duca, with a note, still preserved, addressed to Newman at Oriel, asking him to accept it, and saying it 'was procured by me at Florence.' This must have been in 1841, after the letters by 'Catholicus' in *The Times*. Newman enclosed for Dalgairns, in Hutchison's letter, a draft of the note he thought of sending. See letter of 6 Dec. to Walter.

TUESDAY 3 DECEMBER 1850 Bastard went F Alban past [sic] thro' H W [Wilberforce] and Arthur [Wilberforce]

TO EDWARD BADELEY

Oratory. Birmingham December 3. 1850

My dear Badeley

I was much pleased to see your hand writing, and thank you for your information, which is perfectly satisfactory.[1] At present we are safe, tho' Parliament may pass some more extensive measure, and include us. I had no doubt about it myself, but some furious Protestants here threatened to tear our gowns off us in the street, and, though one felt an action of assault was open to one, if they did so, yet it was desirable to see what the rights of the matter were.

As to the present row, I feel confident what our rulers have done is right, *because* it is done.[2] I have had nothing whatever to do with it, and any one who knows me knows that my line is not that of external manifestation, still I do believe that St Peter has come out of the Flaminian Gate, and not simply Nicholas Wiseman, and that he will be stopped by no 'Domine quo vadis?' outside the walls.

And, to tell the truth, though I hate rows, I hate (I hope) humbug quite as much — and so much had got about lately at home and abroad to the effect that the British Lion had become a lamb, and that John Bull had become instinct with a diviner spirit, that liberals were Catholics, and the race of squires and parsons was extinct, that I do think it is a good thing to have matters put on their true basis. And then those wretched whigs, the $\mu\iota\sigma\eta\tau\grave{o}s$ $\sigma\tau\acute{a}\sigma\iota s$ of Hurrell Froude.[3] I hope we are

[1] Badeley's letter of 2 Dec. began: 'Henry Wilberforce sent me, a few days ago, a letter which he had received from Mr St John, expressing some alarm lest the Oratorians had rendered themselves liable to legal penalties by appearing publicly in the habits of their Order—He desired me to answer his letter by writing to you, and I gladly avail myself of the opportunity thus afforded me for renewing our intercourse, which alas! has been long interrupted— . . .' Badeley went on to explain that since the Oratorians did not take vows, they were not liable to the fine of £50 imposed, by the Emancipation Act of 1829, on those who wore a religious habit. Cf. letters of 16 June 1852 to Faber, and 18 June 1852 to Horatio Spencer Walpole.

[2] Badeley wrote in his letter, 'Altho' I have not joined your Church, I hope you do not accuse me of the insane opposition to the late proceedings of the Pope and Cardinal Wiseman—which appears to me perfectly childish and detestable—as inconsistent with common sense as it is with common Charity—I may have my own opinion upon the wisdom and policy of what has been done at Rome, and in England, by the Heads of your Church but the outcry raised about it is, to my mind, quite disgraceful. . . .'

[3] 'The hateful faction.' See the sonnet against them in *Remains of Richard Hurrell Froude*, 1, London 1838, p. 302. The Prime Minister, Lord John Russell and the Whig

rid of them for ever. And then I suppose it will tend, especially if the row goes on, to bring together and consolidate the Catholic interest all over the Empire. The most serious thing is the collision with the radicals as far as there is one — but that must come — and there is not so much of it as I had expected.[1] One thing the government may be quite sure of, that, though we shall try to escape breaking the law, if we can help, yet if they drive us to bay in a matter of principle, to a certainty we shall, whatever comes of it, though we are sent out after Smith O Brien.

I have often wished to meet you[2] — I called on my return from Rome, but it was Christmas and you were out. It's a shame you are not a Catholic — you have no excuse at all.

Ever Yours affectly John H Newman   Congr. Orat.

TO F. W. FABER

Dec 3/50

My Dear F Wilfrid

For various reasons I could not recommend Bastard to pay F Alban's expences.[3] He does not want a companion but a sort of director — whereas Alban is younger, I suppose, than he is. If Alban would go as a fellow voyager, so that afterwards they would be independent of each other, and see as much or as little of each other as they would, well and good. I dare say Bastard would be very glad — but I don't see what use Alban otherwise can be to him. I inclose a note for B. if he calls in King William Street

Ever Yrs affly J H N

Government had encouraged the popular outcry against the 'papal aggression.' Newman had always disliked the alliance between Catholics and Whigs.

[1] The Radicals not infrequently defended the Catholics. See letter of 12 Dec. to Hutchison.

[2] Badeley wrote '. . . I have never had the happiness of seeing you since we parted at Rome near the Basilica of St Paul [15 Oct. 1847]. . . . How I should like to see you again! I do sincerely hope that you will give me an opportunity when you come to Town. . . .'

[3] Faber had suggested that Wells might be given the offer of going with Bastard to Madeira, in Stanton's place.

TO GEORGE TALBOT

[3 December 1850][1]

My dear Talbot,

The excitement is greater not less — county meetings are spreading through England, and each parish sends up its petition or utters its protest.

Something of course must be done in Parliament, which it is said the Queen wishes to summon for despatch of business sooner than usual. I don't think they can do us any *harm*, but they will *insult* us, which we must bear, and, like mad animals, they will think they have triumphed over us, when *we* have the victory.

Do you think you can learn whether, if 'Bishop of Birmingham,' is made illegal, 'Bishop of the Church in Birmingham,' might be used consistently with Catholic propriety? We ought to have something ready. Don't *talk* about this, because our intentions ought not to get out, else they will forbid our prospective steps.

The Cardinal is firm and vigorous, the effect of his pamphlet has been enormous — the multitude, who dare not confess its truth, only extol his cleverness the more. Our Bishop too has shown the same firm, bold front. Both would go to prison rather than recede. The people of this great country are such (moral) *cowards*, that nothing is likely so to prevail with them as firmness. They will rush forward, if you retreat — but they will be cowed and fall back, if you calmly keep your ground We must not budge an inch — nor will any one, I am sure

Ever Yours most sincerely in Xt

John H Newman   Congr. Orat.

WEDNESDAY 4 DECEMBER 1850   H W [Wilberforce] went

TO J. SPENCER NORTHCOTE

Oratory Bm. Dec 4/50

My dear Northcote,

I am truly glad of your intention. F. Gordon and I have for some months fidgetted about the sort of thing for our own people; *but we have no time*. A set of Tracts is just what *we* want for Birmingham.

---

[1] Dated from diary.

Nothing can be better than to put them under the invocation of St Vincent, but you must have a shorter *working* title than 'Tracts of the Brotherhood of St V. of Paul' — e.g. *we* should have called *ours* 'Oratory Tracts.'[1]

I would tell you what I would promise you, if you would let the performance be delayed on and on till the series is finished and it is too late to write — what I am lecturing on now — a popular sketch of the history of Jansenism, going on with the doings of the Emperor Joseph, the French Constitutional Church, the martyrdom of Pius vi, and the captivity of Pius vii — The downfall of the Jesuits would come in. The general title might be 'Persecution of the Church in the 18th and 19th centuries,' or the like.[2]

I also was going to lecture on 1. Massacre of St Bartholomew. 2 Gun-powder Plot. 3 Titus Oates. 4. James ii. 5 Lord George Gordon. etc. as a series of historical scenes. If any thing came of these, you should have them. But PRAY don't let me grab what others think of — for I am likely to be a dog in the manger at my age — considering Quid brevi fortes etc.[3]

Kindest remembrances to Thompson, and believe me, Ever Yours affectly in Xt

John H Newman   Congr. Orat.

P.S.   My only fear is my History of Persecution would be too *long* for Tracts.

THURSDAY 5 DECEMBER 1850   Bastard came

TO F. W. FABER

Oy Bm Dec 5/50

My dear F Wilfrid,

The more I think of it, the sadder Coffin's case is — and I don't like, nor is it necessary to go into it — he has done a bad thing under

[1] J. S. Northcote wrote on 3 Dec. that he and E. H. Thompson were persuading the Society of St Vincent de Paul at Clifton to publish cheap Catholic tracts, the valuable 'Clifton Tracts,' which began in 1851.

[2] There are preserved at the Birmingham Oratory some notes of the lectures on Pius VII and Napoleon. The writer of Newman's obituary in the *Birmingham Daily Post*, 11 Aug. 1890, remembered having heard one of these lectures, 'in which there was a brilliant sketch of Napoleon and his influence on the national and religious life of Europe.'

[3] Horace, *Odes* II, xvi, 17. 'Why do we whose life is short, so resolutely aim at many things?' Northcote replied that these five lectures were just what he hoped for, but Newman was diverted to other tasks.

bad feelings in a bad manner — and it is this which frightens one about his future — still the mercy of God so wonderfully over rules things, but we must hope it will be well — but what does St Philip say to it?

I find Alban thought me 'wretchedly cold.' I KNEW HE WOULD. It is the way with some of you. *So, I went out of my way* to be kind to him. I ran about the house for him, and talked to him till I had a chance of having no time to read Pius vi's life for my lecture — and, as it was, I lost the Oratory for him.[1] Next time I shall take it easy, and he will say, how delightful I am. The truth is he was *disappointed* I would not consent to B's [Bastard] paying his expences.

As to the furniture of St Wilfrid's, what we should like to do is to see what we want of it, and pay either F Antony or the joint-Congregations for it, as the case may be.

I send two papers, which perhaps you will kindly get filled up, and *anything added* I have omitted, and then sent back to me.

Ever Yours affly J H Newman   Congr. Orat.

TO PHILIP HENRY HOWARD, M.P.

[6 December 1850][2]

for publication

My dear Sir

I am much obliged to you for sending me Dr Tait's second letter, which contains but a fresh proof of what I could not doubt, his frank and honorable mind.[3]

Yet I fear I am not able, much as I should wish, to avail myself of his conditional concession, for I am obliged in fairness to take entirely on myself the report of my Sermon, as it is given in the Times newspaper. I am not speaking of the editor's offensive comment on it, but of the report itself — and I must admit though it is meagre, and gives no idea of the sermon or argument or composition — still there is nothing in it which is not also contained in my Sermon as published, except that

---

[1] i.e. the evening mental prayer in common.

[2] Dated from diary. This letter seems not to have been published.

[3] To Newman's letter of 2 Dec., Tait replied to Howard on 4 Dec. that he had now perused the sermon as Newman published it: 'Certain expressions were given in the report of *The Times* which are not in the published Sermon, and which I understand to be now disclaimed by Dr. Newman. It was to these expressions that I applied the words which have given so much pain. I am bound to state, explicitly, that I should not have thought myself justified in applying these words to the discourse as it is now before the public. . . .'

the reporter says that 'hierarchy' is the 'one *name*' of our religion, instead of 'catholicism.'

And this being the case it follows that I have no clear idea what are the 'certain expressions' contained in that report, which Dr Tait 'understands I now *disclaim*;' And still less I am able to understand how they can give me 'pain,' whatever they are, especially as I have already observed to you that even the extravagant things popularly said of me do but cause me to 'smile.' But perhaps they ought to be a subject of sorrow rather than amusement, and I thank Dr Tait for the admonition.

TO JOHN WALTER

[6 December 1850]

(Let F Bernard send me this back)[1]

Once on a time a young man made his Senior a present in token of his esteem for him. It was a Madonna, and that Senior put her over his bed-head, and whenever any one spoke of it, he used to say 'John Walter gave me that picture,' and he never said so without thinking kindly of him.

And so years passed, and changes came with them, and at length there was a day when the young man made a speech before a whole county; and after speaking by name of that elderly man of whom he once had felt esteem, he said that he wished that all who were such as that elderly man was, were kicked out of the kingdom.

What then could that elderly man do, before he was kicked out, but send back to that young man, who once had an innocent conscience and a gentle heart, that same sweet Madonna, to plead with the dear Child whom she holds in her arms for him, and with her gentle look and calm eyes to soften him towards that elderly man to whom he once gave it and who had kept it so safely.

Yours affectionately John H Newman[2]

[1] Dalgairns thoroughly approved of this letter which Newman sent for his opinion. See letter of 2 Dec. to Hutchison. Dalgairns kept Newman's draft, sending him a copy. The text here is that of the draft, preserved at the London Oratory. The date is established from the diary.

[2] On receiving Newman's letter and the picture, Walter replied:

'40, Grosvenor St Decr 10. 1850

My dear Sir,

It needed not the look of that sweet Madonna to soften the heart of that young man of whom you have spoken towards one whom he once revered and hoped ever to have retained as a teacher and a friend, and of whom, amidst all the changes that have

TO MRS WOOD

Oratory Bm Dec 7/50

My dear Mrs Wood

Many thanks for your kind letter and cheque. We have begun our house (with our own money) and hope soon to begin our Church, for which we are making preparation, so that your gift comes in very seasonable, especially as we have got to pay for the ground, and I will not forget the donor at Hodder or you — or Almeric either, whose illness is certainly a most anxious one, considering the character of Syrian fevers — I hope you will soon have a different account.[1]

You are not au courant with Oratory history. F Coffin never has belonged to this house, nor indeed has he ever really been part of the London House. He has been Rector of our house at St Wilfrid's — which, beautiful place as it is, has been and is so expensive and useless to us, that we are (I suppose) now ultimately parting with it. *It* goes to the Passionists, and its Rector is gone to the Redemptorists.

Miss Giberne is here — I will give her your message, and inquire about St Rose.

I don't agree with you at being troubled at the present row. It is always well to know things as they *are*. The row has not unsettled a single Catholic or Catholicizing Anglican — rather it has converted and is converting many. It has but brought out what all sober people knew, though one is apt to forget it — that the English people is not Catholicly-minded. Many foreigners, many old Catholics, have thought they were — I dislike our smoothing over the nation's aversion to our doctrines, just as I dislike smoothing over those doctrines themselves. The real

passed, he has never ceased to speak as aforetime, even to his own hindrance and reproach, in terms of affectionate regard.

If then, on a second reading of that unlucky speech, it should appear that that young man did not express or imply the wish that has been ascribed to him, but that he only stated his conviction, founded upon his own observation though perhaps too harshly expressed—that if the English people should ever exchange their present feelings of indignation at what they deem an assault upon their Constitution both in Church and State, for those of alarm, they would rise as one man and drive those intruders out—he hopes that the utterance of this Protestant remark may be forgiven him, and not be treated as an act of personal unkindness by one whom he believes to be as willing to pardon an unintentional offence as he has been gentle in rebuking it—

Yours affectionately J Walter

Revd Dr Newman'

[1] Mrs Wood's son, Granville Francis Wood (1818–56), a Captain in the Royal Navy, became a Catholic in 1849, and had just finished his first year as a Jesuit novice at Hodder, near Stonyhurst. His elder brother Almeric was serving with the Mediterranean fleet.

misery is the trouble it has introduced into families, the private persecutions, the alienation of friends, and the bitterness of feeling which the commotion has caused — but all this will turn to good. In like manner, they may insult us in parliament, but I don't see how any act they pass can hurt us

Ever Yours most sincerely in Xt, with kindest remembrances of Miss Wood

John H Newman   Congr. Orat.

SUNDAY 8 DECEMBER 1850   Monsell and Lady A. M. [Anna Maria Monsell] in Birmingham

TO J. D. DALGAIRNS

Oy Bm In fest Concept. [8 December] 1850

My dear F Bernard,

Bye the bye, did you hear that the Roman Gossip is that the present Pope will not define the Immaculata. There has been a sad blow up between Cardinal Fornari and the Archbishop of Paris about Gallican privileges — and I suppose our Lady has got into the quarrel and suffers in consequence.[1]

Ornsby wrote to me some time since, saying I was to be applied to by the Primate to recommend a person as Secretary to the new University Commission: saying he wished if so, I would recommend him. I answered I should be very glad to do so — but have not heard from him again.[2]

As to poor Coffin's matter, it is but a very small and insignificant edition of what we read so often in the history of incipient orders and the lives of Saints — misfortunes which are trying both from their annoyance to the body or the founder, and from the anxiety they inspire about the person who is the subject or cause of them. It is one of the

---

[1] Marie Dominique Auguste Sibour (1792–1857) became Archbishop of Paris in 1849. He was a friend and supporter of Napoleon III, and on 26 July 1850 had written to Pius IX opposing the definition of the doctrine of the Immaculate Conception, being one of the four or five Catholic bishops to do so. Cardinal Fornari (1788–1854) was nuncio in Paris until the autumn of 1850. In Rome he was blamed for reviving the animus between Gallicans and Ultramontanes, and was not made Cardinal Secretary of State, as had been intended.

[2] The University Commission was that appointed to set up the Catholic University of Ireland. Dalgairns on 4 Dec. asked Newman to write for his brother-in-law Robert Ornsby, a testimonial, to the Primate, the Archbishop of Armagh, Paul Cullen.

necessary trials of the present position of the Oratory — but St Philip is greater than it or any loss, and while we have him, we may be content. Its proper effect will be to humble us; make us saints all at once it cannot. We must be content to be despised in (what the Protestant version calls) 'our day of small things.'[1] A shrub must grow before it is a tree — young men in time become old. If we are young, this is a fault which *mends* — but we can't help ourselves — If Coffin declares we are not Saints, there's no denying it; we can but try to be. Meanwhile neither God, nor our Lady, nor St Philip despises his own little ones — and others may as well not despise them either.

I am glad you approved my note to Walter — I have sent it to him with the picture.

Ever Yours affly John H Newman   Congr. Orat.

TO F. W. FABER

Oy. Bm Dec 8/50

My Dear F Wilfrid,

I give you the compliments of the day. Don't make too much of the Roman tattle — It is confined to Dr Grant, depend on it — and he is not Rome, or the Pope.[2] Of course this is a time to weigh our words and actions, as carefully as we can — and, since we are sure to make a number of sbagli any how, to determine and set about making none. It's a nuisance if Dr U. [Ullathorne] is in possession of all our matters, but we must take things lightly and rely on St Philip.[3] Coffin seems to have been oblivious both that there was a St Philip in heaven and a Pope upon earth.

Have you heard Mr Vaughan of Oscott is gone with Coffin to

[1] Zechariah 4 : 10.

[2] Faber wrote on 6 Dec. that Wiseman's secretary 'Searle let out that we are in bad odour in Rome—I think he only means this house—that letters have been written against us; our functions are bad; our irreverence worse; it is a proverb in London, If you want to hear how quick Our Fathers can be gabbled, go to the Oratory; we don't pray for the queen (*the cardinal expressly forbad us*, but has now told Mr Bagshawe he will *make* us do it). This, with Searle's vehemence, and Dr Grant's letter [see Newman's letter of 25 Oct.], and one the Cardinal wrote to me from Rome about our active Crusade against gothicism, are all anxious things. . . .'

[3] Faber added, 'We have also some reason for thinking that one of the 2 catholics of standing, whom Coffin consulted about the Triduo and *other Oratorian affairs,* especially *direction* and *want of confidence in superiors,* was Mgr Ullathorne when he was there to confirm. This explains Dr Grant's letter. . . .'

Belgium? and the report is that McMullen is to follow.[1] McMullen never would do for us — but I suppose Coffin has taken care he should not. It is not uncharitable so to think.

I am not displeased at this row, though the extreme trouble it causes to private persons, domestic persecution, tyrannical efforts at conversions and the like, are most serious and painful matters — but I mean in its public bearing. Humbug is detestable — and at home and abroad such things have been said of the approaching conversion of England, as make one rejoice in any thing, however rude, which destroys the dream.

The report grows stronger and stronger here, that I am married, and have shut up my wife in a convent.

Ever Yrs affly J H N

P.S. On recollection, I think Coffin would have stayed, unless we had given up St W's [Wilfrid's]. He put objections in the way of my removing my closets etc, in saying 'is it certain?' So as to strike me at the time that he was *unwilling* to acquiesce in the settlement. I think he *never* would have gone to London — if the Baron had not been there, he would have consulted Dr U. or Dr Pagani or Dr Morgan etc etc. I suppose now he will turn or return into a furious Goth.

MONDAY 9 DECEMBER 1850 Bastard went F Thomas and A Wilberforce went to Rugby

TO LADY OLIVIA ACHESON

Dec. 9/50

My dear Lady Olivia,

I have had it conveyed to me, I am sorry to say, since F Ambrose spoke to you just now, that there are objections to Lucy Porta's going to Warwick Street.[2] Therefore your self denying intentions must be disappointed. I can't say I am sorry for its own sake, tho' I am sorry for the disappointment, for I have a great fear of your doing too much.

Yours most sincerely in Xt John H Newman Congr. Orat.

[1] Edmund Vaughan (1827–1908), uncle of Cardinal Vaughan, after being at Oscott joined the Redemptorists with Coffin, and became eventually the English Provincial. R. G. McMullen, who had been ordained in 1848, remained in London as a priest of the Westminster Archdiocese.

[2] i.e. the house there, near Alcester Street, where Lady Olivia and other pious ladies were living.

TO WILLIAM MONSELL

Oratory Dec 9/50

My dear Monsell

I am almost amused as well as concerned at what Lady Olivia tells me.

She says that you feel your abstract views of truth insufficient to support you in devotion.

That is, you have *conviction*, but you have not *faith*. Is not this the very state of a person external to the Catholic Church? 'Lord I believe, help Thou my unbelief.'

Let this be your prayer. I will not forget you. Go and be received. You have nothing to hinder you, but your Enemy, who would fain embarrass you

Yours most sincerely John H Newman[1]

TUESDAY 10 DECEMBER 1850   F Austin ill — it turned to small pox   FF Stanislas and Edward examined for the Diaconate.   F Thomas returned   Lady O. A. [Olivia Acheson] ill

TO LADY OLIVIA ACHESON

Oratory Bm Dec 10. 1850

My dear Lady Olivia,

Do not think for an instant there was any thing unkind to me in your note. I am but extremely concerned to think that any thing has happened to distress you. I will not forget to try to do something for Lucy Porta — but you must not and shall not be thrown out of your quiet and peace, since for quiet and peace you came here — and I shall recommend any thing to you rather than that.

I would promise to call on you today, but that I have to go to the Quarant' ore — I shall say Mass for you tomorrow morning

Our Blessed Lord and His dear Mother comfort and console you

Yours affectionately in Xt   John H Newman   Congr. Orat.

WEDNESDAY 11 DECEMBER 1850   Quarant' Ore — sang mass of Exposition   FF Stanislas and Edward went into retreat

[1] See letter of 13 Dec.

TO J. M. CAPES

Oy Bm. Dec. 12/50

My dear Capes

I have nothing to say in my own capacity of theological revisor.

As to the *fact*, *do* you think the Establishment is coming to an end? is it not rather going to be developed, with all its resources, into liberalism? unless the internal conflict of its parties is too great.[1]

Next, can we *at the moment* wish the destruction of the Establishment? As it has got the nation *into* the mess, must it not be used to a certain point in getting it *out*? as you would say to any bad general or minister. Are not numbers kept in a sort of grace of congruity state, which may be the beginning of better things, and who at *this moment* would any how not adopt Catholicism, but go the other way, were the Establishment destroyed?

Does Northcote know that Buonaparte in 1796 or 1797 took the Ancona Madonna into his hand, changed colour, and ordered back its jewels which he had sent off to the hospital? Vid Roscoe's Scipio Ricci.[2]

Ever Yrs affly J H N

PS   Both articles are good — the former too short.

TO F. W. FABER

Oy. Bm Dec 12/50

My dear F W

I suppose you have long ago heard from Philip that it was a false alarm that the Bishop would not let the Passionists go to St W's [Wilfrid's] till the Earl signified his consent.[3] F. Nicholas was going there last Monday to settle the accounts — luckily, I stopped him

[1] Newman is referring to the first article in the *Rambler* for Jan. 1851, 'Catholic Prospects,' in which Capes maintained that the agitation against the new hierarchy had not been taken up by the people nor by the Nonconformists, and that the end of the Established Church was approaching. See also letter of 24 Dec. to Capes.

[2] The second article in the *Rambler*, 'Celebrated Sanctuaries of the Madonna,' was by Northcote, and discussed recent cases of miraculous images in Italy. The Ancona Madonna is mentioned on p. 14, but not the incident of which Newman speaks. For it see Thomas Roscoe, *Memoirs of Scipio de Ricci*, II, London 1829, pp. 112–13.

[3] The following note to W. P. Gordon, at St Wilfrid's, must belong to this period: 'My dear Philip I write in the greatest hurry. I fear your faculties *won't* do. I will see the Bishop tomorrow—Put off hearing confessions Ever Yrs affly J H N.'

thinking he would not have time before the Quarant'Ore — for, behold, the accounts are in London.

I am glad you 'see your way' to the community discipline — *We* have been thinking of it lately — one difficulty is a *room* — but I trust we shall overcome it, nearly as soon as you. It is a fit offering on your part for Coffin's defection — I was afraid you still held to your view of February 1848, which, the more I think of the Rule, the less I can take.[1]

Don't fancy the Cardinal is going to take part against you — and despise the tittle tattle of Rome, and the nonsense written thither about you. I suppose you must go to the receptions, for a while, if the C. insists — but surely having places at his court is quite unoratorian — You may tell him it will lead to Coffinism.

I am going to write to Lord Shr. [Shrewsbury] about the Passionists, as soon as I know his direction. Perhaps our Bishop can give it.

I said Mass for all of you, as well as for us, on the Immaculate Conception — and won't forget what you wish about Eminenza. I think in recreation, you must be much on your guard, all of you, against ridiculing Eminenza. There is a tendency in you all to play out your satire against him and every being besides in the whole world, even each other (which mutual velitation I don't mind) — The consequence is that, when I spoke to Mr Batts something or other seriously about the Bishop (Eminenza) he thought I was ironical — and half timidly and ashamed took the supposed jest up. Nothing makes enemies so much as satire — for it seems like haughtiness.[2]

Stanislas and Edward are in retreat for the subdiaconate — so think of them some of you, or say a Mass, as we will for yours. (N.B. Surely Balston is advancing apace.)[3]

Ever Yours affectly J H N

P.S.   *What in the world* am I to do about the Florence Oratory? Recollect it is an *official* letter they have sent.[4]

---

[1] When Newman set up the Oratory in England and wished to introduce the taking of the discipline three times a week, after the evening mental prayer, in accordance with the Rule, Faber objected. He sent to Newman at Maryvale a paper saying that it would deter people from joining the Oratory, and that it represented 'the ascetic genius' which he thought contrary to St Philip's spirit. On this paper Newman wrote at a later date 'N B. The question of the discipline was suspended—1. in consequence of this paper. 2. in consequence of Dr Duke objecting to the shoulders and F Faber to the thighs. J H N.' Newman also suggested taking the discipline privately. Cf. letters of 18 Dec. 1850 and 20 Jan. 1851, to Faber.

[2] Mr Batts is Charles Batt, the priest at Virginia Street in the east of London. Faber wrote on 13 Dec., 'Thanks for your hint at satire, which we all think very just and true. . . .'   [3] He was to be ordained subdeacon on 21 Dec.

[4] The letter accepted Coffin at Florence, and Newman had to explain (see his letter of 24 Dec.) that he would not be going there.

TO ANTONY HUTCHISON

Oratory Bm Dec 12. 1850

My Dear F Antony,

I hardly know what arrangement you mean, when you speak about the furniture at St W's [Wilfrid's] — have I spoken to you about it? — but I doubt not you mean the same as I do.

There is there *your* furniture — and the *joint Oratory* furniture. I should have liked to have offered to buy the whole, (supposing you in London had consented) but I find it is a general feeling here that we shall not want so much for the new house. What then we *wish* to do, is, if it does not clash with any of your plans, to take what we want for certain — that is, in the first place, to survey the *joint* furniture, and take half of such things as we have a fancy for, e.g. half the sheets, table clothes, napkins, crockery, bedsteads — i.e. if neither we or you have taken off any part of it already without equivalent. I don't think *we* have. Then as to the other moiety, we shall buy them of you or not, according as you do not want them and we do.

As to *your* furniture, what we take, we propose to value and pay for. What we are *not* inclined to take is tables, chairs, wash hand stands, and presses — at least, this is as well as I can make out — but, I confess, to me, it seems like taking two bites at a cherry, and that there is nothing which we should not find useful in a large house.

I congratulate you on your Conception Benediction — of which your Father speaks rapturously.

The grand Protestant meeting here came off yesterday and was a failure — the anti-papal motion or address was lost and a contrary amendment almost carried. We are indebted for this to Mr Sturge the Quaker, Mr George Dawson, and Mr Edmonds, the (?) Town Clerk. Catholics laugh and say that our Protestant friends should not have blundered upon the Octave of the Conception. The Quarant'Ore too, is going on.[1]

Ever Yours affectly John H Newman   Congr. Orat.

[1] The meeting of protest against papal aggression was held at the Birmingham Town Hall on the morning of 11 Dec., at the time Newman was singing the Mass for the opening of the Forty Hours' Exposition. Joseph Sturge (1793–1859), the Quaker philanthropist, who was received with a storm of hooting, objected to the sending of an anti-Catholic address to the Queen. He proposed an amendment, which, in the name of religious freedom, rejected legislative interference with the Catholics. Although no speaker, his arguments stemmed the tide. The amendment was seconded by George Edmonds (1788–1868), the leading Birmingham radical, imprisoned for a year in 1820 because he tried to elect a member for Parliament. He had become Clerk of the Peace

P.S.   I want back my two accounts number 1 and number 2. I am not disposed to give the Passionists any thing but our leavings.

P.S.   I am afraid you *must* write to Lambert. It is a great nuisance.[1]

TO GEORGE RYDER

Oy Bm. Dec 12/50

My dear George,

It is quite true about Coffin. The truth is, it is one of the penalties we have for keeping St W's [Wilfrid's]. When men live out of community, there is a great danger of their thinking that community is nothing to them. Our bonâ fide retirement from St W's revealed to him that he did not belong to the London House, to which he had given himself. He has lost a home and friends, which is not a slight thing — the London House has lost nothing, because it never actually had him; but of course is exceedingly sorry.

This kind of thing is of no unfrequent occurrence — I think I heard the Redemptorists had lost one or two men lately in the same way. One, curiously enough, became an Oratorian, at Florence, I think.

I should like very much to see your Lecture —

Love to the boys — Ever Yours affly in Xt

John H Newman, Congr. Orat.

FRIDAY 13 DECEMBER 1850   F Thomas ⟨Scratton?⟩ went to St Leonard's for the winter

TO WILLIAM MONSELL

[13 December 1850][2]

My dear Monsell,

I congratulate you on your reception, which I suppose has taken place — and pray and am sure that you will be ever kept safely and

for Birmingham in 1839. George Dawson (1821–76), the liberal Baptist preacher for whom the church of St Saviour had been built three years before, also spoke in its favour, claiming for Catholics the right to do what Nonconformists had always done. The Mayor put the amendment, which was lost, but when the original resolution was put, it too was declared lost, thus neutralizing the whole of the proceedings.

'The effect of this meeting was great, not only in Birmingham, but throughout the country. It was the first occasion on which the tide of anti-papal legislation had been resisted and turned.' Henry Richard, *Memoirs of Joseph Sturge*, London 1864, p. 413. Cf. letter of 10 March 1851 to Mrs Bowden.

[1] He had to be asked what his fees were for negotiating about St Wilfrid's.

[2] Dated from diary, and next letter.

happily under the shadow and in the arms of that communion of Saints to which you now belong.[1]

Don't let Lady Anna Maria be received till her way is clearer to her than it seemed to me the other day. She had not a *view* of any thing, did not know many simple truths, and had to think over them, understand them, and familiarize her mind with them. To do this well takes time — and it is not time lost. Let her count the cost. She must learn, and thro' God's grace she will learn, to accept the Church as God's oracle — When she does this, all is done — before it, nothing is done. We cannot precede God — we can but follow, and pray to follow.[2]

Be sure I shall be very anxious to hear tidings of you and her. On Thursday next the 19th I shall say a Mass of Thanksgiving for you, Anderdon, Bastard and some others.[3]

Yours very sincerely in Xt   John H Newman   Congr. Orat.

TO THE HON. MRS A. LISLE PHILLIPPS

Oratory. Birmingham Dec 13. 1850.

My dear Mrs Phillipps,

Lady Olivia has begged me to write to you instead of herself — and the reason I have to do so will also explain why she cannot accept your kind invitation.

The truth is, she is in bed — where she has been confined for some days, and will be some time longer with an attack of bronchitis. She is to be kept very quiet. I wanted her to take measures against it, before the Monsells came, but she was very anxious to see them and talk with them. The doctor says there is no danger, if she will submit to proper treatment — but — naturally enough, she does not like to be persuaded that she is as ill as she is.

Pray give my kindest remembrances to Mr Phillips, and congratulate him on the turn things are now taking. A town anti-Catholic address

---

[1] Monsell replied from Grace Dieu, Leicestershire, on 13 Dec., 'I followed your advice and acted without delay—Yesterday Evening I was received in the chapel here—

This instant your most kind letter has been given me by Mrs Phillipps—

I will endeavour to be patient and not to hurry Lady Ann's mind—

You must allow me to tell you that to you—to your writings—to an indescribable sort of feeling I have long had for you I attribute more than to any other human instrument my present happiness.'

[2] Monsell's wife never became a Catholic.

[3] Anderdon was received at Paris by de Ravignan on 23 Nov., and Bastard by Newman on 30 Nov.

here was defeated on Wednesday in a meeting of 9000 people — and today, instead of our being called by the boys 'candlesticks,' 'Popes' and 'High Priests,' two of our party were saluted with 'Hurrah for the Catholics.'

Yours very truly in Xt   John H Newman   Congr. Orat.

P.S.   Might I beg the kindness of your giving the inclosed to Mr Monsell.

SATURDAY 14 DECEMBER 1850   F William (Penny) went?
SUNDAY 15 DECEMBER   F Philip Gordon came
WEDNESDAY 18 DECEMBER   F Philip went

TO F. W. FABER

Oratory Bm Dec 18/50

My dear F W

Miss Wood of Ryde has just begun to translate the life of St Rose of Viterbo, and wishes to know if you will take it. If you want to correspond with her, her direction is 'St Wilfrid's, Ryde.'

Tell F Antony to add the price of the Illustrated News, which I was to give the Brothers, to the bill between the Houses.

Ask F. Richard on what authority he says we are not to say St Philip's office on the Ferias in Advent and Lent. He is like Sancho Panza's physician — for no days ⟨ferias⟩ are left.[1]

As to the Prayer for the Queen, I don't see how you can resist it — and the simple way (I think) would be to say 'very well — ' and do it in your own way — i.e. deliberately take off chasuble and maniple, and say, not chant, it before going out — or, as the priest went out, and just as the organ was striking up for another to say it. Whether you can do so, after the Cardinal has said that 'it is usual for the celebrant,' I don't know. For myself I positively would not say it in chasuble. I suppose you might say it in *English without* chasuble, and the effect would be better. It would be more understanded of the people, and less respectful. You must run the chance of its getting into the papers any how. Nothing could be more dismally prosaic than 'her most gracious Majesty, their Royal Highnesses and all the Royal family' in England.'[2] My only

[1] The physician condemned every dish, *Don Quixote*, II, Ch. xlvii.
[2] Newman closed the quotation marks here a second time.

scruple is the reverence for the Blessed Sacrament. Would it do *before* Mass, in the midst of some Hail Marys? Why would not it do to say Three Hail Marys for the Queen etc? It would be more Catholic than 'their gracious Majestying' and might mean 'her conversion.' You see I think *you* alone, as on the spot, can say *what* is to be done — but still such is my general view, to obey the Cardinal, *but* in your own way.[1]

Tell F. Antony I wish myself to buy the furniture at St Wilfrid's; if he will suggest a plan how it is to be valued.

Ever Yrs affly J H N

P.S.   I have a paper of yours objecting to the Discipline as un-Oratorian — because it was not a community act (according to the Rule) but an act of the Or. [Oratorium] Parvum — and you deprecate the introduction of asceticism into the congregation as such. For the same reason you were against silence.[2] *My* plan of simultaneous private discipline was an expedient to *overcome* and meet your difficulty.

FRIDAY 20 DECEMBER 1850   FF Stanislas and Caswall came out of retreat
SATURDAY 21 DECEMBER   FF Stanislas and Caswall ordained

TO ANTONY HUTCHISON

Oy. Bm. Dec 23. 1850

My dear F Antony,

While I think of it, let me say that dear good Ambrose Phillipps has some story or other, I know not what, about H Wilberforce having said that I said, or thought, that the London and Birmingham Houses

---

[1] *The Times* on 24 Oct. accused Wiseman of suppressing the Prayer for the Queen in London. Ullathorne wrote to explain that Wiseman had tried to put an end to the 'rubrical anomaly' by which a post-communion prayer, mentioning the Queen by name, was introduced within the Mass, in London chapels. The practice usual nowadays, of praying for the Queen after the principal Mass on Sundays, was the rule, but was not always observed. Even this the Oratorians disliked, as being 'Anglican' and perhaps 'Gallican.' In London they had obtained permission to omit it, as not being a district or parish church. Wiseman considered it more than ever necessary to insist on the Prayer being said after Mass, while the London Oratorians felt that to begin it after eighteen months, in response to popular clamour, would be implying that they had previously been disloyal. They asked to be allowed to say 'Hail Marys' before the Mass, but seem soon to have submitted to the usual rule and custom.

[2] See note to letter of 12 Dec. to Faber. One of his objections to the discipline had been that it was intended for the meeting which laymen attended.

differed in tone — and H. W has written to deny it. I mention it, lest the absurd gossip should get round to you.[1]

Could you not simply do this about the Passionists, make them give you a bond for the very sum which Lord Shr. [Shrewsbury] is bound for to you, and then put his bond into their hands? I mean, is there not some way in which you could oblige them, as a payment for the vast present you make them, to make over the annual £70 odd to you. If you don't like it to look, lest it be misrepresented, like a clear transference of an endowment, alter the sum — and whereas the Earl's bond is for £2000, let the Passionists' be £1900 or £2300, or £3000. Surely there must be some way or other.

This assumes that you have no *moral* difficulty. Here it is so difficult to get at the state of the case. I can't make out from your correspondence with Lord Sh etc *what* precisely was your state of mind about it three years ago. Again, I don't know enough the theological point, whether a builder is bound to endow.

I can't take F Richard's view about the F Minister. My impression was that F Rossi said that the Minister signed the cheques (countersigned by Superior) for *his own* matters — not for Sacristy etc.

I said Mass for your and our disciplines, yesterday morning.

Ever Yours affectly J H N

P.S. Poor Father Lithgow, I have been saying Mass for him this morning.[2]

TO J. M. CAPES

In Vigil N. Dñe 1850

My dear Capes,

A happy Christmas to you and yours, for I suppose we must reckon Christmas begun. Your account of the Oxford movement is very interesting to any one concerned in it, and I suppose to others. I had nothing to say, nor time to write; my only thought was that Pusey's 5 Nov. Sermon was in 1837 — but I suppose this is an hallucination of mine — it was

---

[1] Faber reported to Newman on 10 Nov. a roundabout story 'that the Fathers of the Birmingham Oratory condemn my Triduo, and say (you were not at home) that tho' you looked it over, you did not approve of it; and that the spirit of your house was quite different from ours. . . .' Newman made no comment on this. To this present letter Hutchison replied on 26 Dec., 'Ambrose Phillipps's tale of our Grandfather has not reached us yet.'

[2] Randall Lythgoe, the former Jesuit Provincial, moved to Yarmouth at the end of the year, perhaps owing to ill-health.

but an impression, and I have no argument for saying so.[1] I have received Palmer's pamphlet and thank you.[2]

I don't look on the Church of E. [England] as important, in contrast to *Dissent*, but as a bulwark against Infidelity, which Dissent cannot be. Were the Church of E. to fall, Methodism *might* remain a while — I can't tell, for I don't know it — but surely, on the whole, the various denominations exist under the shadow of the Establishment, out of which they sprung, and, did it go, would go too. I.e. — they would lose their organization, and whatever faint intellectual basis they have at present. Infidelity would take possession of the bulk of the men, and the women, so they had something to worship, would not care whether it was an unknown tongue, or a book of Mormon, or a pudding sleeve[3] gown. Infidel literature would be the fashion, and there would be a sort of fanatical contempt and hatred of all profession of belief in a definite revelation.

Perhaps it is absurd so talking, for the Established Church could not fall without a revolution — and, while it exists in any shape, it so far forth witnesses to a dogmatic and ritual religion, i.e. a revelation — but, in proportion as it is liberalized, it lets in infidelity upon the country, for there is nothing else to stand against infidelity. I can as little triumph then in the decline and fall of the Establishment as take part in the emancipation of the Jews — I cannot, *till* the Catholic church is strong enough to take its place. I don't see that this is inconsistent with my laughing at it, as in my Lectures and Loss and Gain, for such ridicule only disparages it in the eyes of Puseyites who *ought* to leave it, not in those of Erastians and Establishmentarians, who constitute its strength — is this a refinement? I mean, I don't think any thing I have written would *tend* even, to make men such as Lord John or Sir R Peel give up the Church of E. — on the contrary.

If one must speculate, this may happen — not the Church of E. liberalized, but e.g. certain churches in a city given to the Wesleyans, or Free Kirkites, etc etc. Or in the country, the patron being able to chose a parson out of his own persuasion. In this way Puseyism might find a status in the Establishment — If this plan could be adopted, *we* should be cut out both from Establishment and Universities — for 1 we might be unwilling to be bribed. 2. they might plausibly make the oath of supremacy a *test* for occupancy; and then the present movement

---

[1] Newman refers to the second of Capes' articles on the 'Rise, Progress, and Results of Puseyism' in the *Rambler* VII (Jan. 1851), pp. 60–89. Newman was right as to the date of Pusey's sermon, which Capes gave as 1838.

[2] See letter of 17 Aug. 1850 to Capes.

[3] A large bulging sleeve, tied at the wrist.

may be of constitutional use to the Government, even tho' no great legal consequences were to follow, as bringing out that the Queen's Supremacy is a principle of the country, nay rather it would justify a declaration against 'any other prelate, priest or potentate etc' *omitting* mention of the *Queen's* Supremacy, which would be better still for Government. Thus all *religious* tests would be got rid of, political alone imposed. — and 39 Articles etc would be private matters for a particular communion, who might meet in Convocation about it. How easy and unprofitable is it to run on.

Ever Yrs affectly J H N

P.S.   Thank you for your news — Manning is with Hope at Abbotsford — What does this mean?

TO F. W. FABER

In Vig. N.D. [1850]

My dear F Wilfrid

Vix tandem — I send it to you, since I think it should be seen by you, whom it concerns[1] — also because you may like to inclose a line to F Ugolini.

Coffin I suppose is off — he was heard of at Hanley the other day — and has sent me a little parcel since from London, which was a sort of signal. Have you seen him at the Oratory? I hope there is a bargain between S Philip and S Alfonso about him. I am told there is a Redemptorist in the Florence Oratory

Ever Yrs affly J H N

All good wishes of the season. Congratulate the new Deacon Subdeacon etc

TO CHARLES RUSSELL

Oratory Birmingham Dec 24/50

My dear Dr Russell,

I send you the good wishes and thoughts suitable to this sacred time, a season of peace in the Church's bosom, strangely contrasted to the tumult and violence which in this country she is suffering from without.

---

[1] This refers to the letter below to Ugolini, whose date is confirmed by the diary.

You should have heard from me before this on the subject of *The Dublin*, had I any thing to say. I fear difficulties have arisen in the scheme I ventured to suggest to you. One very considerable one, is that rumours are afloat of an English Catholic Newspaper, which would draw off both money and talent in another direction.[1] Moreover, I think I see, or at least I fancy it will be so, that England will be considered ultimately strong enough to have a review of its own. And I cannot deny as much as this, that there are *subjects* enough in England, as well as writers, for a Catholic Quarterly. The Cardinal too naturally wants a centre of thought and action about him.

How wonderfully he has come out on this occasion! never did any one in a more striking way show himself equal to an emergence. When the row first took place, and he had not yet reached England, an intimate friend of his, who had known him long, said, he thought it would be his death. Rather it has turned out his life — I mean, it has brought out his energies in so remarkable a way, that one may say that, if he had only lived for this crisis, it would have been enough. He has still, however, a very difficult part to play and the status of a Cardinal not acknowledged by the Government, is a new problem to be worked out — and he has need of a number of good advisers close about him who would sound the channel and ascertain the current hour by hour.

So some great Irish Nobleman is converted. Can it be the Duke of Leinster, or Lord Kildare?[2] I am glad Monsell is safe.

Ever Yours very sincerely in Xt   John H. Newman

TO TOMMASO UGOLINI, SUPERIOR OF THE FLORENCE ORATORY

[24 December 1850]

Reverendmo Patri Praeposito Congregationis Oratorii Florentinae.

Litteris Paternitatis Tuae acceptissimis, Pater Reverendissime, idcirca non statim responsum dabam, quia quale deceret responsum ad Te mitti, statim perspicuum non erat. Plenissimo utique affectu benevolentiam singularem Tuam et Patrum Tuorum a me paenè impudenter efflagitatam amplectentes, non videbant tamen nostri quâ ratione possent eâ uti ad illum ipsum finem, quocum, litteris meis ad Dominum Russell ante aliquos menses hinc discedentibus, eâdem se uti posse crediderant. Namque eo tempore, quo ad Dominum Russell de Reverendo P. Coffin

---

[1] Cf. letters of 23 and 28 Oct., to Russell, and that of 11 Nov. to Allies.
[2] It is not clear to whom this refers.

in principio scripsi, credidi fore ut ad aures et deliberationem Amplis-
simae Congregationis Florentinae sine morâ veniret epistola mea, cùm
nescirem prorsus urbem Tuam reliquisse amicum meum, quem quidem
speraveram, ore, non litteris à Româ ad Paternitatem Tuam missis, rem
nostram Tibi esse explicaturum. Quare tandem in eam mentem incidi,
ut concluderem litteras meas, ad Dominum Russell missas, ad eundem
non pervenisse, neque esse perventuras.

Quid multa? haec summa rerum est; — scilicet P. Coffin, optimum
virum, alia cepisse consilia contigit, ad alias se applicuisse vias; me
autem cogitationem et curam charitatis Tuae inutiliter exercuisse.

Illud autem a me liceat, Pater Reverendissime, benevolentiae Tuae
suggeri, nos, si imprudenter et temerè Tibi et Tuis nosmetipsos obtuli-
mus, cum id ad exitum ferre nequivimus, quod ipsi a Te ultro postula-
vimus, at saltem id fecisse ob reverentiam et amorem quem gessimus et
gerimus semper, erga antiquissimam et celeberrimam domum Tuam, et
ex desiderio illo, in corde nostro altissimo infixo, ut nos, novissima magni
parentis proles, accederemus propius ad illas Oratorii Congregationes
in Italiâ collocatas, ubi viget intus, et longe lateque resplendet, et
omnium laude et veneratione laetatur, priscus ille Sancti Philippi
spiritus et indoles

J H N

TO JOHN BAPTIST LANS

Oratory Birmingham Dec. 25. 1850

My dear Father Lans,

Your parcel came quite safe, and I thank you for it.

I have been going to write to you for some time, could I have found
an hour to do so in, to thank you for your letter to Father Faber about
our dear friend Coffin, which I thought very sensible and considerate,
if I may take the liberty of saying so.

The truth is, as you know far better than I can, it does not do for
members of a community to live out of community. They lose their
interest in the body, and moreover, losing the stimulus which it supplies
to progress in the religious life, they become slothful, despondent, and
tepid. This seems to have been Mr Coffin's case, from his own avowals;
and then, finding himself without inward life, he judged of others by
himself, and fancied that a disease attached to the body, which was his
own. His mind brooded on itself, and at length he coloured the past, as
well as the present, with hues derived from his own feelings. Besides
this, he could not make up his mind to going to London, when the time
came.

Under these circumstances, nothing else was to be done than what he did. I trust there has been a bargain about him between St Philip and St Alfonso — and that, now that he has a fresh start, he will acquit himself better than he has done with us.

Wishing you and yours all the blessings which belong to this sacred season, and begging your prayers,

I am, My dear F Lans Sincerely Yours in Xt

John H Newman   Congr Orat.

THURSDAY 26 DECEMBER 1850   Monsell passed through

TO MISS HOLMES

The Oratory Birmingham Dec 26/50

My dear Miss Holmes,

I send you a line to wish you a happy Christmas. . . .

Of course you have heard of Mr Bastard's conversion [,] his being a Devonshire man will make the news interesting to you. Mr Dodsworth has resigned his living on the ground, I am told, that the Bishop of London said he meant to put down Puseyism. It is an awful crisis for Puseyism, for if those who are still faithful to it overcome this crisis and think it proves nothing against their position, what is to touch them? They are apparently proof against everything.[1] Many however will apparently overcome it, who will not really. I mean their eyes through divine grace, will be opened — and then if they are faithful to the light given them, it will be but a matter of time with them.

Have you any striking air to recommend me which will do for some of our Oratory hymns? I have got two beautiful ones of Mendleshom (I don't spell his name right) — I dare say there are more of his if I could find them. Beethoven does not condescend to be easy enough for vocal music, or compact enough for a four line hymn

[[Changed my mind here J H N]][2]

[1] Some of the bitterest language in the newspapers and *Punch* during the 'papal aggression' agitation was directed against Puseyites. In his letter to the Bishop of Durham on 4 Nov., Lord John Russell asked: 'What then is the danger to be apprehended from a foreign prince of no great power, compared to the danger within the gates from the unworthy sons of the Church of England herself?' Charles James Blomfield (1786–1857), the Bishop of London, besides taking part in the general outcry, forced W. J. E. Bennett to resign his living of St Barnabas, Pimlico, on 4 Dec.

[2] This sentence must have been inserted much later, but before the autograph was copied.

P.S. I was just signing my name, and your letter comes. I will say Mass for you next Monday, that is, not for toothache only, but for all your aches — and for courage that you may bear them well. All these stories against Catholics though in the case of individuals real stumbling blocks, are on the whole wee¹ excuses. John Bull does not like his wife and daughter to go to Confession.

TO F. W. FABER

[27 December 1850]²

Private
My dear F W

Has Lord Arundel's absence from England and the Cardinal any thing to do with you? or does the Cardinal think so?³

And how did he stomach the 3 Hail Mary's?⁴ I ask because I want to know exactly how the Oratory and I stand with him *at this moment*.

Thanks for the School of St Philip — you will have a letter of thanks from our Brothers⁵

Ever Yrs affly J H N

TO HENRY WILBERFORCE

Oy Bm Dec 28/50

My dear H

⌐The difficulty of answering W F (*and* Mr B)⁶ is first his vagueness,⌐ and next his difference from me in first principles. *I do not think he*

¹ This is clearly a misreading of Newman's 'mere.'
² Dated by Faber's reply of 28 Dec.
³ The Earl of Arundel usually spent Christmas with his father, the Duke of Norfolk, at Arundel, but they were now on opposite sides on the question of the new hierarchy, the Duke having protested publicly against it. Faber replied to Newman on 28 Dec. that 'family unpleasantness' made a visit 'next door to impossible,' and that he had advised the Earl to go abroad, so that his absence from Arundel would be less marked. Faber explained this to Wiseman, who might otherwise have suspected the Earl of deserting him.   ⁴ See letter of 18 Dec.
⁵ Faber had sent copies of his translation of G. Crispino's *The School of St. Philip Neri*, London 1850.
⁶ W. F. is William Froude, and Mr B. is his friend Isambard Kingdom Brunel (1806–59), the railway engineer. Froude had worked under him in South Devon, which Brunel continued to visit regularly, and his views had a considerable effect on the development of Froude's own opinions, as the latter confessed to Newman on 29 Dec. 1859. *Harper*, p. 122. Brunel's latest biographer writes of his religious views, 'the impression we get is of a conventional religious belief weakened by the natural

178

could resist intimacy — but he keeps at arms' length. I have before this expostulated with him for not seeing one — his excuse to himself is, 'Oh, it is so painful to talk with J H N to differ from him — I can't bear it — and I *could* not talk out to him all I felt — ' Yet ⌜I feel certain he could not invelope himself in generalities, if he fairly opened his mind to a Catholic whom he knew and loved. But he is not the only person who has winced from the conversation of Catholics.⌝

As to the argument from the promise, it is but one part of a large question. Take his ⌜'*inexorable* logic' — now how unreal this term is, when you come to particulars — ⌝ Supposing a man tells me that for a certain he will call on me today or tomorrow, and does not come today. Is it inexorable logic which makes me expect him tomorrow? (Who was the father of Zebedee's children? is it inexorable logic makes me say Zebedee?) I mean, there are certain things inevitable, certain principles being granted. On the other hand it is doubtless quite possible to fall into the extravagance of dealing with moral proofs as if they were mathematical — which is really 'inexorable logic — ' But the question is *to which* does our Catholic argument belong? the former kind of logic falsely called inexorable, or the latter? — If to the former, it is a mere *name* fastened on a good argument.

⌜People love to reason *till* they are beaten; then they talk of inexorable logic — as others talk of sophistry, jesuitry etc — ⌝ I don't think the Puseyistic and Transcendentalist 'inexorable logic' (for strangely enough Pusey and my brother Frank, Isaac Williams and Thackeray, agree here) a whit more respectable than the 'sophistry' of Luther on the Galatians, and the 'jesuitism' of the Record or Xtian Observer.

⌜Give a dog an ill name and hang him — our Anglo-Catholic friends enjoyed my logic while it attacked the Evangelicals, Hampden etc etc. but when it went *too far*, then it was inexorable — and I deteriorated.

As to the articles in the Guardian, it astonishes me they are by Rogers — how so clever a man can argue so weakly![1] But besides ⌜they

scepticism of a ruthlessly logical and inquiring mind.' L. T. C. Rolt, *Isambard Kingdom Brunel*, London 1957, p. 324.

[1] Newman may refer to seven articles on 'Anglo-Romanism,' against accepting 'the living authority of Rome,' in the *Guardian* between 24 July and 6 Nov. 1850, or to those on 'papal aggression,' of which that in the *Guardian* of 20 Nov., p. 828, was by Rogers, who said of them all that they 'express pretty much my views.' This was in a letter to his sister on 23 Nov. in which he also said, 'I hear cases of disquiet [people inclined towards Rome] here and there.

However, I don't see any shaking in our clique; Keble is as firm as a rock and stouter in acquiescing in aggression against Rome than I ever thought to see him. There is a degree both of attack and of liberalism in my articles which I feared he would not approve. But he does wholly.' *Letters of Frederic Lord Blachford*, ed. G. E. Marindin, London 1906, pp. 140–1.

are but *negative*. W. F. should be asked *what* he believes — what he
has *positive* in his religion — ⌐ to say that the Roman Church is wrong
does not make the Anglican right — And ⌐this is what I think so unfair
in their argument — that they dare not, won't say, *what* they believe
and *why* — they fence off.⌐ I said to dear W F. about two years ago
'*What* do you believe? and *why*?' and I have got, and believe he can
give, no answer. The unfairness of this, unfairness, I mean, to himself,
trifling with awful matters, is to me *incomprehensible*. The inexorable
logic topos may parry my attack, but how can it satisfy himself? His
'remaining where he is' does not ipso facto give him a creed.

For instance — let me say, as Rogers and others, I suppose, will
say — 'I need not hold Scripture inspired or more than a human
document — but *I see* contained, brought out, in it, a superhuman
character. Did I find that character in Hume's England, or in Livy,
n'importe — here is a fact and a supernatural one — a real person, more
than man — bearing on him the tokens of coming from God — *Him*
I believe, without an implicit submission to *Scripture* as proved infallible — '

Well — I admit this is a view — but I want to see what you *mean*
by it — or how far you carry it — so I must ask you some questions,
not to puzzle you, not to confute you, but really to get *at what you mean*
fully: and thus to see what your view is worth.

You mean, that our Lord's words and works, and history, as making
up His character, are intrinsically supernatural, and recommend themselves as such to our moral instincts. Well then, *do you believe* those
words and works and history? i.e. do you accept them as true. Our
friend looks suspicious, and begins in his heart to suspect I am one of
the [in]exorable logicians. He wants to know more what I am driving
at, before he answers.

I proceed — Of course there must be something *practical* in your
recognition of our Lord — He is not a mere beautiful picture — but a
master, a teacher — else he is nothing. When you say 'Our Lord is
enough for us,' you mean that you have a teacher from heaven, and His
teaching, revealed to you through the medium of Scripture. Well then,
my question is, do you make His words and works and history, therein
contained, a rule to you, a rule of faith and conduct? Our friend at last
s obliged to assent.

1 Then I want to know, do you submit yourself to *all* His words
and works and His whole history, or do you admit some things and not
others, and if so, why?

2. Is His history with His words and works, as a *whole*, clear
enough to teach you definitely what to believe and what to do?

Here at length I shall be sure to be accused of inexorable logic —
yet surely these two considerations are the necessary and immediate
result of turning my mind to the subject. Is there no such fault as what
the Provost[1] used to call 'inaccuracy of mind'? W. F is an engineer —
would he ever dream of assenting to any speculator who offered him a
patent, without applying his mind to see how the machinery worked?
Theories are looked hard at by a clear headed man, and the flaw is then
seen at once. ⌐To use general terms and glowing words is only fit⌐ for
women and ⌐for Sewell of Exeter. It is to sewellize, or to mauricise.⌐[2]

Now I would say that the greater part of our Lord's teaching is *not*
clear — and where it is clearest, it is most startling to the imagination.
Perhaps the clearest doctrine of all laid down is that of eternal punishment. (Is this doctrine to be received as a sole dogmatic truth, like some
promontory coming clear out of a thick sea fog?)

On the other hand, can any one without trifling call the Sermon on
the Mount, the institution and doctrine of the two Sacraments, the
Discourse before the Passion, the institution of the Church Matt xvi.
intelligible without a comment? I do not mean that they have not one
sense — but could we be sure of it? *Why* do we not take the precepts
about turning the face to the smiter etc literally? etc etc — Are we, or
are we not, to take 'This is My Body —' and John vi literally? In
corroboration, does He not expressly refer us to a further teaching, that
of the Paraclete?

Well then, on the whole, *what* is our creed? does any one mean to
say he finds the Anglican creed, and nothing more or less, in our
Saviour's teaching? Does our friend, thus taught, believe in the Atha-
nasian Creed, in the Atonement, in original sin, in the Real Presence, in
Sacramental influence, in etc etc? Surely I have a right to ask him *what*
he believes.

He won't tell; I know he won't — but he will talk of my inexorable
logic — But he has to answer God, not me — it is not a question of
polemics, but of personal duty.

I have brought out what I mean, not at all to my own satisfaction —
but I have set it down to illustrate what I meant by saying 'Take him
off *generals* — bring him down to particulars — bring him to book.'

All I can say is, (not alluding to dear W. F) ⌐I have no sympathy in
such a state of mind — nor ever have had — it is to me simply incomprehensible. I could not feed on words, without ideas.⌐ It is sheer
Sewellism.

---

[1] Edward Hawkins, Provost of Oriel 1828–74.
[2] William Sewell and Frederick Denison Maurice in their different ways opposed
Tractarianism and Catholicism.

As to Mr B. he is so unreal as to be simply ludicrous — 'the Church loved by Whigs and Radicals etc etc'!

As to both of them, ⌜I should say to them, Pray for grace and light — pray to view things *really*.⌝ I have very great doubts, if either of them prays unreservedly to be led into the truth; if they say, 'O my God, I am in darkness — but I wish to be led into the truth — deny me not the truth *at any sacrifice* — I will go through all things for it.' ⌜E.g. *you* were anxious and miserable — if they are so too, I am hopeful about them.⌝ As to dear W F he is continually in my prayers, but I wish he seemed to take things less easily.

⌜Ambrose and I laughed heartily at your Preacher. *He* said 'Sarved him right — ' and I smiled grimly. Charissime, you have from time immemorial, loved me, *and* distrusted me, especially during the last year. You have *gone* to bad preachers, — enjoy them.⌝

Ever Yours affly J H N.

⌜Dec 29. I have been dreaming last night of Rogers, thro' sheer amazement. Wonderful, that to ask 'What and Why?' should be inexorable logic! Why, the AngloCatholicism of 15 years back professed to answer them at once. My Prophetical Office is taken up in the What and the Why.[1] No one called *that* rationalism or inexorable logic. Well, *that* theory, that answer to the questions, broke down under *facts*, historical facts. The question then returns, What do you believe, and why? and now, *since* it involves an action, it is voted rationalism. While the question was to defend a [[an existing]] position, and to justify doing nothing, it was not rationalism. Wonderful indeed! When the treasurer of Candace said, '*How* can I, unless some one teach me?' this too, I suppose, was rationalism.⌝[2] Now is it not a most wonderful trial to one's faith in individuals, to be obliged to believe that they are *sincere* in thus speaking, and that there is not some *deeper* and truer mode of accounting for it. In Rogers, I think it is a deep scepticism, i.e. a shrinking from receiving absolutely what another tells him — an utter suspiciousness of what does not approve itself to his moral feeling — i.e. in substance the very principle which rules my brother, though not so boldly expressed. Of course I don't say all this to any one but you — and can't bring out my meaning of what I feel, satisfactorily to myself.

⌜After coming from before the Tabernacle, after hearing Mass or attending Benediction, what a mere dream and absurdity and talk do these objections seem! *Here* is the reality — Why don't you force me to argue in proof of my having two legs, you declaring I have one a cork one!⌝

[1] *Lectures on the Prophetical Office of the Church*, 1837. *V.M. i.*   [2] Acts 8 : 31.

As to Catholic preaching, the Confessional *makes* it bad. I mean, all seriousness, practicalness, reality, is put there, and the sermon is thought to be a display. (It need not be so — it is not so in Italy — though it *is* there in a number of cases —) Add to this, the utter want of taste, arising from an absence of education, and you have your dish smoking hot. ⟨(theology, as mathematics or metaphysics does not give taste)⟩ Dr Gillis is an able man — at the opening of Cheadle Church he preached a sermon half screaming and bellowing, half whining — and Lady Dormer and other ladies of quality were in raptures with it.[1] The same is seen in a parallel way in the after dinner conversation of priests, and the recreations of nuns. They are to be cheerful and they have *nothing* to be cheerful upon. So they are boisterous or silly

J H N.

2. P.S.   Of course I have not meant to urge above, that if a man discovers the above 'Xt's character' view to be unreal, as not giving the What and the Why, *therefore* he must at once go to Rome. ⌈It is very fair to urge that *Rome* has not [[does not answer]] the What and the Why, and to try to maintain it. [[but the questions themselves are not rationalism.]]

As to the Promise, I think there is a great *difference*, or *harmony*, between the Jewish and the Christian. The Christian is *for a time* as well as the Jewish — the Jewish as well as the Christian is called 'for ever.' But each is expressly fixed *till an event*. The Jewish is to be for ever 'till Shiloh come' — the Christian for ever 'till the end of time,' till the *second* coming.

TO F. W. FABER

Oy. Bm. Dec 29/50

My dear F W

The letter I return is a most absurd one.[2] Yet it is written under a sort of compressed standing irritation — which must have some cause. He actually *may* be annoyed by the idea you are Jansenists, *or* it may be something else.

You must take the letter merely as a private, kind, hint to you and yours and not an expostulation leading to any thing. For he *cannot*

---

[1] This was on 1 Sept. 1846. See Vol. XI, p. 241.

[2] Mgr Vincent Eyre, the priest at Chelsea Chapel, had written to complain that the London Oratorians were severe and Jansenistic in the confessional. See also letter of 12 Jan. 1851 to Faber.

mean to interfere with the Oratory Confessional — if his people get harm there, let them keep away. I don't see what you have to do but compliment him, thank him, and assure him you are not Jansenists or rigorists, and gently hint to him that you trust your Fathers more than the reports he has heard from persons to you anonymous

Ever Yrs affly J H N

P.S. So much to *him* — if you suspect some of the things true, as that about the Bible or grabbing penitents, you can apply the remedy where it is necessary.

TO EDWARD BELLASIS

Oratory Birmingham December 30. 1850

My dear Sergeant Bellasis,

It is with the greatest joy and thankfulness that I have just heard from Oakeley of your reception. Such events are continually recurring proofs of God's love to England and the Catholics who are in it — and witnesses to the truth of Catholicism, considering how carefully and anxiously you have sought the truth.

Neither St John nor I forget the last time we saw you and Mrs Bellasis nor the interest in you and respectful feelings you excited in the good Abate Ghianda of Milan.[1] Some time or other, I hope, a kind Providence will throw us together again — meanwhile, begging your prayers,

I am, My dear Sergeant Bellasis, Very truly Yours in Xt

John H Newman   Congr. Orat.

TO GEORGE BOWYER

Oratory Birmingham December 31. 1850

My dear Bowyer,

The blessings of the Season upon you — so Bellasis is received — good news for Christmas week. But to your letter.[2] I assure you it is no

---

[1] Manzoni's chaplain. See letter of 18 Oct. 1846 to Dalgairns; and for Bellasis's conversion, Edward Bellasis, *Memorials of Mr. Serjeant Bellasis*, 3rd ed. London 1923.

[2] Bowyer wrote on 18 Dec., 'I am afraid the good nature of the Cardinal may induce him to accept invitations where he may meet people who only stare at him like

184

indifference to what is going on, which keeps me from coming forward more than I do. The present struggle is as arresting as any thing can be, of which the ultimate issue is not uncertain. One can't quite feel about the Church's welfare, as about a game of backgammon. The church has no fortunes, she has a destiny. Yet, true as this is, her destiny, I grant, is wrought out by exertions, nor would I willingly be backward in mine.

Every one has his place; mine is where I am. I should be thrown away in a more prominent one. I have ever been as I am, and am too old to take up a new line. Now with the Cardinal it is just the reverse — he is made for the world, and he rises with the occasion. Highly as I put his gifts, I was not prepared for such a display of vigour, power, judgment, and sustained energy, as the last two months have brought out. I heard a dear friend of his say, before he had got to England, that the news of the opposition would kill him; how he has been out! It is the event of the time. In my own remembrance there has been nothing like it. It is an anxious thing, that he is the only one among us equal to the work Providence has laid upon him; yet, again, not anxious, because he is in the hands of that Providence, and because Providence ever works with few instruments.

By the bye there is one thing which does make me rather anxious; though I dare say the Cardinal has thought of it himself. I do think he ought to keep out of society, as much as possible. His line is perfectly distinct from that of ordinary great people; he is in a different sphere. Hard men of the world, in high station, would be delighted to dream he felt a satisfaction in their company, and would draw him on in order to entangle him.[1] Do you recollect Medea's (I think) words, that great

a wild beast. . . . You know what a treacherous thing "society" in London is. If care is not taken about this—the prestige will be lost . . . You are the only man who could exercise the influence which is wanted. . . .' In answer to this appeal, Newman wrote on 25 Dec. a draft of this letter, the final version being sent a week later. On the draft he noted in 1863, 'I th[ink this] was written at Bowyer's wish *in order* to show to the Cardinal. Yes. I am right. vid. Bowyer's letter of Febry 17/51.' This is not to be found, but on 14 Feb. 1851 Bowyer wrote, 'I have not lost sight of the matter on which I wrote to you regarding the Cardinal—and I hope something will be done through Lord Arundel and Surrey. It is most important.'

[1] In the draft Newman wrote: 'By the bye, there is one thing which I can't help being *really* anxious about—if you think it worth while I wish you would give him a hint, though I dare say you will find the Cardinal has thought of it all himself, before you speak—but a lawyer never wants for brass. I do think the Cardinal ought to keep out of society as much as possible,—I think he has a tendency to wish to be in it. I recollect his seeming pleased at the attention shown him by some young men at the Royal Academy dinner,—natural enough indeed. Other things have occurred of the same character. Some Anglican Bishops were present at that dinner, and certainly cut a poor figure. Of course don't mention to him details like this which I should seem to him to have misapprehended. His line is perfectly distinct from that of ordinary great

men, like Pythagoras, should keep in their cave, not to wear off the bloom of their popularity?

Now all this is very impudent — n'importe. The Cardinal and his court must bear the criticisms of little men at a distance

Ever Yours most sincerely in Xt,

John H Newman   Congr. Orat.

TO MISS HOLMES

December 31, 1850.

I think with you that what is called Gregorian is but a *style* of music — viz. before the fixing of the diatonic scale, and the various keys as rising out of it. The Pagan and Jewish tunes are *necessarily* in this style. And in this sense certainly the Gregorian comes from the Pagan *and* the Jewish. The names 'Lydian,' 'Phrygian,' etc., look like Pagan. One should think, however, some *must* be Jewish. I can't answer your question about the genuineness of the professed specimens of Pagan, as in Rousseau's Dictionary. Will Rousseau answer your question?[1]

All true art comes from revelation (to speak generally), I do think, but not necessarily through the Jewish Dispensation. The Fathers look upon Paganism as preserving traditions too: e.g. the Sibyls. It seems to me a very contracted view, and not borne out by facts, to trace Plato's glowing thoughts on the religious rites of Paganism to Judaism.

people—he is in a different sphere. Nothing would men of the world love better than to get him into a scrape, and maliciously laugh at him. I am sure they are saying to themselves, "Give him rope enough etc" Walpole said every man had his price—hard men of the world, in great station, would be delighted to be allowed to dream he felt satisfaction in their company, and would draw him on in order to entangle him.

It is easier to see what he ought not to do, than what he ought, and easier to criticise here than to act in London. All this I grant, yet I go on. I find that persons in the country take the beginning of his second Lecture [on the new hierarchy, delivered in St George's, Southwark, on 15 Dec.] as if he were willing to be bribed—which is absurd enough—but, if *they* think so, so may great and little men in office.'

[1] Jean Jacques Rousseau's *Dictionnaire de musique* was published in 1767 at Genoa, and in 1768 at Paris; English trans. by William Waring, London 1770, 2nd ed. 1779. Rousseau inserted at the end of it what he claimed to be the music of an Ode to Pindar and another to Nemesis. *Œuvres complètes de J. J. Rousseau*, III, Paris 1835, Appendix, page C.

TO J. D. DALGAIRNS

[End of 1850?]

My dear F Bernard

Will you cast your eye, at your leisure, over Conferences 9. 10. 11. 13. 15. to see if there are any bad mistranslations? (for a second edition)

J H N[1]

TO T. W. ALLIES

Oratory, Bm, Jan. 1. 1851.

My dear Allies,

A happy new year to you and Mrs Allies, and your children. Thank you for your good news. You will be a great comfort to Dodsworth, and I am glad you are on the spot. Give him my most sincere congratulations, and assure him how very much I feel the trials he has to bear, but he will have a strength not his own, which will make him more than equal to them.[2]

I wish you had told me something about yourself: It is very shabby of you. Is anything doing about the new Paper?[3]

I do trust the Cardinal will get an efficient staff about him. I don't mean a clerical staff, but of such men as Bellasis, etc. These clever, able, and experienced men must be made something of.

With the best wishes of the season, I am, My dear Allies

Ever yours affectly J. H. N.

TO WILLIAM DODSWORTH

The Oratory, Birmm. January 1. 1851

My dear Dodsworth

I had already sent you a message through Allies, and your kind letter has come, which I hope to answer before the post is gone.

Indeed I do not undervalue the great sacrifices you are making from

---

[1] This letter was written in the fly-leaf of Newman's copy of Gondon's translation of *Mix., Conférences adressées aux Protestants et aux Catholiques*, Paris 1850. Cf. letters of 3 Oct. 1850 to Stanton, and 29 Sept. 1851 to Faber.

[2] Dodsworth was received on 31 Dec. 1850.

[3] See letter of 11 Nov. 1850 to Allies.

obeying the divine call made to you, and it has long seemed to me that these were as great as have been exacted of any one, if not greater.[1] But He who has put on you the burden, will enable you to bear it, and will repay you sevenfold for all you do for Him. Though I have had so few opportunities ever of personal intercourse with you, I look back through many years, and have a history of you in my mind, and now has come the blessed issue of it. I recollect how my and your dear friend Wood first mentioned your name to me, and took me with him to hear you preach at Margaret Chapel about the year 1834 —[2] and how it was to you that members of the Anglican Church were indebted for the call to weekly communion — and then how, many years after you came up with Allies to Littlemore in the Long Vacation, and asked me what was going to become of me — and how lastly, when I was on the eve of reception into the Catholic Church I wrote to you among others to tell it, and how you wrote me a kind answer —[3] and then there was a long silence, and now you are returning the letter of announcement I once sent to you, and, after an interval which to all but the God of grace and the Searcher of Hearts seemed to be barren and uneventful, at length are called and obey a voice which at an earlier time had spoken to me. How wonderful are God's mercies and how inscrutable His ways. Such is the Apostle's exclamation when he is on the subject of God's grace, and it is called out and verified by the events of every day, as it has past, from his time to our own.

And now I will say no more but assure you, what you cannot doubt, that you are in our constant prayers and mementos, and that I am My dear Dodsworth Yours affectionately in Xt

John H. Newman of the Oratory

TO GEORGE RYDER

Oy Bm Jan 1/51

My dear George,

All blessing be with you and yours for the New Year. Give my love to the boys.

Your Lecture, though very interesting, has not enough in it for

[1] Dodsworth, a married man with a large family, wrote 'my outward trials are great.'

[2] This was Samuel Francis Wood (1809–43). Cf. also *Moz.* II, p. 164.

[3] See Newman's letter of 9 Oct. 1845.

publication. Northcote is bringing out a series of Tracts; I think of writing to them about you — Shall I?[1]

Ever Yrs affly J H N

Dodsworth and Bellasis are received

TO ANTONY HUTCHISON

Jan 3/51

My dear F. Antony,

The valuer is going over to [on] Tuesday. Can you suggest how he is to value *yours* distinct from the *Congregation's* furniture? Can George Hawkes manage to enable them?

Another thing — Do you expect I am to pay you *down*? I can't. And don't know when I shall.

Ask F Superior for the sum I owe him for the Brother's Illustrated News.

Ever Yrs affly J H N

A happy new year to you all.

SATURDAY 4 JANUARY 1851   These weeks, F Austin and F Wm ⟨Penny⟩ with smallpox — and Br Frederic (*Godwin*) and Br Aloysius ill

TO T. F. KNOX

Oy. Bm Jan 5/51

My Dear F. Francis,

Your case is a very painful one — at the same time I think the account you send me is considerably exaggerated. This does not make it the less, but the more difficult to deal with, for how shall we convince others that there is any truth where there is evident misapprehension? I have some vague notion as if I recollected there was a touch, not of madness but of fancifulness about the narrator — I mean a tendency to create pictures, be suspicious, jealous etc. Again she is of the *English* cut, and cannot understand a joke.

Also I think the Priests stand excused — I will say presently what I mean — meanwhile, lest I should forget it, I will say at once, that I

[1] Cf. letter of 28 Feb. 1851 to Northcote.

should advise her leaving out every word in her account, (not only which relates to the poisoning, but) to her thoughts or rather reflections on the Priests. She must confine herself to facts, without going into deductions or suspicions.

Her papers are the writing of a serious, correct, single-hearted, pure minded person, and cannot be read without great interest in her. When she spoke to me about that Convent, she told me Talbot had recommended it (or at least her director) and I thought for a place of *retreat*. If I recollect right, it took me by surprise in September, to find she was to be a postulant there.

It is impossible to deny there is at least *one* Sister in the Convent (Sch.) who is now on the verge of mortal sin. Another (Agn.) bad too — I cant make out that there are more. Knowing how difficult it is, as Miss B. herself felt, to keep from laughing at what the conscience condemns, and the taste revolts from, at first sight I have no reason to think that the evil goes beyond these two, though others may *seem* to be in the same sin — Yes 'A little learning etc' If the evil continues, it will ruin the convent.

Then, you must consider the usual lightness of Catholic conversation as contrasted with what serious Protestants may think allowable — there is nothing to show that this was not quite a novelty to Miss B. — and would come upon her as a shock when she had ideal views of the Convent.

Further in recreation a religious house is obliged both by duty and the necessities of the human mind to *relax* — and to relax *by rule* is even more difficult than to be serious by rule. To be bound to be merry, or to relax by rule, is almost a contradiction in terms. All religious houses feel this — we have not escaped the imputation of lightness ourselves — I am not at all certain that Miss B. would not be awfully scandalised, and almost, as she says, doubt whether there is a heaven above us, if she were invisibly present at some of our recreations; especially if we happened to talk of our penitents, more especially our female ones. Yet we are conscious of our innocence, and can offer our breasts to the eye of God.

If this difficulty happens to educated men, how much more to uneducated females! A convent recreation is commonly silly, if nothing worse — for there is nothing to say — they have a certain number of *objects* before their minds — the chapel, the chapter room, the sacristy, confession, the sisters, the priests, and they have nothing else to think or speak about — and if they must not talk of them in the way of business or seriously, nothing is left but to talk of them lightly. It is in consequence a question whether some portion of the reading at refectory, or occasional reading there, should not be of an instructive, and not simply religious character — as travels, histories etc etc which will fill the mind with ideas — or even poetry, if it could be innocent — but this is irrelevant.

Further it must be recollected that coarse minds can no more jest gracefully or innocently, than the donkey (in the fable) could fitly imitate the gambols and endearments of the lap dog. So that certain sisters, without meaning any thing very bad, might show to very bad advantage.

Now these remarks lead to two conclusions which I have anticipated — 1. that things are not so bad as they seem — 2. for that very reason it is a most difficult matter to get them corrected. The charges would vanish under a formal investigation.

Yet there should after all be some way of remedying and preventing such detestable words and insinuations as are some of those your narrative records.

'The Lady Superior,' (why not the Revd Mother?) is represented in the back ground, as almost a mythical personage — how is this? what is she like? *the* simple remedy would be her presence at recreation. Why did she not answer your narrator's letter? did she think her mad?

There is another remark I had intended to make. The nuns evidently intended to *mystify* the poor girl — This is plain especially from the conversation about the Sacristy, ⟨Chapter Room⟩, as far as I can make it out, for Miss B. does but allude; perhaps it is this sort of mystification which has given rise to some of the Protestant stories, of convent horrors, percolated through apostate nuns etc etc.

Now as to the Priests, I dont believe a word they or she implies about the elder. It is a bad coarse joke in them, and a wild misunderstanding in her. They might think it innocent to joke coarsely about a person too old to suggest any thing wrong to their feelings.

The case is different as to the younger. Judging antecedently, and without knowing him, I should say this:— that perhaps he is an Irish priest — I am told, and partly know that some Irish priests have a most light way of conversing with their penitents, which is as contrary to taste as it is to propriety; and which not only might be the occasion of sin, but has perhaps something of sin in it; — yet you must not blame the individual, as if he was actively sinning or taking a step, when he is but passively following a custom. I think he came to persuade her to stop in the convent — and, not at all understanding the sort of person he had to do with, *blundered* in his arguments and persuasions: They on the other hand with feelings three-quarters impure, though *not contemplating* any prospective acts of impropriety between him and her,

as a real fact, nevertheless delighted, such was the state of their imaginations, to view and clothe an intercourse professedly religious, in
this vile garb, as if she ⟨Miss B.⟩ were trembling in his spiritual arms.
All this is detestable — and I do not know whether I can do quite
justice to my meaning I should trust that they would look at any actual
impropriety *occurring* with horror, but who can answer any minute for
those who are putting themselves into the occasions of sin? He on the
contrary without conscious bad meaning, but for want of breeding, was
affecting to be *gallant*. All this is said on the supposition that her facts
are true — if she has exaggerated them, I am doing him injustice. And
indeed after all, I have suspicions of her sanity, ⟨(not an *atom* of evidence
about the poisoning!)⟩ the story of the lumbering sound and scream,
wonderful in itself is made still more of an evidence against her by her
adding that 'the screams *may have* been from the railroad, and the
rolling and lumbering may be caused by a wheelwright!'

I have made some marks in pencil on the MS which can easily be
rubbed out. I propose sending it back by Monday night's post.

And now what is to be done? I see three ways — and I would rather
hear again from you, before I decide on which to take.

1. To bring the matter before the Cardinal. This I should be unwilling to recommend in the first instance. You do not know *what* the
other side have to say. You have but an ex parte statement, and it might
annoy him to have it thus brought before him, if something else could
be done first.

2. For me (leaving you and the London Oratory altogether out of
the matter), as having had to do with her going to the Convent, to bring
it before Dr Doyle.

3. For her to bring it before Dr Doyle, and, if pressed to say from
whom she comes, to say from *me*.

The last way seems to me the best, at least to begin with, if she will
do it — The delicate point will be, lest she mix up her private feelings
about the Priests in her statements to him.

Ever Yours affectly John H Newman   Congr. Orat.

P.S.   On second thoughts I shall keep the papers till I hear from you.[1]

---

[1] Newman's suspicions as to the whole of Miss B.'s story were justified, as his
subsequent letters prove. The Convent was one which did not engage in active work,
was near the railway, and was somehow under the jurisdiction of Dr Doyle of St
George's, Southwark. This suggests the Benedictine Solitaries of the Perpetual
Adoration, London Abbey, London Road, St George's Fields, of which Miss Agnew
was the Superioress.

MONDAY 6 JANUARY 1851   Montgomery and Mr Daly to dinner.

TO T. F. KNOX

[7 January 1851]¹

My dear F Francis

Would this do, though it would be round about? 1. Since the Lady Superior has not heard the matter, to lay it before *her*. 2. For me, as having been consulted by her, ⟨Miss B.⟩ to write you, her director, a letter for her to take to the Lady Superior who would at the same time hear *generally* what she had to say.

My writing the letter will cause her to attend to it — I could not address it to *her* — nor to Miss *B* — but by being written to you I could say just what I chose.

I should *go through* the matter, quoting the strong points of Miss B's statement, omitting the others, and making remarks. Perhaps you can hardly judge about it, till you see what I produce.

It would be a very good thing certainly her going sometimes to the Convent, unless she was thought a spy.

I have said an Hail Mary for the poor lady you spoke of.

Ever Yours affly J H N

P.S.   You may tell her what you will out of my letter. I should advise her simply to *drop* the poisoning, the priests etc — it will throw discredit upon the rest. The point is whether Sister Sch. did not exaggerate the occurrence with the old priest.

How far do her Father and Brother know what has happened

I would write *direct* to the Lady Superior from Birmingham — but I could not relate *to her* the indecent things I might tell indirectly in a letter written to you.

TO RICHARD STANTON

January 8 [1851?]²

My dear F R,

I wish you could contrive to be here on *the Purification*. You would be of use

Ever Yrs affly J H N

¹ Dated from contents and postmark.
² Newman appears to have written in the year in pencil.

TO T. F. KNOX

Oy Bm Jan 9/51

My dear F Francis

I send you my letter.

What I thought of was, Miss B taking it to the Lady Superior stating the facts under which it was written — viz that you her director had encouraged her to send to me her papers, as I had been concerned in her going to the Convent — and that, on my answer coming, you felt you could not do better than give it to her to show the Lady Superior.

Whether Miss B. should herself read my letter first, you shall be the judge. She will leave it with the Lady Superior.

If Miss B. could return to the convent, it would be a very great thing — this depends on how she gets on with the Lady Superior. I suppose the latter, poor thing, has *no hands* — e.g. what a stick the mistress of Novices!

If Miss B. does not return, I dont like Louisa[1] going on, but this is a further matter.

You will see what I have said to obviate the Lady Superior asking for the original papers. If she does Miss B. must say that *I* have got them. If she presses, I will send them and no great harm is done — Rather, it will show that I have made a selection in Miss B's statements Let me know how it ends.

Yrs affly J H N

TO RICHARD STANTON

Oy. Bm January 9/51

My dear F Richard,

I am quite ashamed to give you the trouble, but again I must ask you for the sum you have already given me, viz due to you from me for the carriage of pictures from Rome. My excuse is the arrival of my closets from St W's [Wilfrid's], which with other accidents, have placed all my papers no how, and I can't lay my hand on your letter. I must make the same excuse for having lost a document of F Antony's — of which I petition from him a repetition, viz the sum of interest on his £100 for a year, owing from the Birmingham house, which he gave to F Ambrose, and which therefore that house owes the latter.

[1] An aspirant for the convent, not identified.

Also will you tell F Antony that I cant make out where our Auctioneer is, or whether he has been to St W's or no. Therefore I could send no message, though I gave it up as being past the time. There is no reason F Gaudentius should not have some of the things — but I should like to have a veto on them in detail

This letter is rather for F Antony than you. They say the Duchess of Kent is *certainly* under instruction.[1] Br Frederic is just recovering from the small pox — he has had it worse than F Austin.

Ever Yours affectly J H N

Jan 10.

SATURDAY 11 JANUARY 1851   Miss Bathurst returned

TO F. W. FABER

Oy Bm. Jan 12/51

My dear F W

I congratulate you on your Sermons and on their conclusion — and hope now you will get well.[2]

We can't help fearing that it is to turn out that I am to be a Bishop i.e. as far as a Brief makes me.[3] If so, F Joseph starts off at once to Rome to avoid it. Do any of you wish to go for the lark?

I write about it for this reason:— that you would put together all the things we have to ask for — viz interpretations of Rule — of our Brief — etc etc — privileges, indulgences etc etc. Don't *name* any one (if so) to go with him ⟨Father Joseph⟩ without my hearing of it *first*.

Your letter to Mr Eyre was a good one.[4] It struck F Ambrose, and I think most truly, that 'Jansenism' is being severe with occasions of

---

[1] Victoria Maria Louise, Duchess of Kent (1786–1861), was the widow of George III's fourth son, and the mother of Queen Victoria. The Duchess's father, the Duke of Saxe-Coburg-Saalfeld, was a Catholic, but she, being a girl, was brought up in the religion of her Protestant mother. There appears to be no record of the Duchess having ever become a Catholic, although see letter of 22 May 1861 to M. R. Giberne.

[2] Hutchison wrote on 8 Jan. that Faber was 'still in his room, the sixth day, he has now got a rheumatic headache. He preached for nearly two hours last night and will again I suppose tonight.'

[3] The newspapers were saying, on 'excellent authority,' that Newman was to be appointed to the newly created Bishopric of Nottingham. See also letter of 3 Feb. to Talbot.

[4] See letter of 29 Dec. 1850 to Faber.

sin. Were I a Bishop, I should be a Jansenist in forbidding pretty maidservants in clerical establishments, et id genus omne.

Ever Yours affly J H N

P.S.   Perhaps you may see F Joseph tomorrow seeking a schoolmaster.

TO J. B. MORRIS

Oratory Bm Jan 12/51

My dear Morris,

I dare say you have thought it unkind I have not replied to your most welcome letter till now — but I am so busy and tired. It was certainly wonderful news and I rejoice at it. I inclose a letter for Phillipps.[1]

As to the paper on Monophysism, I fear it is not what you think it to be.[2] Another difficulty is that you must not implicitly trust my facts — This is strange in a *printed* paper, but I believe I wished to give old King a job — I had hardly ½ dozen copies struck off — it was in the days of my wealth and lavish expenditure. Shall I send it you to Prior Park, or where you are?[3]

St John and Bowles send their love

Ever Yours affectly in Xt, John H Newman   Congr. Orat.

MONDAY 13 JANUARY 1851   F Joseph ⟨Gordon⟩ went to Town

[1] The news was that of Robert Biddulph Phillipps's conversion. To the enclosed letter of congratulation he replied on 16 Jan. that Newman's works had 'contributed much to bring me to my present position,' the sermon 'Faith and Doubt' in *Mix.*, having overcome his last hesitations. See also letter of 29 July 1850 to Morris.

[2] This was a printed paper headed 'Monophysite Heresy. August 23, 1839. The following is an abstract of a MS. of this date, with notes and references.' It occupied pp. 17–31 (in double columns), in the pamphlet of which it formed part, the first 16 pages containing the article on 'The Heresy of Apollinaris,' reprinted in *T.T.* pp. 301–28. On a bundle of the pamphlet Newman wrote, 'Note on Apollinarian and Monophysite Heresies The former I have published in "Theol Tracts"—the latter too imperfect to use.'

[3] Morris had been staying with Phillipps at Hagley Park, Ledbury, Herefordshire, but was about to move to Prior Park.

TO T. F. KNOX

Jan 13/51

My dear F Francis

I return all the papers — The Lady Superior's etc notes are inclosed in an envelope, as they came.

I see no harm in the Lady Superior seeing them, if she wishes. There is great simplicity in Miss B's mode of writing — and she will see too that I have not believed every thing, but discriminated.

Should Miss B *return*, I think the Lady Superior *ought* to see them

Ever Yrs affly J H N

TO EDWARD LUMLEY

To Mr Lumley   Jan 14/51
Sir,

Sometime since you proposed entering into correspondence with me about the sale of the existing stock of the Tracts for the Times, which is so considerable, that I wish to get rid of it. At the same time I wish, if possible, to get back, part of the money laid out on the printing — and it is a question how this is practically compatible with my selling the stock to any one. Another difficulty is that the copyrights of some of the Tracts are not mine — and I cannot therefore reprint.

What I can do is this:— I can make up 250 copies of the *whole set* including Number 90 (which I will reprint, and will refuse to sell separate) except however the Tracts on Baptism, Numbers 68, 69, 70 which have long been out of print and will never be reprinted. And I can make up I dare say 500 or 600 of the last 21 Tracts being the Three last volumes, viz from Number 71 to Number 90 inclusive, which contain all the long and important Tracts except the above-mentioned Tracts on Baptism. I thought of advertising this well, and holding out the inducement of Number 90 which is out of print, and I think I should have a chance of selling them.

But I am tempted, before doing so myself, to ask whether you are disposed to offer me any thing, and what, for the 250 copies of the whole, and the 500 copies of the last 3 volumes. Or for any portion of them.

I suppose it is quite certain that, at least in our day, the whole set never will be reprinted — so that, it is now or never for the public. I think the whole set excluding Numbers 68–70 sell for about 1.16.0 in boards, and the last 21 Tracts at 24/ or 25/. I should add that to make up the number of copies proposed, I shall have some considerable reprints to make, which will add to the expence.[1]

I am &c J H N

THURSDAY 16 JANUARY 1851   [W. G.] Ward came

TO W. G. PENNY

Jany 16. ⟨?⟩ 1851

My dear F William

Thank you for your letter and its kind expressions about myself. I trust in all you do you will be guided by God's grace to His greater glory and your own spiritual [?] good. Its purport did not surprise me at all nor would surprise any of us, for the reports you allude to are rife here, and I can only conjecture you must, without knowing it, have let out something to your penitents.[2]

Nor am I surprised for another reason — from the day when at Rome you expressed an intention to live da Cappucino in the Oratory, I felt you had no vocation for the Congregation of St Philip, because the Franciscan Rule is one thing and the Oratory is another. And ever since that time you have deepened that confusion by (I am obliged to say it) systematically and habitually ignoring, or ridiculing or violating our rule, as I have before now intimated to you.

One thing surprised me, that you should have corresponded with a member of another order about your leaving us, that you should have consulted a director on the subject, unless it was done sub sigillo,[3] and that you should have communicated it to a third person, before you told any of us any thing about it.

I have thought over what you ask me as to going to Belgium, and wish I saw my way to consent to it; but it seems to me simply impossible, impossible in idea, i.e. simply selfcontradictory for a member of one

[1] Lumley ended by not taking over any of the *Tracts*. Cf. letter of 9 Feb. to Capes. Newman kept them in the warehouse of Messrs Rivington, who reprinted for him some of the Tracts, a few years later, in order to complete sets. In 1854, he left 300 copies of each volume with Rivington, and stored the rest at the Oratory. In 1878, all that was left of the stock in both places was sold as waste.

[2] Penny had just recovered from smallpox, and was staying with his mother at 23 Dorset Street, London. He wrote on 15 Jan. that, as long ago as the Roman novitiate in 1847, he had wished to be a Capuchin, and that he had recently discussed the matter with a member of that Order and with 'an experienced director.' He wanted, as the best way of testing his vocation, to stay at a Capuchin monastery in Belgium, but secretly, so that he could return to the Oratory if necessary.

[3] Penny replied that this was the case.

body to be a postulant of another. However, the matter does not rest with me, but the Congregatio Deputata, and I will if you wish me, immediately bring the matter before them, indeed I think they would wish it. Of course I do not know, till I make trial of them, but I anticipate they would quite agree with me first that you have no vocation to the Oratory, next that, while nominally a member of it, you cannot try your vocation in any other body.

You may be sure I will not neglect to think of you in this matter in Masses and at prayer, to the best of my power — though I am not in doubt about the matter myself.[1]

SATURDAY 18 JANUARY 1851 Monsell came

TO W. G. PENNY (I)

Oy Bm Jan 18. 1851
(NOT SENT)

My dear F William

You wish me to give you leave of absence for a month, and you let me know the object of it.[2] As I have told you, I cannot approve of that object, and therefore cannot and do not give you leave of absence. I give you leave of absence for a fortnight from today, viz, so that you shall be back here on Saturday February 1, but *on the strict condition* that you drop all conversation or correspondence about your vocation with externals.

If you wish to determine questions about your vocation, this is the place for doing it in the first instance. We in the first instance must be your advisers and judges. Do what you do through us. Take our counsel first. Put the matter before us and we will tell you what to do. To go out of the body for advice is an act of disrespect to St Philip.

Would it were the only one which you have committed, but I grieve

---

[1] Penny had written '. . . let me beseech you, by that kind feeling which I know you must have towards one who has been helped so much by you as I have, to a place in the Church of Christ . . . to assist me by your prayers. . . .' Newman's draft has no conclusion.

[2] Penny wrote on 17 Jan. about exploring his Capuchin vocation while still having 'the earnest wish to hold on to the oratory as long as possible.' He urged that in other Orders a man could leave to try elsewhere, and 'is generally, for the first time at least, received back again.' He then asked, instead, to be allowed to take his annual month's leave of absence immediately. This is the first draft of Newman's reply, to which he gave a second date at the end, 19 Jan. The second letter of 18 Jan. was the reply actually sent.

to be obliged to say that your whole conduct has been one series of insults to the Congregation of which you are professedly a subject. You have now lived three years with us without any token whatever of an Oratorian heart. You have felt no love for the Institution, no reverence for its rules, no devotion to its service. You have done nothing for it except by constraint. You have used its home as a lodging house, for which you paid so much per week grudgingly [,] which gave you a position for hearing confessions, visiting the poor, and evangelizing Protestants. You now stay in it only till something better turns up, which you can take real interest in. In vain have I remonstrated with you again and again; my words were as bullets upon wet sand. You have been simply passive and impassive; have listened, consented, and gone on as before. Your letter of this morning, though you dont know it, shows the deadness which I am describing, as much as any thing has done. I cannot refrain from saying, that, while you are what you are, you cumber our ground. I had been praying, before your first letter came, that God would either remove you from us or give you an Oratorian heart. And now, not without deliberation, I tell you I have taken my resolution, founded on a clear view of my duty, to oblige you, on your return, to lead a more Oratorian life than you have done hitherto.

Moreover, I cannot consent to keep secret from the Fathers what you have told to the whole world. You are not bound, and I must be! I feel no misgivings about this letter — I should reproach myself if I did not show some zeal for St Philip

With my most earnest prayers for you and for ourselves

I am &c J H N

Jan 19/51

TO W. G. PENNY (II)

Jan 18. 1851

My dear F William,

On full consideration, I could not bring myself to keep secret from the Fathers what you have told to the whole world. You are not bound, I do not see that I should be. I have in consequence as a matter of duty laid the matter before the General Congregation, and I found the Fathers quite prepared to take the view I had myself taken, and to come to the following resolution.

They feel with me unanimously that you had no vocation to the Oratory — and they think it will be removing a temptation out of your way, as well as fulfilling their duty to St Philip, if they propose to you to ask for your exeat. At all events they will pass a resolution to the effect of your ceasing to belong to us on Tuesday morning, after the post comes in, the words being only affected by your answer to this.

One does not like to go through the grounds and considerations on which the conclusion has been arrived at. We know perfectly how entirely bent you are upon serving God, but there are many ways of serving Him, and yours is not the Oratorian way, and to mistake one's vocation, spiritual writers tell us, is the way to lose one's election.

Give us your prayers as we give you ours. According to your letter to Brother Bernard your clothes, books and other effects shall be sent to you to Dorset Street — directly — As to any bed, chairs etc which belong to you, they shall be sent wherever you will say

I am &c J H N

Jan 19/51

P.S.   Since writing the above your letter of this morning has come.[1]

Do not be disturbed if I say that my mind is quite made up and nothing can shake it. I should be a traitor to St Philip to take another view. It is neither for your good nor ours that you should continue with us. I have for three years said this 'If F William ought to be elsewhere, we are spoiling a vocation' and you are harming us by being with us. Your thought of leaving us is no 'temptation.' I make my mind up slowly, but when it is made up, it is not easily changed.

I really do not see the good of your coming here tomorrow — and shall not give any direction about your room.

This will all turn to good — believe it, my dear F. William, and resign yourself to the will of God

I am &c J H N[2]

TO F. W. FABER

[19? January 1851]

My dear F Wilfrid,

I will tell our brothers directly about Br Joseph — I am very sorry.[3]

---

[1] In this Penny suggested he should visit Newman on 20 Jan.

[2] Penny replied that he ought not to be dismissed from the Oratory except for contumacy, and asked for a delay of ten days before further steps were taken. This was granted, and he came, after all, to see Newman 'not to argue, but in humility.' On 30 Jan. his withdrawal from the Oratory was accepted. See *Appendix* 2, p. 500, for the Birmingham Oratory decree as to this. Penny never even tried to become a Capuchin, but remained a secular priest, and in 1853 Newman chose him as a tutor for the Catholic University in Dublin.

[3] He was the brother sacristan at London, and died on 18 Jan.

I had not a dream you asked me whether F Bernard should look over the little book. I thought you said that he *would*. I am very sorry for the mistake.

I hope they be not going too fast with their Cardinals, Archbishops, and Synods

Ever Yours affly J H N

P.S.   You don't say how you are.

TO EDWARD WALFORD

Oratory Birmingham January 19. 1851

My dear Sir

Accept my best congratulations on the happy news you tell me about yourself — Those only who have been some time Catholics can understand what good news it is — and no one on earth of course fully — but you must be sensible from the first of what you have gained quite enough to rejoice in it.

We shall be truly glad if you will accept our hospitality, such as it is — and whenever you settle to come for the purpose you have named.[1] I wish I could accept your kind wish that I should stand sponsor for you, but our rule forbids it. However, you will have no difficulty in finding one. Thank you for what you say about myself, and believe me,

My dear Mr Walford, Truly Yours in Xt

John H Newman   Congr. Orat.

TO F. W. FABER

Oy Bm Jan 20/51

My dear F Wilfrid,

I send a letter of F Gaudentius's, part of which concerns you. I will see our Bishop as soon as I can about St W's [Wilfrid's].

I don't understand enough from Lord A's [Arundel's] letter, what his difficulties are. E.g. nothing has yet thrown light on his not signing the address to the Cardinal — was it delicacy towards his father?[2]

[1] Edward Walford came to the Birmingham Oratory on 28 Jan., in order to be received into the Church.

[2] Faber had sent Newman for his comment, a letter of Lord Arundel's, who had not signed the Catholic laity's address of welcome to Cardinal Wiseman. On 22 Jan. Faber reported the London gossip 'that the Duke [of Norfolk] said if Lord A [Arundel] did sign it he (the duke) would abjure the next day.'

We have decided to lose F William and shall pass the decree to that effect tomorrow morning, if all is well. He decided on trying his vocation in a Capuchin Convent in Belgium — and would not take a refusal, but ordered his box up, and fixed the hour of his departure before he had succeeded in getting leave. Afterwards, he was softened a little — why? not from love of the Oratory or devotion to St Philip, but because his mother was distressed at his joining an order which separated him from her. However, this is but the last step of a course. He had corresponded with a Capuchin for some time without our knowing anything of it, and *everyone* knew about it here but ourselves.

Ever Yours affectly John H Newman Congr. Orat.

P.S.   I have found your paper, which I inclose.[1] Do you know anyone who wants a *pupil*, a boy?

TO FATHER GAUDENTIUS ROSSI

Oratory Birmingham, Jan 20. 1851

My dear F Gaudentius,

I have forwarded your letter to F. Hutchison, the property of St Wilfrid's belonging to the London Oratory, not to ours.

Will you kindly send *me* a list of the furniture you wish to take? and I will get a price put on it by the valuer

The *church* furniture, viz candlesticks etc must *not* come *here*. It does not belong to *us*. The six candlesticks which are intended for *funerals* belong to *St Wilfrid's*, and are to go neither here nor to London.

Begging you good prayers, I am, My dear F Gaudentius Very truly Yours in Xt

John H Newman Congr. Orat.

TUESDAY 21 JANUARY 1851 Monsell went

THURSDAY 23 JANUARY F William ⟨Penny⟩ came

---

[1] This was Faber's paper against taking the discipline. See letter to Faber of 12 Dec. 1850. Faber replied on 22 Jan., 'I send you back my paper. It is very shady indeed; but I compliment myself on the *worldly* wisdom of it. . . .'

SATURDAY 25 JANUARY H W [Wilberforce] and Monsell came and Miss Finch French[1]

TO MISS HOLMES

Oratory Bm. Jan 25/51

My dear Miss Holmes,

I certainly ought to have answered you at once, but was busy. Your verses were the expression of a beautiful and poetical idea, and I do not see any one would find fault with the theology of them. The general fault of your composition is what you justly attribute to F Faber's, want of finish. Your thoughts come out in morning dress, with their curls en papillote.

You speak as if I or my friends had something to do with the Catholic Standard — we have nothing at all — and do not know the Editor's name.[2]

Thank you for your news about yourself. I trust and know that God and His Mother will be with you wherever you are.

Yrs affectly J H Newman Congr. Orat.

TO T. F. KNOX

Oratory. Jan 25/51

My dear F Francis,

Thank Miss B. for her kind letter, and say I value the expression of her esteem for me. By the way, is she not a great proser and lecturer? I shall burn I suppose I may, what she has now sent. Also how did you word your letter to the Lady Superior? so as to include me? Else, I will and ought to answer hers.

Yours affectly in Mary & Philip

John H Newman Congr. Orat.

MONDAY 27 JANUARY 1851 Monsell went and H W [Wilberforce] (who had not slept in the House) and F Ambrose with him

TUESDAY 28 JANUARY Mr Walford came

[1] Newman corrected the name, but made no erasure.
[2] Founded in Oct. 1849, the *Catholic Standard* was purchased by H. Wilberforce in 1854, and amalgamated with the *Weekly Register* in 1855.

TO F. W. FABER

Oy Bm Jan 30/51

My dear F W

'Why should I be deprived of you both in one day?' and that the Blessed Sebastian's —[1] but, while we have accepted F William's withdrawal to-day, I have just received a letter from F Thomas to the effect that Dr Duke has declared his health will not allow him to rejoin us.

I will write more another time — but I thought I would give you notice at once.

Ever Yrs affly J H N

SATURDAY 1 FEBRUARY 1851   Penny went for good

TO WILLIAM PHILIP GORDON

Oy Bm Febr 3/51

My dear Philip

I write to the London F Minister in case our Joseph or Nicholas does *not* write to him. In which case my directions must be considered suspended.

1. Aloysius with F. Fred. as his protector, will come to you tomorrow by express train. Can you give them both beds?

2. We fear we shall lose Aloysius — he is in his way to Dr Duke.

3. If F Frederic does not come with him, you must see him ⟨A⟩ lodged in the Hastings Express train — and write to Scratton, (5 Norman Road, St Leonard's) telling him to meet him at the Station, and when.

Ever Yours affectly J H N.

TO GEORGE TALBOT

Oratory Birmingham February 3. 1851

My dear Talbot,

There has been a report some time that my name has been sent to Rome for one of the new Sees. We thought nothing of it till yesterday,

[1] Genesis, 27:45. On 30 Jan. the feast of the Turin Oratorian, Blessed Sebastian Valfrè, Penny's resignation had been accepted, and a letter had come from Scratton, who had been a novice since the previous May, saying he had neither the health nor the vocation of an Oratorian.

when it appears in a leading article of the Tablet.[1] I earnestly trust that nothing will be determined on till *our representations* are heard.

We are all of us in the greatest fright about it. Depend on it, the Oratory is not consolidated enough to do without me. The Holy Father has put me to this work, and I feel that, with St Philip's blessing, this work I could do — I have no confidence that I could do any other work, though God's grace is all in all.

I will not enter into particulars here, for my only object in writing is to arrest proceedings, if there be such. Surely we ought to be heard. Of course *when a thing is done*, I shall bow to it as the act of the Vicar of Christ. But *till then*, I will boldly say, that it would be very inadvisable. My *line* is different — it is to oppose the infidels of the day. They are *just* beginning to attend to me — Every thing shows this. My appointment to a See would take me off this opening field. *My writings would be at an end*, were I a Bishop. I might publish a sermon or two, but the work of a *life* would be lost. For twenty years I have been working on towards a philosophical polemic, suited to these times. I want to meet the objections of infidels against the Church. I saw a letter of Montalembert's lately, in which he expressed pleasure at two of my late Lectures, which were on that tack.[2] A fearful battle is coming on and my place seems to lie in it. Make me a bishop, and I am involved in canon law, rubrics, and the working of a diocese, about which I know nothing. It is a very hazardous thing to put a man of 50 on an *entirely new line*. Do think of this. You cannot think how strongly I feel this. Surely my opinion on the subject is of weight.

Will you let my feeling be known at Propaganda? Pray for me

Ever Yours most sincerely in Xt

John H Newman Congr. Orat.

TUESDAY 4 FEBRUARY 1851 F Fred. and Aloysius to St Leonard's
WEDNESDAY 5 FEBRUARY Mr Walford went

[1] The *Tablet*, XII (1 Feb. 1851), p. 72, reported that the new sees would be filled before the Ecclesiastical Titles Bill put obstacles in the way. 'So we are told that Dr Cox is to be the new Bishop of Southwark; Dr Newman the new Bishop of Nottingham; Dr Errington of Salford . . .'
[2] See letter of 6 Oct. 1850 to Faber.

TO F. S. BOWLES

Oratory, Birmingham February 5. 1851

My dear F Frederic

If your sister has done with it, you may bring with you the 'Constitutiones Societatis Jesu' which she borrowed at Derby, and I think has not returned.[1]

Say every thing kind to her from me

Ever Yours affecty John H Newman

Love to Aloysius and Scratton

SATURDAY 8 FEBRUARY 1851   F Frederic returned from St Leonard's.

TO J. M. CAPES

Ory Bm Febr 9/51

My dear Capes,

I mentioned your plan to H Wilberforce, the only person I could think of — and I almost think he would take it up. Direct to him 'Rugby' and use my name. As he does not like to be 'Esqud' in your *Advertisement*, if he agreed, you might call him Mr H Wilberforce.[2]

I wish I could suggest any thing to you on your subject, which seems to me very promising.

I still shrink from taking up your line of attacking the Church of E. [England] I ask 'Could we supply the place of it and all sects?' See, we have not priests enough for our own body — how much less for England! Besides, I think our game is *not* to return evil for evil, now that the parsons have attacked us so furiously.

Thank you for the Dispatch. I have thoughts of advertising the Tracts for the Times in it and other such publications. They might rescue a remnant of the infidels.[3] Could you give me your opinion on the probable success of this — how to do it — *what publisher to get* (e.g. Richardson?) whether to give him a high percentage, to make it

[1] Emily Bowles had moved with Mother Connelly from Derby to St Leonards, where her brother had just arrived with the ailing laybrother Aloysius Boland.

[2] Capes was organising lectures that were to be given by laymen. Cf. letter of 10 Oct. 1850 to Northcote. Wilberforce, so recently a clergyman, disliked being described as 'esquire.'

[3] The radical and secularist *Weekly Dispatch* had a circulation of 60,000.

worth his while, or how etc etc. I have, say, 250 of the whole work, bating Pusey on Baptism 68–70 — and 500 of the last 21 Tracts (including Number 90) i.e. the last 3 volumes, which contains all the long Tracts but P's on Baptism.

I have not seen, and wish to see, the Battle of the Churches.[1] I have no means of seeing any thing.

I will say Mass for your Lecture Plan soon.

Ever Yrs affly J H N

TO T. W. ALLIES

Oratory, Birmingham Feb. 10. 1851.

My dear Allies,

I have been anxious about you ever since I heard accidentally you were remaining in Town, and had not gone to Paris, which is what, I think, you told me you were going to do. I hoped indeed you were stopping for some good, — certainly the Cardinal's wishes were not sufficient. He is a kind-hearted sanguine man, who never sees difficulties in any thing, and in consequence often promises what in the event he cannot make good.[2]

For myself, I have had no cause for hope in the matter of the Dublin, for any thing I saw, from the moment Maskell showed he was not taking it up. I still think money is the hitch, though I have heard not a word about it from any one. It is useless your undertaking it unless you were independent in the editorship.

I most deeply sympathise in your anxiety; indeed I have all along. Though knowing well it will turn ultimately to a blessing, and that it will only be for a time, yet it is extremely trying, while it lasts. For myself, I have not seen any plan better than that which you naturally did not fancy, undertaking some boys. The worst is, they are scattered now.

Tell me, if I can do anything now in the matter of the Dublin. Can I bring it to a point by asking any question?[3]

Ever yours affectly in Xt   John H Newman   Congr. Orat.

[1] This was the title of an article in the organ of the philosophic radicals, the *Westminster and Foreign Quarterly Review*, LIV (Jan. 1851), pp. 441–96. It reviewed *Diff.* and pamphlets on the papal aggression controversy, and showed an appreciation of the intellectual force of the Catholic revival. Newman quoted from it in *Prepos.* pp. 331–2. George Eliot was a contributor to the *Westminster* at this time, and in Sept. 1851 became assistant editor.

[2] Allies went to see Wiseman again at the end of March, about being employed as editor of the proposed Catholic newspaper, but found that nothing had been *done*, although Wiseman had given the impression four months earlier, that even details had been arranged. See letter of 11 Nov. 1850. The project was never realised.

[3] Cf. letters of 28 Oct. 1850.

TO J. D. DALGAIRNS

Oy Bm Febr 10/51

My dear F Bernard

Thank you much for your letter. The same post brought one from M. Gondon — and since then, good part of his translation has come in type. I suppose it is fair on the whole, with a number of incidental inaccuracies or mistakes.

I don't see harm in his printing the last 5 as the first 5, and the first 7 as the last 7, which he is doing, except that he destroys the drift of the volume, as far as it has any, and makes the advertisement or Preface unintelligible. I suppose he will notice what he has done in a sort of Preface.[1]

On the whole I am indebted to him, for he has got my book into circulation in France.

Only I am fidgetting about poor M. Duferrière [sic], who had so much trouble about the University Sermons. I suppose, if they are selling you would have heard from him.

Thank you for a sight of the Cardinal of Besançon's very nice letter. When you write, be sure to thank His Eminence from me for the souvenir he has so condescendingly sent me. It is very pleasing to be remembered by him.[2]

I am disappointed your Lectures on the Sacred Heart are delayed. I think they will do good. I have read the one you now have sent me, once, but I want to read it again.[3]

Ever Yrs affly J H N

TO WILLIAM MONSELL

Oratory Bm Febr 10. 1851

My dear Monsell,

The last Mass for Lady Anna Maria will be said tomorrow morning — Of course I am very anxious to hear how she is going on, and hope you will write, when you have any thing to say.[4]

It is taking a liberty perhaps to ask you, how you have made up your

---

[1] Gondon's translation of *Diff.* 1, *Conférences prêchées à L'Oratoire de Londres*, Paris 1851, printed the last five conferences first, and contained an explanatory preface of 51 pages, dated 19 March.

[2] Cardinal Mathieu, whom Newman met at Besançon on 16 Sept. 1846, had just written to Dalgairns, and enclosed a small holy picture for Newman.

[3] See note to letter of 29 July 1850. [4] Monsell's wife was ill.

mind about voting on Irish Church questions.[1] Though it did not happen I said much, yet it is a subject on which I take great interest.

Something else I had to say — but though I have given my memory a quarter of an hour's chance, I cannot recall it.

Ever Yours most sincerely in Xt

John H Newman Congr. Orat.

TO F. W. FABER

Oy. Bm. February 11/51

My dear F Wilfrid

I think you must take no notice of Mr Drummond. First because he has the privilege of Parliament, which is, to say what he will — the remedy for which is that it *can't* be published — as this particular case has shown, an action against the newspaper being the prospective remedy, which hinders it.[2] Again, it is our game (if we can keep to it) to ignore the Parliament in these matters, which are not civil but religious. The real quid pro quo, or remedy of the grievance, is for a member to contradict it *in* the House — This many a man ought to have done — Mr B. Hope ought to have done it, and got a retractation — or Lord John M. [Manners] or a score of other persons, — but if they don't and won't, let them enjoy the fetor of the calumny which Dr Reid cannot clear away.[3]

Lord A. [Arundel] was just the person *not* to answer it — from his

[1] i.e. now that he had become a Catholic. Monsell was elected as Member of Parliament for Limerick in 1847.

[2] When the Ecclesiastical Titles Bill was introduced in the House of Commons, on 7 Feb. by Lord John Russell, Henry Drummond, one of the founders and chief supporters of the Irvingites, and a friend of Pierce Connelly, made a long vehement speech in its favour. In the course of it he said 'that fellow Faber went about the country seducing young women.' This remark was reproduced neither in the newspapers nor in *Hansard*, whose privileged position had not been recognised in a recent libel case. Newman asked Faber to verify the remark (letter of 23 July 1851), in view of the Corn Exchange lectures. See *PrePos.* p. 206, where Newman spoke of 'the outrageous language perpetrated in a place I must not name, where one speaker went to the length of saying, what the reporters suppressed for fear of consequences, that a dear friend and brother of mine, for whose purity and honour I would die, mentioning him by name, went about the country, as the words came to the ears of those present, seducing young women.'

[3] Alexander James (later Beresford-) Hope (1820–87) was a devout and anti-Erastian High Churchman. Lord John Manners (1818–1906) was one of the 'Young England' party, also with strong Tractarian sympathies. Both of them had been Faber's friends in his Anglican days. David Boswell Reid (1805–63), the inventor, was at the time applying his ventilation system to the new Houses of Parliament.

connection with you. It would have been infra dig. in him, and perhaps have done you no good.

I suppose the House put it down to anger in the worthy Drummond, and so let it pass.

The only difficulty in such a line of policy is that in this country not to deny a charge is suspicious — but no one could think this of such a charge as Mr D. was angry enough to emit, on the contrary the taking it to heart would have been the suspicious circumstance.[1]

Father Wm [William Penny] dines with us today, and we have some good plum cake for him. We do not hear you have talked to him, but I can't help thinking you have, and have consoled him.

Lord John seems to promise a long warfare — The Conservative measure, I suppose, would have been that synodal decrees in the name of a foreign Power should be treasonable, or the like.

I suppose no government would care for a Concordat which did not give them the Veto

Ever Yours affly J H N

P.S.   I hear you have five fratelli[2] who discipline — Are you not afraid of this getting into Punch, with a picture of F Faber in the act?

WEDNESDAY 12 FEBRUARY 1851   W Wilberforce called   The Bishop called
THURSDAY 13 FEBRUARY   Ryder came for the day
FRIDAY 14 FEBRUARY   F Joseph went to St Leonard's

TO MRS F. R. WARD

Oratory Birmingham February 14. 1851

My dear Mrs Ward,

I congratulate you with all my heart on your reception into the Catholic Church, and pray, and am sure, you will enjoy to the full those blessings which there alone are to be found.

It is very kind in you to tell me about the dear Froudes.[3] How is it possible to doubt that they will ultimately be brought by God's grace to where we are? They have no argument against Catholicism, but it is their imagination which starts back from it. They have all their lives

[1] Faber fully agreed with Newman's advice and wrote 'I hear Drummond is dying to get Lord A to ask him questions, and he will out with Connelly's stories.'

[2] i.e. laymen, who attended the prayer and discipline with the Oratorians.

[3] Mrs William Froude, her husband and children.

been accustomed to something so different — the worship in the Catholic Church is so new to them, the customs, the phrases, the ideas, the tone of thought, that it is like forcing what is square into what is round — And least this is what I conjecture about them. And certainly it is a great trial, but God is all in all.

What she proposes in the way of devotion is very good — Such prayers and hymns as the Veni Creator are most suitable. And the Litany of Jesus, if they get it from the *good* translation, though it would be better if they used it in Latin. To my own feeling no book equals the Latin Paradisus Animae. It is at once so comprehensive and so touching.[1]

Pray remember me most kindly to Mr Ward, and to Mr Walford, if with you

Begging your good prayers, I am, My dear Mrs Ward, Very truly yours in Xt

John H Newman   Congr. Orat.

TO ANTONY HUTCHISON

Oy Bm Febr 17/51

My dear F Antony

I had not forgotten you, but had said Mass for the Wilfridians — in thanksgiving that so sweet a nosegay, or, to speak more poetically, so fair a wreath, had been given me to present to our Lady and St Philip even in the wintry month of February. Your affectionate letter came very apropos, and Nicholas gave the finish by lecturing the Wilfridians in chapter and in presence of the rest on the duty of being worthy of us[2]

What are you all thinking of these Parliamentary matters? As far as they go, they do *us* no harm. If the measures are carried out, they reduce the Church's action to the congregational and the literary, which are just ours; and only impinge on ceremonies, copes, mitres, and Puginism. They do not touch the confessional, the pulpit, or the press. Moreover, considering the great difficulty of getting bishops, it might be right in our making a virtue of necessity, and covering our poverty in function-aries under a show of submission to an unjust law. One thing or other I trust we should do — either totally yield or unequivocally fight — half and half measures, or divided, antagonist action in our Episcopate will

---

[1] *Paradisus Animae* was compiled by Merlo Horstius, a parish priest of Cologne, the first edition appearing in German in 1644, soon followed by many Latin adaptions.

[2] 14 Feb. was the third anniversary of the admission into the English Oratory of the Wilfridians. Hutchison, who had been one of them, wrote to thank Newman 'for having introduced us to St Philip.'

be melancholy — unless it were all England this way, and all Ireland that. There is a talk of a general meeting of bishops of the three king-doms at Dublin, and some joint measure. Judging by his letter to Lord John, I suppose our Bishop would be for resistance.[1] Then follows the question, Can you resist without having the people for you? — e.g. consider St Thomas. Now ascertain this point, before you begin. You will be fined, you will have to go to prison — perhaps you will be trans-ported. At what point will the people stand by you? — how many £100 fines can you bear etc etc? What if English and Irish bishops are indicted simultaneously, will it be any consolation to the English, whom a jury finds guilty, that an Irish jury lets off the Irish? I am not putting all this as an objection, but I do trust the Bishops will take the wisest heads to advise them, and understand simply what they are doing. Our Bishop has gone to town to day on the subject.

I fear Aloysius will not be long with us — he is to come back to us directly

Ever Yours affectly John H Newman   Congr. Orat.

TUESDAY 18 FEBRUARY 1851   Mr Flanagan here.

TO J. M. CAPES

Oratory Bm Febr 18/51

My dear Capes,

I am glad to hear so good a beginning of your lectures. Depend on it, *you* are in the right train, tho' not a member of the Hierarchy. Preaching, confession, publishing, no bill can touch, and these are our proper weapons. The Bill only touches Puginism and its offshoots. We are not ripe ourselves for a Hierarchy. Now they have one, they can't fill up the sees, positively can't. Don't repeat all this — but it really is a question whether one should not look on it as a means of getting us out of a scrape, that this Bill is past. [sic] We want seminaries far more than sees. We want education, *view*, combination, organization. I don't see the lie of things down here, but I am really inclined to think our game is to turn black, silent, and sulky; to suspend the use of those titles which

---

[1] Ullathorne's letter protesting against the speech with which Lord John Russell introduced the Ecclesiastical Titles Bill was printed in *The Times* of 11 Feb. Ulla-thorne asked ' Is it wise . . . to put the religious teachers of a large body of her Majesty's subjects in conscientious opposition to the law . . .' Cf. C. Butler, *The Life and Times of Bishop Ullathorne*, 1, London 1926, pp. 193–4.

the Bishops cannot really lose — to appoint Vicars General, locum tenentes, to the sees not filled up — and to make the excuse of this persecution for getting up a great organization, going round the towns giving lectures, or making speeches, none but Catholics being admitted to speak, starting a paper, a review etc. The great difficulty to this plan would be the Cardinal's status, would it not?

The other plan would be the bold one of all the Bishops of the three kingdoms meeting, and publicly declaring they would not obey the Law. Then they must be prepared to carry this out by submitting to fine, imprisonment, or even transportation, and must have a prospect of carrying the public opinion of Catholics with them.

I think a good deal may be said for either plan — but I earnestly hope there will be a *unanimous* plan of action, and a *view* — or at least that all England may act one way, and all Ireland another. Variety and discord would be miserable.

Also I wish the Bishops would bring out some programme of solemn Masses etc in deprecation of the persecution — and, if they could, make it obligatory to attend. Or perhaps even the Holy Father would have a jubilee, tho' this, I suppose, would be too strong.

Moreover, I think certain acts of retaliation should be practised, unless they looked mean — I mean, if we may not call our Bishops by their titles, our only mode of signifying and intimating our *secret* profession, is to speak of Dr Sumner, Dr Blomfield, *never* calling them Bishops — (at the utmost, Dr Sumner of the House of Lords) etc etc.

I hope your Committee will do something.[1] Is Bellasis on it?

As to the Establishment, what I have written in my Lectures, is addressed to educated men. The more we can weaken its hold upon them, the better. But this does not directly weaken its authority on the masses — nor does it involve any practical measure of *assault* upon it. I thought you were proposing a crusade against the Establishment — now, I think, you must not do so, till you have some thing to give instead. As far as the *people* is concerned, our line is, not to attack the Church of E. [England] which is low game, but to remove prejudices against ourselves, as you are doing at present in your Lectures.

Ever Yours affectly J H Newman

P.S.   Tell me any news, if you think at any time I am not au courant.

Are you constituted as a Committee to *advise* the Bishops? I wish you were. Do they even ask advice? How many country gentlemen, on whose munificence the sees when founded have a claim, do you think they consulted on the subject of the Hierarchy? To come to any decision

---

[1] i.e. Capes's committee of laymen, who were organising the Catholic lectures, etc.

how they ought to act now, you should be in communication with the leading Catholics of Liverpool, Birmingham, Manchester etc and see how they take this or that plan of the campaign. And again, if any thing is done, these must be conciliated. One of the last speakers in the Debate, and Mr Cooper the Chancery Barrister in the Chronicle, depose to the fact of opposition on the part of priests and laymen.[1] All this should be set right as far as possible by interviews. It is a most critical time — when the public has once tasted persecution, it will go on — it will lose its perception that it is persecution — it will get used to it.

To show how cautious it is necessary to be in letter writing, observe the following from Artaud's Life of Pius vii, apropos of Dr U's [Ullathorne's] remonstrance with Lord John. 'M. le cardinal Pacca s'étonne de ce que les étrangers se servent de ces mots, "la cour Romaine." Mais je possède beaucoup de notes où le cabinet de Rome se nomme ainsi à peu près lui-même.' He gives one instance beginning 'dans *la cour de Rome* il n'est pas permis à un ambassadeur etc' from Consalvi.[2]

They say the Bill is to be contracted, and not to apply to Ireland. If so, how can our Bishops stand out by themselves?

Ever Yours affly J H N

P.S.   I said Mass for your undertaking last Sunday

[1] Joseph Brotherton, the reforming Member of Parliament for Salford 1832–57, at the end of the debate on the first reading of the Ecclesiastical Titles Bill on 14 Feb., claimed that he 'had received several letters from Roman Catholics of great influence in Manchester and Salford' in favour of the Bill. *The Times*, 15 Feb. Charles Purton Cooper, barrister, antiquary and pamphleteer, in a letter published in the *Morning Chronicle* (13 Feb. 1851), p. 5, maintained that he had had 'very numerous communications from Roman Catholic laymen and priests' which showed they neither wished for nor approved of the establishment of the hierarchy, but they did not want their names disclosed. 'I have found that laymen allege as an excuse for imposing the condition of secrecy, the disquiet that would otherwise be produced in their families; and the priests allege the grievous consequences of such a violation of ecclesiastical discipline . . .'

Cooper made similar statements in his pamphlets on the establishment of the Hierarchy.

[2] Ullathorne in his letter to Lord John Russell, in *The Times* of 11 Feb., wrote 'Will your Lordship allow me to point out that the phrase "Court of Rome" is an ambiguous and offensive designation, as used instead of "the Holy See." It was invented by state canonists, and statesmen whose designs were directed against the liberty of the Church. . . . It incorporates an error, and is unfair . . . Allow me to refer you to an agreeable work which explains the true sense of this term, "Court of Rome" —Cardinal Pacca's *Memoirs of his Nunciature on the Rhine*.' Newman quotes from A. F. Artaud, *Histoire du pape Pie VII*, 1, 1st ed. Paris 1836, p. 417, note 1. (Consalvi's letter lays down that, in the Court of Rome, ambassadors should present letters of credence not only to the Pope, but also to the Cardinals.)

Oy Bm. Febr 20/51

My dear F Francis,

Miss B again. I have told her to apply to you, as she gives me the choice. Burn her letter.

If you find her quite reluctant to speak, I dont want to force it on you — but you will see she hardly ought to delay till I come to town. I have told her I should *prepare* you, but you had better not say I have sent you her letter, though I have scratched out a part.

I think she is on the point of derangement, though it would do harm to tell her so; you will have to soothe her.

Yet here is a great difficulty. If you show her any kindness, she may be filled with suspicions against you, as she is against the priest she mentions.

You must be kind and cold — from her letter to me I fancy she thinks you somewhat stern, else why should she not at once speak to you? And yet if you give this up, a worse thought about you may come on her.

May our Blessed Lady guide you through it well, secure in your innocence yet compassionate towards the feeble

Ever Yrs affly J H N

TO J. M. CAPES

Oy Bm Febr 21/51

My dear Capes,

I am very sorry to hear of your indisposition — you must get well for the good of the Church. Those who have a *view*, have indefinite power over those who have none. You say too there are good materials among the younger men of all classes. I dare say it may be in the event advisable for our Bishops to do nothing — but for that reason, if for no other, the laity should stir — I like the article on 'How shall we meet etc?' though when I like a thing, I always fear it is imprudent and violent.[1]

I do think you should get a set of fellows who will devote themselves to the cause of the Church — Let it be their recreation as geology or ecclesiology might be — while it is their *work*. Would the 'committee

---

[1] 'How shall we meet the Protestant Aggression?' in the *Rambler* (March 1850), pp. 249–58. The article urged Catholics not to be apologetic, but to resist the Ecclesiastical Titles Bill as an attack on the freedom of the Church.

for supplying members with information' furnish such? Men do with a special gusto what they do themselves — it is an outlet for private judgment. I do wish you could do it — it is a great object — Cannot you name some half dozen or more. It should be quite voluntary and informal at first — (only with the *secret* sanction of the Cardinal and Dr Ullathorne). If I can do any thing in getting them to approve of it, command me.

Ward, I suppose, would not work with other men, or lead them. Is there no old Catholic of sufficient calibre to begin? I would throw over all but energetic men. This you could not do, if the Bishops' names were *openly* given to it, for they would offend respectable or noble nobodies if they did not include them, but if it were voluntary, the choice would be your own.

Why should not half a dozen meet and consecrate their purpose by a religious act? — their object being to stir up their brethren on the duty of maintaining and impressing on the people of England the spiritual independence of the church, as a kingdom not of this world? or take a larger object, not to the exclusion of this, viz of bringing before the laity the position of the church in England and the method of defending it (which last clause brings in your Lectures and all controversial matter whatever) —

If you could get two or three good speakers, you could have public meetings in the principal towns. I know this could not be done without a vast deal of spirit, but surely you might find some young men who would carry it out. We were about 30 in age, when we began the Tracts — have you none of that age? only they must not speak treason. In particular localities, you might get great assistance for a meeting — e.g. I suppose I could get H Wilberforce to speak here, *if* there was a meeting. The *Oratory* ought to have nothing to do with politics — and *I* would not take any very ecclesiastical subject, but Fr Gordon and I would, I dare say, do something, if a sort of club was formed here — though we could not, with our engagements, dream of managing it. But indeed, I should like (as you say) the immediate object, of resistance to the Bill to drop, but the *occasion* to be seized for instructing the young Catholic mind in all Catholic matters. Gradually it would form into shape — each club or association would take a Patron Saint.

I am throwing things out as they occur to me — so you must take them only as stimulants to your imagination and judgment to think of something more practical. I am utterly in the dark as to the materials in various localities, but am going on the suggestion that they are to be found every where. If you thought it safer, you could *discard* the temporary, i.e. the political, side of the agitation — Deprived of that, it would be almost our Oratorium Parvum[1] — and might stand by itself associated to us, without a *Congregation*, or as the nucleus of a future Congregation. We have great indulgences attached to our Or. P.

Supposing meetings were once a month, consisting of a paper read etc. The Lecturer might be supplied from London or elsewhere, if he could not be found on the spot.

The public might be admitted (Catholics gratis — Protestants by tickets — or Catholics by tickets, Protestants on payment), and the meeting advertised. The Lecture would be preceded by a few prayers. *Boys* preach in the Or. Parv. at Rome; so it would be quite free for laymen to lecture.

How many good Lecturers and Speakers could you collect up and down the country? Northcote, Thompson, yourself, Simpson, etc etc. — The thing would be to keep it from being ecclesiastical, (in which case it would fall under the priests of the place, who, if dull, would ruin the whole) and get under ecclesiastical authority. The Cardinal surely would take up this *idea*, (if practical) — The first qualification of a member should be *energy*. If you got six men in London, six in Birmingham, six in Liverpool etc might you not do it? If you could not get six men of talent, they at least must be willing simply to put themselves under those who *had* talent, i.e. from London or elsewhere.

When you begin to work a scheme is the difficulty, I know. We should not get *one* lecturer (layman) here — and our members would be almost poor, though intelligent, men, yet I think they would be enough to make a beginning and to attract others to them.

Or the meetings might be simply confined to Catholics. The subjects might be such as these — 1. how to address oneself to Protestants in controversy — e.g. not sneaking, apologizing etc — 2. how to treat the question of *persecution* — 3 how to treat the question of *truth*. 4. how to deal with objections generally. etc etc. 5. how to bring an adversary to, to grapple, board, and make him strike — 6. how to deal with a Protestant — an unbeliever — an anglo-catholic etc.

Thank you for the information you have given me about the Camden Society — By the bye *Robert* Wilberforce, not Henry, was one of the Trio protesting about the Royal Supremacy. Why have you not mentioned Oakeley? will he not be hurt, if you don't say how ill the Bishop of London treated him — or at least how partially?[2]

Ever Yrs affly J H N

[1] i.e. laymen's confraternity, attached to each Congregation or house of the Oratory.

[2] The references are to the concluding article on the 'Rise, Progress, and Results of Puseyism' in the *Rambler* (March 1851), pp. 228–48, which described the history of

TO JOHN DUKE COLERIDGE

Oratory, Birmingham. Febr. 21, 1851.

My dear Sir,

I have seen a letter of yours addressed to Mr. Wilberforce, and I hope you will excuse the liberty I take in writing to you in consequence.[1]

I seem to myself to have some warrant to do so from the habitual feelings of reverence I have for your Father's name, from the interest I took in your brother as a co-son and co-heir with me of the Catholic Adam de Brome, Founder of Oriel,[2] and for the anxious commendation which a dear friend of mine has lately made of your name to me on his going out of the country.[3]

With those sentiments on my part it is impossible that I should be open to the charge of unkindness towards persons like yourself, which you indirectly convey in your letter to Mr. Wilberforce. In that letter you say things of me far more than I deserve — which you would not say if you knew me better. But as you kindly give me credit for excellence which is not mine, so, for the same reason that you do not know me, you fancy, if you will let me say so, something of uncharitableness to me, and that, founded, as it must be in me who have known the objects of it, on personal feeling, to which I do not plead guilty.

I would not say anything about it, except that I really think it perplexes, as well as distresses you, that you can only account in one way, and that a way which you are unwilling to adopt, for what you impute to me.

When then I use such words as 'hypocrisy,' pray believe me that I use them most advisedly, but not of persons like you. There are two sets of persons in your section of the Church of England. You spoke, I

the Camden Society and how it fostered Tractarianism at Cambridge. The mistake as to Wilberforce was corrected on p. 244, and Oakeley had in fact been mentioned earlier, pp. 160–1.

[1] John Duke Coleridge (1820–94), at Eton, matriculated at Balliol College in 1839, and a Fellow of Exeter College 1843–6, was a friend and admirer of Newman in those years. He remained a High Churchman, and was a frequent contributor to the *Guardian*, founded by the Tractarians who continued as Anglicans. He was now a barrister on the Western Circuit, being made Chief Justice of the Common Pleas in 1873, and in 1874 first Baron Coleridge. By then his friendship with Newman had been renewed and become close.

[2] J. D. Coleridge's father was Sir John Taylor Coleridge (1790–1876), whose second son, Henry James Coleridge (1822–93), at Eton and Trinity College, was elected a Fellow of Oriel in 1845. He was now curate at Alphington in Devon. He became a Catholic in 1852, and later a Jesuit, and a close friend of Newman.

[3] This was Edmund Bastard, like the Coleridges, a Devonshire man.

believe, of *objectors* to Mr. W. and you wrote to him to be able to answer *objectors*. These *objectors* are the *other* set of persons and I cannot help calling their general conduct, as manifested in a hundred similar instances, hypocritical. It is not like men in earnest.

But I will say now; those persons give a colour to the *whole* section or party, and their feeling is its characteristic as a section or body. I say this because it is the tone of your periodicals. A party must be judged by its periodicals, unless its members protest against them. For instance, I have in print shewn my difference of feeling, as regards us[1] Anglo-Catholics from the *Tablet*. On the other hand I cannot find that the *Guardian* is not your esteemed and honoured periodical, a paper, which Catholics may well regard with the most painful feelings, as hollow, unreal, and hypocritical. I do not use these words in declamation.

Every member of the section of the Church of England in question, even those to whom I impute no uncharitable feelings, cuts himself off from converts to the Catholic Church. In consequence such periodicals are the only channels of communication between those who were *friends*, publications which misrepresent converts to those they have left, and are a most painful expression of the feelings of those they have left, when they fall under the eyes of the converts. So entirely is the *Guardian* (and other papers) the medium of intercourse between persons who once knew each other well, that they (those papers) refuse to even advertise the works of those who have left the Church of England for the Catholic Church, which would throw light on their real feelings.[2]

Having thus cut themselves off from all real intercourse with those who were their brethren, they admit any number of idle rumours against them. What has pained myself more than anything else is this — that I suppose,[3] I am the *only* person to whom they have *not* assigned unworthy motives for his change of religion. This is a proceeding so unspeakably mean, that I do not know how to allude to it without saying more than I like to say.[4]

Besides this, every idle tale is taken up and propagated against them. The most improbable stories are believed by friends. Those who have had experience of the gossip of Evangelicals against them, while they were members of the Establishment, forthwith believe and propagate the like of them, now that they are Catholics. The Evangelicals had the excuse of not knowing the object of their attacks — the Anglo-Catholics,

---

[1] This word is inserted by an error, perhaps that of the copyist.

[2] Cf. letter of 27 Jan. 1850 to Mrs Bowden. Coleridge had perhaps heard something of the contents of Newman's letter of 28 Dec. 1850 to Henry Wilberforce.

[3] The copyist misread 'suffer.'

[4] Cf. letter of 1 Aug. 1846 to Henry Wilberforce.

not only have known them, but they have known and laughed at the absurdity of the charges which Evangelicals brought against them. And why all this ungenerousness and unreasonableness? To find some *plea* for their own remaining apart from the Catholic Church.

This surely is want of sincerity, or hypocrisy. I use the word, not from personal feeling, as you imply, but from a feeling I do not know how to suppress; of disdain and disapprobation of such an exhibition.

I really think that it ought to be brought home to the parties in question — those who do not share in it should clear themselves of participation in it — and those who disapprove of such publications as the *Guardian* of which I know not how to speak, should shew they disapprove it.

Pray pardon, if I have seemed to speak harshly — that really is not my wish — though I have spoken seriously.

At all events believe me to feel the greatest interest in such as yourself, and to be

Yours very sincerely, John H. Newman

J. D. Coleridge, Esq.

TO ANTONY HUTCHISON

Oy Bm. Febr 21/51

My dear F Antony,

I will speak of the *site*, since that is the prominent point.[1]

First, I suppose, you cannot hope in so large a place as London to embrace on one spot all the points of attraction which an ideal Oratory might have. You must give up something or other. The rich, the law, medicine, the arts, literature, you cannot open a house for all of them. You must give up the West end, or the law, or art and science.

The plot of ground near Arundel street was admirable for lawyers and the medical schools — but it gave up the West end. I confess I did not think it would do for you, considering your existing connections, etc. I think *we*, who are less aristocratic, were likely to have taken it.

It seems then that you must resign yourselves, *I think*, to *several* Oratories in the Metropolis; and you must choose *whom* you will address, rich or intellectual.

[1] Hutchison wrote that a large chapel in Charlotte Street (now Palace Street), Pimlico, opposite the stables of Buckingham Palace, was for sale. The chapel had been built in 1776 by Dr Dodd, later hanged for forgery.

In Charlotte Street you would be the 'Westminster Oratory.' The site has great qualifications — the highest rank and influence is moored to the neighbourhood. Even if the Queen's palace became a Union Work house, the Houses of Parliament remain for ever. You have a very fair proportion of the fashion of the Metropolis, in spite of the objection of Belgravia's antipathy to the East — (which may have something in it —) you have Westminster Hall, and the Houses of Parliament close to you. You have the poor at your back. Moreover you *get* a place, which seems impossible in the neighbourhood of St James's. And the neighbourhood of the Palace is sure to be progressively improving. Perhaps all the horrid part of Westminster may, in the course of 10 years, when the Parliament Houses are finished, be another Belgravia. (Only beware of two things. 1. that you are not in a *back* street — in which case you have no position, e.g. as *we* have no position here — 2. that a new wide street does not sweep you away, just when you are taking possession)

However, I repeat, you cannot fix on this site without *giving up* a good deal. Except that London is so large, I should say it was rather in a *corner*, and the Parks decidedly cut you off from a good deal. It is not a central place — but I rely on Palace and Parliament improving what lies between them.

This is what strikes me at present — I will write again

Ever Yrs affly J H N

SATURDAY 22 FEBRUARY 1851   Mr S. Flanagan and his wife (*his bride*) here

TO T. F. KNOX

Saturday Febr 22/51

My dear F Francis

I send you the inclosed which I have received this morning, that you may see Miss B's state.

She has a notion that she is the *cause* of every priest she speaks to (so it seems to me) feeling wrongly towards her — which is very unpleasant, and which you must know. You must not be too kind to her

Ever Yours affly J H N

P.S.   Thank you for saying Mass for me. I am 50!

TO F. W. FABER

Oy Bm Febr 23/51

My dear F Wilfrid

As F Richard tells me he only writes as Secretary, I write to you, not to him. I said Mass for you all yesterday morning, and we are following you in your novena, and will do all we can to help you.[1]

I should have liked rather to have conversed (so to say) with F Richard or one of you than to have given my opinion at once, thinking some view would gradually have come out of it — but he seems to wish something distinct from me at once, so I write to you this letter.

1. As to the plan of letting the seats, somehow I do not think you would have St Philip's blessing upon it. I do not see my way to sympathise in it.

2. And there are many most serious objections to the third plan of throwing your properties together for a venture. (1) Could you do it consistently with your duty to keep your ordination titulus? — (2) What such new or greater inducements could you hold out elsewhere to a congregation, as could sufficiently relieve you? e.g. what could you offer them besides a larger church and more doors to enter by without an Irish channel?[2] A large church must be a barn, without internal decorations, which you could not afford — and would not attract them. (3) You have an existing house on your hands with an uncertainty of getting rid of it. If it costs near £600 a year, this represents something like £15.000, taking which from your joint properties leaves, I suppose, nothing for purchasing any new place at all. (4) Changes are bad in themselves without some very good reason, according to the proverb. I think you would lose in reputation by it, and reputation has a good deal to do in filling a new Chapel — It would give your enemies a great advantage. 'These men *cannot* remain quiet — no converts can etc' (5) You would lose all that has been laid out on King Wm [William] Street. The place is turned into a Community House with chapels, sacristy etc etc. and, even to let, must be turned back again — a double loss. This alone has

[1] Stanton wrote on 22 Feb. for advice on the financial plight of the London House, where money given privately by individual members seemed to be wasted, and where it had been decided 'there are to be no puddings, meat less frequently,' and asked Newman to send his reply to Faber. Faber also wrote on the same day that they were living on their members' capital, and asked whether they should let the seats in their chapel, or concentrate on the better class, or take the site near Buckingham Palace. The novena was about this last question.

[2] Faber wrote that 'our tribune people say they can no longer force their way through the crowd of Irish at the lobby.'

struck me under this head — that, if Capes's plan of lectures answered, it might be made a Catholic Lecture Shop; but query. could you not as it is, contrive to turn a penny in this way by letting it to him two or three hours a week? At least this is better than renting the seats.

As to the said renting, I should have asked this under plan 1. viz — would it be impossible to make them pay for *High* Mass — which would also keep the poor from the lobby at such times. This would lead, I suppose, to chairs instead of benches, but I don't see the harm of it.

3. For myself, I think the right and the manly thing is (*if you can*) to live within your present income, and (*if you can*) to cut down to it — and therefore I prefer the plan to which F. Richard's Number 2 points.

The House should support itself — the Chapel should support itself — the two funds should be separate and in different hands.

As to the Chapel, if people won't pay, they should not have. As it is, the Chapel, instead of supporting, *takes from* the Community. Cui bono? — You can give the Catholic public (1) a most decent and presentable room. (2) sermons and lectures the best in London. (3) functions the most exact and devotions the most spirited and kindling — (4) vestments certainly not inferior to those producible any where. This is your permanent capital. You give it all for nothing — you don't ask from your people any thing in return. Of course I ought to add the Confessional, but I speak of the external manifestations of the Chapel.

What you ask your people for is. 1. rent of chapel — 2. lighting. 3. altar candles 4. wine 5 hire of organ. 6. organist. 7 choir. 8. washing 9. new linen, incense etc. Of these rent, lighting, wine, hire of organ, washing, incense, are fixed quantities — It is hard indeed if the offertory does not cover them. But altar candles, organist, choir, are variable, and should vary with the excess of the offertory above the fixed. Your *strength* does not lie in them, but in yourselves, in your preaching and confessing — You *give* your people *yourselves* — it is hard they won't pay for extras — but if they won't pay the extra two pence, they ought not to have its worth.

What is the good of a crack choir bringing together a large congregation, if the said congregation won't pay for their amusement?

It seems to me unlucky you cannot get any one like Capes or Burns to hit it off with you, who might drill an amateur, unprofessional choir, or one semi-such.

Not a penny for the chapel should come from the House. And if the chapel can't be made to support itself, then all I am saying is nothing to the purpose, and I must think the whole matter over again.

Next as to the House, — here of course I shall be at once taking liberties and making failures, for I am talking of what *I do not know*, both as to expences and receipts.

But I put it thus

Dr

20 men at £33 a head, (which is our average for 1 board 2 washing 3 lighting 4 fuel 5 journeys 6 clothing 7 sundries, deducting rent and taxes.)	660.	0.	0
Rent and Taxes (deducting £50 charged on chapel	550.	0.	0
	1210.	0.	0

Cr

Ward	400.	0.	0
1 Father	300.	0.	0
1 Father	100.	0.	0
8, say 7 Fathers at £55 each (viz Francis, Alban, John, Edward, James, Raphael, George, Camillus)	385.	0.	0
Sums at present collected for choir, with leave of donors transferred	100.	0.	0
occasional gifts	50.	0.	0
	1335.	0.	0

Now whether I have exaggerated capabilities or no, and I dare say I have, I should like the expences met in this way, and let us see how things stand, or what deficit.

I should have added, as regards the chapel, that your offertory is (say) £300 a year. Our own expences, exclusive of rent, are £140. Add £50 for superiority of choir — and you have £100 left for rent, whereas I have supposed only £50 taken from the House rent.

Again, tho' I have made mistakes, yet I have not taken into account various items, when there is a *bona fide* wish to give everything to the House. After all allowances for pocket money etc something ought to come from the Mass money. I cannot but think that small gifts would mount up to a tolerable sum (I have put them at £50 overleaf.) e.g. in our first year our gifts (*exclusive* of [Charles Samuel] Stokes's annual donation) came to £76. Last year to £40, and would have been more, had we agitated about it at the end of the year. I have supposed the Arundels to give nothing, nor Fullertons nor Lewis, Zulueta etc.

I should add that if individual members of the Congregation ⟨Community⟩ contributed large sums, as I am supposing, they ought to contribute them only *quarterly* — and ought to be allowed to see the state of accounts so far, as to be sure the House is keeping within bounds. I don't want their full sum sucked and expended in a month or two.

In like manner you must not take Ward's money except *quarterly*.

And if possible, don't let a penny go from the House to the Chapel, or from the Chapel to the House

Ever Yours affly J H N

P.S.   Let me hear from you. This letter of course supersedes what I wrote to F Antony about the Pimlico Chapel.

Tell F Bernard I have not forgot his letter, but have had so many to write that I beg his forbearance.

TO EDWARD LUMLEY [?][1]

Oratory, Birmingham Febr 24 1851

Dear Sir,

Mr Robertson's name stands so high, that I need some apology for what I am going to say, yet I think it best to state simply what struck me after reading your and his letters.

It seems to me most extremely unlikely that through any recommendation of mine, or under any circumstances, Mr Burns will take the poem. I suppose he hardly undertakes any speculation now — I have offered him several works of my own, and he has not taken them. Since then I cannot recommend to him my own with success, I do not expect to be able to persuade him to take the work of any one else.

This answer seems to me quite decisive as far as any influence of mine goes — Nor do I think that Mr Burns would do so under any circumstances. He has, as you know, entered far more into the line of importing foreign books, and articles of devotion, and supplying the ceremonial of worship, than into that of a publisher. He is not likely to engage in any thing where there is a risk.

I do not know then why I should ask to see Mr Robertson's Poem, except for the pleasure of reading what, I know well, would be worth a careful perusal. Such a perusal however, I could not promise myself with my existing occupations, which fill each day, as it comes. I should

---

[1] The diary shows that Newman wrote to Lumley the publisher on this day. James Burton Robertson (1800–77), historian, translator of Schlegel and Möhler, and a friend of Lamennais, wanted a publisher for his poem: perhaps *The Prophet Enoch; or The Sons of God and the Sons of Men*, London 1859. In 1854 Newman appointed him professor of Geography and Modern History at the Catholic University in Dublin, where he remained for the rest of his life.

not like merely to cast my eye over it and do no more. It would be satisfactory neither to him nor to me. If, however, you think it necessary, perhaps you would kindly send me down one canto — but I do not expect I could be of service to him.

I am, Dear Sir, Yours faithfully

John H Newman   Congr. Orat.[1]

TO F. W. FABER

Bm. Oratory Febr 25/51

My dear F Wilfrid

Till F Joseph returns, I can't go — Any how I can't move till *Friday*: if he is back then and all is well, I will come up to you on that day.

I do not *at all* approve of your leaving off your usual quantity of meat — nor can it be necessary. *We* have meat twice a day. Our butcher's bills come to about £2 a week. All our board, (taking in grocer,) our coals, and our washing, comes to the sum I gave you £33 per head. You ought to do nearly the same; your coals and washing, are, I know, dearer. Then as to clothes, our account is £40 about, which added to £660 makes £700, for 20 or 21 persons — whereas your total for 23, *without* coals, is 1105   0   0.

Or to take it more exactly

Bm [Birmingham]				London			
Board — coals	660.	0.	0	Board and clothing	1105.	0.	0
lighting —	20.	0.	0	lighting, coals.	50.	0.	0
clothing	40.	0.	0	23 —	1155	0	0
20 or 21	720	0	0	or £50 a head			

or £36 or £34 a head

It seems to me there must be some great mistake here in your economy.

I do not know how many the £110 pocket money is divided among, but it seems very great, considering clothes are separately accounted for.

Interest on debt, I suppose, goes to members of the body, and therefore ought not to be *lost* to the year's account.

I write in a hurry. Since I began, a letter has come from F Joseph — he is not yet well, and has to stay — how long I don't know — As you may think, it makes him very impatient

Ever Yours affly J H N

[1] For the letter to J. D. Dalgairns of Feb. 24/51 see below p. 495.

TO ANTONY HUTCHISON

Oratory Bm Febr 25/51

My dear F Antony

If I can, I will come up to you — but it depends on F Joseph, whose state of health rather annoys me.

Since I wrote to you, I have studied F Richard's letter, which has made me alter my views about Pimlico Chapel. I think you *can't* do it. On the other hand, you are getting known where you are — You are mentioned in the House. Your present *place* is becoming a position. I think you must not change. A rolling stone gathers no moss.

There is one thing which I observed in the account of expences and receipts, which F Wilfrid sent me — viz that he has not reckoned on your and F Richard's money. Of course you are not bound to give it, but under circumstances, and considering the words of the Rule, I suppose he might have set it down, though from delicacy he has not done so.[1]

I can easily understand one difficulty you may have in letting it go into the common fund — it seems to be absorbed there, and to go for nothing. This I think might be prevented in several ways. You might give it quarterly, and see what the state of account is for the foregoing quarter, before you gave for the next. Or you might give certain articles — e.g. *our* butcher's bill is about £2 a week — you might calculate its yearly expence, and let the butcher's bills be sent to you, as the beer bills go to Lady Arundel. And so with other bills.

I write in a hurry, as I am just going to Lecture

Ever Yours affly J H N

TO RICHARD STANTON

Oy Bm Febr 25/51

My dear F Richard

(Private)   I have written to F Antony, on an *omission* in F Wilfrid's statement — viz he has not reckoned on your and F Antony's money,

---

[1] Decretum LXVII lays down that Oratorians must spend their income each year in good works, and not hoard, 'ne quis scilicet e nostra Congregatione ullam curam ponet in divitiis parandis; imo vero ex censu pro suis cuique facultatibus in commune commodum Congregationis libere conferendum est.' *Instituta Congregationis Anglicae Oratorii S. Philippi Nerii*, Rome 1847, p. 29.

from delicacy. Now unless the House has the said monies, it will ship-
wreck. I felt the difficulty you suggested, and tried to remedy it in my
letter to F Wilfrid — there are other ways of meeting it too. But the
House can't do without you and F. Antony.

You see, I fancy there may be something in the background which I
do not know. Is F Antony unwilling? You must persuade him, if so.

I am afraid the Choir must be done [given?] up, tho' it cant be for
half a year. A *subscription* for it won't meet the difficulty — for it is
really taking the money from the *House*. First make ends meet in the
House, and then accept subscriptions for the Choir.

Is it impossible to give paid tickets for *high mass — 3 o'clock benediction?* — which would at once bring you money, and exclude the poor.

Ever Yours affly J H N

WEDNESDAY 26 FEBRUARY 1851 Penny here[1] McMullen here
THURSDAY 27 FEBRUARY F Lans here.

TO F. W. FABER

Febr 27/51

My dear F W

I did not know, more than you, when I wrote, whether I could go
to town on Friday, since F Joseph's movements are so uncertain.

I will try to come on Sunday, if the trains allow, but I can't tell, till
I hear from him this evening, as I hope to do. I send up some of our
Butcher's bills of last year. We have meat *twice* a day.

Ever Yrs affly J H N
(*Turn over*)

P.S. I am sorry to say I have burnt all the Butcher's weekly bills. I
can but give the sums, and the price of meat.

Oct. 8. Butcher 5 weeks			Butcher	2. 17. 11
bills	8. 16. 10		Butcher 3 weeks	
Butcher	3. 7. 2		bills	6. 11. 9
Butcher	1. 14. 5½		Butcher 4 weeks	4. 19. 1

Beef is /6 mutton /6½ veal /6½ pork about the same 6 PM. A bad letter
from F Joseph — he does not come till Monday — I certainly can't

---

[1] He was now working as a priest at Leamington.

come to you tomorrow. Before I close, I will look at a Train paper as to Sunday.

If all is well, I will start for London by the 9.5. morning train on Sunday, getting to you by 1.15.

TO J. SPENCER NORTHCOTE

Oratory Birmingham Febr 28. 1851

My dear Northcote

In consequence of your former letter, on consideration, I have quite come to your opinion. I don't think the subject you ask about would do for your Tracts. It would run out, if ever done, into an enormous length, and its separate portions would be too long for your Tracts. I think, as far as one article could do it, it will change their character.[1]

I like your Tracts very much, and have been going to write and tell you so. I have seen four of them; it is my fault I have not seen more.

So Neve is to be a white friar — I congratulate him, but I am truly sorry for the diocese. What will the Bishops do, if their clergy leave them? Why, they must form seminaries. Seminaries are more wanted than Sees; for you cannot fill Sees except from Seminaries. I suppose Neve will become one of those stern old fellows, who keep their rule — I hear there is to be a Dominican House of this character in every Province, according to the new reform.[2]

G. Ryder would do something for your Tracts, if you choose to employ him.

Yours affectly in Xt   John H Newman   Congr. Orat.

SATURDAY 1 MARCH 1851   F Joseph returned

SUNDAY 2 MARCH   went to Town

MONDAY 3 MARCH   called on Cardinal and Allies

TUESDAY 4 MARCH   returned to Birmingham   Mr Molloy came

THURSDAY 6 MARCH   Mr Molloy went

[1] See letter of 4 Dec. 1850 to Northcote.

[2] With the appointment of Vincent Jandel as Master General in 1850, the revival of the Dominicans (Blackfriars) gathered momentum. Neve must have altered his purpose, since in June 1852 he was appointed one of the first canons of the Diocese of Clifton.

TO RICHARD STANTON

Oy Bm March 6/51

My dear F R

In a great hurry.

A Mr Harrison, a schoolfellow of yours, a Manx-man a brother in law of W. Greswell, a lawyer, a convert, aged about 26, wishes to become a Brummagem Oratorian. Can you tell me any thing about him?[1]

Ever Yours affly J H N

TO AN UNKNOWN CORRESPONDENT

Oratory Birmingham March 9. 1851

Dear Sir

I wish I had something more valuable to contribute to the Collection you are making for the Brighton Dispensary, than the mere expression of my good will, which you have done me the honor to think worthy of your acceptance.

I am, Dear Sir, Yours faithfully

John H Newman   Congr. Orat.

TO MRS J. W. BOWDEN

Oratory Bm March 10/51

My dear Mrs Bowden

I have constantly been wishing to write to you, especially on last 21st, when you wrote to me, but have never you see, found time. Political events are most curious here — you will read about them — so [I] need not write — We are not quite out of the wood yet — however, whatever comes, so far is certain, that Lord John has struck his foot against a rock and has fallen. A sunken rock, for they did not believe so insignificant a thing as British Catholicism would harm them — but it has shivered them — and, as the Times truly but blindly says,

---

[1] Stanton replied that Charles Harrison came from Cheshire, and had been converted before Newman, by a lady who taught him French or Italian. Nothing came of the proposal that he should join the Oratory. William Greswell was a Fellow of Balliol College, 1818–38, and then Rector of Kilve, Somerset, until his death in 1876.

they have gone down in a smooth sea and under a smiling heaven. They are in again, to their own disgrace; like slaves, obliged to finish their own set work, and drink their own brewing. We do not know what is before us — but the past is past, and the Whigs have caught it.[1] The Queen thought she could lord it over our supremacy [sic], as she lorded it over the poor Anglican Church last year, and the difference is such as, I think, must strike Anglicans themselves.[2]

Thank you for your anxiety about me — Several things which have happened are unpleasant — but one can't be sorry for them. Nothing brings out more strongly that we are a Congregation, have an idea, and need a vocation to be Oratorians, than individuals leaving us. And if some go, others come. It is remarkable that the two Roman Fathers, who have gone, are those who were not with me at Littlemore.[3] The most trying loss has been that of the London *Elton* lay brothers — but London is so very trying a place for country youths, that one can't be altogether surprised.

Our house is rising at Edgbaston — we have been able to build all through the winter. It is quite frightful, the space of ground it covers. We have not yet received the plans of St Martino.[4]

I don't suppose you recollect or knew Br Aloysius — I fear he is dying — just now he is at St Leonard's under Dr Duke; but he will soon return to us. It is consumption. F John Cooke's death was expected when he came to us; he came to die in the Oratory. Aloysius will be great loss — he is the only saintly brother or father we have among us; and he really is that.

I think St Philip has got hold of Birmingham — else, I cannot account for its being one of the few places which have resisted the

[1] The Ecclesiastical Titles Bill passed its first reading on 14 Feb., but Lord John Russell's prestige sank, owing to his attempt to reconcile his liberal principles with the satisfaction he was now giving to the Protestant feeling, which he had encouraged. His Government suffered a minor defeat on 20 Feb. and resigned, but no one would take their place, since that involved continuing with the Ecclesiastical Titles Bill, demanded by popular clamour. On 3 March, Lord John Russell and his colleagues were obliged to resume office, and carry through the Bill of which they were ashamed.

[2] The Queen had lorded it over the Anglican Church in the Gorham case. Although in her Speech at the opening of Parliament on 4 Feb. Queen Victoria was made to speak of 'my resolution to maintain the rights of my crown and the independence of the nation,' her letters show that she did not want Catholics ill treated, but reserved her wrath for the 'Puseyites.'   [3] i.e. Coffin and Penny.

[4] Mrs Bowden was sending Newman the plans of this Roman church, which he wished to be the model of the church of the Oratory at Edgbaston. Owing to the generous contributions to the expenses of the Achilli trial, Newman did not feel justified in making further appeals, and contented himself with a temporary church. After his death, the present church of the Birmingham Oratory was built, as his memorial, on the lines of San Martino ai Monti.

No-popery agitation. Hitherto it has resisted every attempt, though the Exeter Hall party has had down *in succession* Mc Neile, Hobart Seymour, Lord Roden, Dr Cumming, and that great man, I forget his name, a Canon and preacher of Manchester.[1]

You may fancy how the chance of Henry being moved delighted me. It took me quite by surprise — I did not know you had met him at Paris.[2]

As to the rumour of my being a Bishop, it is quite premature; and since, as I trust, it is not to be at present, there is a hope it will never be.

Love to the children and believe me, Ever yours affecty

John H Newman   Congr. Orat.[3]

TO J. D. DALGAIRNS

March 10/51

My Dear F Bernard,

I recollect Father de Montéson well. And have written to thank him for the book he has sent me. If you put it aside, it may come by Aloysius. I inclose an answer to the good Father, for I suppose you are writing at once, from what you say, to M. Gondon. I wrote to him myself lately. You, perhaps, can give him a rowing better than I.

Say every thing kind from me to F Rossi. I have just heard from the Oratorians of Chioggia wishing to cultivate relations.

I think you will find something on a subject you once spoke to me about in John xxii's matter in Benedict the xii's treatise in Raynaldi ann. 1333 59–69 ⟨viz the vision of the humanity of our Lord.⟩[4]

Ever Yours affectionately, J H N.

[1] Hugh McNeile (1795–1879), at this time a Canon of Chester, was an Evangelical, strongly opposed to Catholics. Michael Hobart Seymour (1800–74) was the secretary of the Reformation Society. Robert Jocelyn, third Earl of Roden (1788–1870), was one of the chief members, and later Grand Master, of the Orange Society. John Cumming (1807–81), the Minister at the Presbyterian Church in Covent Garden, was one of the leading agitators against 'papal aggression.' The preacher from Manchester was Hugh Stowell (1799–1865), one of the Evangelical leaders, and incumbent of Christ Church, Salford. 'He was for ever denouncing the "errors of popery."' *DNB*.

[2] Henry Bowden became a Catholic in 1852.

[3] Mrs Bowden was still at Malta, where she had spent the winter for the sake of her children's health. She replied from there on 10 April, saying how delicate John Bowden still was '. . . I know not what he is to do in London—or indeed Charles either, but I hope something will arise to help us.' On this letter Newman wrote long after 'N B If London did not suit the health of either brother, *what* was the obstacle in choosing Edgbaston?'

[4] *Annales Ecclesiastici ab anno MCXCVIII ubi desinit Cardinalis Baronius, Auctore Odorico Raynaldo Congregationis Oratorii Presbytero.* In the Lucca edition (1750),

TO T. F. KNOX

Oy Bm March 10/51

My dear F Francis,

I advised Miss B. to get some steady work, to keep her from writing and thinking. Her excuse is that she steals time from *sleep and meals* — i.e. she sits up half the night. If so, she will soon become mad.

Could she not be set on gaining indulgences — e.g Saying the Stations ⟨Via Crucis⟩, keeping Novenas etc; in fact filling up her vacant time from the Raccolta? That would turn her mental activity to account.

Yrs affly J H N

P S.   Has John [Bowden] sent any box containing drawings of St Martino for me?

TO FORTUNAT DE MONTÉZON, S.J.

Oratory, Birmingham March 10. 1851

My dear Reverend Father,

I do not forget the visit you so kindly paid us here, or the awkward figure I cut by not being able to speak a word of French to you, who conversed in so interesting a strain to us in that language.[1] I make little apology for writing to you in English now — for the Society is of all languages, truly Catholic, and you doubtless have at your elbow Fathers who understand it very well, even if you cannot make out what I am writing yourself.

I prize very much the book you have sent me.[2] It is truly a precious gift. I have long wished to have it — it relates to a most deeply interesting subject, and a most glorious one for your great Society. Give my most respectful thanks to M. Crétineau Joly — assure him of the esteem in which I hold his name, and of the service which his learned book has rendered to the cause of truth and of Holy Church. I do not forget the share you have had in it.[3]

Vol. v, pp. 575–81. The treatise is on the knowledge of the blessed before the resurrection of the body.   [1] See the diary for 23 Aug. 1850.

[2] *Clément XIV et les Jésuites*, by J. Crétineau-Joly, 2nd ed. Paris 1848. On the reverse of the title-page of the copy in question is written, 'A Monseigneur Newman hommage respectueux de l'auteur J Crétineau Joly paris 20 février 1851.'

[3] The Jesuits helped Crétineau-Joly with his book, which was attacked by Theiner and then defended by de Ravignan. It was thought to reflect covertly on Pius IX. See letter of 19 March to Stanton, and also that of 15 Sept. 1847 to Mrs John Mozley.

I could not help smiling at the notions which have got abroad about me from your Reverence's address. I am no Monseigneur, but a humble priest of St Philip, a great Master, whose scholar and son I hope to be for such years as I have still to live and who, I trust, will not forget me in the hour of death.

Meanwhile, give me your good prayers, my dear Father, that, whether I live or die, I may be found a worthy disciple of his school and believe me, With profound respect, Yours very truly in Xt

John H Newman, Congr. Orat.

The Reverend Father de Montézon, S.J.

TO HENRY WILBERFORCE

March 11. 1851.

William Anderdon is *likely*, I think, to join the Jesuits. I have not heard from him, since he was a Catholic.

As to my doctrine, C. substitutes 'utter' for 'ultimate.'[1] It is no absurdity to say that a man is in God's favour and in advanced holiness, yet may ultimately fall away; but it is (not 'horribly false,' but) a contradiction in terms to say that he is all this, *yet* at the time in utter damnation.

But it suggests another thought, which is brought home to me again and again. He does not hold the utter, infinite separation between the Creator and the creature; but, like the elder brother in the Parable, or the Pharisee, thinks that we have claims on God, and are something more than what grace makes us. I suspect this is at the bottom of a vast deal of Puseyism. It is a curious fact that my original Evangelical-Calvinistic bias has kept me personally (whatever I may have *written*) from feeling the force of this temptation; but I find instances continually of minds rising up in pride, and exclaiming, or being tempted to exclaim against the injustice of the Catholic system.

If we once realize an eternal self-dependent God, from whom an impassible gulf separates all creatures, all mysteries vanish ⟨are as nought⟩. If C. would meditate for a year on this great Sight, this Allglorious, Ecstatic, though most awful Vision, he would be a Catholic. O my Lord, keep me to the thought of Thee, and I am safe.

[1] C. is presumably J. D. Coleridge. See letter of 21 Feb. Newman's doctrine is that of *Mix.*, especially the sermon on 'Perseverance is Grace.'

235

C. is in the way to be a liberal. I wonder whether he holds eternal punishment.

TO J. M. CAPES

Oy. Bm March 12/51

My dear Capes,

Our Bishop spoke about your Lectures, but he might think I had something to do with them. He is a cautious man, and rather looks to what people will say. I should doubt if he liked them in his heart, at least at present. He said you were 'all safe, because you had the Cardinal with you.' I think he did not like it being in Chapel, nor the applauding.[1] I am very glad you are invited to Liverpool, and I hope you will accept the invitation. See, however, that it is not against the feelings of the *majority* of the Priests there.

Did *you* send me the Westminster? I suppose Ward bought a new one and sent it.[2]

March 19. I am very much concerned about Mrs Capes's eyes — and have put her name on our private prayer list. I wish you joy sincerely. I suppose you will think you have got a victory if you only have to budge from the Chapels. Your articles are very interesting — the Novel is very clever and good — but it will be too short.[3]

I wish some one or other would take in hand the organization of the London Catholics. It is miserable at present — A freemason's Hall meeting, and the speakers *Irish* — a most Irish mode of showing off the London Catholics.[4] Are there no lawyers who can drill them? The Bishops cannot do any thing effectively, without a powerful body of laity to back them. In Ireland they can do any thing just for this reason

Ever Yrs affly J H N

[1] There was criticism of the lectures Capes was organising, on the ground that they were by laymen, and in chapels, where there was applause. John Kyne, the priest at Clerkenwell, where Capes was the lecturer, wrote to defend the 'lay preaching,' in the *Tablet*, XII (1 and 15 March). See also the *Rambler*, VII (April 1850), pp. 366–70, and letters of 6 and 10 April to Capes, below.

[2] See letter of 9 Feb. to Capes.

[3] The *Rambler* for April contained the fourth instalment of a novel 'Passion, Love, and Rest; or the Autobiography of Basil Morley.' There was also a moving account of the Irish poor in London, and three long reviews, 'The Church and the Antiquarians,' 'B. Ippolito Galantini, the Apostolic Silk-Weaver,' and 'Lord Holland's Foreign Reminiscences.'

[4] There had been a meeting at the Freemasons' Hall, on 10 March, to petition Parliament against the Ecclesiastical Titles Bill, at which the chief speeches had been made by Irishmen.

TO J. SPENCER NORTHCOTE

Oratory, Bm. March 19/51

My dear Northcote

I wish you had mentioned the particular objection which you or your brother Editor takes to the extract you sent me.[1] I have read it carefully twice — and I do not discover anything to find fault with — Whether it is 'the best and most profitable way' of treating the subject, I really cannot say, but I do not know to the contrary — and it seems to me good and profitable.

The doctrine of the passage is, that the honor paid to the Image passes on to the Prototype — which I suppose is true.

Write to me again, if I have overlooked the point

Yours affectly in Xt   John H Newman   Congr. Orat.

TO RICHARD STANTON

Oy Bm 19 March 1851

My dear F R

Thanks for your hint about Cretineau Jolly — I hope I am safe. F Montéson told me when here, he was commissioned (I think) by the F General Jesuits [sic] *to correct the work*; and the second Edition which he sent me is authentic and authorized.[2]

As to the office, it is what we have wished here some time — i.e. *devotions* to St Ph's [Philip's] heart. Nothing can be better than an office — if they will grant it.[3] The objections to the Ante vigil is that it may coincide with May 26 — and is any how likely to be close upon it. E.g. from 1851 to 1868 we have the Ante-vigil on June 2, May 25. 9. 29.

[1] Newman deals with this question, which concerned one of the *Clifton Tracts*, in his letter of 25 March.

[2] Stanton wrote on 11 March, 'There is a report that M. Chretineau Jolie has sent you his book on Clement XIV, because you told Père Monteson . . . that you liked it.' See letter of 10 March to de Montézon.

[3] Stanton asked Newman to write an office, and suggested keeping the feast on the day before the Vigil of Pentecost. St Philip's intense devotion to the Holy Spirit was closely connected with bodily symptoms. When he was praying in the catacombs at Pentecost 1544 he felt his heart expand, in a way that caused a permanent swelling and left him subject to continual palpitations. It was found after his death that two of his ribs had been broken and forced outwards. See Louis Ponnelle and Louis Bordet, *St. Philip Neri and the Roman Society of his Times*, English translation, London 1932, pp. 127–31.

21. June 8. May 25. 17. June 6. May 22. 13. June 2. May 18. June 7. May 29. that is, calculating on the variation of Easter, you could not hit on a day which would on the average so synchronize with May 26. Still I don't deny it is in itself on the right day, and I can't think of another.

As to making the office, let us all contribute what we can — I will try to get Nicholas and Edward to attempt hymns. Your Father Superior Father Francis and others could do so too — then let your F Superior take the symbola and make an office out of them — and then I and others will criticize

Ever Yrs affly J H N

P S Can Hope's disgust and that of others arise from such displays as James's life of St J Colombino? Ask F Wilfrid about this. He seemed to me casting pearls before swine, and stumbling stones before seekers if 'tis true what's said.[1]

TO GEORGE RYDER

Ory. B. March 21/51

My dearest George,

I do not forget this season.[2] I shall say a mass for your intention to-morrow morning. I must put it off some days if I wait for a black Mass.

All good be with you and yours. As to composition, I would rather speak to you than write. I hope every thing came right about the boxes — we did our part with great exactness.

I have no news to tell you. Tell the boys I fear we shall lose Aloysius, though not immediately — he is at St Leonard's. Our new house is rising. It will be fit for habitation on Michaelmas day — but I don't suppose we shall think it prudent to inhabit it till this time year

Ever Yrs affly J H N

[1] James Hope had expressed to W. G. Ward a strong dislike of the London Oratory, which Newman was inclined to attribute to a sermon of James Rowe, relating extravagant miracles in the life of Blessed John Colombini. See letter of 26 March to Faber.
[2] Ryder's wife died on 21 March 1850.

TO HENRY WILBERFORCE

Oy Bm March 23/51

Charissime

I shall not write Miss M. a word more — I have not time to tell you why. I have *told* her 'her general' and particular 'duty already.'[1]

The other letters are very interesting indeed. I should like much to see you — but after Easter is a better time, and I shall be more ready for you. ⌐I am writing on Persecution, and when I have done, I should like your judgment on what I have written.

It is *cruel* that so many able men are doing *nothing* — but our Lord has some purpose — perhaps he wishes you all to be longer in the Church before he uses you.⌐ If you wanted a *work*, for which there are ample and most interesting materials, there is an important one, which, had I ever so much time I should not be tempted with, and which I could hardly recommend to *you*, viz a life of Dr Milner. It ought to be done by an old Catholic — but there is none to be found equal to it.[2]

⌐It seems to me pretty plain I shall be left quiet here for some time, unless some very strange turn up took place. I have the matter of 5 or 6 volumes in my head — but *composition* is the labour — These Lectures on Persecution date from December last at latest — yet I have not written the second yet!⌐ [[NB. They came to nothing]]

Ever Yrs affectly J H N

P.S. Father Joseph said Mass on Friday, I yesterday for dear Sophia [Ryder].

P.S. I am rather puzzled at dear Robert's question. He ends the 2nd of his two points with a quotation of Andrewes's against Bellarmine, which does not give promise that the statement he makes is Catholic; (viz that Xt's presence is not local.) — B. (I think) says it is both local and with outline: and whether this be taken or not, *substance*, tho' not material, implies more than energy. I suppose the Catholic doctrine is, that nothing is, but is a thing or reality. What we see then, if more than an optical delusion, must be a *thing*, of which what we see cannot be more than the accidents, for they change. They are but tokens of what is not seen, or the substance. Whether we ever can analyse down to the

---

[1] This probably refers to Miss Mason, a convert at St Leonards.

[2] John Milner (1752–1826), zealous Catholic apologist and Vicar Apostolic of the Midland District from 1803, was an extreme ultramontane, who aroused the opposition of many of the English clergy and laity. F. C. Husenbeth's *The Life of John Milner* was published in Dublin in 1862.

substance, or make it cognizable to the senses, I cannot tell; (I suppose *not* from the nature of the case) but a substance or thing there must be, to which what we see does but belong, but is not identical. This substance is changed into the Body of Christ in the consecration of the Eucharist. Give him my love when you write.[1]

J H N.

TUESDAY 25 MARCH 1851 Mr Flanagan here Bathurst admitted *novice* to first probation and year of first probation.

TO J. SPENCER NORTHCOTE

Oratory Bm March 25/51

My dear Northcote

I fear I shall not send you a satisfactory answer on so difficult a question. Indeed I expect it falls under a very large subject, which requires much consideration to settle duly.

It would seem as if the Church suffered the mind to expatiate in devotion and imagination, as it will — but then when it comes to reflect on these exercises in the way of reason and science, it is forced to speak guardedly and by rule, and *it interprets* devotional feeling its own way, as Dr Johnson interpreted for Goldsmith Goldsmith's poetry.[2]

Thus in a parallel case — Theology tells us that faith is *more certain* than demonstration — this is a theological truth — it *must* be true — but it is not deduced from experiment, from testimony, from feeling. *A man's consciousness does not attest it.*

So again, 'Mites fac et castos'[3] — this is the natural outpouring of the mind. Yet, when that same mind, which has so relieved itself, comes to consider what it has said, it reflects 'Well, after all, I don't mean that our Lady is the *giver* of grace, I know it comes from God alone, yet somehow I can't help so expressing myself.'

And so again, I conceive the image is put as a sort of veil or rather simulachrum (as the Epicureans, I think, say) flying or steaming off from the real form of Christ, and, according as you take it, you may either say (according to the exploded opinion) 'I don't worship the image *at all*, my eyes pass on to that I do not see thro' that I do see —'

[1] Robert Isaac Wilberforce published his *The Doctrine of the Holy Eucharist* in 1853.
[2] Boswell's *Life of Johnson*, ed. Birkben Hill, III, London 1950, p. 253.
[3] 'Make us gentle and chaste,' words addressed to our Lady in the hymn 'Ave maris stella.'

or 'I *identify* it with the reality, I see the reality in it, I worship the reality in it, I worship what is unseen *in* what is seen or *through* what is seen — that is, I worship the seen as the visible form of what is unseen, and therefore with λατρεία.' Then theology comes, and makes its calm distinction — 'Yes, you worship it with λατρεία, but *improprié*, as your own words go to show.' Or in other words λατρεία, as applied to images, is a devotional word, not a theological, controversial, didactic, or homiletic.

Such is the theological view of St Thomas — but it is not de fide — accordingly Bellarmine thinks it fair to analyze the devotional act in another, and (to my mind) less natural and real way. If I understand him, he *separates* the image from the Archetype, as two distinct things — and says that an image is to be honored as a *Bible*, from its deductive, not immediate, relation to the Archetype. (I say all this under correction) This seems to me unnatural, for it does not do justice to the devotional feeling, or adequately analyze it — however I can *assent* to it, tho' I like St Thomas's analysis better — yet withal, assenting to so great an authority as Bellarmine that it is better not to *teach* the ascription of λατρεία to images of our Lord, since it is but given in *devotion*, *improprié*.

March 26. As to the Paper you sent me[1] I looked carefully if I could detect Bellarminism, which I don't like — but I could not. I took the argument of the writer to be this — '*Adoring the Cross* — that's your objection is it? well, do you object to the *word* or to the *thing*? — to what we say and do, or to what we think? If to the *word*, it is what is applied to almost the usages of civil society, as when Abraham adored the sons of Heth. If it is the thing, it is not the wood we adore, but Him whom we see in it.'

I am only giving you my *impression* of what you sent me. As to the sense of the word 'Adoratio' in the Office for Good Friday, I should answer that it was used in the sense of λατρεία *but improprié* — (I *can't* understand here Bellarmine's view, because no one, in adoring, even wishes to think of the material image, whether beautiful or plain, gold or ivory, Spanish or Italian, but of *Christ*) And therefore I think in a penny Tract it *might* be called 'improper latria,' but as this would be *perfectly unintelligible*, as much as if you spoke of 'consubstantial,' 'circumincession,' 'communicatio idiomatum,' or 'concomitancy,' you must not use the word at all.

We will not forget Mrs Northcote — I am much concerned at what you say.[2]

---

[1] See letter of 19 March.
[2] Her health was failing. She died on 3 June 1853.

I hope Dr Hendren takes the Times easy.[1] When will men in authority learn that Newspapers are not to be recognized as accusers and judges of their religious responsibilities? What would be thought of a prime minister explaining to the Times that a certain appointment was not a job? It was so easy, if he must speak, to have said 'As the case is taken into the Court of Chancery, Dr H may dispense with any explanations of the charges brought against the Convent.'

I think I shall take advantage of your offer to send you a letter or two for persons in Rome

Yours most sincerely in Xt   John H Newman   Congr. Orat.

WEDNESDAY 26 MARCH 1851   Stanislas and Henry went into retreat

TO F. W. FABER

Oy Bm March 26/51

My dear F W

Do I understand that you have done for £60 a month, what you calculated would be £80? If so, it is a most important saving — enough to keep your choir. But one day does not make a summer — and you must watch each month, as it comes.

Thank you for your specimens of the Office. I suspect and trust that F Nicholas will do something — Can't you get F Francis to give a hymn? As far as you have done it, it seems to promise very well.

I did not write to F Antony about St Wilfrid's, because I had nothing to say. I return his letters. Dr Ullathorne has promised me Lord Shrewsbury's to you.

What James Hope said to Ward has been sticking in my throat — at last, what I heard James had said to your people about St John Col. [Colombini] seemed the *sort* of thing which would *account* for it. I mean, I find it so difficult to analyse *what* it is which offends people in you — for they *are* offended. I wrote a word to F Richard about it[2] —

---

[1] Augusta Talbot, a minor and heiress of £80,000, had been placed by her guardians, the Earl and Countess of Shrewsbury, in the Convent at Taunton. Her stepfather feared that she would become a nun, and her money go to the Convent, and petitioned the House of Commons to prevent this. The case was taken into the Court of Chancery. *The Times* had violent leading articles on the subject on 17 and 21 March, on which day also appeared a long defensive letter from Bishop Hendren of Clifton, explaining how completely free Miss Talbot was. On 22 July 1851 she married Lord Edward Fitzalan Howard, brother of the Earl of Arundel. She died in 1862.

[2] In the letter of 19 March.

but since then a new light has been thrown upon the view taken of that discourse. Protestants don't believe you CAN believe such miracles — so that they at once charge you with hypocrisy. They would as lieve believe an educated man to believe in Baron Munchausen, as in St John's miracles. I heard of one person, to whom it was a relief to find himself able to believe that the speaker credited them.

We admitted Bathurst yesterday under the name of Father Philip. Stanislas and Henry are going into retreat, the former for the diaconate, the latter for the sub-diaconate. Don't forget them.

Ever Yours affectly John H Newman   Cong. Orat.

THURSDAY 27 MARCH 1851   F Ambrose went to London   Richard Ward and Mr Crawley called[1]

FRIDAY 28 MARCH   R. Ward called

SATURDAY 29 MARCH   received Crawley

TO F. W. FABER

Oy Bm. March 30/51

My dear F W

Thank F Francis for his beautiful verses — they will do capitally. The narrow minded Nicholas of New,[2] recognising nothing in poetry but longs and shorts, objects to the *scansion*. Am I right in supposing the following to be the types of the verses? If so, F Francis will perhaps make a few alterations.

$$\smile - / \smile - / \smile - / \smile - /$$
$$- - \qquad\qquad - -$$
$$\smile \smile \smile$$
$$\smile \smile -$$
$$- \smile \smile$$

I will write about F Richard's plan as soon as I can — Today I am in haste to ask you a question. The Leeds St Saviour's party have put

¹ Richard Ward (1813–69), a former Vicar, and George Crawley (1820–74), a curate, at St Saviour's, Leeds, came to be received, the former at Oscott on 28 March, the latter at Alcester Street on 29 March, by Newman.

² i.e. Nicholas Darnell, for ten years a Fellow of New College. Knox's verses were for the Office of St Philip's Heart. Newman contributed a Latin hymn, which he sent to Faber some while later, together with other suggestions for the Office, heading them 'First package of goods for the Industrial Exhibition of all Oratorians.' See also letter of 28 March 1853 to Faber.

themselves into our hands, to be turned into an Oratory, if St Philip, as time goes on, sees good. I am going to Leeds, if all is well, some day after Tuesday to receive as many clergymen as I can — not to say nuns, penitents, and id genus omne. Dr Briggs has given me faculties, and is to have a talk with me on the subject.[1]

The plan, as it stands, is this:— we should keep them together at Leeds, something as we were at Littlemore and Maryvale, bringing over some of them by relays here as our novices. By the end of a year we should see how matters stood, and whether their vocation lies for the Oratory.

There is just *a* CHANCE of conversions coming on so rapidly at Leeds and work being so thrust on us, that we should be obliged to open a chapel there at once, or very soon. What is the chance of our receiving assistance from you, now or in six months time, for three months or six months, in the shape of one priest or two, alternately or priest and novice etc etc? Alas, it is no change of *air* from London.

Ever Yours affectionately J H N

P.S.   How is it you have not seen me in Punch before, 4 or 5 or 6 times at least.[2]

MONDAY 31 MARCH 1851   Crawley went

TO F. W. FABER

Oy Bm March 31/51

My dear F W

I think a lb a person a good deal for meat still, *if it is* to be doubled after Lent. I can't understand why it should be so much. Do you mean to say that a father eats more than $\frac{3}{4}$ lb of meat daily — then, allowing $\frac{1}{4}$ lb for waste in cooking (bone etc is already allowed for) the average

---

[1] St Saviour's, Leeds, had been built by Pusey and was consecrated on 28 Oct. 1845. It was to be served by a college of unmarried clergy, and was to show Tractarianism at work amid the horrors of an industrial town. Three of those serving the church had become Catholics early in 1847. The Bishop of Ripon and Dr Hook, Vicar of Leeds, objected to the sacramental teaching at St Saviour's, and now a second group of converts was coming over, in spite of a last-minute visit from Pusey. The Leeds Oratory plan did not materialise, although one of the converts, William Paine Neville, joined the Oratory at Birmingham. See John Hungerford Pollen, *Narrative of Five Years at St. Saviour's, Leeds*, Oxford 1851, pp. 197–200, and Anne Pollen, *John Hungerford Pollen*, London 1912, pp. 213–15.

[2] See *Punch*, Vol. XIX, pp. 185, 223, 229, 243, 263 Vol. XX, p. 125, etc.

should not be above a lb. John Lewis ought to make this reduction *his work*, by which he is to get to heaven — else *he* will be cooked in Purgatory, till he comes out as wasted as his meat.

F. Francis's calculation was £85 a month. So you have £5 for additional meat and Manciple.[1]

Now as to the Father of the O [Oratory]. I suppose the one and sole object he has is *to make* money.[2] If so, he does not bring it out enough. To exclude ladies is not the way to make money. And it should be recollected that women are certainly provided for in *what was*, tho' not now, the Oratory Proper. The Oratory consisted of *Sermons* and *Prayers*. The prayers are made over to the Orat. Parv. — the sermons remain, at 4 o'clock, in possession of the women (and men). — Whatever then *answers* in 24 K. Wm. Str. [King William Street] to the 4 o'clock quadripartite or bipartite Ragiomento [sic] belongs to women as well as men — and if you are considering the ministrations of the chapel under the strict type of an Oratory, should be open to women. In like manner, according to the same type, you should not at all (not even for a *bribe*, as the Father modestly and gently suggests) give admittance to women in the evening.

When he talks of the 'proper' work of the Oratory, I can't see how he provides for it more than at present. If Sermons are proper work, admitting women is proper.

Very likely I don't enter into his idea — his *object* is to frame a theory for making people pay. I don't see that he *does* — and besides, I think that some one, say F. Bernard, should stand up for the 'rights of women.' Dr Ullathorne has already begun that line. Are women alone to be taxed? And if they are submitted to it, would it provide a revenue?

I still don't see why the ticket plan would not do. Those who did not bring tickets, and were very urgent, might be put into a sort of ghetto under the gallery.

Ever Yrs affly J H N[3]

[1] The manciple is the servant who purchases provisions for a college or religious house.

[2] This refers to Stanton's plan for men's confraternity services, which he hoped would produce increased offertories. For the ticket plan (for High Mass) see letter of 23 Feb. to Faber. On 16 Jan. 1852 Newman noted on a paper of accounts sent him a year earlier from London: 'Both ends not meeting, at the end of January 1851, plans were devised for raising more money—viz by changing their locality, or by altering their services, so as to increase contributions or diminish expences (e.g. of choir) or by getting donations from rich friends. I said "*Reduce your Butcher's bills*, which are monstrous or John Lewis (the cook) and all of you, will boil in Purgatory."'

[3] The autograph of the following is preserved at the London Oratory among Newman's letters to Faber, and must have been sent to him not later than this period:

Please, write me some verses.

Answer. I can't, They won't come. A poet is not a 'maker,' but a 'finder', a

WEDNESDAY 2 APRIL 1851   went to Leeds with F Nicholas   (Aloysius returned to Birmingham from St Leonard's)   began receiving converts

THURSDAY 3 APRIL   received Minster, Coombes, Nevil, Rooke etc.   public reception — I preached[1]

FRIDAY 4 APRIL   F Nicholas went to Dr Briggs at York

SATURDAY 5 APRIL   Stanislas deacon   Henry Subdeacon   Philip tonsured came off with F Nicholas to Birmingham   Mrs Nicholson came

SUNDAY 6 APRIL   (Manning and Hope received in London)

TO J. M. CAPES

Oy Bm April 6/51

My dear Capes

I have just heard that Dr Ullathorne has said this: 'Mr Capes has uttered rank heresy, for he says that a layman can do any thing which a priest can do, with the leave of his Bishop, but offer sacrifice.' Have you said this any where? (You *have* said 'Sacrifice *and* SACRAMENTAL grace' — that is another matter)[2]

'retriever.' Igneus est ollis vigor, et caelestis origo Seminibus. [*Aeneid*, VI, 730–1] However, must I? Well then, here goes:—

Could I hit on a theme	When the chance-seed
To fashion my verse on	Is piously nursed,
Not long would I seem	Brighter succeed
A lack-courtesy person;	In the path of the first.
But I have not the skill,	One sighs to the 'Muse,'
Nor talisman strong,	One speaks to his 'heart;'
To summon at will	One sips the night-dews
The Spirit of song.	Which moon-beams impart.
Bright thoughts are roaming	All this is a fiction;
Unseen in the air;	I never could find
Like comets, their coming	A suitable friction
Is sudden and rare.	To frenzy my mind.
They strike, and they enter,	What use are empirics?
And light up the brain,	No gas on their shelf
Which thrills to its centre	Makes one spout lyrics
With rapturous pain.	In spite of oneself!

[1] Thomas Minster was the Vicar of St Saviour's, Leeds. He died in 1852. Henry Combs and Seton Rooke were his curates, and William Paine Neville was Manager of St Saviour's Orphanage. For Newman's sermon see *Sayings of Cardinal Newman*, London, n.d. [1890], pp. 5–11. Rooke became a well-known Dominican and Neville was Newman's support in his last years and his literary executor. Combs, was matriculated at St John's College, Oxford, in 1834 at the age of 18, and was a fellow there until 1851. He became B.D. in 1848, and was Perpetual Curate at Summertown, Oxford, before going to Leeds.

[2] The article, 'B. Ippolito Galantini, the Apostolic Silk-Weaver,' in the *Rambler*, VII (April 1851), pp. 337–49, began: 'It is always a token of the spiritual prosperity of

This is *intended* to be a *set off against Pugin's heresies*.

I think you had better write to him and bring him to book; — not for an *opinion*, in which you have a right to differ from him, but for the *charge* of *heresy*. You might say that you are sensible that you might have said things which all might not assent to, and feel this was the inconvenience of publishing at all, but the question was altered when a charge of *heresy* came in, which you would gladly set right, if you had expressed yourself ill.

You must not mention your informant

Ever Yrs affly J H N

So Manning is received

TO F. W. FABER

Oy Bm April 6/51

My dear F W

I write a hasty line. The *end* of the Oratory of Brothers is doubtless to *save the soul*. If any one or any Oratory, can arrive at this end by no means or by any means (allowable), let him do it.

One can't prescribe one's own means to others. If you can attain the end directly and immediately, by all means do it and use no means.

I think I may say for certain that here we shall not be able. Here I shall try to bring a number of people together in a mob, on no religious principle at all — and I trust, out of them Stanislas will be able to strike sparks here and there — which said sparks will be the nucleus of the Oratory of Brothers.

I certainly mean to use the brothers ⟨fratelli⟩, if I can, as decoy ducks —

We shall begin with *very* few, and more in order *to say* we have a Brotherhood than for any thing else. A number may be ἀκροαταὶ,[1] as yours are at present. If you mean to make the Oratory entirely spiritual, I think you should drop your ragionamenti on primitive history.

Ever Yrs affly J H N

So Manning is received.

any portion of the Church, when the laity emulate the clergy in their zeal for the salvation of souls. . . .

In fact the distinction between the clergy and the laity as Evangelists is quite different in kind from that which exists between them by virtue of the *sacerdotal* character of the former. It is by virtue of their *priesthood* that a line which never can be passed is drawn between them and the people for whom they offer sacrifice, and to whom they are the channels of *sacramental grace*.' See also letter of 10 April to Capes.

[1] Listeners or pupils.

TO T. W. ALLIES

Oratory Birmingham April 7. 1851.

My dear Allies,

I should have answered your letter before this had I not been away from home (at Leeds). I had lately written to Dr Russell about the Dublin, and I enclose you what he says in answer.

Your trial is one of the severest which can befall a man, but be sure that all who take the step we have taken, in some way or other have to pay for it to the world. The world asks a price to let us go. Your trial is *care*, which is a most exceedingly great one, but those who are unmarried have their own. They are solitary and thrown among strangers more intimately and intensely than married people can be. You have a home. We have not had one. The very object aimed at has been, first, to separate us from each other, secondly to bring us individually under discipline, thirdly to mortify us. I believe all this *in substance* is right, but it may be trying when it *is* right, and it may be done untenderly and rudely when the substance is good. We have been (necessarily) located as children being grown men. This is *not* a trial to one's pride, in the common sense of the word, but it is to one's desire of sympathy, and to those habits of refinement and good breeding and mutual consideration which University Life more or less creates.

Can I do any thing in consequence of the enclosed letter? — As to your taking boys, you seem so averse to it, that I doubt whether it would succeed. It would involve an outlay at beginning, force you to take a house etc. Is it impossible for you to get even for some months, one or two pupils, e.g. such as attach themselves to Gower Street College, or who read for the honors at London University? If you could get occupation for six months or so, you would not have formed engagements inconsistent with the Editorship whether of a newspaper or of the Dublin. This seems to me best, if it can be done.

I will write to Ward anyhow, not from you.

Ever yours affectly J. H. Newman

TO RICHARD STANTON

Oy Bm 7 April 1851

My dear F Richard

The only ground, on which so strong a change as that you throw out, is defensible, would be, (I think) *necessity* — i.e. want of money.[1]

[1] See letter of 31 March to Faber.

But I do not *feel* the money ground. First I think the expences of board etc have been *immoral* — and that you will all suffer in purgatory, if you don't diminish it. To increase means of getting money, which you are to squander, is but to increase your purgatory, and not relieve your need. You will squander *up to* the supply, and still cry, Give, give, with the horse leach.

This view is both confirmed yet alleviated by Father Wilfrid's return of expences of March — which (unless there is some awful cooking) shows both that you have been, and need not be, extravagant. F Francis estimated the month's expences at £85 — and this, I think, as a *reduction* on what had been. This sum took in butcher, baker, grocer, green grocer, fish monger, butterman milkman, beer, washing, candles, poulterer, charwomen, brandy, clothing, crockery, coals, medicine, postage, sundries, and £3 for mistakes — Now in the month of March all these items came to £61 odd — to which had to be added manciple, say £2 or £3 — making £64 — and, in order to make it a fair average, extra meat for the extra-Lent months — which ought not to be more, on the above calculation, than £7, making it £71 — This is a gain on starting of £14 on F Francis's calculation, making in the year £168 — which goes a great way towards your choir.

But this is *on starting* — and you must reduce *now* — The first and second weeks of the above month were not under the manciple, whereas I have charged him, though the account has not his reductions. Br John Lewis must learn economy — else he will be sinning. I cannot understand, after allowance for loss in cooking, your eating more than $1\frac{1}{4}$ lb a day — now even in Lent (after allowance for bone etc) you eat 1 lb— in the above calculation I have allowed $1\frac{1}{2}$ lb out of Lent.

All I can say, if you tell me, that there is some fallacy in these calculations, is that there *ought not to be* — and if you are spending what I think extravagant sums, you have no right to make money in order to meet them.

As to the Offertory, I calculated it very low, you will find, in the scheme drawn up when I was in London.

Directly I found what extravagance there was, I *gave up* all plans of tickets etc, viz as thinking you had no right to make more money, till you spent better what you had.

2. I agree with you that a fratellanza would strengthen the Philippine Congregation beyond any thing else — but I don't think you must act violently or undo, in order to it.

3. I did not explain myself about the women — I said that *when* St Philip's original meetings took their *permanent* shape, then at once they were open to women. They consisted, in germ, of Sermons and prayers;

— the Sermons (in Church) were put at 4 the prayers (in Oratory) in the Evening — the Sermons were then open to women, and you had no right to keep them out.

Women are twice and twice only in the year (I think) admitted into the Roman Oratory, on the Assumption and on St Cecilia.

Were all to begin over again, I am not certain I should not recommend you to begin simply with the Oratory and *without* the Church — but then, 1. what would the Cardinal have said? 2. where would your Lady penitents have been? e.g. Lady Arundel, would she have been converted?

Ever Yrs affly J H N

P.S. The inclosed is for your F Minister

WEDNESDAY 9 APRIL 1851   Mr Collins came (F John's Executor)
THURSDAY 10 APRIL   [William Paine] Nevill came   F Henry went to see his Father at Derby.

TO J. M. CAPES

Oy Bm April 10/51

My dear Capes

I liked your first letter — but your second (as yet unsent) might be a better one. I will make a running comment on the Bishop.

Letter 1st (public)[1] The Bishop (*entre nous*) used the term 'rank heresy' to FF Flanagan and Bathurst. Flanagan is indignant that the fact should be doubted. This at Oscott. The day before, in Lander's shop,[2] before one or more, the Bishop said to Caswall, that the last Rambler contained 'heresy.' You might say you fancied he had spoken 'in Birmingham and in a public place;' but you must try not to commit our men.

2. It is very offensive he should talk of reconciling '*conflicting*' opinions — where do *we conflict*? where have *we* spoken against Gothic? much less you. We only ask that we should be *suffered* — Pugin won't suffer us. I think you should find some way of inflicting on him this — e.g. by asking him *what* the extreme opinions are, unless this brought you into a controversy, and *who* are the persons who hold them.

3. I think you should simply ask him whether he considered it wrong to say, as the Cardinal had said, 'that he had preached before the

[1] Following Newman's advice on 6 April, Capes had written to Ullathorne, who sent him a reply which was intended for publication.
[2] Lander Powell and Co., Catholic Repository, 108 New Street, Birmingham.

Pope when a layman —' that, as was commonly said at Propaganda, the Alumni 'preached' before the Pope — that Mr Kyne is wrong in his use of the words 'lay preaching' etc in his letters.[1]

4. You must not *argue* with him, and therefore you must *not* say what is the case, that the heretics, against whom the Canons are written which he quotes, took 'preach' to mean, proclaim *with authority*, as priests etc.

5. But I think you may introduce it in a notice which you ought to introduce into the next Rambler — *and which the Cardinal should see*, IF HE WILL. I think you had better say that, to prevent misapprehension, you wish it understood that you did not use the word 'preach' as a word of authority, answering to the Latin 'praedicare,' but for such exercises as B. Ippolito, St Philip Neri etc. were permitted as laymen, such too as the preaching before the Pope of members of the English College, Propaganda etc etc.[2]

6. I think this should be a lesson to you to avoid categorical or dogmatic statements. E.g. you should merely have referred to the *instance* of B. Ippolito, leaving it to others to give the *theory*. E.g. 'However special and incommunicable are the prerogatives of the priesthood, yet they do not imply a prohibition of such exercises etc as etc. —'[3] You are perhaps apt to be categorical.

7. Why did not I notice it, you will say. Why, I think I *ought* to have noticed just the word 'preach;' but I do not consider myself answerable for the *expediency* of what you say, else I should be exposed to be carried into space, — but for the theological accuracy. No other line can be drawn for my office but this.

Private Letter 2. His words 'Oratorian controversy,' are to me

---

[1] See letter of 12 March to Capes.

[2] Capes followed this advice, and thus no doubt managed to avoid printing Ullathorne's 'public' letter. See p. 464 of the *Rambler* for May: 'The writer of the remarks in pp. 337–9 in the last *Rambler* [see note to letter of 6 April to Capes] is desirous of adding, in order to prevent misapprehension, that the word "preaching" as there used, in reference to religious exercises given by laymen, is, of course, to be understood in the *popular* sense of the term, and not as including that *authoritative* teaching which is exclusively committed to the Clergy. The opinion, broached by certain heretics in former times, that the latter kind of preaching is committed to the laity, is condemned by the Council of Constance and other authorities. The actual practice of the Church, which permits the alumni of the Propaganda, Roman College, etc., to preach before the Pope (Cardinal Wiseman did so when seventeen years of age), and which sanctioned the instructions given by St. Ignatius Loyola, St. Philip Neri, B. Ippolito Galantini, etc., when laymen, shews in what sense the canons alluded to are to be interpreted. The instructions are generally, if not always, described as "preaching;" as also are those other instructions given by laymen to confraternities, etc., which are not unfrequent in Italy to this day.'

[3] See note to letter of 6 April to Capes.

offensive — tho' that is not to the purpose, it being a private letter. We have pursued our own way, without attacking others. Pugin has twice insulted us in print, in a gross way — we have taken no notice of it. What can we do less than we have done, except give up our practice? i.e. *submit* to Pugin. I have never written a word in the Rambler (in prose) or suggested an article — Dalgairns has written several — some notes of Hutchison were accidentally inserted — this is the whole of it. Yet the Bishop *deplores* a *quarrel* in the face of enemies.[1]

You, again, have not alluded to this last outbreak of Pugin's — on which side has been the violence? *who* is it has not borne an opposition of opinion? who has made it a quarrel, if it is one.

His writing a dogmatic epistle for insertion in the Rambler is of a piece with his dogmatic tome in the Tablet 'de rebus Domuum S. Mar. in Valle et S. Wilfridi prope Ceaudulum,' two years ago.[2] I am unaffectedly sorry about it — I fear there is a deep gulf, poorly covered over, between us. He has a horror of laymen, and I am sure they may be made in this day the strength of the Church.[3] Curiously enough, I have been at this very time lecturing in their favor, up to last night, apropos of our Oratorium Parvum — which he will be sure to look after most jealously.

His paralleling you again to Pugin in his postscript is an additional insult — as if you and Pugin were equally extravagant. In your answer I think I would *ignore* Pugin

Ever Yours affly in Xt   J H Newman   Congr. Orat.

FRIDAY 11 APRIL 1851   MRG *Giberne* returned from retreat   Mrs Gordon came   Mr Collins went

SATURDAY 12 APRIL   Miss Mason came.

[1] See letters of 7 April 1850 to Miss Holmes, 13 Oct. 1850 to Faber, and 18 and 20 April 1851 to Ullathorne. For Pugin's two insults, in *Remarks on Articles . . . in the Rambler relating to Ecclesiastical Architecture*, and in *An Earnest Appeal for the Revival of the Ancient Plain Song*, both London 1850, and his last outbreak, in *A Treatise on Classical Screens and Rood Lofts*, London 1851, see letter of 18 April to Ullathorne.

[2] For Ullathorne's letter of 22 Nov. 1848, published in the *Tablet* on 26 Nov., see Vol. XII, *Appendix* 7, p. 405.

[3] This is the only sentence of this letter to be reproduced in *Ward* I, p. 259. Although he wrote more than twenty years after Ullathorne's death, Wilfrid Ward did not allow his readers to know to whom Newman was referring.

TO F. W. FABER

Oratory Bm April 12/51

My dear F Wilfrid,

I wish I could say something to your purpose — I have two strong feelings in limine. First I have a great dislike and suspicion of change of any kind, and I seem to feel that your House has not the same quite. The present question comes in, I suppose, thus:— 1. 'as we have actually begun, (as St Ph. [Philip] would have us,) the Or. P. [Oratorium Parvum], *what place* is it to hold in our services?'. 2. 'Since, for economy, we must retrench our Chapel expences, e.g. our choir, can't we cover the ill-look of it with this fair pretence, the introduction of the Or. P?'

Secondly, I feel vividly that what does for one place, does not do for another, and that no one can know your place but yourselves, and that I can do no more than deal with generals.

This leads me to say what F Bernard and you have said something about; viz that due account is to be taken of what F Perrone calls the ordo historicus ⟨chronologicus⟩ and the ordo logicus. It does not follow that what is more important or characteristic in the Oratory, should be introduced first. Nothing varies so much in the history of Oratories as the mode in which they got into position — sometimes the narrow end of the wedge, sometimes the broad. In one city I think they started with the convitto — in several a convitto, established without reference to St Philip, is changed into an Oratory. Elsewhere the Exercises come first — elsewhere the Parochial work. This being the case, *possession* has the greatest weight of argument for it, and innovation has on its side the burden of proof.

Further I don't think it follows because this or that is *distinctive* of the Oratory, that therefore it is to take the lead, or other things to be sacrificed to it — else you might cut off a camel's head, without prejudice to its life, so that you were religiously tender of its hump.

All this being considered, supposing your present services were prospering, I certainly should not be disposed to alter them for the Orat. P., though I acknowledge it as the differentia of the Oratory — it is only because you have an opportunity of change without the blame of not 'letting well alone,' that the introduction of the Or. P. into Church comes allowably into contemplation.

Next comes the question, in what respect the present plan *does not* answer, or whether a change does not involve a *sacrifice*. In money certainly not — but there are other things besides money, though that, up to a certain sum, is indispensable. E.g. it would not be a sufficient reason for giving up the present plan of services, *merely* because you must cut off your choir. The question is whether you are doing your *work*. Now it must be considered that the Holy Father has distinctly sent you to the upper classes (whatever else he has done) — does this mean gentlemen only, or ladies also? I cannot doubt it means ladies as well. If then you are (I don't say you *are*) but *if* you are exerting a certain influence on families in a certain rank, it is no reason for destroying it, that these persons cannot belong to the Orat. P. and your duties to them interfere with it.

Again, if you think that the Orat. P. will draw more upon your intellect than these gentlemen and ladies, and that such demands on the intellect are unoratorial [sic], that is a reason (so far forth) for not supplanting these people with the Orat. P. which is addressed to a more stirring class of minds. For I cannot but think that the Oratorium P. will claim more intellectual work than your present services. And it is certainly a curious fact, as if St Philip considered his original Oratory required more mental energy than he could promise himself in his Congregation on the long run, that, when he gave it its normal form in the Chiesa Nuova, he cut off the ragionamenti, historical discourses, disputations etc.

On the other hand, if you feel that intellectual work is allowable, and that the organisation of a good Orat. P. is a work desirable both for yourselves and for London, and that you are rather preaching to poor than to rich at present, then you will have a good reason for letting the Orat P. supplant your present services.

All that I have been saying comes to this:— were I you, I would not change my plans without a distinct and trustworthy reason — *What* is your reason? Keep to it, if you give it — let it be one you have so maturely taken up, and have so clear a view about, that you can promise yourselves it will last, and that you will not be undoing in a year to come what you are doing now.

Another consideration is this — I may be too sanguine, but you seem to me in the way to weather your pecuniary difficulties. As you don't say to the contrary, and have diminished your house expences by (at the rate of) £170 a year, I trust the House is going on well. As to the Chapel, its debt is simply referrible [sic] to the choir, which you are going to put on a right footing. If this be so, and you will be paying your way, it would be wrong to make any experiments, if they are such as to interfere with your present fair prospects. But you will tell me perhaps, as I have assumed above, that the prospect is *not* fair — or secondly if it were, yet that a substitution of the Orat. P. for the open services on certain days would not interfere with it. This is another matter.

But again will there not be an awkwardness in practice in *excluding* women 2 or 3 days in the week? *Will* they be excluded? How will they recollect what nights they can be admitted? Nay, can you *legally* excluded [sic] them from a public chapel?

While then I look upon the Orat. P. as the distinctive peculiarity of our work, I should not be inclined, were I in your place, to bring it into Church, unless there are reasons I have not mastered.

On the whole, I agree with F Bernard's paper, which will be seen best by my going on to say what we *propose* to do here, though it is difficult to talk of what as yet only exists in intention.

(Sunday 9 P.M. Dear George [Hawkes] is said now to be in his agony.) I have begun a letter to F Richard, but shall hardly have time to finish tonight.

What we are think[ing] of doing is this:— not at once to receive any one but ourselves into the Orat. P. — but to take ½ a dozen or a dozen of our most pious men and make them *candidates* for admission. To bring them together in our upper chapel at 7 on Sunday mornings — give them and help them through a meditation — then to say Mass with them and for them — ending (1) with a short, (10 minutes,) address on some distinct point of practice and duty. Again to have them together in the afternoon — to read them a short passage from saint's life etc — and then discuss one out of a list of difficulties or objections, which they are allowed to enter in a book, to Catholicism or Catholic doctrine or precept etc.

I don't expect to do more than this at present — but to watch if any thing germinates sponte suâ from this.

But further, if I can, to get a room in the Town — and advertise 'Father Newman's Lectures to the Brothers of the Oratory —' putting a small price on tickets of admission, the Brothers, however, being allowed to take a friend. These Lectures once a week and on some historical subject.

I have no time to write more

Ever Yrs affly J H N

TO RICHARD STANTON

Or Bm 12 April 1851

My dear F R

Your questions are not new to me, but have always been puzzles — I mean, we seem very much in the dark as to the history of the transition of the Oratory from its original to its normal state — and also as to the reasons of the transition.[1]

Perhaps St Philip thought that his ragionamenti etc etc required more spirit to keep up than he could reckon in his Congregation — Perhaps he found he had no one to succeed him at Chiesa Nuova in them — Perhaps he was advised to drop them, (for is not the change contemporaneous with the Bull of foundation?)

Certainly, did I judge by my private judgment, I should say that the whole idea and thing simply *went*, when, for St Philip's swinging on a bench, there were four half hour Sermons in a Church. Who could stand them? I should like to know, as a matter of fact, whether they have ever succeeded. (Of course they would in St Philip's time.) Still such is the fact, that, letting alone the *number* of sermons, a sermonization, and that in an open Church, is a real portion of the Oratorian Father's duty.

As to your other question, I suppose they shifted, as they could, in the Chiesa Nuova ⟨St Maria in Vallicella⟩, as they could, till, House, and Church and Oratory were successively built.

These very variations in St Philip's time show by what a series of experiments and experiences we shall find what is best or practicable for England. Our Rule has been left open for this very purpose. I confess, if I were asked what was best for England, and most feasible in time to come, considering the efforts the Hierarchy will make to bring all Churches into their own system, i.e. to make us take *missions*, it would be, to let our staple work be the Oratorium Parv., with general confessionals for men and women, irrespective of these public services — and Church Services only on Sundays and great festivals. This, however, would require, to avoid idleness, that the Fathers gave a good time to the preparation of intellectual amusements, instructions etc, for the Fratelli. But this is a theory, about which I may change — I only mean we *don't* yet know *what* form the Oratory will take in England. One almost insurmountable difficulty of introducing the exact Ordo for the day of the Chiesa Nuova is this, that since in England we cannot, as in Italy, command a congregation in the afternoon, the Church sermonising *must* clash with the Oratorium Parv. so that, either the two must be at the same time, or one of the two omitted.

I am very suspicious of change without very good reasons — but at first sight I dont see an *objection* to giving up the present sermons some nights of the week for the Orat. P ⟨i.e. if you can make women understand it, as I have said to F Wilfrid.⟩

Ever Yrs affly J H N

[1] On this see Louis Ponnelle and Louis Bordet, *St. Philip Neri and the Roman Society of his Times*, translated by Ralph Kerr, London 1932, chapters v and vii.

April 14. G. Hawkes died today. We talk of his being buried at St Wilfrid's.

TUESDAY 15 APRIL 1851   H and L R *Ryder* came   Mr Simeon came   Mr Fullerton came
WEDNESDAY 16 APRIL   Mr Simeon went[1]

TO ARCHBISHOP CULLEN

Oratory Birmingham April 16. 1851

My dear Lord,

I feel exceedingly the honor you have done me by asking me the questions contained in your letter[2]

I write at once to acknowledge it — but I cannot of course say any thing to your Grace's purpose, without some thought.

One difficulty is this — that the leading men and authorities in the University would necessarily be priests — and England as your Grace knows, has none to spare. I do not know how far the Professors would fall under the same rule — perhaps those who filled the chairs of Classics, History, Mathematics etc, need not be. Of course my own acquaintance chiefly lies with married converts, who have been clergymen in the Protestant Church, such as Mr Allies.

I hope soon to write a second letter on the subject and meanwhile

Begging your Grace's blessing, I am, My dear Lord, Your faithful Servant

John H Newman   Congr. Orat.

[1] John Simeon (1815–70), who succeeded his father as 3rd baronet in 1854, was later one of Newman's close friends. He was about to become a Catholic, being received by Fr Brownbill at Farm Street on 21 April. He then resigned his seat in the House of Commons, where he had represented the Isle of Wight since 1847. He entered Parliament again in 1865 and was an active supporter of Newman's Oxford plans.

[2] Cullen wrote on 15 April to Newman that the collecting of funds 'for the purpose of establishing a catholic university in Ireland' had been 'very successful.' Cullen added, '. . . we must now proceed a step farther. I suppose the first thing to be done is to select a fit and proper superior. In this matter your advice would be of the greatest importance. Would you be able to recommend us any one that would give a character to the undertaking. We shall also have to appoint a vice president and professors Would you be so kind as to give us any suggestions you may think useful in this business . . . It is now time to make some effort to have at least one college for the higher branches of science and litterature [sic]. . . . Should you have any intention of coming to Ireland this season, your presence at the meeting of our committee in Dublin would be most useful. Indeed if you could spare time to give us a few lectures on education, you would be rendering good service to religion in Ireland. . . .' Newman replied fully on 28 April.

P.S.   I ought to have noticed your Grace's very flattering invitation of me to Ireland. There is nothing at all which I can feel more interest in than the subject of Irish Education — yet I do not know how I can possibly promise myself the pleasure of the visit in question.[1]

GOOD FRIDAY 18 APRIL 1851   went up to the new House with Mr Fullerton[2]

TO BISHOP ULLATHORNE

Oratory April 18. 1851

My dear Lord

Thank you for your kind note.[3] As to the controversy about Skreens, the members of the Oratory have had really nothing to do with causing it. I believe it took its rise in a letter of F Lockhart to the Rambler, written without any intention at all of making mischief.[4] For myself, I signified my dislike of it from the first; not however, from any insensibility to the haughty and domineering tone adopted by Mr Pugin. Nor had the Oratory any share in the actual controversy, when it had arisen, except this:— that a paper of authorities and references against the use of skreens, not intended for insertion, was by a mistake published in the Rambler.

Mr Pugin, however, who, when at Rome, poured contempt upon the very notion which I suggested to him of building a *Gothic* Oratory, because an Oratory is not a Medieval idea, and who told me that St Philip's institution was nothing else than a mechanics' institute, on his return to England, so far from letting me and mine alone, has ventured

---

[1] It was Robert Whitty, writing to Cullen on 12 April, who suggested that Newman should be consulted about the proposed university, and should be invited to lecture on education. *McGrath*, pp. 104–5, *Culler*, p. 131.

[2] To the new Oratory at Edgbaston.

[3] On 17 April, Ullathorne, after looking at his copy of Pugin's *A Treatise on Chancel Screens and Rood Lofts*, wrote a note to Newman, marked *private*, about its 'language so unwarrantable against the opponents of screens . . . I think it is high time that some one having authority should interfere. It only remains therefore for me to consider how that ought to be done. . . .' But see postscript to letter of 11 May to Capes.

[4] This was presumably the letter signed 'A country priest,' in the *Rambler* of 15 July 1848, p. 263, which, after the severe criticism the previous week of the rood screen at St George's, Southwark, asked what were the 'theological objections to them.' For an account of the controversy see Bernard Ward, *The Sequel to Catholic Emancipation*, II, London 1915, pp. 261–78, and M. Trappes Lomax, *Pugin a Mediaeval Victorian*, London 1932, pp. 221–46.

to say that we have mistaken our way and ought to have put up at Geneva — has associated us with immoral livers and, I think, with heretics, and all this *in print*.[1] Under these circumstances, I am quite curious, if it is right to be curious in such a matter, to know, how he can have outdone himself, — in his new publication, when he has already said such things *of priests*.[2] The scandal of all this is so great, that, if it had not been a personal matter, I think I should have been tempted to speak about it — and it is with great pleasure and gratitude that I find your Lordship is determined to put an end to it.

I am, My dear Lord, begging your Lordship's blessing Your faithful Servt in Xt

John H Newman   Congr. Orat.

[1] In *Some Remarks on Articles . . . in the Rambler relating to Ecclesiastical Architecture and Decoration*, p. 24, Pugin wrote, 'To rescue religion from the miserable degradation into which its externals have fallen, is one of the grandest objects to which a Catholic life can be devoted. It is not inferior to the rescuing of the Holy Land from the Infidels: for the artists of the latter centuries . . . are little better.' This was in 1850, and at the end of the year, in *An Earnest Appeal for the Revival of the Ancient Plain Song*, pp. 3 and 4, Pugin complained of buildings erected for divine worship 'as similar as possible to dissenting conventicles in their arrangement, only rather more offensive than their meagre prototypes, by the meretricious decoration of their interiors. Now, monstrous as these suggestions must appear to Catholic-minded men, they become light when compared to the changes that are proposed in the divine service itself, and which have been lately put forth in a publication that is the recognised organ of the party from whom this miserable system of modern degeneracy emanates.' This was a reference to Capes' article 'Popular Services' in the *Rambler*, Oct. 1850, pp. 315–51, reviewing Faber's *The Spirit and Genius of St. Philip Neri*. Pugin continued, 'No Catholic is compelled to assist at their maimed rites or to enter their conventicle-looking chapels' where prevailed 'the doggrel rhymes and poetical effusions of a few individuals whose tendencies and principles should have led them down to Geneva' rather than to the Catholic Church, where they used 'the ancient liturgy as a mere vehicle for the display of their Methodism.' He also protested against 'the erection of churches, whose appearance is something between a dancing-room and a mechanics' institute.'

[2] In his book on Screens, just published, Pugin wrote (pp. 98–9), with a veiled reference to the controversy in the *Rambler*, and the Oratorians, that the party opposed to screens were first heard of after the consecration of St George's, and 'It has been asserted that their first dislike of screens arose from a desire of literary notoriety, and . . . they profited by the occasion to increase the sale of a periodical. But this may be mere calumny; and, indeed it is very probable that it is a case of pure development, as at first they did not exhibit any repugnance to pointed churches . . . but they speedily developed other propensities and ideas, and latterly have exhibited symptoms almost similar to hydrophobia at the sight, or even mention, of pointed arches or pillars.' They have 'an inordinate propensity for candles and candlesticks,' 'require great excitement in the way of lively, jocular, and amatory tunes at divine service,' and try to realise 'a somewhat Italian atmosphere.' Cf. p. 8, 'It has been most justly said, that there is no legitimate halting-place between Catholic doctrine and positive infidelity, and I am quite certain that there is none between a church built on Christian tradition and symbolism and Covent Garden theatre with its pit, boxes, and gallery.'

SATURDAY 19 APRIL 1851   Mr Fullerton left

TO J. M. CAPES

[19 April 1851][1]

My dear Capes

I am not quite reconciled to your expression 'pretended Catholic Roman Empire,' p 374 as I think it is generally accounted the 'Holy Roman Empire,' or am I mistaken? Such is the tone of 'respice ad Romanum benignum imperium, ut gentes, quae in sua feritate confidunt, potentiae tuae dextera comprimantur' in yesterday's function.[2]

The Article on Loretto is good and interesting, as the rest of the series[3] — but I think it might be more rhetorically convincing. It seems to me not to be adapted to the state of men's minds. One point which should have been thoroughly discussed is the *material* of which the building is made — a great deal turns on this. It should have been shown more distinctly that the stone is of the same kind as that at Nazareth — and not likely to have been brought from the quarries in the neighbourhood. Also I think the antecedent probability, or not-improbability, should have been discussed at length — since the evidence is so small. What makes me anxious is that at this moment, unless you make a strong case, you are putting arms into your enemies' hands. e.g. when the Popes are mentioned as committing themselves to the miracle. The arguments in p 390 against the invention of the legend seem to me hardly strong enough, though p 391 is striking.[4] Is the argument of the Paper this: 'The translation is to be received on the authority (not strictly infallible) of the Church — therefore all that is to be done is to see that no facts can be brought *against* it —' This seems implied in p 397 — but if so, it should have been brought out more clearly.

Easter Day. The blessings of the season on you and yours. While I am criticising, I will say, that, without denying, I have not made up my mind to agree with, the argument of your first article.[5] The problem is

[1] This letter is headed in another hand, 'date on envelope April 20. 1851.' It was evidently begun the day before.

[2] i.e. the old Morning Office of Good Friday. Capes altered this phrase in the first article of the *Rambler* for May, 'Our Position and Policy.'

[3] *ibid.* pp. 383–408. It was one of J. S. Northcote's on 'Celebrated Sanctuaries of the Madonna.'

[4] It showed the belief in the legend among the people of Dalmatia, whence the shrine was said to have come to Loreto. Newman shows himself already more cautious than in his letter of 19 Jan. 1848 to Henry Wilberforce.

[5] This article ended by saying, p. 382, that 'if . . . we *must* choose between state favour and persecution, we a thousand times prefer persecution.'

how can the Church be made to do most good — now a time of persecution separates from the Church vast numbers who otherwise would die Catholics in a state of grace — it is depriving numbers of the hope of salvation, perhaps of the donum perseverantiae — many never know the truth, many lose the truth, with whom it *would* have been otherwise. What does the Church gain instead? an elevation in the tone of those who remain firm? I doubt it *as a whole*. Recollect the scandals among the Confessors in St Cyprian's time, and the low tone among us now. And great as the sanctity of the Martyrs is, I suppose the sanctity of St Ignatius and St Theresa, subjects of the Most Catholic King of Spain, may be compared to it. Then again in times when religion is established, you have schools of all sorts, of doctrine, of ritual, of antiquities and histories — it is the age of *doctors* — who are formed by the very heresies which then germinate — Think on the contrary of the miserable state of the Church from 1780 to 1830, during the temporal misfortunes of the Holy See, from which we have not yet emerged. At this moment, where are our schools of theology? a scattered and persecuted Jesuit School — one at Louvain — some ghosts of a short lived birth at Munich — hardly a theologian at Rome. And recollect independence and persecution go together — the state must either be our friend or our enemy. Now, consider the confusion every thing is thrown into, by the Pope's absence from Rome — the destruction of records — the dispersion of libraries, the suspension of the Sacred Congregations — think of Pope Pius vii shut up from the Church for five years. *What is to put against all this?* You cannot pick and choose — you cannot have all the advantages of freedom and none of the disadvantages of being outlawed. You may say that we are in the worst state possible now, being neither one thing nor the other — the Pope bound to the world without corresponding benefits — but I am not defending any *view*, I am only anxious that things should be calmly looked at. As to a Concordat, the difficulty would be, when we came to the point, *what could we give up*, which the civil power would care to accept?

Thank you for Dr U.'s [Ullathorne's] letter — having inflicted his criticism on you, he is now (I am glad to say) turning round upon Pugin — whose book on skreens has at last shocked him. I don't know what he says

Ever Yrs affectly John H Newman   Congr. Orat.

TO T. W. ALLIES

Oratory Bm Easter Sunday [20 April]/51.

Private

My dear Allies,

A Happy Easter to you and yours.

What would you think, if an offer was made to you, of undertaking a Professorship in the new Catholic University in Ireland?

A greater field of usefulness cannot be. It will be the Catholic University of the English tongue for the whole world. And I shall think I have [done] much, if I can accomplish the settlement of you and other Saxons in it, to do the great work.

I am supposing such Professorships as Classics, History, Polite Literature, etc. Is there any one you would like more than another.

Ever yrs affly J. H. Newman   Congr. Orat.

P.S.   As to the pay. I know no more than you, but it *must* be enough to keep a married man, or they will get no one to come.

TO J. D. DALGAIRNS

Oratory Bm April 20/51

My Dear F Bernard,

Your account is very promising and full of interest.[1] Certainly you must do something with those youths.

I seem to think this, but throw it out for discussion. What the Ragged Schools are, or what position or function your youths would take in them I know not — but this seems to me a principle — *such good works must be propter Oratorium, non Oratorium propter illa.* I mean, St Philip had in view as his *object*, had he not? the sanctification of his children, and used good works simply as means towards that end, in subserviency to it, and therefore in moderation. St Philip took his youths to the Hospitals, but he did not set up a hospital and he left the care of the sick, as such, to St Camillus. He did set up the Pellegrini,[2] before he was in his own work as Oratorian — but he gave it over when

[1] Dalgairns had collected 'forty two men most of them artizans,' a nucleus of the *Oratorium Parvum*, and instead of St Philip's visits to a hospital, wondered if they might conduct a Ragged School.

[2] An organisation for the care of poor pilgrims in Rome.

he was in his own work, and merely took his people there. He looked on all things as merely trying, humbling, subduing, diverting his penitents — and, so that he saved their souls, it mattered not whether it was by making them eat lemons, dance jigs, listen to Baronius's annals, or visit the hospitals; but he no more contemplated hospital work as an end, than dancing jigs.

The simple question then is, how you can sanctify your youths — If they are to attend the Schools only as disciples of St Philip attended the hospitals, well. If as St Camillus and his people, to me they are no longer Philippines — but I speak under correction. I do not see my way to say that any Brothers of the Oratory can in any sense *undertake* the schools, consistently with St Philip's idea.

This is what I say in opening the subject — and I cannot say more in answer to your question, till I have the point I have dwelt on settled.

Best Easter Greetings in return — F Joseph is at Leeds to bring matters to a final *decision*.[1] If we think the plan bids fair, and your house takes it up, he means to ask for *you* to help him.

Ever Yrs affly J H N

P.S. Bastard of Devonshire, who is proceeding from Madeira to Spain, wants a line of introduction to the Bishop of Marseilles, the Cardinal Archbishop of Besançon, the Bishop of Langres.[2] Could you write just a line to each and send them me here? You may call him one of the country noblesse; and a distinguished Oxford scholar, lately converted.

TO BISHOP ULLATHORNE

Oratory Easter Day. 1851

My dear Lord,

I beg your Lordship's blessing upon me and mine on this greatest and most joyful of days, and I assure you that we pray constantly that your pious and zealous labours for the advance of religion among us may receive an abundant answer from our Almighty Lord.

Just now the inclosed letter was brought me, which I think your Lordship ought to see. It was addressed, as you will observe, by Mr Pugin, some six months ago to one of our *novices*, Mr Caswall; not to

[1] This refers to the plan of founding an Oratory in Leeds, with the converts there.

[2] These were Charles Eugène de Mazenod, founder of the Oblates of Mary Immaculate, Cardinal Mathieu, and Pierre Louis Parisis, who was translated this year to Arras.

any intimate friend of his, for he addresses him as 'Dear Sir,' so it is not confidential, but to a friend and subject of *ours*. He does not scruple to tell our novice, and thinks it '*only honest* to tell' him, that he 'holds the new system,' by which he means the architectural tradition of Rome and Italy, 'in nearly as much *horror* as the *principles of Voltaire*, for an architectural heathen,' (such as a whole line of *Popes*) 'is only one remove from an *infidel*, and in his way more dangerous.'

This applies not only to the Popes of at least three centuries, but to St Philip, St Ignatius, and a host of Saints. After this, it is little to say, as I mentioned in my late letter to your Lordship, that he accounts *us* but 'one remove from infidels,' and our principles almost as horrible as 'those of Voltaire.'[1]

I am, My dear Lord, Your Lordship's faithful Servt

John H Newman   Congr. Orat.

EASTER MONDAY 21 APRIL 1851   H Bethell came — and his father etc.[2]

TO F. W. FABER

Oy Bm April 21/51

My dear F Wilfrid,

A happy Easter to all of you — I hope you don't feel the change of weather — they talked of thunder yesterday.

You ask me the very question which I said in my last letter (to F Richard I think) I *could not* answer.[3] *The* crux about the Oratory, I said, was this, that, owing to the hours of business in England, the Oratorian Sermons, which in Italy are at 4 PM., are put off here till the evening, and thus run against and into the Oratory of Brothers. I said I did not see my way out of this at present. It follows that I can give no answer at all to the question, whether you should substitute the Oratory for the Sermons once or twice a week. All I can say is, that, since the Sermons are in possession, you should not do so without a *good* reason. For what I know, you *may* have a good reason, but I don't know what it is. If you *do* substitute, I shall be content, as supposing you *have* a good reason.

As to the two Musical plans, which I have now looked at, I don't like hiring an orchestra — and think the F. Ceremoniere's remark has

[1] Pugin's letter to Caswall is quoted also in Bernard Ward, *op. cit.* II, pp. 272–3.
[2] Henry Slingsby Bethell (1836–1908), at school at Eton, son of John Bethell.
[3] That of 12 April to Stanton.

great weight, that it is important that all the members of the Congregation should have a familiar acquaintance with the sacred Functions, which cannot be if they are seldom. Besides, since the rule looks for weekly etc High Mass, the question is whether Mass with second best Music is not a sufficient fulfilment of it.[1]

As to Leeds, the plan is on one of those intermediate phases of difficulty which may be got over or may capsise it — I will write when there is any thing to say.

Ever Yrs affly J H N

TUESDAY 22 APRIL 1851   Minster came

WEDNESDAY 23 APRIL   Minster went   Manning and H W *Wilberforce* came for a few hours

THURSDAY 24 APRIL   Penny to dinner

TO BISHOP BRIGGS

April 25/51

Extract of answer[2]

'An Oratory implies men and means. . . . Men and money are not enough — Oratorians are required. To determine their Vocation, they must be tried *here*, as postulants. . . .

Our duties are incompatible with missionary work. We are required to preach 6 days in the week, and to form the Oratory of Brothers. . . . Two Priests could not possibly get through the work of the mission in addition to all these duties. . . .

We should offer, if we send two Fathers to Leeds, not to take care of existing Catholics, but to aim at making new ones. . . . Preaching and taking confessions would be our principal occupations.'

J H N.

TO EDWARD BELLASIS

Oratory Birmingham April 27. 1851

My dear Sergeant Bellasis

Your kind letter gave me the sincerest pleasure. How great a blessing is it to you, over and above the blessing to them. Say every thing from

---

[1] It had been suggested in London that they might have High Mass six times a year and hire an orchestra for this.

[2] Bishop Briggs wrote on 20 April, that he would welcome two Oratorians to take charge of a mission near St Saviour's, Leeds.

me kind to Mrs Bellasis.[1] Did I tell you, in answer to your former announcement, how our meeting at Milan has dwelt in my memory? I am sure the good Ghianda has given you some prayers. He liked you and Mrs B. so much.

I wished very much to get at you when I was for a day in London some time back. If I come again, I shall have a double inducement.

Ever Yours most sincerely in Xt

John H Newman   Congr. Orat.

TO F. W. FABER

Oratory Bm. 27 April [1851?][2]

My dear F Wilfrid,

You don't say a word about the two letters you inclose. I don't see you have anything to do at the moment. It is great disappointment to you of course, but think how things might have been worse. I suppose the marriage is in good faith on both sides, at least you did not I believe, tell her contrariwise. Thank you for sending them.

If you could spare a day or two, which I think you might, could you not run down to Frank?[3] No news here

Ever Yrs affly J H N

TO T. W. ALLIES

Oratory, Birmingham April 28. 1851.

My dear Allies,

I cannot answer your question better than you can yourself; and can but say what strikes me.

People seem to think the University will open at or after Christmas next, but it depends, I suppose, upon their getting Professors, etc, etc,. All I know is that they are at work upon it already.

A more serious question for you perhaps is, when can you get an answer or promise as to an appointment. All I can say is that I have written about you, saying just what I felt, but of the movement of the

---

[1] Mrs Bellasis became a Catholic on Easter Tuesday, 22 April. Her three eldest daughters had been received on the previous Thursday. See E. Bellasis, *Memorials of Mr Serjeant Bellasis*, 3rd ed., pp. 95–7.

[2] There is no year in the date of this letter, but it appears to be 1851.

[3] Faber's brother Francis, Rector of Saunderton.

Committee I know nothing. Of course you shall hear directly I have anything to tell you.[1]

    Yours affectly in Xt   John H. Newman   Congr. Orat.

TO ARCHBISHOP CULLEN

Oratory Birmingham April 28. 1851

(*Confidential*)

My dear Lord

  I send your Grace the names of those persons who at present strike me as fit candidates for Professorships in the New University. I say Professorships, for there is no one strikes me who would fitly fulfil a place which involves the duties of government and oversight, though several of those I am going to mention would have been equal to them under other circumstances.

  Mr Morris is the only Priest I have to name. He was a Fellow of Exeter College, Oxford — and was received into the Church five years ago last January. He was the first Syriac scholar in Oxford, and one of the first Hebraists. He is a man of genius — besides a great talent for languages, (for I think he knows French, Italian, and German, perhaps Welsh, besides the classical languages) he is a metaphysician, a poet, a carpenter, and a chemist. He is now publishing, with Mr Waterworth's supervision, a learned work of a Patristical nature, based principally on the Syrian school of St Ephraim, on the Blessed Virgin.[2] He has never found his place since he has been a Catholic — he has been at Oscott, St Edmund's, and is now at Prior Park. He is docile and amiable, but has the deficiencies of a man of genius, having little judgment, and being somewhat eccentric in his habits. He may be 35 years old.

  Of the laymen, I have to mention, all but two are married, and all but one have been Anglican clergymen.

  Mr Ornsby requires to be mentioned first. His wife[3] has cast him off and returned to her parents, and he cannot claim her, because he

---

 [1] Not until 1854, after Newman had become Rector, was Allies offered a professorship. He declined the post as being too insecure, since, if Newman were removed, 'all would go to pieces.'

 [2] This was J. B. Morris's *Jesus the Son of Mary; or The Doctrine of the Catholic Church upon the Incarnation of God the Son, considered in its bearings upon the reverence shown by Catholics to His Blessed Mother*, London 1851, 2 Vols. 'Before publication, Mr. Morris entrusted his MS. to Fr. Wm. Waterworth, S.J., whose approbation of the treatise was of the warmest and most unqualified sort.' *Gillow*, v, p. 131. But see also letters of 7 and 17 Dec. 1851 to Capes.

 [3] Elizabeth, sister of J. D. Dalgairns.

cannot maintain her. At least I *suppose* this is the state of the case. He is subeditor of the Tablet. He was a Fellow of Trinity College, Oxford — ⟨(perhaps he is 30)⟩ and distinguished himself highly. I do not recollect his various honors etc, but I once had an opportunity of examining him at Oxford, and know him to be a man of great ability. He is an excellent person, and a gentleman. He was received in May or June 1847.

There are two persons, each of whom would make a first rate Professor of history — viz Mr Allies and Mr Henry Wilberforce. I doubt whether Mr W. would leave England — he is one of my most intimate friends, I have known him as a brother these 25 years. He is a man of great talent, extremely quick and penetrating in matters of thought and argument, with considerable knowledge of history and turn for politics, an easy writer and an eloquent speaker. He was received in Belgium last Autumn with his wife — and gave up a living of (I suppose) £900 or £1000 a year. He is 43 or 44 — and has just published a Letter to his late Parishioners, which will give a general idea of what he is.[1]

Mr Allies has also given up a rich living, and, with a wife and family, is almost reduced to poverty. He is perhaps not quite so old as Mr Wilberforce. He was received last Summer. I think he would be willing to accept a post in the New University, and his own choice would be the Professorship of History. He was the first man of his day at Oxford. He came from Eton with the highest character for scholarship — I suppose he is well versed in philosophy — and, as your Grace knows, he is a powerful and eloquent writer — and has of late years devoted himself to the study of the Fathers. He would be invaluable as Greek Professor, or Latin, or Professor of Ancient History or of Modern, or of Metaphysics. He is a person I value very much, and take great interest in, from the painful difficulties in which he is at present. Should there be any notion of strengthening the Dublin Review, he and Mr Wilberforce would be most important accessions to the staff of writers. As to Mr Wilberforce, in mentioning his name, I am doing violence to my own feelings, for I love him so much, that after being separated from him so many years, it would be a sad disappointment to me, if he left us for Ireland.

Mr Northcote, your Grace might know at Rome, where he was with his sisters in law, Mrs Anstice and the Miss Pooles, for several years. He was received in 1845. He is a man of exact and careful thought — of great application, and sound judgment. I suppose he would be considered thoroughly Italian in his views and feelings. I do not know him

[1] *Reasons for submitting to the Catholic Church: a Farewell Letter to his Parishioners*, London 1851, 6th ed., 1855.

well — but I have a high respect for him. He got the highest honors in classics, was on the foundation of Corpus Xti College Oxford, and is about 30, I suppose. He has great reputation as a *Tutor*, and I expect would thoroughly drive into a class of young men any thing he had to teach them.

Mr Walford is a young man, whose wife is dying — He was a scholar of Balliol College, Oxford — and has a great name among his contemporaries as a classic. He is an amiable man and docile I should think — but of unformed mind. Though I have but seen him for a day, I feel as desirous that he should be employed in this new undertaking, as of any one — as he seemed to me a man of active, energetic mind, willing to learn, and of an age when impressions are possible and lasting.

Mr [Joseph] Simpson was a scholar of Trinity College, Cambridge, where he came from Eton. I believe he was one of the most rising men of his day. He seems to me about 30 or under. He is a man of refined and gentlemanlike mind — and a first rate classic, I suppose. He lived in our house at St Wilfrid's for a time, having been converted by one of our Fathers three years ago. At present he is at St Sulpice, and is on the point of being tonsured. He is not strong in health. He is just the person for the Professor of a College, and his name would give eclat to any Institution — but I do not know him enough to say whether he would turn his thoughts to that kind of life. He has not been in Anglican orders.

These are the persons whom I should name to your Grace in the first instance. However, I will add one or two others.

Mr Lewis is a man of considerable legal and historical reading; he was received about 5 years ago, had been Fellow of Jesus College, Oxford, and assisted Mr Lucas in the Editorship of the Tablet, when it was published in England.

Mr Thompson is of the University of Cambridge — and has the reputation of a very able man. He is very pleasing in his manner, and is the author of a book on Papal Jurisdiction in answer to the former work of Mr Allies.[1] He is Co-editor with Mr Northcote in the Clifton Tracts.

Mr Seager was Dr Pusey's Lecturer in Hebrew, is a man of original mind, thoroughly in earnest, and deeply religious. But he is certainly eccentric in his manners and ways. He has been of late Tutor to Mr Kenelm Digby's sons.

Mr Scratton was a Student ⟨(synonymous with *Fellow*)⟩ of Christ

---

[1] Edward Healy Thompson, *The Unity of the Episcopate Considered, in Reply to the Work of the Rev. T. W. Allies, M.A., entitled, 'The Church of England Cleared from the Charge of Schism,'* London 1847.

Church, Oxford — He is a man of pleasing manners, about 30 — very fond of boys and of tuition — and much given to the classics. He is made for University life. He is unmarried.

I fear I have tired your Grace with this long letter — and perhaps I have taken a liberty in going into details, which from the nature of the case are of a confidential character. Let my zeal for the great object you are undertaking excuse any excess or mistake in this matter; and in the trust that it will do so, I will not hestitate to add any thing further, which it may occur to me to mention. At present, begging your Grace's blessing, I am, My dear Lord Your Grace's faithful Servt in Xt

John H Newman   Congr. Orat.

P.S.   I know that Mr Allies and Mr Wilberforce are forming plans for the future, and cannot tell how long they will be disengaged.[1]

TUESDAY 29 APRIL 1851   F Joseph went to Leeds

TO F. W. FABER

Oy Bm April 29/51

My dear F W

Persons have been representing to our Bishop that your Translator of St Camillus has spoken of 'his adorable Crucifix,' when it should be 'his adorable crucified one.' I have turned to the original and find your translation quite right.[2]

I write to put you on your guard, for at this moment *every thing* will be caught at — and persons who are not our friends are making out that Pugin and Rosmini are in one extreme, the Rambler and we in the other. In the case of such passages it might be well to put the original text in a note at the foot of the page.

Who revised the Volume? It would not have mended matters, tho' it would have been more literal, if the translation had run 'Camillus did not forget that beloved Crucified Lord . . . so he took the image in his arms. . . . They [sic] people ran to see — Camillus carried his Crucified Lord to the Madonnina. He was all the time imploring the assistance of

---

[1] No reply to this letter is to be found. Of those mentioned in it, only Ornsby and Scratton eventually held resident posts at the Catholic University.

[2] *The Life of S. Camillus of Lellis*, London 1850, 1, p. 45. See also letter of 1 May to Monsell, and 23 May to Faber, and cf. that of 11 Sept. 1850 to Faber. The primary meaning of 'Crocifisso' in Italian is 'Crucified One.'

his adorable Crucified Lord. Monsignor Cusano, seeing that Camillus had taken with him his crucified Lord,' I think this *is* the real meaning, the mind of an Italian going to the Prototype, and the image not existing *as* an image — 'Crucifix' *ought* to mean the original, but English Catholics have contrived to fix the word to denote the material image. Can you get instances in Italian of 'un crucifisso,' as we say '*a* crucifix.' I suppose you can certainly.

How have you settled about the Orat. Parvum?

Ever Yrs affly J H N

6. P.M. F Bernard's letter just come. Tell him I will write to him soon.

TO F. W. FABER

Oy Bm May 1/51

My dear F W

There is an article ⟨a letter⟩ in the last Catholic Standard abusing the Rambler under the name of *Oratorian*.[1] They say that Richardson has a share in the property of the Paper. If so, I really think you should write to him, to hinder such liberties being taken with our name. It will do us serious harm, if it goes on. Pugin, the C. St. Ambrose Ph. [Phillipps] etc etc., if they talk on a certain line, people will not only believe their doctrines (for that is their own look out) but believe us violent, abusive etc. like those worthy individuals — *because* they are violent, and because they assume or assert we are violent too. At length it may be said, that, whether we are right or wrong, at least we give scandal, for we provoke angry feeling etc etc.[2]

Just think of this

Ever Yrs affly J H N

[1] This was the second part of a review of the *Rambler* for April, and appeared in the *Catholic Standard*, IV (26 April 1851), p. 11. Newman evidently had not read it, and his letter of 6 May to Capes implies as much. It began, 'The *Rambler* announces on its front that it is a "Catholic Journal"; but we have as yet only known it as an Oratorian Journal. . . . it is not right in the Oratorians to get hold of particular reviews, monthly and quarterly, belonging to Catholics in general, and to plant everywhere they can a sly article, to bring about a CONSPIRACY to turn the whole Church into an Oratorian asylum. . . . They have no doubt that he [St Philip] is "in England," and that he is the *sole* "Representative Saint" of modern times. In fact, if we may judge from Father Faber's Triduo, "The Three Days' Entertainment," we cannot discover the difference of honour and veneration to be paid to St Philip during the last three centuries, and to Our Blessed Lord as the Representative of the first three. . . .' The review then went on to attack Faber for his disapproval of Gothic architecture.

[2] See letter of 3 May to Faber, who thought the *Standard* article 'very amusing.'

TO WILLIAM MONSELL

Oy. Bm May 1./51

My dear Monsell

Thank you for your account of Lady Olivia [Acheson], and thank her too for her letter. If you make her well, I shall be very glad — if you do the reverse, I shall call you a bad doctor, who has not let well alone. If she is really better, I am sorry you are leaving so soon.

I spoke to Penny at once, but he did not entertain the notion at all — He said he had given up his Mathematics. H. Wilberforce is a good mathematician, and, I know, has not given up the idea and the love of the study. Would *he* listen to you?[1]

All blessings on your first month of Mary. Say every thing kind from me to the Phillippses.

Lady Olivia, by the way, tells me that the good Ambrose has begun a second course of preachments against F. Faber — founded on a passage in his Edition of the (translated) Life of St Camillus. I have looked at the original — where it is not 'Il crocifisso,' but 'Il *suo* crocifisso.' Il suo crocifisso he *takes* to the Maddelena [sic], he has in his room, he is very fond of, etc etc when then he says that he acknowledged 'the almighty power of his adorable Crucifix,' the word crocifisso means *just what* it means in the other adjoining phrases, which are all found in the same page.

The truth is Catholics in England have become Protestantized, and look on 'the Crucifix' as a thing of wood or ivory — but abroad they speak of it as the Prototype. E.g. in the Prayer in the Raccolta, which the Pope has indulgenced, 'Quando (viz on the bed of death) le mie *mani* tremole ed intorpidite non potranno piu *stringervi Crocifisso*, e mio mal grado lascierovi *cadere* sul letto etc'[2] And St Thomas expressly tells us that the *adoration* we pay the Crocifisso is the *highest*, latria — viz because we contemplate *in it* the Prototype. The only reserve on this doctrine is, first, that such latria is of course *impropria*, viz because it is not for its own sake (of course) — secondly that preachers for prudence-sake are not [to] exhort to latria or call it so — Still we speak of the Adoratio Crucis on Good Friday.

I wish Mr Phillipps would content himself with not approving of things, which he has a right to do, without *preaching* against them. He has a right to mention a thing to the Bishop — he has no right (*as he will do*) to repeat it to every soul whom he sees for a year to come

Ever Yours affly John H Newman

---

[1] Monsell was helping to find professors for the proposed Catholic University.

[2] *Raccolta di orazioni e pie opere*, Rome 1844, p. 275.

Ryder and his boys went.

TO F. W. FABER

Oy. Bm. May 3/51

My dear F Wilfrid,

The Oratory of Brothers here is occupying my thoughts at present, and if I wrote lectures, it would be for them. I could not possibly *write* lectures for London. I have got on *very* slowly with the subject which I showed you in part — and find it will make rather essays than lectures.

I do not see how any one can *publish* a disclaimer of the Rambler, without implying something positive, or taking an offensive line against it. This I should not myself wish to do.[1]

As to your question about the Ragged Schools, I did not know how to do justice to it, since I did not distinctly know *what* they are, or what part you proposed taking in them. However, I have since written to F Bernard about them. At first sight, I feared the undertaking, as too great.

I am glad you have all got a holy day — tho' I wish you seemed better for it — but our Lady will carry you through May — and your subject for Lectures is particularly important.[2] What you say about 'growing —, not forcing' is a point I was going to lecture about myself, the day before yesterday, but did not come to it.

Joseph is at Leeds, to bring matters there to an issue. He has nothing of a definite character there yet to tell us. He does not return for near a week yet.

Ever Yours affly J H N

P.S. Have you found you can give some days of the week to the Orat. Parvum?

[1] In consequence of Newman's letter to Faber of 1 May, the London Oratorians wanted a public disclaimer of any connection between the Oratory and the *Rambler*. See letter of 6 May to Capes, of whom Faber complained that he 'goes about blackguarding us and our music, why should we be responsible for him, specially as in this house we prefer Pugin to Capes architecturally?' This was from Faber to Newman, on 2 May.

[2] Faber wrote on 30 April, 'I am wanting to show why B.V.M. occupies such a different place in St Alphonso's works e.g. from what she does in S. Chrysostoms . . .' and how a convert 'must *grow* in not force, this devotion.'

TO RICHARD STANTON

Oy Bm 3 May/51

My dear F R

Your gift is most exceedingly kind and welcome — tho' I am unwilling and ashamed to accept it — but I suppose you have made up your mind.[1]

What I should like it to go for, would be some *definite necessary* ornament of the new Church — say a Tabernacle or crucifix or 6 Candlesticks for the high altar — which might have 'Orate pro etc' on them. So, we would make a memorandum to that effect, that it was only *lent* for bricks and mortar — and must be repaid by the building fund to the Committee of Taste.

I have answered F Wilfrid about the Rambler.

As to the Orat. Parv. in *my eyes* it is more important than any thing else. You know perhaps a private memorandum of mine, when we came here, which got up to Burns's instead of Our Lady's Litany, and got printed by mistake — to this effect — 'however flourishing our mission here might become, yet, unless we established at length the Orat. Parv. the *Oratory* would have failed.' I feel this still. But I dislike uncommonly *change without a view* — I dont like new experiments if they involve interference with what is.

(I inclose for F Bernard, if he can't find one, a copy of a Chiesa Nuova admission to Orat. Parv.) a failure — I have not found it.

Ever Yrs affly J H N

SUNDAY 4 MAY 1851   Sleet, and even lying in patches on the ground and roofs, as snow.   Sleet etc for 10 days past at intervals.   Today good honest snow and large flakes

TO ANTONY HUTCHISON

Oy Bm. May 4/51

My dear F Antony,

Much may be said for your project, and I don't like the chance of stopping your contribution towards a work so imperatively necessary as is the education of our poor children. What I am now going to say, is, in the way of *discussion*. If I were giving my decided opinion, I should take

---

[1] Stanton sent £25 from a legacy he had received.

more time about it — but at present I would rather set before you what appears on the first blush of the matter.

It seems to me then that the Orat. Parv. is intended as a *recreation* — and that is especially needed in London — where 'all work and no play etc' Now your plan gives it the most serious of works. It is a substantive work in itself, the setting up of a Ragged school — not a divertimento.

The Orat. Parv. has nothing of *work* in it. Its meditations, according to the School of St Ph, [Philip] are on easy subjects — even its penances are fun. Hence Music has so much to do with it. It is, I think, an out-bidding of the world — in all ways a doing what the world does, on Christian principles.

This is the only light in which I have viewed the exercise of the *intellect* in it. ⟨(Your papers imply I am bent on exercise of the intellect, *as such*)⟩. This is why Mechanics Institutes might fairly be imitated. I never dreamed of puzzling the fratelli, e.g. with mathematics, meta-physics, or any thing fatiguing — but what would strictly be a recreation.

I conceive the visits to the Hospitals at Rome are of that nature — they are not frequent, done by lot, and are of the nature of a lark. I mean, there is something out of the way and exciting in a hospital, nothing in teaching children. It is bonâ fide hard work. And so again, washing pilgrim's feet, is, me teste,[1] most odious, and so far a good penance, but it has something picturesque about it, which a Ragged School has not.

Now then does a Ragged School come under the notion of recreation? — that, in my view of the Orat Parv. is the point. Bring it under this category, and it is Philippine.

What I have said suggests another view of the subject, closely connected with the above. It is a work which will *run away* with you. At least it seems to me that you could not do it, or take it, by halves.

At the utmost then, I do not think I can see my way to say more than, 'Engage yourselves in it only for a time — fix a term — so that you may not let the occupation get hold of you'

Ever Yours affly J H N

MONDAY 5 MAY 1851   Mrs and Miss Phillipps went.
TUESDAY 6 MAY   Lord Dunraven (*formerly Adare*) came[2]

[1] See diary for 2 April 1847.
[2] See letter of 29 July 1851 to Monsell.

TO J. M. CAPES

Oy Bm May 6/51

My dear Capes

I am going to write to you on rather a difficult subject.

Some of our people in orbe terrarum are fidgetty at the way it is taken for granted that we are the conductors virtually of the Rambler. They think it unfair to you, and to them. There has been a late article, I believe, in the Catholic Standard, distinctly calling the Rambler 'Oratorian.'

Again, I think we all feel that it is doing us disservice as far as this — that it makes it appear as if we were neglecting our proper work and becoming partizans.

I wish you would turn this in your thoughts, and see if you could not put a few lines in the Rambler, stating what the fact is — or, if you think it better, I will write you a note for insertion in the Rambler on the subject.[1]

Ever Yours affectly John H Newman   Congr. Orat.

TO GEORGE CRAWLEY

May 6/51

My dear Crawley

. . . . F Gordon gives me little hope of being able to do any thing at the moment at Leeds. Should any of you ultimately see your way to join the Oratory, either absolutely, or with a reservation in favour of Leeds, if ever practicable, we should rejoice. But I shall hear all about it from F Gordon[2]

J H N

TO F. W. FABER

Oy Bm May 6/51

My dear F W

F Joseph has written to me this morning from Leeds and returns here tomorrow. It is plain from what he now says that there is no

[1] See letter of 11 May to Capes.

[2] Gordon wrote on 5 May from Leeds that the recent converts were hesitant about forming an Oratory there. Crawley became a priest and worked at Newcastle upon Tyne. In 1858 he tried his vocation at the Birmingham Oratory, but left after a year.

chance of our doing any thing at the moment at Leeds, that is, things are not in that state of forwardness, that we can pledge ourselves to *begin now*.

As to your other question, I cannot say anything more than I have said, till F Antony writes to me in answer to my letter of Sunday.

Congratulate James from me. As to dear John, he will arrive, I conjecture, before his box with our church plans.[1]

Ever Yours affly John H Newman

TO ANTONY HUTCHISON

Oy Bm May 7/51

My dear F Antony

I have nothing to say against your proposition now on the main ground I took. You seemed to me to put it on the ground, first of *work*, secondly of *piety*, whereas I thought *the* ground ought to be *recreation*. But if, as you now say, it *is* recreation, which *I* cannot feel myself, but am no judge about others, you quite remove this objection.

My other objection, that it is too much of a thing, as a system, and will run away with you, remains. ⟨Opera propter Oratorium, non Oratorium propter opera.⟩ Therefore I should say, if you begin it, be careful not to commit yourself to it more than you can help — not to commit yourself for good. Could you not propose to a missionary priest to *set up for him* a ragged school?

As to my own Lectures, they would be essentially and primarily *recreation*. I had intended to read the fratelli bits of a romance, quite original, but unwritten. *This* would be my intellectual training for them

Ever Yrs affly J H N

TO F. W. FABER

Oy Bm May 8/51

My dear F Wilfrid,

My difficulty in answering you, F. A. [Antony] F. R. [Richard] and F. B. [Bernard] is, that you are accustomed to move so much more rapidly and completely than I, that I seem to be saying neither one thing nor the other, because I do not write decidedly. What seems indecision or obscurity in me is but the expression of a habit of *gradualness*.

[1] Faber had just received into the Church one of James Rowe's brothers, and John Bowden in Sicily was expected home in June.

I am not *at all* criticising you. I am only stating a difference in order that you may not think me indirect or shilly shally when I am not.

Now all your papers mark the difference between your House and ours in this matter. You bring out Programmes of Lectures and Services — systems of preaching and celebrating you post up over your recreation fire place. You print copies of works by the 1000, you revolutionise chapels, sacristies, and refectories as by a magician's wand, and a choir, nay a double choir, starts up, like Cadmus's men, only more harmoniously, from as scanty and unlikely a sowing.

Hence, when you would have an Orat Parvum, you ignore it except in its integrity — you will not let it be born and grow as human beings are — but it comes forth, or ought to do so, like the goddess of wisdom from the brow of Jove, totis numeris.

Now I repeat most sincerely, I do not say all this, simply as criticising it — for every one has his own way — and to find fault with another's would be like Pugin's intolerance about Roman devotions — still it would not be wonderful if Pugin could not draw as well as Michael Angelo, and as I, so far like Pugin, am a man of details, I cannot sketch a Moses off or Half a dozen Sibyls.

At present you are tormented in mind because the Orat. Parv. will not issue from your brain fully armed and instructed, to do battle — and you may think me difficult, when it is the thing itself is so.

With this Preamble, which is nearly all I have to say, I will put down such bits of wisdom as your proposed scheme suggests to me.

As to the Brief requiring us to form the *Orat. Parvum* of the higher classes — I do not see that, because the Orat. Parv. is not the whole of the Oratory. If without *any* chapel (*supposing* it) you merely, as F Brownbill did for years, open your house, or room, for *confessions* of gentlemen and ladies, you most fully answer the brief.

I like your plan very much — as far as I can enter into it. Parts of it may fail in working, but never mind. You must distinctly get the Cardinal's leave for the laymen lecturing in CHAPEL. I wish it — but let him quite see what he is doing. Capes's opponents take the ground that it is in *chapel*.

Ever Yours affly J H N

TO F. W. FABER

Oy Bm May 9/51

My dear F W

It is certainly a better thing that the Ragged Schools should *not* be *set up* by the O. P. [Oratorium Parvum], according to your plan — but then you give the *Congregation* that task — and is it not too great a one for it? I am only afraid of your doing too much for mind and body — instead of waiting to let things grow. I am not at all insensible of the value, as a matter of expedience, of the Oratory's beginning the Ragged Schools — only, count the cost.

I don't recollect your allusion when you say 'I do not at all, as you seem to think, wish or expect the O. P. to be of the upper classes.'

I am glad you are getting a separate room.[1]

If I *understand* your expence paper — it is a wonderful improvement. It seems you have done, in successive weeks, for £16. 8. 0, £10. 17. 3 (here is some omission? the Butcher being put at 18/9½) and at £17. 0. 5, ⟨i.e. an average of £15 per week⟩ what beforehand you calculated at £85 per month, i.e. at £21 per week — That is, it is a saving of (£21 — £15) £6 × 52 = £312 a year

When I spoke of your 'playing too bold a game,' it was your sweeping substitutions, I spoke of, not your additions

Ever Yrs affly J H N

SUNDAY 11 MAY 1851   Oratorium Parvum began — I saying mass up-stairs and Stanislas giving the Meditation

TO J. M. CAPES

Oy Bm May 11/51

My dear Capes,

The Paragraph will do very well.[2] I think you might add two or three words to it for greater distinctness — Look at my pencil marks;

[1] i.e. for the Oratorium Parvum, so that there could be no complaints that laymen were preaching in a chapel.

[2] This was the note for the *Rambler*, referred to in the letter of 6 May to Capes, disclaiming a connection with the Oratory. It appeared in the *Rambler*, VII (June 1851), p. 452, as follows:

'The Editor of the *Rambler* is desirous of correcting an impression which appears to prevail in one or two quarters, to the effect that this journal is in some peculiar way the organ, or under the influence, of the Oratory of St. Philip Neri in England. The impression is totally without foundation; being so far from true, that from the commencement of the *Rambler* till the present time, not more than six or seven articles or reviews, and those almost wholly on historical subjects, have appeared on its pages from the whole number of the Fathers of the Oratory. It has, indeed, been often a cause of regret to the Editor, as, no doubt, to the readers of the *Rambler*, that the incessant labours of the Fathers of the Oratory should have left them so little leisure for literary occupation. A similar contradiction must also be given to ideas entertained in

if possible, I should like the word influence, suggestion, inspiration (as our neighbours say) or some similar term, to be introduced, else the whole will be looked on as an evasion. The point of your last sentence of all, 'The merits etc' is not brought out clearly enough (as a matter of criticism) for the ordinary reader.

Ever Yrs affly J H N

P.S. Dr U. [Ullathorne] has changed his mind about his letter to P. [Pugin][1]
P.S. Let me have the inclosed sad letter back.

TO WILLIAM MONSELL

Oratory Bm May 11. 1851

My dear Monsell

I have no business to write to you about the Conelly [sic] Petition, except that the Bishop has shown it me.[2]

It will not be *safe* to take up Mrs C's cause too warmly. She is a Yankee, I suppose this is the reason, but any how, though she is a very good woman, it is difficult for an Englishman to follow her. Our Bishop is afraid of being called in, lest his words should tell against her, and so apparently against the Catholic cause.

As to Conelly, it is an extreme impertinence in a Yankee, not naturalized, to petition about an English matter — viz the suppression of Monasteries. He can get divorced too in America with the greatest ease.

other quarters; in one case attributing the management of this journal to his Eminence Cardinal Wiseman, and in another regarding it as the organ of the Fathers of the Society of Jesus. In reference to all such reports the Editor is anxious to state that he alone is responsible both for the opinions from time to time advocated in the *Rambler*, and for the expediency of putting them forward. The merits of the journal, and the merits alone, he is desirous of sharing with his coadjutors.'

[1] Ullathorne was to have rebuked Pugin. See letter of 18 April to Ullathorne.
[2] Mrs Connelly's appeal against the decision of the Court of Arches that she must return to her husband, was not given in her favour by the Privy Council until June. Meanwhile Connelly, at this period the guest of Henry Drummond, presented a petition to the House of Commons for the abolition of convents. The allegations in this petition were so extraordinary that it was decided, on 8 May, in the then state of public opinion, only to print copies of it for members of the House. On 12 May, the Earl of Arundel and Surrey moved unsuccessfully that the Petition be published generally. He wished to show that the calumnies would refute themselves, and that Catholics were not afraid of them. On 14 May the Religious Houses Bill was thrown out, at its second reading.

You alone will know how to treat it in the House of Commons. As to the public, I suppose the Petition will do Titus Oates's work — The only way I can think of for meeting it, is to *damage Conelly*. I suppose some of the facts of his Petition are simple *lies* — again, if it is fair and will tell, I suppose there is no doubt that he is a disappointed man.

Ever Yrs affly J H Newman Congr. Orat.

TO RICHARD STANTON

Oy Bm May 11/51

My dear F R

Our Bishop told me, the evening before your letter came, the Cardinal's intentions for St Ph's [Philip's] day. I have thought over it, and don't see what can be done. Dr U's [Ullathorne's] words to me were that the Cardinal said 'he was going to pour some oil on the troubled waters.' So I trust it will be rather a condescending sop or patting on the back to our modern-antiques, than any thing reflecting upon us.[1]

Ever Yrs affly J H N

MONDAY 12 MAY 1851 Mrs Wilberforce went.

TUESDAY 13 MAY Penny slept here

TO RICHARD STANTON

Oratory Bm May 13. 1851

My dear F Richard,

What I feel about the Ragged Schools is this, that it is so great an undertaking and you have all so much to do, that I *dont see my way* to say 'Undertake them.' Yet, not being on the spot or in mediis rebus, I dont like the responsibility of utterly extinguishing the idea.

What I should have thought best was this — to let *others* set them up — and, by way of encouraging them, to promise to throw the Orat. Parv. upon them, when set up, as St Philip threw his people into the

---

[1] Stanton wrote, on 9 May, that Wiseman had told Faber that morning, 'I have heard from Mgr Ullathorne who now gives up Pugin—we must therefore now put an end to these differences on *both* sides—I shall therefore take this for my subject at the London Oratory on St Philip's Day, and bring a man to take down the sermon for publication.' See letter of 6 June to Stanton.

existing hospitals, and that, say, for 2 years or so — and at the end of that time you would see how matters stood. But to undertake an indefinite responsibility seems to me dangerous.

Father Wilfrid has sent me the whole House expences of three more weeks — and I must say, unless the accounts are infamously cooked, they present a most satisfactory reduction. F Francis's calculation was £85 per month — they are short of this by at-the-rate-of £24 or £25, i.e. £300 a year.

This brings you safe — but you must not on that account relax your retrenchments in the Sacristy and Ceremonial and Music. I can't say I am sorry the Choir is going — I am not at all clear St Philip is not knocking it up. The music I have heard, Haydn and Beethoven, has not pleased me, either at the time or in retrospect. I am as fond of scientific music as any one — but if any music is theatrical, theirs is such, judging by what I heard. I doubt whether a thorough *instrumental* composer will ever compose good *sacred* music. I mean, he will consider spiritum propter instrumenta, not instrumenta propter spiritum. As scientific music is, (as I have 'elsewhere' said,) like Gothic architecture, so is the temptation it occasions to its professors. Architects sacrifice the rites of the Mass, and musicians the words.

Ever Yours affly John H Newman   Congr. Orat.

WEDNESDAY 14 MAY 1851   day at Sedgely Park[1] — FF Austin and Nicholas there

THURSDAY 15 MAY   Parsons in Birmingham[2] Penny went out with F Joseph to Leamington   Lady Olivia brought Miss St John[3]

TO THE EDITOR OF THE MORNING CHRONICLE

Oratory, Birmingham, May 15. [1851]

Sir,

The *Times* newspaper has just been brought me, and I see in it a report of Mr. Spooner's speech on the Religious Houses Bill. A passage in it runs as follows:—

'It was not usual for a coroner to *hold an inquest*, unless when a rumour had got abroad that there was a necessity for one, and how was

---

[1] Boys' school and junior seminary near Wolverhampton.

[2] Daniel Parsons (1811–87), who went to Oriel College in 1828, and after taking Orders, became a Catholic in 1843. He lived at Malvern.

[3] Georgiana, daughter of George St John, Rector of Warndon, Worcestershire, and a cousin of Ambrose St John.

a rumour to come from the *underground cells* of the convents. Yes, he repeated, *underground cells*; and he would tell honourable members something about such places. At this moment, in the parish of Edgebaston, within the borough of Birmingham, there was a large convent of some kind or other being erected, and the whole of the *underground* was fitted up with *cells*; *and what were those cells for?* (hear, hear).'

The house alluded to in this extract is one which I am building for the Congregation of the Oratory of St. Philip Neri, of which I am Superior. I myself am under no other Superior elsewhere.

The underground cells, to which Mr. Spooner refers, have been devised in order to economize space for offices commonly attached to a large house. I think they are five in number, but cannot be certain. They run under the kitchen and its neighbourhood. One is to be a larder, another is to be a coal-hole; beer, perhaps wine, may occupy a third. As to the rest, Mr. Spooner ought to know that we have had ideas of baking and brewing; but I cannot pledge myself to him, that such will be their ultimate destination.

Larger subterraneans commonly run under gentlemens' houses in London; but I have never, in thought or word, connected them with practices of cruelty and with inquests, and never asked their owners what use they made of them.

Where is this inquisition into the private matters of Catholics to end?

Your obedient servant, John Henry Newman.[1]

TO ANTONY HUTCHISON

Oy Bm May 16/51

My dear F Antony

I should have written before but I have been so busy.

I don't see why you should not commence the plan as you state

[1] The speech of Richard Spooner, M.P. for North Warwickshire, and uncle of Henry Wilberforce, was made during the second reading of the Religious Houses Bill, and reported in *The Times* of 15 May. Already on 6 May, William Scholefield, M.P. for Birmingham, had put questions to Spooner in the House of Commons about the supposed cells. Scholefield intervened again on 6 June, to say that 'a great deal of odium had been raised in consequence [of Spooner's accusations], and at last the mayor was called on to inspect the premises. The mayor had done so, and . . . there was no truth whatever in the statement. . . .' On this occasion Spooner, who received no support, read in the House, amid ironical interruptions, Newman's letter of 15 May, as a confirmation of his suspicions. Newman made play with the episode in *Prepos.* pp. 118–25.

it, with the understanding you undertake it only for a limited time, stated.[1]

Is there any one, who has *experience*, who could tell you whether or not it is an absorbing matter?

Ever Yrs affly John H Newman

P.S.   Thank F Richard for his letter and say I will write soon.

TO GEORGE RYDER

Oratory Bm May 18/51

My dear George

I will tell you just what I think.

1. It was *imprudent* in the priest to give an opinion uncalled for. The point was just one of those, where, if there be sin, it is well to leave persons in *material* sin, and say nothing (lest greater difficulties should follow) — tho' one cannot deny what the state of the case is, *when asked*.

2. Well, I think there *is* sin in dancing the polka, both from what I hear of the dance, and because *all* the books say so. At least it is a most grave occasion of sin to others, to men, even if particular women may not find it to be so themselves.

3. Moreover, I very much doubt whether there is any one who can be sure that it *might* not be, any day, an occasion of sin to him or her in fact, even if it has not been hitherto.

4. Since then I am asked, I must say that Miss C. should not dance it.

5. Even if she has danced it hitherto, yet I doubt whether she would ever like to dance it again, now that the Priest has put such thoughts into her head.

6. When I say it has been sin to dance it, observe, it is only material sin — i.e. the *thing* has been sin, but it has not been sin *in her*, because she did not know it. Yet I think it would be best to confess it, as one might confess material heresy.

Ever Yrs affly J H N

[1] Hutchison proposed employing a paid master for the Ragged School, in which members of the Oratorium Parvum would visit, and teach the Catechism.

MONDAY 19 MAY 1851   Rooke came

TO DAVID LEWIS

Oratory Birmingham May 19. 1851

My dear Lewis,

As I hear you are living in London, I am tempted to ask you to do me a favor. It is to make me two extracts from books which I fear are not in your library — if not, I must ask you if you can do it without inconvenience, to find them out at the Museum or elsewhere.

The first is Doblado's (Blanco White's) Letters upon Spain. In that work there is a puff of the Jesuits at the time of their suppression — it is that puff I wish copied.[1]

The other work is White's Bampton Lectures — in it, I suppose a note, there is a censure of the famous sermon of St Eligius. I want, please, White's words extracted about St Eligius, and to know whether he refers to Mosheim or any one else as his authority.[2]

I am sorry even to propose to you this trouble — but must thank you when you come down next year to see our new House. N.B. We won't put you into the cells so graphically described by Mr Spooner

Yours affectly in Xt   John H Newman   Congr. Orat.

Was there any contradiction ever brought out to Dr Gabriel's charge and proofs that White's Bampton Lectures were written by Mr Badcock[3]

WEDNESDAY 21 MAY 1851   Rooke went

[1] Newman wanted this for his *Lectures on the Present Position of Catholics in England.* See *Prepos.* pp. 18–19 and 404–06, where the quotation is given from *Doblado's Letters* in the *New Monthly Magazine,* vol. II, 1821, pp. 157–8, in which they originally appeared. Lewis could not find at the British Museum the volume into which they were later collected.

[2] The words of White, who does quote Mosheim, were transcribed by Lewis and are to be found in *Prepos.* p. 102.

[3] See the next letter to Lewis on 21 May.

TO J. D. DALGAIRNS

Oratory Birmingham May 21/51

My dear F Bernard,

I am of course very sorry you are in this trouble — but it is well you will so soon be out of it — and it does not matter much.[1]

F Joseph saw the new article in the C. S. [Catholic Standard] I have not. You must not attend to *it*, if you can help. *We* thought it was Ambrose Ph's [Phillipps'] corrected by our Bishop I will look over every thing you send me — I had better not write it

Ever Yrs affly J H N

(Turn over)
P.S.   I will tell *you* all I feel. I don't write to F Wilfrid, because he is so very sensitive — but I wish to put you in possession of just what I feel.

I was displeased about the Triduo[2] — F Wilfrid said to me, 'Will you just look over this which is coming out, as censor? for Father B is busy etc etc —' So I took it simply *as* censor — and it did not come into my mind to ask '*Is* this to be *published*?' AFTERWARDS, I was told, when the row took place, that Lord Arundel *had* before the resolve to publish doubted the *prudence* of publishing. *This I ought to have been told*. It struck me uncomfortably, as if he had been getting my *sanction* without my knowing what he was at —

Well, I think he has in his heart both fretted and laughed at the *selection* of Lives which followed the row with the Bishop at the end of 1848, St Alfonso etc. as slow, and said to himself 'O it is all fudge — publish strong, and people won't mind — or if there is a row what's it to me?'[3] So out comes St Camillus, he, observe, being *recommended* to leave out certain passages, and pooh poohing the recommendation. I suspect this passage is one of those objected to by the revisor. I know F Wd [Wilfrid] said before the volume appeared, that some strong things were coming out. Now I know the rule is, that *nothing* should be

[1] The trouble was over the translation of the *Life of St Camillus*. See letter of 29 April to Faber. The translation had now been criticised a second time, in the *Catholic Standard*, IV (17 May 1851), p. 5, where the 'adorable crucifix' passage was one of those animadverted upon. It was proposed to publish a correction. Before Newman had finished his letter, one arrived from Dalgairns saying that Wiseman wished a retraction to appear in the next volume of the *Saints' Lives*. See second postscript.

[2] *The Spirit and Genius of St. Philip Neri*, published in July 1850. See letter of 2 Aug. 1850 to Dalgairns.

[3] See letters of 14 Oct. 1848 and 4 Aug. 1849 (last paragraph) to Faber.

suppressed — but it does not follow therefore that a remonstrance should be utterly unheeded. The passages ought to have been looked at again — and, I think, *a note appended*. I put a note to the passage in Bl. Bened. [Benedict] Labré, to which Dr Newsham objected, and nothing was said against the passage, when published.[1] The other day I said to F Wilfrid, apropos of A. Phillips, something about a *note* on such passages[,] he answered 'Will *you* put one?' — The words rose to my lips, as I read his answer, 'No indeed, it's not my business.' It was as if he said, 'As *you* have put the difficulty, you may please *yourself.*'

I cannot help thinking the scrape (as far as I understand the circumstances) arises from a certain recklessness and wilfulness, which showed itself also in the publication of the Triduo.

Ever Yrs affly J H N

P.S.   Your letter has only just come. Let me hear from you again. I *do* hope the Cardinal does not want many words.

TO DAVID LEWIS

Oy Bm May 21/51

My dear Lewis

Thank you for your letter. I need not trouble you, I find, about Mr Badcock. I have a volume containing Dr Gabriel's document, and White's *admissions*. And I know just what Badcock and Parr did for White. Badcock took orders and was Curate in the West. I *believe* he was a Dissenting Minister before, but am not sure[2]

Yrs affly in Xt, John H Newman

THURSDAY 22 MAY 1851   F Stanislas began to preach

[1] *The Life of Benedict Joseph Labré*, London 1850, p. 98, note about his dirty clothes, explaining how other saints preferred cleanliness.

[2] Among the books Newman brought from Littlemore to Birmingham was a volume of the pamphlets in the controversy over the authorship of Dr Joseph White's Bampton Lectures, 1784, on Christianity and Mahometanism. Samuel Badcock was a dissenting minister who took Orders towards the end of his life and died in 1788. After his death, Dr Gabriel, whose curate he had been, showed that Badcock had given Dr White considerable assistance, and had written one whole lecture. Samuel Parr came to the defence of White, but only by claiming to be responsible himself for a fifth part of the lectures. See *DNB* s.v. Badcock, Parr, and White.

FRIDAY 23 MAY F Joseph went to Leamington with Lady O. A [Acheson]. Walford to dinner

TO J. D. DALGAIRNS

Oy Bm May 23/51

Charissime,

I am very sorry to have brought you into a fix[1] — I have written to F Wilfrid, and said something about the Triduo — not quite so much as I said to you. You had better burn this, or at least don't let it lie about. I know your talk.

What you have hinted to me has pained me a good deal.[2] F Ambrose says a mass every week for my intention, and that intention is your and our sanctification. I say a mass for you personally every now and then, tho' I have no opportunity of telling you — and have lately for your Orat. Parvum with ours.

I wish you were not so knocked up. Pass a year, if all is well, and really I think we shall try to tempt some of you to recruit at Edgebaston.

Ever Yours affectly in Jesus, Mary and Philip,

John H Newman   C.O.

P.S.   We are a good deal anxious about F Frederic's health — but don't mention this. He does not know it himself. Aloysius gets weaker. Of course we shall be said to have poisoned him, and Mr Spooner will demand an inquest.

TO F. W. FABER

Oratory Bm May 23/51

My dear F Wilfrid,

I know well you *could not* publish the translations we selected, for they were not forthcoming — but I think you have been careless in what you *did* publish. This is all.[3] You said F Buggenoms gave you a

---

[1] Dalgairns had let Faber know that Newman was displeased over the Lives of the Saints, but had not dared tell him what was contained in the first postscript of Newman's letter of 21 May, about Faber's 'Triduo.' Faber had surmised that the letter contained more than he was told. Hence the fix Dalgairns was in, as he explained on 22 May.

[2] Dalgairns added that *he* could not tell Faber his faults, 'at the same time in real and sincere charity I wish he had someone to tell them to him. He rules so absolutely in this house, at all events, as far as opinion goes, that none would venture to do so. . . . You alone in the world can do so; and he listens to you as he would to no one else.'

[3] Faber, on 22 May, apologised for whatever in him had annoyed Newman, and specially for not publishing certain of the Saints' lives. In the postscript of his letter of

hint — this might have been attended to, not to leave out, but to reconsider the passages.[1] Had this been done, the false translation would have been detected. A note too might have been added. When I mentioned the matter to you 10 days or a fortnight since, you still in your answer treated the matter with indifference, as if you did not think it worth while to consider the feelings of people. This I do think you do not — but I really think you ought. It was so with the triduo; I doubt whether you asked any one's opinion, before it was in type, whether you should publish it. Many heard it, and might have had an opinion. I have heard, I forget from whom, that, before St Camillo was published, you said there were passages in it which would startle people.

Don't make too much of it — what is now happening is no great thing — A. Phillips gets no triumph — but it just is sufficient to warn one that trouble may happen, if the world's opinion is neglected

I think what you propose to put is quite enough, and will do very well. I say this, however, not knowing precisely *what* the Cardinal's objection is. I suppose it is [sic] to lie against the translation as *inaccurate*. How did he find it out [?]

Ever Yrs affly J H N

P.S.   I suppose the notice comes in the conclusion of your Preface to the new volume — and does not stand by itself.

Why do you change 'mighty' into 'powerful?' I don't say 'powerful' is not better, but it was quoted to me '*al*mighty' — if then you put 'powerful,' this misconception will continue. Would it not be better to *quote* your words as they stand in print already? — but perhaps you mean to do so.[2]

TO RICHARD STANTON

Oy Bm May 23/51

My dear F Richard,

I must still put off the music question. I write selfishly about our own matters.

14 Oct. 1848, Newman had laid down that the lives of active saints should come out first, when the English Oratory made itself responsible for Faber's series.

[1] Faber wrote, on 30 April, that he had inserted in St Camillus's *Life*, passages omitted in the version approved by Fr Buggenoms. See also letter of 11 Sept. 1850. Faber now replied that the latter was opposed to omissions.

[2] This postscript refers to the retraction about St Camillus 'imploring the mighty assistance' of his adorable crucifix. Faber followed Newman's advice. See *The Lives of Father Antonio Talpa . . . Eustachio . . . and Prever*, London 1851, pp. xi–xii.

Inclosed you have a beautiful drawing, which is so precious I must have it back. Let me have the criticisms of any who care to give them, though, till Monday is over, I suppose you are very busy.

When Eminenza comes on Monday, ⟨(dont show *him* the drawing)⟩ I want you to get hold of him, and ask him if he knows of any Italian or Spanish architect or man of taste now in London, some one above par, who could give us hints and criticisms. Nothing strikes my fancy in style more than the sort of Roman style I inclose the specimen of; it has a smack of moorish and gothic — and has all the beauty of Greece with something of the wildness of other styles — yet without the extravagance of the moor and the gloom of the Goth. The simple Basilica style is heavy — we have got a model made which looks inside like an omnibus.

If Eminenza knows of no one, perhaps Mr Doyle[1] could name some accomplished person, whom I could meet and have a talk with. Mr Flanagan is a most capital *architect* — every one is admiring the strength of our building, which they say will last for ever (we are using 1,700,000 bricks) but I dont suppose he has much taste.

Tell F Antony, if the Sacristan has an ear for any light matter on the Eve of St Philip, that the other night, during discipline, Brother Charles lost his place, and spun about amid the whips and against their wielders, till, when the Nunc dimittis and the light came, I found him deposited in a vacant space which, reverentiae ergo, they leave just before me.

Ever Yrs affly J H N

SATURDAY 24 MAY 1851   F Joseph and Lady O A [Olivia Acheson] returned

SUNDAY 25 MAY   Dr Dollinger and Sir John Acton called[2]

MONDAY 26 MAY   to dinner the Bishop Dr Dollinger Sir John Acton Mr Jeffreys, O Sullivan, Dr Weedall, Formby, Estcourt[3] Mr Poncia, Bretherton, Jephson.

TUESDAY 27 MAY   Dr Jones came down to see Lady O. A.

[1] This was Henry Doyle (1827–92), who was among the guests of the London Oratory on 26 May. He had made a study of art, and was later Director of the National Gallery of Ireland. He was the son of John Doyle, the political caricaturist, and the brother of 'Dicky' Doyle of *Punch*.

[2] Acton, who had been a boy of eleven at Oscott in 1845, when Newman first visited the place, went to Munich in 1848 to study under Döllinger, and remained with him for the next six years.

[3] These five were Birmingham priests, and the remaining three, Birmingham laymen.

TO LADY OLIVIA ACHESON AND OTHERS

May 27 [1851][1]

We the undersigned in all humility entreat our kind and indulgent
father not to deprive our thirsting souls of the conclusion of his most
attractive sermon on the comparison of the saints of different nations —
but to continue it for our instruction, from where the bell interrupted it,
viz: The Seraphic St Francis —

Olivia Acheson if she will contrive to hear me, sitting at home in her
easy chair.

Elinor French as soon as she can go through the Saints of the names
of Colman, Finian, Kieran, Kentigern, and Kebby.

C. A. Bathurst when her school can show a Saint younger than St
Rose and wiser than St Theresa.

M. Georgina S
St John must learn first to chirp, and must have a little down
on her wings.

Elizabeth Moore when she has made and illuminated vestments of the
Spanish, Italian, cockney, and every other cut.

M. R. Giberne if she will be good enough to canonize half a do[zen
on occ]asion, and give me their measure.

J H N.

TO LADY OLIVIA ACHESON

Friday[2]

My dear Lady Olivia,

I hope you quite understood that I thought that *sofa*, which I saw,
would not do for you. You must get another. I mentioned it to Miss
Bathurst yesterday, but I find from her today that nothing has been
done about it.

We will come on Sunday and give you communion, and to Miss
Moore too if she is not well enough to come to Church

Ever Yrs most sincerly in Xt J H N

[1] This paper is undated, but 1851 is the only year in which the ladies concerned
were together in Birmingham. The comments after each signature are in Newman's
hand, the text of the letter in that of Miss Giberne.
[2] This letter is undated, but appears to belong to this period.

THURSDAY 29 MAY 1851   F Joseph went to Brighton for a month and more
FRIDAY 30 MAY   Recollect the Bond of the Debentures
MONDAY 2 JUNE   Miss Mason went
TUESDAY 3 JUNE   Shortlands came
THURSDAY 5 JUNE   still cold wind and rain — and fires

TO MRS LUCY AGNES PHILLIPS

Oratory Birmingham June 5. 1851

My dear Madam,

I fear you have thought me neglectful in not acknowledging your letter, but I have been ever wishing to answer it, without finding time. Be sure I take great interest in what you say, and will not forget you. I have put you (without mentioning your name) on our private prayer list.[1]

It is quite true that the Catholic Church claims your absolute submission to her in matters of faith — Unless you believe her doctrines as the word of God revealed to you through her, you can gain no good by professing to be a Catholic — you are not one really. At the same time she does not ask your confidence without giving reasons for claiming it — and one mode of proving her divine authority among others, certainly is that which it has occurred to you to adopt — viz to see whether certain of her doctrines are not *like* truth, or reasonable, or scriptural, or conformable to the state of the world. You certainly may gain a ground for believing her, through the *vraisemblance* of her doctrines — but you cannot *fully* prove them — you can only see their excellence to a certain point — else, what the need of a *revelation?* a revelation implies the grant of something which could not otherwise be known. If then you have chosen this way of approaching the Church, you must think it enough to prove her doctrines *to a certain point* — and then your argument will be this, '*Since* I have been able to prove the Catholic doctrines *so far*, I will take the whole on faith —' just as you trust an informant who has in other matters already shown he has a claim to be trusted.

The more *obvious* reasons for believing the Church to come from God are its great notes, as they are called — such as its antiquity, universality, its unchangeableness through so many revolutions and controversies, its adaptation to our wants. The more you think on these

---

[1] Lucy Agnes Phillips, sister of C. J. Vaughan the Headmaster of Harrow, and widow (left with a son and two daughters) of George Peregrine Phillips, an evangelical clergyman, had been first drawn towards the Church four years earlier by a remark of Dr Duke, who was attending her dying husband, at St Leonards.

subjects, the more, under God's grace, will you be led to see that the Catholic Church is God's *guide* to you. How ignorant we are! do we not *want* a guide? is the structure of Scripture such as to answer the purposes of a guide? How can a bare letter, written 2000 years ago, though inspired, *guide* an individual now? Every thing has its use — God uses it according to its use — Is it the use of a written Word to answer doctrinal questions starting up to the end of time? as little surely, as it is the use of a spade to saw with, or a plough to reap with. If then Divine Mercy has given individuals, you and me, a revelation, *how*, in what *channel*, does He bring it home to us? Even the Jews, whose doctrinal system was so simple, had a visible church.

All this does not involve a denial of grace being given to those who are external to the Church. All we say is this, that grace is given them in *order* to bring them into it — for that reason it has been mercifully given to you.

You ask me whom to advise you to apply to — I do not know what Miss Bowles's engagements are (of the St Leonard's Convent) — but she is a person who would quite enter into your difficulties. If you know Dr Duke too, he would be of great use to you — but then I suppose he is busy all day in his profession. Should you know him, pray give him my kindnest regards, and thank him for his attentions to F. Gordon when at St Leonard's —

I am, My dear Madam, Very faithfully Yours

John H Newman   Congr. Orat.[1]

TO RICHARD STANTON

Oratory Bm. June 6/51

My dear F Richard

Thank you for your remarks on the plans I sent you. The place of the *altar* is as it is at the Oratorian Church at *Naples* — testibus me et P Ambrosio, who assisted at Vespers there — Also the F Superior has sent me a plan of it, which I could show you. The choir is behind the Altar. I suspect it is so also at the Chiesa Nuova — and, if there *were* a choir in the Gesù, would it not be behind the altar? I wish you could learn for me which are the best engravings of Churches in Spain e.g. Robert's?[2] — and whether it would be possible to get a second hand

---

[1] Mrs Phillips visited Birmingham, where she was received at the end of Aug. 1851. She settled there, and worked for the Oratory until her death on 3 March 1857.

[2] David Roberts's *Picturesque Sketches in Spain*, London 1837.

copy cheap — Considering that every thing is going the way of Gothic (for the Tablet shows there are two sides to the Cardinal's sermon)[1] it is very important we should do something really good. The Spanish and Sicilian style seems to me one, which *must* strike; whereas the Roman, or most ancient Basilica, is somewhat like an omnibus. The Cardinal says there is *no one* in London who could help us. Is this *possible?*

Congratulate F Wilfrid on the Cardinal's sermon, and thank him for sending the C's letter.[2] The title (considering what our Bishop said) should be 'Oil upon the waters —' and the motto from Pugin's last work, 'He who says he likes Gothic yet does not like skreens, is a *liar.*'

Do you think Doyle, or any one he would recommend, has studied *colour* so as to be of assistance to us in the church. Since we do not distinguish ourselves in *form*, we must make much of colour. E.g. how beautiful the colouring of St Peter's is! If the Apse does not show well in this way, it will be counted a failure. I am very glad to see the adaptations of glass are progressing so much — here is a great opening for colour.

As to the Music, it seems to me quite possible to decide *what* is theatrical and what is not in the particular case. And I do not see why you should prescribe *composers*, but compositions. E.g. Mozart may write things which are not theatrical. I don't wish to make light of a difficult subject, or to slur over it, but this is what appears to me. Write again on the subject, if you have ought to say

Ever Yrs affly J H N.

---

[1] The *Tablet*, 31 May, p. 347, reported Wiseman as saying in his sermon at the London Oratory, on 26 May, that the Churches after Constantine were built 'without much art,' while in the Middle Ages there were 'erected temples that rivalled those of Solomon.' He asked 'Shall we revert to the old examples of our ancestors, or shall we import the changed style of those countries where the Church has never slumbered? The Cardinal owned he preferred the former, but only if adapted to the changed spirit of modern times. Thus no pinnacle of cold stone round the tabernacle . . . all things must give way to the exigencies of the rubrics of the Church and to the spirit of modern devotions.' The *Tablet* concluded by calling this an 'important *pronouncement* . . . evidently called forth by the recent tirades of the ultra-Goths.' Faber, on 27 May, had quoted Wiseman as saying: 'St. P [Philip] was the type of modern times and modern charity—no carved pinnacles should interrupt our view of Philip's love, Jesus in the Eucharist—no longer could we pray in dark corners of Churches intercepted with pillars—we in England have been in chaos, now that we are emerging we must look at Rome and Italy and see what the Bridegroom has been whispering to the Bride these 300 years—'

[2] Faber also described the effect of the sermon, 'Manning who was in choir was much affected, F. Bernard whimpered, I in my grand cope nearly cried in Eminenza's face, and old Ward blubbered freely in the tribune.'

SUNDAY 8 JUNE 1851   Shortlands received in Church   Monsell to dinner
MONDAY 9 JUNE   F Fred. [Bowles] went home

TO RICHARD STANTON

Oy Bm. June 9/51

My dear F R

Thanks for your hints — I am amused at your notion that we shall finish down to the façade before the electric telegraph can convey your hints, or at least my reply. 'Twill be well if our third generation decide about it. We have two or three thousand pounds — and all we aim at, is a shell of a head and shoulders.

As to the place of the Altar, think what a remarkable fact it is that the Naples Church should have the choir behind it. Mr Flanagan has got the plan, or I would trace it out for you. You dont therefore fancy, I suppose, that the *presbytery* is behind. The Sacred Ministers sit in *front*. It runs this way.

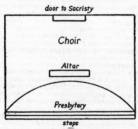

As to the Italian architect, the thing would be to see if his *plans* are in London.[1] If we sent to him, we should have to pay for his plans. I am intensely of opinion that foreigners do such things infinitely better than we. Look at the public buildings of London and Paris. But at present we shall be doing very little — viz an apse and testudo, which only requires due measurements. At the same time I covet very much some foreign opinion. I wonder whether there is any good architect in Paris who would assist us. Before I can say any thing about Bulmer,[2] I

---

[1] Wiseman reported 'that an Italian architect had sent in a very beautiful design for the Italian Church in London.'

[2] A decorator recommended by Stanton.

must get from Mr Flanagan the probable cost of the bricks and mortar of the shell of the apse — one shall then see how much is over to lay out in ornament.

Don't trust F Frederic's facts — they are always imaginations. He told me you wanted to change the cloke to the foreign one — I said I saw no objection to it, but could not pledge ourselves at once to do the same, as it would involve expence — as to the hat, I am open, as Prince Albert is, to improvements — but I have not yet heard of one — The common hat seems to me more ridiculous than our present — would it do if our present were made less stiff? i.e. the *angles* not so mathematical, which a less rigid material or a different kind of beaver would effect. I dont think you should *strikingly* differ from us — Else the habit ceases to be a uniform.

Ever Yrs affly J H N

TUESDAY 10 JUNE 1851   Archbishop Nicholson called

TO HENRY WILBERFORCE

Oratory Bm. June 10/51

My dear Henry

I am sorry to have kept you in suspence — I return the MS. I did not know you were in a hurry.

Will you let me say it? I don't think you *ought* to be. The first reason of my delay was my want of time — but I had another — I could not get myself to enter into the *spirit* of your project. No one can be more intensely devout (in *intellect* ⟨appreciation⟩) towards the psalms than I am — nor more intensely sensible of the deficiencies of the Catholic version — but ⌜the duty of all converts is to throw themselves into things as they are, not to carve out devotions for themselves any more than creeds, but take and use some or other among those which they find.⌝[1] I think in various respects you need to [be] put on your guard here.

Excuse this hasty and abrupt note

Ever Yours affectly in Xt   John H Newman   Congr. Orat.

---

[1] When copying this sentence twenty-five years later Newman began '[[I think it]] the duty of all converts to throw . . .' The outer sheet of the letter has in Newman's hand 'The Revd H W Wilberforce'

TO JONATHAN HENRY WOODWARD

Oratory Birmingham June 13. 1851

My dear Mr Woodward

I should be rejoiced to see you here at any time, and to make your acquaintance. We could give you a bed.

Let me congratulate you, as I do most sincerely, on your reception into Catholic communion. I earnestly trust and pray that Robert Williams will not be left behind. I have had no good information whether Mrs Woodward has been received or not.[1]

As to your inquiry, it would be a great pleasure to me, could we help you — but we are quite unable. The account you give of your parish is interesting, yet anxious. I could say more than I can write — but do not encourage rapid conversions, till you have obtained for them the presence of a priest who is likely to *understand* them. Else you may have defections after a while.[2]

Excuse this shabby bit of paper. I have no other at hand — and beg for me your Bishop's blessing

Yours very truly in Xt   John H Newman   Congr. Orat.

TO RICHARD STANTON

Oratory Bm June 14/51

My dear F Richard

I wish you could beg, borrow or steal for me, Bellasis's pamphlet — was it not his? which Mr Reynolds read out of in the house and Sir James Graham. It had a *list* of the epithets the Anglican Bishops gave the aggression — atrocious, insolent impure [?] etc. You shall have it back.[3] Tell F Antony I said Mass for him yesterday

Ever Yrs Affly J H N

[1] Jonathan Henry Woodward (1805–79), at Trinity College, Dublin, and Vicar of St James's Bristol, had just become a Catholic. His wife, Mary Susannah Woodward (1818–1903), daughter of J. W. Cunningham, Vicar of Harrow-on-the-Hill, appears to have done so at the same time. Robert Williams (1811–90), at Oriel 1828–32, a banker, had been a Tractarian, but after Newman's conversion became an Evangelical. He is referred to in *Apo.* p. 116 as 'very dear to me, a Protestant still.'

[2] Woodward wanted help in the reception of some of his former parishioners into the Church, similar to that given at Leeds. His bishop was Joseph Hendren, of Clifton.

[3] Stanton sent the pamphlet on 16 June, *The Anglican Bishops versus the Catholic Hierarchy: A Demurrer to further Proceedings*, London 1851. J. Reynolds, M.P. for Dublin City, read from it, in the debate on the second reading of the Ecclesiastical

SUNDAY 15 JUNE 1851   Dr Jones here
MONDAY 16 JUNE   Lady Olivia [Acheson] went to town
TUESDAY 17 JUNE   Wm Froude called

TO J. M. CAPES

Oy Bm June 17/51

My dear Capes

I did not at all neglect your letter. I wrote off at once to F Gordon, and am really sorry he returns the answer I inclose. It has disappointed me. It has just come.[1]

As for myself I am just commencing a set of Public Lectures at the Corn Exchange and going to Press with them. They run on till the end of September.[2] It is well if I get through them without great exertion. I would help you, if it were physically possible — but it is a physical, if not a metaphysical, impossibility.

No one deserves to be helped more than you — but I don't know where to look about, to help you. As to K. Wm Str [King William Street] they have abjured literature as sinful — and as to Sermons even and Lectures, F Dalgairns promised in print a set of Lectures on the Sacred Heart, which he has not had time yet to write.[3]

Is it impossible to get Allies or H Wilberforce to do any thing for you? I will write gladly to either of them, but fancy you are likely to have anticipated me.

I conclude in a great hurry

Ever Yrs affly J H Newman

P.S.   I have not expressed to you my great concern at your state of health, tho' I can't be surprised at it with your work —

THURSDAY 19 JUNE 1851   C C [Corpus Christi]   F Edward went for holy day
FRIDAY 20 JUNE   Mr Flanagan here

Titles Bill, on 14 March. Sir James Graham refused to join the Ministry because he disapproved of the Bill. Newman seems not to have made use of the pamphlet. See note in *Prepos.* p. 77. See also Edward Bellasis, *Memorials of Mr Serjeant Bellasis*, 3rd ed., pp. 105–10, who, however, gives a wrong date.

[1] Gordon was convalescing at Brighton.

[2] *Lectures on Catholicism in England*, now *Lectures on the Present Position of Catholics in England*. They were delivered weekly, from 30 June to 1 Sept., except for the first Monday in August. Each lecture was on sale separately, a week after delivery.

[3] See letter of 10 Feb. 1851 to Dalgairns.

SATURDAY 21 JUNE   Mr Woodward came
SUNDAY 22 JUNE   Mr Woodward went at night

TO LADY OLIVIA ACHESON

Oratory Bm June 22/51

My dear Lady Olivia,

It was very kind in you writing to me. I don't know quite whether to be glad or sorry the Chapel is so far off — glad, I think — for it makes it clearer to you, as you would wish it to be, that you must return soon. I certainly think you right to have determined as you have.

Your hint about Miss Munro is a good one — it is a shame I have not spoken to Miss Moore yet — I shall this very day — but I am getting into the dreadful whirlpool of those Lectures — three months! I dread it very much.

And now, to complete my state of confusion, your letter has walked away, and I cannot see if there is any thing to reply to. It will come to hand, I hope before the post.

F Stanislas's cousin comes on Friday, or Friday week — he seemed much pleased at your message.

I don't think our procession went off in our best way. It wants a burst of voices, and a week day does not provide them. We have had, and have, some beautiful flowers.

Pray say every thing kind from me to Lady Georgiana [Fullerton] when you see her — I am so glad she is in London, and well. I am surprised you don't know Manning.[1]

See how stupid I am, still I am Ever Yours most sincerely in Xt

John H Newman   Congr. Orat.

TO RICHARD STANTON

June 22/51

My dear F Richard

I can't tell whether I have written to tell you *not* to get Roberts' Spain, thank you — for Nicholas says it will be no use to us.

As to the Secret Corrector, it would be dangerous, it seems to me, to consult with '*an*other —' yet I am not prepared to say it would be

---

[1] Henry Edward Manning was received on 6 April, and ordained a Catholic priest on 15 June, giving Benediction that evening at the London Oratory.

wrong to consult with F Superior or with F Director — or again with F Novice Master in certain cases — but I dont like to pronounce at once[1]

I am in a *whirl* of composition, alas —

Ever Yrs affly J H N

MONDAY 23 JUNE 1851 Mr Flanagan went F Frederic went to Mr Eyston
TUESDAY 24 JUNE F Fred. returned F Henry went for holiday
WEDNESDAY 25 JUNE F Fred went to his brother's marriage

TO LADY OLIVIA ACHESON

Oy. Bm. June 26/51

My dear Lady Olivia,

I hope you will find some priest to come to you — for, as you are under an express medical course, which has been one purpose of your going up, I think you should follow Dr Jones's advice about not going out before breakfast.

Your letter perplexes me on one point, which is nothing to the purpose however. I can't construe the word 'faith' — 'because of the faith —' 'if interfering with my faith.' I have turned the sentences all possible ways, and quite smile at my own stupidity

Excuse haste, and believe me, Ever Yours most sincerely in Xt

John H Newman Congr. Orat.

FRIDAY 27 JUNE 1851 F Stanislas went to fetch his cousin
SATURDAY 28 JUNE F Stanislas returned

TO J. D. DALGAIRNS

St Peter & St Paul. [1851]

My dear F B

I have told the Printer always to send you the *revise.* which 1 please compare carefully with the proof, for it does not come down to me. There are many faults in this first Lecture. 2 Return it to them

[1] Stanton asked whether the Corrector, whose duty it was to warn members of the Community privately of their faults, might consult with another before correcting.

directly, if you possibly can, for each Lecture is to come down to me for *sale*, the Saturday after you receive it. I hope this will not try you.

I am fidgetted. I fear these Brummagems will take my first Lecture as serious — and then, to make up for it, all my others, which (alas) are getting prosy for irony

Ever Yrs affly J H N

P.S.   Tell Father Wilfrid I wish to write to him, but am so busy.

MONDAY 30 JUNE 1851   Manning and H W [Wilberforce] here   My Lectures began in the Corn Exchange[1]   (I think they were once a week)

TO DAVID LEWIS

Oratory Bm June 30/51

My dear Lewis

I have not answered your Pontifical question, but cannot make up my mind, and am very busy.[2] And now I say so, because I am obliged to make some excuse, since I am writing to you some more questions. As Jacob was obliged to send down Benjamin.

First, I am told here that Blanco White's Poor Man's Preservative against Popery is out of print. I cannot believe it. I believe it to be on the Christian Knowledge List. It would be a great kindness, if I had it by return of post.[3]

Also could you turn to the columns of the Standard Newspaper of April 1836, for that paper's lament over the unhorsing of King William ⟨It was blown up April 8⟩ on College Green, which I thought at the time less Protestant than became an opponent of the *idolatry* of Rome.[4] Should they seem to you good, will you copy out a few sentences for me?

---

[1] The Corn Exchange had been opened in 1847, in High Street, Birmingham. It had desks and counters at the side, but the floor was open. If a painting of Miss Giberne may be relied on, Newman delivered his lectures, on a dais, seated, with a reading desk for his manuscript, on his left.

[2] Lewis asked on 23 May, 'Is it true to say that a christian is a subject of the Pope before he is a subject of any particular Bishop?'

[3] J. Blanco White, *The Poor Man's Preservative against Popery*, London 1825. See *Prepos.* p. 144, where Newman explains that because the book was based on facts, it had not made an impression against Catholics; and so was withdrawn from the list of the Society for Promoting Christian Knowledge. Cf. letter of 6 July to Lewis.

[4] Lewis could not find the passage in the *Standard*, but Newman had among his papers a copy made by a friend of an account in the *Dublin Annals*. See *Prepos.* p. 181, where Newman used the episode to defend the veneration of images.

Also can you give me any information about a debate on the Coronation Oath, in Lord Grey's time, in which Lord Brougham advocated a dispensing power *somewhere or other*?[1]

I give my first of a course of Lectures to-day in the Corn Exchange — and have got a hoarseness. I shall be satisfied, and ought to be, if I get two hundred hearers[2]

Ever Yours, J H Newman

TUESDAY 1 JULY 1851   Manning and H W [Wilberforce] went

TO LADY OLIVIA ACHESON

Oy Bm July 1/51

My dear Lady Olivia

I write in great hurry, as I am just setting-to my Lecture — but I won't delay a moment. I have been very anxious to hear from you.

It is my full conviction you should return here at once — i.e. the very first day you think you can do so with convenience. The mind makes the body ill, as well as the body the mind, at very least.

Would not Mr Monsell gladly bring you? Of course you don't mind asking him — else, I will write to him, or (to save time) if you like it, lest you should be delicate would beg you to ask him from me — I am sure, he would *rejoice* to do you any service

Ever Yrs most sincerely in Xt   John H Newman   Congr. Orat.

P.S.   Miss French told me yesterday she wished you back exceedingly. She has been *most* kind about copying for me, and done me a great service. I was ashamed to ask her. I have had no letters which you anticipated.

WEDNESDAY 2 JULY 1851   news of appointment of four bishops[3]

[1] Lewis replied on 7 July, 'I have hitherto failed about the deposing power,' and on 24 July 'nobody but you knows anything of the Brougham debate.'

[2] The audience was described as 'large and respectable.'

[3] i.e. James Brown (1812–81), to Shrewsbury, Thomas Burgess (1791–1854), to Clifton, George Errington (1804–86), to Plymouth, and William Turner (1799–1872), to Salford.

TO F. W. FABER

July 2/51

My dear F Wilfrid,

Thanks for your news; which *was* news.[1]

As far as I recollect, it was Mr Cotter of St George's, who called here and said that after the Cardinal was gone the people in Golden Square took the red books we were sending as a present to the Pope out of Stewart's boxes, did them up with other things, and directed them to the Vatican.[2]

Ever Yrs affly J H N

FRIDAY 4 JULY 1851   F Frederic returned

TO J. D. DALGAIRNS

Oy Bm July 4/51

My dear F Bernard

Your criticism is a very important one.[3] See if the following approves itself to you.

1. Burning is *not unlawful*. This is implied in Leo the 10th's condemnation of Luther's proposition.[4] (I don't know of any other decision — Is there any thing in the Council of Constance?)

2. Burning etc. are not *necessary*.

3. Burning etc. vary with the age, *as penances do*.

4. It is not necessary *because* they burned in the middle age to burn now, any more than because they imposed swinging penances then, to put them on now.

5. I don't suppose we should return to a thousand medieval practices, *though we could*.

[1] See diary for this day.

[2] The Oratorians were presenting a set of Newman's works, bound in red morocco, to Wiseman. The books were taken out of the bookseller's boxes and sent, in error, to Rome, where they were found nearly three years later. See letters of 13 Oct. 1850 and 28 April 1854 to Faber. Jeremiah Cotter was one of the priests at St George's, Southwark.

[3] Dalgairns, at Newman's request, was looking over the second of the 'Lectures on Catholicism in England,' to be delivered on 7 July. In it Newman laid it down 'that Catholics would not burn Protestants if they could,' *Prepos.* p. 79. Dalgairns evidently hesitated as to whether this could be asserted absolutely.

[4] Luther's proposition reads: 'Haereticos comburi est contra voluntatem Spiritus.' The proposition was condemned by Leo X in his bull, *Exsurge Domine*, 15 June 1520.

6. Therefore I think *we should not burn, if we could*

7. Observe, I rest it on the utter, certain, inexpediency of it.

8. I believe, when you examine it, *the Church* has burnt etc very few. *Innocent II* and others are strongly *against* violence.

9. And it never has been declared right, or praised by the Church — it has only been said *not to be wrong.*(?)[1]

You make a most cruel mark of unintelligibility, on what I thought one of my best hits? 'Let the Protestant paint up Popery, and the profligate will mistake it for virtue —' Should it be 'take'? or what is the matter?[2]

Ever Yrs affly J H N

Thank you for the pains you are taking.

SATURDAY 5 JULY 1851   Lady O A [Acheson] returned from London with Monsell

TO DAVID LEWIS

July 6. [1851]

My dear Lewis

I am ashamed to give you so much trouble.

I am bringing in Blanco White — and my notion is, from his '*Life*' and '*Evidences*,' the two works I have,[3] that he only speaks on his *personal knowledge* to 3 *infidel* clergymen besides himself — (In his Life, however, we hear of a Sotomayor turned Protestant, and 3 canons, who, I suppose, were so too) — Now I want to know how far Doblado and the Poor Man's Preservative *enlarge* this evidence, and floor me.[4]

---

[1] Dalgairns agreed, on 8 July, that Newman's assertion in the lecture was fully justified, but thought he underestimated 'the number of persons burned by the Church.'

[2] Lecture II, *Prepos.* 1st ed. p. 65. Newman's point was that the profligate comes to believe virtue 'is nothing else than hypocrisy grafted on licentiousness,' and this is the picture Protestants paint of Popery. Dalgairns replied on 8 July: 'I beg your pardon for not understanding your hit about the "Profligate." After a considerable deal of study I have made it out; but I beg leave to state I am the only member of the London Oratory who has made it out. It is a hit, but I must say not a palpable one.' Newman omitted the phrase in later editions, *Prepos.* p. 67.

[3] *The Life of the Rev. Joseph Blanco White . . .*, edited by *John Hamilton Thom*, 3 vols., London 1845, and *Practical and Internal Evidence against Catholicism . . .*, London 1825.

[4] For Doblado's *Letters from Spain* and *The Poor Man's Preservative from Popery* see letters of 19 May and 30 June to Lewis, who sent Newman extracts from these works. Their evidence was inconclusive, and not relevant to Newman's argument, as he explained in a footnote, in *Prepos.* pp. 153-4.

Also I should like very much to have the heads of chapters of the Poor Man's Preservative.

Thank you for the trouble I put you to about the Standard. I have a lively recollection of a passage in the Standard compassionating the Statue — it might be the Irish Correspondent, or a letter[1]

Ever Yrs affly J H N

TO ANTONY HUTCHISON

Oy Bm July 7/51

My dear F A

Excuse great haste. F Gaudentius wrote to me lately to say he meant to *take* the furniture — And inclosed a huge list, comprising every thing of consequence — all the iron beds, the towels, napkins, chairs, etc etc[2]

So F Ambrose went over last week — and sure enough, they have taken above £200 worth. F Ambrose says that what remains is not *worth* my taking — old tea cups, tops of vegetable dishes, a priedieu etc

I write you word without delay — for F Ambrose only returned Saturday evening. Those monks have a queer and holy simplicity

Ever Yrs affly J H N

TUESDAY 8 JULY 1851   Dr Cullen came, and slept.

TO ANTONY HUTCHISON

July 8/51

My dear F A

What do you think of this? — you and *we* ⟨(London and Birmingham)⟩ are altogether owed £340 in furniture at St W's. [Wilfrid's] Now suppose we tell the Passionists they may pay *interest* for it, taking the whole? the interest is about £10 at 3 per cent. They could discharge it in Masses for Mrs Caswall.[3]

---

[1] See letter of 30 June to Lewis.

[2] The Passionists were taking over St Wilfrid's from the Oratorians, and had transferred most of the furniture elsewhere. See letter of 17 July to Hutchison, and cf. letter of 20 Jan. 1851 to Fr Gaudentius.

[3] Edward Caswall's wife was buried at St Wilfrid's, and he arranged for masses to be said for her there.

As they have already taken some Masses for her, it will be no new idea to them.

Ever Yrs affly J H N

WEDNESDAY 9 JULY 1851   Bastard came

TO T. W. ALLIES

Oratory, Bm July 9. 1851.

My dear Allies,

The Primate left this place this morning. Between ourselves, there is no doubt he feels Dublin to be the place.[1] And it is now only a few hours from England, from London.

He is in *London*. I wish you could see him. I wish Hope could see him. You have much to bear up against, but all will turn out well.[2]

In haste Ever yours affectly J H. N.

P.S.   He is gone to Town to *talk* about the University. Say everything kind from me to the Bellasises.

TO MRS J. W. BOWDEN

Oy. Bm. July 9/51

My dear Mrs Bowden

I should like to write you a long letter, but, as usual when I wish to do so, I am cruelly busy. I shall only write about Marianne, which of course is so very important.

I hope she will not be hasty. She ought quite to understand what she is doing. F Brownbill of course will be so careful, that it is only my anxiety makes me speak.

In any convent worth any thing, she would have something to go thro' at first — and this might startle her. A convent worth any thing, and which is not a boarding house, has a *system* — and to get *assimilated* to the system is a process. And it is not like *home*; it is *meant* as a morti-

---

[1] Dr Cullen, Archbishop of Armagh, Primate of All Ireland, visited Newman in order to discuss the establishment of the Catholic University, and favoured Dublin as the site for it.

[2] This is a reference to Allies' poverty and inability to find a position, since his conversion in Sept. 1850.

fication; a young woman is thrown on herself; she has no dear mother to go to; she feels as if no one sympathised in her; and then some of the rules are so strange or so distasteful — thus she is tempted to despond and go back.

I dare say dear M. has not fully brought out her meaning to me — but she does not give her *object*. It is *not* teaching, *not* works of mercy. What is it? Life must have an *object* — She will soon get sad, and her mind will prey on itself, especially in inclosure, without an object. Contemplation indeed is abundantly an object — but 'inclosure and the divine office,' which alone she mentions, are not sufficient objects.

Young people are apt to deceive themselves in this point, viz: They feel a distaste to (which is called) settling in life — but this is not a vocation. The vow of obedience is the difficult vow. It is very complex — it is not merely obedience to one Superior, but to a state of things, resignation to companions she may not like etc etc. An intense devotion towards the Blessed Sacrament will overcome every trial, and that, I am sure, will grow in her more and more, but still it is well she should anticipate things a little.

I should not say all this, if it were not she is *silent* about her object — and then my anxiety comes in to make me say more perhaps than I have a right to do. I don't think it will be easy for her to find a convent to suit her. You will do me a kindness, the more you tell me about her

Ever Yrs affly in Xt   J H N

P.S.   They tell me you are not well.

TO MARIANNE BOWDEN

Oratory. Bm July 9/51

My dear Marianne

I have thought of you a good deal since your letter — and shall say Mass for you (the Mass de B.M.V.) on Friday next — my only vacant day. —

Of course you are in such good hands as being under F Brownbill's direction, that I have little really to say.

We are not likely to set up any Convent here. You must not be discouraged if you do not find any one to suit you at once — I know a Lady who has just joined one, who was at least a year and a half looking about — perhaps much longer.

You do not mention the *end* of the order you wish to join — but I suppose, by your cutting off works of mercy and teaching, it would be contemplation. Most orders, however, which are contemplative, have, I think, austerities, which would be too much for you.

There are Communities which teach, which yet do not oblige every one who belongs to them to teach. There is a Convent of English Benedictines at Ypres, I hear a good deal of, the Mother Superior, I believe, is a Lady of family, English.[1] Teaching is their object, but I believe all do not teach. The same may be the case of Taunton ⟨⟨(Franciscans)⟩⟩ — I am told Westbury, (St Fr de Sales) is the only English Convent, where there is no teaching (i.e. — besides Sisters of Charity etc) — it has various recommendations.[2] Perhaps something else may strike me Love to Emily

Ever Yrs affectly in Xt   John H Newman   Congr. Orat.

FRIDAY 11 JULY 1851   Mr Crofton came

TO JAMES HOPE

⌐Oratory Birmingham July 11. 1851

My dear Hope,

Shall I be very unreasonable in asking an answer to this question, and, if possible, by return of post?

I am going to say in a public Lecture on Monday, that if Mr Spooner had said about us elsewhere, what he is reported to have said in the House of Commons, his words would have been actionable[3]

Is this contempt of the House, and can I be had up to the Bar?

I asked Monsell when he was here, and he made light of it — I showed him Mr Anstey's attempted motion about the Freeman's Journal, and he had no explanation to give.[4]

[1] By exception, the Irish Benedictine Dames at Ypres had an English abbess, Mary Winifred Jarrett, elected in 1840.

[2] Marianne Bowden entered the Convent of the Visitation at Westbury-on-Trym, Bristol, in Aug. 1852.

[3] See Newman's letter to the Editor of the *Morning Chronicle*, 15 May 1851.

[4] Thomas Chisholm Anstey (1816–73), English convert, Member of Parliament 1847–52, was an advocate of the extreme Irish party. His motion of 30 June 1851 proposed that the printer of the *Freeman's Journal* should be called to the bar of the House of Commons for publishing a misrepresentation of a statement Anstey had made in a recent speech there. It concerned the Maynooth Grant, and the Irish bishops had taken exception to it. See the *Freeman's Journal*, 2 July 1851.

The proof has come down this morning, and some of us are rather nervous.[7]

Excuse this trouble,[1]

Yours affectly in Xt   John H Newman   Cong. Orat.

SATURDAY 12 JULY 1851   Bastard went

TO SAMUEL MINTON

Oy Bm July 13/51

Revd Sir,

I beg to acknowledge your letter just received.[2] I suppose I shall have in due time Aris's Gazette with your letter addressed to me. Whatever are its contents, I hope you will feel it no disrespect if I say I am not likely to feel myself called upon to give any direct answer to it, as I could not devote [?] my attention to it without neglecting prior arrangements and existing duties.

Yrs &c J H N

TUESDAY 15 JULY 1851   Mr Crofton received

TO ARCHBISHOP CULLEN

Oratory Birmingham July 15. 1851

My dear Lord

Your letter dated Sunday has only just come. I reply to it by the early Post.

I feel exceedingly the kindness of your wish that I should come up to London, and both in obedience to it and from my zeal in the matter

---

[1] Hope, writing on 12 July, advised only an indirect allusion to the House of Commons such as: 'a statement had in the newspapers been attributed to Mr Spooner which, if not protected by some special privilege, would have been actionable.' Newman spoke even more vaguely in the lecture, and omitted Spooner's name. *Prepos.* pp. 118 ff. (1st ed. p. 115).

[2] Samuel Minton, a Liverpool clergyman, wrote to Newman on 12 July to say that he had addressed a letter to him which would be published in *Aris's Birmingham Gazette* on 14 July. In it, by way of answering Newman's first lecture, which had been reported in *Aris's Gazette* on 7 July, he attacked the Catholic doctrine of intention in the administration of the sacraments. Ambrose St John's reply was published on 21 July. See also letter of 20 Aug. to Minton.

to which it relates would wait on your Grace at once, could I possibly do so, as I am situated here. But I really cannot.[1]

I have to get *written, and transcribed* for the Press, by Friday Morning a Lecture of 40 printed pages, of which not one half is written — and I have now waiting below one of the Professors of the Queen's Colleges in Ireland to make his confession for reception — and am so driven and hunted, I do not know which way to turn.[2]

Most gladly would I make myself useful in so great an object as the Catholic University, but at this very moment I deeply regret, for I know what an important moment it is for the University, I am literally tied here

Begging your Grace's blessing I am, My dear Lord, Your faithful Servt in Xt

John H Newman   Congr. Orat.

P.S.   I do not know how your Grace feels about such matters, and you may have rules which make it impossible, but, if I might without a liberty ask the favor, I should wish to be allowed to place my Volume, when it is finished, under the Patronage of your Grace. It would be dedicating it to St Patrick, qui in haerede suo vivit ad huc.[3]

TO JAMES HOPE

⌐Oratory Bm July 16/51

My dear Hope,

I wish I could write to you about the University; I wish I had not to bore you with my present matters. But at present I am a man of one idea. The Printers are upon me; by the morning after next I must have copy finished and transcribed to the amount of 40 pages close type; and it is not near ready.

Could you off hand answer me a question? Can I be had up for a libel, in criminal court or civil, for saying against Dr Achilli the contents of the article in the Dublin, since published as a pamphlet?[4] I can't

[1] Cullen had written, asking Newman to come to London to discuss with Manning, Hope, and Monsell the setting up of the Catholic University.

[2] This was Morgan William Crofton, Professor of Natural Philosophy at Queen's College, Galway.

[3] Newman dedicated *Prepos.* to Cullen. See H. Tristram, *Newman and his Friends*, London 1933, pp. 144–8.

[4] Giacinto Achilli, an ex-Dominican, who had been condemned by the Inquisition in Rome for immorality and for preaching against the Catholic religion, had been

make out he has answered it. It contains the gravest charges, about his seducing women etc *with many of the legal documents* proving them.[1]

I am too dull and stupid to say more⌝

Ever Yrs affly in Xt   John H Newman

TO JAMES BURNS

Oy Bm July 17/51

Dear Mr Burns,

Various persons have pressed me to have simultaneously a cheap edition of my Lectures now delivering. I have had some printed off which I sell (without loss) at *2d* apiece *in* the Lecture Room, i.e. to those who attend — but they are not *published*.

The type must be broken up at once, so I must make my arrangements *without delay*.

Are you willing to undertake, at your own risk, any number of these cheap copies? I have had several offers. If they were sold for *3d* to the public there would be a gain of 1d on each copy or £ 4 the 1000, which you might think not worth the trouble.

I shall protect my 1/3 edition, — thus:— by having no title pages to the cheap Lectures, no preface, no dedication, no notes. So that they could not be made a volume of. In this way the cheap Lectures would, not only get among those who will not buy the dear, but will be advertised to those who will —

What do you think of this?[2]

Yours very truly John H Newman

lecturing in England to enthusiastic Protestant audiences since the early part of 1850. Wiseman wrote an article in *D R*, XXVII (June 1850), pp. 470–511, exposing in great detail Achilli's offences against morality. The article was revised and issued as a pamphlet, entitled *Authentic 'Brief Sketch of the Life of Dr. Giacinto Achilli,' containing a Confutation of the Mis-statements of Former Narratives. Extracted from the Dublin Review No. LVI, with additions and corrections*, London [n.d.]. The month of publication of the article in *D R* is generally given as July, as in *Ward* II, p. 278, and by Newman himself in *Prepos.* p. 207, note 5. This is probably due to an error on the cover of the June issue, which carries the imprint 'July, 1850.'

[1] Hope replied on 17 July, ' If you publish libellous matter, although it has been published before, you are open to an action. But as in this case the Challenge has been fairly made by others and no notice taken I do not think you would be in much danger. I have also been assured that abundant proof is forthcoming of the allegations against Achilli, and if you are satisfied on this point it is an additional security.'

[2] Burns did not accept this proposal, and the cheap edition of the lectures was published in Birmingham. Burns was already bringing out the lectures, as they were delivered, at 1/3 each, in the same form and pagination as the first edition, but each with an additional heading, and without the title-page and dedication.

TO ANTONY HUTCHISON

Oy Bm July 17/51

My dear F Antony

I have had a long letter from F Gaudentius, which is all nonsense, and a simple misunderstanding. But I have not answered him, *as waiting* for you to answer my *second* letter, which I sent the day after the first.[1]

It was to the effect, that, since they had made such inextricable confusion in the arrangement, they should *buy the whole*. And *till* they could pay us the money, pay us the *interest* on it. They could pay the interest by taking Mrs Caswall's Masses.

Your sum is	£154. 3.	9
The two houses —	177. 16.	9
	332. 0.	6 — adding valuation
		makes £340.

£340 at 3 per cent is about £10. I do not consider they would be giving rent for the furniture, but interest for our money.

Say what you think of this, and I will write to F Gaudentius at once

Ever Yrs affly J H N

P.S. F Gaudentius *refused* to take the whole, when he heard the price — then he said, 'May I have a few little things, at least for the present?' to this I said — Yes[2] —

They actually have taken the wool out of the matresses, put in straw, kept the matresses, and left me the wool *piled* up! they have taken the vegetable dishes, and left me the covers!

P.S. Your second letter is just come. We here have always been *against* taking the furniture. I *have been sincerely for it*, and meant to buy it on my own spec. But when F Gaudentius sent the list of things he meant to take, for which I asked him, and I found it swallowed up nearly all the available furniture, and sent F Ambrose in consequence, who reported as I have told you, since, I really do not see how I *could* take it, though I wished to do so. I doubt whether you could charge your lodging House with the full sum,[3] which we *may* fairly charge the passionists. I should say that Br Frederick carried off some linen some time ago, which we therefore *owe*.

[1] These were the letters of 7 and 8 July.
[2] Fr Gaudentius had defended himself to Hutchison by saying he had taken the furniture with Newman's knowledge and consent.
[3] A committee had been formed in London to open a lodging-house.

FRIDAY 18 JULY 1851   Dr Cullen dined with us[1]

TO MRS J. W. BOWDEN

Oy Bm July 19/51

My dear Mrs Bowden

I read your letter, 'the 28th —' but whether or not, I am right, any day almost will do for me. I am always engaged much on Friday, when my MS goes up and proof comes down — also somewhat on Monday — but else, e.g. Tuesday morning, would suit me any week. Do you know that the consecration of two Bishops is on the 27th at Oscott?[2]

I am quite overpowered with work. There is the Catholic University. Of all things I wish to help — not a week should be lost; and they will not move without me — and I physically *cannot* till these Lectures are done; and I cannot *hurry* the lectures — It would be like attempting to run 50 miles an hour on the narrow gauge.

Then there are endless letters on my table, each thinking itself the only letter unanswered. And there is this St Wilfrid's furniture teasing me. So you see I have a peck of troubles.

I am so glad about Henry, though not much surprised after what you told me before.[3] You don't think it best then for Charles to go on reading with Allies — I suppose he would have no home.

You must see our new house when you are here

Ever Yrs affly in Xt   J H N

P.S.   I have not forgotten your and Marianne's letters.
P.S.   *If* I stop the Lectures a week as I think of doing, Monday the 28th *will be the best possible day for me.*[4]

---

[1] Newman wrote in 1870, at the beginning of his 'Memorandum about my connection with the Catholic University,' 'In the conversation he (Cullen) had with me, he proposed to me to be President (Rector) of the proposed University, I replying that, should I be able to serve the undertaking in any way, I should be glad to do so, but I thought that for this end it would be sufficient if I was Prefect of Studies. I believe too, that I felt such an office as the latter would commit me less to an institution which had its seat in another country, and which on that account threatened, if I had the highest post in it, to embarrass my duties to the Birmingham Oratory.' *A.W.* p. 280.

[2] James Brown was consecrated for Shrewsbury, and Thomas Burgess for Clifton, on 27 July.

[3] The reference is to the intended conversion of Henry Bowden, Mrs Bowden's brother-in-law, which took place in 1852.

[4] The Bowdens came on Monday 28 July, when Newman gave his fifth lecture. On the following Monday, 4 Aug., he gave no lecture.

TO RICHARD STANTON

Oy Bm July 19/51

My dear F R

I will send a letter for Theiner on Monday ⟨Sunday night⟩ — please to get from Burns copies of 1 Loss and Gain, and 2 my Lectures of last year, and 3 such Lectures, as are published, of my present course — and from Longman 4 my Discourses — for Theiner.[1] Of course I will make a present of the books he wants. Stewart, I suppose, can furnish them. Will you get them?[2]

I am *dreadfully* oppressed with work.

As to the Malta House, it is very tempting.[3] We and you have members who would profit by it. The difficulty is this — 1. either we expatriate Fathers for good, which neither we or the fathers themselves would allow — 2 or we throw Fathers out of community and unsettle them. Moreover, when we come actually to the point, I suspect there will be *difficulties*, either with the Bishop of Malta, or Propaganda (though Father Cesarini and Dr Grant are away) — or as to the Funds etc etc.[4]

Yet could such a proposition as this be thrown out? 'We (i.e. Philippini of England) will engage to keep three Fathers at Malta, nine months in every year.'

This would be as *guests*, I suppose — but so as to enable the House to remain Philippined under Father Lebrun, and to cherish it *till* it got subjects and could keep up itself.[5]

I shall send you my letter to read — I suppose you will not be able to answer this *tonight*, at *least* by *parcel*.

Ever Yrs affly J H N.

---

[1] i.e. *Diff.* 1, *Prepos.* and *Mix.*

[2] On 1 July Theiner sent a letter to Newman, through Stanton, asking for a copy of Joseph Mendham, *Memoirs of the Council of Trent . . .*, London 1834–6. This he required for his continuation of the *Annals* of Baronius, and it was now sent to him. Origen's *Philosophoumena* which he also asked for, Newman sent out later. See letter of 20 Sept. to Theiner.

[3] Theiner was again urging the English Oratorians to take over the Oratory at Malta, which Fr Lebrun, one of its last members, offered them. See Newman's letters at the end of April 1847.

[4] Pacifico Cesarini, Superior of the Roman Oratory, and Thomas Grant when Rector of the English College had acted unco-operatively in the difficulties over St Wilfrid's. See letters of 24 and 25 Nov. 1849 to Faber.

[5] Paul Lebrun, the only remaining Oratorian at Malta, had a reputation for 'apostolic zeal.'

P.S.   Tell F Bernard that, as I find there *is time* for me to see the
Revise, I shall take them instead of him. It sometimes gives me things
to correct which I can only do *in* revise.

SEND ME BACK THEINER'S LETTER

MONDAY 21 JULY 1851   Lecture at Corn Exchange (4)

WEDNESDAY 23 JULY   Shortlands left us   Coopes [sic] to dinner   Dr Whitty
passed through   Coupe about this time

TO MRS J. W. BOWDEN

Oratory Bm July 23/51

My dear Mrs Bowden,

Westbury and Taunton had occurred to me.[1] Of the two Taunton
seems to me preferable — but they *teach* — I don't know whether all of
them — but they have a boarding school. At Westbury they have not,
and I suppose it is one of the easiest rules in England, but I have understood, though I do not wish it repeated, there are two sets among them,
one more educated than the other, which makes a sort of separation.

They say now the Consecration next Sunday is to be in London, not
at Oscott.

If you tell me where you are to be found, I had better come to you
next Monday — for we may be interrupted in this small house.

Ever Yrs affly in Xt   John H Newman   Congr. Orat.

TO ARCHBISHOP CULLEN

Oratory Bm July 23./51

My dear Lord,

I am going to say something to you which will make you smile.

Our Fathers here feel reluctant that I should be any thing but Rector
of the New University, as your Grace kindly proposed to me; under the
notion that since I am *their* Superior, I ought not to have a subordinate
place elsewhere.

I do not feel this *at all* myself — and I hope you will over rule it by
showing them what the way of doing things is at Rome. But since they
urge me, I write to you on the subject.

[1] See letter of 9 July to Marianne Bowden.

315

What I should desire is, to do as much work for the University as possible with *as little absence as possible* from this place. This problem being satisfied, I do not care what you are pleased to make me

Begging your Grace's blessing I am, My dear Lord, Your faithful Servt

John H Newman   Congr. Orat.

TO F. W. FABER

Oy Bm July 23. 1851

My dear F Wilfrid,

I should like nothing better than a long gossip with you — but I am in a mill, I hope I shall come out with bones unbroken.

We do not say Masses for Secular Priests — i.e. we have suspended them, *till* we get some satisfaction. We should be glad to get it.[1]

As to Brother Frederic, I don't think we can spare him.[2] We have very few brothers. Aloysius is dying (by degrees) — Charles is away, his sister being ill — and is going again — and then perhaps to the funeral. Bernard has to visit his friends in Ireland. And Francis is a poor fellow as to hard work. Edward too cannot do much. Frederic and Lawrence are our only strong ones, and Frederic besides sings.

I rejoice to hear so prosperous an account of you, and it was very good in you to write. You should throw Polycrates's ring into the sea.[3]

Tell me, what Drummond said in the House was, 'That fellow Faber went about seducing young women.'?[4]

I suppose I shall have some office in connection with the Catholic University[5]

Ever Yrs affly J H N

[1] The secular priests had an agreement each to say a Mass for any of their number who died. Notifications of their deaths were not being sent to the Oratorians, perhaps because their status as secular priests was not understood.

[2] Faber wished Br Frederic to go for a fortnight to Bonchurch in the Isle of Wight, where Mrs Bowden had promised holiday accommodation for the Oratorians of London.

[3] Faber's long letter of 13 July described the success of the London House, and its good internal state. Polycrates, Tyrant of Samos, was so fortunate in all things that he was advised to interrupt a run of luck that could not last. He threw a very valuable ring into the sea.

[4] See note to letter of 11 Feb. 1851 to Faber.

[5] By return of post Faber wrote that all at the London Oratory were 'in favour of the rectorship over the prefecture.'

TO JAMES HOPE

Oratory Bm July 23. 1851

My dear Hope,

⌐I am tempted to ask when you leave Town¬ — for though I don't see the smallest prospect of my being able to leave Birmingham for weeks and weeks, I should like to know. ⌐Dr Cullen wished me to be Rector of the new University[1] — I thought that Prefect of Studies would take up less time and so settled with him — but now my people here declare it is infra dig. in the F. Superior of an Oratory, and clamour for my being Rector.

But, as to you, I want your full thoughts on the whole subject, and if you could put them on paper for me I should be glad. But I don't want to tax you.¬[2]

Ever Yours affly in Xt   John H Newman   Congr. Orat.

TO T. W. ALLIES

Oratory, Bm July 25. 1851

My dear Allies,

You have had and have a great deal to bear, but you will be rewarded for it. As to Dr Cullen, it is quite impossible a new institution should move at once, — *how* it is to move is the *question*. At present I believe they have not decided *who appoints* Professors. I told Dr C. I would be any thing he pleases which did not interfere with my duties here. I threw out Prefect of Studies as taking less time and absence than Rector, which he wanted me to be. Since that, our Fathers have been clamouring for my being Rector.

I am expecting daily a long letter from some person connected with the scheme, proposing details, and you may be sure I will do what I can to hasten matters.[3] You must get the Dean and Chapter to meet in another room. Can't you do this?[4] I can't bear the thought of your giving

[1] See diary for 18 July.

[2] Hope's reply of 24 July that Newman should be, 'both in name and fact at the head of the institution,' and therefore rector, is quoted in *A.W.* p. 281, and in *McGrath*, p. 108.

[3] Evidently James Hope, who was an authority on the constitution of universities and whose advice Newman had just asked.

[4] Allies was living with his family in lodgings in Golden Square, two doors from Wiseman's house. It seems that the newly created Chapter of Westminster was meeting in these lodgings of Allies.

up the Irish Scheme, though you will of course have up hill work there at first.

Yours affecty J H N.

TO DAVID LEWIS

Oy Bm July 25/51

My dear Lewis,

I am very sorry you have had so much trouble about Lord Brougham. I can do without it.[1]

As to the Times, I quoted the St Gudule case as a *warning* which ought to have startled it, not as the *basis* of what it said.[2] I neither meant nor have said otherwise. It is atrocious that they should not have learned *caution*, by such an experience. The Spanish case was the Concordat — which proved nothing as to selling leave to sin; it simply confirmed my view, for I think *fees* are spoken of — by the Times correspondent.

I am in a great stew lest what I say of Dr Achilli be indictable on Monday next.[3] 1. is it a libel to say what has been *proved* in courts of justice? 2. is to accuse a man of seduction a libel, he being at the time *not* what he is now? It might be actionable to accuse a clergyman here of seduction; would it be to accuse a military man, as such? or if so, is it libel to accuse one who, not *is*, but merely *has been* a Catholic Priest — for *his present utility* is not injured. I fear this is special pleading — but the first ground I hope is sound. It would be such nuts to have me in court — but Achilli has not had Dr Wiseman up. How solemn the Times would be! Could you throw any *off hand* light on this?[4]

Ever Yrs J H N

[1] See note to letter of 30 June to Lewis.

[2] Newman discusses the St Gudule case in the third Lecture of *Prepos*. A Protestant clergyman thought that the listing of prices for seats in St Gudule's in Brussels was a list of sins to be forgiven for the payment of a fixed fee. In the same Lecture, Newman quotes a statement from *The Times*: 'It is the practice, as our readers are aware, in Roman Catholic countries, for the clergy to post up a list of *all the crimes* to which human frailty can be tempted, placing opposite to them the *exact sum* of money for which their perpetration will be indulged.' *Prepos.* p. 110. Lewis objected, on 24 July, that the quotation from *The Times* referred not to St Gudule but to a notice (concerning the Concordat) put up in the Nuncio's house at Madrid, and that the failure to bring this out could provide grounds for a quibble.

[3] The fifth Lecture, which contained the denunciation of Achilli, was delivered on 28 July. See *Appendix* 3.

[4] Lewis's reply on 26 July deserves to be quoted in full: 'As for my offhand light it is not favorable, unless you put yourself forward as a reporter of the trials. The Judges will allow a fair report, in good faith of a public trial, but if there be unfairness it is libel, and if Achilli's friends can make sport of you they will borrow a leaf from the

TO JOHN EDWARD BOWDEN

Oy Bm July 26/51

My dear John

I write in a wonderful hurry. We shall rejoice to give you a bed.

On second thoughts I had better not see your Mother till *Tuesday*. But I advise her and all of you to go up to the 'Plough and Harrow,' Edgebaston, to have a look at our house on Monday[1]

Ever Yrs affly J H N

TO J. M. CAPES

Oy Bm July 26/51

My dear Capes

Will you kindly give a second thought to this matter, whether I have said any thing in my Lectures against the *sacred rites and objects* of Protestantism? If I have, leave what you say about my attacking its 'idol —' If I have *not*, I think the word Idol will do me harm, as (unhappily and most inconsistencly [sic], if so) I am *attacking* ridicule of sacred objects in Lecture 5![2]

p 151 'St Dionysius the Areop:' I suppose, has not written a word — grave authorities think the works attributed to him to have come from the Monophysite school — and I think almost all critics assign them to the 6th century or thereabouts.[3]

Ever Yrs J H N

Philistines, and do it. But, apart from your legal liability, you are pretty safe because you will never be called upon to justify the matter. This certainty of a most perfect justification prevented the information against the Cardinal who otherwise would have had to pawn the Dublin to make up the damages. I suppose you will also be able to prove that Dr Achilli is none the worse for your attack and that the protestant beef is not a bit the more scarce. I think it is Lord Campbell's act which enables a libeller to justify, which before could not be done, and under the present state of the law you are, I think, perfectly safe. It will be a marvellous evidence of your great deterioration, if you should go down to posterity as a convicted libeller. You asked for offhand light, so I have obeyed in the dark.'

[1] The Plough and Harrow Hotel, still in existence, is close to the Oratory, on the Hagley Road, Edgbaston.

[2] The *Rambler*, VIII (Aug. 1851), p. 161, contained a short notice of Newman's Lectures. It is clear that, as a result of his request, the notice was revised and a more measured tone adopted.

[3] Newman's criticism of the testimony of the Pseudo-Dionysius seems to have been ignored by Capes. See 'Thoughts on the Festival of the Assumption of the Blessed Virgin Mary,' *ibid.* p. 151: 'St. Dionysius the Areopagite, who saw her [the Virgin Mary] at this advanced period of life, has left us his testimony . . .'

TO ARCHBISHOP CULLEN

Oratory Birmingham July 26. 1851

My dear Lord,

We are very grateful indeed for the unexpected mark of your Grace's kind thought of us which came a post or two ago, and which, considering the many calls upon you, is especially friendly. I should have acknowledged it at once, but knew you were from home.[1]

Your Grace does not need any thing to recall you to our thoughts, but now you are strictly among our Benefactors, and come into the weekly Mass which we offer for them.

Begging your Grace's blessing I am, My dear Lord, Your faithful and affte Servt

John H Newman   Congr. Orat.

TO ANTONY HUTCHISON

Oy Bm July 26/51

My dear F Antony

F Rafaelle has just been here from St Wilfrid's.[2] The Passionists give up *all* the furniture — and wish it all removed by the middle of August.

The simple thing would be for *us* to see what we should like to take and send you a list of it — and let the rest go up to your lodging house, unless you see a better way. It seems as if about a fourth belongs to us, but I must inquire what Frederic carried away

Ever Yrs affly J H N

SUNDAY 27 JULY 1851   Coupe here

MONDAY 28 JULY   Bowdens came   *Mrs Bowden and her girls and John ⟨?⟩ came.* Lecture at Corn Exchange (5) (*the Achilli one*)

TUESDAY 29 JULY   Bowdens went

---

[1] Cullen sent a donation on 22 July, expressing the wish to have 'a place among the benefactors of the Oratory.'

[2] Fr Raphael Gorga was the Superior of the Passionist House at St Wilfrid's.

TO WILLIAM MONSELL

Oy Bm July 29/51

My dear Monsell

I never read a more distressing letter than Lord Dunraven's — but suspence seems to me as little to kill Lady D. as a crisis[1]

Yrs affly in Xt   John H Newman   Congr. Orat.

WEDNESDAY 30 JULY 1851   Allies came and went.   Dr Kirby came[2]
THURSDAY 31 JULY   Dr Kirby went   F Nicholas went

TO MRS T. W. ALLIES

Oratory, Bm July 31. 1851.

My dear Child,

You will let me call you so. I need not answer your letter in words. Be sure I take the greatest interest in you and your husband. God and His dear Mother bless you both.

Yours affectionately in Xt   John H. Newman   Congr. Orat.

TO F. W. FABER

[31 July 1851]

My dear F W

I take Eminenza's annoyance as a compliment to the Lectures.[3] *They are cheaper than last year.*[4] Then they were 1/ per 27 pages, now 1/ per 34. I printed two thousand of my St Chad's Sermon, and *lost by the*

[1] The third Earl of Dunraven was on the point of becoming a Catholic but, held back by his wife's opposition, did not take the step until 1855. On 6 May he had visited Newman and shortly afterwards told A. L. Phillipps (who wrote on 14 June to Lady Olivia Acheson) that he 'had left everything, i.e. as to the period of his reception into the Church etc.,' in Newman's hands.

[2] Tobias Kirby (1803–95), of Waterford, appointed in 1835 Vice-Rector of the Irish College, Rome, succeeded Cullen as Rector, holding the post from 1848 to 1894.

[3] Faber reported on 30 July that Wiseman was annoyed at the dearness of the lectures, saying it prevented many leading Catholics from giving away large numbers.

[4] i.e. *Lectures on Certain Difficulties felt by Anglicans in submitting to the Catholic Church*, London 1850.

2000.[1] If there is a *demand* for cheap, I will sell cheap, hitherto *cheap does not pay expences.*

I know about F de Vega. There *could not be* a more charitable office than to attend such poor fellows. St Philip did.[2]

Ever Yrs affly J H N.

TO R. B. SEELEY

Oratory, Birmingham, July 31. [1851]

Sir,

I have this morning received a copy of the *Morning Herald*, of yesterday, containing in it a letter addressed by you to me. I beg to thank you for the courteous way in which it is written. Since I have not time to enter into controversy, I trust to your kindness to be content with these few words in answer to it, which I think will be to the purpose.[3]

I am grieved you should have permitted yourself to say that 'you believe we have not a dozen of priests in any town, without there being among them at least one such as Blanco White, at least one who doubts.' How can I meet an assertion except by a counter-assertion? Perhaps, you wish so to be met; perhaps, you think I cannot so meet you. If so, alas! how you are mistaken; but you will be pleased to be set right.

I assure you, then, upon my word, that nothing so struck me when I first became a Catholic as the simplicity and reality of belief in all the Catholic doctrines which I found among the priests. Some I liked personally more than others; but I saw a simple, natural, unaffected faith in all. I have now been nearly six years in the Church; I never heard of a single priest who doubted or disbelieved. It comes to my mind as

---

[1] 'Christ upon the Waters,' preached on 27 Oct. 1850 in St Chad's, Birmingham.

[2] Faber had written, 'I should like to show you in the life of F. Vega, of the Seville Oratory (Blanco White's F. Vega) the gusto with which he assists at burnings for heresy. . . . And he used to preach on the spot as soon as they were dead.' Faber was referring to Newman's argument in his fifth lecture, that the Spanish Inquisition was a political not an ecclesiastical institution. *Prepos.* p. 210.

[3] Seeley's letter was a reply to the contention in Newman's 4th lecture that Blanco White's inward disbelief, before he externally left the Church of Rome, did not reflect upon the whole of the Catholic clergy and religion, any more than the existence of unbelieving Protestant clergymen would reflect upon Protestantism. Seeley denied the parallel on the ground that the validity of the sacraments depends, in the Catholic view, upon the intention of the administering priest, and, therefore, many Catholics would be deprived of grace, if they received the sacraments from an unbelieving priest. Moreover, he personally believed that many priests like Blanco White existed in England. Newman referred to this controversy in his 8th Lecture. See *Prepos.* p. 352.

possible that there was one, whom I never saw, whose name I never heard, who was *said* to doubt or disbelieve. If this is an exception, take it as such; but my memory is so indistinct upon it that I could not positively assert it. And I heard at Rome of one, who was so profane, that I must conclude he was an unbeliever. As to myself, I assure you solemnly that I have not had a single doubt of the truth of the Catholic religion and its doctrines ever since I became a Catholic. And I have an intense certainty that the case is the same with my friends about me, who have joined the Church with me.

Under these circumstances, I feel your statement, that you believe at least one in twelve of our priests is an unbeliever, like Blanco White, or at least doubts, as (excuse me) *very cruel*. What should you say if a Catholic, who knew nothing of the establishment, said in print he believed that one in twelve of Protestant clergymen was an adulterer? Yet where is the difference of the two cases? It is shocking so to be treated, but it is our portion.

As to your difficulty about *intention*, there is, according to our doctrine, no weight in it at all; and I have a right to rule it so, for you appeal to a Catholic's intellectual *consistency*. There is abundant proof all through the volume in which Mr. Blanco White records his feelings that his *intentions* were ever valid. Belief in the truth of the Church was not necessary in order to his intending to do what the Church did. Nothing is more remarkable than the way in which he insists on his always having been faithful in all points to his duty. He makes a boast of it. He does not call ordination a farce, but meditation; nor did he call meditation a farce at the time he practised it, but at the time he wrote his book.[1]

Certainly every now and then an instance may turn up, though I know of none, and do not much credit those which Protestants report, of a priest distinctly withholding his intentions. And so, some priests may have sold themselves to the devil; I think one as likely as the other. Where such a case occurs, I believe that the extraordinary providence of God, which works by miracle in the Church, as well as by fixed laws, takes care that no harm ensues.

I am, Sir, Yours very sincerely, John H. Newman.[2]

[1] *The Life of the Rev. Joseph Blanco White, written by himself* . . ., London 1845. Newman's references are given in *Prepos.* pp. 147–58. Blanco White began to write these memoirs in 1830.

[2] This letter was published in the *Morning Herald* on 2 Aug.

SATURDAY 2 AUGUST 1851   H. W. Wilberforce passed through

TO MRS JOHN MOZLEY

Oratory Birmingham August 2. 1851

My dear Jemima

Thank you for your news about John.[1] He is a dear boy, and I never think of him without affection. Give him my love.

This weather is sadly against my Aunt's exercise which I suppose is necessary for her head. Give my love to her.

I am very well, thank you — though quite oppressed with work.

Ever Yours affectly John H. Newman

SUNDAY 3 AUGUST 1851   Father Ambrose went at night.   Mr Glenny to dinner
MONDAY 4 AUGUST   Father Frederic went.   F. Joseph returned   *No* lecture at Corn Exchange

TO R. B. SEELEY

Oratory, Birmingham, August 5, 1851.

Sir,

I am very sorry you should not withdraw the statement contained in your former letter, that it is your belief that we 'have not a dozen of priests in any town, without there being among them at least one such as Blanco White; at least one who doubts the value of the mass, the efficacy of prayers for the dead, and of the other inventions of the Romish Church.' This you said with a special allusion to *Birmingham*. 'Who,' you said, 'but the Great Searcher of Hearts can tell whether you have not priests at *Birmingham* who feel now just as poor Blanco White?'

No man has a right to make assertions reflecting on his neighbour without proof. What is your proof here? That certain priests in Spain, France and Bavaria, were, in the *course of the last century*, unbelievers.[2] How does this prove the like of England in 1851? Last century was the century of unbelief. Would you allow the present established clergy to be judged by stories told in Fielding and Smollett, or by Bishop Butler's

---

[1] Jemima's son, John Rickards Mozley (1840–1931). This must refer to John's acceptance at Eton as a Colleger.

[2] Seeley, in his reply of 2 Aug., *Morning Herald* 4 Aug., referred especially to the French bishops and priests who left the Catholic Church at the time of the French Revolution. Newman's answer appeared in the *Morning Herald*, 7 Aug.

remark when he refused the Anglican primacy, that 'it was too late for him to try to support a falling Church?'[1]

As to your quotation from Blanco White, I consider it irrelevant to your purpose of proving the Spanish infidel priests *many*. His 'knowledge' was *limited*; but I do not go into the question, because I am determined to keep to the point between us. I refer you, in explanation, to p. 145, and note 7, p. 146 of my Lectures.[2]

You add, that you know of '*several*' who are inquiring whether the Protestant Church would receive and employ them. I wish you had said *how many*. Also you have heard from clerical friends of *many* such. I wish you had stated *of what country*. Make out your list; sum them up; I do not wish them hidden, only give us your *evidence* in full. You will find them, I am sure, few among many. They are not samples of any beyond themselves. Who would judge of the state of health of the swarming population of London by the fever wards of its hospitals?

On the other hand, I adduce a fact, and a great one — *my own evidence*. This does not go the length of proving there are *no* priests in England who doubt, but it goes a pretty step in the way of refuting your astonishing assertion, that at least one in twelve of our priests disbelieve or doubt, and your insinuation that such are in Birmingham. I affirm that in the course of six years, one of which was spent in Rome, I never heard of one single instance of an unbelieving priest.

I am speaking of my own *private experience*, which is far from limited. I also add that (by the grace of God) I and my friends *living in Birmingham*, have never had a single doubt since we became Catholics. My witness from *sight and knowledge* is better surely than your *inference*.

However, you answer that I am perhaps like 'an amiable and devout clergyman in Lancashire, who was firmly convinced of the divine mission of Joanna Southcott;'[3] also, that I am '*surrounded* by all that is suited to confirm my new faith,' and that everything else[4] is 'kept from my view.' Here, again, as is ever the case with Protestants, *assertion* and *hypothesis* stand for *proof*. But adhere to the assertion; it will amuse my friends.

However, we at the Oratory are, I suppose, excepted; therefore the

---

[1] On the death of Archbishop Potter in 1747 an offer of the archbishopric of Canterbury was made to Joseph Butler, author of the *Analogy*, at that time Bishop of Bristol, but he declined on the ground quoted here by Newman. This remark is vouched for by two people closely connected with Butler, see Thomas Bartlett, *Memoirs of the Life, Character, and Writings, of Joseph Butler*, London 1839, p. 96.

[2] *Prepos.* pp. 152–3 and 153 note 3.

[3] Joanna Southcott (1750–1814), the well-known religious fanatic.

[4] This word is added in Newman's handwriting in a printed copy at the Oratory. The word also occurs in Newman's draft.

priests at Birmingham who are unbelievers are some of the following:—
The Right Rev. Dr. Ullathorne, Dr. Weedal, Mr. Jeffreys, Mr. Leith,
Mr. Bond, Mr. Penny, Mr. Ivers, Mr. O'Sullivan, Mr. Fornby.[1] Were
it not that I have been witness and subject of reckless slanders for near
20 years, I should feel deep indignation at this. But, though I am
schooled into patience from experience, do not suppose I have not
keen sentiments, though I have not warm feelings. I repeat it is our
portion.

The second and main point between us was, whether the intention
of infidel priests is good. You did not know we held that it was. You
appeal to my *consistency*. You wish me, 'if possible,' 'to make my
system *consistent* with itself.' I answer that you have utterly misconceived our doctrine. We hold that an unbeliever's intentions *may* be
valid. I think there is proof that Blanco White's were. I have no doubt
at all he meant to do what the Church did. Indeed, he sometimes boasts
of his strict performance of his priestly duties; and sometimes, again,
apologises, as if ashamed of his fidelity. In both ways he proves the fact
of his seriousness, and that, under these circumstances, a priest's intention is valid, is the doctrine of St. Thomas, not invented by me for
the occasion. Non obstante infidelitate potest (minister) intendere facere
id quod facit ecclesia, licet aestimet id nihil esse. Et talis intentio sufficit
ad sacramentum, quia minister sacramenti agit in personâ totius
ecclesiae, ex cujus fide suppletur id quod deest fidei ministri.[2]

These are the two points to which your first letter gave rise. I am not
going into others to which you invite me. Whether St. Peter died at
Rome and founded a succession of Popes there, is as foreign to our
subject, as whether our Lord died on the Cross — on which subject I
received an annonymous challenge a few days ago. 'The new Trial of
the Witnesses' just as much concerns me at present as Barrow, or any
other anti-Catholic.[3] Else, I might have to go on to prove something
about Pontius Pilate, or the Jewish High Priesthood. I invite you back
then to your two points; first, that at least one in twelve of our priests
in large towns, not excepting Birmingham, disbelieves or doubts;

[1] These were all the priests other than Oratorians, in Birmingham in 1851. They
served St Chad's Cathedral, except Dr Weedall at the Handsworth Convent, Ivers and
O'Sullivan at St Peter's, and Formby at St Joseph's Cemetery, Nechells.

[2] *Summa Theol.* III, 64, 9, ad 1.

[3] Anon, *The new trial of witnesses or the resurrection of Jesus considered on principles
understood and acknowledged equally by Jews and Christians; with an enquiry into the
origin of the Gospels, and the authenticity of the Epistles of St Paul*, London 1823. This
work is thought to be modelled on the earlier one by Thomas Sherlock (1678–1761),
Bishop successively of Bangor, Salisbury and London, *Trial of the Witnesses of the
Resurrection of Jesus*, 1729. Barrow means the posthumous *A Treatise on the Pope's
Supremacy*, 1680, by Isaac Barrow (1630–77), Anglican divine and controversialist.

secondly, that Catholics consider the intentions of an unbelieving priest invalid.

I am, Sir, yours sincerely, John Henry Newman.

P.S.   I find I have omitted one remark I had intended to make. As to my system, as you consider it, of extraordinary providences, not 'neutralising,' as you assert, but *completing* fixed laws, it is on a large scale the system of the world.[1] The whole divine system is a system of compensations and recapitulations. Revelation itself is an extraordinary system compared to nature. And so, to speak of human matters, equity is the compensation and completion of law. This is too large a subject to draw out here, but Bishop Butler would show how to do so.

TO F. W. FABER

Oy Bm Aug 7/51

My dear F W

Thanks for your book. I may use it in a note at the end of the Volume. Is there nothing but internal evidence to go on?[2]

Can you get me, or tell me, where to look for information about the *Roman* Inquisition. I half distrust Balmez[3] — I could put a note at the end of the Volume

Ever Yrs affly J H N

---

[1] Seeley complained of Newman's appeal to the extraordinary providence of God, to help the Church out of difficulties such as those arising from her doctrine of intention.

[2] This book appears to be, Le comte Joseph de Maistre, *Lettres à un gentilhomme russe sur l'Inquisition Espagnole*, Paris 1822, which was written in the summer of 1815. Newman inserted a note at the end of his 5th lecture, 'Since this Lecture has been in type, I have been shown de Maistre's Letters on the Inquisition, and am pleased to see that in some places I have followed so great a writer.' *Prepos.* p. 222.

[3] Jaime Balmes (1810–48), Spanish philosopher and apologist. Newman quotes Balmes, *Protestantism and Catholicity, compared in their Effects on the Civilization of Europe*, trans. C. J. Handford and R. Kershaw, London 1849, p. 166, as saying that the Roman Inquisition never shed blood. In a note, *Prepos.* p. 210, Newman expresses surprise 'that this is stated so unrestrictedly.' Cf. Hugh A. MacDougall, *The Acton-Newman Relations*, New York 1962, pp. 148 ff.

TO R. B. SEELEY

Oratory, Birmingham, August 9 1951.

Sir,

I do not think I need trouble you with reading many words more on the subject to which you called my attention. Our correspondence is brought close upon a termination by your third letter.[1]

On the main question between us — that of intention, what I have shown, and what I repeat is, that you *misconceived* our doctrine, and thought you had an argument against me, when you had not. You thought we did not hold the validity of the intention of an infidel priest; we do. Now, having discovered this, you say we hold an *impossibility*. That is a new question; but when you talk of scholasticism, I would observe to you that all theological words are terms of science, and, like those of other sciences, have a sense of their own.[2] I suspect the sense of the Protestant word *faith* is in like manner not obvious to the apprehension of the uninitiated. The simple fact is, you have not apprehended *what* intention theologically is.

As to the other point between us, your believing that in the great towns of England, and in Birmingham as well as others, at least one in twelve of our priests disbelieves or doubts, in proof of this assertion of yours you have nothing to say at all. I did not, as you seem to think, ask for any evidence which would lead to the ascertaining of individuals. I never asked for names, as you say I did; I never dreamed of doing so. I wanted the *cases* not hidden. Since you said you knew *some* priests who doubted, I asked *how many*; and since your friends knew *more*, I asked *of what country*. These are simple questions; you cannot answer them satisfactorily to your argument.

You have given to the world a statement seriously reflecting on given individuals in Birmingham and elsewhere, *without* evidence; you have persisted in it *in spite* of evidence the other way. And you have hid from yourself the real state of the case by hiding yourself in the history of France, Spain, and Bavaria, during the last century. While I grieve at prejudice such as yours, I am not sorry you have put it on record. It is a memorial for the twentieth century what an English gentleman thought

---

[1] Seeley wrote on 7 Aug., *Morning Herald* 8 Aug., defending his belief that one Catholic priest in twelve entertained doubts as to his religion.

[2] Seeley attacked Newman's explanation of the doctrine of intention as an absurdity, and made the charge that Newman's adherence to the doctrine could be explained only on the supposition that his once brilliant mind had been impaired by scholastic subtleties.

of the Catholic priests about him in the nineteenth. Time is the proof of all things.

I am, Sir, yours sincerely, John Henry Newman.[1]

TO WILLIAM FROUDE

Oratory Bm August 11/51

Charissime,

I should have written to you by the first post, after the receipt of your letter from Mrs Ward,[2] were I not in such suffocation of business, from the lectures I am delivering. And now I cannot say much more than express my thankfulness to Him Who has brought you so far, and will surely bring you on still. Your ideas about confession are most unreal and romantic. The Priest is nothing — God is everything. They are the greatest friends who know each other most intimately. The Confessor's sympathy so flows out upon a penitent that it is as if he were making, not hearing a Confession. I can only repeat, you are making bugbears.

What I should *like* would be, if you could come and live with us for a week, pledged to nothing. You would see Catholicism to a disadvantage so much as this, that we profess nothing. We have nothing high about us — you would be sharp enough to see this — we do not profess it — what we profess is to do hard work for the sake of Xt — to be busy, and to be cheerful. You might see things to shock you — never mind. I want nothing hid from you. It would try you — if you overcame it, it would be a test to you, where your heart lay and what was God's will. If your romantic idea continued, charissime, I would not quarrel with it — but send you up, if you were disposed, to the Cistercian Convent at Mount St Bernard, where every one wears a white habit, and fasts till 12 or 3 in the day — and whom you need never see again. Charissime, pardon and forget it, if I seem to be light. Here am I, worked beyond my powers, just now; but if you would bring work, you could mix with us naturally, tho' no one has time on his hands. On Friday or Saturday comes a French architect with suggestions for a Basilica, and our own architect who is of your own trade, being the

---

[1] Newman's letter was published in the *Morning Herald* on 12 Aug. Seeley replied, at length, next day, in a letter published on 14 Aug., which Newman left unanswered.

[2] Mrs F. R. Ward. See Newman's letter of 14 Feb. 1851 to her; also that of 20 Oct. to Mrs William Froude.

Engineer on the Blackburn Rail.[1] Tres faciunt Collegium. We should be sure to have a good plan, if you joined them.

   Write to me, please, and say you forgive me, if I have written freely
     Ever Yrs affectionately John H Newman Congr. Orat.

P.S. I said Mass for you directly your letter came.

TO MISS HOLMES

             Oratory Bm Aug. 16/51
My dear Miss Holmes,

  I saw your niece's name in the paper before your letters came.[2] It rejoices me greatly. It shows how our Lord and His dear Mother love you. I am busy almost to suffocation — I am delivering and printing nearly 50 pages a week. I assure you it is very hard work. I meant to have written to you in London. F Stanton is a gentle nice person, take my word for it. When we get into our new Church, if you *can* exist in any thing which has not a pointed arch, I shall look out for your coming and seeing it.

  Your new publication has come to me — and thank you very much for it.[3] I look forward to the pleasure of reading it as soon as these most trying Lectures are over. Every book I write add[s] certain wrinkles to my face, and certain pot hooks to my handwriting

    Yours affectly in Xt John H Newman Congr. Orat.

 [1] i.e. Terence Flanagan. William Froude had worked as a railway engineer under I. K. Brunel.

  The French architect was E. E. Viollet-le-Duc (1814–79), see letters to Mrs Bowden of 28 Aug. and to Joseph Gordon of 7 Dec. 1851. The plans which were brought to England on 18 Dec. (see diary) were for a kind of Byzantine church. They were found to be too elaborate and expensive.

 [2] The niece of Miss Holmes was received into the Church.

 [3] This was a little book on music, which Thackeray tried to promote, but which did not sell. He offered to help to pay for the printer's bill. (See letters of Thackeray to Miss Holmes, 5 Feb. 1852, and to Mrs Carmichael-Smyth, 26 Feb. 1852, in Vol. III of *The Letters and Private Papers of William Makepeace Thackeray*, collected and edited by Gordon N. Ray, London 1946.)

TO ARCHBISHOP CULLEN

Oratory Birmingham August 19. 1851

My dear Lord

I hear from Mr Allies, that Dr Leahy proposes to come here this week.[1] If it would be possible for him to delay two or three days, it would be all I should require. I am now just beginning my last Lecture, and I hope it will be finished on Saturday, but not till then, I fear.

I propose going to Ireland September 2. Would this save Dr Leahy the trouble of coming?

Begging your Grace's blessing, I am Your affte Servt in Xt

John H Newman

TO THE EDITOR OF ARIS'S BIRMINGHAM GAZETTE

Oratory, August 20, 1851.

Sir

A Clergyman of the Establishment says of me in your last week's paper, that 'the whole of my public life' has been 'one unmitigated lie.'[2] That is, in other words, either he or I am a liar. It is not I.

Were I well known at Birmingham, he would not dare to say it; or, if he did, all men would laugh at it, as I do.

He has professed to quote two passages from me, in support of his charge. He does so in the received Protestant fashion on such occasions; for he has *cut off the beginning* of the first sentence of the former of the two; and he has *cut out the middle* of the latter. Let him, if he can manage to be so fair, quote both *entire*; and *then* I pledge myself, not

[1] Patrick Leahy was a member of the Committee set up at the Synod of Thurles in 1850 to establish the Catholic University of Ireland. This Committee passed a resolution on 12 Aug. 1851, 'that the Rev. Dr. Newman, the Rev. Dr. Leahy, and Myles W. O'Reilly Esq., be requested to draw up a report on the organization of the University . . . and that Mr. Allies be requested to act as Secretary.' *Campaign*, p. 76.

[2] *Aris's Birmingham Gazette* reported on 18 Aug. a lecture Samuel Minton had delivered the previous week at Liverpool: 'From Dr. Newman's own confession they had it, that when he was at Oxford, and for many years before he joined the Roman Church, the whole of his public life had been one unmitigated lie, believing Popery in his heart, and repudiating it with his tongue. He taught the principle of economy—which was another word for lying—he ate the bread of Protestantism, and when he subsequently denounced it, and was taunted with his inconsistency, he replied he was not inconsistent, "for it had been necessary for his position—"' On this see the letter of 20 Aug. to G. S. Faber, and on the economy that of 26 Aug. to F. A. Faber.

to answer *him*, but to explain them, if they still need explaining, to your readers.

A friend of mine has been carrying on in your paper a controversy with him, which luckily he had already brought to an end; else I should have advised him, and he would have wished, to stop it.[1] A person who can say that another habitually lies, ought not to wish to correspond with him or his friends.

Strange to say, he feels this so little that he has just had the impertinence to send me a letter by post; I have returned it unread.[2] I shall burn the next; and the third, if it comes, I shall nail against the wall. I will have no private dealings with such a man.[3]

Your obedient servant, John H. Newman.

TO GEORGE STANLEY FABER

August 20 1851

I think you will not be displeased, since the charge is revived in this place of my having held one thing and taught another in the Establishment, founded on what you have printed [?], if I say publicly that you are convinced your impression was erroneous.[4] But I should any how be pleased to have your concurrence in express terms.[5]

J H N.

---

[1] This was Ambrose St John, whose controversy did not end until Sept.

[2] See letter to Minton of 20 Aug.

[3] The editor of *Aris's Gazette* refused to insert Minton's reply, describing it as 'a long and personal tirade' against Newman. Minton then came and lectured at the Birmingham Town Hall 'Against Romanism' and Newman, on 12 Sept.

Years later, on 1 Nov. 1870, Minton wrote a letter of apology to Newman. He had read in its context Newman's statement that denunciation of the Roman Church was 'necessary for our position,' and offered to explain in the Birmingham press that he had grossly misrepresented him. On 7 Nov. he wrote to thank Newman for his 'exceedingly friendly and Christian letter' in reply. Newman sent him one of his books, probably *A Grammar of Assent*.

[4] See letters of 22 Nov. and 6 Dec. 1849 to F. A. Faber. G. S. Faber had criticised Newman for saying that he had attacked the Roman Church as an Anglican, because it was necessary for the position of the Church of England. Newman's statement ran, 'I am not speaking my own words, I am but following almost a *consensus* of the divines of my Church. . . . I wish to throw myself into their system. While I say what they say, I am safe. Such views, too, are necessary for our position.' *Dev.* p. ix, and *V.M.* ii, pp. 432–3.

[5] G. S. Faber refused Newman's request. See letter of 26 Aug. to F. A. Faber.

TO SAMUEL MINTON

Aug 20/51

(copy)

To Revd Samuel Minton

Revd Sir,

I return your letter unread. If you write again, I shall not be at even this trouble. I can have no private correspondence with a person who accuses me of lying.

Yr well wisher John H Newman

TO T. W. ALLIES

Oratory, Bm Aug. 25. 1851.

My dear Allies

Dr Leahy and another come here on *Wednesday* morning from Ireland, to talk about the University.[1] Could you meet them? say by 11. o'clock?

Ever yrs affecty J H N.

TO F. A. FABER

Oratory Birmingham August 26. 1851

My dear Faber,

Thank you for your kind letter. The charge, which your Uncle put forward and withdrew, having been renewed in this place by a Liverpool clergyman of the Establishment, I wrote to him to tell him I meant to mention his withdrawal of it, asking in addition for a line from him to that effect.[2]

He wrote me answer that he had fallen back from the admission, which, in the simplicity of his heart (or some such phrase) he had made two years ago; — that my explanation of my words *might* be true, *but*

[1] This was the first meeting of the sub-committee of three appointed by the Catholic University committee. See *A.W.* p. 281.

[2] See letter of 20 Aug. to G. S. Faber.

1. A Romish priest always lies for the good of his Church, I am a Romish priest (and this lie was for the good of my Church?) therefore this *need* not be true — and I must take the *liabilities* of a Romish Priest with resignation.

2. That he had seen a passage in which I advocated lying — the famous passage *in my Arians* published in 1833, and brought forward quarterly by old Golius for some years at Oxford, NONE OTHER!!![1]

I sent his letter back the next hour — I will not have a word to say to him, till he recants. Neither *now*, nor ever, have I had any bad feeling against him — but he ought to be told, as I should tell him, if I had the opportunity, that it will not be satisfactory for him to appear before a divine tribunal with so gross an injustice and untruth unretracted in his hand.

It is not worth going into less matters — but what makes his conduct more inconsistent still is, that my letter took the form of an acknowledgment to him for his pamphlet which he sent me, in which he calls me 'our *friend* Mr N.' 'our ingenious friend —' 'our friend N.'[2] He goes out of his way to make his friend one whose word he does not believe

Ever Yours sincerely, John H Newman

P.S.   You will recollect that his letter to me was a private one, written, as you would find, if you saw it, in a *friendly tone*. It was not a controversial letter. You must also understand I am in a very different position from what I was at Oxford. Then 1. I was *known*. 2. I was a private person; so no matter what people said of me. But now at Birmingham 1. I am *not* known. 2. I am *not* a *private* person; so I cannot afford to let people speak against me —

[1] The passage in *Ari.* occurs on pp. 73–4. Newman was explaining the doctrine of 'Economy,' that the truth must be put before people as they can bear it. After warning that the doctrine could be abused, and that some of the Fathers had applied it improperly, he quoted a passage from Clement of Alexandria, *Stromata* VII, that a Christian will sometimes lie, 'as a physician for the good of his patients, he will lie, or rather utter a lie, as the Sophists say. For instance, the noble Apostle circumcised Timothy, while he cried out and wrote down, "Circumcision availeth not" . . . Nothing, however, but his neighbour's good will lead him to do this.' Newman thought Clement meant that a partial truth was in some sense a lie. See *Apo.* pp. 269 ff., and notes F. and G. On the charge made by Charles Portales Golightly (1808–85), Newman's eccentric but indefatigable opponent during the Oxford Movement, see letter of 24 Dec. 1835 to R. H. Froude, *Moz.* II, p. 148.

[2] G. S. Faber's pamphlet was *Papal Infallibility, a Letter to a Dignitary of the Church of Rome . . .*, London 1851.

TO WILLIAM FROUDE

Oratory Bm August 26/51

My dear William,

I have only time to send you a hasty acknowledgement. Do you not confuse between conversation and writing? A writer about the Arians, A.D. 1833, spoke of 'the unfitness of books, compared with private communication, for the purpose of religious instruction —' p 152[1] and this, I suppose, applies to letter writing. It is a paradox to say that we cannot communicate our ideas by words — and what you say seems to come to this — though I may make the perplexity greater if I go on — so I shall [fall] back upon the writer about the Arians

Ever Yours affectly John H. Newman

TO MRS J. W. BOWDEN

Oratory Bm August 28/51

My dear Mrs Bowden,

I am glad to say I am sending up my last bit of MS to the press tonight (excepting the Preface etc) I inclose a letter about Westbury, which I meant to have sent you long ago — Though Marianne does not like to have a choice, I think you might have for her — and I wish there was some way of *your* seeing the place —

We have had a French Architect here — and I trust shall lay the foundations of our Church before winter. Two Irish friends, sent by the Primate, have just been here, laying plans with me. I go over, if all is well, in three weeks to see things — and we shall commence in January, I suppose — Nothing is settled yet about place — Thurles seems likely as a commencement, to remove at a fixed time, say in a year or two, to Dublin.

There is a rumour still that Dr Achilli is to indict me — my Lectures are making the extreme party so very angry, that they will do all they can.[2]

I should have said that the Pope, through Mgr Talbot, has signified

[1] *Ari.* p. 137.

[2] As a result of the Lectures, besides Newman and St John, Joseph Gordon was now involved in fierce controversy in *Aris's Birmingham Gazette,*—with Josiah Allport, incumbent of St James's, Ashted, Birmingham, on the subject of 'Maria Monk.'

his pleasure, at the notion of my helping in Ireland — this is very satisfactory.[1]

Two facts I have just heard on good authority — 1. that the Catholics are continually increasing in the Irish Police, owing to their proving so much better officers than the Protestants. 2. that they are declaring they will resign rather than act against their coreligionists.[2]

TO ARCHBISHOP CULLEN

Oratory Birmingham August 28. 1851

My dear Lord,

I have had great pleasure in making Dr Leahy's acquaintance — he went today. Mr O Reilly is still here. I trust our conference was very satisfactory. We settled to meet at Thurles in about three weeks time from this. Dr Leahy seemed to think that this would be a better time for my going to Ireland than next week.

Begging your Grace's blessing, I am, My dear Lord, Your affecte Servt

John H Newman   Congr. Orat.

TO F. A. FABER

Oratory Birmingham August 28. 1851

My dear Faber

Thank you for the trouble you are taking about me. Certainly, I have no objection at all that you should send my letter to your Uncle — not of course *from me*. I know perfectly well he is a generous man — and I cannot believe he will not see his injustice. You may be quite sure I will apologize to him for returning his letter, *directly he* recalls an act which has hurt me so much.

Ever Yours very sincerely John H Newman

P.S. In the passage from the Arians a sentence of St Clement *is omitted* in Mr Minton's version — viz St Paul's crying out against

---

[1] Talbot wrote on 6 Aug., 'He [Pius IX] told me yesterday with pleasure that you had agreed to take upon yourself the superintendance of the Irish University.'

[2] The conclusion and signature have been cut off.

circumcision *yet* circumcising Timothy — *which shows what Clement meant by 'false.'*[1]

TO MISS HOLMES

Oy. Bm. Aug. 28/51

My dear Miss Holmes,

This very sudden blow must be a great affliction to you[2] I have no vacant day for a time, but on Saturday, St Rose's day, I will add you and *your intention* to the two persons I then say Mass for. You know that the more common opinion is, that it is quite as much to you as if I said Mass for you by yourself. There is nothing at all to show that your father was not in invincible ignorance.[3] Your letter came to me only this morning.

I am truly glad to hear that your niece is gone to the Wards[4]

Ever Yrs affly in Xt   John H Newman   Congr. Orat.

TO ANTONY HUTCHISON

Oy Bm Aug. 28/51

My dear F Antony,

Thank you for your letter just come — it will make a capital note at the end.[5] By all means write to the Abbé Donet. I suppose, if we leave out her name, there will be no libel. I have enough on my hands, if Dr Achilli is to indict me

Ever Yrs affly J H N

F Joseph has another story which he must set down for you

TO J. SPENCER NORTHCOTE

Oy. Bm. Aug. 28/51

My dear Northcote

What are you doing about the abridgment of my Lectures? From what some one said here, after you were gone, I fear you have been kind

---

[1] *Ari.* p. 74. See letter to F. A. Faber of 26 Aug.

[2] The death of Miss Holmes's father.

[3] i.e. as to any duty of entering the Catholic Church.

[4] She found employment in the family of either W. G. Ward or F. R. Ward.

[5] Newman is replying to Hutchison's letter of 27 Aug., which gave information about the impostor Miss Garside, author of *The Female Jesuit*, a work much in demand. Newman had considered this type of fraudulent material in his fourth Lecture. The Abbé Donnet of St Gudule's, Brussels, had received the 'female Jesuit' into the Church, before she was exposed as a fraud. Newman did not mention the case in *Prepos.*

enough to undertake what you did not like; which has annoyed me. You can fight off at once, you know.[1]

The immediate cause of my writing is this, that there is a report (*which do not repeat*, lest it should tend to bring it out into a fact) that Dr Achilli's friends are going to prosecute me, for what I have said of him in Lecture 5, though I have only repeated the Cardinal's words, which he let pass. Of course you had better leave out the whole passage in an abridgment

Ever Yours John H Newman   Congr. Orat.

TO EDWARD BADELEY

Oratory Birmingham August 29. 1851

My dear Badeley

Your letter was most kind and friendly.[2] I deliver my last Lecture on Monday — I will come to Town Tuesday morning, if I can see you. Appoint your hour and I will come to you, rejoiced indeed that even an unpleasant matter brings me to the sight of you.

Before doing what I have done, I thought a good deal and was very anxious. I wrote to Hope and Lewis. Cardinal Wiseman having published *all* I have said in the Dublin first, then in a pamphlet without any notice being taken of it gave me a certainty no attempt would be made. Now, however, I wish quite to prepare for the worst. I shall try to get the Cardinal's documents and will bring them to you. Have you seen his pamphlet? I send it you. One of our fathers will go out to Italy at once, if you recommend it. Would bringing *one* case home to him, so damage him as to dispense with the necessity of other evidence? He must make an affidavit, I suppose, if he proceeds by *action*. If so, the wording of it would be a guide, would it not?

What is the *maximum* of damages he is likely to get? You will smile at this question, but I always like to make up my mind for the worst.

Ever Yours affecty John H Newman   Congr. Orat.

[1] Northcote undertook the abridgment. The abridged Lectures appeared weekly in the *Lamp*, III, 6 Sept.–1 Nov. 1851.

[2] Badeley wrote on 28 Aug., 'I am sorry to hear that you are threatened with a Prosecution, but I certainly am not surprised. When I read your 5th Lecture, (for which, and for the others, accept my *very best thanks*,) I thought that such a result would not be unlikely. . . . If Dr Achilli brings an action against you for a libel . . . I fear it will be almost impossible for you to prove the truth of your Charges, from the extreme difficulty of collecting the necessary evidence. . . .'

MEMORANDUM.   Aug 29. 1 51[1]

What you have said has taken me by surprise. I took great pains to do what was safe before I published the passage, but I almost think I need not have done so, I mean, things seemed to me so clear. Are you not looking at the matter simply as a Lawyer?

Dr Wiseman some time since preached a sermon against Achilli. Why did he not publish it? he had not yet his documents. We send up to him for documents last winter when Dr A. [Achilli] is *here* — he does not send them — why? because he has not yet got them all.

At length his article appears in the Dublin with portions of the documents. There is a report Achilli means to prosecute — some say he attempted it.

An *answer* of some kind from Achilli's friends comes out — not a prosecution.

Next, Dr Wiseman commits himself to an additional act of publishing in a Pamphlet his Dublin article. Still no answer, and the Catholic papers jeer, and defy Achilli to prosecute.

I send up to town to Burns to inquire whether Achilli ever put out an answer. He replies 'We have inquired and cannot hear that Achilli ever answered the article in the Dublin.'

I buy the only book I can find he has published since. There is an allusion to the heap of filth which Dr Wiseman has cast on him, but, I believe, nothing more definite.

At the end then of *six months* after these transactions, or rather a year perhaps, or 9 months, I do nothing more than *repeat* what Dr Wiseman has said, *referring* to him as my authority. And first I write to Hope, who says nothing like 'it is dangerous —' or 'I'd advise you not.' 'don't meddle' etc

Now I am not going to the *legal difficulty or responsibility* — but first, will not these circumstances tell in court in mitigation, to say the least, that I only said what has before been said, and not prosecuted? Then again I think it tells against the *chance* of prosecution, which of course is another thing. *Why* did they not prosecute Dr Wiseman at so exciting a time, and when he was such a mark? This thought weighed with me a good deal, and weighs still.

As to the present state of things, a hint has been conveyed to me that they are *trying* to do something — next, I should add that there is certainly a curious silence as to answering or noticing what I have said, which looks like an intention.

By the bye an additional thought weighed with me. The Times etc

----

[1] Newman added in pencil the date of this memorandum, which he enclosed with his letter.

never took him up, the Evangelical clergy here did not take him up, when he came down, and, I think, were said to have had too much experience of him a year or two back. *Further the Record has attacked him.*

J H N[1]

TO EDWARD BADELEY

Oratory Bm Aug 31/51

My dear Badeley,

From the inclosed, I fear I shall be proceeded against.[2] I suppose it will take the Catholic body utterly by surprised [sic], and I trust I shall

[1] Badeley replied on 30 Aug., 'From what you tell me today, I incline to think that you may be in less danger of an action—but how did you learn that you were likely to be prosecuted? On what ground did your information rest? If the rumour is only vague, and not capable of being traced to any authentic source, it may perhaps be scarcely worth while to go to any great trouble or expence by way of anticipation.

But you cannot well be sure of Achilli's intentions—he may wait for some time, and then issue his writ, and if you are to justify your publication on the ground of its truth, nothing but direct and regular evidence of the facts in question will suffice— you will have to prove them in the same manner as if you were prosecuting him by an Indictment—secondary evidence will not do—I mean, *as a defence to the action*—' Badeley then explained that the question of damages was a different matter, and that if some of the charges against Achilli were proved and he was shown to be a villain, the jury would not be likely to impose heavy damages in the case of the charges that could not be proved.

Badeley continued, referring to Achilli, 'He need not make any affidavit in order to *bring his action*, as you seem to suppose—if he were to proceed against you by means of a *Criminal Information*, it would be necessary for him to deny specifically, on oath, in the first instance, each of the offences imputed to him—But for this very reason he is not likely to attempt such a remedy—My notion certainly was from the first that he would be disposed to bring an action, from the chance of your not being able to prove the truth of your charges, and then make your failure an argument to prove his own innocence—your telling me that you were threatened with a prosecution confirmed this notion—and I want much to know what foundation there is for what you told me—' In fact Achilli did bring a Criminal Information and denied on oath all Newman's allegations.

Badeley added that Hope had been quite right in saying that an action for libel was possible, although the libellous matter had been published before. 'All that he could tell you was that you were probably *not in much danger*—and this, under the circumstances, it was natural to suppose—But you must remember that you have alleged specific facts, *as facts, not as mere rumours*, nor as matters resting on certain Documents before you—you refer in a note to the Dublin Review, and to Wiseman's Pamphlet— but this may be taken rather as *a verification of your own allegations*, as corroborative evidence, not as the sole foundation or ground of your charges—His not suing Wiseman may have been because he could not fix Wiseman himself with the authorship or publication, for the Cardinal's name does not appear—Your's does—and you have given a fresh sanction and impetus to the charges. . . .'

[2] This was a letter of 29 Aug. from Michael Maher, who was told by one of the speakers at an Evangelical Alliance meeting in Birmingham that evening of the intention to prosecute Newman.

have their whole energy to get me evidence. I happened on Friday to mention to our Bishop the chance of a prosecution — and he laughed it to scorn quite. I could not get him to enter into the notion, tho' I returned to it. I should mention this and other instances, to show that I have as little said what is private or local, as if I said that there was an anti-Catholic agitation in England. That is, a trial will rather be against the Catholic body than me.

If, as I suppose, *authoritative* (e.g. legal) statements alone will avail from a foreign country, I fear I must give up *Viterbo*.[1] Mr Cass, the American minister, could do something, but, I fear, not more than what is secondary.[2] I am writing by this post to Dr Cullen, who may give me some information where to apply.

As to Naples, I suppose the Neapolitan authorities in London can authenticate Neapolitan police statements, if they are producible in Court.

Dr Hadfield of Malta may be subpoenaed or any better man to give evidence about Achilli's goings on there.[3]

As to Corfu, there is an unpleasant difficulty about identity — Achilli is called Achile Giacinti in the statement of the Civil Court.[4]

It was said at the time that Cardinal Wiseman's publication was put out with the express purpose of *forcing Achilli* into court — and I think he did it with legal advice.

I have told Burns to send you whatever has been put out on his side.[5] As to his book *since* the charge was made, a writer in the Rambler for September, whom we (perhaps) both know, confirms what I have said of the absence of any defence in 500 pages.[6]

Most sincerely Yours John H Newman

[1] Newman knew from Wiseman's article that Achilli's offences at Viterbo had not been brought before a legal tribunal.

[2] Lewis Cass, Junior, was appointed chargé d'affaires to the Papal States in 1849, and in 1854 promoted to the rank of Minister resident in Italy.

[3] George Horatio Hadfield, an Evangelical clergyman, had been appointed Principal of St Julian's Protestant College at Malta in 1846. In 1847-8, at the request of the Committee of the College in London, he investigated the charges of immorality brought against Leonini and Saccares, apostate priests, who lived for a while with Achilli in a Mission House connected with the College. *Finlason*, p. 93.

[4] Cf. letter to St John of 4 Nov. (1), note 3, and letter of 5 Nov. to Badeley.

[5] Newman wished Badeley to see all that had been printed in favour of Achilli. Burns sent three pamphlets: *Brief Sketch of the Life of Dr. Giacinto Achilli*, Sir C. E. Smith, *Imprisonment and Deliverance of Dr. Giacinto Achilli*, and Lewis H. Tonna, *Letter to Dr. Wiseman*.

[6] This was the review of Achilli's *Dealings with the Inquisition; or, Papal Rome, her Priests and her Jesuits: with important Disclosures*, London 1851, in the *Rambler*, VIII (Sept. 1851), pp. 235-52, 'Dr. Achilli and the Inquisition.' The reviewer was presumably J. M. Capes.

P.S.   I think of coming up to Town on Sunday next September 7 in the fore noon. I have taken your hint about Burns and Rivington — and *am going to stop* the sale of the particular Lecture in the Lecture *room* here, where it has been sold hitherto, *tomorrow.* But what am I to do? may not I sell the Lecture here again? the London copies can be easily got? May I sell it in the *shops* here, but not from myself? or must I withdraw it from circulation?[1]

9 P.M. I have just heard they are trying to find some one who will swear to my words.[2] This shows they are in earnest. Achilli gave it ⟨his intention⟩ out last Monday to the Evangelical Alliance. It is said that his friends now wish to bring it to a point, and to white wash him or discard him. There is no doubt Achilli or his friends are driven to bay — they *must* act.

I am growing very cautious. Tell me if this passage in my dedication to Dr Cullen is *extravagant*, in point of truth.

'A subject of the United Kingdom may with impunity expose the Scriptures to contempt, ridicule the Apostles' Creed, speak against revealed religion, nay, deny the existence of a Supreme Judge; but should he be a Catholic Bishop, he may not ascribe to himself that office of his religion, to which he has been called by its constituted authorities according to its ⟨their⟩ immemorial usage ⟨prerogative⟩. To reject the Saviour of man is a far less political offence than to acknowledge His earthly Vicar; and atheism circulates unmolested while it lives in peace with the established Protestantism.' Of course I am not asking your opinion of the sentiment.[3]

                                                                J H N

TO ARCHBISHOP CULLEN

Oratory Birmingham August 31. 1851

My dear Lord,

There is a report I am to undergo a prosecution from Achilli, on account of what I have said of him in one of my Lectures. Can you give me any hint, from your knowledge of Rome etc, where I had best apply

---

[1] Badeley, on 28 Aug., had recommended Newman to tell his publisher and printer not to show the MS of the Lectures to anyone, and to answer no enquiries.

[2] Maher wrote to Newman on 30 Aug. that a solicitor was trying to find press reporters who would swear to what he had said about Achilli.

[3] Badeley advised Newman to modify this passage, since blasphemy was a criminal offence, and it was not an offence in law to acknowledge the Pope. See letter of 3 Sept. to Badeley.

for evidence — for the best evidence will be needed, and I am told no time is to be lost in looking about for it.[1]

It has just struck me that, under these circumstances, your Grace might think it inexpedient that I should dedicate the Volume to you. Only say half a word to that effect, if you feel this, and I shall quite understand it.[2]

Begging your Grace's blessing, I am, My dear Lord, Your affectte and faithful Servt

John H Newman   Congr. Orat.

TO J. D. DALGAIRNS

Oy Bm Aug 31/51

My dear F Bernard,

I heartily wish you would turn St Cyprian into a second St Stephen.[3] Some years back I had thoughts of making a sort of romance in which he should come. I got up the locale of his province; I mean as to woods, mountains etc. I wish you would. If I find any of my notes, I will send them to you.

Charissime, you know *I* think it is *the* line in which St Philip wishes you to profit the age. Think how much young Catholics want information about Church history.

They say I am to be prosecuted by Achilli — any how, I am obliged to prepare for it. *Don't let this go beyond the community*, for it may bring about the very thing, if it does. I should esteem it a great favor, if any one would say a Mass with the intention that it may not take place, or may turn out well, saving the 'Fiat laudetur' etc[4]

Ever Yours affly J H N

[1] Cullen suggested on 3 Sept. that Newman should apply to Wiseman who 'had all the police reports,' and added, 'Here we will endeavour to aid you in paying any expenses.'

[2] Cullen replied, 'About the dedication of the book, I leave everything to yourself. For my part the very fact of your being prosecuted for exposing an impostor and telling the truth, would make me more ready to accept the dedication.' Thus *Prepos.* was dedicated to Cullen. See also postscript to letter of 15 July to him.

[3] Newman wished Dalgairns to write as successful a life of St Cyprian as he had of St Stephen Harding, in the *Lives of the English Saints*, London 1844. The romance of which Newman next speaks appeared in 1856 as *Callista*. See letter of 23 May 1848 to Burns.

[4] 'Fiat, laudetur, atque in aeternum superexaltetur justissima, et amabilissima voluntas Dei in omnibus.'

P.S.   I expect to come to Town this day week, Sunday the 7th.

Could your Edward do any thing with his Father about the Cardinal's evidence against Achilli?[1]

TO GEORGE TALBOT

Oratory Birmingham Sept 1. 1851

My dear Talbot,

I am entering on a most anxious matter, in which I shall have to act, I may say, for the whole Catholic body. You know the Cardinal accused in the Dublin, and then in a pamphlet, Dr Achilli of certain crimes. I have repeated what he, ⟨the Cardinal⟩ said — and he ⟨Dr A⟩ is going to bring an action against me; not willingly I believe, but his friends, the Evangelical Alliance, force him.[2] They wish to bring the matter to a point. In a little while I shall write again — at present I write to prepare you. It is a most important crisis. I have a *most difficult* thing to do, yet a great thing, if I do it. First you must get me the Holy Father's blessing. Next I must have all the assistance you can give me, from documents etc. Achilli is charged of three (at least) sins with women at Viterbo about 1831–33 — a sadly long time ago. Witnesses may be dead now, but there must be documents, police and other. However, I am now speaking generally, I shall write again to tell you *what* to do; now I write merely to *prepare* you. The evidence must be primary, *not secondary* — this is the great difficulty. I must produce evidence as good as if *I* were bringing a charge of crime against an innocent man, instead of being on my defence. I have written to the Cardinal, who is in the north, and has not yet answered me. Badeley tells me I have a work of *extreme difficulty*; but I rely on our Blessed Lady and St Philip to carry me through. Indeed it is not my cause, but the cause of the Catholic church. Achilli is going about like a false spirit, telling lies, and since it is forced upon us, we must put him down, and not suffer him to triumph.

Thank you for your very consoling letter about [?] my helping the

[1] Edward Bagshawe's father, Henry Ridgard Bagshawe, was the friend and joint editor with Wiseman of *D R*.

[2] The Evangelical Alliance was founded in 1846 as a non-denominational body, to work for religious liberty, and to ' associate and concentrate the strength of an enlightened Protestantism against the encroachments of Popery and Puseyism, and to promote the interests of a Scriptural Christianity.' It made arrangements to bring Achilli to England. (*Evangelical Alliance. British Organization. Abstract of the Proceedings of the Fourth Annual Conference, held in Liverpool, October* 1850 . . ., London 1850.) It is now known as the World's Evangelical Alliance.

new University. It was more pleasant than I can say, as you may imagine, my hearing the Holy Father was pleased at the idea.

Say a Hail Mary for me sometimes at some holy place, and believe me, Ever Yours most sincerely in Xt

John H Newman Congr. Orat.[1]

TO JOHN HARDMAN

Oratory Sept 2. 1851

My dear Mr Hardman

I am exceedingly obliged to you for your letter.[2] It has given me great gratification and encouragement. To have done any thing which deserves the approbation of the Catholics of the Town, I account a great gain — After the praise of God above, there is nothing which would support me more than the good will and sympathy of the Catholic body, especially here.[3]

I cannot but feel anxious at the threat of Dr Achilli — for it would, if fulfilled, stake very great issues on a single decision — but I trust in a good cause — and am rendered quite cheerful and happy at the news of your sympathy and promise of assistance.

Yours very sincerely in Xt   John H Newman   Congr. Orat.

TO EDWARD BADELEY

Oy Bm Sept 3/51

My dear B

I see you consider me one of [the] maddest headstrongest fellows that ever a man of 50 was — and I retort that you are a mere unimaginative

---

[1] Talbot replied on 14 Sept. promising all help.

[2] On 2 Sept. Hardman wrote, as an old Catholic, to thank Newman for his Lectures. He promised the support of the Catholics of Birmingham should there be a prosecution, and later, he headed the Newman Indemnity Fund.

On 5 Sept., at a meeting in the Corn Exchange, presided over by Ullathorne, Hardman seconded a resolution approving the Lectures, of which the proposer was Dr Weedall.

[3] On the previous day Newman had delivered the last Lecture in *Prepos.*, which ended with the often quoted appeal for 'an intelligent, well-instructed laity,' 'not disputatious,' but 'who know their creed so well that they can give an account of it.' Ullathorne wrote his reservations to Newman on 3 Sept., 'I think your advice to the catholics the right thing, but knowing the habits of the poorer classes especially the Irish, will they not think, however erroneously, that it supports and encourages their love of religious controversy which some of them like to carry on in pot houses, unless they have a word of explanation?'

blue bag. As to my dedication, think of my poor brother's book, and similar ones.[1]

I inclose the real authority about Dr Achilli's movements.[2] You comfort me in not *at once flooring* the chance of the Naples Police account being received in court. You will see Dr Achilli's line is to *protest against all foreign trials and decisions* as unfair.[3]

I will, if all is well, come to Town on Tuesday next the 9th. If you send a line to 24 King William Street Strand, I will come to you — at any hour you name.

Ever Yrs affly J H Newman

P.S.   The Lecture has for three several nights been sold in *the Lecture room* — which, I fear, fixes it on me without any trouble.

I have put the passage thus, which considering books like my Brother's, Morell's, and Chapman's other publications, the works of Unitarians, etc. the Weekly Despatch and a host of others,[4] really seems to me likely to pass your legal mind without offence:— 'There are many things which the Queen's subjects may say with impunity: ('so far well — ') they are suffered to deny the Christian faith, and to impugn the authenticity and sacredness of its inspired documents; they are allowed, for whatever cause, to make even further aggressions upon it; but should etc'[5]

TO F. W. FABER OR W. P. GORDON

Sept 4/51

My dear F Wilfrid or F Philip

Thank you for the Masses which have been said for me.

Perhaps Mr Bagshaw had better do nothing except what the Cardinal

[1] See letter of 31 Aug. to Badeley, and postscript here. The work of Francis William Newman referred to is *The Soul, her Sorrows and her Aspirations: an Essay towards the Natural History of the Soul as the true Basis of Theology*, London 1849.

[2] Enclosed was a newspaper cutting, reporting an address by Achilli before the Evangelical Alliance, in which he stated his intention of bringing Newman to trial as soon as the courts were opened for the next term.

[3] 'He (Dr Achilli) was in England—in a free country, where good laws were in force, and this time it would be as well to bring his adversary before the Courts of Law.' (From the report of Achilli's address.)

[4] John Daniel Morell (1816–91) wrote a liberalising work, *The Philosophy of Religion*, London 1849.

John Chapman (1822–94), the publisher, became editor and proprietor of the Positivist *Westminster Review* in 1851, and also edited and published 'Chapman's Library for the People,' 1851–4.

The Weekly Despatch, with a circulation of 60,000, was radical and secularist.

[5] Newman ended by dropping the passage entirely from the dedication of *Prepos.* to Cullen.

mentions — so say no more about it to him. *I don't hear from the Cardinal* — it is a week tomorrow since I wrote to him.

I am coming up *on Tuesday.*

If any of you can *make* the Cardinal *look out the Achilli papers*, it will be doing me an inestimable favor

Ever Yrs affly J H N

TO WILLIAM PHILIP GORDON

Oratory Bm. Sept 6. 1851

(Private)

My dear Father Philip or any one,

Is there any one who is bold enough to tell the Cardinal I come to town on *Tuesday*, and will call in Golden Square, as I come from the rail, *for the documents* about Achilli. If he has them not, will he tell me *where* to find them, AT ONCE.

I suppose not even F Wilfrid would be bold enough to hint what pain his silence has given me. I wrote to him yesterday week. Not a word yet. Hardman etc have taken me up most handsomely. So has the Primate of Ireland. The Origo mali is silent[1]

Ever Yrs affly J H N

TO ARCHBISHOP CULLEN

Oratory Birmingham Sept 7. 1851

My dear Lord,

I fear your Grace will think me very troublesome. First I must thank you for your very kind words about the Achilli matter, which were a great encouragement and consolation to me.[2] Next I see by the Papers that the F General (or Visitor?) of the Dominicans is at Drogheda[3] — and I have just had a message from the Cardinal to the effect that I had better apply to *him* on the subject. Will you then kindly ask him a question for me?

It is whether he would do me the great favor of directing me to some *primary* sources of evidence for Achilli's misconduct. E.g. I suppose documents drawn up at the time would be such — episcopal registers or the records of the Cancelleria — (which I am told were

---

[1] The Origo mali was, of course, Wiseman. See below, letter to W. G. Ward of 26 Nov., and note 2 there.　　[2] See notes to letter of 31 Aug. to Cullen.
[3] Robert Augustine White, O.P., Assistant to the General of the Dominicans.

burned at Viterbo by the Republicans two years ago!) or living witnesses to which a commission, if sent from England, could get access. *Secondary* evidence, such as general report, I fear will not be enough.

I am to join Dr Leahy and Mr O Reilly in Ireland in a week or two. We got on very satisfactorily

Begging your Grace's blessing I am, My dear Lord,

Faithfully and affectly Yours

John H Newman   Congr. Orat.

P.S.   I am at '24 King William Street, Strand, London' from Tuesday (9th) to Friday.

TO FRANCIS RICHARD WEGG-PROSSER

Oratory Birmingham Sept 7. 1851

My dear Sir,[1]

I was glad to have your letters and have pleasure in saying what I can in answer, but I have so little time for controversy that I cannot say as much as I should like. But I will say what comes uppermost.

I will lay down this principle, and perhaps shall not get further than to illustrate it, that, in moral questions, it is unreasonable and un-philosophical to insist on *all* objections being removed before coming to a definitive conclusion. According to an observation of Dr Johnson's quoted somewhere by Dr Whately, 'There are objections against a plenum, and objections against a vacuum, yet one or other must be true.'[2] Unanswerable objections *need* not interfere with a moral proof. I believe that God is all good, yet I *cannot* reconcile this belief with the existence of misery in the world.

This last instance will show that I do not mean by a moral proof a mere balance of probabilities, the greater weight carrying the day. On the contrary a proof is something such, that it can only be on *one* side; it is something specific; *yet*, consistent with unanswerable (if so be) objections. All that *can* be said against a proof is that there *are* difficulties in it; but those difficulties or objections do not form a proof of some contrary or incompatible conclusion; they are simply negative and barren; they weaken what they oppose; they create nothing of their own.

Now I really do think before going into any particular argument on the question of Catholicism, this important principle of proof should be

[1] Wegg-Prosser wrote on the autograph: '(This letter is a reply to one written to Dr. Newman, in which were enclosed the extracts relating to the Papal Infallibility etc—*F R W P.*)'

[2] Richard Whately, *Elements of Logic*, London 1826, pp. 197–8.

348

carefully looked into, and, if fallacious, exposed. It must be shown that it is not necessary for the proof of a Creator and Governor, and of revealed religion generally [that there should be no unanswerable objections]. For myself, I think the only ground why we are not Manichees, is, because the existence of evil is *only* an objection to the being of a God, and not sufficient to introduce a contrary hypothesis; as (I would also say) the cases of Liberius, Honorius, etc. are *at the utmost* only enough to embarrass the proof of Catholicism, not to prove Protestantism.

And so again I know no *satisfactory* answer to such objections against our Lord's divinity as Mark xiii, 32 'not the Son, but the Father.' Yet I cannot allow an isolated text to stand against the conspiration of the whole of Scripture. It is not a mere balance of probabilities, that our Lord's divinity is in the inspired word.

There is a passage of Bishop Butler on a parallel subject, human nature, which seems to me much in point. He says in his 15th Sermon (in a note) 'Supposing that, upon a very slight and partial view which (a spectator) had of (a great) work, several things appeared to his eye as disproportionate and wrong, others just and beautiful . . . there is a probability that the right appearances were intended, there is no probability that the wrong appearances were.' etc[1] And so in the same way, if out of a vast number of historical facts, 9/10ths go to one conclusion, and the remaining 1/10th neither to that one conclusion, *nor* to *any other*, the unaccounted and inexplicable 1/10th does not destroy the proof from the 9/10ths.

This, I consider, to be the case with the historical argument for Catholicism; and I have expressed it in my Essay on Development ⟨p 388⟩ thus:— 'It may be said that we are connecting together for a *particular purpose* certain opinions or practices, which are found *among others* in primitive times, and which are really unconnected and *accidental*. It may be urged, moreover, that there are many things in the documents or the history of the period which have a *contrary* bearing; that the Fathers *also* speak against idols, and invocation of angels etc etc . . . and that, by putting all these together, we might form as imposing a catena against the Catholic doctrines as can be formed in their favor. But this is to misunderstand etc etc. If there be but an *hypothesis*, which has never been realized, with which they fall in, which interprets *more consistently* than the Catholic creed the whole mass of Antenicene testimony, (even) this will have its weight, though it rest on no historical foundation. But this is not the case. STRAY heterodox expressions, Platonisms, argumenta ad hominem, . . . omissions in practice, silence

---

[1] Joseph Butler, *Sermons*, 'Upon the Ignorance of Man,' in *Works*, ii, Oxford 1835, pp. 232–3, note b.

in public teaching . . . CAN MAKE UP INTO NO SYSTEM. They are a rope of sand . . . not a catena. — On the other hand the Catholic anticipations . . . are parts of a whole etc etc'[1]

This is the principle, on which I have not mentioned in my Essay (which has sometimes been objected to me) St Gregory's refusal of the term Ecumenical Bishop, St Chrysostom's language about our Lady etc.[2] my object being *to make out the system* or whole, to which and which only the phenomena of history point. And I maintain that the Catholic system, as we now have it, is that to which the *mass* of historical phenomena point — and what remains of fact not taken up by it, consists of odds and ends, and is amorphous, pointing to nothing at all; — that when you confront Catholicism before the facts of history, they are seen almost all tending, converging, absorbed in it — but that place *Protestantism, Anglicanism* etc before the same facts, and there is a simple discord, no sort of relation and sympathy at all existing between the doctrinal system and the phenomena.

It is as entertaining this view of the case, that I am so much pained at the general mode of arguing, which Anglicans adopt. *They have nothing to say positive*; they only carp at those historical facts which *we* are unable (if so) to take up and locate in our system. Theirs is an 'argument from odds and ends —' i.e. an *objection* — nothing more. I could enlarge on this at great length.

Before then I go into your specific objections, let me ask first, whether you have *any view* yourself of history at all — whether with Mr Allies you take the patriarchal view; or the Protestant view with Bishop Newton;[3] or no view at all — *which is saying that Christianity has never been a revelation.* If you take Bishop Bull's view, how do you, who stumble at Honorius, account for his admission that 'nearly all the ancient Catholics who preceded Arius have the appearance of being ignorant of the invisible and incomprehensible nature of the Son of God?'[4] If you consider exceptions, which are insoluble, are decisive refutations of a doctrine, why [do] you believe in a God or a Christ, etc etc.

It is for Dr Cumming and Exeter Hall to think they have a right to

---

[1] This passage is omitted in the 1878 edition of *Dev.* 1st ed. pp. 388–9.

[2] On these see letter of 5 Nov. 1849 to Mrs Lockhart, and *Letter to Pusey, Diff.* II, pp. 128 ff.

[3] T. W. Allies, *The Church of England cleared from the Charge of Schism.* Thomas Newton (1704–82), Bishop of Bristol, in *Dissertation on the Prophecies*, 1754, taught that the Pope was Antichrist. Cf. *Apo.* p. 7.

[4] 'Veteres Catholici pene omnes, qui Arium praecessere, Filii Dei invisibilem atque immensam naturam ignorasse videntur.' George Bull, *Defensio Fidei Nicaenae*, Oxford 1685, IV, 3, 1.

attack Catholics without professing what they hold themselves and what they do not, but I confidently expect you are of those who feel they have no right to demolish without building up — or to attack *in the dark*. Each combatant surely must show himself. I claim, to use my own words in the work already quoted, 'those who find fault with the explanation here offered of its historical phenomena, will find it their duty to provide one of their own.'[1]

I should put the state of the case then thus:— both Anglicans and we confess the Primitive Church to be a Divine Ordinance to last for ever. Anglicans moreover say that the Church of England is a continuation in this present age of that Ordinance; and that our communion is also a continuation but with great differences from it, which in consequence they call corruptions. Now I am prepared to maintain, that, set an infidel (if you will) to *draw* the Church from the primitive records, he will produce a picture, toto coelo different from the Anglican Church, looked at as a *concrete whole*; a picture different *in parts* from the modern communion of Rome, but with an unmistakable and intimate resemblance to it. In thus stating the case, I have put it much less advantageously for the Roman communion than I conceive to be the fact, for argument's sake.

This being my way of viewing the matter, I consider the *first* thing to prove is, the *identity* of the present Roman Church, *or* the Anglican Church, with the Primitive Church. *When* this is proved of the Anglican Church, I will take its doctrine of 'Scripture being the whole rule of faith' *upon faith*; and, when it is proved of the Roman Church, you ought to take the 'necessity of communion with the Pope' on faith.

Lord Bacon in his Advancement of Learning or Novum Organum, shows how to draw up an investigation, the arguments for one conclusion being in one column, those for the other in another. When the arguments, pro and contra each body, are put in separate columns, we shall be the better judge of the matter.

Excuse the freedom, with which I have been writing, and believe me, Very faithfully Yours

John H Newman   Congr. Orat.

P.S.   My object of course is to ask the favor of your telling me your view of the above, *before* I proceed to such cases as that of Honorius. I go to town on Tuesday, and my direction will be '24 King William Street, Strand.'

[1] *Dev.* p. 31. 1st ed. p. 29.

TO EDWARD BADELEY

Oratory Bm Sept 8/51

My dear Badeley,

I will come up to London on Thursday morning — and, if all is well, will make my appearance in Paper Buildings about three o'clock.

The Catholics here have taken up my cause with great enthusiasm — and, though not a *very* wealthy body, will go to great expence — and assure me nothing shall be wanting. Dr Cullen writes me the same from Ireland — in neither case did *I* or any friend of mine mention the matter to them.

I shall bring the Cardinal's documents with me, which he is to have out in Golden Square.[1]

One bad piece of news I have heard — viz the records of the Cancelleria at Viterbo were burned by the republicans two years back.

It seems that Richardson (the publisher) offered his name to Achilli, and he would not take it, because it was not Dr Wiseman's — but Richardson was prepared to stand the action, which implies, one should think, some sort of legal advice.[2]

There is a meeting of the Evangelical Alliance here tomorrow, when we expect their plan of operations will be published.

People here are confident it cannot be brought home to me — but the selling in the room is surely a strong fact.

Ever Yours affecty John H Newman

P.S.   On second thoughts I shall come up Wednesday afternoon, and so will come to you about 11 or 12 (noon). If this won't do, please, drop a line to me at '24 King William Street Strand.'

[1] This Newman must have asserted on the basis of Philip Gordon's letter of 6 Sept., 'I went to the Cardinal's this morning to ask about the time of Fr John's ordination. The Cardinal came into the room where I was, and seemed to take for granted that I had come from you, and came up to me and said that he was very sorry to hear that you were not coming to Town till next week, as he had hoped to have seen you, but he was then on the point of leaving for St. Leonards by order of the Doctors. He said he had given orders for his papers about Achilli to be sorted for you, that he would write to Naples, Viterbo, and Corfu for more official documents, . . . He said that he did not think Achilli would press the matter . . . He said that he had many more papers sent to him since his article in the Dublin—I suppose he will have these papers out for you.' The documents, however, were not found until it was too late. See letter of 26 Nov. to W. G. Ward.

[2] Newman is replying to Badeley's letter of 2 Sept., 'I should doubt whether the Cardinal really acted under legal advice in putting forward the article [on Achilli in *D R*]—if he did, it implies considerable confidence, on the part of his adviser,' for each case would have to be proved. Richardson was the publisher of *D R*, and of the pamphlet on Achilli reprinted from it.

TO F. A. FABER

Oratory Birmingham Sept 9. 1851

My dear Faber,

Thank you for the trouble you have taken with your Uncle; and for what you say of me.

You speak of 'two sections of Christians using language so hard of each other;' does this mean your Uncle and me? I have called him 'generous,' he has called me a *liar*. God will to a certainty judge between us.

Yours very truly John H Newman.

TO MRS LUCY AGNES PHILLIPS

Sept 9. 1851

My dear Mrs Philipps,

You must have thought it very strange I did not answer your very kind letter last week. But from some stupid mistake of mine I fancied you had gone the day after you wrote it, and only discovered my mistake on Sunday, when, to my great surprise and hardly trusting my eyes, I saw your children on the Oxford Road.

Now then let me, though so late, express my thanks to you for it — and to congratulate you, as I do with all my heart, our loving Lord, who is so rich in mercy, has brought [you] and your dear children, within the True Fold. The longer you live, the more you will praise and bless Him for this gift

Yours most truly in Xt   John H Newman   Cong. Orat.

P.S.   I had intended to call to explain my mistake, but am going to Town this morning, and am so busy that I think you will excuse me.

TO FRANCIS RICHARD WEGG-PROSSER

24 King Wm Street, Strand Sept 10. 1851

My dear Sir,

I prefer to send you a few hurried lines to postponing my answer, till I return, which will be on Saturday.

Did I not in my letter make the infallibility of the Pope a *doctrine* to be taken in faith on the Church's word (so far as the Church says it)? If I have not said so clearly (at the end of my letter) it is what I meant to say. The way I wished to put the question is this:— 1. There must be ever in the world a continuation of the Primitive Church. 2 that continuation is infallible. 3. It is no other than the Roman. 4. What the Roman says is to be received. 5 The Roman teaches (if so) the infallibility of the Pope. — I mean, submit yourself to the Roman Church, and *then* take the infallibility of the Pope, if the Roman Church teaches it.

As to the Greek Church, a writer in the Guardian accused me of understating its numbers, but his account agreed with mine, mutatis mutandis, except as regarded the Asiatic Greeks, about whom Mouravief, I suspect, knows nothing.[1] I think I followed Malte Brun. But I expressly said, as *you* say, the numbers are little to the purpose.[2]

The great argument against the Greek Church is that it is in no sense *Catholic* — it is national. It lives where it first found itself, when the Schism began. There are some striking passages of St Augustine quoted in Dr Wiseman's article in the Dublin Review on Donatism and the Anglican movement in the year 1839.[3] It was one of the chief instruments of destroying my own faith in the Anglican Church — and it applies to the Greek. I wish you would read it. 'The kingdom of heaven' is a polity, which implies *political* life, activity, history, progress, development, warfare etc etc. All this the Roman Church has — the Greek has not — and the more it is known, the less it is seen to have. It has in Russia *sunk into the Erastian* heresy — when has the Roman Church done this? What *centre* is there in the Greek Church? What *real* intercommunion between Russia and Syria? a sympathy, nothing more.

Very truly Yours John H Newman

P.S.   I *don't* go the lengths of what is said against the Fathers in the extracts you inclose me — and cannot believe any of our Priests would *write down* what they are said to have uttered.

---

[1] A. N. Mouravieff, *A History of the Church of Russia*, trans. R. W. Blackmore, Oxford 1842.

[2] Newman is referring to his treatment of this question in Lecture IX of *Difficulties of Anglicans* I, where, p. 335, he cites Josiah Conder, *An Analytical and Comparative View of All Religions now extant among Mankind . . .*, London 1838. Conder appeals on p. 39 to Conrad Malte Brun (1775–1826), Danish geographer, who published *Géographie mathématique, physique et politique de toutes les parties du monde*, 1803–27.

[3] 'Tracts for the Times: Anglican claim of Apostolic Succession,' *D R*, VIII (Aug. 1839), pp. 147 ff. Cf. *Apo.* pp. 116–17.

TO ROBERT ORNSBY

24 K Wm Street Sept 11/51

My dear Ornsby,[1]

I have already spoken of you to the Primate. What power I shall have to nominate, I cannot yet say. You may be sure I will do what I can for you

Ever Yours John H Newman   Congr. Orat.

P.S.   Say a Hail Mary for me now and then, for this miserable Achilli has the power of annoying me.

TO MRS HENRY WILBERFORCE

24 K Wm Str. Sept 11/51

My dear Mrs Wilberforce,

Thank you for your kind note. I would come if I could, were it merely to excuse my rudeness the other day — but that apparent rudeness was caused by the rudeness of another person.

But I can't come — for I don't leave this till Saturday. ⌈I have been with Badeley 5 or 6 hours today, and see him tomorrow again. This Achilli will, by his mere threat, put me to a deal of trouble and expence — for I suppose I shall have at once to send out some one to Italy to collect evidence, for precaution's sake — even though in the event he does nothing. In the present want of money this is a great nuisance.⌉

Pray for me, I earnestly ask you, My dear Mrs Wilberforce, and believe me, Ever Yours very sincerely in Xt

John H Newman   Congr. Orat.

Tronson was the name of the writer — but, recollect, he is uncomfortably rigid, and has no tact or accommodation.[2]

---

[1] Newman's spelling 'Ornsby,' which was the more usual with him until 21 July 1854, has been everywhere corrected.

[2] Evidently *Examens particuliers sur divers sujets*, by M. Tronson (1622–1700), the third Superior of St Sulpice. A copy of this work is among the books in Newman's room.

TO EDWARD CASWALL

Oy Bm Sept 12/51

Charissime

I am not going to plague you with many words. Be sure we think of you a good deal. I shall give you a weekly Mass.[1]

Ever Yrs affectly in Xt   John H Newman

TO T. W. ALLIES

29 King William Street Saturday [13 September 1851]

My dear Allies,

I should not have known how to speak to you today even had I had time. Of course, if I am autocrat, my first wish will be to try to persuade you to come to Dublin but my offer may be limited by what the Commission has already past, and it *must* be after the day, when the School[2] matter here is decided.

Ever yrs affectly J. H Newman

TO MRS J. W. BOWDEN

Oratory Bm Sept 15. 1851

My dear Mrs Bowden,

I inclose a letter I received some little time back. What it says about chanting should be thought of. I can fancy it a trial — at least it would be to me a trial to have to chant as they do at the Good Shepherd, a bad imitation of French Latin through the nose. Also the strictness of the enclosure is a very serious matter. But something or other there must be strict, if it is to be a convent. Considering that Marianne has before now been delicate, and may require change of air, inclosure itself is an anxiety. Of course it is my line here to take the office of the Advocatus diaboli, and to urge every thing against any step, which deserves consideration.

---

[1] Caswall was ill at Malvern. Newman was still in London when he wrote this letter.

[2] This letter is dated only by its contents, and 'School' is almost certainly the copyist's error for 'Achilli.'

There are symptoms already of Achilli shrinking back — and the more I go into the subject, the more wonderful it seems he should persist in his threat — But men do odd things; Badeley whom I have gone to see, tells me of a man who went on with an action, in spite of his Counsel (Scarlett)[1] twice warning him, as the trial proceeded, that, if he went on with it, he would be hung — and he *was* hung. I fear the very threat will put me to expence.

F. Joseph is going to Italy for three months for his health — and will reconnoitre the ground — but if it goes on, we must have a Commission appointed, which will be an expensive job — We do not wish it mentioned that F. Joseph is going on any other ground than his health.

I have never thanked you for the beautiful aspersorium you left, and now I have to thank you for the £100 in addition — which, as you leave it to me, shall go to the new Church — unless Achilli presses us very hard, and then thankfully, though very grudgingly I shall apply it in opposing him — but I don't think this likely.

Ever Yours affly in Xt   John H Newman

P.S.   I don't forget your message about Sir John.[2]

TO ARCHBISHOP CULLEN

Oratory Bm Sept 16/51

My dear Lord,

Not any one answer has come to the letters of inquiry we have addressed to the members of the Consulting Committee — and I have written to Dr Leahy to ask his opinion what had best be done under the circumstances.[3]

As to your Grace's proposal, I will most readily accede to it — but I consider I ought to know better than I do the state of public opinion and knowledge in Ireland on the subject of education, and your own

[1] James Scarlett, first Baron Abinger (1769–1844), was, according to *DNB*, 'by far the most successful advocate of his day.'

[2] Sir John Swinburne, Bart. (1762–1860), of Capheaton, Northumberland—Mrs Bowden's father.

[3] When Leahy and O'Reilly met Newman on 27 Aug. they brought with them a list of questions, which Newman revised slightly, and sent to various Catholics who were authorities on University education, Mgr de Ram of Louvain, Dr Döllinger, Dr Jerrard, Dr John O'Hanlon of Maynooth, and others.

ideas what Lectures ought to be about, in order to be useful. I do not see I could do them well, unless I did them with a good deal of thought. But, as a first condition, I should like to have the *definite* subjects to be treated of from your Grace.[1]

Have you seen the good Abbé Gaume's book?[2] It is a startling one, to judge from a very partial inspection of it. He seems to wish to give up the Classics altogether. Is Aristotle to be given up with the rest?

I will certainly let your Grace know when I come to Liverpool. Begging your blessing, I am, My dear Lord Primate, Ever Yrs affecty

John H Newman   Congr. Orat.

TO THE FATHER IN RESIDENCE[3]

Oratory Bm Sept 17/51

My dear Father in residence,

Please look into the Clerical ⟨Clergy⟩ List at Stewart's, and let me know if there is a clergyman of the name of J. Berrington there — who has a living in Gloucestershire, and lives at Clavenage House, near Tetbury.

Also if there is a Revd J. de Carteret, Waddesdon Rectory Aylesbury and a Revd Edward Coupland Fellow of St John's College Oxford, now at Thurlby, Alford, Lincolnshire[4]

If you *could* give me a line by the *early* post tomorrow, I should be obliged

Ever Yrs affly J H N

[1] For Cullen's reply see letter of 22 Sept.

[2] Jean Joseph Gaume (1802–79), *Le Ver rongeur des sociétés modernes ou le paganisme dans l'éducation*, 1851, in which he attributed the moral deterioration of the modern world to the use of the pagan classics in education. The book provoked a controversy in France. See *Culler*, pp. 263–4. Gaume was disowned by his own Bishop at Nevers, and later was to be found on the side of Veuillot against Bishop Dupanloup.

[3] Many of the London Oratorians were absent during the holiday period.

[4] None of these names is in the Clergy List for 1851. John Berrington, born about 1809, had been at St Edmund Hall, Oxford, and Caius College, Cambridge. He took Orders in 1835, but was later suspended by the Bishop of Ely. From about 1843 he lived as a swindler, among other things raising money by offering titles for ordination, in advertisements. He was sentenced to 15 years' penal servitude in 1873 for obtaining money by false pretences. Edward Coupland, whose father lived at Boston, went to St John's College in 1846, at the age of 18. Newman was evidently following up some information he had received in connection with Achilli.

TO RICHARD STANTON

Oratory Bm Sept 17/51

Charissime,

We have been hoping for you some time.

As to myself I *wish* to go to Ireland next Monday, *but I don't think I shall.* If I don't, I am engaged to go to Rugby on Tuesday to come back at night.[1] Now you know my engagements. I shall be truly disappointed not to see you.

I used John's note directly — but have not yet had a word from F Esmond.[2] Nor from F White, the Dominican. People are sadly slow in writing.

FF Joseph and Nicholas are going abroad till Christmas — *F Joseph's health requires it* — They will try to get evidence against Achilli — but *this must be kept secret,* for, the Mazzini people being all about, they may get stuck, were it known.

Ever Yrs affly in Xt   J H N

P.S.   Think if our Fathers can do any thing for you at Rome.

Stewart is to send Origen, for F. Joseph to take to Theiner. It is to be sent to your House for him.[3] Where are *my books*, which were got several months ago? He will take them too.

TO F. A. FABER

Oratory Bm Sept 18/51

My dear Faber,

Thank you again for your kind letter.

Most certainly do I wish you to read Loss and Gain, whenever you have an opportunity, and would send you a copy, if I had a spare one; so utterly conscious am I, not only that I have not, as you say, written 'a satire on my old Oxford friends,' but that I studiously avoided every

---

[1] Newman wanted to go to Ireland for the meeting of the sub-committee of the Catholic University, but did not do so until 30 Sept. On Monday 22 Sept. he went to Rugby (see diary), and Stanton arrived for his visit.

[2] Stanton wrote on 15 Sept., 'Did you get a note from F. John Bowden which he wrote to tell you that F. Esmond the Jesuit got up the whole Achilli case when in Malta. F. Esmond is now in Dublin.' Bartholomew Esmonde had been a missionary in Malta 1848–50.   [3] See letters of 19 July and 19 Sept. to Stanton.

thing connected with them. This I have expressed in the advertisement, where I say, 'It must be added, to prevent a further misconception, that no proper *representation* is intended in this tale, of the religious opinions which had lately so much influence in the University of Oxford.'*

As to my recent Lectures, what you have heard is an absurd misrepresentation.

Very sincerely Yours John H Newman

*   *   *

* I have only ridiculed the *abuse* of those opinions, as I laughed at it, when in the Anglican Church, viz persons going by outside show, pompousness, flippancy, unreality — etc — against which my *Protestant* Sermons are strong.

TO FRANCIS RICHARD WEGG-PROSSER

Oratory Birmingham Sept 18. 1851

My dear Sir,

I consider I CAN give to 'those historical cases, which seem to contradict the Ultramontane theory of Papal Supremacy a solution beyond the answers' which seemed to you insufficient, but it seemed to me there was a *previous question*, which inquirers were *bound* to consider, viz what *is* a sufficient answer? — is that sufficient in the Catholic argument, which is sufficient in the Trinitarian? — It is no use to argue with different canons of argument from those of one's opponent. The writer of the letters you were good enough to send me[1] was 'determined *to get to the bottom* of the Papal Theory,' and I was determined to get at the bottom of the argumentative process which was the principle of his investigation. And I seriously think this ought to be done; it seems to me, if you will let me say it, that inquirers are not fair to themselves *till* they do it.

When a person will fairly put down the *idea* he has of a good proof and defend it, I will gladly consider it with him, and then go on to further points of detail. I assert that the proof of the Papal Supremacy is as good as that of the Divinity of Christ, by which I mean that it is the same *in kind*. Let us then settle what the proof must be *in kind* whether of the Papal claims, or of the Divinity of Christ, or of the

---

[1] This was Wegg-Prosser's friend, Robert Campbell, with whom Newman soon began to correspond directly. See letter of 27 Sept. to Wegg-Prosser, and 21 Oct. to Campbell.

Being of a God; whether the same or different. Till this is done, argument is but time and thought wasted.

I still am obliged to repeat, I cannot see that the Papal Supremacy *is* at the bottom of the whole question. I still would say, — the existence of the Church. The Church proclaims the Papal Supremacy (in whatever degree she proclaims it), as she proclaims the Divinity of Xt — She supports the Papal Supremacy by a body of proof (moral) — and she supports the Divinity of Xt by a body of moral proof. The great point then to be proved by us is that the present Church which the voice of mankind calls Catholic is the continuation of the Primitive Church. This I think can be proved over-poweringly (without any reference to or assumption at all of Papal Supremacy) to those who admit that a Church, one and the same, from first to last there ever will be. This I think can be proved as clearly as, more clearly than, the Divinity of Xt can be proved; it being more *argumentatively* certain that the modern Catholic Church resembles the Primitive as no other body does, than that the present Trinitarian doctrine resembles the Antenicene doctrine concerning the Son and Holy Ghost

Yours very truly John H Newman

TO T. F. KNOX

[19? September 1851]

My dear F Francis

Thank you for your information, which is much to my purpose.[1]

I write to prevent the Origen going down to Philip.[2] Joseph will call for it in a day or two in his way to the continent.

I wish you would ask Stewart, who will not be suspected, to get me,

1. The Two Reports of the Malta Protestant College about Dr Achilli referred to in the following

2. Report of the London Committee for the religious improvement of Italy and the Italians, on the Charges made against their agent, Dr Achilli, by the Malta Protestant College committee, adopted at a meeting on March 27, 1851.

The latter of these Reports is printed as an advertisement in the Record of April 7, 1851[3]

---

[1] This may refer to the letter of 17 Sept. to the Father in Residence.

[2] Newman was afraid that his present for Theiner would go to Philip Gordon, who was taking a holiday with other London Oratorians near Southampton.

[3] This letter is incomplete.

TO RICHARD STANTON

Oy Bm Sept 19/51

My dear F Richard

I do *not* go to Ireland next week. If Origen's Philosophumena has travelled down to Southampton, perhaps it may travel up with you to lie in King Wm [William] Street for F Joseph to take with him

Ever Yrs affly J H N

TO ALEXANDER BARNABÒ

Dabam ex Domo Birmingham die Sept 20. 1851
Domino Reverendissimo et Excellentissimo Alex. Barnabò &c. &c.

Ea est Tua erga nos benevolentia, Domine Reverendissime et Excellentissime, ut credam Te benignè esse recepturum duos è nostris Patribus, quos per hasce litteras Excellentiae Tuae commendo.

Consilium et patrocinium à Te humillimè expetunt in re molestiori, quam illi melius Tecum vivâ voce tractaturi sunt, quàm ego litteris possem explicare.

Accipias, Domine Reverendissime, professionem obsequii mei;
Excellentiae Tuae observantissimus Servus

Joannes H Newman   Congr. Orat.

TO AUGUSTINE THEINER

Dabam ex Domo Birmingham die Sept 20 1851.
Patri Reverendissimo et Charissimo
Augustino Theiner, Congr. Orat. Presb.

En Tibi commendo, Pater Reverendissime et dilectissime, duos è nostris Patribus Philippinis Domûs Birminghamiensis, Nicolaum Darnell et Josephum Gordon. Illi secum portant opuscula mea recentiora, quae, pro Tuâ erga me benevolentiâ, accipias velim, venerationis ergò et obsequii, ab humilitate meâ. Origenim vel Pseudo-origenim mitto simul, de quo mentionem fecisti. Alterum librum, quem à me ante aliquot menses petiisti, jam ad Te per amicum Tuum, miseram.[1]

---

[1] See letter of 19 July to Stanton.

Acceptissima mihi erant opera Tua, quae ineunte anno a tè ad me venerunt

Valeas, Pater amicissime, et memento mei. Tui et Tuorum observantissimi

Joannis H. Newman   Congr. Orat.

MONDAY 22 SEPTEMBER 1851   Went to Rugby to H W's *Wilberforce's* to consult Mr Babington   FF Joseph and Nicholas set off for Rome ⟨*Naples*⟩ (*on the Achilli matter*)

TO MRS J. W. BOWDEN

Oratory Bm Sept. 22/51

My dear Mrs Bowden,

It seems to me really best that Marianne should go with you.[1] She cannot possibly dispose of herself so suddenly. As far as my experience goes, which of course is not much, nothing of the kind is done well in a hurry. I wish she had more of a taste for external duties — I mean it would be less difficult and anxious for her to make her choice — The cloister is a trial. Miss Ryder (or Miss Lockwood) has undertaken it.[2] She tells me she quite bears it now — but the first year it tried her a good deal. As before, I am looking at it in a merely human aspect, as her director will be able to look at it in a higher.

As to Charles, I confess I wish our Irish matters were so far advanced, that I could press you to send him to us. He would have no where more friends.

I don't *think* any thing will come of the Achilli matter — he is showing (apparently) the white feather already. However, we are collecting evidence. F. Gordon and F Darnell are gone to Italy, ostensibly for F Gordon's health, which (I regret to say) is quite a real reason, but to collect evidence and to procure official documents. (We do not wish this known, for Achilli, I suppose, belongs to the secret societies of Italy.) As any how they would have gone abroad some time or other, and this is as good a time as any other, we cannot call this any expence — and I really trust we shall have to spend nothing at all, except for the mere copying of some police etc. reports. However, some of us wish to *push* the matter, if we get our evidence, at all risks — and challenge Sir Cullen Smith to proceed — as willing even to risk a *legal* defeat for the

[1] The Bowdens were to spend the winter in Malta.

[2] Sophie Ryder and Harriett Lockwood, both of them converts, entered the Good Shepherd Convent at Hammersmith in 1849.

moral exposure of A. and its moral effects[1] — This is so bold a game, I should never think of doing it, without the concurrence of the Catholic body here, and in other localities.

I have heard of Lisbon as a place to which invalids go — but recollect, *unless* lodging keepers are prepared for it, a foreign climate may be worse than England. I can bear witness to Naples, Palermo, and Corfu, when I travelled with Hurrell Froude. Lisbon is said to be a very dirty place — and I fear the Church is in a miserable state there. There seems almost a disorganization of Catholicism. Some of the Bishops are free masons, having taken the Pope in — and the Government would gladly see the Church destroyed, judging by appearances.

I expected to go to Ireland this week — now I expect to go next. I very much fear there is not a chance of my seeing you — but no one can tell.

We have heavy hearts just now. FF Nicholas and Joseph left us for the Continent yesterday. F Edward Caswall is seriously ill at Malvern, and F Stanislas attending him. Br Aloysius is dying (of consumption) and F. Philip (Bathurst) is sufficiently indisposed to be going with me to Ireland for change of air.

Ever Yrs affly in Xt   John H Newman

Love to the dear girls.

TO ARCHBISHOP CULLEN

Oratory Birmingham Sept 22/51

My dear Lord Primate,

I fear there is no chance of Dr Leahy sending for me, while your Grace is at Liverpool; at least, time is getting on so quickly.

Thank you for the subjects you mention for Lectures.[2] They are

---

[1] Sir Culling Eardley Eardley (1805–63), only son of Sir Culling Smith, second baronet, and Charlotte Elizabeth, daughter of Lord Eardley, was at Eton and Oriel College. He changed his name in 1847, on becoming the representative of the Eardley family. In 1846 he founded the Evangelical Alliance, was chairman of its Executive Committee 1850–1, and a member of the deputation 'to free Achilli from the Roman Inquisition,' and to bring him to England. He published *The Imprisonment and Deliverance of Dr. Giacinto Achilli, with some account of his previous history and labours,* London 1850, one of the books reviewed by Wiseman in his article on Achilli in *D R,* June 1850. When the evidence against Achilli was brought to Eardley's notice, the latter challenged him with it, and was satisfied with Achilli's word that he had never been guilty of immorality.

[2] Cullen replied on 20 Sept. to Newman's request of 16 Sept.: 'What we want in Ireland is to persuade the people that education should be religious. The whole tendency of our new systems is to make it believed that education may be so conducted as

most important ones — but will take a long time thinking out — and I ought to know some thing of the state of feeling of my audience before I actually do any thing. But I will turn my mind to the subject at once.

I am now waiting to hear from Dr Leahy; as I said, unless something unforeseen happened, I would be at his disposal any time.

Your Grace's affecte Servt John H Newman   Congr. Orat.

TO T. W. ALLIES

Oratory Bm Sept. 24./51

My dear Allies,

Dr Leahy has fixed next Monday for my going to begin business at Thurles next morning. But I have to see the Primate at Liverpool first, so I shall write about it by this post. You shall hear from me as soon as I have any thing to say.

Ever yours J H N

TO FRANCIS RICHARD WEGG-PROSSER

Oratory Birmingham Sept 24. 1851

My dear Sir,

I must protest with all my might against what *I* consider an assumption, that the infallibility of the Pope is the *basis* of the Catholic Religion looked at controversially, and I will not meet you on a point, the admission of which seems to me a mistake. I will not put myself in a false position, as I have said already in two letters.

For me, I maintain it is a *doctrine of the church*, (whether a dogma or not, I am not going into) but I mean, as far as it is to be received, it is to be received on the church's authority. What do you think of an Evangelical who will persist in arguing with a Catholic, only on the basis of the

to have nothing at all to do with religion. Moral philosophy, law, history are proposed to be taught in this way. The project is in itself absurd and impossible, but it is necessary to instruct us a little upon the matter. To do so however I suppose the whole question of education should be reviewed—The subjects or some of the subjects might be the advantages of educating the people and the sort of education they ought to receive—Mixed education—Examination of the education given to Catholics in Trinity College and its effects—education in the Queen's Colleges, or education without any religion—The sort of education which Catholics ought to seek for—' Newman now acknowledges the receipt of these suggestions. See also *Culler*, p. 137, and letter of 4 Feb. 1852 to Cullen.

Scripture being the Rule of faith, and cries out 'a victory' if the Catholic refuses so to meet him? In like manner I will not grant, I will not meet the Anglican on, the point that the Papal Infallibility is the ultimate resolution of the controversy between us and him. I deny it, and I will maintain my denial by arguments.

Of course this is no fine or subtle question, but a most important one. Suppose a man planted himself against the *walls* of Rome and declared he would not go round to one of the *gates* — for he had a fancy to enter the city at that particular point. Equally unreasonable is it, to attempt to become a Catholic *through* one particular doctrine, instead of through those which Providence has appointed.

One modification only is necessary to this illustration, if you will allow me to continue it. In a moral question what is a gate to one is a wall to another, and vice versâ. There *are* persons who have found Papal Infallibility to be the gate; let them, if they will — our minds are so differently constituted that proof and difficulty change places in the case of separate persons — However, to you and to me, Papal Infallibility is *not* a proof. *I* say, Very well, go to that which *is* a proof — *You* say (excuse me) 'No, I will not come into the Church except in my own way — Unless Papal Infallibility be my gate, gate for me there shall be none.'

I hope you will excuse my freedom, but I wish to bring out my meaning.

I conceive that the fundamental proof of Catholicism, (i.e. the basis according to *my* conception of Catholicism,) is the promise that the Primitive church shall continue to the end, the likeness of the (Roman) Catholic church to the Primitive, and the dissimilarity of every other body — The (Roman) Catholic church then, being proved to be the organ of revelation, or infallible in matters of faith, will *teach* the Pope's Infallibility, as far as it is a doctrine, just as it teaches the Divinity of our Lord, or original sin — and its teaching must, as regards the one doctrine and the other, be received on faith.

Either of two things then a person, who thinks like me, will be willing to do — 1. to *prove* the divinity of the Catholic church. 2. to *defend* against objections her doctrines, and among others the Papal Infallibility. BOTH of these things may be required of her, to *prove* the church, to *defend* the Papal Infallibility — but I will not prove the Papal Infallibility, and that however, not as denying it *can* be proved, but as confessing that *I* will not do so — for it is not *my* way of looking at the evidence, as to which the most absolute private judgment is (primâ facie) allowable.

Now it is very plain how very differently objections look *after* the

366

point has been proved and before. To *defend* the church's doctrines, when she is proved to be the divine *oracle*, is a very different thing from *proving* those doctrines nakedly by themselves. You yourself stated the difference in a former letter; when I said that there were difficulties in the historical proof of our Lord's divinity, you answered, 'Yes, but I receive the doctrine on the church's word —' i.e. without *denying* that there were difficulties, you did not make much of them, as receiving the doctrine on the Church's authority — Now why will you not receive the Papal Infallibility just in the same way, viz a doctrine, to be received so far as the church teaches it? Why will you not rather address yourself to the proof of the (Roman) Catholic church's *mission*?

I do not deny, far from it, that there are objections to a doctrine *so great* as to be sufficient to overturn the authority of the person who propounds them. Did the (Roman) Catholic church say that impurity was a virtue, there would be no way of solving the opposition which our moral sense would make to it — there would be arguments so decisive against so monstrous a position, as to suffice simply to overturn the Church's authority — all proofs for that authority notwithstanding — and so doubtless there might be historical arguments against our Lord's Divinity or Papal Infallibility such as to destroy the credit of the oracle which asserted either. On the other hand there might be arguments against the doctrines of the church, unanswerable, yet insufficient to overturn the authority propounding them, which had a just claim to be believed in its propounding, in spite of those arguments; and this, whether against its moral precepts, or its theology, or the economy of grace.

I fully agree to your distinction that historical objections against one doctrine may be more intelligent and pertinent than against another. You wish this to tell in favor of your non-acceptance of Papal Infallibility, — in comparison of our Lord's Divinity etc — I cannot perceive the justice of this application.

The difficulty in the way of receiving the Papal Infallibility is, that certain Popes seem to have erred, and to have been recognized by the church as erring. See what a number of distinctions are obvious at once, in explanation of this difficulty, e.g. 'err' — granted, *but* not in matters of *faith* — or 'err' granted, but not *ex cathedrâ*; 'seemed to err,' granted, but the church has never so recognized etc etc. I mean the force and edge of the objection is not at first sight *decisive*.

On the other hand, observe the three following difficulties in the proof of *other* doctrines. I say they are evidently, in the very form of the objection, greater — i.e. in the logical force of the wording.

1. God is all good and all powerful — *yet*, He has allowed evil to exist.

2. The Son of God is incomprehensible and immense ⟨vid Athan. [Athanasian] Creed⟩ — *yet* Bishop Bull says that 'nearly all the ancient Catholics who preceded Arius have the appearance of being ignorant of the invisible and incomprehensible (or immense) nature of the Son of God.'

3. The Son of God, even in His human nature, has ever known all things which are to be; *yet* He says Himself of the day of judgment, 'Not the Son, but the Father.'

I consider then that, even though I said not a word to soften the difficulties about Liberius, Honorius etc. a Protestant opponent would have no cause to complain.

1. Because *if* I have brought a *real ⟨positive⟩ proof* from the historical documents of the church for Papal infallibility, I am not bound to answer objections; so that the question is, *Have* I brought a real proof?

2. Because, *since* the church (*granting* it does) asserts the doctrine, (and the Church is infallible) the onus probandi is with my opponent — and *I* have not to answer *his* objections, but *he* to prove *his* point.

3. Because so little is this doctrine the basis of our system, that any Catholic may in fact *deny* it — and this is bringing the matter to the shortest issue, viz for me to give up the doctrine to you. — As a controvertist, (though not in my own belief,) I *grant to you* that the Pope is not infallible. Now what will you say?

I ought to apologize for saying that I have not finished my subject, but shall resume it, except that you have encouraged me. It is useless to answer your question, unless I explain from what point of view alone I will *consent* to answer it

Yours very faithfully John H Newman

TO J. M. CAPES

Oy Bm Sept 25/51

My dear Capes,

I doubt if it is prudent to be quite so strong in your condemnation of Animal Magnetism — I mean, *as deducing* from the Reply of the Penitentiary.[1] I don't mean your private opinion.

'as the *above* facts stand —' or 'would seem to be prohibited' etc —

---

[1] This was in Capes's review of William Gregory, *Letters to a candid Inquirer on Animal Magnetism*, the *Rambler*, VIII (Oct. 1851), pp. 296–326. The book was concerned with mesmerism and hypnotism, and Capes based his judgment, not quite accurately, on a Roman reply, pp. 322–4.

would, I think, be safer — For is it certain that every one would grant that an absolute command over a patient is involved and necessary for curing him? or that the account sent to the Penitentiary is co-extensive with the Science?

Professor Nardi of Padua has been here today and wished to know you — he was frightened at the notion of seeking you in the country, and I did not encourage him.[1]

I have written to the printer not to print off the sheet till he hears from you. Most unluckily I have mislaid the sheet with all the extracts from Dr Gregory,[2] which I had most carefully put aside to read.

Ever Yrs affly in Xt   John H Newman   Congr. Orat.

TO FRANCIS RICHARD WEGG-PROSSER

Oratory Birmingham Sept 25. 1851

My dear Sir

I continue my letter of yesterday. Supposing a person said 'I will believe in Christianity on one condition, that you prove to me historically the darkness at the Passion:' what should we say? — We should believe it ourselves, we should know that, *did* he believe in Christianity, he *would* believe it — but we should know also that, as Gibbon says, history does not mention it, and therefore it cannot be proved by history — and in consequence we should say that he was unreasonable, and trifling with serious things. So I say of any one who *insists* as a sine quâ non, on the Pope's infallibility being proved to him as the medium of his conviction to the Catholic Faith. It is true — he will believe it, when he is a Catholic — but it is not the necessary instrument of conviction.

Coming then to the question which you ask 'How I solve certain historical facts bearing on the question of the Pope's Infallibility', I say

1. There is an Infallible Church.
2. The (Roman) Catholic Church is it: —
3. All points of doctrine which the Church teaches are to be believed.
4. If the Church teaches this, it is to be believed.

Therefore I approach these alleged historical facts with the Papal Infallibility already *proved* (as far as it is certain) by the authority of the Church — and I will consider these historical facts simply as objections,

---

[1] Francesco Nardi (1808–77) was professor of philosophy and canon law at the University of Padua, and later secretary to the Congregation of Bishops and Regulars. On 23 Aug. 1867 Nardi again visited Newman, who wrote a witty account the next day. *Ward* II, pp. 188–90.   [2] In the *Rambler* article, pp. 298–319.

and in no other way. And observe, I will consider them in no other way, for the same kind of reason that I will not prove (e.g.) purgatory from Scripture to please the Protestant. Not that I dont think purgatory is in Scripture, but I will not do any thing to seem to grant to the Protestant that Scripture is the *whole* Rule of Faith. So I will not profess to prove the Papal Infallibility *merely* from historical facts, lest I seem to grant to you, which I cannot, that it is the cardo of the whole question — that, till and unless it is proved, nothing is proved by us.

Assuming then (what I am bound to prove, if called upon) that the (Roman) Catholic Church is that Church which is promised authority in matters of faith, and that if Papal Infallibility be a point of faith, it is so because the Church teaches it, I can only look at your objections as objections to a conclusion *already proved* — and the question simply is, whether these objections are *sufficient* to set aside a point already proved on the Church's authority, (and the Church's authority with it.) I say they are not: —

1. For first, if *nothing* could be said in explanation of them, *even then* it would be a very grave question whether they interfered with the proof from the Church's evidence at all; — any more than *the fact* of evil in the world (which is nothing à priori, as you say it is, but a *fact*) overturns, *though it does in words contradict*, the Church's doctrine that God is All good and All powerful. (There is nothing à priori here, it is a question of the contradiction of two statements)

2. Next a great deal may be said in their explanation. I will take the two which seem most formidable. (1) Liberius's fall. (2) Honorius's prevarication.

(1) As to the first, it is most difficult to determine that he asserted ex cathedrâ any wrong doctrine. What he seems to have done, though the history is confused, is, by *not* positively confessing the Nicene Symbol, to *give a sanction* to the heretical party — as St Peter in Galat. 2. This is a sin, but not an ex cathedrâ error of faith. I shall be acting fairly, if I quote my own words in my work on the Arians published in 1833.

'A creed was compiled, that of the *orthodox* Council against Paulus, (A.D. 264) that of the *Dedication* (A.D. 341) and a third *lately published at Sirmium*, on the condemnation of Photinus. (AD. 351) Thus carefully composed, it was signed by all parties, Eusebians and Semiarians, as well as Liberius.'[1]

Now of these three formularies which made up the creed, you see the first is distinctly *called* orthodox. As to the second, I say of it, where mention of it historically occurs (p 308), it 'was that ascribed to the

[1] *Ari.* p. 322. 1st ed. p. 344.

martyr Lucian, though doubts are entertained of its genuineness. It is in itself almost unexceptionable — and, had there been no controversies on the subjects contained in it, would have been a satisfactory evidence of the orthodoxy of its promulgators. . . . An evasive condemnation was added of the Arian tenets; sufficient, as it might seem, to delude the Latins etc.'[1] — As to the *third* formulary, I cannot find in my volume any definite description of it, but I recollect that it is thought an orthodox Creed of *St Hilary* (*I* recollect the Creed quite, but I am not giving you my present ideas, lest they should be suspicious) and various encomiums are passed on it by ecclesiastical writers.

Granting then that Liberius by his *acts* encouraged heresy, that as little implicates his ex cathedrâ decisions, as David's adultery and murder compromise his Psalms.

2. As to Honorius, I have not time to look at my books, but I recollect it was clearly proved to my mind that Honorius's fault lay in committing himself to an unlawful economy. In matters of conduct and discipline, the Church has ever economized greatly. It allows the Greek clergy in marriage, tho' it thinks celibacy the proper state of a priest. It has not pushed its rights upon monarchs, when more evil would come of it than good. But it has never dared to compromise the faith. Honorius countenanced an heretical party. Here again he was like St Peter in Galat 2. He cannot be proved to have issued any dogmatic tome on the doctrine in dispute — To take the lowest ground (which is enough in *the case of an objection* to a point already proved, viz by the Church's authority) he *need not* have done more than commit a practical error — the extant documents *admit* of that interpretation.

Now, after speaking of Liberius and Honorius, let us suppose fifty similar objections — (for you will say they are but specimens) — let me, for argument's sake, admit also that I am not able *perfectly* and *completely* to destroy any one of them — let us grant in consequence, that, as Davison says in the beginning of his work on Prophecy, these remnants, after being enfeebled and attenuated, are thus able to cumulate into one aggregate objection.[2] Very well — they form a *probable case* against the Infallibility of the Pope. *But* on the *other* hand there are arguments too — put them at their lowest — still they too cumulate into a probable argument *for* the Pope's Infallibility. On *neither* side then is any thing proved. It is probability against probability. It is like Dr Johnson's 'There are objections to a plenum, and objections to a vacuum — yet

---

[1] *Ari.* p. 286.

[2] John Davison (1777–1834), *Discourses on Prophecy*, 2nd ed. 1825. See the first Discourse, 'On the Connexion of Prophecy with the other evidences of the Christian Religion.'

one or other must be true.' Well then — here the Church comes in — the Church declares (if it so declares, for it is not actually a point of faith) that the Pope *is* infallible. What become then of your cumulated objections, if they do not *reach* the point of utterly and imperiously establishing the Pope's fallibility? which I do not understand you to claim for them.

Again, I beg you to excuse my freedom of style, but I have not time to write with much ceremony.

Praying that God will bring you into all truth, and knowing perfectly that all conviction is from him

I am, my dear Sir, Very truly Yours

John H Newman   Congr. Orat.

P.S.   I am quite ready to go into the question of the exclusive divinity of the Roman Catholic Church, which is the basis of argument in my view of the controversy, after hearing your opinion on what I have said.

TO FRANCIS RICHARD WEGG-PROSSER

Oratory Bm Sept 27/51

My dear Sir

I wrote to Mr Campbell on receipt of his letter. I can't tell whether I directed right. I read his direction some place in 'Isle of Cumbrae.' I did not know the place.[1]

Do not suppose I said or alluded to any view of mine about Developments of doctrine in what I have said.

I think I understood you quite well — if you will let me say so — I *knew* you thought that '*if* the Papal Infallibility was given up, the Eastern Church was a Catholic Church or a branch of it.' But *this is the very point* I am *sure* you could not maintain in argument. Nor do I think you will long be able to maintain it to yourself. It is [the] very point I have wished you, in all I have said, to *reconsider*. I do not think there was any want of clearness in what you said. I wished with all my heart to consider with you the case of the Eastern Church, *separate* from the Pope's Infallibility. I think its ⟨Catholicity⟩ such a dream.

---

[1] None of Newman's letters to Campbell is to be found earlier than that of 21 Oct. 1851. Campbell was perhaps staying at the Episcopalian College of the Holy Spirit, founded in 1849 by George Frederick Boyle, afterwards Earl of Glasgow, on the island of Great Cumbrae in the Firth of Clyde.

Please to excuse me if, in any part of our correspondence, in writing quickly and offhand, I have written rudely

and believe me Very truly Yours John H Newman.

TO HENRY WILBERFORCE

Oy Bm Sept 27/51

My dear H

You were quite right in writing to Dr Weedal.[1]

I *thought* you were tiring out your wife, but I recollected 'You fool, said Mrs Bowman.'

I fear there is not much chance of our going together to Ireland, but don't know. As it stands, I am to visit the Primate at Liverpool. On the other hand, they have put me off at Thurles from Monday till Thursday. I will let you know.

Ever Yrs affly J H N

MONDAY 29 SEPTEMBER 1851 FF Nicholas and Joseph set off for Naples this day week. F Stanislas was ordained Priest on the 27 Br William Neville admitted to his year of 1st Probation.

TO ARCHBISHOP CULLEN

Oratory Bm Sept 29/51

My dear Lord Primate

As Mr Allies and I have now made our arrangements with Dr Leahy,[2] I think it will be best, since you seem to have no strong opinion to the contrary, for me to proceed at once to him, which I do, via Holyhead tomorrow. I will find out your Grace, wherever you direct me, after our conference.

I am, Yr Grace's affte Servt John H Newman C. O.

P.S. I do not think we need be *many* days with Dr Leahy and Mr O Reilly. If we finished our work by Friday night, I should find you at Drogheda on the 4th or 5th. I have engagements here just now, which make me wish to get back soon if I can.

[1] Wilberforce was living at Rugby in the Birmingham diocese, of which Dr Weedall was the Vicar General.

[2] The arrangements were for a meeting at Thurles of the sub-committee of the Catholic University.

TO F. W. FABER

Oy Bm Sept 29. 1851

My dear F Wilfrid

I should almost be glad your ailments took a tangible shape like gout.[1]

As to J.M., if he is a *professor* at Prior Park, I should suppose he must say so — but not if he is a lodger.[2]

Tell F Bernard M. Gondon will come towards the end of the week to take back some corrections of mine which are not ready and which I must send him.[3] I am off to Ireland tomorrow. My direction is 'College, Thurles.'

Perhaps F Bernard will also tell M. Gondon that the good Priest's of Carcasson's question was answered by me months and months ago

Ever Yrs affly in Xt   J H N

TUESDAY 30 SEPTEMBER 1851   set off with F Philip (*Bathurst*) and Allies for Ireland by Holyhead   got to Dublin by 1 A M

WEDNESDAY 1 OCTOBER   set off for Thurles, being joined by Mr O Reilly where got about noon

TO LADY OLIVIA ACHESON

Thurles. Oct 1/51

My dear Lady Olivia

Your letter has made me anxious how I am to answer you. I have an extreme repugnance to having the disposal of property, tho' I suppose it is what most persons would feel as well as I — and besides I think it very inexpedient just now that clergy should mix themselves up in such matters. If I understand, what you so kindly say, (of which be sure I do feel the extreme kindness though I do not use many words) you mean, that when Mr F.[4] asks me 'what shall I do with so and so?' I should answer 'Do this or do that.' I have not my ideas as clear as I should like, but hope I am not wrong in going as far as this; — that, if you define

[1] Faber's ailments had now taken the form of pains in both wrists, which the doctor thought was gout.

[2] J. B. Morris was consulting Faber as to whether he should remain at Prior Park. Newman perhaps meant to write 'stay so.'

[3] This presumably refers to the second edition of *Conférences adressées aux protestants et aux catholiques*, Paris 1850, which appeared in 1853. See letter to Dalgairns at end of 1850.

[4] Evidently Alexander Fullerton, who was Lady Olivia's executor and trustee.

the object etc *as far as ever you can*, I will suggest to Mr F., if he asks me any question in detail, what occurs to me — but still subject to his final decision. — You must tell me, if I have not answered to your satisfaction, or hit your meaning.

Tell them, please, at the Oratory, that we got here quite safe, at 11 this morning. We had a bad passage, and Stanislas will be glad to know that I abjure Holyhead. We got to bed at Dublin between one and two a m — my two companions knocked up. Tell Miss Bathurst that Philip[1] will not pick up till after a good night's rest — and tell F. Ambrose, that I, with my usual infelicity, spilt I can't say how much of my precious medicine over the amice, and other contents of my portmanteau, owing to the stiffness of the leather cover, making every thing very sticky, and going the way to take the skin off my hands. If the nitric acid had been pure, I suppose my hands would have been of a bright yellow.

All good Saints and blessed spirits be with you and around you, now and ever, is the fervent prayer of

Your affte friend John H Newman   Congr. Orat.

TO SAMUEL HINDS, BISHOP OF NORWICH

Thurles, Ireland, Oct. 2. [1851]

My dear Lord,[2]

A slip of a Norwich paper has been sent me which purports to give a speech of the 'bishop of the diocese,' delivered in St. Andrew's Hall, at a meeting of the British and Foreign Bible Society. Though the name of the diocese is not stated, I cannot be mistaken, under these circumstances, in ascribing the speech to your Lordship. Yet I know not how to credit that certain words contained in it, which evidently refer to me, should have been uttered by one who is so liberal, so fair, and temperate in his general judgments, as your Lordship.

The words are these: 'My friends, I have heard, and I am sure all of

---

[1] i.e. the brother of Catherine Anne Bathurst.

[2] This letter began a correspondence with Samuel Hinds, who, in 1827, had succeeded Newman as Vice-Principal of St Alban Hall, Oxford, Whately being the Principal. Hinds, who became Bishop of Norwich in 1849, criticised what Newman had said about ecclesiastical miracles in *Prepos.* Lecture VII, p. 312, 1st ed. pp. 298 ff. The correspondence was published in the *Morning Chronicle* (21 Oct. 1851), in the *Tablet* (25 Oct. 1851), and in the *Rambler*, VIII (Dec. 1851), pp. 444 ff. It also appeared as a pamphlet, *A Correspondence between the Rev. J. H. Newman, D.D., and the Bishop of Norwich on the Credibility of Miracles*, Birmingham 1851, and was added by Newman as a note at the end of the 1872 and subsequent editions of *Prepos.* The text now reprinted is that of the pamphlet. Cf. also Newman's *Essays on Miracles*.

you who have heard of it will share with me in the disgust as well as the surprise with which I have heard of it, that there is a publication circulated through this land, the stronghold of Bible Christianity — a publication issuing from that church against which we are protesting, and which is, on the other hand, the stronghold of human authority — a publication issuing from one of the most learned of its members, a man who, by his zeal as a convert, and by his position and acceptance with that church, speaks with the authority of the church itself, and represents its doctrines and feelings — a publication, as I have heard with dismay, read, admired, circulated, which maintains that the legendary stories of those puerile miracles, which I believe until now few Protestants thought that the Roman Catholics themselves believed — that these legends *have a claim to belief equally* with that word of God, which relates the miracles of our God, as recorded in the Gospel, and that *the authority of the one is as the authority of the other, the credibility of the one based on a foundation no less sure than the credibility of the other.*'

The statements here animadverted on are as contrary to the teaching of the Catholic church as they can be repugnant to your own views of Christian truth.

Should I be right in supposing that you did not really impute them to me, I beg to apologise to you for putting you to the trouble of disavowing the newspaper account. But if, contrary to my expectation, you acknowledge them to be yours, I take the liberty of begging your Lordship to refer me to the place in any work of mine in which they are contained.

You will not, I am sure, be surprised, if, at a moment like the present, when so many misrepresentations are made of Catholicism and its defenders, I should propose, as I do, to give the same publicity to any answer you shall favour me with, as has been given to the speech, the report of which has occasioned my question.

I am, my dear Lord, yours very faithfully, John H. Newman.

TO ARCHBISHOP CULLEN

Thurles. Oct 3. 1851

My dear Lord Primate

We seem to have finished our work here, as far as we can do it[1] — and I purpose coming to your Grace tomorrow (Saturday) night by the

---

[1] The work in question was the 'Report of the Sub-committee on the Organization of the University,' printed in *Campaign*, pp. 77–87. See also *McGrath*, pp. 116–18, and *Culler*, pp. 133–4. It formed the basis of the University as actually constituted.

Dublin 7.15 PM train. I do this on the idea, which I gathered from your letter, that you would be at Drogheda till Monday morning — I proposed going to Maynooth on Monday, and then back to England.

I have a friend with me, one of our Oratory, whom I hope I am not over bold in bringing with me to Drogheda.

Mr Allies is here, and hopes for an opportunity of paying his respects to your Grace before he leaves Ireland

Begging your Grace's blessing I am, My dear Lord Primate, Your affectte & faithful Servt

John H Newman   Congr. Orat.

TO AMBROSE ST JOHN

Thurles. Oct 3/51

Charissime,

In the greatest hurry, of course — It distressed me I had not taken leave of Aloysius — I had thought again and again of it, but it escaped me at the moment. Give him my love, and tell him it has made me think of him the more. Philip not well, and distresses me — I don't think Dr E. [Evans] has fathomed him.[1] I shall get back as soon as I can do nothing more; but, if I *can* be of use here, I shall. I *might*, according to appearance, get back on Tuesday next. Do not send me any more letters. But, alas, I can't conceive how I am to remain quiet at Bm [Birmingham] when I return. I fear I shall have to come again before Christmas. ⌈The quantity of work I shall have is enormous, and grows on me.⌉ The very patronage I shall have, will be a business. ⌈All things are parts of a whole and must be done on an idea —⌉ hence, willingly as I would give up (e.g.) culinary matters to some procurator or other absolutely, I don't think I shall be able. ⌈I trust we shall have an Oratory in Dublin — which is the only thing I can bribe St Philip with [[for coming here]]. W. Wilberforce dropped in here yesterday night, and then dropped off.

(Entre nous) this would never do for a site — a large fine building si,[2] but on a forlorn waste, without a tree — in a forlorn country, and a squalid town.⌉

---

[1] George Fabian Evans (1808?–73), after being at Caius College, Cambridge, built up a large practice as a doctor in Birmingham.

[2] Italian for 'yes,' 'I grant you.' Leahy was in favour of Thurles as the site for the University. See *A.W.* p. 282.

I must, if the trains allow of it, run over to Limerick, to see the Bishop.[1]

Ever Yrs affly in Mary & Philip   J H N

P.S.   Your letter has just come. I am *not* going to Limerick. Probably to Dublin tomorrow (Saturday)

I shall think myself well off if I have the appointment of 5 Professors out of ten.

I thought Miss Giberne was going to the poor Clares *tomorrow*.

⌈I generally am careful about strange houses — but, alas, slept with my window open the first night here — which has given me such a cold in my tongue that I can hardly speak a word, and seem half drunk when I attempt to make a speech.⌉

I suppose I shall be at 'Maynooth Dublin' on Monday, to which place you may direct my letters on *Sunday* night — but not later. Tuesday ⌈I propose⌉ to pass in Dublin, to embark on Tuesday night — and ⌈to get to you on Wednesday.⌉

TO FRANCIS RICHARD WEGG-PROSSER

Thurles Ireland Oct 3. 1851

My dear Sir,

Your letter has been forwarded to me here. Thank you for it, but I am so busy, that I will not offer to write more just now. I seem to feel that, were I talking to you, I could set right (if I may say so) many things you say — but letter writing is endless.

The theory of development of doctrine is but a method of *answering objections*. At least this is the primary view I have taken of it in my Essay. Then, in the next place, it becomes an *evidence*, when you see it proceeds on a *law*, which obtains, as now, so in the earliest period. Further, in drawing out the state of the case in the way of *defence*, the *unity* of the Church *throughout* its apparent changes, is an additional (and to me) most strong evidence. For instance, (and this, from memory, I would recommend for your perusal) my chapter on the 'First Test' — it is divided into three parts.[2]

---

[1] John Ryan (1784–1864) was consecrated Coadjutor to the Bishop of Limerick in 1825, succeeding in 1828. For a description of him see letter of 28 Feb. 1854 to Flanagan.

[2] *Dev.* Ch. vi, pp. 207–322; 1st ed., chaps. iv and v, pp. 204–317.

I cannot write more. The God of grace and truth be with you is the prayer of

Yours very truly John H Newman

P.S.   I propose to return to Birmingham next week.

SATURDAY 4 OCTOBER 1851   left with Philip [Bathurst] for Dublin   thence to Drogheda *to Dr Cullen with Philip* where arrived about 9 P M

SUNDAY 5 OCTOBER   with the Primate   (Tyler died)

MONDAY 6 OCTOBER   went with Philip to Dublin   to Dentist, Drumcondra, the Dominicans then back to Drogheda to dinner

TUESDAY 7 OCTOBER   to Dublin with Philip and Marshall   called on Ornsby and Dentist and Vincentian Hospital and Sisters of Mercy   dined with Jesuits then to Maynooth with Philip and Marshall

TO F. S. BOWLES

Dublin. Oct 7/51

My dear F Frederic,

We trust to start by Holyhead Steamer on Wednesday (tomorrow) at 1 PM. and, as far as I can make out, shall get to Birmingham, favente S. Raphaele, by about mid-night—to keep the day of my reception at home.[1]

We go to Maynooth in 2 hours time, where I hope to find letters from all of you. Philip does not pick up — I write from Ornsby's lodgings — Love to all

Ever Yrs affly J H N

WEDNESDAY 8 OCTOBER 1851   after Mass set off to Dublin with Philip [Bathurst] and Marshall — and breakfasted with Ornsby, meeting Lucas and Mr Cooper[2] who with Marshall went with us down to Kingstown   whence *with Philip* to Holyhead and got to Birmingham by 1 A M

TO MRS WILLIAM FROUDE

Oratory Bm October 9. 1851

My dear Mrs Froude

I returned from Ireland early this morning, and since your letter is dated the 29th September think it better to write a hasty line, than delay.

---

[1] i.e. 9 Oct. St Raphael was the Guardian of travellers.

[2] Peter Cooper (c. 1798–1852), a priest at the Pro-Cathedral in Dublin, and one of the secretaries of the Catholic University Committee.

379

Thank you for all it contains — what you say about yourself, Wm and Hurrell is very interesting to me.[1] I will attend at once to your hint about E. Bastard. As you would suppose, I know nothing whatever of his money matters, or his disposition of money. *One* application was made to me from a most excellent and useful Institution, to intercede with him for a subscription, but I snubbed the applicant, though a very dear friend of mine, and refused her. I have also generally cautioned him against letting his money go in large plans — but, as he has not spoken to me in detail, I have said nothing to him. From what you say, I am almost sorry I did not say more — but, as you would suppose, and as our Founder St Philip strictly enjoins, I have little or nothing to do with money matters of my penitents.

Excuse this very short letter ⟨answer⟩ to your very pleasant one & believe me

Affectly Yours John H. Newman

P.S.   I see poor old Tyler's death in the Paper. This is the anniversary of my reception into the Church, St Denys's day

TO EDWARD HAWKINS

The Oratory, Birmingham Oct 9. 1851

Dear Mr Provost,

It is with the most unfeigned concern I see in today's paper an announcement of the death of one whom I know to be very dear to you, Tyler — and I cannot resist the feeling which leads me to send you a line of condolement, however insufficient.[2] It is just two years, I think, since you suffered a deprivation as heavy.[3]

Death indeed has been busy lately with those I have known and respected. Scarce three weeks have passed, since I read that Dr Kidd had been taken away — and I had intended, though I have not done so, to write a line in consequence to the President of Trinity.[4]

[1] Presumably Newman's Hurrell Froude is meant and not Mrs Froude's son, then only 9 years old.

[2] James Endell Tyler was Dean of Oriel at the time of Newman's election as a Fellow in 1822. He resigned his tutorship in 1826, when Newman was appointed. See *A.W.* pp. 60–3. Tyler died on 5 Oct. 1851.

[3] i.e. the death on 14 Oct. 1849 of Edward Copleston, Bishop of Llandaff, who was Hawkins's predecessor as Provost of Oriel.

[4] John Kidd (1775–1851), Regius Professor of Physic at Oxford, died on 17 Sept. John Wilson (c. 1790–1873) was President of Trinity 1850–66.

As to dear Tyler, I have been for some months intending to call upon him in London, being encouraged by the kind way he spoke of me to Mr Spencer — Now it is too late. Thus one puts off things — nearly the same thing occurred as regards poor Kinsey, whose death I saw some months since.[1]

With the kindest remembrances of past times, I am, Dear Mr Provost,

Very sincerely Yours John H Newman[2]

FRIDAY 10 OCTOBER 1851   F Ambrose went off to Belgium with Mrs Phillips[3]

TO F. W. FABER

Oratory Bm Oct. 10/51

My dear F Wilfrid,

Thank you for your congratulations — I have been kept from writing you a sedate answer by the Little Bear who has kept me in controversy all my spare hours this day. I have a right so to call him, for he talks of my 'disgusting' him.[4]

We have had a deed drawn up, but it could not be executed till this July, for my money had not come in — and we have not had time since. Mr. Tarleton, the Catholic Lawyer, did ours — I would have you go to some one who understands Catholic matters. 'A joint tenancy' is an intelligible form to a Catholic.[5]

As to Dr Grant, I don't think much of it.[6] I cannot trust him, nor

[1] William Kinsey (1788–1851) was Dean of Trinity when Newman was an undergraduate. See *A.W.* pp. 34, 54, 59 ff.

[2] Hawkins wrote on the autograph '(to be kept)' and 'Answered Oct. 11/51.' In his answer he wrote, 'Your kind letter met me on my arrival in Oxford, and I am truly obliged to you for it.' Hawkins then gave an account of the deaths of Tyler, Kidd, and Copleston, and ended 'Once more thanking you for your kind letter which I was sincerely glad to receive, and with the kindest feelings tho', I need not say, the saddest thoughts, I am always, my dear Newman, Yours very sincerely, E. Hawkins.'

[3] See letter of 14 Oct. to Joseph Gordon.

[4] See letter to Hinds of 2 Oct. Hinds was known at Oxford as the white bear, Whately being the black one. Cf. letter of 22 Sept. 1849 to Bowles.

[5] Newman is replying to Faber's question of 8 Oct., 'Whom did you consult about your joint trust? Might not we save ourselves the expense of an opinion, and follow your lead?' The London Oratorians were about to buy land and a villa at Sydenham.

[6] Faber wrote of Bishop Grant, whose scrupulousness was well known, and who had just come to England as Bishop of Southwark: 'He is constantly here, and affectionate beyond every thing; but there has been quite a little disturbance at S.

have — but I suspect the truth is, he comes and finds my influence spreading, and is fidgetty, because timid. He merely wishes people not to go ahead after me. *Where* have I the phrase you quote? I wish you could tell me the page. It sounds like mine. All I can say is that Father Cook, an old Catholic, revised it — and it shows with what jealous eyes some critics have looked thro' my book. 'Tis well they have found nothing else. On the other hand have you seen our Bishop's puff of me? it is absolute.[1] The Primate of Ireland too has been puffing me at his Conference, and I had to make a speech in answer — so I can bear the Little Bishop.

I am glad you are better

Ever Yrs affly J H N

TO ARCHBISHOP CULLEN

Oratory Birmingham Oct 11 1851

Private

My dear Lord Primate,

I want to put down two or three thoughts I have on paper, that I may state them more distinctly than I could in conversation, unless they have gone out of my head.

It strikes me that the only right way of beginning the University is that which your Grace proposes, experimentally — The Rector, (with a constant subordination of course to a board,) (say of the Archbishops,) should be autocrat. Two authorities will ruin the attempt. And he ought, with the same subordination, to have the choice of his associates,

---

Edmunds from his telling the divines that you taught "heresy" in your Mixed Discourses: e.g. "He vouchsafed to accept Mary as the teacher of His Infancy."' This phrase is not to be found in *Mix*. Faber also reported Grant as saying that Newman's doctrine of development was viewed with suspicion, and 'you can never trust converts.'

[1] The extreme anti-Catholic (evening) *Standard* in a leading article on 28 Sept. claimed that the converts 'have not been received by any means with the expected fraternal cordiality of the Popish priests, among whom they have taken shelter. Newman, the most eminent of them all, is, we are assured, a standing jest among the Romish priesthood. We should like to have made public the opinion of him entertained, and in private freely expressed, by his new bishop Doctor Ullathorne.' Ullathorne, who was out of England, replied only on 4 Oct., 'I will take the liberty of saying that I know of no dignitary in the Catholic church whom I consider more sound in orthodoxy, more solidly formed in the ecclesiastical and Christian virtues, or more deferential to church authority than Dr. Newman. I love him as one of my dearest friends; I have often consulted his judgment, and admired his prudence; and I have nothing either in my mind, or my heart, that I could have the slightest wish to conceal from his knowledge.' Ullathorne added that 'The charge of want of confidence in the converts has no more truth in it than the one of which I have just disposed.'

and the power of choosing, especially, *lecturers* and *tutors*. I think it is more necessary that he should choose lecturers and tutors even than Professors — by lecturers and tutors I mean a sort of informal (or, so to speak, Propaganda) system, as contrasted to a normal state of things, (or, to continue the illustration, a Diocesan Episcopacy or Hierarchy). Whether he should have the choice of Professors is a further question, and scarcely an initial one — but I think he ought to have 1 the *decision* whether there *should* be (as yet) Professors in this or that department — 2. the *choice* of Lecturers and Tutors.

A Rector, with a number of Professors at once assigned him by others, nay with the necessity of choosing them himself, could do little. I say 'even did he choose them himself,' because he *must* choose eminent men, i.e. men who would have a right to exert a distinct and personal influence on the management of things. E.g. were I Rector, and had to choose a Professor of History, I might think it a point of duty to make an attempt to get so distinguished a man, as Dr Dollinger — yet not knowing his views etc. how can I tell if I should work well with him? (and so again Dr Jerrard in Classics)[1] When a University is *once set up*, and a system established, different influences are beneficial; they are fatal in its commencement. I think then I must stipulate for an autocracy of this kind — and say for 2 or 3 years.

I inclose a sort of plan of what I should propose.

There are two difficulties to this arrangement

1. We want to be doing something at once to meet the Queen's Colleges in the way of *demonstration*, to show we are not a mere school etc. — To meet the difficulty, would it not be possible (1) to name a definite time, e.g. October 1853, by which the University would be constituted in form. (2) to purchase ground at once. (3) to set about building at once. (4) to publish a code of *elementary* statutes etc. (no matter tho' they *are* eventually modified) (5) actually to appoint some Professors, though of course (since they would not come into their office for 2 or 3 years) they might draw back when the time came. (Would this last be impracticable? I wish it may not be) etc etc.

2. If I had the provisional appointment (i.e. for the first two years) I should naturally take my own friends — i.e. I should bring in *too much* of an English and convert element into the commencement of the Institution. This, I feel, to be a great difficulty, yet I do not know how to

---

[1] Joseph Henry Jerrard (1801–53), Scholar and then Fellow of Caius College, Cambridge, 1824–44, first Principal of Bristol College 1831–8, and Examiner in Classics at London University from 1838 to death, had become a Catholic in April 1851. He was one of the educationalists from whom the Sub-committee sought suggestions for the organisation of the Catholic University, and his letter to Allies on the matter, 15 Oct.–10 Nov., is still preserved among Newman's papers at Birmingham.

dispose of it. The Deans of discipline would be Irish, and some of the Lecturers — but I fear I might create remark by the number of those who were not.

Hoping your Grace will excuse the freedom with which I have written, I am, begging your blessing, Yours faithfully & affectly in Xt

John H Newman   Congr. Orat.

P.S.   I may seem inconsistent in *first* agreeing to the joint report we made at Thurles, and now writing this — but it is not so — I write this *because* your Grace seemed dissatisfied with that Report.[1]

I shall send this first to Mr Hope to see if he has any thing to remark on it.[2]

TO SAMUEL HINDS, BISHOP OF NORWICH

Oratory, Birmingham, Oct. 11. [1851]

My dear Lord,

I thank you for the kind tone of your letter, which it was very pleasant to me to find so like that of former times, and for the copy you enclose of your answer to Mr. Cobb.[3]

Your Lordship's words, as reported in the Norwich paper, were to the effect that I believed the ecclesiastical miracles to have 'a claim to belief *equally* with that word of God which relates the miracles of our God as recorded in the gospels;' that I made 'the authority of the one as the authority of the other,' and 'the credibility of the one as based on a foundation no less sure than the credibility of the other.'

You explain this in a letter to Mr. Cobb thus: 'I did not say that Dr. Newman asserted for the miracles related in the Romish legends a credibility based upon the foundation of divine revelation, no less than those of scripture. What I said was, that he claimed for the miracles related in the legends, the authorship of which was human, the same amount of *credibility* as for the miracles and divine revelations recorded in scripture, the authorship of which was divine.'

---

[1] Since Cullen and Newman agreed that at first there should be no staff of Professors, the Thurles Report was amended on this point, before it was brought before the University Committee on Nov. 1851. See *A.W.* p. 282.

[2] See letter of 11 Oct. to Hope.

[3] William Cobb, S.J., formerly the priest at Norwich, had sent a letter of enquiry to Hinds, similar to Newman's of 2 Oct. For Hinds's reply to Newman and his answer to Cobb see *Prepos.* note 11, pp. 409–12. Hinds concluded his reply to Newman, 'your handwriting has brought back on my mind other days, and some dear friends, who were then friends and associates of both of us.'

Will you allow me to ask you the meaning of your word 'credibility?' for it seems to me a fallacy is involved in it. Archbishop Whateley [sic] says that controversies are often verbal. I cannot help being quite sure that your Lordship's difficulty is of this nature.[1]

When you speak of a miracle being *credible*, you must mean one of two things: either that it is 'antecedently probable,' or *verisimile* — or that it is 'furnished with sufficient evidence,' or *provable*.[2] In which of these senses do you use the word? If you describe me as saying that the ecclesiastical miracles come to us on the same *evidence* as those of scripture, you attribute to me what I have never dreamt of asserting. If you understand me to say that the ecclesiastical miracles are on the same level of *antecedent probability* with those of scripture, you do justice to my meaning, but I do not conceive it is one to raise 'disgust.'

I am not inventing a distinction for the occasion; it is found in Archbishop Whateley's works; and I have pursued it at great length in my *University Sermons*, and in my *Essay on Miracles*, published in 1843, which has never been answered as far as I know, and a copy of which I shall beg to present to your Lordship.

First, let us suppose you to mean by 'credible,' antecedently probable, or *likely* (*verisimile*), and you will then accuse me of saying that the ecclesiastical miracles are as *likely* as those of scripture. What is there extreme or disgusting in such a statement, whether you agree with it or not? I certainly *do* think that the ecclesiastical miracles *are* as credible (in this sense) as the scripture miracles — nay, more so, because they come after scripture, and scripture breaks (as it were) the ice. The miracles of scripture begin a new law; they innovate on an established order. There is less to surprise in a second miracle than in a first. I do not see how it can be denied that ecclesiastical miracles, as coming *after* scripture miracles, have not to bear the brunt of that antecedent improbability which attaches, as Hume objects, to the idea of a violation of nature. Ecclesiastical miracles are *probable* because scripture miracles are *true*. This is all I have said or implied in the two passages you have quoted from me, as is evident from both text and context.

As to the former of the two, I there say, that if Protestants are surprised at my having no *difficulty* in believing ecclesiastical miracles, I have a right to ask them why they have no difficulty in believing the Incarnation. Protestants find a difficulty in even listening to evidence adduced for ecclesiastical miracles. I have none. Why? Because the

[1] Richard Whately, *Elements of Logic*, London 1826, pp. 253–8, 'On Verbal and Real Questions.'

[2] For Newman's explanation of the term 'antecedently probable,' as he uses it here, see *Prepos.* note 11, pp. 407–08.

admitted fact of the scripture miracles has taken away whatever *primâ facie* unlikelihood attaches to them as a violation of the laws of nature. My whole lecture is on the one idea of 'Assumed Principles,' or antecedent judgments or theories; it has nothing to do with proof or evidence. And so of the second passage. I have but said that Protestants 'have no *difficulty* at all about scripture miracles, which are quite as difficult to *reason* as any miracles recorded in the history of the saints.' Now, I really cannot conceive a thoughtful person denying that the history of the ark at the deluge is as difficult to reason as a saint floating on his cloak. As to the third passage you quote as mine, about 'revelation through nature,' and the 'Romish system,' and the 'legendary statements,' I know nothing about it. I cannot even guess of what words of mine it is the distortion. Tell me the when and where, and I will try to make out what I really said. If it professes to come from my recent lectures, all I can say is, that what I spoke I read from a printed copy, and what I printed I published, and what is not in the printed volume I did not say.[1]

But now for the second sense of the word 'credible.' Do you understand me to say that the ecclesiastical miracles come to us on as good *proof* or *grounds* as those of scripture? If so, I answer distinctly, I have said no such thing anywhere. The scripture miracles are credible — *i.e.*, provable, on a ground peculiar to themselves, on the authority of God's word. Observe my expressions: I think it '*impossible to withstand the evidence* which is brought for the liquefaction of the blood of St. Januarius.' Should I thus speak of the resurrection of Lazarus? — should I say, 'I think it impossible to *withstand the evidence* for his resurrection?' I cannot tell how Protestants would speak, but a Catholic would say, 'I believe it with a certainty beyond all other certainty, *for* God has spoken.' Moreover, I believe with a like certainty every one of the scripture miracles, not only that apostles and prophets 'in their lifetime have *before now* raised the dead to life,' etc., but that Elias did this, and St. Peter did that, and just as related, and so all through the whole catalogue of their miracles. On the other hand, ecclesiastical miracles may be believed, one more than another, and more or less by different persons. This I have expressed in words which occur in the passage from which you quote, for, after saying of one, 'I think it *impossible to*

---

[1] Hinds in his letter to Cobb, after criticising *Prepos.* p. 312, and *Mix.* p. 205, quoted Newman as saying 'We have no higher proof of the doctrines of natural religion —such as the being of a God, a rule of right and wrong, and the like—than we have of the Romish system,' and added 'including, I must presume, all those legendary statements which he so strongly represents as part of that system.' On 17 Oct. Hinds explained that he took this quotation from a letter in the *Spectator* of 27 Sept., which Hinds felt accorded with his impression of Newman's speech as reported.

withstand the evidence for' it, I say of another extraordinary fact no more than, 'I see *no reason to doubt*' it; and of a third, still less, '*I do not see why it may not*' be; whereas, whatever God has said is to be believed absolutely and by all. This applies to the account of the ark; I believe it, though *more* difficult to the reason, with a firmness quite different from that with which I believe the account of the saint's crossing the sea on his cloak, though *less* difficult to the reason; for one comes to me on the word of God, the other on the word of man.

The whole of what I have said in my recent lecture comes to this — that Protestants are most inconsistent and onesided in *refusing to go into the evidence* for ecclesiastical miracles, which, on the first blush of the matter, are not stranger than those miracles of scripture which they happily profess to admit. How is this the same as saying that *when* the grounds for believing those ecclesiastical miracles *are* entered on, God's word through His church, on which the Catholic rests the miracles of the law and the gospel, is not a firmer evidence than man's word, on which rest the miracles of ecclesiastical history?

So very clear is this distinction between verisimilitude and evidence, and so very clear (as I consider) is my own line of argument founded on it, that I should really for my own satisfaction like your Lordship's assurance that you had carefully read, not merely dipped into, my lecture before you delivered your speech. Certain it is that most people, though they are not the fit parallels of a person of your dispassionate and candid mind, judge of my meaning by bits of sentences, mine or not mine, inserted in letters in the newspapers.

Under these circumstances, I entertain the most lively confidence that your Lordship will find yourself able to reconsider the word 'disgust,' as unsuitable to be applied to statements which, if you do not approve, at least you cannot very readily refute.

I am, my dear Lord, with very kind feeling personally to your Lordship, very truly yours,

John H. Newman, Congr. Orat.[1]

TO JAMES HOPE

Octr 11. 1851

⌐Will you forward the inclosed to the Primate at Drogheda, adding 'to be forwarded.' The meeting is on the 15th.[2]

---

[1] See letter of 17 Oct. for Hinds's reply.
[2] See letter to Cullen of 11 Oct. The University Committee was to meet on 15 Oct.

I need not tell you about my visit to Dublin Quot homines, tot fuere sententiae; but the Primate is strongly with you and me. After reading the inclosed, add any thing you have to say to the Primate.[1]

TUESDAY 14 OCTOBER 1851 Philip Bathurst went away with his sister to Scarborough

TO ARCHBISHOP CULLEN

Oratory Bm Oct 14/51

My dear Lord Primate

I wrote to your Grace on Saturday, but, as I sent it round by Abbotsford, it strikes me too late that it will not reach you in time for the meeting — Therefore, at the risk of troubling you, I write again, directing to the Committee Rooms. I wrote to Dr Leahy on the same subject on Sunday.

It strikes me that nothing will be done well by a *number* of minds, *except* as regards the final form of the University — as regards its provisional state, it must be committed entirely to one person.

To satisfy the public expectation, the Committee might proceed tomorrow to take measures for 1 buying ground, 2 building — 3 appointing Professors etc. It might *pledge itself*, e.g. that the normal state of the University should be completed by October 1853 — But Meanwhile, *till* it is constituted normally, all must be put into the hands of one person, acting under the sanction of (say) the Four Archbishops. For myself, great as is the responsibility, and fool as I should be if I did not get all the advice I could and listen to every suggestion, yet I do not see how I could have a chance of beginning any thing well, unless I did it in my own way. I should begin with very few Professors and

---

[1] Hope wrote to Cullen on 13 Oct. that he concurred 'heartily in Dr Newman's opinion as to the best mode of commencing the University,' and that if something had to 'be done by "*way of demonstration*"' to counteract the Queen's Colleges, 'I would endeavour to confine it within the narrowest limits which would satisfy the public mind. . . . I may add that as regards our Opponents, and especially the Government, I cannot doubt that the moral effect which will be produced on them by the appearance of deliberation and care, will be much greater than could be attained by any forced attempt at immediate display.

Of Dr Newman's provisional scheme I heartily approve. The Autocracy of the Rector however is the principal Article, and beyond allotting the sum to be annually expended by him I should recommend that the Board leave him wholly unfettered during the provisional period. Dr Newman himself is the best security that we can have, and as the Rector's responsibilities will be very great it is but reasonable that his powers should be ample.' (This letter is preserved in the Diocesan Archives, Dublin.)

tutors, enlarging the number according to the need; but I should like a good large sum for *exhibitions* and *prizes*, which would diminish the expence to the deserving students and create a sort of model set of men, who would form the nucleus of a good tradition.

Excuse bad grammar and other mistakes; I write in a great hurry to save the post[1]

Ever Yr affecte friend & servt in Xt

John H Newman   Congr. Orat.

TO MRS WILLIAM FROUDE

Oratory Bm Oct 14/51

My dear Mrs Froude

I am not going into controversy — but I could not help smiling at your argument against Indulgences from William's observation.[2] I will give you a parallel. A Frenchman, who had travelled through England, said what struck him most, was the extreme munificence of the Inn Keepers, he saw every where put up 'Entertainment for man and horse' — not a word about paying. He had been told we were a nation of Shop Keepers — but he never was so agreeably disappointed. He had never indeed entered an inn *himself*, but had slept sometimes in his travelling carriage, sometimes in friends' houses — but he could vouch for the fact — and he recorded it in a letter he sent home during his travels. In his next letter he added a further pleasing trait of character of a similar kind — viz he found on every third door, as he walked through the private streets and squares of London, written, 'Ring the bell' — he had never indeed rung it, but *there* were the hospitable words, and they could not be explained away. — Read my 8th Lecture on this subject.[3]

I suppose in a few days I shall know what is decided on in Ireland about the University. It is a most daring attempt but first it is a religious one, next it has the Pope's blessing on it. Curious it will be if Oxford is imported into Ireland, not in its members only, but in its principles, methods, ways, and arguments. The battle there will be what it was in

---

[1] For Cullen's reply see letter of 5 Nov. Cf. also *A. W.* p. 286.

[2] William Froude, who was travelling abroad, wrote that at Marseilles he had seen notices about the grant of indulgences, without any conditions attached. See letter of 20 Oct. to Mrs Froude.

[3] 'Ignorance concerning Catholics the Protection of the Protestant View.' Newman added in the later editions the illustrations in this letter. Cf. *Prepos.* p. 346, and 1st ed. p. 330.

Oxford 20 years ago. Curious too that there I shall be opposed to the Whigs, having Lord Clarendon instead of Lord Melbourne — that Whately will be there in propriâ personâ —[1] and that while I found my tools breaking under me in Oxford, for Protestantism is not susceptible of so high a temper, I am renewing the struggle in Dublin, with the Catholic Church to support me. It is very wonderful — Keble, Pusey, Maurice, Sewell, etc who have been able to do so little against Liberalism in Oxford, will be renewing the fight, alas, not in their persons, in Ireland.

God bless you all, and believe me Ever Yours affecty

John H. Newman   Congr. Orat.

TO JOHN JOSEPH GORDON

Oy Bm. Oct 14/51

My dear F Joseph,

I find from F White that the S. Maria Maggiore he spoke of is the Roman Basilica, not at Naples — but I dare say you have found out this yourselves already.[2] I was a week in Ireland — and all was well except Philip [Bathurst], who is seriously unwell, and has gone away with his sister to Scarborough. He makes me anxious — he hardly smiled once all the time we were in Ireland. The University Committee meet tomorrow, then I suppose something will be done — but nothing is done as yet. The Bishop has put a most kind puff of me in the Standard, on its having a leading article in which it said I was the jest of all Priests, and all the converts were looked on as fools.[3] Poor old Tyler is dead — I wrote to Hawkins and had a very kind answer. And Dr Kidd is dead. Lady Arundel has been here a week, chiefly while I was away, and Lord Arundel on Sunday. F Ambrose has run off to Belgium with Mrs Phillips, (whose children were pursued by a wicked giant called Chancery and their two cruel uncles) and just now writes

[1] George Villiers, fourth Earl of Clarendon (1800–70), Lord-Lieutenant of Ireland 1847–52, was the strong supporter of the Queen's Colleges, which the Catholic University was intended to supplant. Lord Melbourne was Prime Minister during most of the Tractarian period, and appointed R. D. Hampden Regius Professor of Divinity at Oxford in 1836. Whately, enemy of the Tractarians then, was now one of the chief supporters of mixed education in Ireland, which would, he hoped, be a solvent for Catholic beliefs. See *McGrath*, pp. 36–9.

[2] The Dominican Fr White was assisting in the search for evidence against Achilli. Newman's present letter was addressed to Gordon at the Poste Restante in Rome. He had landed at Naples and only reached Rome on 12 Nov.

[3] See letter of 10 Oct. to Faber.

me word that he likes Belgium better than six hours a day in the Con-fessional.[1] He is larking away to Paris. The Library in the new house is not quite roofed in — all the rooms to be plastered and floored by Christmas — The plans of M le Duc not yet come — it's F. Ambrose's excuse for going to Paris.[2] F Richard is ordered to Malta with the Bowdens for his health. F Edward does not pick up. I think it is anxious. I have been calculating how much money we have altogether for the church, and find we have collected between £1700 and 1800 — and have been promised, about £3700, making a total already of near £5500. Love to Nicholas

Ever Yrs affly J H N.

List of things to be done.

1. The Chiesa Nuova at Rome gives away its vestments. Bag [Beg?] some of them of the good Fathers for us. Dr Cullen is my informant.
2. Bring home an impression, if they will let you, of the Chiesa Nuova seal.
3 Bring home an accurate rubric of the Chiesa Nuova Benediction.
4. Do the Lay brothers have any after dinner recreation.
5. If the F Superior is ill and leaves home — e.g. for six months, does the Dean take his place, or is a Rector to be appointed, and if so, by *whom*?
6. Does the Padre Sagristano or the Cerimoniere appoint the inferior Ministers at Benediction etc
7. In saying Mass ought one to kiss the altar stone itself
8. Ought one to cross oneself while saying Fidelium animae etc[3]

TO RICHARD STANTON

Oratory Bm Oct 14/51

My dear F Richard

How I should like to see you, John, and the Bowdens off! but it seems impossible.[4] With F Ambrose in Belgium, FF Nicholas and

---

[1] Lucy Agnes Phillips had become a Catholic in Aug., and her two elder brothers, both clergymen, were evidently trying to make her children wards in Chancery, and to prevent their mother from bringing them up as Catholics. These brothers were Edward Thomas Vaughan (1813–1900), Vicar of St Martin's, Leicester, 1845–59, and Charles John Vaughan (1816–97), Headmaster of Harrow School 1844–59.

[2] Cf. letter of 11 Aug. to William Froude.

[3] Questions 6 and 7 are by Austin Mills. He and William Neville wrote to Gordon on the same sheet as Newman, Neville's letter being dated 21 Oct.

[4] John Bowden, with his family, and Richard Stanton were going to winter in Malta for their health. Both were to give valuable assistance in obtaining evidence against Achilli.

Joseph in Rome, F Edward at Malvern, F Philip at Scarborough, who is left? Stanislas has not his faculties yet.[1]

I don't like your plan of the candlesticks — gilt wood I do not take to — either for the material, or the chance of bringing it from Rome safely. And then how can you tell if the size would be right. I should have thought you might have had large brass candlesticks electroplated with gold, for the same money, and no hurry for getting them.

You will have a pleasant time, and do St Philip's work in one way or another

Ever Yrs affly J H N

WEDNESDAY 15 OCTOBER 1851   FF Antony *Hutchison* and Bernard *Dalgairns* came down about F Wilfrid's (*Faber's*) going to the Continent (*N.B.*)

TO F. W. FABER

Oy. Bm Oct 15/51

My dear F Wilfrid

All is well — and St Philip knows what he is at — but it is very mysterious that both your house and we should have so many invalids. You are quite right in not going with the Arundels.[2] Depend upon it, a priest must not be familiar with his secular penitents — you must not live with them. Indeed I have doubts whether (except under a special dispensation) a Father should live in a family at all. I certainly mean to *try* never to sleep a night under a gentleman's roof.

— The two Fathers have just come[3]

Ever Yrs affly J H N

[1] Ordained priest on 27 Sept., Flanagan had not yet received faculties for hearing confessions.

[2] Faber wrote on 14 Oct., 'Mr Tegart is apprehensive about the state of my brain, from long excitement and overwork, and insists on my leaving the Congregation for not less than 6 months, or he won't answer for it.' Faber was invited to stay with the Earl of Arundel at Fontainebleau, but wrote, 'Mr T [Tegart] says a month at Fontainebleau would do me little good, and that I must have external excitement. This may be so. For grave reasons I am not drawn to Fontainebleau: to live with my own penitents, of such high rank, being ill and irritable . . . would I think be unwise . . .'

[3] Hutchison and Dalgairns had come from London to discuss what should be done about Faber.

TO ROBERT JOHN GAINSFORD

Oratory Bm Oct 15/51

Dear Sir,[1]

I have been absent from home, or should have acknowledged your letters sooner. I thank you for your quotation from Mr Arthur's Pamphlet, which I will keep by me, as it may be useful.[2] There are some good examples of similar methods of controversy in the last Dublin. I do not know who has furnished them.[3]

As to what you say in your former letter about yourself, it is quite intelligible. It is very difficult for individuals to act any where, and in few places are Catholics in force.

I am, My dear Sir, Very truly Yours in Xt

John H Newman   Congr. Orat.

TO GEORGE RYDER

Bm October 15/51

My dear George,

We are indeed a disabled house just now. F Joseph has been ill the whole year, (not, I trust, seriously) and is now in Italy with F Nicholas. F Caswall has had a bad fever, and is still at Malvern — F Bathurst has gone off to Scarborough with his sister. He went with me to Ireland, but it did him no good. F Ambrose is in Belgium.

The Committee meets at Dublin today when something will be decided about the University.[4]

[1] At the foot of this letter there has been written in pencil 'To Rob. Jos. Gainsford.' Robert John Gainsford (1807 or 8 – 70), educated at Oscott, lived at Darnall Hall, Sheffield, and practised as an attorney. He employed Miss Holmes as a governess, and James Stewart as tutor to his sons, but as late as 1865 had not himself met Newman. In politics he was liberal, and agitated for the Reform Bill of 1832. He wrote a pamphlet, *Reformatory Schools: how and why they should be established and maintained*, which he sent to Newman in Jan. 1859. He founded a Catholic reformatory for boys at Market Weighton, and another for girls at Sheffield, in 1861, in favour of which he asked Newman to preach.

[2] William Arthur (1819–1901), Secretary to the Wesleyan Missionary Society 1851–68, was the author of a number of anti-Catholic pamphlets.

[3] The article, 'The Guardian and a "Theory of Lying,"' *D R*, xxxi (Sept. 1851), pp. 201–17, gives examples of one standard being applied to Catholic and another to Protestant controversialists.

[4] At this meeting of the Catholic University Committee Newman's appointment was deferred. On 12 Nov. he was appointed 'President of the Catholic University of Ireland.'

You speak too humbly when you call me only Chancellor or Rector. I mean to be Chancellor, Rector, Provost, Professor, Tutor all at once, and no one else any thing.

We can receive Harry and Lisle well, but they will find an empty house, and no one knowing Greek and Latin enough to floor them — so it is their time. Is it not absurd, building a large house, and so few to fill it? They must in time go to Dublin, and prove themselves some of the first fruits and flowers of the University.[1]

Bathurst thought at one time of coming for [sic] you for change of air, but I think he has decided well. He is to be in the open air all day, either on the sands, or rocks, or horseback, or in the sea — any where but on himself.

Love to the children, & believe me, Ever Yrs affly in Xt

J H N

TO RICHARD STANTON

Oy Bm Oct 15/51

My dear F Richard

Your and your Father's letters have just come (6 PM)[2] It is very mysterious — St Philip must have a hand in it — F Joseph knocked up by work — and our Edward and Philip both (don't repeat it) in a state of mental excitement very anxious. I suppose it is the want of holydays — at Oxford near half the year is Vacation.

If Stanislas had faculties, I certainly would go to London. I can't, as it is — I am nearly the only person here. And I am taking F Ambrose's Sermon. I wish you were not going quite so soon. Now that two of you are going, I think you might cut the Bowdens, and go by yourselves.

I like the plan of F Wilfrid going about for 6 weeks,[3] and then returning. It is a great evil, he cannot control his mental activity — else, to a certainty he will wear himself out. Who is Mr Tegart? is he an oracle? He has found out two new complaints in F. Wilfrid, gout and insanity.[4] He should have some real first rate advice. Voyaging is the best thing certainly, if he must go. Why does he not think of Spain? his voyaging

---

[1] Both Ryder boys eventually studied in Dublin.
[2] The superior of an Oratory is known as 'the Father.'
[3] A slip for 'months.'
[4] Stanton wrote on 13 Oct., 'Mr Tegart, who has been attending him lately, says that besides the gout and headaches . . . his nervous system is completely shaken by mental exertion; and that unless he has complete repose for a considerable time, he fears the most serious consequences, and that his brain will be affected.'

course might take him to Seville, without effort, and to Lisbon — I am afraid the Church is in a wretched state in Portugal. I hope you won't be going quite so suddenly — but it can't be helped

Ever Yrs affly J H N

THURSDAY 16 OCTOBER 1851   FF A [Antony] and B [Bernard] returned to London

FRIDAY 17 OCTOBER   Ryder came with his two boys?

TO J. R. BLOXAM

Oratory, Birmingham October 17. 1851

My dear Bloxam,

I am now able to pay you the £20 which I consider I owe you for the ground at Littlemore.[1] Also I am going to take the liberty of asking you to receive and pay two sums for me, which on looking over my accounts I find to be due to two friends of ours; the sum of £5. 5. 0 to Copeland for the school at Littlemore, being the College donation which (the last year, I suppose) I did not transfer, and the sum of £2. 15. 0 to Barrow of Queens, whom I have never paid for a Saints' life he wrote for Toovey. He ought to demand interest.[2]

There is another favor you can do me. I had always hoped to pay these debts from the large sum which Mrs Tombs owes me, but I get nothing of it. Now will you kindly call on Mr Betteris of Grove Street, and ask him a question, which I asked him some months ago and he did not answer — viz. have I *secured*, by my late proceedings against Mrs Tombs, the payment on her death of my money? or shall I have another suit to gain it? In fact how do things *stand*?[3]

I suppose I shall be right in paying the sums above spoken of (£20 + 5. 5. + 2. 15) £28, to your account at Messrs Parsons and Co.

Yours very sincerely John H Newman

[1] See letters of 20 and 27 Oct. to Bloxam.

[2] John Barrow (1810–80) was Tutor and Librarian at Queen's College 1835–46. In the *Lives of the English Saints*, published by Toovey, he wrote those of St Herbert and St Ninian. Barrow declined to accept Newman's £2. 15, saying that he never expected any remuneration, and that if it was really due to him, he wished Newman to put it to some good use. Barrow was appointed Principal of St Edmund Hall in 1854, but resigned in 1861 and became a Catholic three years later.

[3] See letter of 3 July 1849 to Betteris.

TO J. M. CAPES

Oy Bm Oct 17/51

My dear Capes

I have nothing to remark on your sheets down to p 406 — except that I hardly know whether or not to notice the words '*Anglican Church*' in pp 369 etc This is so much the ecclesiastical title of the Establishment that Mgr Palma at Rome would not put into our Brief 'Anglicana Congregatio Oratorii' but altered it to 'Anglica C.O.'[1]

Ever Yrs J H N

Nothing yet from Ireland.

SATURDAY 18 OCTOBER 1851   F Wilfrid set off for Jerusalem.[2]   F Ambrose returned

SUNDAY 19 OCTOBER   F Austin went away

TO MRS J. W. BOWDEN

Oratory Bm Oct 19/51

My dear Mrs Bowden,

I have not been unmindful of you all, though I have not written. So you are going to Malta after all — What F Richard means to do, I have not heard — but very likely Malta will not agree with him as well as it does with John.

It disappoints me to find by the papers that the Catholic University decision is put off for a month, so we are all at sea what is to be done. I have not heard a word from Ireland yet on the subject. I know, great matters *will* take time — but this suspence is a great nuisance. Of course I have my own views about its setting up — and would not go to Ireland for the responsibility of what I considered would be a failure. Then, if I do not go there as Rector, I should not deliver Lectures there — and thus a damp and doubt is cast on the preparation of the Lectures, to which I am now turning myself; and time is too precious to waste on what will come to nothing. It is a most serious trouble to Allies, and worse, to be kept in suspense.

[1] In 'State Encroachments on the Church before the Reformation,' the *Rambler*, VIII (Nov. 1851), Capes proposed thus to describe the pre-reformation Church in England. He altered it to 'English Church.' In the *Rambler*, Oct. p. 259, however, he had spoken of it as the 'Anglican Church.'

[2] This was Faber's first plan, altered to Italy.

Every one was abundantly kind to me in Ireland, and would wish to be — but, when we come to the working of a system or a view, it ever must be an anxious thing how matters will be adjusted.

No movement yet on the part of Achilli — but the time is now drawing near when he must make up his mind. We have not yet heard from our absentees at Naples.

F Richard will give you the latest news of us and the new house — All good angels be with you all — I shall not forget you, as before

Ever Yours affecly John H Newman

TO SAMUEL HINDS, BISHOP OF NORWICH

Oratory, Birmingham, Oct. 19. [1851]

My dear Lord,

I thank your Lordship with all my heart for your very kind and friendly letter just received, and for your most frank and candid compliance with the request which I felt it my duty to make to you.[1]

It is a great satisfaction to me to have been able to remove a misapprehension of my meaning from your mind. There still remains, I confess, what is no misapprehension, though I grieve it should be a cause of uneasiness to you — my avowal that the miraculous gift has never left the church since the time of the apostles, though displaying itself under different circumstances, and that certain reputed miracles are real instances of its exhibition. The former of these two points I hold in common with all Catholics; the latter on my own private judgment, which I impose on no one.

If I keep to my intention of making our correspondence public, it is, I assure you, not only as wishing to clear myself of the imputation which has in various quarters been cast upon my lecture, but also, in no slight measure, because I am able to present to the world the specimen of an anti-Catholic disputant, as fair and honourable in his treatment of an opponent, and as mindful of old recollections, as he is firm and distinct in the enunciation of his own theological view.[2]

That the Eternal Mercy may ever watch over you and guide you, and fill you with all knowledge and with all peace, is, my dear Lord, the sincere prayer of

Yours most truly and faithfully, John H. Newman.

[1] Hinds wrote on 17 Oct. that he was reprinting his speech at Norwich and would omit the word 'disgust' in reference to Newman's lecture in *Prepos.*, but maintained his view that to consider later miracles as a continuation of those in Scripture tended to throw great doubt on the latter.

[2] See first note to letter of 2 Oct. to Hinds.

TO RICHARD STANTON

Oy Bm Oct 19/51

My dear F Richard

I missed Friday's post, and now write in the greatest hurry, a penitent waiting for me.

I doubt whether it will do for you to continue long at Malta. If you move, *beware of the weather*. I know from experience in 1832–3, that the Mediterranean is a *wretched* winter birth [sic]. At Naples in February we were worse off than ever in England — cold, piercing winds, profuse week-long rains, brick floors, no furniture, no fires. Corfu the same. Palermo may now be a little better — but Messina was as bad. I earnestly caution you of this. Is not Rome your safest place?

I shall say a weekly Mass for the Invalids

Ever Yrs affly in St Ph. J H N

MONDAY 20 OCTOBER 1851   The Bowdens with F Richard *Stanton* set off for Malta

TO J. R. BLOXAM

Oratory Bm October 20/51

My dear Bloxam

The reason of the £20 is this — There was a loss upon the Littlemore property — At first I made you partake of the loss, according to your share — then it struck me that, whereas you had no part of the interest accruing from the field, this was not fair. So now I have made up the full £100.

This is according to my *recollection* — for I have not thought of the matter for so long, that I cannot be very accurate[1]

Yours very sincerely John H Newman   Congr. Orat.

TO MRS WILLIAM FROUDE

Oratory Bm Oct. 20. 1851

My dear Mrs Froude

I never can be hard upon you whom I love so well, and it is a great shame you should say so. I thought, in alluding to what Wm said, that

[1] See letters of 17 and 27 Oct.

no *conditions* were *mentioned* on the notice of Indulgence at Marseilles, that you concluded '*Therefore*, the Wards are wrong, for they said there always *were* conditions.'[1] I answer '*So there* are — there are in that Marseilles one.' You object, 'They are not *written down*,' — I reply, 'Certainly not, we do not write down what every one takes for granted.' Then followed my innocent parable — viz it is *as* preposterous to suppose there are no conditions *because* they are not written down, as that there are no conditions to 'Entertainment for man and horse,' viz *paying* or for 'Ring the Bell' viz, needing to call. Life would not be long enough for it, if we put down in writing what every one knew. And this was part of the subject treated in my 8th Lecture — viz that to know the meaning [or, bearing] of Forms (e.g.) of Indulgences, you must not go by what Hurrell used to call 'textises' (texts) but, instead of fancying what *must* be, ask Catholics what *is*. I meant that the Wards' *assurance* was not at all impaired by William's *eyes*. What, dear Mrs Froude, is 'hard' in this? As to the *theological* question I did not dream, nor do dream, of going into it. I said quite enough in former letters to show how I disapprove the plan of thinking that every thing must be level to reason when you are called to a system of faith. The single [or, simple] question is, 'have I *reason enough* to resolve to place faith?'

Get 1. 'The Life of St. Ignatius, in two duodecimos, Richardson, Fleet Street —' 2 'The Life of St. Camillus of Lellis, ibid.' 3 'Father Claver' ibid.

As to Ranke's Popes, it is a work a *Protestant* gains a great deal from, for it is much in advance upon common English notions.[2] On the other hand it has so many grave faults and imputes motives so shamefully that it has been put upon the Index. (i.e. it has been marked as an untrustworthy book) — I think you would be pleased to read it, but that it would be above the comprehension of a child — It is short, sententious, and almost antithetical. It is not a *history* — Butler's Lives of the Saints I suppose you know.

Ever Yrs affectly J. H Newman.

P.S. Do not suppose I have not ever the kindest and most considerate and loving thoughts of you.[3]

---

[1] See letter of 14 Oct. to Mrs Froude. The F. R. Wards were her close friends.

[2] Leopold von Ranke, *Die römischen Päpste, ihre Kirche und ihr Staat*, 3 vols. 1834–6, English translation by Sarah Austin, London 1840.

[3] On 7 Nov. Mrs Froude was writing, '. . . I am daily expecting to be in bed,—and am anxious, before I retire, to hear something of this trial about Achilli,—that is, whether it is likely to occasion you greater inconvenience than the expence which must attend it.—

I fear there is not much justice to be hoped from a Protestant court,—or jury. Still I cannot feel regret that you said what you did of him—as I know his testimony was thought much of by many,—who have now begun to doubt . . .'

TO T. W. ALLIES

Oratory, Bm Oct. 21. 1851.

My dear Allies,

Till we hear more about it, I can't tell whether the news is as bad as it seems.

If they appoint a Rector, I suppose he will at least have a *Secretary*. Indeed that was the original idea. Can they make you such? And then, *if* the Professorships are *none* of them at once appointed, a definite salary must be assigned for the Secretary.

The delay of a month is the nuisance, else it *may* be they are proceeding quite in the right way. To appoint a Rector as a nucleus, and to show they are not idle, and to make him go to Dublin, lecture, talk, look about him, and gradually make appointments, would, I really think, be the best thing for the University. The nuisance is that men like Manning etc may get their places fixed elsewhere, if they are not engaged at once.[1]

Ever yours J H N.

TO ROBERT CAMPBELL

[21?] October 1851

Dear Sir

I know so well that you do not dream of my aiming at a disputation or a victory, that I will ask your permission to say nothing in proof of my agreement with the Catholic de Maistre or the Dublin Review, or my consistency with the Anglican writer of the Church of the Fathers however dear to me. And for a like reason I will ask your leave to abandon your Sulpician to such judgment as you may wish to pass on him — I am not concerned with him — doubtless he can defend himself better than I have done, the true solution of your two questions on which I have failed, shall be left to him[2] — and for a like reason one

---

[1] Manning wrote affectionately to Newman, this same day, but declined to commit himself. On 3 Nov. he started for Rome, to study at the Collegio de' Nobili.

[2] Robert Campbell, Edinburgh lawyer, and a friend of Wegg-Prosser, had begun to correspond with Newman in Sept. See letter of 27 Sept. to Wegg-Prosser. On 18 Oct. Campbell wrote Newman an immensely long letter, explaining that his difficulties had not been met, 'The question at issue between us, is, whether the Nicene (or Anti Nicene) Church was a political unity. . . . The world's accusation is, that it was certainly "political" in a sense, but not that it was a political unity. . . .'

Campbell had quoted passages from de Maistre's *Du Pape*, to argue that great sovereignties grow slowly, from Newman's account of St Basil in *The Church of the*

which does concern myself, I will take the liberty, instead of following you sentence by sentence which would savour of controversy, merely to put down on paper some heads of the proof as I consider it, of the political nature of the unity existing in the Early ⟨Nicene⟩ Church; meaning by political unity, that unity which consists in unity of Government.[1]

Argument of letter sent to Mr Campbell Oct. 1851
Whether the Nicene Church had a political unity.

———

In all things so much lies in understanding the words made use of, that I will first put down what you and I respectively mean by the Church and its unity. Thus I consider it to be the Anglican, that is, your view, that the Church is the aggregate of certain visible congregations, which are descended from one stock (this by ordination from the Apostles), marked by a certain government, episcopacy, and professing one faith (Apostles' or Nicene Creed) — When then the Catholic Church is spoken of, the word Church is not analogous to a singular noun, as John or Thomas, marking an individual, but a general term as man or Englishman or again as manhood or humanity. The Church of Jerusalem, or the Apostolic College in the beginning, was the only instance of a Church meaning a social individual or corporation. Ever since Christianity spread into the world, it denotes a collection of small and real corporations, which are severally individual Churches, and viewed all together make up a generalized or Catholic Church.

On the other hand the present communion of Rome, and the Catholic Church according to Roman theology, is a social individual, answering to a singular noun, or corporation, having intercommunion in a political form.

It is true that the Anglican idea admits of the holding of general

Fathers, and from an article in *D R*, for Dec. 1847, on why Catholics could not go back on their grounds of adhesion to the faith (presumably 'Mr Brownson on Developments' by W. G. Ward). Campbell also referred to the Sulpician test as to whether a doctrine was part of the Catholic faith, namely that it could not be shown to be against the mind of the primitive church.

[1] Newman did not send the long reply, of which this is the covering letter, at once. See letter of 22 Oct., which Campbell answered on 28 Oct. On 16 April 1852 Campbell wrote, asking for an explanation of minor difficulties against the Papacy, but evidently convinced by Newman as to the main question. He later became a Catholic.

councils, which seem to throw the whole aggregate of (real) Churches into a momentary unity, but so did the Congress of Vienna throw together England, France, Russia etc but no one considered it made three nations *one*: It is no duty to meet in Council, but a voluntary and accidental act, issuing in engagements which there is no one to enforce. General Councils then do not enter into the idea, or the essence of the Church of the Anglicans.

What [is] in our view the Catholic Church, is in the Anglican view the particular diocese. The Church of Smyrna, or of Exeter does precisely in the Anglican view answer to that idea to which the whole collection of dioceses answers in our view. By Catholic Church we mean a thing, and the Anglicans a name. When we call the Catholic Church one, we mean it to be one in the same sense in which we popularly speak of a body of men being one; e.g. there is one Royal Society [,] one Royal Academy, one British Association, viz a social or political unit; when Anglicans call the Catholic Church one, they mean it in the sense in which we might call Whigs and Tories one, because they both are loyal subjects to the Monarchy, or England and the United States one because their race and language are one.

We call the Church one in a sense analogous to that in which the Nicene Catholics called the Father and Son one, viz one individual; Anglicans call the Church one in the sense in which the Arians called the Father and the Son one, viz in will and love and (according to the high Semi-arians) nature.

If I have not described you fairly, it is because I have had to do what I might have expected from yourself. I have distinctly stated in what I consider the unity of the Church [consists]: I wish you had defined your terms, and said what you meant by *degrees* of unity. What you call degrees, I should call kinds.[1]

My first argument is this: —

A   Unity was in nicene times a note of the Church; it is not a note now in the Anglican view; but notes belong to the essence of the Church; therefore unity was of the essence of the Church, in the Nicene view ⟨Scripture and Antenicene⟩, and it is not of the essence in the Anglican view. Therefore unity in the Anglican view differs in kind from unity in the Scripture and Nicene view. On the other hand unity is a note now in the Roman view; therefore Roman unity agrees in kind with Nicene unity. Thus the Roman idea of the unity of the Church so far agrees, and the Anglican simply differs, from

[1] Newman added in pencil, apparently intended for insertion at this point: 'Now I said to you or to Mr Wegg Prosser [words illegible] which of these two Ideas then is patristical etc yours or mine'

the Scripture and Nicene idea of the Church; and though this does not at once prove the Roman idea to be precisely the same as the Scripture and Nicene idea, it puts the Anglican idea hors de combat.

We insist on that which is clear — it was the *idea* under which they would present the Church to the heathen — unity is its badge. Is unity as a badge impaired now or lost — what unity does Barrow maintain except by cutting off 5 sacraments here, 4 or 2 orders there, and some points of faith everywhere.

B 2. Next, the Church is one *body*, according to Scripture and the Ante-nicene and the Nicene period; by body is meant an organized individual, vide St Paul; it is *not* one body according to Anglicanism, it is one body according to the Roman view: therefore the Roman view agrees and the Anglican disagrees with the Scripture and Nicene view.

Also, in the nature of the thing, so far as members form one body, rules are involved and the enforcement of rules. Who can fancy a commission, a club, an association, a congress, without rules — and an arbitrating power — so far as it could not take a means of enforcing them, it would not be a body. A mere multitude, a collection, or mental generalization does not come up to the idea of a body. In the Anglican view there are as many bodies as dioceses, excepting the accidental and occasional union of sees by the state or otherwise.

The various denominations collected at a meeting in Exeter Hall, might call them one spirit, could they call themselves one body? in what sense are Nestorians, Greeks, Monophysites, Copts, Armenians, Anglicans and Romans one, in which those denominations are not one. In what sense is England and Rome one body in which the Establishment and Wesleyans are not one [?]

C 3. Further, Scripture calls the Church 'the pillar and ground of the truth —' The Fathers take the same view of its function. If all the separate sees all over the world or the greater mass of them had ever preached the same doctrine, then the collection of them, which is the Anglican 'Catholic Church' may be said to have fulfilled like a jury this scope, which is so essential to the Scriptural and Patristical idea of it — But this is so far from having been the case that at one time Arian hierarchies and establishments for years and years covered the face of Europe; and at another the numbers of Nestorians and Monophysites about equalled the number [of] those who united in opposing their separate errors. Some arbitrating power then is requisite between the sees in order that the aggregate 'Catholic Church' may be the 'pillar etc' Councils are not such, for what is a General Council, has there ever been such, what discriminates, who decides it? Have all Bishops a seat in it? can they appear by proxy? do they decide by majority? was the second so called General, when there was not a single Latin? etc etc. When then Scripture and the Antenicene and Nicene era, calls the Church 'the pillar of the truth,' it must have spoken of the Church in such a sense as is consistent with its being so, and, when individual sees have and do differ from each other, the oracle must lie in something else than the concurrent witness of independent Churches, for such is not found; nor do I see in what it can lie but in an arrangement similar to that which gives a voice, not to a jury, but to a diocese; that is, the Anglican idea of the Catholic Church does not and the Roman does come up to the requisitions of the Scriptural and patristical idea of it. It must be recollected that Bramhall, Laud etc have felt this difficulty so strongly that they more than incline to consider that the Nestorian and Mono-physite heretics are to be reckoned part of the aggregate Catholic Church — there being no power on earth, in the Anglican view, to hinder them giving their testimony, whether it agreed with the orthodox doctrine of Bull, Pearson, Beveridge etc or not.

D 4.   Scripture and the Fathers call the Church a 'kingdom'; the Roman idea of a Church *is* a kingdom; the Anglican idea is not a kingdom. Now a kingdom is essentially a political unity.

In like manner the birds of the air are said to lodge in it, the very description of Nebuchodonosor's visible kingdom.[1]

In the prophets too it is spoken of as the continuation of the Mosaic Church, with different subjects, Gentiles for Jews; but the Mosaic Church was a polity.

And so too the prophets promise 'princes,' 'judges,' a 'rule,' a 'rod,' etc all which imply a polity.

And there are a number of texts to the effect that David was never to want a man to sit upon his throne, which St Paul claims for his Church ⟨gospel⟩ the re-construction of the throne of David; and Hooker says, with Catholic writers, that etc (when it *may* be literal, we must not go to figures.)

E 5.   Take in detail passages in Fathers which describe it as a body politic —   e.g.

7. [6]   Having now got the idea or form of the Church, in Scripture and the Fathers, we are in a condition to apply the observation quoted by me in a former letter, either to you or to Mr Wegg Prosser — in the note to his Sermon '   '

[1] Daniel 4 : 12.

that is, those passages which *fall in* with the idea tell for it in a sense in which those do not tell against it which seem to oppose it.

F 8. [7] Those which tell for it — such as Victor etc etc.

9. [8] I believe very few will be found to oppose it — such, e.g. as Meletius.

G And then, though taken by themselves they are primâ facie evidence of the Anglican theory, yet taken in connection with the idea and the proofs which I have been drawing out, must rather be taken as only *apparent* not real exceptions to that idea. E.g. I should hypothesize without but not against facts that Meletius was in involuntary ignorance and was reconciled to the Bishops he quarrelled with on his death bed or adopt some other supposition — Roman controversialists generally consider that there is historical evidence of his being reconciled in his life time — but I take the facts at the least advantage — and that on the ground that it was easier to imagine as a fact some such possible occurrence, than to suppose that the idea set up by Scripture and the Fathers was wrong. Just as I say there is *some way* of explaining consistently with infinite love the Almighty's dealings with Esau, his knowing and permitting Judas's sin, his allowing eternal punishment, though we may not see how. In the case you put the prisoner at the bar was *proved* in spite of his good life, to have committed an offence; whereas historical fact cannot be made to go further than to make it seem probable that S. Meletius died out of Roman communion.

10. [9] Gibbon — Neander etc. and è contrà Barrow not unbiassed.

11. [10] If you write now, say what you mean by *unity* — and by *degrees* of unity. I should say *species* of unity.

TO ROBERT CAMPBELL

Oct 22/51

My dear Sir

I had begun a letter in answer to yours, and then after getting some way it occurred to me that I could not profitably proceed unless I knew more distinctly some of your opinions

I have told you in what sense *I* spoke of the 'unity of the church —' viz as being that real and literal unity in which we call a kingdom or a Parliament or a club one, viz as consisting in intercommunion of its members and a common authority.

Well then let me in turn ask you, as I have a claim to do 1 What you mean by the church's unity? 2 is it visible?[1] 3 what do you mean by its '*degrees*'? (I suppose I should call them kinds or species.) 4 in what sense the Church is 'the pillar of the truth?' 5 in what sense it is one 'body'? 6 in what sense a civitas or 'Kingdom.' I shall be answering you quite wide of the mark, as you seem to think I have done already, unless you tell me where you *stand*

I am &c.

THURSDAY 23 OCTOBER 1851   M. Abbé [Labbé] called?
FRIDAY 24 OCTOBER   F Austin returned.

TO WILLIAM PHILIP GORDON

Oy Bm Oct 24/51

My dear Philip

I want you to do me a favor. Will you ascertain for me if Brodie is in London — when he will be — and at what hours is he visible. If I can see him, I shall ask you to give me a bed.

Don't tell this — or I shall have a paragraph in the papers to the effect that I am dying[2]

Ever Yrs affly J H N

TO JOHN YOUNG

The Oratory, Birmingham October 24. 1851.

Dear Sir[3]

You ask me what is to be thought of a Baptism administered by a layman to the little children of a family where all means of grace are ridiculed. You add that the Baptism was private, and consequent upon the refusal of the Protestant Rector of the Parish, circumstances which I shall not notice as being irrelevant in the particular case.

[1] Newman erased these three words in the draft.
[2] Newman's own doctor, G. G. Babington, wished him to consult Sir Benjamin Brodie. See diary for 6 Nov.
[3] John Young (1829–92) was an architect in the city of London, and from 1854 until his death a deputy alderman of Tower Ward. When sending this letter for William Neville to copy in the autumn of 1890, he explained that he became a Catholic some time after receiving it. He was later a prominent layman and a Knight of St Gregory.

You ask me, first whether such a baptism is valid, next whether it is licit (justifiable)

It is *valid* — because, as I understand you to say, the administrator, while he applied the water, also said the words, 'N. I baptize thee in the Name of the Father, and of the Son, and of the Holy Ghost;' and as the case supposes, with distinct intention of baptizing. I am assuming that the water was natural or common water, that was applied to the head or forehead, and that it ran down the skin.

I doubt whether it was *licit* — and consider the doubt turns on the question whether the administrator had any security that the children, who were not in danger of death, would be brought up in a knowledge of the rudiments of the Christian faith, viz in a belief of the Blessed Trinity, in Jesus Christ as the Son of God and Saviour of man, and in a future judgment.

A third question relates to its expediency, which is a question which does not fall under doctrine.

There is no doubt that the administrator acted for the best — and I trust his act will be accepted and blest and made a step towards bringing him into the Catholic Church.

Yours faithfully John H. Newman   Congr. Orat.

TO SIMEON LLOYD POPE

Oratory, Birmingham Oct 25/51

My dearest Pope,[1]

I was so glad to see your handwriting. I often think of you and of my godson. How could you fancy it was necessary to make the apology you so kindly have done? but I know how old notions stick by one and tease one, and so quite understand you. Any how it has been my gain.

Ever Yours affectly John H Newman   Congr. Orat.

---

[1] Simeon Lloyd Pope (1802–55) was at Trinity College, where he and Newman became close friends. He was ordained deacon in 1825 at the same time as Newman received priest's orders. In 1829 he became Vicar of Whittlesey St Mary. They corresponded regularly until 18 Sept. 1845, when Newman wrote to confirm that he was about to leave the Church of England. The present letter is the only one known to exist after that date. When copying from a letter of Pope's years later, Newman added a note: '(I have kept whole a few letters of this dear friend, so simple, so affectionate, so true, so cheerful. Most of his letters I must destroy, as of no interest except to me.)' Newman was godfather to Pope's son, Henry Edmund, born in 1838.

MONDAY 27 OCTOBER 1851   Dr Grant came and went in evening   notice came
about Achilli's legal move   *legal notice served on me by Achilli's lawyer*.

TO J. R. BLOXAM

Oratory Bm Oct 27/51

My dear Bloxam,

I am taken by surprise at your kind refusal to accept the £20. It is yours. I propose then, if you do not object, to put it as a subscription from you (your name will not appear) to our new Church at Edgbaston.

Thank you also for your trouble in re Tombs. I have availed myself of your kindness to inclose a cheque for Copeland and Barrow[1]

Very Sincerely Yours John H Newman

TO GEORGE TALBOT

Oratory, Birmingham Oct 27. 1851

My dear Talbot

Many thanks for the kind trouble you have been at. Our Fathers (Darnell and Gordon) are, I suppose, by this time at Rome. Achilli has moved this day — it is to be by criminal information.[2] If you could send me *at once an attested copy* of his Confession, of which you spoke, it would be most valuable.[3] It must be attested by Englishmen or Irishmen such as yourself — or by known Americans, — two witnesses, I suppose. Then how will *you* prove it genuine? This must be considered. He will say it is a *lie*. Who can swear to his signature? can any Irish Dominican swear to his handwriting? Any other proof, short and direct, of any of the facts mentioned by me against him, would be to the point. E.g.

---

[1] See letters of 17 and 20 Oct. to Bloxam. Bloxam wrote on 1 Nov. agreeing to Newman's suggestion, and saying that Copeland had not replied, while Barrow wished Newman to keep what was said to be owing to him.

[2] The information was a charge presented to the Court of Queen's Bench, in order to the institution of criminal proceedings, without formal indictment. This, as Newman explained in the memorandum of 22 Dec. 1851 (see *Appendix* 5, pp. 508-10), forced him to give in his name, which a civil action would not have done, and brought him before the Court as a criminal.

[3] The confession mentioned was the one that Achilli made before the tribunal of the Roman Inquisition in 1841, and which was, after great difficulty, put in as evidence at the trial. It contained a precise list of Achilli's crimes in Italy. See *Finlason*, p. 113. Talbot wrote to Newman on 4 Sept. that he had obtained this document from the Holy Office of the Inquisition. See also letter of 26 Nov. to Gordon.

Keosse's evidence, well attested, to any crime he did in Malta.[1] It might be an answer to his affidavit, and stop proceedings at once.[2]

Ever Yrs most sincerely in Xt   John H Newman

P.S.   I fear they will not let me pay postage for my letters; I must ask you to trust me, if so.

[1] It was from Wiseman's article in *D R*, June 1850, that Newman learned about Keosse, an Armenian priest, who abandoned the Catholic Church. He became Professor of Turkish and Armenian at the Protestant College of Malta, lodging at St Julian's Mission House, which was attached to it, and 'which was designed for seceding Romish priests professing to love and seek the truths of the Bible.' He withdrew in Sept. 1847, when he made the charges mentioned below against the two apostate priests, Leonini and Saccares, and was present in Dec. 1847 at their accusation, and that of Achilli who had returned to Malta, before Dr Hadfield. In June 1850, Keosse came back to Catholicism, and was employed in the Propaganda College at Rome as a teacher of languages. His account is corroborated by the *Report of the Committee of the Malta Protestant College on the removal of Dr Achilli from the College*, Malta College Office, 3 St James Street, 2 Dec. 1850, and by *Finlason*, p. 93.

Keosse's testimony, in Joseph Gordon's words, who interviewed him at Naples, and reported it in his letter of 21 Oct., which reached Birmingham on 3 Nov., ran: '1. When he came to Malta he was received into the Mission House 1847. There he *saw* the immoralities committed by Achilli's companions. On speaking to them they told him that Achilli (who was then in England) not only did the same, but *justified it* as necessary. 2. In consequence he left the Mission House, went to Valetta and wrote to the London Committee of the College accusing Achilli and his companions of the sins of *fornication* and *adultery*. 3. An enquiry was made in consequence into the truth of these charges before Dr Hatfield President of the College and Dr Bryan Vice President—and he (Kösse) was warned that if the charges *were not proved he* would be dismissed. 4. The result was Achilli and his companions were dismissed—and Kösse retained his office in the College till June 1850—Copies were taken down of the evidence given before Dr H. and Mr B—and were in the possession of Dr H. Mr B and two others. K. himself once had a copy. K. says that two gentlemen Mr Innes and Dr Bonavia who began by being A's [Achilli's] friends were in the end fully convinced and he is sure would give evidence against him. He is going to write down for me the names of those who could give evidence. Could not Dr Hatfield be put into a witness box and forced to give evidence? What a case! Kösse was himself the accuser—Dr Hatfield etc the Judges—Lord Ashley and the London Committee the Supreme Court. The crimes charged against Achilli were distinctly *fornication* and *adultery*— He was condemned—and is yet allowed to play the Saint and Confessor in the Evangelical Alliance. If this could be brought out! I shall get Kösse's evidence sworn to before the English Consul.' See also last note to letter of 16 Nov. to Cullen. Lord Ashley succeeded his father as Earl of Shaftesbury in June 1851.

[2] Achilli, in his affidavit, swore that *all* Newman's charges against him were false. At this stage, clear proof of one of them would almost certainly have stopped the case.

409

TUESDAY 28 OCTOBER 1851   Mr Terence Flanagan here?

TO BISHOP ULLATHORNE

Tuesday Morning [28 October 1851]

My dear Lord

It was a great mortification to me to find you had gone yesterday, before I well knew you had come. I hardly knew whether you had got out of your car, or whether you were coming into the Refectory. It will make you smile to say it, but my mouth was not empty, before F. Flanagan said you were gone.[1]

And now I have missed your Lordship by waiting for him. I have brought him up to be examined for faculties, if you would have kindly done so, and he *would* go on looking over his books till 11 o'clock.

I heard yesterday from Dr Achilli's lawyers that he was going to move by criminal information — that involves (I believe) an affidavit on his part, swearing to the falsehood of each particular allegation

Begging your Lordship's blessing I am, Yr faithful Servt

John H Newman   Congr. Orat.

P.S.   F Flanagan leaves a book for M. l'Abbé. [Labbé]
The Rt Revd
    The Bp of Birmingham

THURSDAY 30 OCTOBER 1851   Stanislas went off to see Mgr Nicholson (*about Achilli*)[2]

TO GEORGE RYDER

Oy Bm Oct 31/51

My dear George

For the present, I would leave the S. case, were I you, and see how F Hutton works.[3] I go to London Monday about this Achilli matter. It

---

[1] Ullathorne explained that he had not meant to stay, having a train to catch.

[2] Francis Joseph Nicholson, at Malvern, was Coadjutor to the Archbishop of Corfù, and was to help in procuring evidence from that island. See letter of 4 Nov. to St John.

[3] Ryder, who lived near Whitwick, seems to have had some disagreement with the Rosminian missionary priest for that district, Fortunato Signini. See letter of 11 Feb. 1850. The latter's place was now taken by Peter Hutton (1811–80), President of Ratcliffe College.

will soon, I suppose, be in the papers. You must give me a prayer sometimes

Ever Yrs affly in Xt   J H N

TO MESSRS LYON, BARNES, AND ELLIS[1]

Nov. 1. 1851

Gentlemen,

In answer to your letter of the 24th ult. received by me on the 27 I beg to refer you to my lawyer, Mr Lewin of Southampton Street, Strand, who acts for me in the business to which your letter relates.[2]

I have to apologize for my delay, but I thought it more respectful to you, as well as more usual, to reply to a legal letter through a legal medium, than otherwise and I was not at the moment provided with one

I have the honour to be &c J H N

Messrs Lyon, Barnes, & Ellis
   Spring Gardens, London.

TO MESSRS JOHN AND GEORGE WHATELEY[3]

[1 November 1851]

Gentlemen,

I believe the letter I received last Monday from Messrs Lyon etc came from you. I have the honor to inclose a copy of the answer I have this day written to them.

MONDAY 3 NOVEMBER 1851   went to Town early   called on Mr Lewin and Badeley and Bowyer who was out

---

[1] These were Achilli's lawyers.

[2] This was a letter calling on Newman to give up his name, in order to prevent a criminal information being laid against Burns and Lambert, the publishers of the alleged libel. See Newman's Memo of 22 Dec., *Appendix* 5, p. 509.

[3] These were attorneys at 41 Waterloo Street, Birmingham.

TO AMBROSE ST JOHN

⌐Nov 3/51⌐

My dear F Ambrose

⌐Hardman might know in confidence that, as far as we *can* judge, which is most difficult, the expences *up* to conviction (supposing it) cannot be more than £1000.[1]

Sir F Thesiger and Sir Fitzroy Kelly are retained for Achilli: the Attorney General ⟨[[Cockburn]]⟩ for me⌐

B. [Bowyer] was not at home!

Ever Yrs affly J H N

TUESDAY 4 NOVEMBER 1851   Thesiger moved against me in Court   with the lawyers

TO AMBROSE ST JOHN (1)

Nov 4/51

Charissime

My hand is cold, and I have so little time for writing that I don't know how I can write or you will read.

⌐On the whole I was relieved yesterday (Monday)

1. We shall certainly be able to put off our reply to Achilli till the beginning of Hilary Term.

2. The greater part of the trial *in fact* is in the affidavits on both sides — when the Rule is made absolute and the matter goes to a Jury, the case is half lost.[2] Thus you see *the Judges by themselves settle nearly the whole before it goes to a jury.*

3. A jury would and must be fair in the case of the substantiation of great *facts.*

---

[1] John Hardman had promised Newman the support of the Catholics of Birmingham. See letter of 2 Sept.

[2] A rule absolute is 'an order following a rule *nisi* and changing a conditional direction into a peremptory command.' A rule *nisi* 'is a rule *unless*, i.e. unless cause be shown to the contrary, as distinguished from a rule *absolute*.' Thus, when Achilli swore to the untruth of the charges brought against him, Lord Campbell decreed the passage was clearly libellous, and a rule *nisi* was granted to Achilli. Sir Alexander Cockburn, Newman's counsel, obtained a cross rule *nisi*, for enlarging the rule *nisi*, for a criminal information, until Easter Term, in order to afford Newman time to answer the matters in the affidavit of Achilli, and to show cause against the rule. But the rule for time was subsequently dismissed, and the original rule made absolute on 21 Nov.

4. One fact PROVED would be enough, and we seem to think we *shall* be able to prove one or other.

5. By means of English agents on the spot, we shall escape (the expence of) a commission at Corfu and Malta.

6. The expences *need* not be more than £100 or two — though they may be more. (Dont tell Hardman this)

Meanwhile Thesiger has this morning moved against me.[1] I have not yet heard about it — Achilli *may* break down in his affidavit — or something unexpected may turn up against me.

The truth is, our cause and case seem *too clear almost*. I mean I am frightened lest something should be in the back ground. But if I possibly can, I will send you news before I close this — but the post goes so cruelly early

We have a consultation with the Attorney General tomorrow

Ever Yrs affly J H N

5 PM. (Thesiger moved this morning — nothing new — he was considerate — said nothing against me)

Things look bad today. Badeley either has no opinion, or he thinks gloomily. He said 'Well, I really do not think it *impossible* the judges may refuse Achilli his rule —' compare this with what I have said above of the effect of the rule being made absolute. I asked him whether much did not turn on the *judges* being able to take a *moral* not a *legal* view of the matter in granting or refusing the rule — he said Yes — and at first seemed to think they *might* take a moral view — but afterwards relapsed. Lewin too seemed to think that *evidence* of the *adultery* and *seduction* was necessary, or almost so — and he thought Garamone's affidavit did not (nor does it) prove adultery.[2] Much seems to turn on delay. *If* we could put it off till *Easter* Term on first day of Hilary,[3] Achilli might be out of the country. Then the trial indeed would be granted, (if the rule was made absolute) but it would be put off till he came back.

He seemed to think if the worst came to the worst, I should be had

---

[1] Strictly speaking Thesiger moved against Burns and Lambert. See next letter.

[2] Nicholas Garamone (or Garimoni), a tailor in Corfu, had presented a petition to the Civil Tribunal, in July 1843, to be freed from paying alimony to his wife, on the grounds that he had surprised her in her mother's house, 'while she was in company with a certain *Sig. Achile Giacinti*, and that the time, the manner, the circumstances, and the conversation that followed the surprise, prove that the said wife is unfaithful to her conjugal duty.' (Garamone's affidavit, as quoted by Wiseman in *D R*, June 1850, pp. 495–6). Archbishop Nicholson had been called on officially in the case, and now gave Newman a copy of Garamone's affidavit. (See letter of 11 Nov. to Badeley.) This affidavit, and that of Keosse, were the only items of evidence Newman had in his possession at this moment. See also *Finlason*, p. 115.

[3] [[If we could on first day of Hilary put it off till Easter Term]]

up to the bar and sentenced, but to nothing very grievous under the circumstances. I assure you there is need of prayer⌉

J H N.

TO AMBROSE ST JOHN (II)

⌈Tuesday Night [[Nov 4 1851]]

[[London]]
My dearest A

Two things I omitted today — one that *my name* is to be substituted for Burns's tomorrow morning — the other, that Achilli was actually present in court to hear my libel read — and incurs transportation (for perjury), if any one of my charges against him is proved. Is it not incomprehensible? I fear he knows *just what* evidence *is* producible against him, and knows it cannot be produced. The consultation with the Attorney General is fixed for 4 tomorrow, and nothing takes place till then — So I shall not be able to let you know any thing of tomorrow's proceedings tomorrow. On Thursday I may come down to you, if Brodie lets me.

Hitherto every thing has gone, as I feared, in the worst way for me. I say now, as I said two months ago, that nothing but a good deal of prayer will deliver me.⌉ I don't expect I shall have a bit of news to send you tomorrow.

⌈Wednesday — Cardinal Wiseman's *Pamphlet* is out of print. Secure a copy, if you can. I have secured Badeley's.⌉[1]

Since it is now in the Papers, I think you may speak to the Brothers about it. The two points I should wish you not to exclude would be 1 that I knew what I was doing when I did it, tho' I did not bargain for his swearing so many lies — 2. that it is a battle not with men, with [but] distinctly with the evil spirit, 'we wrestle not with flesh and Blood etc'

I may in pencil add a line at the Attorney General's

Ever Yrs affly in Mary & Philip J H N

P.S.   Will you remind me to look at Theiner's work, to see if Achilli confessed any thing to him?[2]

[1] i.e. Badeley's copy of Wiseman's pamphlet, *Dr. Achilli. Authentic Brief Sketch* . . ., reprinted from the article in *D R*.

[2] When Achilli was in the hands of the Inquisition in 1849, Pius IX asked the Oratorian Fr Theiner to try to persuade him to return to the Church. According to Theiner's account, Achilli said: 'If I submit, what will become of me? What will the Pope and Cardinals do to me? How shall I live?' To remove these fears, Theiner promised, on his word as a German, which he told Achilli was as good as an oath, to share his last penny with him, and even, if necessary, to appeal to the Prussian Embassy,

⌐I am much better and worse, as if some one were praying for me from time to time.⌐

I speak under correction, but ⌐it seems to me that *suspence* is a trial to which our Blessed Lord could not be subjected.

3 P M. The consultation with the Attorney General put off till tomorrow.⌐ Alas! another day of suspence — I can't come till Friday.

WEDNESDAY 5 NOVEMBER 1851   with the lawyers

TO EDWARD BADELEY

24 King Wm Street Wednesday [5 November 1851]
My dear Badeley

Should a stranger call on you, saying he had been in the Ionian Isles etc, and can give names etc. ask him to do one thing, which he *can* do, to come forward to *identify* the Achilli of Westminster Hall with the Cavaliere Achilli.[1]

Ever Yrs J H N

TO F. S. BOWLES

5 PM Wednesday [5] (Nov 51)[2]
My dear F Fr

ὡς ἄρκτου στροφάδες κελευθοί

Now it is good.[3]

A stranger has called on Burns to give his own minute references to persons in the Ionian Isles (where he himself has lived) who can prove

rather than that Achilli should suffer in consequence of his apostasy. Agostino Theiner, *Dell' introduzione del protestantismo in Italia*, Naples and Rome 1850, pp. 248 ff.

St John replied to Newman on 6 Nov. 'I have looked again, (I had looked before) over Theiner's book. There is not a word to hint that Achilli was even an immoral man before relapsing into Apostasy. Theiner certainly wrote his account to move *him* and abstained purposely from saying anything to offend him. He says Achilli cried over his misfortune, and that he offered himself to support him. It is all a most affectionate appeal to the confidence Achilli placed in him. I think he almost seems to say Achilli confessed sacramentally to him. He says "You opened his [your] whole heart to me," which will quite explain his saying nothing of Achilli's character.'

[1] See letter of 31 Aug. to Badeley. According to the record of expenses, the stranger told the lawyers of rumours about Achilli, and said they should get into touch with Larkin Reynolds at Zante.   [2] '(Nov 51)' is added in pencil.

[3] Sophocles, *Trachiniae*, 130, Joy succeeds grief, 'like the orbit of the circling Bear,' now low, now high, on the horizon.

Achilli's guilt there — having only seen the notice of proceedings in the Papers.

This is excellent in itself, and I hope an omen and first fruit of many such — He is a Protestant, but felt indignant

Ever Yrs affly J H N

TO ARCHBISHOP CULLEN

24 King William Str London. Nov 5/51

My dear Lord Primate,

I began a letter to your Grace a fortnight since, and then I thought I should be only teasing you, and gave it up. Your letter has been a great satisfaction to me;[1] everyone is likely to have his judgment biassed by the feeling of what is congenial to him, and what he is used to — Now it has been so entirely my way of doing things ever, to begin on a small scale and without pretence, that till I see such a mode of setting about our work in Ireland approved by your Grace, I seem to fear it may be merely a way of my own and nothing more. Another anxiety remains behind — such a mode of proceeding throws far more work as well as responsibility on one or two individuals. I trust, through God's mercy, I shall be equal to any which the Committee puts before me — but at my age, when strength and spirits and vigour and health fail, one may well feel alarmed about it. I do earnestly trust my spirits may not go, or rather that grace may take their place — but, my dear Lord, I need your prayers, and those of all whom I can get to think of me.

I am here on unpleasant business, as the Papers will tell you. Dr Achilli has actually made an affidavit, declaring *on oath* that every one of the things I have charged against him is false. If I prove *one* against him, he subjects himself to transportation for perjury! Yet the proof on my part is both difficult and expensive. Nothing, I fear, will quite do, but *primary* evidence, which it is most difficult to get. You were kind enough to say some time back, that you thought *something* could be done for the expences in Ireland. If I can't get the money, I must knock under. It will cost not less than £1000.

[1] Cullen wrote on 28 Oct., ' I fully agree in all your sentiments, and I hope we shall be able to carry them into effect. At our meeting [on 15 Oct.] all present expressed a desire to get an opportunity of examining for some time the Thurles report—so the consideration of it was deferred till the 12th Nov next—Every one however appeared quite decided that the University should be in Dublin—When the meeting comes on I think I will succeed in getting your views adopted, and then I trust the matter will go on well. . . .'

Begging your Grace's blessing I am, My dear Lord Primate Your affte Servt in Xt

John H Newman

P.S.   I expect to return to Birmingham tomorrow.

TO BISHOP ULLATHORNE

24 King Wm Street Nov 5. 1851

My dear Lord,

I am afraid this Achilli matter will prove a serious one. So it has seemed to me from the first, the more so, because I knew how serious it was before I involved myself in it, though of course I thought the risk so small as not to be regarded. I did not do it without a good deal of thought and anxious prayer. However he has denied on oath every one of the charges; and if I cannot prove some of them against him I shall be liable to fine and imprisonment.

I have written to the Cardinal and the Primate of Ireland about the expences, as well as to Mr Hardman. The matter will be put off till January — and then again, if necessary, till after Easter — but I suppose, if it proceeds, it will be all over by the Long Vacation. I expect to return to Birmingham tomorrow.

Please get some prayers for me, and give me your blessing, and believe me, My dear Lord, Your faithful Servt

John H Newman[1]

THURSDAY 6 NOVEMBER 1851   called on *Sir B*. Brodie to consult him (*as Mr Babington wished me*.) consultation with Attorney General (*Cockburn*) at Westminster

TO AMBROSE ST JOHN

⌜London Nov 6/51

Charissime

I now know the worst, and it is very bad — but I am not so troubled as I was, and hope the calm will continue.

[1] Ullathorne replied on 6 Nov. 'My faith is not at all shaken in the success of your, and our cause. It will be an anxious thing, and expensive, but that is all—. . . . I will set all my convents to pray, and neglect no means in my power to help you.'

I have just returned from the Attorney General [[Cockburn]] — he is the first *impartial* person who has given an opinion,⌐ for Badeley and Lewin are friends — ⌐next, he is so near the judges, that he speaks *their feeling*, (so Lewin said)

1. Observe, that Lord Campbell showed a bias, by calling it ribaldry.[1] And Lord C. is very likely to have the decision.[2]

2. The Attorney General evidently was indignant [[with me]]. He called it a bitter libel etc — (it imputed a pretence of religion as a cloke for bad practices etc) Asked whether I had thought of knocking under etc. if so, the quicker the better.

3. He said we *must prove the* [[*our*]] *points*: i.e. bring primary evidence; secondary, without primary, would do more harm than good.

4. He said the Judges would send on the matter to trial, if they could.

5. That there would be no chance at all with a jury.

6. that they would come down more heavily upon me than upon Burns.

The alleviation was this — first, that they think they can get the matter postponed till Easter Term: yet what a time for suspence! next, that IF Achilli's confession is made good, it will go a very great way indeed⌐

The Attorney General was evidently hostile. If I go to Ireland to the new University *doubtless* I shall be doing myself an injury — but it must be.

⌐And now, Charissime, you know the whole — things can't be worse — they may be better. I said this morning I never would be sad again; I will try not to be. May He⌐ who was on the Cross, ⌐enable me to bear whatever He gives me, in love, of His sufferings⌐[3]

Ever Yrs affly J H N

⌐P.S.   Brodie pronounces very well of me.⌐

Thanks for F Joseph's letter.[4] I propose to come down tomorrow (Friday) and may have to come up here next week.

---

[1] When the passage concerning Achilli in Newman's lecture was read in court on 4 Nov., Lord Campbell said: 'The ribaldry with which the passage commences would not be a sufficient ground for the Court to interfere; but it certainly imputes specific and gross breaches of morality, which justify our interposition.' *The Times*, 5 Nov., p. 6.   [2] Altered to [[the trial.]]

[3] [[May He support me, who in love gives me to suffer.]]

[4] That of 21 Oct., which reached Birmingham on 3 Nov.; quoted in note to letter of 27 Oct. to Talbot.

FRIDAY 7 NOVEMBER 1851   breakfasted with Badeley   went down to Westminster to swear affidavit   came down to Birmingham

TO EDWARD BADELEY

Oy Bm Nov 9/51

My dear Badeley

When you see the Cardinal tomorrow, please try to get from him the
name of that person connected with the Police of Naples who gave that
account of Achilli's offence with the child of 15 which is *not* in the
Police Register; because we could apply to him. Get from him too any
other names and references he can give.

There is a young Catholic barrister of the name of Warren, at Number
3 Paper Buildings, knowing French, Italian and German well, who ought
to be got (I think) if he will go, to proceed at once to Italy and thence to
Malta and Corfu. I have various letters from a distance on the subject
of my case, from persons who do not know *my* especial risk in it, showing
me how entirely the Catholic body will take it up as *their* matter. We
must not do the matter then in a way which they would call by-halves.
I wish exceedingly to employ the agents Mr Lewin may find *on the spot*,
at Malta and Corfu — but that will not supersede our engaging a man
such as Mr Wallis.[1]

Ever Yrs affectly John H Newman

MONDAY 10 NOVEMBER 1851   NB[2]   1. we have been looking for a cross.
2. the Psalms all thro', being in prison and in a snare, and only getting out
thro' prayer.
3. The Law God's Ordinance (duty of submission to it)
4. Only broken (when laws of nature) for a good in a higher order.
5. Our Lord before the Jewish Court, His own ordinance
6. I have had so little trouble in life
7 I have been so carried thro' trouble
8. I have such great comforts in friends etc
9. I have people to pray for me, in a way I never had in other troubles.
10. It is my lot thus to be cast off, (as in former instances)
11 It is not a light thing to beard a country — to oppose its prejudices and I
may be called on fairly to suffer.

[1] Newman wrote to Lewin suggesting that John Wallis, editor of the *Tablet*
1856–68, should be engaged to go abroad and collect evidence. In the event, neither
Warren nor Wallis was engaged.

[2] This is a dated note at the end of the diary.

Molloy and his sister went to Paris?[1]

TO EDWARD BADELEY

Oratory Bm Nov 11. 1851

My dear Badeley,

I was bitterly amused at the way the Cardinal, in his usual sanguine way, was taking you in.[2] With Dr Nicholson I have been in correspondence these two months — ten days ago one of our party actually went to Malvern to him. The affidavit of Garamone came from him — and he has had nothing to do with Achilli personally. With F Esmonde I have both conversed and corresponded. Mr Lewin has both his letters and Dr Nicholson's. Depend on it, you will get nothing from the Cardinal, except indeed you get the papers — which I do not expect. He *might* just have remembered the name of his Naples Police man, whose letter he has lost. Since he can't do even that, he can do nothing.

Be sure, we have all the information we can get in England from Catholics. Protestants indeed may come forward as Burns's anonymous visitor — and there may be information from some virtuous Recordite, or some secret source as that to which you alluded, but that is all.[3]

At the same time, it seems to me most important that the Cardinal should write to the Pope — and get him to do every thing he can. If the

---

[1] See letter of 19 Nov. to Gordon.

[2] Badeley wrote on 10 Nov., 'I have seen the Cardinal, but he could not tell me the name of the Person connected with the Police at Naples which you ask for. But he has promised immediately to see the Bishop of Southwark, and to try and ascertain from him all he can to help you, as well as to search among his own papers for every thing that may help. He says Father Esmond at the Jesuits' Church in Gardiner Street in Dublin will know all about Achilli at Malta, and be able to speak about his doings— he was at Malta with him all the time—Archbishop Nicholson is at Malvern, and will probably be able to state the facts which Achilli confessed in his presence—Probably an affidavit from him will be important—Can you write to him? The Cardinal is ready to write to the Pope and get him to allow original Documents to be sent, as well as to induce him to set other People to work. . . .

I read the Cardinal the latter part of your letter to show him the interest taken about the matter, and put before him strongly the serious consequences to you and the whole Catholic Cause, if you were not enabled to meet Achilli satisfactorily, and I think I rather alarmed him—'

On 31 Oct. Wiseman had written to Newman saying, 'I cannot make out where all my papers about Achilli are, though they must be together somewhere. Many things got misplaced when I was at Rome. However I have no originals, but only copies from Propa [Propaganda] and Corfu. . . .'

[3] See letter of 5 Nov. to Badeley, who must have alluded in conversation to some secret source of information. A Recordite is a supporter of the Evangelical weekly, the *Record*.

Cardinal would get the Pope to *influence the Naples Police*, it would be a great gain.

Lewin writes me word he thinks I should *not reprint the libel*. Give me your opinion. The second edition is now going through the Press. I am sorry to think it is not to be reprinted. I think the moral effect will be bad. Already I have been charged with shirking and putting forward Burns. There is an article against me in a Birmingham Paper on this score, and in the Record.[1] However, if you confirm Lewin's judgment, of course I will omit it. I inclose what I wish you to look over, as its substitute. You shall see it again in type, if you do not pluck it. Send it me back.[2]

Ever Yrs affly John H Newman

P.S.   No one could *know* that the continued publication was *my* doing. It might be Burns's to whom I had sold the book

[Enclosure]

And in the midst of outrage etc. p 197 and so on to 'Mothers of families,' he seems to say, 'gentle maidens, innocent children, look at me, for I am worth looking at. You do not see such a sight every day. I am he, who for a whole year past have lived under the heaviest accusations, and have suffered them to remain on me, as if I cared not for them.[3] I am he, whose history has been blackened by opponents, and that with the

---

[1] This was when Achilli obtained a rule *nisi* against Newman's publishers. It was complained that '. . . when it comes to the point, and he is asked merely to admit, legally, that which every one knows to be the fact,—he gives no answer—thus forcing the aggrieved party to proceed against the mere agent, and to put, it may be, Mr. Burns into prison, for an offence committed by Dr. Newman. We believe that even among worldly men, there is scarcely a precedent for conduct like this.'

[2] Badeley wrote on 12 Nov. agreeing with Lewin. It would be a serious matter to continue to circulate what the Court thought a proper subject for a Criminal Information, and Newman could not be accused of cowardice for holding his hand out of deference to its authority. Besides, Newman should consider what he could prove, before reiterating such heavy charges. Badeley added: 'With respect to the proposed substitute, I can only say that it is less dangerous and objectionable than the original attack—But I don't think it likely to *improve your position* in the Queen's Bench.'

The pages in Lecture v, dealing with Achilli, were left blank in the second edition of *Prepos.*, except for being marked with asterisks, and except for the sentence 'De illis quae sequebantur posterorum judicium sit. In fest. Nativ. S. Joan. Bapt. 1852.' This was the day, 24 June 1852, on which Newman was found guilty of libel. The second edition of *Prepos.* has the date 1851, when, except for the above pages, it was printed. There is also a copy of *Prepos.* at the Birmingham Oratory, dated 1851, and not marked 'second edition,' which nevertheless contains the asterisks and sentence quoted above.

[3] vid. the accusations urged against Dr Achilli in the Dublin Review for July 1850; and Authentic Brief Sketch of the Life of Dr Giacinto Achilli, Richardsons. These two works are the grounds for every thing that is said in the text. [Newman's note]

circumstances of date, place, and persons, who have been denounced in published works, not once but twice, and the second time in a popular form, for general circulation, and, though defied and braved to answer them, have met them neither by ⟨with⟩ legal proceedings, nor with intelligible refutation, nay, nor with minute and detailed denial. I am he, who, charged with these many crimes, have not satisfied my friends more than my enemies; who have been laden with the repute of profligacy and hypocrisy, of treachery, of seduction, and an unprincipled course, have yet seen my path clear to come forward against others, and accuse my late communion, and her members, and her chief pastor of the most hideous wickedness, as if I had already proved to my hearers that I had a claim to be believed. And now attend to me, such as I am, and you shall see what you shall see about the barbarity and profligacy of the Inquisitors of Rome.'

You speak truly, O Achilli, and we cannot answer you a word. You are a Priest; you have been a Friar; you are, it is undeniable, the scandal of Catholicism, and the palmary argument of Protestants, by your extraordinary courses. You are, it is true, covered with the gravest imputations, which you have not given us the means of disbelieving. You come forward, it is true, as the accuser of your own brethren, though you yourself are under accusation. You speak of their religious tribunal as 'sacrilegious'[1] when sacrilege is already charged against yourself. You say their religion allows them 'a life of pleasure,' when they have done their utmost to turn you from such a life. You speak of your church's system as 'a mystery of abomination' and her earthly head as 'the man of sin, the son of perdition,' when sins abominable, and leading to perdition, have been laid to your door without your striving yourself for their removal. She is to be proved a 'fallen and corrupt Church' by one who has not yet proved himself upright and pure; she is 'a Church of Satan,' but you are not to have partaken in Satan's deeds. How then do you prove her so evil, except by the force, not of your words, but of yourself? She is guilty because you are her child. Yes, you are an uncontrovertible proof, that priests may fall, and friars break their vows. You are your own witness; but, while you need not go out of yourself for your argument, neither are you *able*. With you the argument begins; with you too it ends; the beginning and the ending you are both. When you have shown yourself, you have done your worst and your all; you are your best argument and your sole. Your witness against others is utterly invalidated by your witness against yourself. You leave your sting in the wound; you cannot lay the golden eggs, for you are already dead.

[1] Dealings with the Inquisition p 4. [Newman's note.]

TO AN UNKNOWN CORRESPONDENT

Oratory Birmingham Nov 12. 1851

Dear Madam

Of course my only answer to you can be that the Catholic Church is the true fold of Christ, and that it is your duty to submit to it. You cannot do this without God's grace, and therefore you ought to pray Him continually for it. All is well if God is on our side. Excuse the brevity with which I am obliged to write, and believe me,

Dear Madam, Faithfully Yours John H Newman

TO EDWARD BADELEY

Oratory Bm November 13/51

My dear Badeley,

I have stopped the publication of the Lecture, as you recommend.

The Cardinal's letter is satisfactory, as far as it goes. You have succeeded in rousing him. What a wonderful gift it is to be a Lawyer! Put your screw on once more, and he really will wake up. I send the letter back.[1]

Entre nous, I have a suspicion of his man, as such — though I don't

---

[1] On 13 Nov., before returning it, Newman copied parts of this letter: 'Extract from the Cardinal's letter to Badeley of Nov 12.

1. The Extract from the Naples Police was given him ⟨Dr Grant⟩ by Cardinal Patrizi in his own handwriting. It is from the records of the Secret Police, which is not easily accessible. He thinks the father of the child may be discovered. I will write to Cardinal Patrizi on the subject. [Patrizi was the Pope's Vicar General].

2. The depositions of Garamone at Corfu are in the legalized copy at Propaganda. The Bishop of Southwark will write about them.

3. The accounts of the crimes at Viterbo are from the depositions in the Holy Office, and were procured by the Pope's orders from its archives by Cardinal Patrizi. They were sent to me in the handwriting of Mgr Stella, one of the Pope's four chamberlains. . . . No doubt it was thus that he ⟨Mgr Talbot?⟩ saw the original of Achilli's confession. I write also to Mr Talbot.

4. There is another document by a judge at Viterbo, the original of which was in the possession of Mr Wigley, a Catholic architect now in the East. A new deposition could be procured.

5 All the documents sent passed through the Pope's hands.'

Wiseman wrote on 13 Nov. to Newman, promising to give every assistance, and to write to Pius IX.

know Mr Hartin at all.[1] At the same time it would be a great thing to *bring the Cardinal* into the matter — which to take Mr H. would do. Besides Mr H. would far surpass Wallis in ferreting out evidence.[2] On the other hand he evidently cannot speak Italian, which Wallis (I am told) does fluently; this is a great objection. How can he ferret, who cannot speak? The matter of expence is secondary to doing the matter well.

Is it an absurdity to send both? perhaps they would not pull together — which would be awkward when you had a young barrister and an older attorney. Could they go together as far as Italy, leaving Hartin to go by himself to Corfu and Malta? but I fear Burns's friends Pelagio Runi etc do not speak English more than the Viterbites.[3]

Ever Yrs affly J H N

TO J. D. DALGAIRNS

Oy Bm Nov 14/51

My dear F Rector,

I wrote to you telling you of my suspence. I can't conceive why my affidavit has not been brought before the Court by the Attorney General. I send you the cover of your letter, just received. You will see 'too late' on it. Your box, I suspect, acts under the law of 'Too late.'

I send James a letter — and beg him to buy for me at John Chapman's 142 Strand, 'No 731, Nonnotte ou les erreurs de Voltaire, 2 vols. duod. calf 4. sh. A.D. 1770.'[4] If you print your Sermon, as I mine, you won't get a penny on it. I lost by the first 2000 — and did not gain (at least have not yet) on the next 2000, for one of the London sellers of it failed, and my money is irreclaimable. It is [a] good idea, the Clifton way.[5] Whether you should do it at all, I cannot possibly say. It would

---

[1] Wiseman, in his letter, suggested that his own legal adviser, James Vincent Harting, solicitor to the Westminster Archdiocese 1850–83, should be sent out to Italy to collect evidence.

[2] Wallis, who was a barrister, while anxious to serve Newman, wondered whether etiquette did not require the business to be handled by an attorney. Badeley reported Lewin's opinion that Harting 'would not be so good or efficient a Person as Mr Wallis . . .' However, on 19 Nov. he told Newman that Cockburn had decided that for professional reasons Wallis could not be sent out.

[3] Pelagio Runi was Catholic Chaplain at Cephalonia.

[4] Claude François Nonnotte, *Les Erreurs de Voltaire*, Avignon 1762, enlarged edition 2 Vols., Paris 1770. This was one of the most effective of the replies to Voltaire, who was extremely angry with the book. Newman wanted it for the preparation of his Dublin Lectures.

[5] The Provincial of the Jesuits suggested that Dalgairns should publish as one of the 'Clifton Tracts' the sermon he had preached on 2 Nov., in honour of the beatification of Peter Claver.

be a compliment to the Jesuits. It depends on the time it takes you. I have been appointed President of the New University — and am expecting the official intelligence.

I am much disappointed about F Wilfrid — and certainly do not think it the way to get well — but you must ask the Doctor. If he disapproves, I will write to him.[1]

I am expecting to be summoned, as much as ever; indeed I must be. The Cardinal is beginning to be frightened. Badeley has stuck it into him — and he has said what, in spite of my extreme incredulity as to all Cardinalitian statements, if said two months ago would have been of use to our two fathers and a comfort to us. He is in great trouble about the Monmouth Bank[2]

Ever Yrs affly J H N

SATURDAY 15 NOVEMBER 1851   Mr Flanagan here?

TO ARCHBISHOP CULLEN

Oratory. November 16/51

My dear Lord Primate

The news of my appointment conveyed to me by Dr Cooper, and now your Grace's letter of this morning have affected me with a great deal of pleasure and gratitude in spite of the anxiety which the responsibilities I am entering on occasion.[3] Unless I have the prayers and the good advice of those who have thought me worthy of so high a post, I shall have no hope of acquitting myself well — but I am encouraged by the thought, that so great an undertaking, suggested and sanctioned by the Holy See, and commenced with such deliberation by the Hierarchy of Ireland is not destined to come to nothing. Would there be any way

---

[1] Dalgairns wrote on 13 Nov. his anxiety about Faber, his Superior, 'We have heard from him from Malta. He is going to stay there to visit Father Richard. Meanwhile he is preaching at the Gesù there. I am so afraid of his getting into work there again, and coming back just as bad as he went. He has also got an Italian master. He has given up going to the Holy Land and intends spending the time in visiting Oratories in Spain and Sicily. Does not it strike you that all this will keep his brain in excitement . . .'

[2] The Monmouthshire and Glamorganshire Banking Company, of which the liability was not limited, failed in the autumn of 1851. Wiseman held shares in it, in trust for the mission at Radford in Oxfordshire. The shares were transferred to Bishop Ullathorne and Dr Moore, who were, as a result, imprisoned for debt in 1853. See letter of 1 June 1852 to Bowles, and note there.

[3] Newman was appointed President of the Catholic University on 12 Nov. For Cooper's and Cullen's letters see *McGrath*, pp. 122–3, and *A.W.* p. 283.

of putting the University under the patronage of our Blessed Lady, for it would be most desirable?

The Achilli matter is a great annoyance — for I fear the Court will be *rigid* in the documents it requires. You spoke of De Sanctis being a bad character at Rome — could you refer me to any means of tracing what passed between him and Achilli then? for the Cardinal, in his pamphlet, says that Achilli corrupted his morals as well as his faith.[1]

Begging your Grace's blessing I am, My dear Lord Primate Your faithful & affte Servt

John H Newman   C.O.

MONDAY 17 NOVEMBER 1851   Attorney General asked enlargement of the Rule in my favor[2]

TO J. D. DALGAIRNS

Nov 17 [1851]

My dear F Bernard

I have written to F Wilfrid. As to Mr Strickland, I have long been looking out for him. I wish by all means you would send him to Lewin in Southampton Street, *Strand*.[3] I am looking out for a summons to

---

[1] Luigi De Sanctis (1808–69), parish priest of the Church of the Maddalena in Rome, apostatised in 1847 and fled to Malta, where he became a resident in St Julian's Mission House, at the Protestant College of Malta. Cf. letter of 9 Oct. 1847 to Wiseman. Newman is referring to Wiseman's statement: '. . . to him [Achilli] was attributed the sad fall *first* in morals, and *then* in faith, of F. Desanctis . . .,' *D R*, XVIII (June 1850), p. 490, and *Dr. Achilli, Authentic Brief Sketch*, p. 24. Newman's concern, in connection with the Malta College, was to prove that Achilli had been dismissed ostensibly for disobedience, really for immorality. This he was not able to prove legally. Sir A. Cockburn pressed the point at the trial, saying: 'The question is on what grounds the committee really proceeded.' Lord Campbell, the Judge, replied: 'The resolution states them, and you cannot go further and enter into other grounds.' Cockburn complied, saying: 'Then we are shut out from proof plainly applicable to the issue.' *Finlason*, p. 98. The Committee of the Malta College, while admitting that Achilli was 'the object of many grave personal objections,' dismissed him because he prevented an investigation into the immorality of others. Cf. note to letter of 27 Oct. to Talbot.

[2] Cockburn obtained a cross rule *nisi*, delaying the trial until the Easter Term, but this was set aside on 20–21 Nov.

[3] This was evidently Edward Strickland (1820–89), educated at Stonyhurst, who entered the Commissariat branch of the British Army, becoming eventually Commissary General. He came on 22 Nov. to see Lewin, whose expense account for that day has 'Attended Mr Strickland when he said he had been resident at Corfu and other places and explained various matters relating to Achilli and conferring fully with him—' Strickland served in the Crimean War and was Commissariat Officer in

London every day. A fortnight has passed, and not a line from Naples. The poor Cardinal is now at length frightened and making amends — but what a different state things would have been in, had he moved two months ago! The hitch at Naples is for want of his stirring himself — This is proved.[1]

Ever Yrs affly J H N

TO W. G. WARD

Oy Bm Nov 18. 1851

My dear Ward

I thank you very warmly for your kind letter. Should I be pressed for money, I will gladly take your £50 *when* you offer it; else I would take it at a later date, but perhaps this will only inconvenience you.[2]

I have felt the seriousness of the matter from the beginning of September, when I could not get any one else to do any thing but laugh at it. The Cardinal has neglected it for two months, in spite of all I could do — and now is beginning to awake. I hope he will not go into the opposite extreme, which Dr Grant's language seems to imply. Our Fathers at Naples (*entre nous*) have been able to do nothing, though evidence lay all around them, because the Cardinal had not exerted himself. However, so far is clear that Achilli is even worse than we knew — and it is impossible therefore, if every one does his duty, but we shall be carried safely through the trial. I suppose, we shall have four months — but I cannot understand today's report in the Times. Properly *one* proof of perjury, and he has committed himself in the most absolute way, would be enough to put an end to the proceedings — but the Judges, I fear, *will* not do what they *might* — and will demand a good broad refutation — it must be *primary* evidence, there is the difficulty. But our friends must not despair, else we shall certainly be dished.

I sent about for prayers 2 months ago — but it is difficult to keep people up to the mark for a long time. Give me yours and your wife's. If it goes to a *jury* I am certainly done for — but the judges *may* stop it, and I trust will, before it gets so far.

Do not repeat what I have here said — but urge every one who can to pray.

charge of the British Army of occupation in Greece, 1855–7. He published in 1863 *Greece: its condition, prospects and resources.*

[1] See second note to letter of 19 Nov. to Joseph Gordon.

[2] W. G. Ward had heard from Bishop Grant of the serious danger to which Newman was exposed in the Achilli trial, and offered £50 in Jan. 1852 towards the expense.

Will you excuse me, for any shabbiness, to Mr Dolman? I should have written except that I have so much on my mind[1]

Ever Yrs affly John H Newman

TO JOHN JOSEPH GORDON

Oy Bm. Nov 19/51

My dear F Joseph

Your letter from Naples dated November 5 with the prospect of Mr Fortunato's Sunday information and the affidavit came yesterday.[2] We have sent several letters to Rome in the course of the last 6 weeks, which I trust you have found at the Post Office, we expecting you to be only a fortnight in Naples. Your failure, which must have teazed you much is simply owing to our good Cardinal not having given you sufficient instructions and introductions.[3] He has been in a dream, now he is awakened, and every one is horribly frightened and very earnest and busy, when two good months or rather three have been lost. I felt it so much a fortnight ago that I made Manning take a hint to Rome that I would give in, if nothing were done. I am threatened with fine and imprisonment. However, they are awake now. I keep delaying writing to you from day to day, for the lawyers are in as great suspence in London, as you have been at Naples. I have been expecting a summons to London daily for the last ten days, in order to send Hartin, the Cardinal's attorney, off to Rome. He is to go every where with the most pressing introductions, and to take evidence in the shape of affidavits. This day it is to be decided in Court *how long* time is to be allowed me.

---

[1] Alfred Dolman, a priest at St Edmund's, had, at Ward's suggestion, collected some passages bearing on pagan classical education, to help Newman with the preparation of his Dublin lectures.

[2] Gordon wrote from Naples on Wednesday 5 Nov., 'We have been to Fortunato the Prime Minister this morning—and he has promised that we shall have the documents on Sunday morning.' The documents came three days later and proved to be '*the notes* which the Police keep of notorious and bad characters.' See second letter of 30 Nov. to Gordon. The affidavit enclosed in Gordon's letter was that of Keosse about Malta. The liberal-minded Giustino Fortunato (1777–1862) was Prime Minister from 1849 to 19 Jan. 1852, when he was dismissed by Ferdinand II, for having failed to warn him of Gladstone's attack in July 1851 on the Neapolitan prison system.

[3] Gordon had arrived in Naples on 30 Oct., and wasted a month because he relied on Wiseman's introductions which were not addressed to the right persons, and were so general that the police would not release information. The Cardinal Archbishop of Naples was unwilling to intervene. When Gordon realized that Wiseman ought to have written to the King or the Prime Minister for the documents, he approached the latter himself, and obtained what was required, but too late to prevent the trial.

The lawyers expect till Easter, but I am prepared for Hilary Term January 14. No time must be lost, that is clear. Your work is done, when Hartin comes, except to give him your impressions, information etc. And now I have nothing more to say about the matter except to lament your anxiety etc and hope it has not hindered the expedition from doing your health good.

It is good news to know that dear Nicholas is well; but look to his windows at night etc etc for I know well he is longing to catch a second fever. What does one go abroad for, but to play the John Bull, to dismiss all advice, to sleep in the white vapour, and to bask and toil in the hot sunshine? I never will believe he is not bent on mischief. I am appointed head of the University. There are no signs of my being wanted in Ireland till the beginning of January. I think you should set off immediately after Christmas; St Stephen's Day, if possible; else you won't catch me here, unless indeed my matter comes on January 14. Edward [Caswall] is with his mother — he had a bad skin after he got well — however, his handwriting is not his own yet. Philip [Bathurst] is *not well*. Francis is *forcibly* taken away from us by his mother.[1] I shall give him a month's furlough — and if he does not come back then, he must not at all. Aloysius [Boland] lives, and, I think, without much pain. Stanislaus [Flanagan] looks pale from not eating and sleeping enough. Molloy is taking his sister to Paris.[2] William is *doubtful* — I have not dared let him be tonsured.[3] Miss French goes with Monsell to Ireland next week. The plastering goes on rapidly at the House — all is to be done and floors down by Christmas. Poor old Tyler is dead. I am beginning to sketch my Lectures on Education for Dublin — but, easy as they ought to be, find them difficult from not knowing sufficiently the lie of the ground in Dublin. Enjoy yourselves as much as you can. I consider your labour over now. I have sent you *many* questions etc. to get answered at the Chiesa Nuova;[4] I hope all the letters will turn up. You will not have to go to Viterbo. I consider all over, if the judges let it go to trial. So think my lawyers, and do not mean to send a commission. Every thing will be done by affidavit.[5] I doubt not I shall be sustained, whatever is God's will — my comfort is I have not lost a day, tho' I

---

[1] The mother of Francis Davis, laybrother, insisted on his returning to her.

[2] Philip Molloy's sister was to try her vocation with the Sisters of Charity at Versailles.

[3] William Neville, who, to the end of his days, found difficulty in making up his mind, was admitted to his first probation at the Birmingham Oratory on 29 Sept. 1851. He was tonsured on 5 June 1852, but not until 30 Oct. 1861 was he ordained priest.

[4] Letter of 14 Oct.

[5] Newman meant that it would not be worth while sending a commission to collect witnesses for a trial, at which the prejudice would be overwhelming.

could get *no one* to take it so seriously as I did. The week before the legal proceedings commenced, I said to Ambrose and Stanislas, 'Now you must pray, for this is the critical time —' They both laughed, as if I were fond. Plenty of zeal among Catholics, now, but as yet money does not *flow*. I heard from F Wilfrid yesterday — not a word of allusion to my matters. Depend on it, he has not said one Hail Mary for me since he set out.[1] Love to Nicholas

Ever Yrs most affly J H Newman

THURSDAY 20 NOVEMBER 1851   The Enlargement argued and given against me summoned up to London by Telegraph   called on Badeley
FRIDAY 21 NOVEMBER   The Rule made absolute[2]

TO ARCHBISHOP CULLEN

London. Nov. 21/51

My dear Lord Primate,

I am going to put a sort of responsibility upon your Grace, which you may not think you can undertake, but I am obliged to write round about to Catholics, lest I should be betraying interests not mine.

The Judges are against me, and a Protestant bias pervades the whole

---

[1] Faber wrote on 9 Nov. about his own health, and about his plan of making a tour of Sicily and then spending a month in Rome, and about his fluency in Italian, without a mention of Newman's troubles. On 25 Nov. he wrote again from Palermo, 'My dearest Padre,

The air of Sicily has done wonders for me. I sleep like a top, and eat ferociously. I am perfectly well, and feel as if I had never been ill. So I pine for home and work again. I shall start for Naples in 10 days, and go straight to Rome; then come home, visiting the principal Oratories—so as to reach home by the beginning of Lent. In the Livre des Etrangers at Catania I saw—John H. Newman, well satisfied with Signor Abbate's kind attentions after a fatiguing journey. May 1 1833.

I have visited the Congregations at Messina, Catania, and here. This is said to be the *largest* in the world. Its magnificence is really wonderful.

In haste Yours affly & obedly F. W. F.'

Faber wrote again on 31 Dec. 1851, 10 and 18 Jan. 1852, almost entirely about his health, and without ever a reference to the Achilli trial.

[2] The rule for the enlargement, or extension of time in which to put in justifying evidence by affidavit, having been refused, the rule *nisi*, granted to Achilli to bring a criminal information, was made absolute. Newman was crippled because he could not yet produce evidence to counter Achilli, not having the documents which Wiseman had collected in London (see letter of 26 Nov. to W. G. Ward), nor those which Talbot had collected in Rome. (See letter of 26 Nov. to Joseph Gordon.) He was unable even to *name* the witnesses he would produce, given time. (Cf. second letter of 30 Nov. to Joseph Gordon.)

Court. It seems certain I cannot get the justice which a Protestant would, though this must not be said publicly. Hence my lawyers are disposed to wish me to submit, if I can do it with truth and honor — and thus I should escape fine or imprisonment, and have *no* expences. Mr Badeley thinks that, if it goes on, there is a chance of my having a year's imprisonment.

On the other hand, if I submit, I betray a great Catholic interest. Catholics may say to me, Had you gone on, at least you would have most considerably damaged Achilli — whereas now you make us all seem as slanderers and liars. And *if* you damaged him, you would reduce your *sentence to nothing*.

Should persons of weight and authority tell me to go on, I will — Is there any one you would like to send this letter to, in case your Grace has not time or materials for forming a judgment yourself? I suppose I ought to decide soon. I expect to return to Birmingham tomorrow.[1]

Begging your Grace's blessing, I am, My dear Lord Primate, Your affte friend & servt

John H Newman   Congr. Orat.

TO JAMES HOPE

⌜London Nov 21 [[1851]]

My dear Hope

Will you give me your *wide* judgement?

The Judges are against me and there is a Protestant feeling over Westminster Hall altogether, tho' this must not be said. Lewin, my lawyer, calls the Judges prejudiced. It is impossible I can escape before a Jury — what I *can* do is to lighten the judgment [[(verdict?)]] and to blacken Achilli.

Lewin wishes me to submit (if the opposite side will let me) — i.e. I suppose, say I did not speak on personal knowledge, but on the Dublin Review etc.

Now there are two questions I wish you to consider for me.

1. how it will look *in me*? of course I could do nothing inconsistent with truth and honor. I could not withdraw the charges in such sense as to imply I did not believe them, or was sorry for saying them. Still

---

[1] Cullen replied on 25 Nov., 'In my humble opinion you cannot retract the charges against Achilli—there is no doubt of their truth. It would give him a triumph, and inflict a wound on the Catholic cause in this Empire—'

what shall I think of the whole matter, how shall I wish to have acted, *ten years hence*? I want a *broad* judgment.

2. its effect on the Catholic body — it is *giving them up* as (apparently) liars and slanderers. I am writing to several of the Bishops.

Of course it would be pleasanter to me to submit, (if possible) for 1. I have no expences. 2. I have no punishment.

But if I go on, 1. I have the chance of damaging Achilli's character. 2. and in the same degree, tho' found guilty, I diminish my sentence. Badeley fancies I may have a year's imprisonment.

Write to me soon, to Birmingham — give me your prayers — and may you be guided to give me a good, honest, and sound opinion on the point. (I shall not go *simply* by *it*)⌐1

Ever Yrs affly John H Newman   C.O.

(I return to Bm tomorrow 40 Alcester Street, Bm)

TO AMBROSE ST JOHN

[[London]] ⌐Nov 21/51

Charissime

The Judges are clean against me — will grant nothing — determined to bring on a trial and to have witnesses in the box instead of affidavits, the people present humming assent. As a last effort we are trying to present another affidavit from me today, to gain to Hilary Term — but Lewin says it is hopeless.[2] Badeley last night said he thought I should

---

[1] Hope replied on 24 Nov. that although Achilli might be glad to let the matter drop, his supporters would only do so in return for an acknowledgment that he had been traduced. 'My opinion then is—
1. that you cannot avoid fighting except by retracting.
2. that a complete legal victory is not essential to the cause of the Church or to your own justification—But I do not forget the two points which personally affect you—expense and punishment. As to the former of these we ought all to help you, and I for one am ready. As to the second I cannot see that, short of retractation, you can hope in any way to escape so lightly as by proving all you can against Achilli . . . and if you can prove him a fornicator or adulterer I doubt much whether an English jury will consider his theology.'
Hope ended 'Mean time I have prayed for you and shall continue to do so—Would that I had better prayers to give.'

[2] Lewin was right, and the rule was made absolute later in the day. On this same day St John wrote to Gordon not to think that Newman was 'in any way breaking under the trial, he is coming out more and more and one sees a special providence in it for his sanctification, and he half feels it will eventually raise him up. He says "don't suppose I shall be damaged by it. It is my fate to fail and rise out of failure."'

have a year in prison. Lewin wishes me to submit at once. I answer, it does not depend on me: Catholics would say you are betraying *our* interests. Had you gone on, you at least would have made play, and shown up Achilli, as well as made your own judgment light.

Go and talk to the Bishop — *for* going on is 1. the chance of bringing damaging facts against Achilli. 2 the chances of war, e.g. Achilli may abscond. It ⟨the trial⟩ would not probably come on till Easter.⸥ ⟨and if I damaged him considerably, I should reduce punishment to nothing.⟩ ⸢On the other hand, if the opposite party will *accept* my submission. 1 I should escape without punishment. 2. We should have *hardly any* expences. I should like Mr Hardman's opinion too and Dr Moore's. I shall also consult Dr Cullen, the Cardinal, Dr Grant, and any one else⸥ who strikes me.

Ever Yrs affly J H N

I hope to return tomorrow (Saturday)

SATURDAY 22 NOVEMBER 1851   went down to Birmingham
SUNDAY 23 NOVEMBER   called on Bishop   Mr Hardman, Mr Lambert etc came to me.

TO EDWARD BADELEY

Oratory Birmingham Nov 23. 1851

My dear Badeley

A thought has risen in my mind, which I think it right to ask you to think over. Is the Attorney General heart and soul enough with us to conduct a matter as important (though in a different way) as the Gorham case? Would he not wish to get out of it, and some one like Hope substituted?

Perhaps such a change is unprecedented and the notion absurd. Excuse my mentioning it, if so.

I can well believe that a perfect knowledge of the Court, the tact which such experience as his gives, the ear of the Judges etc are of extreme importance — but in so grave a matter we want enthusiasm. The Attorney General seems to me desirous to bring 'an unfortunate affair' to an end.

I will illustrate what I mean. Speaking in ignorance, still it strikes me, that my appearance in the witness box would be of importance. 1. because a jury, as all men, are more prejudiced against a person they never saw, than one they have seen. 2. because I could bear (I trust)

433

turning inside out, as to my motives, i.e. on the point whether (as Lord Campbell's act gives opportunity, I suppose, of inquiring) I had private and personal or public motives for what I did. Now suppose Mr Attorney either set himself against calling me — or examined me carelessly and badly. Hope, I suppose, would draw me out.[1]

Ever Yrs affly John H Newman

TO J. M. CAPES

Oy Bm Nov 25/51

My dear Capes

As to the story about the crabs, are you certain it is not true? I have heard of frogs being allowed to hop about the Altar abroad. Of course the frogs, (not the crabs) were not supposed really to be souls.[2]

We are attempting a compromise, the event of which is known in London, I suppose, by now. I don't expect much from it. Since the middle of August I have thought *most seriously* of the whole matter. I trust I am prepared for any thing. The pranks (*entre nous*) of Cardinal and Attorney General are incredible.

Ever Yrs affly J H N

TO JAMES HOPE

⌜Oratory Bm November 25/51

My dear Hope

If I do not use many words to thank you for your most kind letter, it is because I have to put you au courant of the matter it is about.

When I got here, and put before the Bishop and others the state of the case, they were decided in favor of a compromise, as I was myself.

My own reasons are contained in papers I inclose.

[1] Badeley agreed that 'some one with more energy and zeal' was desirable, but ruled out Hope as unused to such proceedings, and explained that Cockburn could hardly be got rid of unless he abdicated voluntarily. In 1852 Newman again tried to dismiss Cockburn, see letters of 2 May 1852 to Cullen and 3 June 1852 to Hope. Cockburn's speech for the defence, at the trial, was masterly, but Newman was not called as a witness.

[2] In a review, in the *Rambler*, VIII (Dec. 1851), pp. 487–8, of *Quakerism; or the Story of my Life*, 'by a Lady who for forty years was a member of the Society of Friends,' her account of an Irish priest who arranged for crabs to be manipulated in the dark, to make his parishioners think that they were souls released from Purgatory, was dismissed as quite absurd.

The compromise offered, (Lewin, too, kindly pressing for it,) was this

1. a declaration that my charges were grounded upon the documents set forth in the Dublin Review.

2 the withdrawal of the passages in the Lecture.

Certainly this does not seem to me much to grant — so little that I have no idea it will be accepted.

But supposing it accepted, I did not mean to tie up my hands from saying in my Lecture, in the new Editions (and telling them I meant to say), that I had withdrawn it because I wished to avoid the expence and difficulties of law, not as if my affidavit had been rightly interpreted as denying the charges.[1]

I cannot conceive their accepting these terms — do you think they would commit me to any thing unworthy?[2]

Our great difficulty is this, that *at present we have no one good piece of evidence in our hands* — We cannot get any thing, *people are so dilatory. I believe* there is good evidence, but I have *nothing to show* to the lawyers.

I suppose I shall hear from Lewin tonight or tomorrow. If a negociation is commenced, I shall at once go up to London; so, please, direct to me at 24 King William Street, Strand. What you say will guide me, in many ways.⌐

                Ever Yours affecty John H Newman

[Enclosure]

⌐1. Since the charge, if not true, is a most scandalous libel, directly there is a verdict of guilty, a most heavy punishment follows.

2. For instance, imprisonment for a year.

3. The charge cannot be proved, except by evidence as good as if I were actually prosecuting Achilli for seduction, adultery, etc.

4. Thus it is undertaking a series of separate indictments.

5. It will not be enough, *nearly* to prove *every one*; some at least must be fully brought home to him.

6. They are of a nature proverbially difficult to prove.

7. They will require a number of witnesses, at a great expence.

8. The most trustworthy witnesses break down in the witness box.

---

[1] Newman's rule for the extension of time, in order to collect witnesses, was dismissed partly on the ground that he did not believe the truth of the charges he had made. See letter of 30 Nov. to the editor of the *Morning Chronicle*, and *Finlason*, pp. 43–5.

[2] A draft of Newman's includes three further possible points of a compromise: 'that it was wrong to say, what, tho' I thoroughly believed, I had not proof of already in my hand.' 'that I am sorry if I stated facts in an insulting way.' 'that I will publish no other explanation of my conduct but this.'

9 We are in a state of extreme uncertainty what our evidence amounts to. We have at present no evidence at all, and do not know whether we shall get even what might be got.

10. The Judge will certainly find me guilty, if he can

11. And the Jury is certain of giving it against me.

12. And my own lawyers, as being lawyers, are obliged to go by legal forms and traditions, not aiming at moral effect

13 The person put on his trial is one who has a great deal to lose.

14. E.g. my Irish engagement would be completely disarranged by a year's imprisonment.

15. We must then look *defeat* in the face.

16. In cases like this, the Catholic Church has commonly given way, if she could not make a point. It is a question of expedience.

17. Her bishops flee in persecution.

18. St Ambrose would not have resisted Justina, unless he knew he should be backed up by the Catholic people.

19. Mr Weale was sent to prison, and excited no popular (Catholic) feeling.[1]

20. Dr McNeil and Mr Stowell said priests deserved death, and roused no popular (Catholic) feeling.

21 The Judges, to guard against the chance, might merely insult me with a lecture, and cripple me with a fine.

22. It is not right to suffer for the mere sake of suffering, when Catholic interests are involved.

23. Suffering only tells, when it is also a *fact*, as intimately influencing and shared by the whole Catholic body.

24. I will gladly take the whole risk, if the Catholic body will make my cause theirs. Is this likely? [[i.e. I meant *I* could not 'start a spirit' or create an interest for myself in the Catholic body.]]

25. If then it can be done honorably, a compromise is expedient.

26. There is nothing dishonorable in yielding to necessity, e.g. running away from a wild beast.

27. It is not fair to bring a great Catholic question before a Protestant Judge and Jury.

28. To submit at this moment is explained to the world by the fact of the Judges having refused me time.

29 Achilli will be detected on the long run without our trouble.

---

[1] William Weale, a convert and the master of Islington Catholic Poor School, was sentenced to three months' imprisonment for beating a boy who stole and lied. The trial appears to have been unfair. See Frederick Oakeley, *Statement of Facts relative to the Case of Mr. William Weale, Master of the Poor-School at Islington*, London 1851, and letter of 20 Dec. 1851 to Capes.

30. A withdrawal of the passage is not a recantation.

31. It must any how be withdrawn shortly, for conviction involves it.

32. It is withdrawn already, for the Lecture is put out of circulation.

33. A compromise does but anticipate what will soon be done with worse concomitants.[11]

TO SISTER MARY IMELDA POOLE

Oratory. Bm Nov 25. 1851

My dear Sister

Just now is a most critical time, since you ask, but for what I know the crisis was over yesterday, and before this letter goes, we may know about it. We have an exposition of the B.S. [Blessed Sacrament] on the matter this evening.

What is going on is an attempt at a Compromise. It was offered yesterday, — it may have been rejected at once — if not, the negociation will go on for several days. Thus I have not known whether to write to you at once or wait. Perhaps it is refusal, and then there is urgent need of a triduo[2] — again, if it goes on for several days it is a most urgent time for one — so that in either case I should thankfully accept it.

The need, if it is refused, for a triduo, is that we all may have strength to bear God's blessed will. Tomorrow we begin a Novena to the Holy Ghost for that object. Your good Mother[3] may if she will, and I will thank her, *add* the intention of my deliverance from the snare of the hunter, but let the main intention be, that we, — that I, may have fortitude, patience, peace, to bear His sweet will withal.

Since the middle of August I have been saying with St Andrew, O bona Crux, diu desiderata. I was going to bring mention of it into my concluding Lecture, but found it would not be in keeping — and now it is coming as we approach St Andrew's Day.

You will see I expect the matter will go on. I hope, I pray it will *not*. I may be fanciful, but I cannot divest myself of the notion that it *will*. I have anticipated evil from the first: — i.e. if it can be called evil — anyhow it is no harm to offer myself in expectation and in will, a sacrifice to Him who bore the judgment seat and the prison of the unbeliever. Lawyers tell me that the chance is, I shall have a year's imprisonment.

---

[1] Newman also sent a shorter list of points to Ullathorne, headed 'As to taking the bold step of resisting to the last,' and made up of numbers 15, 16, 18 to 24 above, and finally '10. What did the English Bishops say last week? what would the Irish Bishops say?'   [2] i.e. three days of prayer.

[3] Mother Margaret Hallahan, then at Clifton.

Everything has gone so wonderfully hitherto — as if our dear Lord were taking the matter into His own hands, and utterly destroying all human means. He has let me be bound as in a net, and, as I said to Sister M. Agnes Ph.[1] near three months ago, with intense conviction, nothing but prayer can break the bond. It will be prayer has unlocked the fetter if we can say Laqueus contritus est, et nos liberati sumus.

When it flashed on my mind in the beginning of September that I might go to prison, I said 'May I come out a Saint!' I don't say that now when things are more real, but 'May it be accepted for my Sins.' I have all my life been speaking about suffering for the Truth, — now it has come upon me.

Yours affly in Jesus & Mary   John H Newman   C.O.

WEDNESDAY 26 NOVEMBER 1851   F Fred. [Frederic] wrote to F Joseph at Rome and I   Began our Novena de SP. S. [Spiritu Sancto][2]

TO ARCHBISHOP CULLEN

Oratory Birmingham. November 26/51

My dear Lord Primate

I am sorry to be obliged to teaze you with another letter.

You need only answer 'Yes' or 'No' — and please to direct to me at *24 King William Street, Strand, London.*

Do you call it a wrong compromise if I 1. simply left the passage out of my Lecture — or 2 added to the omission a *note* stating I omitted it, not from not believing what I said, but to avoid an anxious law proceeding. or 3 agreed to publish a statement to the effect that I withdrew it 'without prejudice to my view of its truth.'

I suppose, if I go on I am nearly certain of far worse terms than these — viz to be imprisoned as well[3]

---

[1] Elizabeth Moore, sister of John Moore, entered at Clifton on 2 July 1851, receiving the names Agnes Philip.

[2] Newman kept the details of the Novenas he and his friends made at this time, 26 Nov.–4 Dec. to the Holy Spirit, 'for fortitude, patience and peace'; 10–18 Dec., of our Lady, 'for a good deliverance'; 24 Dec.–1 Jan., of St Antony, 'for the discovery of evidence'; Jan. 7–15, of the Apostles, 'that the Church may gain advantage.' See also *Appendix* 6, p. 511, for a litany Newman composed for the emergency, dated 22 Dec. 1851.

[3] Cullen replied on 29 Nov., 'I think there can be no evil done by admitting any of the three propositions which you mention. It will be most desirable to get out of the lawsuit so easily.

If Achilli still presses the matter, we must get up a subscription . . .'

Begging your Grace's blessing, I am, My dear Lord, Yrs faithfully & affectly

John H Newman   Congr. Orat.

TO JOHN JOSEPH GORDON

The Oratory, Birmingham. Novr 26th 1851.[1]

The cruel suspence, day after day, the post coming in, and no letters from abroad. You cannot *conceive* it. We cannot make affidavits that any thing is coming even, for we have not been told minutely what. O that we knew what was *meant* by 'Achilli's Confession,' — *what* he confessed — whether in his *hand writing* etc etc.[2] We are thrown upon God simply — for man has deserted us. I wrote to Talbot on the 27th October for all his documents — not one has come yet November 26![3] It's three months since Badeley *told* me we should be driven into a corner. His words have been fulfilled.

J H N.

TO CHARLES NEWSHAM

Oratory Birmingham Nov. 26. 1851

My dear Dr Newsham,

I have been exceedingly touched by your kind letter just received. O what a surpassing compensation will it be for any trouble which may come on me of this world, if I have the masses, the prayers, and sympathy of brethren, of whom I am so unworthy![4] As to this trial, certainly it is likely to be severe — but 'they who play at bowls, must expect

---

[1] The address and date are taken from Bowles's letter to Gordon, on the 'turn up' of which Newman wrote, adding also the outside address to Gordon in Rome.

[2] Talbot announced on 4 Sept. that he had secured an attested copy of Achilli's confession before the Inquisition. See Newman's letter of 27 Oct. begging him to send it at once.

[3] Newman's letter of 27 Oct. reached Rome on 5 Nov. On 14 Nov. Talbot wrote, 'In answer to your last note . . . I have given all the papers and documents I have collected to Father Gordon, who will do all he can to get them properly attested and send them to you as soon as possible.' This letter reached Birmingham on 21 Nov., the day the rule was made absolute. For Joseph Gordon's letters, which arrived on 27 Nov., see second letter of 30 Nov. to him.

[4] Newsham wrote on 25 Nov., 'We feel that this is the cause of God and religion, and that He is our only hope. Accordingly the whole of this college [Ushaw] is now making a novena for you . . .'

rubbers —' I deserve it, and shall have strength (I trust) given me to bear any thing. I have looked forward to it, since the middle of August, and said with St Andrew, O bona Crux, diu desiderata — and now with St Andrew's day it comes — for I am told that the day after, the first steps are to be taken for the trial.

I took advice, and thought a good deal before I put out the passage which has been laid hold of. I ought to have reflected that a man guilty of what I laid to his charge, was not likely to scruple at an additional sin — He has sworn, not only that each fact is false, which I have stated, but that he never committed any such sins any where or at any time. When he has once got himself to do this, justification is exceedingly difficult, for one must get oaths to refute his oath, and that on the part of persons who know as much about each case as he knows.

I am perfectly clear, that, if trouble is to come on me, it is for some greater good in a higher order. May I continue prepared for any thing! and I shall, if you support me with your prayers. Give my most sincere thanks to your kind friends and pupils at Ushaw who are at present assisting me — and to the good nuns too — My enemies will be doing me abundant good, where they meant harm — and accept yourself the most heartfelt acknowledgment of

Yours affectly in Xt   John H Newman   Congr. Orat.

P.S.   I am attempting a compromise (not of course on the ground of denying what I have said) but of suppressing the passage. If you have any thing to remark on it, will you drop me a line at once to *24 King William Street, Strand, London* If the matter goes on, I suppose I shall have, not only to suppress it, but to be imprisoned.[1]

TO W. G. WARD

Oratory Bm Nov 26/51

My dear Ward

The marvellous mistakes which have been made show most strikingly that God's hand is in the whole matter. As to its hurting my influence, it is absurd, but it will be a most severe cross.

I have anticipated it since August last and said with St Andrew O bona crux, diu desiderata — Nothing has been wanting on my part in point of vigilance and promptitude.

[1] Newsham, on 27 Nov., advised strongly against a compromise, but added that he wrote with great pain 'for your sufferings would be my deepest anguish.'

Lewin had *nothing to do* with the Affidavit.[1] I will tell *you in confidence* the origines mali.

1. The Cardinal, who *did not look* for his documents till the *hour* when the Rule was made absolute and it was too late.[2] In that hour he looked and he found. F Hutchison brought them me. I took up my hat and went to Lewin. He had just returned from Westminster. It was all over.

2. The Cardinal ditto; who sent our dear Fathers to Naples with introductions not *strong enough* to open the Police books. They were told there that every thing would have been done, had the Cardinal been more alive.[3]

3. The Attorney General, who said confidently that we should gain till Easter — who took it for granted, and threw us off our guard completely. *Consequently* the Affidavit was drawn up as a form, and the Attorney General had it with him several days, before he brought it into Court. When it was unsuccessful, Badeley drew up other and stronger affidavits, but the Attorney General would have nothing to do with them.

4. Lord Campbell, who from the first has been against me.

I brought the point of the Dublin Review before my lawyers, but they said that it would only tell in mitigation of punishment — as indeed Hope had told me *before* I published the passage.[4]

I cannot help thinking matters will go on to conviction and imprisonment; but for three months I have been saying 'nothing but prayer will

[1] Ward forwarded to Newman a letter he had received on 24 Nov. from Frederick Oakeley, who wrote in great distress, having heard that Newman's case was being 'messed,' and that Lewin was inexperienced. Oakeley added 'Altogether I am grieved beyond description at the idea of N's sufferings and of his influence being weakened.' The affidavit was that in which Newman affirmed that he could prove the truth of the charges, if given time to collect the evidence.

[2] Wilfrid Ward, in *Life and Times of Cardinal Wiseman*, II, London 1897, pp. 39–40, claims that Wiseman did look for the papers, but cites no documentary evidence. His account of an interview between Philip Gordon of the London Oratory, and Wiseman, differs completely from the only interview for which evidence exists. See note to letter of 8 Sept. to Badeley. Even on the hypothesis of another interview, for which there is no evidence, Ward's account is highly suspect, for he claims that Wiseman, in the greatest distress of mind, said: 'I dare not write to him [Newman].' All the evidence indicates that it was only after Badeley's interview with him (see letters of 11 and 13 Nov. to Badeley) that Wiseman became alarmed, and, by that time, he had already written to Newman, on 31 Oct., saying he did not know where the documents were. The cavalier tone of this latter letter (see letter of 11 Nov. to Badeley, conclusion of first note) can as little be said to represent 'the greatest distress of mind,' as the weak introductions given to Joseph Gordon and Nicholas Darnell, can be interpreted as the vigorous action of a man who was as deeply concerned as Wilfrid Ward maintains.

[3] See letter of 19 Nov. to Joseph Gordon.

[4] Oakeley feared that the fact of Achilli's having noticed yet not followed up the attack on him in *D R* had not been brought to bear.

save me' — and I have been a Cassandra — my words have fallen idle —, men have but laughed

Ever Yrs affly J H N

THURSDAY 27 NOVEMBER 1851 F Ambrose went to Town in preparation for Hartin's going off to Rome wrote to F Nicholas F Joseph's letter came[1]

TO J. M. CAPES

Oratory Bm Nov 27/51

My dear Capes

The series of strange occurrences connected with this matter, it is impossible to convey to any one who is not with me. If the devil raised a physical whirlwind, rolled me up in sand, whirled me round, and then transported me some thousands of miles, it would not be more strange, though it would be more imposing a visitation. I have been kept in ignorance and suspence, incomprehensibly, every now and then a burst of malignant light showing some new and unexpected prospect.

This morning, when I thought a negociation for a compromise coming on, suddenly I have a letter not even *alluding* to this, but saying the trial is to come on in February, and that Mr Hartin, the Cardinal's Lawyer, is to go abroad in two days, to get evidence.[2]

Last week I was whirled up to Town by Telegraphic despatch, to be told that the Attorney General had quite taken us in, and that we were to have *no* time granted us, whereas he assured me of a period till Easter Term to answer Achilli's affidavit.

For three months I have been solliciting information from abroad — but I can't get people even to *write* to me.

The Cardinal said he had lost the papers — he never had *looked* for them. He looked for them for the first time in the hour when the Rule was made absolute — it was impossible to use them. He looked and immediately found. I seized them, and ran off with them to my Sollicitor's — It was just too late; all was over at Westminster.

All this shows it is God's hand — I have abundance of prayers — I shall have more. If people would but have believed me three months

---

[1] See second letter of 30 Nov. to Joseph Gordon.

[2] Badeley wrote on 26 Nov., 'I understand there is no chance of the trial before February, probably the middle of that month—and of course if our witnesses are not arrived, we must postpone it—Lewin is cramming Mr Harting, who I suppose will start in two or three days.'

ago, it had been well — but they laughed at my fears — but all is well, victory or defeat. The Church is never more dangerous, than when she seems helpless. Thank you extremely for your sympathy[1]

Ever Yrs affly in Xt   J H N.

TO EDWARD BADELEY

Oratory Bm Nov 28/51

My dear Badeley,

Judge Ball of Ireland wishes us to buy off Achilli, arguing that the fact of his allowing himself to be bought off, if it be known, will be a proof of his guilt. But *how* is this to be done? — 1. It does not rest with Achilli. 2. Where am I to raise the money for an issue so selfish? 3. how can we secure Achilli's not refusing — and — telling? However, I don't like to pass by any thing that comes to me[2]

Ever Yrs affly John H Newman

SATURDAY 29 NOVEMBER 1851   F Ambrose returned

TO J. D. DALGAIRNS

Nov 29/51

My dear F Rector,

There is a difference in your question as viewed as a *new* one, and one which once before was determined on — for now the onus probandi is on the side of *not* taking the House.[3]

Viewing the question in the first blush of it, however, I should say, that the *term* of 20 years renders the matter impossible, considering how large a sum the rent is. At the same time I grant that, in so good a

---

[1] Capes had written on 26 Nov., 'I don't think I ever felt anything so much, beyond the range of my wife and children.

You are in the hands of *the world*, which one sometimes foolishly flatters oneself loses its hatred of the Church, when it gets on the judicial bench.'

[2] Badeley dismissed this on 2 Dec., 'as to Judge Ball's suggestion, surely nobody but an Irishman would have thought of it. . . . It would *of course* be made public . . . That Ass Sir C. Eardley would take care not to let his Hero be bought off . . . the whole scheme appears to me chimerical.'

[3] It had been proposed to rent the house next to the London Oratory for £90 a year. The owner at first refused to accept these terms, but had now changed his mind.

situation, it will not be difficult to let the house again — Shall you be *allowed* to underlet

Ever Yrs affly in Xt J H N

SUNDAY 30 NOVEMBER 1851 wrote to F Joseph

TO EDWARD BADELEY

Nov 30/51

My dear Badeley

1. Achilli was *nearly* brought over by F Theiner to confess his sins, when he was in prison at Rome — His difficulty was 'how shall I live?'[1]

2. He is said to have been seen in Warwick Street Chapel, or in the Oratory, within this year, weeping.

3 He has been a year *resisting* his friends, and could not be brought to the scratch.

4. He has lately said in print, that he was going off.

Could nothing be made of all this? I believe him to be in *thraldom* to the Evangelical Alliance[2] — and if he had the wherewithal he would leave England. I am not certain that he could not be brought, by proper treatment, to do something in our favor. Is it absurd to ask you to think of this? I am sure he hates the people he is with.

Ever Yrs affly J H N

P.S.

1. I will write another letter to the Chronicle, if the inclosed will not do. By all means send it me back.

2. 1. Would it not be well to make Hartin send you a *specimen* of his work, when he has done one piece

    2. How will his papers get through the Customs House?

    3. I postpone F St John going, since Clifford is at Rome[3]

    4. Mr Canning takes up a curious letter from me.[4] Is it *impossible* to

---

[1] See note to second letter of 4 Nov. to St John.

[2] See letter of 1 Sept. to Talbot. Badeley replied that it would be impossible to make approaches to Achilli.

[3] William Clifford, ordained in 1850, Bishop of Clifton in 1857, one of Newman's staunchest friends.

[4] Walter Canning, the Birmingham lawyer, writing to Newman on 4 Dec., mentioned this letter which he brought up to London. It was from Mrs Wise [or Wyse] and told of witnesses to Achilli's offences in London. See last note to letter of 11 Dec. to Badeley.

bring Achilli's *present* conduct in, under my general heading of 'extraordinary depravity —' and 'ravening after crime' etc?

Again, may it not be an opening to negociate with him through Italians? I declare I think he would run off, if means were given him to go.

J H N.

1. The women, I suppose, should be *kept apart* from each other — or Thesiger will make out they took their cue from each other.
2. Would not the Belgian convents be a good place for them? the said convents are poor.
3 Time has so got on, that *I am not eager* to send the inclosed to the Chronicle. I mean, Act according to your judgment.[1]

TO THE EDITOR OF THE MORNING CHRONICLE

Birmingham, Nov. 30. [1851][2]

Sir

There is an impression abroad, founded on what took place in Court, that I do not believe what I said in the passage of my Lecture which is the ground of legal proceedings against me. I should have noticed it sooner, except for reasons which it is not necessary to go into. I believe *heartily* what I have said; I have never wavered in my belief of it;[3] and certainly should not have said it at all, or persisted in saying it, unless I believed it.

Whatever I have said had been said already more fully and in detail, and with extracts of original documents, a full year before I wrote, in an article in the *Dublin Review*, and again in a separate pamphlet, which was in substance a reprint of that article; nor had it been met or answered by the person who is the subject of it.

[1] Newman was enclosing the second draft of this letter about which Badeley wrote on 2 Dec., 'I thought it did very well, and was likely to be of use—'

Badeley had drastically revised Newman's first draft, saying on 28 Nov., 'I think, as it stood, it was far too "*bumptious*"!'

[2] This letter was printed in the *Morning Chronicle* for 2 Dec. On 5 Dec. Newman sent a copy of it to *Aris's Birmingham Gazette*.

[3] In the first draft Newman wrote at this point, 'I have had no repentance or misgiving about what I have done, nor am I likely to have. Legal forms are no measure of inward convictions.

I must gain from what is before me any way; and, though it was my duty to prevent it, if possible, I welcome it, since it is to be. If I succeed, I shall have unmasked an hypocrisy. If I fail, I do but fail in legal proof; I do but fail, till time brings out the truth; I suffer for a truth, and for what all men who inquire will find to be a truth'

And what I said against him I said simply in self-defence. It was an answer to the imputations which, in this town, he had cast upon persons whom I revere, and on a religion which I hold to be divine, to the prejudice of every Catholic here. These charges rested on his personal *testimony*, that testimony on his former *position* in the Catholic Church. I was desirous of pointing out, as I expect to be able to prove, what his *testimony*, founded on his *history*, was worth.

Your obedient servant, John H. Newman.

TO JOHN JOSEPH GORDON (I)

Oy Bm Nov 30/51

My dear F Joseph

You will find Mr Hartin the bearer of this, full of good hope and spirit — just the person for your work. You must help him; and *witness* with your own eyes, (for you *may* have to witness in Court) the fidelity of all his extracts from Books of Inquisition etc — I suppose you have got on with Italian; therefore I am wavering about sending F Ambrose, whom our friends wish to be sent. Besides, you have Clifford and Patterson at hand.[1] I shall write to you by post as well as by Hartin — and so shall *repeat*, I dare say, much. Tell dear Nicholas that I think he should come back at once. I grudge his stopping over Christmas, since we are so few here — but I think he really ought to start on St Stephen's day at latest. As to you, *stay on* and come back with Hartin. The trial will be in the middle of February.

It is an awful crisis, but the *only thing* we want is prayer. If we duly pray, we must succeed in one way or other. In that case defeat will sure to be victory. The boys here have begun to cry out 'Six months in quad.' It will be a trial — but all will be well. Suspence is what tries one; but the greatest suspence is over now that the documents have come. Till then *no one* knew what we had to say for ourselves — it was a land of clouds. The lawyers looked blank. They still promise nothing better than a verdict of guilty — but we shall, I trust, have a *moral* victory — i.e. *if* our documents are admitted in Court, and *if* we can bring witnesses over

Ever Yrs affly J H N

[1] James Laird Patterson (1822–1902), who was at Trinity College, and then curate at St Thomas's, Oxford, had become a Catholic in 1850 and was studying in Rome. He was President of St Edmund's College, Ware, 1870–80, and then auxiliary bishop of Westminster.

TO JOHN JOSEPH GORDON (II)

Oy Bm Nov 30/51

My dear F Joseph

I have just written a letter for you by Hartin.[1] *You* must go about with him as the *paid agent* with him of the Committee at home.[2] Our friends are exceedingly desirous that F Ambrose should go, as knowing Italian. If he does, we have no one left at home — I must think more about it.

Your letters as of last Thursday were [of extr]³eme comfort, and altered the state of things.[4] Our lawyers, and therefore we, were in a *simple fog* — We did not know, till they came, that we had any evidence at all. I wrote to Talbot October 27. He must have got it by the 6th November yet your letter did not start till the 19th — thus Talbot was 12 days *dispatching* what is dated September 22![5] The delay has been *fatal* — the papers came 6 days too late. They would have told powerfully in Court, and *might* have quashed the whole proceeding[6] — but it

---

[1] This second letter Newman sent by post.

[2] i.e. of the committee which had been set up to collect funds for the trial.

[3] Paper torn by seal.

[4] Joseph Gordon's letters of 14–19 Nov. to Newman and 19 Nov. to St John reached Birmingham on 27 Nov. The former told Newman about the documents he forwarded on 20 Nov., first, the one he had obtained through the Neapolitan Prime Minister (see letter of 19 Nov. to Gordon), ' *the notes* which the Police keep of notorious and bad characters—it is the information which they have to give to the Minister concerning A [Achilli]—from the notes or records they have kept of his conduct. It is in no sense a judicial document. . . . Another document Talbot has put into our hand is, in connection with this, of the greatest consequence. It is the *very letter* written by the Minister of Police to the General of the Dominicans demanding the recall of Achilli on account of the notoriety of his crimes, and particularly of the seduction case. It *proves* the facts *alluded to* in the other document . . . Another document of still greater importance, is that which has been furnished by the Holy Office with the Pope's seal, and in which A's confession is not the most important part. It is a statement of the crimes with which A. was charged, *including all those mentioned in the Lecture*, in this country, and others, and the sentence passed on him . . . The difficulty here again is to get it *attested*.' See *Finlason*, pp. 112–14. Gordon added, ' I suppose Talbot has told you of Monsignor Scandella's letter from which it appears that there is ample and positive testimony to the Corfu cases in Corfu.'

[5] i.e. the document from the Holy Office. See letter of 26 Nov. to Gordon.

[6] This was Badeley's first reaction. St John who was in London 27–29 Nov., wrote to Newman by way of consolation, that he 'thinks the documents *might* have stopped the whole proceedings; he does not speak confidently that they would.' On 28 Nov. Badeley himself wrote to Newman. 'So we have got the Documents at last— I doubt whether they would have been sufficient even if they had arrived sooner—what unpardonable delay, when the Paper relating to the proceedings of the Inquisition was ready at the end of September!'

is God's will. We have plenty of money — we shall gain a *moral* triumph if our documents are admitted into court and once witnesses can be persuaded to go to England. The more witnesses, the better — *so that they be good ones.*

I must gain either way — either I unmask an hypocrisy, or I suffer for a truth, and what all men will feel to be true; — but Monsell, Judge Ball, Bowyer, Mr Langdale and such descriptions of persons are most cruelly cut up about it — they say it will dish my influence for ever, if I go to prison for a day. I don't think so — but of course it will be a severe trial to us. I am parting with all my property, and arranging my papers as if I were to die — that I may be quite expeditus. We are getting all the nunneries etc. to pray for us, we can. The poor clares have put on themselves extra austerities! Dr Newsham has had a novena for the whole College, and said Mass for me every day last week. Mother Margaret [Hallahan] has carried her favorite image in procession for three days. I trust the whole Catholic Body will be roused. Dr Cullen, Dr Newsham etc seem to fear nothing so much as compromise — Judge Ball etc say Compromise *any how*, i.e. — buy him off. Monsell, who is here, says that Aubrey de Vere can be of great use to Hartin, and would be glad to be.[1] He understands Italian and would go about with him. Will you bear this in mind, if there is any hitch. *The* difficulty is getting the women to come, and I suppose each must be accompanied with Brother, husband or father. Belgium would be a good rendezvous for them — the monasteries there — and then they ought not to be allowed to talk together — lest they should mix up each other's evidence. *How* will you persuade them? will the Pope's special blessing bring them? I suppose they will be asked in the witness box, *what* induced them to come, whether an indulgence or threat — *what they know of oaths* etc etc. I think this about oaths important. You must send an officer of the court to swear that it is the *proper court* for such persons and such offences. I am impatient to see Nicholas. We want the *sacristan*, Francis having taken to his heels — besides, I suppose we shall want a Rector, if I go to Ireland, and I wish, as far as the looks of things go, to disconnect myself with the Oratory, till the storm is blown over. I am afraid of a mob bullying us.

Don't mind F Frederic's military epistle[2]

Ever Yrs affly with love to idle Nicholas J H N

---

[1] Aubrey de Vere the poet had become a Catholic at Avignon on 15 Nov.

[2] Bowles had written a rather peremptory letter on 26 Nov., telling Joseph Gordon to write frequently, even if there was no news.

TO JAMES HOPE

[[The Oratory]] ⌐Nov 30 [[1851]]⌐

My dear Hope

There is no settlement, but a fight, as Badeley and I, not to say you, expected. It is a great comfort to be out of suspence, and out of responsibility, on the point.

Another comfort in this last three days is, that money seems to be amply forthcoming. A number of persons have undertaken to guarantee the expences and have opened an account.

And a third cause of satisfaction and thankfulness is, that documents have come from Rome. They promise well, if they *are received in Court*. The lawyer employed, Mr Hartin, goes off tomorrow — there is abundance of evidence, but the difficulty is bringing it across the continent

Ever Yrs affly J H N⌐

TO JOHN BUTT

Oratory Bm Dec 1. 1851

My dear Mr Butt

Thank you very much for your kind and welcome letter just received. I shall be very grateful to you for your Masses.[1] Since the middle of August I have been seriously anxious about my present trial, and have said from that time to this, and feel it more and more strongly, that nothing but prayer would get me through it — you may think then how very acceptable your letter is to me.

If we pray enough, we must gain by this unpleasant matter. Should I succeed, I shall have unmasked a piece of hypocrisy. If not, I shall suffer for a truth, which the common sense of the world, certainly the good sense of all who inquire, will feel to be a truth, or at least will eventually discover to be a truth; and that again, tho' a trouble to me at the moment, will be on the whole and on the long run a gain. I have had no misgiving about what I have done, and I am full of hope, for I did not do the original act without a great deal of consideration, and I have a clear conscience. But we must pray. The trial comes on in February

With many thanks, Yours most sincerely in Xt

John H Newman   Congr. Orat.

[1] John Butt, at Mortlake (later Bishop of Southwark), wrote on 30 Nov., promising to say two masses each week for Newman, until his trial was over.

THURSDAY 4 DECEMBER 1851   Hartin went off to Rome   sent a letter by him to
F Joseph

TO ANTONY HUTCHISON

Dec 4/51

My dear F Antony

Can you set any one to get me information, (if possible, by return of
post) what is the best way for an unprotected female to go to Rome by?
Will she be made a barricade of in Paris just now? Or can she get
through the snows of Germany which the papers speak of? — In short
how should she go? And if she must go thro' Germany, can you send
me a small foreign Rail road book?[1]

I do not wish it known — for we must be quite secret in all our
movements — but Miss Giberne is on the point of setting out for Italy
— she is to pounce on one woman at Naples, another at Viterbo, and
forthwith to return with one in each hand.[2]

Ever Yrs affly J H N

I have just heard from F Richard — a fair account of himself, an
unpleasant one of F Wilfrid.[3]

TO RICHARD STANTON

Oy Bm Dec 4. 1851

My dear F Richard

Let Mrs Bowden take this as addressed to her too. Thank her for
her letter. There was a message to you in mine to F Wilfrid. We got off
our lawyer, Mr Harting, to Rome the day before yesterday — and I was
just going to write to you — when your welcome letter comes. I have
been very anxious since the middle of August. Things are about as bad

---

[1] The *coup d'état* of Louis Napoleon was on 2 Dec. Hutchison's final advice was
on 6 Dec., 'By tonight's paper it appears that the insurrection in Paris is quite put
down—If this is the case I suppose the route through France will be in every way the
best.'

[2] These were Sophia Maria Balisano (née Principe) of Naples, who testified at the
trial to having been violated by Achilli in the Sacristy of St Peter's Church at Naples,
Finlason, pp. 81 ff.; and Elena Valente now married to Vincenzo Giustini, from
Viterbo; *Finlason*, pp. 77 ff.

[3] Stanton wrote on 26 Nov. of Faber, 'While here I am sorry to say I did not
think him at all better—he was certainly *not less* restless and excited than when in
London, and I fear more so.'

as they can be. The previous stage of the affidavits is past — the Judges
to *the utter surprise* of our lawyers would give *no time* to get them.
Talbot delayed at Rome. I wrote him the most pressing letters. I urged
him to send off at once *what he had*. He kept *what he had* 12 days —
they came six days too late. Now, we go on to trial; it comes in February.
Humanly speaking, I am certain of being found guilty, for *any one point*
unproved is enough. I have three things against me — three things for
me. Against me, the Judge who will give it against me, if he can — the
Jury, who any how will give it against me (unless there is *one* honest
man to stick out) and the next to impossibility of getting evidence — I
have to bring the very women across Europe in this season! On the
other hand I have for me 1 the truth. 2 prayers. 3 money. A load of
prayers are being discharged daily, and if they don't do something, it is
strange. It is strange if our Lady and St Philip do nothing — but, I am
most thankful to say, (O that it may continue, and I only say it lest you
should be anxious about me,) I have not had any interruption to the
simple feeling, that I am in God's hands, who knows what He is about,
and that every thing will be well, and that I shall be borne thro' every
thing — I cannot at all divine the event, but that it will be good in
some way or other, I am *sure*. We must prepare ourselves for prison.
Badeley said for a year — but considering the circumstance of mitigation, I can hardly conceive it. But recollect, the world is let loose against
the Church. They will do what I can. [sic] But you must all pray —
thanks for the masses you have got for me — It was very thoughtful —
I have sent to get £20 worth at Rome. Nothing will be done without.
Mr Butt wrote to say that he should give me two a week — Dr Newsham
that his whole College was having a Novena — and he saying Mass
every day thro' that week — Convents here, and in Ireland, are praying
on all hands. Hardman, Zulueta etc etc. have come forward for the
expences. I have none. I am sorting my papers, and making up my
affairs, just as if I were going to die; and having all my effects made over
to others. All through the year, I have said we should have some cross
on account of our new building, and when the report of this matter
came in August, I said 'Behold, the cross.' — I did what I did most
deliberately. I went before the Blessed Sacrament and begged to be
kept from doing it, if wrong. I have no misgiving. I cannot wish it
otherwise. It is God's hand; it is His purpose. We shall see in time why.
Many people think it will hurt my influence. It will not. I have said in
print more than once, 'Willingly would I suffer, if the Church is to
gain —' I seem to be taken at my word.[1]

I have been formally elected President of the new University and a

[1] See *O.S.* p. 160.

committee appointed to build. Little more will be done at once — I expect to be summoned to Dublin (where it is to be) to beat up, give Lectures etc etc. and hope (were my Lectures ready) to go in the middle of January, but you may think how all this Achilli business takes up my time. Our house is getting on — floors putting down.

Dec 5. The criminal information is not yet filed, and we wonder at the delay. *I* think it is, that they wish to keep us from setting about our work in good earnest, till the last moment. We shall show up the Maltese College most awfully. Go to Mgr Casolani or Father Tonna, the Dominican, and get from them all the information you can, *preparatory* to Harting's coming.[1] If you could ferret out any thing about Achilli's misdeeds, it would be a great thing. There is a Dr Bonavia, who could tell you a great deal. Write down any *names* he gives you.[2] Mind, what we want is *personal*, primary evidence. We shall not only show up the Record and Shaftesbury party, but (whatever happens to *me*) we shall show up Achilli singularly.[3] Fancy our having *witnesses* to his profligate doings in *London*! while he was in favor with the Parsons! but our object is to get as much evidence as ever we can — There *is* abundance, if we can bring it to bear. I hope you will hear again from us soon.

I rejoice to hear so good an account of your health — You say nothing of John, which is well — I *wish* we could seize on the Malta Oratory. *Can* we? *Who*, alas, will consent to live there continuously even five years? Yet what a great thing it would be for English soldiers and sailors!

Ever Yrs affectly in Jesus and Mary   J H N

Love to all the Bowdens.
I like your plan of travel. Get all the traditions of the Chiesa Nuova you can. It would be a gain, if you could get to their MSS in the Library etc.[4]

[1] Mgr Annetto Casolani, Bishop of Mauricastro, Vicar Apostolic of Central Africa, was a Maltese, and, according to a memorandum of Newman's, resident at that time in Malta. Fr Tonna was Assistant to the Dominican Provincial of Naples. Newman had been told he was in Malta and knew about Achilli's immoralities at Viterbo.

[2] Dr Vincent Bonavia, a Maltese lawyer, brought up as an ecclesiastic, who had become a Protestant, was professor of Latin and Italian at the Malta College. He testified against Achilli at the trial, *Finlason*, p. 98. He was reconciled to the Church in London in 1854, and seems to have entertained hopes that Newman would find him employment at the Irish University.

[3] The *Record* was the weekly Evangelical paper. Lord Shaftesbury, the leader of the Evangelicals, was Chairman of the London Committee for the Protestant College at Malta. See note to letter of 27 Oct. to Talbot.

[4] Stanton proposed to take three months for the journey home, spending half that time in Rome.

TO THE EDITOR OF ARIS'S BIRMINGHAM GAZETTE

Oratory, Dec. 5, 1851.

Sir

I should be obliged by your inserting the following, which has appeared in the *Morning Chronicle,* in your next *Gazette.*[1]

Your obedient servant, John H. Newman.

TO GEORGE RYDER

Oratory Bm Dec 5. 1851[2]

My dear George,

It *cannot* be other than a good and commendable object to get money to keep up your mission — my main difficulty, however, in considering your circulars, is, that you do not state this object.[3]

In the one I return, you vaguely speak of 'relief of *spiritual wants,*' and then go on to speak of '*stockings.*' Even if the reader is not perplexed at the juxtaposition, it will only be to infer that under the *pretence* of 'spiritual wants' you wish to insinuate your stockings.

I think you should say — 'I want to keep up the Mission — it will take £30 (e.g.) to do this — I find if I can get off a certain number of stockings ⟨e.g. 180 pair or 500 pair⟩ at such a price, I *can* raise £30 — therefore will you help me to get them off?'

Ever Yrs affly J H N

TO HENRY WILBERFORCE

Dec 5 [1851]

Charissime,

Your letter is a good one — and it is right you should send it to the Priest of the place. It just occurs to me to ask you, will *he* understand its fun? or *how* will he take it?[4]

¹ There followed the letter to the Editor of the *Morning Chronicle* of 30 Nov., printed above.

² Newman wrote 'Nov', but this has been crossed out and 'Dec' written in pencil.

³ Ryder was trying to help the Catholics around Whitwick, Leicestershire, where he lived, who were in the stocking trade and were out of work, by offering to get orders for them from convents and other Catholic institutions. He sent a draft of his circular to Newman for criticism.   ⁴ It is not known to what this refers.

I shall be truly honored by a visit from Lady Lothian[1] — I am not so oppressed by this montebank Achilli, as to be unfit for ordinary duties — tho' I thank you for your consideration Thank F Pagani too.[2] We shall at least be like Samson — seize the two pillars, Lord Shaftesbury and Sir Cullen, and pull at once the Malta College and the Evangelical Alliance, about our ears, to grace the catastrophe[3]

Ever Yrs affly J H N

SATURDAY 6 DECEMBER 1851   Stanislas went off with sub poena to find F Vincent[4]

TO EDWARD BADELEY

Oratory Bm Dec 6/51

My dear Badeley

Miss Giberne passes through London in her way abroad on Monday next the 8th. She will stay the night, and wait till post time next morning. I inclose the instructions I have given her. If any thing strikes you, to observe or to add, please to write her word, (according to the direction I shall write on the instructions;) and please to send the instructions back to *me*.[5]

Of course the subpoena is served on Dr Hadfield? This is very important. I suspect his Sub, Mr Bryant is in Malta.[6]

As Keosse testifies that, when he went to Malta, he was told that Achilli, who was in *London, did* the same that *he* found the rest (Sacchares etc) did at Malta, surely the evidence of the Regent's Street people about 1845 (the very time I think Keosse speaks of) which Mr Canning brought you an account of, will be important as clenching Keosse's deposition. And besides, will it not come in under the general head of 'profligate'?

Why have they delayed till now filing the Information? is it to get their agents fairly in Italy before ours start.

[1] See diary for 16 Dec.

[2] J. B. Pagani was the Provincial of the Rosminians. Wilberforce was still living at Rugby, which was served by that Order.

[3] See letter to Mrs Bowden of 22 Sept. for Sir Culling Eardley, founder of the Evangelical Alliance.

[4] The Passionist, Fr Vincent Grotti, had been a Canon of Viterbo and knew two of Achilli's victims there. He was stationed at Broadway, but was evidently sent away so that he might not be subpoenaed. See letter of 7 Dec. to Joseph Gordon.

[5] See at the end of this letter.

[6] Hadfield was the Principal of the Protestant College in Malta. See letter of 31 Aug. to Badeley. Bryan was the Sub-Principal.

A parcel of papers have just come from Corfu to Dr Nicholson, and have been forwarded to the Cardinal. I will write to Lewin at once, lest they get into the Cardinal's closets[1]

Ever Yrs affly John H Newman

P.S. Sunday. Lewin has sent me a letter of Messrs Lyon and Co to answer! how can *I*? I have referred him to you. Act for me and I shall be satisfied. Left to myself, I should make no answer at all, but tell them to fish for one; *unless* it compromised the Chronicle.[2]

As their game seems to be to terrify, and ours to be undaunted, on second thoughts I think it might be best boldly to say that I am the author — but you are the judge.

[Enclosure][3]

1 You are absolutely under Mr H's [Harting] orders, and must not act without him.

2 Your work is nothing else but to *persuade* and to *bring* such persons as Mr H. shall point out to you.

3 Go to them, if possible, with a servant of the Borghese family; and use the influence of the family as far as they allow you.[4]

4 Perhaps the Prince will allow his name to be used in promising a safeconduct, a safe return, and proper remuneration.

5 Perhaps he may use his influence with their own landlord to persuade them.

6 Perhaps he will allow them to pass a night in his palace.

7 Perhaps he will let the one remain in his palace while you go to get the other.

8 When you first go to them, do not speak of their coming to England, but of their taking an oath before a magistrate.

9 Thus accustom them to the idea of *giving witness* — If they consent, then leave it, making them some little present, a picture or the like.

10. Leave the matter there at first for three reasons: 1. you will be breaking it to them gradually. 2 you will hinder what you are doing being known, or the opportunity of their being tampered with or frightened and changing their mind. 3 you will have a *hold* over them without *fixing* the time of their coming; for it *may* be as late as May.

[1] The parcel contained documents concerning the Garamone and Coriboni cases. For the former see first letter of 4 Nov. to St John. Albina Coriboni was a chorussinger at Zante, with whom Achilli consorted.

[2] Messrs Lyon and Co., Achilli's lawyers, had written to Lewin, asking if Newman would admit to having written his letter of 30 Nov., which appeared in the *Morning Chronicle.*   [3] These are Newman's instructions for Miss Giberne.

[4] Miss Giberne had been a friend of the Borghese family during her previous stay in Rome, and travelled with them as far as Paris, when she returned to England in 1850.

11. Next, when the proper time comes, first ask them if they would come to *Rome* to take oath.

12 When they consent, break it to them and to their friends, that they must come to England.

13. Urge the Pope's authority, and promise the relations all you can.

14 When they come to Rome, gain an interview for them with the Holy Father, and obtain for them his benediction.

15 As to the *route*, Mr H. must decide it.

16 And so also, their *destination* — but I think some convent in Belgium desirable.

17 Keep us au courant, and, when Mr H. leaves Rome, go by my instructions.

18 Direct to me thus 'Henry Lewin Esqr, Southampton Street, Strand' with J H N in the corner.

19 I will direct to you at Mgr Talbot's, Vatican.

SUNDAY 7 DECEMBER 1851   wrote to Talbot?

TO J. M. CAPES

Oy Bm Dec 7/51

My dear Capes

I am told Morris's book, *part 2*, is so exceptionable, that there is a chance, if it remains in publication, of its getting on the Index — so I advise you not to meddle with it just now.[1] Perhaps the Cardinal will in[terfere?][2] Part one, and good part of Part 3, are excellent, I hear — For me, I have not seen the book yet.[3]

[1] John Brande Morris, *Jesus the Son of Mary, or the Doctrine of the Catholic Church upon the Incarnation of God the Son, considered in its Bearings upon the Reverence shown by Catholics to His Blessed Mother*, 2 Vols., London 1851. Part of the Second dealt with 'The Influence of the Incarnation on the Blessed Virgin.' See also note to letter of 28 April 1851 to Cullen, and letter of 17 Dec. to Capes.

[2] The paper has been cut, for the sake of the signature.

[3] Newman was evidently passing on what he had heard from Ullathorne, who denounced the book to Wiseman. There is at the Birmingham Oratory a copy of a letter from Wiseman to Capes of 11 Dec., sending on one from Ullathorne; who, Wiseman writes, 'has strong feelings on the subject [of Morris's book]. I do not agree with His Lordship in his censures, though I do not like Morris's phraseology.' Wiseman warned Capes to be cautious in reviewing the book, for fear of possible errors in it, 'tho' I cannot believe any grievous ones and certainly not any intentional ones, will be found.'

Capes's review in the *Rambler*, IX (Feb. 1852), pp. 140–54, gave Morris high praise, but made a reservation as to the crudity of his illustrations and language.

The Information is filed against me — and the trial will come on in February. Every effort of course will be made to keep my evidence from *coming into Court*. There will be the battle, I suppose — but if they will not let my witnesses *speak*, how can they expect me to prove *any* thing? How *can* I prove foreign transactions except by foreign evidence?

Ever Yrs affly in Xt[1]

TO JOHN JOSEPH GORDON

Oy Bm Dec 7/51

My dear F Joseph

Proceedings have commenced against me. The trial comes on the beginning of February. Miss Giberne sets off tomorrow, an auspicious day, for Rome. *Tell Talbot* I shall direct my letters to her, to *him*, with *M R G* in the corner. She comes to act simply under Harting's directions. Let *the Borgheses* know, if you can manage it, that she is coming. F Ambrose is not going out.

She comes to *take to England* at once any women who can be got, and prior to this, to *persuade them*. A woman can do this better than a man — and men will be *watched* by the opposite party. The *Naples case* is the most important. Her going out would be abundantly successful, if she could lay hold of that *one* woman.[2] As women are likely to change their minds, *I* should think it best to strike while the iron is hot, and to carry off such women as she got at once — but Hartin and you are judge. *She* will break it to the women much better than Hartin, and it should be done very gradually. They should be accustomed to the idea of making an affidavit, or bearing witness, before *England* is mentioned; — but you on the spot know best. Could not the Pope give his benediction to those who go? The opposite party is most exceedingly sharp, and I dare say, not very scrupulous. Her movements had better be as quiet as possible. I have nothing more to tell you. We are on the look out for news from *you*. Till we get something substantial from Italy, we are not sure of escaping a complete break down. Materials are abundant, but it is difficult to bring them to bear, as Hartin will tell you. *Beware of talking* to *Freeborn* — or any one else.[3]

Aloysius still lives and without much distress. We are terribly anxious about Lady O.A. [Acheson] [who][4] seems to have not many

[1] Signature cut out.

[2] Sophia Maria Balisano, née Principe. See letter of 4 Dec. to Hutchison.

[3] John Freeborn was the British Consular Agent in Rome, before whom Gordon had authenticated some of his documents.   [4] The paper is torn here.

months to live. Say a Hail Mary, theirs [sic] a good fellow, for a friend of yours, not Mrs Phillipps or Marie [?], who is in a deplorable way. I have no right to tell you.[1] They say Morris's book in part is very good, and in part so bad, that some people talk of the Index. No news about the University. I rely on Nicholas coming back immediately after Christmas Day. Bad account of F Wilfrid who is in Sicily. Fair accounts of Richard at Malta. Molloy is at Paris. The plans are to come in 10 days. He says it is a fine church and according to our directions. It will cost £20.000, and may be built in three portions. The flooring goes on at the new House. I told you Francis suddenly stripped himself and left the House, while I was in Town. We have heard nothing of him since.

The Convents in England and Ireland are praying at a great rate for me.

Ever Yrs affly J H N

The Father General of the Passionists and Father Ignatius ought to know that the *only* persons who have not befriended me, but have thwarted me among Catholics, are the English Passionists.[2] This very day dear F Stanislaus is running over England *chasing* F Vincent who is running away from our lawyers, to a great expence and the murder of the Vespers of the Immaculate Conception! We have not deserved this at their hands. We literally cannot find him, and from what has past, it is not uncharitable to surmise they had said of him 'Not at home.'[3]

J H N

I said in a former letter that your expences would be paid by Hartin directly you joined him.

MONDAY 8 DECEMBER 1851   M R G [[Giberne]] went off to Rome

TO MISS HOLMES

Oratory Bm In fest. Concept. Imm. 1851

My dear Miss Holmes,

Tho' a priest cannot introduce the name of your dear Father *into* the Mass, yet he can say Mass for *your intention*, and that intention may

[1] The reference has not been traced. Mrs Phillips had fled to the continent to prevent her children becoming wards in Chancery; see letter of 14 Oct. to Gordon.

[2] Ignatius Spencer was in Rome with the General of the Passionists, Anthony of St James.

[3] Flanagan eventually found Vincent Grotti on 8 Dec. at Taunton. He agreed to go out to Italy to collect evidence, and testified at the trial. *Finlason*, p. 80.

be the repose of your Father's soul.[1] If you like, you shall have 2 Masses for your ½ sovereign one 'for your intention' — the other 'for the soul nearest to its release.'

As to this Achilli matter, I have no right to complain. I have challenged the world and the devil, and they are trying to fetch me a sharp blow. If I catch it, it will turn to good, as all blows do. And as I do not deserve it *morally*, I need not be very anxious about it — However, say all the Memorares you can for me — for I don't mean to catch it, if I can help.

As 'stone bars do not a prison make,'[2] so stone walls do not make a University. At present I am head, not of a material, but of an intellectual and moral body — which in course of time will develop into buildings.

I have got a great number of your letters — and it has just struck me you might like them as a record — I am nervous about keeping things of this kind at my age, lest they should fall into other hands.[3] *I have burned at the time, the most private of them.*

Ever Yrs affly J H N.

TUESDAY 9 DECEMBER 1851   F Stanislas returned

TO GEORGE TALBOT

Oratory Bm Dec 9/51

My dear Talbot

F Vincent the Passionist ⟨(Canon Grotti of Viterbo)⟩ has at last turned up — after being pursued by one of our Fathers for 3 days, including yesterday's feast our great day. His information is most important, and it is a cruel thing that his Superiors have kept him out of the way so long. I write it to you at once, that you may *give it to our lawyer Mr Harting*, before he starts for Viterbo.

The victim whom Achilli ruined at Viterbo in the Sacristy is called *Gippina*[4] — she used to live in the Parish of S. Sisto, vicolo detto il

---

[1] Newman was following the common opinion of moral theologians at the time. They are no longer so exclusive.   [2] Richard Lovelace, *To Althea from Prison.*

[3] Although Newman made a parcel of these letters, he had not sent them when he wrote to Miss Holmes on 16 Jan. 1852. It is probable that they were never sent, for on 6 May 1863 Newman began to transcribe those of her letters which he thought should be kept as a record. This transcription, *The History of a Conversion to the Catholic Faith, in the years 1840-1844, exhibited in a Series of Letters,* is still preserved at the Oratory, together with a memorandum of the reasons for making it. The original letters were burned.

[4] Gippina (or Giuppina) was the familiar name of Elena Giustini, née Valente. She testified at the trial. *Finlason,* pp. 77 ff.

Bottalone. Information may be got of Dr Mencarini, of Canons Ceccotti Nevi, Frontini, Bergasi, Mgr Fratellini, Marge.[1]

The Judge was Anselmi — Cancelliere Canonico Piermartini — Secondo Cancelliere Rosati

Miss Giberne started yesterday, and was to cross to France today — on the mission of persuading the women, either at Viterbo or Naples, or elsewhere — a most difficult job, but necessary, if we are to ensure success. Nothing will resist such a witness, but nothing short will be sufficient — though many things will *mitigate* the sentence, when pronounced against me. If I am to be acquitted, we must have the women or some of them in court. Miss G. is very eager the Borgheses should know the fact of her coming. She hopes to convey her charges, if she succeeds, to Belgium, and lodge them in some convent there. I assure you that, when the Judges confirmed the Rule for a trial, (from the want of Affidavits producible on our side) Badeley told me he thought I should not get off with less than a year's imprisonment.

Perhaps F Vincent will go out to Italy in order to accompany Mr Hartin about; but this depends on the Lawyers and Mr Hardman's committee. I shall send him to you, if he goes out — if you will kindly introduce him to Mr Hartin.

The less our Fathers talk of our plans, witnesses etc the better; else it will all be picked up by the correspondents of London Papers and so be published in England[2]

Yours very sincerely in Xt   John H Newman

WEDNESDAY 10 DECEMBER 1851   letter from F. Richard.   began our novena de B M V [Beata Maria Virgine]

TO VINCENT GROTTI

Oratory Birmingham Dec 10. 1851

Dear Revd Father

I beg to return my thanks to your Very Revd Father Provincial,[3] for his kindness in allowing you to be at our disposal in this unpleasant

---

[1] Newman placed a question mark over the name 'Marge.' The original memorandum of Fr Vincent would seem to read 'Marzi.'

[2] Talbot replied on 19 Dec., 'Your letter of the 9th Inst. reached me here yesterday most fortunately before Mr Harting and Gordon started for Viterbo this morning at 5 o'clock, so that I gave them all the information and names in it. I have also let Princess Borghese know that Miss Giberne will shortly be in Rome. . . .'

[3] Eugene Martorelli, Provincial of the English Passionists 1851–7, and again in 1866.

matter. And I beg also to acknowledge your kindness in being willing to second our wishes.

I have just had a long conversation with Mr Hardman and Mr Canning. They agree with me in thinking you had better at once go to London — Accordingly I have written to the Oratory in London to find you a bed and to pay your expences.

Will you then have the kindness, Revd Father, on the receipt of this letter, without any delay, to go to London — to *Number 24 King William Street*, STRAND (mind, *Strand*, for there is *another* King William Street, two miles off)? There you will be received by our Fathers, who on Friday morning will take you to my friend, Mr Badeley, in the Temple, who will decide whether it is better to ask you to go to Viterbo or not.

Begging the prayers of your holy community, I am, Dear Revd Father, Very truly Yours in Xt

John H Newman   Congr. Orat.

TO FREDERICK FORTESCUE WELLS

Oratory Bm Dec 10. 1851

My dear Alban,

Please receive Father Vincent, the Passionist, who will make his appearance tomorrow (Thursday) — and give him, or find him, a bed. Also let him be taken next morning (Friday) to Badeley in Paper Buildings. Also, please, pay him what he has spent in coming up from Broadway. Badeley will decide whether he is to go to Viterbo or not.

Miss Giberne is full of the praise of your mock turtle — but the poor Passionist will be content with the scraps.

Let James keep the account. I already owe in this Achilli matter to the London House

Imprimis 1, for a cab to Burns — — —
2. a cabman who called — — —
3. a telegraph — — — —

Besides this, I owe on my own score some medicine at Godfrey's.

I write to you because I can take the opportunity of assuring Mrs Hope I never officiated in the reception of any Protestant nun or sister of charity — or heard any woman's confession while I was a Protestant — nor had any thing to do with them. I have referred to my memorandum book of the said Trinity Sunday, and find it runs thus:—

'June 6. did duty morning and afternoon. Church and Marriot

461

assisted me in Sacrament. Lucy Pusey received Sacrament for first time.

preached No 536
dined in rooms.'[1]

Ever Yrs affly J H N

THURSDAY 11 DECEMBER 1851   first letter from Mr Reynolds[2]

TO EDWARD BADELEY

Oy Bm Dec 11. 51

My dear Badeley

Father Vincent, the Passionist, will call on you tomorrow (Friday) morning. If you cannot see him, please, make an appointment with him, He is at 24 King Wm [William] Street.

Mr Hardman, Mr Canning and I, think you should see him. I do not know him. I believe you will find an intelligent, zealous man — he is a man of education and has been a Canon of Viterbo, his native place. He says all I have said is as true as the gospel. One draw back there is that he was not above 13 or 14, when Achilli's offences there were committed — but listen to him yourself.

Till I heard his age, I was for keeping him in England (he is subpoenaed) considering a bird in the hand is worth two etc. but others are for sending him to Viterbo. He has perfect knowledge of the place and people — and being an Italian and a priest would have much influence with those whom we want as witnesses. But then will not Hartin have left the place before he gets there?

You have no need to trouble yourself with writing to me — but give *him* your answer, and let him or whoever comes with him, write to me.

[1] Wells wrote on 9 Dec., 'Mrs H. [Anne Hope, Catholic writer] says in her letter [thanking for Newman's offer to say Mass for Miss Hughes], Fr Newman "can scarcely have quite forgotten Marian Hughes, daughter of the rector of Shennington . . . whom he in conjunction with Dr Pusey and Mr Seager made a sister of charity on Trinity Sunday 1841." Is all this a myth?'

Newman wrote at the bottom of Wells's letter, 'N B. *I* had nothing [more] to do with making her a sister of charity than this, that Seager brought her one Sunday to the ordinary Communion, and told me the *intention* with which she was offering herself to it.'

Marian Rebecca Hughes (1817–1912), daughter of Robert Hughes, Rector of Shenington, Glos., was the first woman to take religious vows in the Church of England, which she did in Charles Seager's house in 1841. In 1849 she founded 'The Society of the Holy and Undivided Trinity' in Woodstock Road, Oxford. See Liddon's *Pusey* III, pp. 10–11, and Peter F. Anson, *The Call of the Cloister*, London 1955, pp. 289–97.   [2] See letter of 12 Dec. to Badeley.

There is another point which I want you to give an opinion on. The said 'who ever' will expound it, and convey your answer to me — It is about Malta.[1]

I am not certain that Lewin is active enough about the subpoenas. This Father Vincent he had instructions from me to find three weeks and more again [sic] — He did nothing, but sent his clerk (I think) to make one call at the Hyde in the Edgware road[2] — One of our Fathers pursued him about the country for three days, found him at last at Taunton, and served the subpoena on him. It seems to me [of] great importance to find Hadfield — I inclose you a note from John Bowden to one of our people — you will see by it, that we have nothing to hope from any voluntary communications of the Maltese College people

Yours affly John H Newman

P.S. I send a second letter, with a notice of Wm Froude.[3]

I am disappointed you considered Castellani's evidence (through Mrs Wyse) only going to *general* profligacy. I accuse Achilli of detestable doings which was the cause of his being sent away from Malta — and *Castellani deposes to some of them.* (which took place in England.)[4]

TO MISS HOLMES

Oy Bm Dec 11. 1851

My dear Miss Holmes

Thank you for your affectionate letter. I will take care that your three Masses are said. As to the 1/ for the postage of your letters, I cannot take it, and return the stamps.

Yrs affly in Xt   John H Newman

[1] It was a question of employing a Maltese lawyer to send witnesses to England. See letter of 11 Dec. to Hutchison. The lawyer Newman had in mind was Dr Adrian Dingli, who was actively helping John Bowden to collect evidence, and who was to become the leading personality in Malta.

[2] This was the house of the Passionists in London.

[3] John Bowden's letter of 2 Dec. reported that the Protestant College of Malta would give no help. The second letter was from Stanton to Dalgairns of 2 Dec., and announced that William Froude was in Malta, 'He seems to have a great affection for him [Newman] and wishes to serve him—He proposes to go and see whether he can get anything out of the people at the protestant college.

He is most indignant at the account he has seen of the trial, particularly at the insinuation that the Padre does not believe what he has said.'

[4] Castellini was working in Achilli's house in London in March 1850, when Harriett Harris, Achilli's servant, mentioned the advances he was making to her at this time. Harriett Harris testified at the trial. *Finlason*, p. 99.

TO ANTONY HUTCHISON

Oy Bm Dec 11/51

My dear F Antony

I am a good deal anxious about Dr Hadfield, whom we want to subpoena, and cannot find. Would Stewart help us or would he peach? Every one must buy books, he could learn his bookseller — perhaps Seeley. Might not some anonymous pamphlet of an anonymous author be found, (say Mr Finlayson's?) which its author wished to present to Dr H.? This would elicit his address. But make something better.[1]

Another thing. It is *impossible* Harting can get through all his work by February — yet I do not like to bore Badeley. Some one will have to go to him with F Vincent tomorrow (Friday) morning. I wish he would propose the following to him, and report his answer, (so that he would not have to write to me.)

'What if F. Stanton were to employ a Maltese lawyer, (so that he knows something of English law,) to send *at once* witnesses to England, *in case* Hartin did not make his appearance at Malta by a certain day — say January 14? — Perhaps, if Mr Badeley came into this notion, he would write down on paper two or three lines of instructions to guide the lawyer and send them *at once* to me.'

Ever Yrs affly J H N

P.S.   Thank F Rector for Mr Lorain's zeal, etc.[2]

FRIDAY 12 DECEMBER 1851   Quarant' Ore set up in our Church   letter from Mr Reynolds Malta which I answered at once and wrote to F Richard   letter from F Joseph   Hartin got to Rome

TO EDWARD BADELEY

Oy Bm Dec 12/51

My dear Badeley

F. Vincent's not making his appearance after our race after him shows *it is dangerous to trust him out of our sight*.[3] Either his Superiors

[1] Stewart wished to try this plan only as a last resort. Hadfield was found about the middle of Dec. F. W. Finlason was a convert, a lawyer and prolific writer.

[2] Canon Lorain of Langres wrote that he was getting convents to pray for Newman's success in the trial.

[3] The Provincial of the Passionists wrote on 13 Dec. to explain that the non-appearance of Fr Vincent was owing to Newman's letter having been delayed in the post. He promised every assistance in the future.

may *keep* him in Italy, or at least he or they may so little understand the value of time as to be *too late for the trial*. So, with deference to your better judgment, I should be against his quitting England.

The letter from Mr Reynolds (whose name is one of those the anonymous informant gave Burns a month ago) is, I suppose, a very important one.[1] Recollect, my view of the whole matter *must* be different from *yours*. You, as a lawyer, look to proving the Viterbo etc cases, as *the* thing — *I* look to the moral question; and if I can prove morally, the Garomone and Coribone adulteries, I am morally acquitted.[2] Therefore I beseech you not to be so absorbed in Italy, as to neglect Malta, Corfu, and London.

Hardman is as urgent as I am that you should *employ* Mr Reynolds for Corfu and Malta. A post goes off (to Malta) on the 18th inst. another on the 23rd I hope Lewin will manage to get a letter off to Mr Reynolds by the 18th or by the 16th — he will receive it on 26th. Two difficulties occur to me in employing him. 1. how will he know what is evidence. ⟨cannot [Dingli],[3] Bowden's Maltese lawyer, tell him?⟩ 2 how will he give *assurance* of safe conduct, payment etc to witnesses?

Another question arises, whether *his* own evidence and those of the other persons he refers to, will not *suffice* without going to Corfu at all?

Then again, will he be useful as interpreter?

At all events Hardman and I hope — 1 that Mr Reynolds will be engaged as a witness for the trial. 2. that Lewin should by the 18th *tell him so* and promise him ample remuneration.

What *more* he ⟨Mr R.⟩ is to do, you must decide.

We are not easy Dr Hadfield is not found and *we* think *we* could have found him sooner

Ever Yrs affly John H Newman

P.S.   I have heard today from Rome. No news, for they think the trial over and I in prison.

---

[1] William Larkin Reynolds, former collector of public revenues at Zante, wrote to Burns and Lambert from Malta, where he had retired, on 30 Nov. and again on 22 Dec. He offered to give evidence as to Achilli's relations with Albina, wife of Vincenzo Coriboni, and to procure documents at Malta and Corfu. He testified at the trial. *Finlason*, pp. 87 ff.

[2] For the Viterbo cases see letter of 4 Dec. to Hutchison, and for Garamone, the first of 4 Nov. to St John. Garamone was brought over to testify, but returned to Naples because of the delay in the trial. Antonio Russo, a carpenter, and Giovanni Patriniani, a jeweller, both of Corfu, testified regarding the Garamone case.

[3] Newman wrote a hardly legible name, with a question mark above it.

TO J. R. BLOXAM

Oratory Birmingham Dec 12. 1851

(*Private*)

My dear Bloxam

I wish you silently to do me a favor.

First see if Hatfield's name is on the Pembroke books. If not, there is an end of the matter.

If it is, go to Pembroke, and get his address. (You may say a person wishes to send him a parcel.) If they say they do not know, because he is in Malta — answer, that he is in England just now. Get from them at least, how a letter would reach him, e.g. what Club he belongs to, what bookseller he deals with, or what religious societies he has to do with. Perhaps Parker could tell.[1]

'Dr Hatfield, Head of the Malta College —' but be quite sure *my* name does not appear in the matter.

This is an urgent matter

Very sincerely Yours John H Newman

P.S. Old Churton, if still at BNC. would know.[2] Perhaps Browell, late Tutor of Pembroke, now in Essex, would know.[3] Or Mr Hill of Edmund Hall — but if *I* am smelt out, you will never get it.[4]

TO ANTONY HUTCHISON

Oy Bm Dec 12/51

My dear F Antony

I have written to Badeley about the non-appearance of F. Vincent.

I wish you *quietly* to do something, and am sorry to bother you, who have duties enough. Entre nous, Lewin (Southampton Street, Strand) must move faster. He ought to have found Hatfield. He *did not* find F Vincent.

Well, now about this important letter of Mr Reynolds's, for which

---

[1] i.e. the Oxford bookseller.

[2] Thomas Churton, Fellow of Brasenose College, 1821–52.

[3] William Robert Browell (1806–67) was a Fellow and Tutor of Pembroke College from 1828 until 1839, when he became Rector of Beaumont-cum-Mose, Essex.

[4] John Hill (1787–1855), Vice-Principal of St Edmund Hall, 1812–51; Rector of Wyke Regis, Dorset, from 1851. Hill replied that he did not know where Hadfield was, and Bloxam offered to make further enquiries.

thank F Rector and two novices. *Lewin must answer it* by the mail which goes out the 16th or 18th. He *must be forced* into this, and you, please, must see he does it.

As to *what* the answer is to be, Badeley must determine, and I have written to him about it.[1]

Let some one, when a letter comes here, give me the Bowdens' *definite* direction.

Ever Yrs affly J H N

P.S.   Ask Lewin to send me *at once* a parchment blank Sub poena — (as I may have to sub poena some one)

TO MISS MUNRO

Oratory Bm Dec 12/51

My dear Miss Munro,

Your letter explains what was a disappointment to me — that you had not been here in November, as you proposed; — that you did not hear from Birmingham, was not my fault, nor Mrs Wootten's. I can only suppose that my matters have so filled the heads of our people, that they have forgotten other duties.

I am very glad to find you write from St Catherine's Clifton. I wish Dr Whitty would find you a vocation there — for it is a really good community, and a sure gate to heaven.[2]

Shall I speak again about your coming here?

Many thanks indeed for your prayers. I *trust* to succeed in this serious anxiety which has visited me, but *solely by prayer* — for 'all things are against me' at first sight. Yet I think prayers have done a good deal already, and will you tell Revd Mother, with my best respects, that things are somewhat brighter than they were three weeks back.

Ever Yours affectly in Xt   John H Newman   Congr. Orat.

Your letter came this morning.

---

[1] Badeley replied on 13 Dec., 'I have seen Lewin and Canning, and given full directions for immediate communication with Mr Reynolds, with Harting, and with Dr Dingli the Maltese lawyer whom Bowden mentions.'

[2] This was Mother Margaret Hallahan's community. Miss Munro had made a promise to consult Dr Whitty about her affairs. She still had thoughts of working under the Oratorians in Birmingham.

TO GEORGE RYDER

Dec 12/51

My dear George

I am sorry that, by mistaking you, I have given you the trouble to write *three* circulars or addresses. Neither the *first* nor *second* will disadvantage you 'spiritually;' so you can send which of the two you will[1]

Ever Yrs affly J H N

My 'suit' is no 'suit,' but I am tried as a criminal.

TO RICHARD STANTON

Oy Bm Dec 12/51

My dearest F Richard

How hard it is that you and Mrs Bowden will not give me your *full* direction, when I want so to write that you may not lose a single post in the delivery. A most important person has turned up, Mr Reynolds of Number 73, Strada San Cristoforo. *Go to him at once*, and say we will gladly employ him. Have a talk with him, and, *if no instructions come by the posts of the 26th ⟨25th⟩ and the 30th*, send him off to get evidence in the Ionian Islands. Furnish him with the text of my libel from the papers — The two cases there are the tailor Garamone and Coriboni's wife. He knows all this. Give him the following references* — as persons who will assist him. Tell him, *we* are told to *avoid* the police in the Islands, for Government is for Achilli —[2] but he will know better than we. *All this is on supposition you do not hear by the 26th or 30th from our lawyers.* If they do not write, *engage him* to come to England as a witness. The trial is in the beginning of February. He must bring Garamone and another witness† to Achilli's being caught with Garamone's wife, and real evidence (which he is *himself*) of the Coriboni case. BUT MIND, the lawyers' letter of the 25th 26th or 30th supersedes all these directions.

Ever Yrs affly Love to the Bowdens J H N

* Pelagio Runi, Priest Catholic Chapter [Chaplain]⎫
   Cefalonia   ⎬ for information.
  P. Gerardini Chaplain to troops, Zante ⎭

† Piperi and Giovanni two carpenters. And another carpenter in the Calle Santa Croce, Corfu.
  At Malta — inquire of Stefano Aignea a broker. Padre Marchetti.

[1] See letter of 5 Dec. to Ryder.
[2] From 1815 to 1864 the Ionian Islands were under British protection.

I wonder you have not found out at Malta the Dominican, Father Tonna, who knows all about Achilli's early life. Send us *at once* an abstract of what he knows, that we may determine whether to send for him or not.

Thanks for your zeal. Your letter is come.

We are getting on pretty well. But, *as yet*, not in the *heart* of the matter, Italy.

SATURDAY 13 DECEMBER 1851   H W [Wilberforce] here

SUNDAY 14 DECEMBER   F Wilfrid got to Rome from Naples   F Nicholas left Rome for England

MONDAY 15 DECEMBER   H W went and F Ambrose with him

TUESDAY 16 DECEMBER   letters from F Joseph and F Nicholas   F Vincent went off to Rome and Viterbo   H W and F Ambrose returned   Monteith here   Lady Lothian in Birmingham[1]

TO ANTONY HUTCHISON

Oy Bm Dec 16/51

My dear Antony

It is provoking about L. and the servant — but it can't be helped.[2] I hope he will think right to subpoena Dr Crawford.[3]

One thing has made me anxious, tho' I don't know it is any good just now to put it before the lawyers — but I wish your Fathers would keep

---

[1] Cecil Chetwynd Talbot (1808–77), only daughter of the second Earl Talbot, married in 1831 John William Kerr, seventh Marquis of Lothian, who died in 1841. Encouraged by Manning, she was received into the Church on 11 June 1851 by Fr Brownbill at Farm Street. Lady Lothian described this visit to Newman, in a letter to her brother-in-law Lord Henry Kerr, soon afterwards: 'He was most kind. I was nervous, but without cause, for he is so full of sympathy and Christian love that he is the last person one need be afraid of. That which struck me most was his childlike sympathy and humility, and next to that, the vivid clearness with which he gives an opinion. He is a very striking looking person. His saying of Mass is most striking. I do not know what makes the difference, but one is conscious of a difference. It appeared to me very unearthly.' *Cecil Marchioness of Lothian a Memoir*, edited by Cecil Kerr, London, n.d., [about 1920], p. 111.

[2] Hutchison explained on 12 and 15 Dec. that Lewin sent a clerk to Miss Lambert, to question her as to statements her servant had made about Achilli, but Miss Lambert put him off. The servant, Catherine Gorman, testified at the trial that Achilli tried to take liberties with her. *Finlason*, p. 103.

[3] Dr A. Crawford was a member of the London Committee of the Malta College. Lewin finally found him at Brighton, on 10 Jan. 1852, but noted in his *Record of Expenses*, 'it appeared that the Reverend Mr Watt was the person who managed the correspondence' concerning Achilli's conduct at the College.

it in mind in their prayers. (*We* are to begin a Novena next week to St Antony for the finding and securing of evidence — when our Novena to our Lady is over)

It is this:— we are told on good authority 1. that Achilli's party is well organized. 2 that it has been preparing for a year and is now quite prepared for every thing we can do. 3 that it intends to *expose* the state of the Catholic Church.

Then comes the report you forward me in Burns's anonymous letter, of their destroying evidence.

This has made me recur to my original suspicion of a secret society — and I fear

1. *at the moment* when they are to set out, witnesses vanishing from Viterbo etc.

2. *counter* witnesses (Italian refugees etc) brought to swear black white, that they have seduced the women before Achilli etc etc. that the priests are all villains etc etc.

Now this makes me feel, more strongly than I did some time back, the necessity of Miss Giberne coming back *instantly*, if she can persuade any of the women — which (unluckily) I gave up in my instructions to her in consequence of what Badeley said.

And secondly it makes it necessary we should have present *at the trial* men who know the state of things, as F. Vincent and other Italians, or F Esmonde, who could refute on the spot, any lies which Achilli's witnesses may tell.

I wish you would have all this in your mind, and see if any thing occurs to you. On the latter point, the Cardinal might suggest.

Ever Yrs affly J H N

P.S. When next you see Lewin, you might (obiter) ask him if he had subpoened Crawford.

TO HENRY WILBERFORCE

Oy Bm Dec 16/51

My dear H

You cannot decide *in a moment*. You must ask the Primate. It will any how be an unenviable office — but Marshall wants to get the whole concern into good hands evidently — and the Primate might be obliged to you. You must know who will be your colleagues — you [who] will support you — whom you will have to fall back upon. I will write a line to Marshall by this post.[1]

I forgot to talk to you yesterday about Miss French — which I now do in confidence. Lady Anna Maria M. [Monsell] *asked* her most kindly to Ireland — then put it off. Monsell comes here — talks little about — she is in fright lest she should be de trop — or Monsell and his wife quarrelling about her. *Can you get at the real state of the case?* does Lady A. M. *wish* her to come.

Ever Yrs affly J H N

WEDNESDAY 17 DECEMBER 1851   H W [Wilberforce] went   Mr Hadfield sub-poenaed about now

TO J. M. CAPES

Oy Bm Dec 17. 1851

My dear Capes,

I have read over Simpson's article once — and will read it again before I write about it.[2] He is the only one of your writers who puzzles me. I wish his Redemptorist friends would give their Imprimatur — and that would exonerate *you*. Perhaps they do.

Jack [Morris] *would* puzzle me too, but he is not one of your writers. I cannot get past his Dedication, which is the only thing I have seen of his book.[3] 'The Mother of Jehovah,' is inadmissible, first as being novel. The word 'Jehovah' is not Catholic — We say 'Javeh' or the like. Still it is unheard of to say 'Mother of Javeh.' Think of the Scythian Monks whose formula 'Unum de *Trinitate* passum esse' found no favor from Pope Hormisdas. 'Mother of Jehovah' seems to incur the same suspicion, for Jehovah is the Name of the Divine Substance, not of Personality — and Morris implies thereby that our Lady is Mother of the Divine Nature. *Till* he justifies the expression by precedent, I think it a

---

[1] Henry Wilberforce had been invited to become Secretary of the Catholic Defence Association, set up by Irish and English Catholics, in view of the Ecclesiastical Titles Act. Henry Johnson Marshall, the former curate of Robert Wilberforce, had just joined the staff of All Hallows College, Drumcondra, and was greatly esteemed by Archbishop Cullen, the Primate of All Ireland. See also letter of 19 Dec.

[2] 'Galileo and his Condemnation,' in the *Rambler*, IX (Jan. 1852), pp. 1–25. Simpson lived near the Redemptorist House at Clapham.

[3] See letter of 7 Dec. to Capes. The dedication was to Wiseman, and spoke of his 'zeal in promoting devotion to the Blessed Mother of Jehovah.'

grave offence — and ought to be withdrawn at once. Did Father Water-worth see it? I doubt it.[1]

I am told he constructs a dialogue or scene, as taking place under the Cross, in which, by way of realizing the circumstances, he throws what is most sacred into the most distressing associations — so as deeply to scandalize pious ears.

To me certainly it is not a question of right or wrong doctrine, but of scandal. If there are such things in the book, (and you allow it) I fear we must have them all brought out in Protestant Reviews etc. of every shade of opinion, with the additional fact, that the book is dedicated to the Cardinal and subscribed for by the dignitaries of England and Ireland.[2]

As to my own matters, if it were not for the marvellous unfairness of the Court in their announcement, I should have hope; for in one way or another we are getting on. But Lord C's [Campbell] conduct has been so astounding that I can believe his suppressing evidence to any extent — and then of course I shall be dished.

Yrs affly John H Newman

TO J. D. DALGAIRNS

Oratory Bm Dec 17/51

My dear F Bernard,

Your most anxious letter has just come,[3] and I reply to it without delay, having first commended the matter to our Lady and St Philip before the Blessed Sacrament.

1. You must not dream of deposing F. Wd [Wilfrid Faber]. You have chosen him for three years — St Philip will not bless you in un-doing *his* arrangement. Three years is no intolerable period — if it be a trial, you must get him to teach you to bear it. Every thing will go wrong, even as a matter of human calculation, if you depose F. Wd. It will be like private judgment, and like waters running out. It will be imitating the restlessness you complain of. The community will crumble into units. If F Wd is not good enough for you, no one will be.

2. I am willing to write (if I know where) to hinder his returning yet, if you think best. I have written once against his *preaching*, and can

---

[1] In the preface Morris thanked his friend William Waterworth, S.J., for reviewing the sheets as they passed through the press. See also first note to letter of 28 April 1851 to Cullen. [2] Newman himself is listed among the subscribers.
[3] Dalgairns's letter is not to be found.

do so without any suspicion. The *expedience* of this step has to be considered. It is staving off the evil, to increase the seriousness of the crisis, when at length he does return. I cannot be a judge of course, but yet I *can* fancy that staving off may be a gain.

3. Can you at all suggest how the F Superior's power should be *limited*? Are there grievances to be arranged?

4. I am much concerned at F. Ay. [Antony Hutchison] having talked over the matter with F. Fs. [Francis Knox]

5. You must not droop. I feel this strongly. You tend to make matters worse than they are. Beware of this.

6. When you were here with F Ay you talked of a basis or formation existing of Fathers who perfectly understood each other. I will not believe this is not a basis of *carità*. I will not believe this is not sufficient to preserve the Congregation. They are as follows, as I understood you; yourself, A. [Antony], R. [Richard Stanton], Ph. [Philip Gordon], James [Rowe], and E. [Edward Bagshawe]; six. Whatever be the state of others, even the F Superior six are, under God's blessing, abundantly sufficient as ballast, and as a principle of life and conservation. Your business is to strengthen the bonds, and deepen the feelings, which unite these Fathers to each other. You may be prepared for any thing, and may defy any one, and surmount all perils, if as many as six remain true to each other. And I think you may avoid the appearance of a clique, or congregation in the Congregation, by prudence and caution of an ordinary kind.

You have every thing in your favor — Your only enemy is loss of self confidence. You must all be firm in your devotion to St Philip, and jealous of the symptoms of disloyalty, and prompt and energetic against wavering, restlessness etc in *any* one.

I wish I could say Mass for you at once — I will as soon as I can. Let me hear again.[1]

Ever Yrs affly in Jesus, M. and Ph   J H N

TO MRS WILLIAM FROUDE

Oratory Bm Dec. 17. 1851

My dear Mrs Froude,

I had heard of Wm's kind zeal for me from my friends the Bowdens at Malta.

---

[1] Dalgairns did not reply to Newman until 27 Dec., when he wrote: 'From your using the word "deposing," I cannot help thinking, you may have mistaken me. What

It is strange that neither he nor John Bowden fell in with a Mr Larking Reynolds, who is helping us very energetically there, and who will go, either by himself or with our lawyer, Mr Harting to Corfu and Zante *Keep his name* secret, except from Wm, for we have no confidence that the opposite party is not doing its utmost abroad in every place to thwart us.

I will add the name of some persons who can be used as *sources of information* — I do not know how long Wm stops in the Ionian Isles — but he had best, if possible, cooperate with our lawyer and Mr Reynolds, if they get there in time.

The time for affidavits is over. The Judges would not give me a day to get affidavits in, tho' I am brought to trial on an affidavit of Achilli's — In spite of my counsel urging that they might be making the Court the tool of a perjurer, they refused me what would have enabled me to prove him so, on the pretence that I did not believe what I said, and was seeking, without knowing of evidence. My first legal notice of the proceedings against me was on October 27. They sent me to trial November 21st — thus allowing less than a month for getting a lawyer and communicating with Corfu, Malta, and Italy — nay it was less than 3 weeks — for the matter did not come into court till November 4.

However, the time of Affidavits is over — and nothing will do but witnesses in court, and they must distinctly bear witness, not to what they have heard, but to what they know personally.

The names I spoke of above are as follows:—

Father Pelagio Runi, Catholic Chaplain, Cefalonia.

Father Gerardini Chaplain to Troops Zante.

Dr Scandella, Malta.[1]

With many thanks and all kind wishes

Yrs affectly John H Newman

F. Antony wanted was your asking him to resign on the ground of ill health. I dare say my letter conveyed the idea of deposition because I felt that what was at the bottom of it was a strong disgust at F W.'s restlessness. I agree to every word you say . . .' Dalgairns went on to say that Hutchison thought Faber acted overbearingly and interfered too much. Dalgairns thought the opposite, and that Faber consulted others excessively, 'he consults us; he is opposed and then he chafes and is irritated. . . . He brooks no opposition.'

[1] John Baptist Scandella, a Spaniard, had been chaplain to British Troops in Corfu. In 1857 he was consecrated in London as Vicar Apostolic of Gibraltar.

TO GEORGE TALBOT

Oy Bm Dec 17/51

My dear Talbot

As our Fathers will probably have left Rome, by the time this gets there, I write to you.

Miss Giberne ought to arrive at it [?] by two days hence — We have not heard of her since she left Paris. In conversation I told her to seize and bring *at once* any women, whom Harting pointed out — afterwards, in her written instructions, I told her, not to bring them *till* she heard from me. I said so under uncertainty *when* the trial would take place. Since she has gone, it seems *plain* it will be in February, and that she cannot be too soon. If then our Lady prospers her so far as to make her persuade any women, she must come with them *at once* — and take them, by such route as she thinks best, to Belgium. We meanwhile will inquire about Convents in Belgium which will take them in.

A letter from Miss Giberne has just come, dated Marseilles — where she has just escaped a boiler which burst in the steamer. I trust her good angel has brought her to Rome by today, or will by tomorrow. She must be put in communication with Father Vincent, Passionist of Viterbo, who left London for Marseilles yesterday (16th) Her one object is to persuade and bring the women. Nothing has yet been said to *her*, how she is to get money for her and their journey to England, but I think Mr Chomleigh is to find it.[1]

I told F Gordon he was to come back with F. Darnell directly after Christmas Day, *unless* he really was wanted in Rome by Harting or any one else. If he is wanted let him stay of course.

At present I am anxious about two things — first lest our opponents should hinder us bringing over our witnesses — for I suspect they are in league with the secret societies in Italy — next, lest they should bring false witnesses to contradict our witnesses, to lie about the *state* of the Church, the priests etc, to swear an alibi, etc etc. We ought to have two or three men like F. Vincent in Court to meet emergencies of this kind. *This* difficulty has struck me, viz. that he ⟨Achilli⟩ may deny that he is *the* Father Giacinto who committed the offences, the witnesses not knowing his surname. I suppose Harting will provide for the proof of identity

---

[1] Lewin's record of expenses shows that the reference is to Messrs Plowden and Cholmeley, Bankers, 234 the Corso.

We shall have judge and jury against us, I fear. Still, they say there *is* a proof which is irresistible, if we are prepared to produce it[1]

Ever Yrs most sincerely in Xt   John H Newman

THURSDAY 18 DECEMBER 1851   Molloy returned from Paris, with the plans (*of the Church?*)[2]

TO MRS WILLIAM FROUDE

Oratory Bm Dec 19/51

My dear Mrs Froude

There is one thing which William could do. We know, Mr Reynolds, late in the Police or Customs at Zante, to be a most respectable man — but of course our opponents will be saying every thing they can to impeach his motives etc when he comes forward against Achilli.

It would be a great gain if William could quietly get information about him, his relation to Government, to Achilli etc — that we may be prepared with *answers* to any attack on him.

Do not mention his name except to William.

Ever Yrs affectly John H Newman.

TO HENRY WILBERFORCE

[19 December 1851][3]

My dear Henry

Your letter to a dead certainty went in time — at least quite as much in time, as if it went 3, 4, or 5 hours earlier; *for* it went between 9 or 10 and the box does not close till 10. There's no doubt of it — See whether *this* gets to you tomorrow (Saturday) morning.

⌈You must accept — but I advise you to go at once to Dublin and *make terms.*⌉

It is lucky you did not go on Tuesday night — for then you must have said Yes or No — now without having that responsibility — you

¹ Talbot replied on 29 Dec. that the two witnesses from Viterbo had come to Rome. Elena Valente and her husband were willing to go to England, but Rosa di Alessandris and her husband peremptorily refused, on the ground that they had six children and that she was pregnant.

² Those of Viollet Le Duc for the proposed church at Birmingham.

³ This undated letter must refer to Wilberforce's election, on 17 Dec. 1851, as Secretary of the Catholic Defence Association. Had Wilberforce left for Ireland on Tuesday 16 Dec., he doubtless would have attended, on the following evening, the meeting in Dublin, at which he was elected Secretary.

can secure things your own way. ⌜Write to Monsell, and get his advice⌝ directed to you at Dublin

Ever Yrs affly J H N.

P.S. ⌜Call here in your way to Dublin, and I can tell you one or two things.⌝

SATURDAY 20 DECEMBER 1851 M R G [Giberne] got to Rome H W [Wilberforce] came?

TO J. M. CAPES

Oy Bm Dec 20/51

My dear Capes

As your article on Mr Weale, is evidently meant in kindness to allude to my matter, I will speak about it.[1] Could you speak, without any suspicion whatever that you represented the same principle and party which I do, it would be useful to adopt the tone you do against the Judges — but I fear, as matters stand, its hurting me. I fear its irritating people against me. The Judges have done one wrong — there is a chance of their coming to their senses, and feeling their injustice, if let alone — none, if they are taxed with it. After it is all over, I should [be] disposed (did I consult my own feelings) to let out, whether I succeeded or not — but we must bide our time.

Mr Weale's case hardly came before *Judges* — it was the counsel apparently and the Home Secretary who were in fault.[2]

Ever Yrs affly J H N

TO GEORGE TALBOT

Oratory Bm Dec 20/51

My dear Talbot,

There is one point of evidence — about which I am anxious, and which we can get evidence of from Rome — viz Achilli's corrupting the *morals* of priests and others, as well as the *faith*.

[1] In 'Protestant Justice and Royal Clemency,' a review of *Statement of Facts relative to the Case of Mr William Weale, Master of the Poor-School at Islington*, in the *Rambler*, IX (Jan. 1852), pp. 79–84, Capes made an attack on English magistrates and juries for their unfairness towards Catholics. See also note to letter of 25 Nov. to Hope.

[2] Weale's barrister apparently made no defence whatever, and when the case was referred to the Home Secretary, with a petition that the sentence should be remitted, the memorial remained unanswered for nearly a month, and then the refusal was announced by means of a printed circular.

De Sanctis is the most obvious of his victims.[1] His brother is or was organist at Propaganda — and might give or point to good evidence on the point. I think people in Rome ought to be able to make good this point

Has *Father Borg* the Dominican, one of the Penitentiaries at St Mary Major been used as much as he ought? He knew Achilli at Viterbo.[2]

Where is Father *Tonna*, who knew him well at Viterbo? — he seems not to be at Malta now.

I do not write this, to give *you* all the trouble; but that you may put this letter into the hands of Father Vincent, or Mr *Hartin*, if he is still at Rome.

When you see Miss Giberne, tell her I have nothing yet to write to her. F Vincent left London for Rome on the 16th.

Dec 22. We send in our *Pleas* tomorrow, and are sadly crippled by having had no news at all from *Capua*. F. Salzano of Naples was to have sent a number of papers from the Archbishop of Capua.[3] None have come. Our great trouble all along has been that we have not known *what to promise* the Court. This lost us our first application, and has thrown us into a trial. I know how occupied your time is. Give this letter to *Gordon, Clifford*, or *Harting* to attend to — but it is *important* that the points I have put down, *should* be attended to.

9. P.M. Darnell not yet come — but I don't like to delay this longer.

Ever Yours most sincerely in Xt

John N Newman   Congr. Orat.

Dec 23. Miss Giberne's letter from Leghorn, giving the frightful account of her accident, came last night; and Frs Gordon and Darnell's letters of the 12th We are expecting Darnell but have not yet heard of him.

Another thing — We want more *proof* of Achilli being, what I have called him, an *infidel* while professing Catholicism. Can De Sanctis, the organist, or any one else, furnish it?

---

[1] See letter of 16 Nov. to Cullen.

[2] Fr Augustine Borg, according to John Bowden's letter of 9 Dec. to the London Oratory, 'was professor of the seminary at Viterbo with Achilli, and was ejected from it by Cardinal Pianetti at the same time for the same reason, although he was afterwards proved completely innocent, and reinstated by the Cardinal. This Borg lives, I believe, in the Penitenzieria, but may be heard of at the Minerva.'

[3] Michael Thomas Salzano (1810–90) was Provincial of the Naples Province of the Dominicans. He was a professor of Theology and canon law 1834–50, and in 1854 was named titular Bishop of Tanensis, and in 1873 Archbishop of Edessa.

MONDAY 22 DECEMBER 1851 F Ambrose went to Town for the day to be at Badeley's during the drawing up of the Pleas H W [Wilberforce] went to Ireland about the Secretariship

WEDNESDAY 24 DECEMBER F Nicholas returned from Rome

TO ANTONY HUTCHISON

Buona Festa   Oy Bm Dec 24/51
My dear F Antony

I am sorry I have subjected you to any thing so unpleasant.[1]

Blunder has attended every step of our proceedings hitherto — and unless prayer get us out of our difficulty in the event, I don't know what we have to rely on.

The Bm [Birmingham] Lawyer has been very eager, I should go up to be present at the deciding on the Pleas — Badeley has been against it. They were drawn by the *first Special Pleader*, Chitty,[2] — when they came down here on Saturday, I found them so full of defects and errors, that, in spite of Badeley, I sent F Ambrose to him. The Pleas were to be given in as *yesterday* at latest

When Ambrose got to Paper Buildings, he found Badeley as angry with the legal aspect of the Pleas, as I with the common sense aspect. He expressed no pleasure at seeing him — *nevertheless* Ambrose did essential service, *when only* a priest *could*; for tho' Badeley knows a great deal of ecclesiastical matters, a priest knows more. Badeley was in a state of great discomfiture at the *corner* into which they were driven. For *the Pleas decide the whole course at the trial.*

When Ambrose came back here, I found there was still so much to do, and such delicate work, that I said — 'How in the world will they finish?' 'Will they have the sense in a difficulty to apply to King Wm [William] Street?' At last I thought it best to secure your presence, as an *appeal* in points of difficulty. (E.g. [Ambrose] had to tell them the nature of the vow of chastity at the Subdiaconate.)

It has been a failure, and it cannot be helped. The Pleas are now *in*, and St Philip must supply what is wanting.

---

[1] Hutchison had received a telegraphic message from Newman on 23 Dec., telling him to 'go to B and Co and wait till 3 p.m. and to take Nicholas there too.' This Hutchison took to mean, as he wrote the same day, that Nicholas Cardinal Wiseman was to be taken to Badeley, but he decided to go and ask Badeley if he wanted the Cardinal. The latter replied 'Cardinal, no, he can't draw the pleas, can he?' and sent Hutchison away. Newman's letter explains what he intended.

[2] Thomas Chitty (1802–78), legal writer; special pleader, 1820–77.

'Nicholas' meant, as usual, F. Nicholas, who I heard by Monday's Post was to be in Paris on Sunday, and here yesterday or today.

Ever Yrs affly J H N

P.S.   Nicholas just come — he does not bring promising news. Hartin cannot get from Rome the documents Badeley wants.

THURSDAY 25 DECEMBER 1851   sang midnight mass

TO EDWARD BADELEY

Oratory Bm Christmas Day 1851

My dear Badeley

The best blessings of the Season to you — I am concerned to hear your eye still tires you — of course it is rest you want. I am not certain yet whether you want the draft of the Pleas back by return of post. I suppose you do.

One of our Fathers returned here from Rome yesterday, and he says that no one seems to anticipate any difficulty in getting the women — however, he brings one uncomfortable piece of news. I fear we shall not get any more from the Inquisition. What annoyed me more than this apprehension, however, was the *readiness* with which Harting acquiesced in this. He was going off to Viterbo, thinking his Roman work done.

There is plenty of time to take further measures. 1. Shall we prime Manning to have a talk with Talbot, whom I have some fear I may be urging too hard and rudely?[1] 2. Will a priest, if not Harting be allowed to see and take a copy? 3. Would it be any good if the priest, who made the affidavit, were to come over, and swear to the contents of the Records in *court*? 4. Could an affidavit be prepared, or a person brought to testify, that it was against oaths etc. to produce the Records — so that second hand evidence was the best that could be got?

I hope to say Mass for you, in all those various aspects in which you

[1] This must have been a report Darnell brought from Rome. On 19 Dec. Talbot himself wrote, in a letter which reached Birmingham on 26 Dec., 'I was sorry to hear that you had expressed an opinion that I had been dilatory in the execution of your commissions to me, for God is the only witness of the trouble and anxiety I have been put to in doing all I could to serve you.' But Talbot did not explain his delay in sending the document of the Inquisition. See also Newman's reply on 26 Dec.

have a claim on me, tomorrow, St Stephen's Day. What a sad thing you cannot get to Hope by Christmas Day![1]

Do not suppose I am recommending *getting rid* of the Attorney General, unless we saw something *much better*. I *suppose* he will exert himself. Bellasis thought so. Why don't you take Mr Watson as a second?[2]

Ever Yrs affly J H N

P.S.   With the respect to the word 'infidel,' of which you say little enough in the Pleas, will the following thought do any good?

I call A. [Achilli] an infidel — well, it is answered, '*my* sense is not the popular sense of the word —' my sense is a technical sense and will not stand. Still — *if* he says there was a time, when he had not *faith*, *was* he not *then* by *his own showing* an infidel? You will answer 'Ah, but he meant something else by faith, he meant, he had not faith in its evangelical sense.' But surely I may retort — Here, *you too* are technical. If *he* says that from 1830 to 1835, he was without faith, surely *I* have a right to infer that during that time he was an unbeliever or infidel.

Now he asserts it in such passages as the following.

'They (his enemies) undertook to explain to others my *profession of faith*, which I had *not yet been able to make out clearly* to *myself*.' p 37[3]

'I possessed the understanding of faith, *but not faith itself* . . . I stood midway between the old and the new man; the old man was already buried, but the *new man had not yet come to life*.' p 25 What is this but saying (to the *popular* apprehension) 'I disbelieved *Catholic* doctrine, without believing as yet *evangelical*?'

Again, 'I was already a Protestant,' (i.e. I had given up *Catholic* doctrine) '*but not yet sufficiently a Christian* . . . My virtue arose from self love, and not *from faith*.' p 183

I *know*, all this is an Evangelical sense of the word faith — but has he a right to put his interpretations of the word 'faith,' and I no right to put my sense upon the word 'infidel?'

NB.   Father Darnell brings word that Achilli's *signature* occurs several times in the Inquisition Records of his trial.

P.S.   I am too tired to send the Draft up tonight.

---

[1] Badeley was planning to go to Hope at Abbotsford for a rest, and also to discuss Newman's trial, and the possibility of finding someone to assist or supplant Cockburn.

[2] William Henry Watson (1796–1860) had been present at the battle of Waterloo. He was a well-known barrister, who became a Queen's Counsel in 1843.

[3] The quotations are from Achilli's book, *Dealings with the Inquisition; or Papal Rome, her Priests and her Jesuits: with important Disclosures*, London 1851.

FRIDAY 26 DECEMBER 1851   Lady Olivia Acheson ill — confined to her room
and bed — her last illness

TO EDWARD BADELEY

Oratory Bm Dec 26/51

My dear Badeley

A happy Christmas to you, if I have not already said so. — 1. Would
it be prudent in me to write a private letter to Mr Hadfield, whom I
knew a little in Oxford, saying how sorry I was to put him to the inconvenience of a subpoena — that I did it because it was the easiest and
readiest way in which I could bring out the information I want — but
I would dispense with him, if I could — that he might be hindered by
honor etc. from giving me information as to sources which would dispense with him, but if this were not the case I appealed to his sense of
justice. etc.

Though I have so put it, I should not put the subpoena in the *fore
ground*, but rest my letter on the *justice* which he owed to a person like
myself suffering for what *he* knew to be a truth, and *apologising* for the
subpoena.

Would this be unsafe, or absurd?[1]

2. I have some notion I have seemed uncivil at Rome for not sending
some *formal acknowledgment* to the dignitaries etc. who went to Freeborn
to make affidavits.[2] This may be causing a hitch. I propose then at once
to write to Manning to say that the papers in question had gone to the
lawyers, and that *I* had never seen them, but that I wished him to go to
Talbot at once to ask him how he (Manning) could from me convey
thanks etc. And it strikes me secondly that if *you* followed up this letter
by a letter, as a *lawyer*, (*not from me*) written to Manning, urging on him
the importance etc of what you want, which he may show to Talbot.

One thing I will add to what I said yesterday. Would not personal
evidence of the mere *verdict* of the Inquisition, and of Achilli's signature
in the books of the Inquisition, be a *confirmatory* evidence? if we could
not get primary.

Ever Yours affectly John H Newman

Miss Giberne got to Rome the 20th
P.S.   I don't wish to bore you about the *London* offences; do the Pleas
admit of their *possible* introduction in evidence? — The case seems to

---

[1] Badeley approved. See the letter sent to Hadfield on 31 Dec.
[2] These were Angelus Argenti, notary of the Inquisition, and Vincent Leo Sallua,
O.P., his assistant.

me strong. Achilli, a *servant* of the Malta College, comes to London to collect money for *it* — and *during this visit*, if I understand the dates right, (1847?) he commits the excesses of which Mr Canning has notice; his friends meanwhile, at Malta, acknowledging and defending him to Keosse.

P.S. Could not something be brought out as to the Malta College charges, by subpoenaing some of Achilli's own friends, as Tonna?[1]

(My definition of infidelity is '*disbelief against authority*' and this I think *is* the common use of the word.)[2]

TO JOHN EDWARD BOWDEN

Oy. Bm. Dec 26/51

My dear John,

I write to John, for Richard may be gone, and I don't write to your Mother, because I am going to write upon business. Buona Festa to you all. You ought to have got a letter this morning (i.e. F. Richard) about a Mr *Larkin* Reynolds, late in the customs of Zante, who is the *only* important person who has not yet turned up. I have just got a letter of F Joseph's who will be with you before you get this, (F Joseph's is of the 19th) telling me of failures; he was starting for Viterbo.[3] However, tell him Sacchares is found to be in Rome, and may do something for us.[4]

I write to you at once, for fear Hartin, who is our agent, may miss Mr *Larkin* Reynolds. The latter will undertake the Corfu matter for him, if he has not time — and Hartin is to be paymaster.

Tell F Richard, if he is still with you, that I think Malta does not agree with him; and perhaps Rome would. He should give a long trial

[1] This was Lewis H. Tonna, not to be confused with Fr Tonna, O.P. He was secretary of the 'Committee of the London Society for the religious improvement of Italy and the Italians,' who sent a memorial to the French Government on 4 Oct. 1849, to ask for help in 'freeing Achilli from the Roman Inquisition.' Lewis H. Tonna also wrote a *Letter to Dr. Wiseman*, in defence of Achilli.

[2] For the reasons why Newman called Achilli an infidel see *Appendix* 4, p. 505. In the pleas the term was left undefined, and Badeley wrote on 28 Dec. that the lawyers had come to the conclusion that it was better to leave it so.

[3] Gordon's letter is dated 18 Dec. One failure was the impossibility of getting a copy of the record of Achilli's trial before the Inquisition. Harting obtained only an extract which included Achilli's confession. Another failure was the inability to secure as a witness the girl Achilli had seduced at Naples. Gordon returned to Rome from Viterbo on 23 Dec.

[4] See letter of 31 Aug. to Badeley. Saccares did not testify at the trial.

to Rome — I should have prosed to him, (did I write to him) about his posting himself in Chiesa Nuova, with the leave of the F. Superior, remaining there till he got well. He might do the English Oratory an immense deal of good by being at head quarters.

Aloysius is still alive very cheerful and without much pain — F Nicholas returned to us Christmas Eve. Joseph goes with Hartin to Malta. We have got our plans for our church, and are much pleased with them, except that the architect makes the aisles and nave too narrow.

I am so much obliged to your Mother and the rest of you for the Masses, Novena, prayers etc. Of course good *must* come of it. I cannot fancy *justice* being so overpowered that I should not gain at least a *moral* victory. But if it is to be not even this, depend upon it, it is for some greater good; and I have no right to complain because it is what I have said, not once only, 'The preachers of religion suffer, but their cause succeeds —'[1] and I have said that I gladly resign myself to the operation of this principle. *If* we go on steadily praying till the matter is over, all must be well. And please, pray for me that I may be blessed with evenness of mind and serenity, whatever befalls me. If we give up prayer, we are done; actum est. Love to all of you

Ever Yrs affly in Mary & Philip J H N

(I received F Richard's letter this morning)

TO GEORGE TALBOT

Oratory Bm Dec 26/51

My dear Talbot

Your letter of the 19th has just come, and I write instanter, (wishing you a buona festa) to assure you how very sensible I am of your extreme kindess, and the zeal with which you have taken up my matter. I am only truly sorry to have given you and other friends so much trouble — and should have felt I had no right at all to do so, were not Cardinal Wiseman, and the cause of English Catholicism, involved in a blow aimed against me.

Your letter suggests two things — 1st Is Sacchares *really* in Rome? *would he come to England*, and bear witness against Achilli — his evidence would be *decisive* if either he could *witness* to Achilli's irregularities or could depose to *avowals* which Achilli had made him. If he felt reluctant, why, it would be the best of penances — it would be a reparation.

[1] 'Christ upon the Waters,' *O.S.* p. 160.

2nd F. Vincent started the 16th. Harting and F Gordon were to start for Naples, at latest today, the 26th. Therefore the chance is he will never see them. Will you then see that he proceeds to Viterbo, and tell him what they have done there, and what they have left to be done — and what use he can turn Miss Giberne too? [sic]

I have just got Miss Giberne's letter of the 20th and would write to her, except that I have nothing to say, except to thank her, which I do heartily.

F. Faber has given me an account of the feeling manner in which his Holiness has condescended to speak of me. It is a great support to me under my trial — nothing can be wrong, if St Peter is for me.[1] I also feel deeply the kindness of the F General of the Dominicans[2] and others who have exerted themselves for me

Yours most sincerely in Xt   John H Newman

P.S.   I am anxious about another thing. A *most* important letter from our lawyer to Hartin went from London the 16th — about a person at Malta of the name of Larkin Reynolds — it ought to be got to Hartin at once.

TO ANTONY HUTCHISON

Oratory Bm Dec 28/51

My dear F Antony

I think we *have* sent you the kind wishes of the season — else I do now. What I write about has been on my mind some days, but I have been so busy. Father Nicholas brings the news of F Wilfrid having got to Rome — nay he himself, I ought to say, has since written me word from Rome that he is to be home by the Epiphany. I am very sorry for this, and would write to him, were it possible to catch him. St Philip always obeyed his physician — as far as I know, *he* has done nothing but disobey his. I wrote to him to Malta, by the suggestion of some of you, to hinder his preaching — the next I heard of him, was his preaching at Messina in Italian. Suddenly he is at Rome, and as suddenly he will be in England.

I must say I wish I had power over him — but a physician surely

---

[1] This letter is not to be found.

[2] Vincent Jandel (1810–72) was one of those Frenchmen who, with Lacordaire, restored the Dominicans in France. He was a reformer, who was appointed Vicar-General of his Order by Pius IX in 1850, and in 1855 General.

has; and if his medical men persist in the anxious opinion they gave in October, I am quite ready, if your Fathers think it right, to urge upon him as strongly as possible to follow out their advice. His letters to me have been far from satisfactory. I like his assurance that he is quite well even less than his saying, if he said it, that he was very ill. It has struck me some time, that it would be a good plan, as well as a buona penitenza, to make him go to America — He would have a good deal of sea, a country with little to excite him, and an opportunity of doing a great deal of good by showing himself. But any how, his life and powers are too precious, to let him throw them away, which he will do, if allowed. It is not often a Superior has an opportunity of obedience, in following the directions of his physicians, he is making one.

But how will things go on without him? How have they gone on since he went? I wish you would let me know how — 1. the whole house has fared. 2. how the novices. 3. how the lay brothers.

Ever Yours affectly J H N

P.S.   If you think it worth while, I wish you would ask F Bernard to answer me the 3 questions at the end as well as you.[1]

TO J. D. DALGAIRNS

Oratory Bm Dec 29/51

Charissime,

I know how difficult it is to rouse and raise the mind, when it is floored and prostrate, and I see perfectly how much you must have had to beat all spirit out of you, yet I still think you exaggerate, and let

---

[1] Hutchison replied on 29 Dec. '1. As to how the *House* has gone on since his absence—I think really very well on the whole—there have been no rows—. . . . 2. As to the Laybrothers, they I think are in a good state and are improving. . . . 3. As to the Novices—this department is not quite in so satisfactory a state. . . .'

Hutchison added that if Faber returned no better than he went, he could not be allowed to stop at the London Oratory. Hutchison approved of the idea that he should travel to America, and suggested as an alternative that Newman should ask him to resign, on the ground of ill-health.

Dalgairns also replied on 29 Dec. as to Faber, 'If he comes back as ill as he went, he certainly is better away. He only remained in his room, creating rows in the house and living apart from the Community.' Dalgairns, however, feared the effect of being ordered away again on Faber's spirits, and on 30 Dec. suggested he might remain, with his work regulated by Newman. '. . . you must help us, for he certainly *will* not and cannot be under obedience to any one here.' Newman, meanwhile, had written to Faber.

despondency to bear hard [sic] upon reason and good sense, as I think I can show you from your own words.[1]

It is not necessary for carità, even humanly considered, that the objects of it should be strong minded or should agree with us in opinion, but that they should be *amiable*. Now you say of A. [Antony Hutchison] 'I love him much, but I disagree utterly in his views about Philippine government.' Surely here is a sure material of a *basis* — where hearts are one, things find their place, and where there is a will, there is a way. Then again you say of Ph. [Philip Gordon], he 'has not the slightest strength of character —' Still, I think he is a person whom you could easily *love*. And why are James [Rowe] and Edward [Bagshawe] non-entities? because they are still novices? but what hindrance is that to your loving them and they you? If you mean any thing else, I do not know enough to understand what you are aiming at. F. Richard again is away — but, I trust, not for ever. I think any one could love him who tried. There is a chance of life and health as regards *every* one, but still I do think I have named five persons whom you could love — five persons who could love each other. And I do not see at all why such six might not 'swear an eternal friendship,' and stand by each other, whatever happens. So clear does this seem to me that I think your difficulties do *not* lie here — but that you mean — 'Yes, but there are *other* inconveniences and troubles, some of which I have *not* named, which are insupportable.' This, I fear, is the real state of the case — and, it being so, nothing but a firm loyalty to St Philip will keep things going, but I think *it* will.

Your complaint about the want of tenderness, gentleness, courtesy, and sympathy, in your congregation is, alas, most true, and I think most unphilippine, as you describe. Had you not said it, I should not have ventured to have a clear opinion that it was so — but directly you say it, you collect together all the scattered surmises of my own mind as in a focus, and throw from my own impressions a clear light upon your own testimony. Yet here again A. is very different from what he was — this is a matter of common remark. Again, I am sure Ph's turn of mind is not such, but, whatever be his faults of character, he is gentle like yourself. Nor do I think that James would be otherwise. Certainly not Richard — It would seem then as if some overbearing influence, or some bad habit, or youngness, or want of experience of trouble, has

[1] Part of Dalgairns's letter of 27 Dec., to which this is a reply, is quoted in last note to Newman's of 17 Dec. Dalgairns also wrote in his letter, 'You say I take a gloomy view and you talk of a basis of carità. I acknowledge my gloom, and disbelieve in the carità. Of the six you mention, James and Edward are non-entities. Philip has not the slightest strength of character.' Dalgairns added, 'I am broken in spirit. . . . All this has filled me with temptations to leave the Congregation.'

been here or there the cause of this, in those who are its promoters. I trust in time the evil will work out. F. A's change is a happy token that it will.

However, nothing I have been saying interferes with my acknowledging how much must be done to put the Congregation on a better footing. On this subject I will not write today — but in conclusion I will remind you that all *Acclimation* is painful, and acclimation in a religious body as much as any one. No one but a Jesuit or a Trappist, knows what a Jesuit and Trappist goes thro' in becoming a Jesuit or Trappist — but the vow binds them and they must go thro' it. What do women go through in accommodating their lives to the will of a husband! when they have done it, it is their happiness. *We* have no vows — and there is an urgent temptation to break away from that from which we can break away. We are able to speculate on want of peace and rest, for we have no vow to hinder us. But will our impatience benefit us? What religious order would suit us better than St Philip's light yoke? As to the secular clergy, see how all our own friends, and those who seem most like them, rush away into the ranks of the regulars — (Amherst passed through this place yesterday, in his way to St Domenic)[1] — You indeed *could* go to France — but somehow I do not think you could feel you had a call to desert poor benighted England — however, I will say no more today[2]

Ever Yrs affly John H Newman

P.S.   Many, many thanks for all your Masses on Saturday.

TO ARCHBISHOP CULLEN

Oratory Birmingham Dec 30/51

My dear Lord Primate

You may think with what interest I waited for the result of the proceedings which attended the appointment of Mr Wilberforce, and how

---

[1] Francis Kerrill Amherst (1819–83), a priest at Oscott, had decided to try his vocation as a Dominican, entering the Novitiate in 1853. His health obliged him to leave two years later, and in 1858 he was made Bishop of Northampton.

[2] Dalgairns replied on 30 Dec. 'You did not suppose that I had any formed design of leaving St. Philip. What I did mean was that if this state of outward restlessness and interior suffering continued, it seemed in my present mood as though it would turn out to be unbearable. . . . Would it not be well for you to say to F.A. what you have said to me about a "basis of carità," about rudeness to each other etc. How can we thank you enough for all this thought expended on us amidst your troubles.'

rejoiced I was at their happy termination.[1] I will talk with Mr W. on the subject your Grace names without delay.[2]

As to myself, you may rely on it I do not *forget* the Lectures — but alas! with my present most troublesome affair hanging over me and constantly making calls on me, how shall I find time? Every thing looks very gloomy just now. If we could have got the proceedings of the Inquisition, our lawyers thought they would be a smasher, from knowing the number of offences they would embrace — but it is against all precedent to grant them to us, and the Holy Father, who has been most condescending in the whole matter, says he cannot in conscience go further. Mr Badeley has all along looked on the matter most seriously — and thus the news from Rome is but the fulfilment of his forebodings. However, there have been so many, many prayers and Masses offered for me that it will be a most extraordinary thing if I fail — or if I do, it must be for a greater good.

The trial is to come on in the middle of February — and nothing takes place before it (as I understand) till the following term. Directly after it I hope to go to Hodder for retreat — and then, by the 1st of March I could come to Dublin to deliver the Lectures — I should be called up for judgment (if unsuccessful) after Easter — and then if I am put in prison, I *am* put in prison, and the difficulty must provide for itself.

On the whole then, saving those contingencies which must attend on this annoying affair, and which may overturn all one's calculations, I should be able, I trust, to come to Dublin in Lent — if it suits your Grace's ideas, whatever happens after it.

I was very much concerned to hear of your illness, and attribute it to Drogheda, which I am sure cannot suit you after Italy.

Begging your Grace's blessing, I am, My dear Lord,
Your affecte Servt John H Newman C.O.

---

[1] Wilberforce's appointment as Secretary of the Catholic Defence Association was opposed by some Irishmen on the ground that he would not understand Irish affairs. Writing to Newman on 27 Dec., Cullen described the opposition as 'factious and unprincipled.' Cullen also publicly deprecated the opposition to Wilberforce. See the *Tablet* (27 Dec. 1851), pp. 824–5.

[2] Cullen wrote on 27 Dec. to Newman, 'I am quite anxious that he [Wilberforce] should prepare for us an address to the people of England on Proselytism, showing that the efforts made to pervert the Catholics of Ireland are only calculated to produce hypocrisy and infidelity.'

TO F. W. FABER

Oy Bm Dec 30/51

My dear F Wilfrid

I am going to write you a very ungracious letter, that is, to express my *sorrow* at your return.

The truth is, I have been fuming ever since you went, at the way you have been going on. I wrote to Malta to protest against your preaching — the letter missed you, and next I heard of you as lecturing an Orat. Parv. in Italian.[1] The tone of your letter from Palermo pleased me not at all — I had no confidence in your sudden restoration, and I thought your letter excited.[2] Then suddenly you were making for Rome, which was *forbidden* you — and before [a] letter could hit you, you are, against all medical orders, in England.

St Philip used to obey his physician. Have you taken one of the few opportunities a Father Superior has for obedience? I saw his letter — he prescribed six months for you.

You are *not* recovered — the very impatience with which you have come back shows it. As far as I can see, you are still bound to obey your medical adviser, and explere numerum. Your life is precious

This, I know, is very ungracious but I am bound to say it.

Ever Yrs affly J H N

P.S. As *I* am like to have to submit to ’Ανάγκη[?][3] so must you.

TO HENRY WILBERFORCE

Oy Bm Dec. 30/51

Charissime

1. The Primate wishes me to talk to you about an *Address* you are concocting. Can you come over?

2. Have you any view of the good of Miss French going to Ireland to Monsell’s?[4]

3. When you come here, bring with you my papers on Faith. I know you are the most careful man in the world, but I know too that

---

[1] *Oratorium Parvum*, Little Oratory, the confraternity for men.
[2] See last note to letter of 19 Nov. to Joseph Gordon.
[3] ‘Restraint.’ See letter of 1 Jan. 1852 to Faber for the latter’s reply.
[4] See letter of 16 Dec. to Wilberforce.

Papers delight in hiding themselves — especially if no duplicate exist of them[1]

I congratulate you on your success — it is a buona festa.

⌐We are going on very badly in *our* affairs — but I cannot think the many Masses and Prayers which have been offered will not do something after all¬

Ever Yrs affly J H N

TO G. H. HADFIELD

[31 December 1851]

Revd Sir[2]

I do not know whether I am addressing the gentleman I knew at Oxford years ago — but though to have once known you will explain the liberty I am taking in writing, it will not in any way alter the substance or scope of my letter, which is an appeal, as you will see, not to your kindness, but to your sense of justice and your generosity

Most unwillingly have I engaged you as a witness at the trial in which I am concerned; most unwillingly because I know how annoying it is to any person, much more a person of refined mind and retiring habits, as a clergyman must be, to be subjected to a legal examination. But I am forced to do it as a matter of duty.

To myself indeed I feel it will matter very little, putting the question of pain aside, whether I am found guilty or not; or rather with the certainty (thank God) which I possess that I have but spoken what was true nay within the truth, in the matter which forms the subject of the criminal information, I am quite sure that He who has never failed me, will but bless me the more in all true blessing, if it is His good pleasure that I should be condemned. But it is my duty to do my utmost not only to justify myself, but even to save His own ordinance, the Law, from being made the instrument of injustice

It is then simply to your sense of justice that I wish to appeal in this letter. I know well I am addressing a religious man, and though you may possibly be bound in honor and in duty to a charge to keep from doing for me even what you can do, still I take the chance of putting the facts before you, and of claiming of you, for as far as you can, to do

[1] These are presumably the notes of Newman's lectures on faith, given to the novices at the Oratory in the spring of 1848, and to be published among Newman's theological papers.

[2] This letter is printed from Newman's draft, which is much interlined and extremely difficult to decipher.

your part in preventing the defeat of the innocent and the triumph of the guilty. There is a Judge above us, before whom eventually we all must appear.

The case stands thus. After charges most grievous and very definite had been made in print against the person whom I am accused of libelling [,] more than a year, after he had been challenged to refute them, after some of his supporters had left him in consequence of his silence, I repeat in print a portion of them. On his making an affidavit against me, swearing his innocence of all the crimes I had mentioned and moreover *all such* crimes, when I ask of the Court for just so much time as will enable me by writing abroad to prove him perjured by means of counter affidavits (which is the usual course) the Judges refuse me even a week or a day, and that on the ground most untrue and most injurious to my character, that I do not believe what I have said, nay, and that moreover without suffering, or rather directly hindering, my counsel to set right this misapprehension. This decision throws me at once on the necessity of bringing together in one spot and at one time, a great number of witnesses from very different places, (an operation always most difficult), and still more in such a matter, to substantiate charges which have for a whole year made their way through the community, virtually uncontradicted.

Now the appeal I venture to make to you is this; — to be so good as to inform me, if you are at liberty to do so, of any sources of information at Malta about the guilt of the person in question which may happen to be known to you. You may probably know of evidence better because more direct than your own; and, while it would be a gain to me to obtain such, it also would save me from the pain of rudely calling you to undergo an examination in the witness box, in relation to matters so disagreeable as those which are the subject of the present trial.

I beg to say in conclusion that I write this at my own suggestion — and that, should you wish me, I will put your answer at once into the fire.[1]

I am &c J H N

---

[1] Hadfield replied on 2 Jan. from Whitchurch, Hants:

'I beg to acknowledge your letter of the 31st ult. received this morning. I am the same whom you knew at Oxford, having been examined by you for my degree in 1827, and having experienced more than one act of kindness at your hands afterwards.

On the subject of your letter, it has hitherto appeared to me to be my duty to say nothing before the trial, but then to state truly and unreservedly *what* I wrote officially from Malta to the Committee in London concerning the parties referred to, and *why* I so wrote, so far as my reasons are producible in evidence.

The farthest extent to which I can now go, in compliance with your appeal to me to furnish you with "any sources of information at Malta, which I may happen to

TO ANTONY HUTCHISON

Dec 31/51

My dear F Antony,

I *still* think F Wilfrid should absent himself longer.[1] It will not do for him to spoil what he has gained by using it up at once.

Please, *attend to the following*. The Malta post goes out the 6th (or 7th?) and the 7th (or 8th?) If then a letter comes for me on the 7th open it, take it to Lewin, and let it be answered to save the post without coming down to me

Ever Yrs affly J H N

P.S.   I think you and F Rector should make *no secret* to F Wilfrid that I have recommended his going abroad again. I am pretty sure I have written to that effect to F Richard.

TO ROBERT MONTEITH

Oratory Bm Dec 31. 1851

My dear Mr Monteith

I will not let the year die out without answering your kind letter. How I should like to be able to take advantage of your suggestion: but it is impossible. Mr Stothert had been so very kind as to send me his work on its publication.[2] I had never answered him in acknowledgment, hoping first to read it — which as yet I have not had time to do. Much less have I time to write. In like manner I was asked to review Mr Morris's book,[3] but was obliged to decline. I have not written a Review for years — only one since 1843 or 1844 — and that was in the Dublin,

know, and evidence more direct than my own,'' is to give you a list of the persons of whose evidence I should wish to avail myself, if I were in your position.

As I wish to say nothing but what duty calls me to say, I must decline describing what evidence I should expect from any of them, but if my evidence in Court is given before theirs, there will be no difficulty in afterwards obtaining theirs.'

Following on this correspondence, Newman's solicitor Lewin had two long conferences on 19 and 20 Jan. with Hadfield, who also testified at the trial. *Finlason*, p. 93.

[1] Faber reached London on 31 Dec., and Hutchison wrote at once to say he was looking much better than had been expected, and suggesting that, 'if a small country-house could be got at once, that might be sufficient to re-establish his health.'

[2] Monteith had evidently asked Newman to review James Augustus Stothert's *The Glory of Mary in conformity with the Word of God*, London 1851. Stothert became a Catholic in 1844.   [3] J. B. Morris, *Jesus the Son of Mary*.

and the only one I ever wrote in it. As to the Rambler, I never wrote a line for it, though some verses of mine have appeared in it.[1] At this moment, besides my duties here, and this provoking trial, I have my thoughts full of the new University. I heartily wish justice were done to Mr S.'s work — but it will meet with it in time.

I feel the extreme kindness of your zeal for me in getting the prayers you mention. It is the only way of doing me good, for the matter, on its human side, is dark enough just now.

Could you give me any distinct information on the subject of the granite columns you mentioned? or tell me whom to apply to? We are soon commencing our Church, and we shall have in it about 16 pillars, with shafts 16 feet high; we should be very glad to have them rose coloured granite, if the expense were not too great.

With every kind wish for the ensuing year for you & yours, I am, My dear Mr Monteith, Yours Very sincerely in Xt

John H Newman

[1] See *D R* (July 1846), a review of Keble's *Lyra Innocentium*, now *Ess.* II, pp. 421–53. One or two of Newman's hymns were published in the *Rambler* in 1850.

LETTER OF J. H. NEWMAN TO J. D. DALGAIRNS[1]

Oratory Bm Febr 24/51

My dear F Bernard

I have not answered you before, because I have had a great lot of letters to write, and nothing to say to you — nor have I now.

Some happy inspiration, I hope will give us a view about the Orat. Parv. [Oratorium Parvum] — meanwhile the only thing to do is what you are doing, viz to feel your way.

Stanislas, our Prefect, will attempt something too, and I shall advise him to do what you are doing. I altogether approve of your principle, viz of beginning in a general free and easy way, and not going to *Rules* for a time.

The great problem is this — what is the object or form of the Institution? as to Confraternities, one tends the sick, another buries the dead, a third prays for England, and so on. You must find out this, and I think it is a puzzle — not to visit the 7 Churches, for there are none — not to tend the Hospitals, for we are debarred. To visit occasionally the poor, or to meet once a week for a mass, is not definite enough.

Dr Acquerone says that 'to keep young men from sin' is its object — but this is rather the reason for *establishing* the O.P. than the O.P's reason. Yet it may suggest a good deal — It suggests that no object is to be selected which does not tend, and objects are to be selected only so far as they tend, to this end. Lord Brougham and Co I do believe, (as far as Lord B. is serious about any thing, or is capable of an end,) have set up Mechanics' Institutes, to give men something better to do than abandon themselves to low vice.

E.g. *this* would be an object such — 'to spread knowledge about Catholicism, intelligent views, controversial skill etc etc. among our Catholic Youth — ' Considering the power and force of the Catholic system, as a philosophy, had we a number of well trained youths they would be the best of missionaries — quite irresistible among medical students, lawyers, merchants' clerks, artists etc. — and if a gentle rule were added, it would serve to keep them from making theology a literature, while the occupation itself would, please God, keep them from sin. In saying this, I may perhaps be influenced by my own way of doing things — for I have always found I have best insinuated Catholic

---

[1] This letter was discovered too late to be included in the chronological sequence.

principles through literature and by the intellect. However some *object* you should have, chosen and regulated by Dr A's canon.

As to the discipline, so that it is quite secret, and those who use it are as much in the moral dark about each other, as in the physical, it does not much matter.

Poor old Woodmason, I fear I don't sympathise enough in him not to be glad he is so far off. Yet he has done his family an immense benefit — One of the girls is dying of consumption

Ever Yrs affly J H N

Appendixes

Appendix 1

Letter signed by Wiseman, giving his sanction to the London
Oratory. (See letter of 14 August to Stanton.)

AT the head of his draft of this letter, Newman later wrote in pencil:
'This I drew up in August ⟨15th?⟩ 1850 for Dr Wiseman's signature,
on his going to Rome for the Cardinalate, with the uncertainty who
would be Bishop of the Westminster Diocese. He signed it.'

August 16. 1850

Cùm, per litteras Apostolicas in formâ Brevis Romae die 26 Novembris 1847 datas, Sanctissimus Dominus noster, Pius Papa ix, Con-
gregationem Oratorii Sancti Philippi Nerii, Romae 1575 ⟨?⟩ fundatam,
Birminghamiae in centrali districtu Angliae erexerit et instituerit, eâ
autem mente, ut, sicut in iisdem litteris continetur, decursu temporis
per totam Angliam ejusdem Congregationis domus, juxta normam Insti-
tutorum anno 1847 pro earum regimine in supradictis litteris appro-
batorum, in urbibus amplioribus fundarentur:—patres autem nonnulli
ejusdem Congregationis Birminghamiensis Londinii jam per annum at
amplius commorati, laboribus suis in salutem animarum summopere
nobis se commendarint, hoc autem tempore ad nos adierint, suppliciter
rogantes, ut ibidem consensu nostro domus ipsorum formaliter tandem
et canonicè erigatur:

Nos, perpensâ eorumdem Patrum supplicatione, quò devotionem
nostram erga S. Philippum, et approbationem et amorem quo filios ejus
antedictos respicimus, evidentius commonstremus, his litteris nostrâ
manu subscriptis, (quantum ad ordinarii auctoritatem spectat,) domum
Londiniensem à Congregatione Birminghamiae jam jam erigendam
⟨juxta litteras Apostolicas⟩, ex corde et libenter suscipimus et sancimus.

499

Appendix 2

Decree of 30 January 1851 accepting W. G. Penny's Departure from the Oratory[1]

DECREED . . . unanimously that whereas it is the traditional maxim of the Oratory that 'chi vuol vivere al suo modo non e buono per la Congregazione,' and that all things must be subservient to 'santa communità,' that 'all should accommodate themselves to the good of the community, which rule of conduct includes a treasure of merits,' that the first degree of charity is to the Congregation which is our mother, our nurse, and our guide to heaven; and that 'whoever aspires to sanctity must heartily follow holy community,' and whereas the experience of three years, the ordinary period of the Noviciate, though shortened of necessity in the commencement of our Congregation, has shown that our dear Brother F. William Penny, in spite of his unusual gifts and most exemplary correctness of moral deportment, and high aspirations after sanctity, is nevertheless, from an indifference to community life, which is injurious and detrimental to the body, unsuited to our particular Institution; and whereas, on this feeling being made known to him, he has himself expressed a wish to obtain its permission to retire from it; we, with real sorrow at the loss of so highly endowed a Father, yet from love to him as well as from loyalty to St Philip, and with the special advice of our Father, John Henry Newman, whom the Sovereign Pontiff has by Brief charged with the establishment of the Oratory in England, hereby accede to his request, and pronounce that he is no longer a member of our body.

[1] From the Decree Book of the Birmingham Oratory.

Appendix 3

Extract from Lecture V on the Present Position of Catholics.
The Denunciation of Achilli which was held to be a libel,
28 July 1851

AND in the midst of outrages such as these, my Brothers of the Oratory,
wiping its mouth, and clasping its hands, and turning up its eyes, it
trudges to the Town Hall to hear Dr. Achilli expose the Inquisition.[1]
Ah! Dr. Achilli, I might have spoken of him last week, had time admitted of it. The Protestant world flocks to hear him, because he has
something to tell of the Catholic Church. He has a something to tell, it
is true; he *has* a scandal to reveal, he *has* an argument to exhibit. It is a
simple one, and a powerful one, as far as it goes — and it is *one*. That
one argument is himself; it is his presence which is the triumph of
Protestants; it is the sight of him which is a Catholic's confusion. It is
indeed our great confusion, that our Holy Mother could have had a
priest like him. He feels the force of the argument, and he shows himself
to the multitude that is gazing on him. 'Mothers of families,' he seems
to say 'gentle maidens, innocent children, look at me, for I am worth
looking at. You do not see such a sight every day. Can any church live
over the imputation of such a production as I am?[2] I have been a
Catholic and an infidel; I have been a Roman priest and a hypocrite; I
have been a profligate under a cowl. I am that Father Achilli,[3] who, as
early as 1826, was deprived of my faculty to lecture, for an offence which
my superiors did their best to conceal; and who in 1827 had already
earned the reputation of a scandalous friar. I am that Achilli, who in the
diocese of Viterbo in February, 1831, robbed of her honour a young
woman of eighteen; who in September, 1833, was found guilty of a
second such crime, in the case of a person of twenty-eight; and who
perpetrated a third in July, 1834, in the case of another aged twenty-four.
I am he, who afterwards was found guilty of sins, similar or worse, in

[1] From this point up to and including the final paragraph below, Newman omitted
in the second edition of *Prepos*. The text reproduced here is that of the first edition,
pp. 197–201.

[2] From this point until 'Yes, you are an incontrovertible proof, that priests may fall
and friars break their vows,' is omitted in *Prepos*. pp. 207–8.

[3] Vid. Dublin Review for July, 1850; and Authentic Brief Sketch of the Life of
Dr. Giacinto Achilli.—Richardsons. [Newman's note.]

other towns of the neighbourhood. I am that son of St. Dominic who is known to have repeated the offence at Capua, in 1834 or 1835; and at Naples again, in 1840, in the case of a child of fifteen. I am he who chose the sacristy of the church for one of these crimes, and Good Friday for another. Look on me, ye mothers of England, a confessor against Popery, for ye "ne'er may look upon my like again." I am that veritable priest, who, after all this, began to speak against, not only the Catholic faith, but the moral law, and perverted others by my teaching. I am the Cavaliere Achilli, who then went to Corfu, made the wife of a tailor faithless to her husband, and lived publicly and travelled about with the wife of a chorus-singer. I am that Professor in the Protestant College at Malta, who with two others was dismissed from my post for offences which the authorities cannot get themselves to describe. And now attend to me, such as I am, and you shall see what you shall see about the barbarity and profligacy of the Inquisitors of Rome.'

You speak truly, O Achilli, and we cannot answer you a word. You are a Priest; you have been a Friar; you are, it is undeniable, the scandal of Catholicism, and the palmary argument of Protestants, by your extraordinary depravity. You have been, it is true, a profligate, an unbeliever, and an hypocrite. Not many years passed of your conventual life, and you were never in choir, always in private houses, so that the laity observed you. You were deprived of your professorship, we own it; you were prohibited from preaching and hearing confessions; you were obliged to give hush-money to the father of one of your victims, as we learn from the official report of the Police of Viterbo. You are reported in an official document of the Neapolitan Police to be 'known for habitual incontinency;' your name came before the civil tribunal at Corfu for your crime of adultery. You have put the crown on your offences, by, as long as you could, denying them all; you have professed to seek after truth, when you were ravening after sin. Yes, you are an incontrovertible proof, that priests may fall and friars break their vows. You are your own witness; but while you *need* not go out of yourself for your argument, neither are you *able*. With you the argument begins; with you too it ends: the beginning and the ending you are both. When you have shown yourself, you have done your worst and your all; you are your best argument and your sole. Your witness against others is utterly invalidated by your witness against yourself. You leave your sting in the wound: you cannot lay the golden eggs, for you are already dead.

For how, Brothers of the Oratory, can we possibly believe a man like this, in what he says about persons, and facts, and conversations, and events, when he is of the stamp of Maria Monk, of Jeffreys, and of

Teodore, and of others who have had their hour, and then been dropped by the indignation or the shame of mankind? What call is there on Catholics to answer what has not yet been proved? what need to answer the evidence of one, who has not replied to the Police reports of Viterbo, Naples, and Corfu? He tells me that a Father Inquisitor said to him, 'Another time,' that you are 'shut up in the Inquisition,' 'you' will not 'get away so easily?' I do not believe it was said to him. He reports that a Cardinal said of him, 'We must either make him a Bishop, or shut him up in the Inquisition.' I do not believe it. He bears witness, that 'the General of the Dominicans, the oldest of the Inquisitors, exclaimed against him before the council, "This heretic, we had better burn him alive."' I don't believe a word of it. 'Give up the present Archbishop of Canterbury,' says he, 'amiable and pious as he is, to one of these rabid inquisitors; he must either deny his faith, or be burned alive. Is my statement false? Am I doting?'[1] He is not doting, but he is false. 'Suppose I were to be handed over to the tender mercy of this Cardinal (Wiseman), and he had full power to dispose of me as he chose, without losing his character in the eyes of the nation, . . . should I not have to undergo some death more terrible than ordinary?' Dr. Achilli does not dote; they dote who listen to him.

Why do I so confidently assert that he is not to be believed? — first, because his life for twenty years past creates no prepossession in favour of his veracity: secondly, because during a part of that period, according to his own confession, he spoke and argued against doctrines, which at the very time he confessed to be maintained by the communion to which he belonged; thirdly, because he has ventured to deny in the general, what official documents prove against him in the particular; fourthly, because he is not simple and clear enough in his narrative of facts to inspire any confidence in him; fifthly, because he abounds in misstatements and romance, as any one will see who knows any thing of the matters he is writing about; sixthly, because he runs counter to facts known and confessed by all.

[1] Dealings with the Inquisition, pp. 2, 27, 46, 75 [Newman's notes].

Appendix 4

Newman's Memoranda for his lawyers — written probably
towards the end of 1851

1. Circumstances under which I published the alleged libel.

THERE was a great excitement against Catholics all thro' England last year.

A variety of calumnies had been circulated one after another against Catholics in this place.

Two years ago an impostor of the name of Jeffreys had circulated the grossest lies of a monastery in the district, which had excited a great ferment, till they were detected, and he sentenced to the house of correction.[1]

Afterwards some Poles, who professed to have been Catholic priests, came into the place, and told still more abominable stories of our priesthood. They spoke against our house here specially, not from knowledge but from what they were sure was the case from their general knowledge of the Catholic Church, they said our hands ran with blood, etc — till at length they too were detected and sent about their business.

Besides this it was distinctly asserted, or reported to be asserted, in an august assembly by a person high in station, and a relation of my intimate friend, who might be supposed to know, that I was building a house in the neighbourhood of Birmingham with cells for the purpose of secret murder.[2]

And lately new editions had been issued of the notorious work of Maria Monk, against a Convent in Mon[t]real in Canada, which, though again and again shown to be an impudent imposture was largely circulated in Birmingham making people believe that all priests and nuns were profligates.

These and other calumnies I had referred to and exposed in Lectures I publicly delivered last summer. One remained of great importance to which I had not alluded. In the course of the foregoing year, Dr Achilli came down to Birmingham, and made a speech in the Town Hall against the Roman Inquisition. This speech had its weight as coming from one who had been a Priest and Friar in the Catholic Church, and professed to be witnessing what he had known. It had raised a great deal

---

[1] See letter of 11 July 1849 to Ryder.
[2] See letter of 15 May 1851 to the Editor of the *Morning Chronicle*.

504

of odium against Catholics, and in particular attacked individuals who could not defend themselves. Moreover, it had actually perplexed some of our own Catholic congregation, who did not know how to disbelieve stories which came from what seemed so good authority.

Soon after this speech of Dr Achilli in Birmingham, i.e. in June 1850 there was an exposure of his character in an article in the Dublin Review, which, with great minuteness of detail, and quotations from original authorities, police reports, and the like, said all that I have said against him and a great deal more. This article was shortly after published as a pamphlet, and excited a great deal of notice. Friends of his own called on the publisher, and threatened him with an action; who said he was prepared for it and defied them to do it. Neither his friends however or he took any legal measures to vindicate his character. However, a friend of his, a Mr Tonna, wrote a pamphlet, in which he slurred over the main charges. Next Dr Achilli wrote a book, which, while it was professedly an attack upon the Roman Inquisition, was covertly an answer to the Dublin Review, yet with no bold statement or examination of the charges against him, but a sort of rhodomantade and declamation.

This was the position of things when I delivered my Lecture, in which I repeated some of the charges detailed by the Dublin Review, and which is the subject of the present prosecution. It has appeared that I was urged to do so by the following motives

1. by the desire to set right Protestants who relied on Achilli's authority.

2 to defend and inform Catholics who were at once perplexed themselves and abused by Protestants, in consequence of what he said.

This became still more necessary from the circumstance that I *had* been noticing other calumnies against Catholics. For it might have been inferred that, had I left this alone unnoticed, it was because I could say nothing to refute it. As then in my 3rd Lecture I had noticed the calumny against ⟨the cathedral of St Gudule⟩ our New House in Birmingham, as in my fourth Lecture I had noticed the calumnies of Jeffreys, the Poles, and above all Maria Monk, so in my 5th, in which [I] was treating expressly of the Inquisition, I directed my attention to Dr Achilli in the passage which is the ground of the prosecution.

N B. For the provocation he gave in his speeches and book vid other papers I have sent up.

2. A Priest and an Infidel.

If I have called him an Infidel, it is only what he calls himself, i.e. if an infidel is a person who has no *faith*. I have said he *professed* faith, but *had* it *not*. Now what does he say of himself? — as follows:—

'I was already a Protestant,' (i.e. as *not* holding the *Roman* faith,) 'but *not yet sufficiently a Christian*. . . . My virtue arose from self love, and not from *faith*. I had acquired some practice in the habit of well-doing, but was not yet guided by divine inspiration. . . . O how delightful is the life of a *believer*! *He* lives by *faith*.' Dealings with the Inquisition p 183[1]

Now he may have some technical meaning in the word *faith*, (as I had in the word *infidel*) but the question is what the general or popular impression would be, of an avowal on the part of a person that he had not *faith*. This state of mind lasted for *five* years from 1830 to 1835. In 1830 he *disowns* the *Catholic* Faith, but not till 1835 did he *embrace* the *Evangelical*.

(He says the same thing in p 25; 'I possessed the understanding of faith, but not *faith itself* . . . I stood midway between the old and the new man: the old man was already buried, but the new man had not yet come to life.')

Speaking of his enemies, he says. 'They undertook to explain to others my *profession of faith*, which *I had not yet been able to make out clearly to myself*.' p 37

Is it wonderful, that, with such avowals, he should be called by others 'an infidel'?

If you insist upon the *impression* of my word 'infidel,' why may I not urge the impression of his word 'faith'?[2]

3. On the *Notoriety* of the charges, or that I am not the *first* to make them.

1. In Corfu. 'It appears that both of them (his accusers) had a miserable pittance allowed them, for which they amused themselves in inventing and promulgating their abominable falsehoods. I know that the director general of the police, Captain Lawrence, twice summoned before him one of these detractors, a Neapolitan tailor, and severely reprimanded him; and I also know that this tailor confessed he had been paid for his slanders.'

'Several of the Maltese, who constitute the most vile and wretched part of the population of Corfu, had, at one time, taken it into their heads to follow me in the streets, with insulting and threatening words.' p 269

2 Malta. 'A Maltese journal, notorious for its bad and abusive character,

---

[1] This and the subsequent quotations are from Achilli's *Dealings with the Inquisition* . . ., London 1851.   [2] Cf. letter of 25 Dec. 1851 to Badeley.

thought fit to publish several articles against me — In one of them, written by a *Portuguese*, probably connected with some foreign *policy* etc . . . Another writer, who I believe had been an *English Clergyman* . . . pp 282, 3

'He (Keosse) had the art to *induce some English* clergymen, and others who *called themselves Protestants*, to *oppose themselves to my proceedings*' p 288

It is suspicious when charges follow a man wherever he goes, in Italy, Corfu, Malta, England — urged by Italians, Maltese, Portuguese, English — by Catholics and Protestants. Is it wonderful one person in addition should assert them?

Appendix 5

Newman's Account of the first stages of the Achilli Trial

December 22. 1851.

IN the middle or towards the end of August came the news that Dr Achilli had pledged himself to take legal proceedings against me for the passage directed against him in my Lecture delivered in the Town Hall on July 28. I wrote to Badeley, and, his view of the matter being serious, I went to Town, as soon as his engagements permitted, to consult with him. In consequence I sent abroad FF Nicholas Darnell and Joseph Gordon, to get documents ready to meet any measures which might be taken against me. They started September 21.

Badeley advised their going abroad; lest, if a sudden movement was made against me in November when the Law Term began, I might be driven into a corner, if I had nothing to produce. This was the more necessary, since Cardinal Wiseman's documents, on which I had relied, were, as he said, mislaid. I had relied on them, when I published the passage in my Lecture in question; I had relied on the time which had elapsed since he had published the Article in the Dublin, and Achilli's continued silence. Also I had written to a legal friend before publishing, as to the risk I ran, and he had not discouraged me. I had thought a good deal about it, and been very anxious. I had presented it before the Blessed Sacrament, and I kept saying to myself, 'There is nothing comes to stop or dissuade me.' I knew Achilli might prosecute, but I thought that, if he attacked any one, it would have been the Cardinal, under the peculiar circumstances of last year, ⟨(viz. the Cardinal's prominence and unpopularity)⟩ and I thought to myself that no good would ever be done, if we were stayed by possibilities. Directly that I found he promised to prosecute, my view *simply changed*, for my sole ground of confidence had been that he would not. Then at once I saw the whole prospect of what was to be as a present fact; sensi medios delapsus in hostes.[1] I had put my foot into a snare; I could do nothing; my enemies had nothing to do but to pull the noose tight at their leisure. Man could do nothing; accordingly from the first I kept saying 'Prayer alone will bring me out.' I could not get any one to feel with me; every one thought

---

[1] *Aeneid* II, 377.

me needlessly frightened, and laughed at the idea of any trouble happening.

The two Fathers proceeded to Naples, with the intention of at once getting from the Police an authenticated copy of what was the grossest case among Achilli's offences. They were to send it to me at once, and then go on to Rome, where Mgr Talbot meanwhile had been collecting evidence from various quarters. To their disappointment they found that the Cardinal, who had made light of the whole matter and could not be got to give his mind to it, had given them letters of introduction of so general a nature that they could not obtain from the Police the documents they wanted. The Cardinal Archbishop of Naples would not sign the necessary order, and at last in despair they introduced themselves to the Prime Minister, who did for them what, had it been done sooner, would have been of essential use in my behalf.

Such was the state of things on the 27th of October. Nothing from Naples, nothing from Rome, nothing from Naples,[1] nothing from Corfu, where also I had applied through Dr Nicholson, when I received a lawyer's letter, calling on me to give up my name to prevent a criminal information being laid against Burns and Lambert, the publishers of the alleged libel. Dr Achilli had made an affidavit, declaring on oath he was innocent of every one of the crimes with which I had charged him. This affidavit enabled him to contemplate a criminal information, which had the effect 1. of obliging me to give up my name, which a civil action would not have done — 2 of putting me in the bar as a criminal. Had he but brought a civil action, he would have no certainty he had got the right person; for, though I had written the alleged libel, Burns might have bought it but he might not — but, whether he had or not, it would have been invidious to proceed against Burns instead of me, and he could not get proof that I had spoken or written the Lectures — but of course I could not let another be submitted to a criminal sentence, and perhaps be sent to prison instead of me. However, I made no answer at the moment — said I would answer through my lawyer, and by that post wrote off to Rome to Talbot to send us whatever documents we had without any delay.

The criminal information against Burns and Lambert was moved for in Court, a week after, November 4 — and then, when it was inevitable, I came forward and got my own name substituted for theirs. We had a meeting with the Attorney General our Counsel on November 6. when he said that there would be no doubt of our obtaining till Easter Term to answer Achilli by counter affidavits, that time being necessary

---

[1] Newman evidently meant to write 'Malta.'

for communicating with foreign places. All that was necessary was for me to make a short affidavit, begging for time on the ground of the necessary delay in collecting evidence. Accordingly a short common-place affidavit was drawn up for me to swear. I had asked whether nothing could be said to the effect that I had taken what I had stated from the Dublin Review, but was told that that point would only come in in mitigation of the offence when proved. I had received a letter from a lawyer, saying that that fact alone would hinder the Judges granting Achilli the Rule; but, when I showed it to my lawyers, they passed it over, and, when I urged them, one of them distinctly said it was not to the point. When the affidavit was drawn up, there was one thing I objected to; it stated that I promised to *prove* every thing that was said; this I said I could not swear to, considering the documents had not come, or any account of what they contained. We were as yet quite in the dark what we could do; an affidavit of Garamone's, and another of Keosse's, neither sufficient for any legal purpose, as Mr Badeley said, were all I had at the moment to produce. Consequently the affidavit was altered so as to say, that I verily believed I should be able, if time was granted me, to bring evidence which would prevent the Judges from making the Rule absolute. Having sworn this affidavit, I returned to Birmingham on Friday the 7th.

The Attorney General was to have appeared in Court to gain me the delay at the beginning of the following week, but I found there was a delay from the circumstance of the opposite party refusing to let my name to be [sic] substituted for Burns and Lambert, and they did not give in, till the week had run out. The next week (beginning the 17th) the Attorney General brought it on — Judge Earle suggested an arguing of the point, on the ground that the delay might be an injury to Achilli's character. It was argued before the four Judges, Campbell, Coleridge, Patteson, and Whitman [Wightman] on Wednesday the 19th. Our lawyers were quite secure, heard that there was to be an opposition to their action, but laughed at the idea.

Appendix 6

Litany for the Achilli Trial

Dec 22/51

Educes me de laqueo hoc quem absconderunt mihi.

Litany

God, the Father, of heaven, have mercy upon us.
God, the Son, Redeemer of the world, have mercy upon us
God, the Holy Ghost, have mercy upon us
Holy Trinity, one God, have mercy upon us
Jesus, God and man, bound in swaddling clothes by Mary
      in Thy infancy, have mercy upon us
Jesus, God and man, tried and imprisoned by Thy enemies
      in Thy passion, have mercy upon us
Jesus God and man, imprisoned by love in Thy most holy
      Sacrament, have mercy upon us.
St John Baptist, imprisoned for thy true witness,
                pray for us
St John the Evangelist, cast without harm into a cauldron
      of hot oil, pray for us
St John, Pope, thrown into a loathsome dungeon, pray for us
St John Chrysostom, victim of an unjust sentence,
                pray for us
St John of Egypt, for 40 years shut up in thy cell,
                pray for us
St John of God, seized and confined for mad, pray for us
St John Nepomucene, imprisoned for the law of Xt,
                pray for us
St John of the Cross, imprisoned by the envious, pray for us
St John Capistran, born anew in prison, pray for us
St John of Matha, deliverer of captives, pray for us
St Philip, my Father, Apostle of Rome, pray for us
St Dominic, Confessor and Patriarch, pray for us
St Januarius of Naples, pray for us
St Rufus, first martyr of Capua, pray for us
St Spiridion of Corfu, pray for us

St Julian, honored in Malta, pray for us
St Rose of Viterbo, pray for us
Sts Mellitus and Erconwald of London, pray for us
St Edward King and Confessor, pray for us
St Chad, Bishop of these parts, pray for us
Lamb of God etc.

Let us pray.

God, who didst break the chains of Thy Apostle, and hast delivered Thy saints in every age from bonds and imprisonment, grant to us Thy servants in this our present trouble so to persevere in prayer that we may be pleasing in Thy sight, and obtain what we desire, through Christ etc.

List of Letters by Correspondents

List of Letters by Correspondents

Abbreviations used here in addition to those given at the beginning of the volume.

A.	Original Autograph.
C.	Copy, other than those made by Newman.
D.	Draft by Newman.
Georgetown	University of Georgetown, Washington, D.C.
H.	Holograph copy by Newman.
Lond.	London Oratory.
Magd.	Magdalen College, Oxford.
Oriel	Oriel College, Oxford.
Pr.	Printed.
Prop.	Archives of the Congregation of Propaganda, Rome.
Pusey	Pusey House, Oxford.
Rankeillour	The Lord Rankeillour.
S.J. Dublin	The Jesuit Fathers, 35 Lower Leeson Street, Dublin.
S.J. Lond.	The Jesuit Fathers, 114 Mount Street, London.
Stoke	The Dominican Convent, Stoke-on-Trent.

The abbreviation which describes the source is always the first one after the date of each letter. This is followed immediately by the indication of its present location or owner. When there is no such indication, it means that the source letter is preserved at the Birmingham Oratory. It has not been thought necessary to reproduce the catalogue indications of the Archives at the Oratory, because each of Newman's letters there is separately indexed, and can be traced at once.

After the source and its location have been indicated, any additional holograph copies (with their dates) or drafts are listed, and then, enclosed within brackets, any references to previous publication in standard works.

Lastly, when it is available, comes the address to which the letter was sent.

Correspondent	Year	Date	Source	Location, Owner, Address
Acheson, Lady Olivia	1850	27 Sept	A	
		9 Dec	A	
		10 Dec	A	
	1851	27 May	A	(*Trevor* I, p. 544)
		End of May	A	
		22 June	A	
		26 June	A	
		1 July	A	
		1 Oct	A	
Allen, John	1850	7 Nov	A	Trinity College, Oxford
		10 Nov	A	Trinity College, Oxford
Allies, T. W.	1850	22 Aug	C	
		21 Sept	C	
		30 Sept	C	
		8 Oct	C	(T. W. Allies, *A Life's Decision*, London 1880, pp. 332–3)
		11 Oct	C	(T. W. Allies, *op. cit.*, pp. 333–4)
		11 Nov	C	
	1851	1 Jan	C	
		10 Feb	C	
		7 April	C	
		20 April	C	
		28 April	C	
		9 July	C	(*McGrath*, p. 106)
		25 July	C	(*McGrath*, pp. 108–9)
		25 July	C	
		25 Aug	C	
		13 Sept	C	
		24 Sept	C	
		21 Oct	C	
Allies, Mrs T. W.	1850	3 Aug	C	
	1851	31 July	C	
Bach, Pedro	1850	19 Nov	A	The Oratory, Vich, Spain.
			D	*Ad.* Al R./Padre Bach, Filipino/ Vich/Cataluna/Espana/*L'Espagne*
Badeley, Edward	1850	3 Dec	A	National Library of Scotland (*Trevor* I, p. 535)

Correspondent	Year	Date	Source	Location, Owner, Address
Badeley, Edward	1851	29 Aug	A	
		31 Aug	A	
		3 Sept	A	
		8 Sept	A	
		5 Nov	A	
		9 Nov	A	
		11 Nov	A	
		13 Nov	A	
		23 Nov	A	
		28 Nov	A	
		30 Nov	A	
		6 Dec	A	
		11 Dec	A	
		12 Dec	A	
		25 Dec	A	
		26 Dec	A	
Barnabò, Alexander	1850	12 Aug	A	Prop.
	1851	20 Sept	A	Prop.
Bellasis, Edward	1850	30 Dec	A	
	1851	27 April	A	
Bloxam, J. R.	1851	17 Oct	A	Pusey, 'Cardinal Newman' volume
		20 Oct	A	Pusey, 'Cardinal Newman' volume
		27 Oct	A	Pusey, 'Cardinal Newman' volume
		12 Dec	A	Magd. MS. 307
Bowden, John Edward	1851	26 July	A	Lond. Vol. 15 *Ad.* The Revd John E Bowden/ 17 Grosvenor Place/London
		26 Dec	A	Lond. Vol. 15 *Ad.* Via Marseilles. French Packet/The Revd John E. Bowden/ 72 Strada S. Lucia/Valletta./*Malta*
Bowden, Mrs J. W.	1850	29 July	A	Lond. Vol. 14
		21 Aug	A	Lond. Vol. 14
		30 Sept	A	Lond. Vol. 14
	1851	10 Mar	A	Lond. Vol. 14
		9 July	A	Lond. Vol. 14

Correspondent	Year	Date	Source	Location, Owner, Address
Bowden, Mrs J. W.	1851	19 July	A	Lond. Vol. 14 (*McGrath*, p. 108)
		23 July	A	Lond. Vol. 14
		28 Aug	A	Lond. Vol. 14 (*McGrath*, p. 110)
		15 Sept	A	Lond. Vol. 14
		22 Sept	A	Lond. Vol. 14
		19 Oct	A	Lond. Vol. 14 (*McGrath*, p. 112)
Bowden, Marianne	1851	9 July	A	Lond. Vol. 14
Bowles, F. S.	1850	2 Aug	A	
		9 Sept	A	
	1851	5 Feb	A	
		7 Oct	A	
		5 Nov	A	
Bowyer, George	1850	31 Dec	A	(*Ward* 1, p. 256)
			D	
Briggs, Bishop	1851	25 April	D	
Burns, James	1851	17 July	D	
Butt, John	1851	1 Dec	A	
Campbell, Robert	1851	21 Oct	D	
		22 Oct	D	
Capes, J. M.	1850	5 July	A	
		17 Aug	A	
		23 Aug	A	
		28 Aug	A	
		6 Sept	A	
		13 Sept	A	
		16 Sept	A	(*Ward* 1, p. 249)
		14 Oct	A	
		28 Oct	A	
		14 Nov	A	(*Ward* 1, p. 249)
		16 Nov	A	
		12 Dec	A	
		24 Dec	A	(*Ward* 1, p. 259)
	1851	9 Feb	A	(*Ward* 1, p. 260)
		18 Feb	A	(*Ward* 1, pp. 260–1)
		21 Feb	A	(*Ward* 1, pp. 262–3; *Lord Acton and his Circle*, ed. Abbot Gasquet, London 1906, pp. xxviii–xxxi)

Correspondent	Year	Date	Source	Location, Owner, Address
Capes, J. M.	1851	12 Mar	A	
		6 April	A	
		10 April	A	
		19 April	A	(*Ward* 1, pp. 250–1)
		6 May	A	
		11 May	A	
		17 June	A	
		26 July	A	
		25 Sept	A	
		17 Oct	A	
		25 Nov	A	
		27 Nov	A	(*Ward* 1, p. 287; *Trevor* 1, p. 567)
		7 Dec	A	
		17 Dec	A	
		20 Dec	A	
Caswall, Edward	1851	12 Sept	A	The Newman Preparatory School, Boston
Circular Letter	1850	19 July	Pr	
Coffin, R. A.	1850	4 Sept	A	
		3 Oct	A	The Redemptorist Fathers, Clapham
			D	
		4 Oct	D	
		22 Nov	A	The Redemptorist Fathers, Clapham
			D	
		24 Nov	A	The Redemptorist Fathers, Clapham
			D	
Coleridge, John Duke	1851	21 Feb	C	(*Trevor* 1, p. 522)
Crawley, George	1851	6 May	D	
Cullen, Archbishop	1850	5 July	A	Diocesan Archives, Dublin
		6 July	A	Diocesan Archives, Dublin
		9 July	A	Diocesan Archives, Dublin
	1851	16 April	A	Diocesan Archives, Dublin
		28 April	A	Diocesan Archives, Dublin
		15 July	A	Diocesan Archives, Dublin

Correspondent	Year	Date	Source	Location, Owner, Address
Cullen, Archbishop	1851	23 July	A	Diocesan Archives, Dublin
		26 July	A	Diocesan Archives, Dublin
		19 Aug	A	Diocesan Archives, Dublin
		28 Aug	A	Diocesan Archives, Dublin
		31 Aug	A	Diocesan Archives, Dublin
		7 Sept	A	Diocesan Archives, Dublin
		16 Sept	A	Diocesan Archives, Dublin
		22 Sept	A	Diocesan Archives, Dublin
		29 Sept	A	Diocesan Archives, Dublin
		3 Oct	A	Diocesan Archives, Dublin
		11 Oct	A	Diocesan Archives, Dublin
		14 Oct	A	Diocesan Archives, Dublin
		5 Nov	A	Diocesan Archives, Dublin
		16 Nov	A	Diocesan Archives, Dublin
		21 Nov	A	Diocesan Archives, Dublin
		26 Nov	A	Diocesan Archives, Dublin
		30 Dec	A	Diocesan Archives, Dublin
Dalgairns, J. D.	1850	29 July	A	Lond. Vol. 12
		2 Aug	A	Lond. Vol. 12
		1 Oct	A	Lond. Vol. 12
		8 Dec	A	Lond. Vol. 12
		End of 1850?	A	
	1851	10 Feb	A	Lond. Vol. 12
		24 Feb	A	Lond. Vol. 12
		10 Mar	A	Lond. Vol. 12
		20 April	A	Lond. Vol. 12
		21 May	A	Lond. Vol. 12
		23 May	A	Lond. Vol. 12
		29 June	A	Lond. Vol. 12
		4 July	A	Lond. Vol. 12
		31 Aug	A	Lond. Vol. 12
		14 Nov	A	Lond. Vol. 15
		17 Nov	A	Lond. Vol. 12
		29 Nov	A	Lond. Vol. 15
		17 Dec	A	Lond. Vol. 12 (*Trevor* I, p. 573)

Correspondent	Year	Date	Source	Location, Owner, Address
Dalgairns, J. D.	1851	29 Dec	A	Lond. Vol. 12 (*Trevor* I, pp. 574–6; R. Chapman, *Father Faber*, London 1961, p. 254)
Dodsworth, William	1851	1 Jan	C	
Editor of *Aris's Birmingham Gazette*	1851	20 Aug	Pr	*Aris's Birmingham Gazette* (25 Aug. 1851), p. 3
			D	(Two)
		5 Dec	Pr	*Aris's Birmingham Gazette* (8 Dec. 1851)
Editor of the *Morning Chronicle*	1851	15 May	Pr	The *Morning Chronicle* (17 May 1851), p. 4
		30 Nov	Pr	The *Morning Chronicle* (2 Dec. 1851)
Editor of the *Tablet*	1850	20 Oct	Pr	The *Tablet*, XI (26 Oct. 1851), pp. 676–7
Faber, F. A.	1851	26 Aug	A	The late Sir Geoffrey Faber
		9 Sept	A	The late Sir Geoffrey Faber
		18 Sept	A	The late Sir Geoffrey Faber
Faber, F. W.	1850	5 July	A	Lond. Vol. 9
		9 July	A	Lond. Vol. 9
		11 July	A	Lond. Vol. 9
		18 July	A	Lond. Vol. 9
		22 July	A	Lond. Vol. 9 (*Trevor* I, pp. 524–5)
		2 Aug	A	Lond. Vol. 9
		12 Aug	A	Lond. Vol. 9
		21 Aug	A	Lond. Vol. 9
		23 Aug	A	Lond. Vol. 9
		30 Aug	A	Lond. Vol. 9
		1 Sept	A	Lond. Vol. 9
		3 Sept	A	Lond. Vol. 9
		4 Sept	A	Lond. Vol. 9
		5 Sept	A	Lond. Vol. 9
		11 Sept	A	Lond. Vol. 9
		19 Sept	A	Lond. Vol. 9
		22 Sept	A	Lond. Vol. 9
			D	
		30 Sept	A	Lond. Vol. 9
		1 Oct	A	Lond. Vol. 9

Correspondent	Year	Date	Source	Location, Owner, Address
Faber, F. W.	1850	3 Oct	A	Lond. Vol. 9
		4 Oct	A	Lond. Vol. 9
		6 Oct	A	Lond. Vol. 9
		9 Oct	A	Lond. Vol. 9
		13 Oct	A	Lond. Vol. 9
		23 Oct	A	Lond. Vol. 9
		25 Oct	A	Lond. Vol. 9
		31 Oct	A	Lond. Vol. 9
		4 Nov	A	Lond. Vol. 9
		6 Nov	A	Lond. Vol. 9
		9 Nov	A	Lond. Vol. 9
		11 Nov	A	Lond. Vol. 9
		22 Nov	A	Lond. Vol. 9
		23 Nov	A	Lond. Vol. 9
		26 Nov	A	Lond. Vol. 9 (*Trevor* 1, p. 529)
		28 Nov	A	Lond. Vol. 9
		2 Dec	A	Lond. Vol. 9
		3 Dec	A	Lond. Vol. 9
		5 Dec	A	Lond. Vol. 9
		8 Dec	A	Lond. Vol. 9 *Ad.* The Very Revd/The Father Superior/London Oratory./
		12 Dec	A	Lond. Vol. 9
		18 Dec	A	Lond. Vol. 9
		24 Dec	A	Lond. Vol. 9
		27 Dec	A	Lond. Vol. 9
		29 Dec	A	Lond. Vol. 9
	1851	12 Jan	A	Lond. Vol. 9
		19 Jan	A	Lond. Vol. 9
		20 Jan	A	Lond. Vol. 9
		30 Jan	A	Lond. Vol. 9
		11 Feb	A	Lond. Vol. 9
		23 Feb	A	Lond. Vol. 9
		25 Feb	A	Lond. Vol. 9
		27 Feb	A	Lond. Vol. 9
		26 Mar	A	Lond. Vol. 9

Correspondent	Year	Date	Source	Location, Owner, Address
Faber, F. W.	1851	30 Mar	A	Lond. Vol. 9
		31 Mar	A	Lond. Vol. 9
		End of Mar	A	Lond. Vol. 9 (Poem)
		6 April	A	Lond. Vol. 9
		12 April	A	Lond. Vol. 9
		21 April	A	Lond. Vol. 9
		27 April	A	Lond. Vol. 9
		29 April	A	Lond. Vol. 9
		1 May	A	Lond. Vol. 9
		3 May	A	Lond. Vol. 9
		6 May	A	Lond. Vol. 9
		8 May	A	Lond. Vol. 9 (R. Chapman, *Father Faber*, p. 248)
		9 May	A	Lond. Vol. 9
		23 May	A	Lond. Vol. 9
		2 July	A	Lond. Vol. 9
		23 July	A	Lond. Vol. 9
		31 July	A	Lond. Vol. 9
		7 Aug	A	Lond. Vol. 9
		4 Sept	A	Lond. Vol. 9
		29 Sept	A	Lond. Vol. 9
		10 Oct	A	Lond. Vol. 9
		15 Oct	A	Lond. Vol. 9
		30 Dec	A	Lond. Vol. 9 (*Trevor* 1, p. 576; R. Chapman, *Father Faber*, p. 255)
Faber, George Stanley	1851	20 Aug	D	
Father in Residence	1851	17 Sept	A	Lond. Vol. 9
Feilding, Viscount	1850	4 Oct	C	
		12 Oct	C	
		15 Nov	C	(*Ward* 1, pp. 256–7)
Froude, William	1851	11 Aug	A	(*Harper*, pp. 112–13, where it is dated 1857 and ascribed to William Froude's son, R. H. Froude)
		26 Aug	C	
Froude, Mrs William	1851	9 Oct	C	
		14 Oct	C	(*Harper*, p. 90, *Ward* 1, p. 312; *Trevor* 1, p. 561)

Correspondent	Year	Date	Source	Location, Owner, Address
Froude, Mrs William	1851	20 Oct	C	(*Harper*, pp. 90–1)
		17 Dec	C	(*Harper*, p. 92)
		19 Dec	C	(*Harper*, p. 93)
Gainsford, Robert John	1851	15 Oct	A	
Giberne, Miss M. R.	1850	3 Aug	A	
		4 Oct	A	
	1851	6 Dec	A	(Enclosure in letter to E. Badeley)
Gordon, John Joseph	1850	Beginning of Dec	C	
	1851	14 Oct	A	*Ad.* Al Signore/Il Signore Gordon Inglese/Posta Restante/*Roma*/*Italia* Postmarks: Birmingham 21 Oct; Rome 30 Oct.
		19 Nov	A	*Ad.* The Revd Father Gordon/to the care of Monsignore Talbot,/Palazzo Vaticano/Roma/*Italia*. Postmarks: Birmingham 19 Nov: Rome 29 Nov.
		26 Nov	A	(*Trevor* I, p. 567) *Ad.* Revd J. J. Gordon/care of Monsignore *Talbot*/Il Palazzo Vaticano/Roma/*Italia*. Postmarks: Birmingham 26 Nov: Rome 6 Dec.
		30 Nov (I)	A	(*Trevor* I, p. 568)
		30 Nov (II)	A	*Ad. Via Marseilles*,/The Revd. J. J. Gordon,/care to Monsignore *Talbot*/Il Palazzo Vaticano/Roma/*Italia*
		7 Dec	A	*Ad.* Revd F Gordon/care of Monsignore *Talbot*/Palazzo Vaticano *Roma*/*Italia*
Gordon, William Philip	1850	12 Dec	A	Lond. Vol. 11
	1851	3 Feb	A	Lond. Vol. 11
		6 Sept	A	Lond. Vol. 11
		24 Oct	A	Lond. Vol. 11
Grotti, Vincent	1851	10 Dec	A	St Gabriel's College, Blythe Hall, Ormskirk
Hadfield, G. H.	1851	31 Dec	D	
Hanmer, A. J.	1850	19 Sept	A	S.J. Lond.
Hardman, John	1850	8 Aug	A	*Ad.* John Hardman Esqr/166 Great Charles Street,/Birmingham
	1851	2 Sept	A	

Correspondent	Year	Date	Source	Location, Owner, Address
Hawkins, Edward	1851	9 Oct	A	Oriel. Vol. 4
Hinds, Samuel	1851	2 Oct	Pr	*A Correspondence between the Very Rev. J. H. Newman, D.D., and the Bishop of Norwich on the Credibility of Miracles*, Birmingham 1851, pp. 2–3. (*Prepos.* pp. 408–09)
		11 Oct	Pr	*Op. cit.*, pp. 5–7. (*Prepos.* pp. 412–414)
		19 Oct	Pr	*Op. cit.*, p. 8. (*Prepos.* pp. 415–16)
Holmes, Miss	1850	12 July	C	
		31 July	C	(*Ward* II, pp. 326–7)
		26 Dec	C	
		31 Dec	Pr	*Moz.* II, p. 479
	1851	25 Jan	A	
		16 Aug	A	
		28 Aug	A	
		8 Dec	A	
		11 Dec	A	
Hope, James	1850	20 Nov	A	Rankeillour (Robert Ornsby, *Memoirs of James Robert Hope Scott*, II, p. 67)
			H	1873
		29 Nov	A	Rankeillour (*op. cit.*, p. 68)
			H	1873
	1851	11 July	A	Rankeillour
			H	(two) 1873
		16 July	A	Rankeillour
			H	(two) 1873
		23 July	A	Rankeillour
			H	1873
		11 Oct	H	1873
		21 Nov	A	Rankeillour
			H	1873
		25 Nov	A	Rankeillour (*Ward* I, pp. 284–5)
			H	1873
		30 Nov	A	Rankeillour (*Ward* I, p. 287)
			H	1873

Correspondent	Year	Date	Source	Location, Owner, Address
Howard, Philip Henry	1850	24 Nov	Pr	The *Carlisle Journal* (28 Nov 1850)
			D	
		2 Dec	Pr	The *Carlisle Journal* (5 Dec 1850)
			D	
		6 Dec	D	
Hutchison, Antony	1850	21 July	A	Lond. Vol. 9
		30 July	A	Lond. Vol. 9
		2 Aug	A	Lond. Vol. 9
		8 Aug	A	Lond. Vol. 9
		26 Aug	A	Lond. Vol. 9
		4 Sept	A	Lond. Vol. 9
		6 Sept	A	Lond. Vol. 9
		8 Sept (i)	A	Lond. Vol. 9
		8 Sept (ii)	A	Lond. Vol. 9
		10 Sept	A	Lond. Vol. 9
		17 Sept	A	Lond. Vol. 9
		9 Nov	A	Lond. Vol. 10
		19 Nov	A	Lond. Vol. 9
		2 Dec	A	Lond. Vol. 9
		12 Dec	A	Lond. Vol. 9
		23 Dec	A	Lond. Vol. 9
	1851	3 Jan	A	Lond. Vol. 9
		17 Feb	A	Lond. Vol. 9
		21 Feb	A	Lond. Vol. 9
		25 Feb	A	Lond. Vol. 9
		4 May	A	Lond. Vol. 9
		7 May	A	Lond. Vol. 9
		16 May	A	Lond. Vol. 9
		7 July	A	Lond. Vol. 9
		8 July	A	Lond. Vol. 9
		17 July	A	Lond. Voi. 9
		26 July	A	Lond. Vol. 9
		28 Aug	A	Lond. Vol. 9
		4 Dec	A	Lond. Vol. 9
		11 Dec	A	

Correspondent	Year	Date	Source	Location, Owner, Address
Hutchison, Antony	1851	12 Dec	A	Lond. Vol. 9
		16 Dec	A	Lond. Vol. 9
		24 Dec	A	Lond. Vol. 9
		28 Dec	A	Lond. Vol. 9
		31 Dec	A	Lond. Vol. 9
Knox, T. F.	1851	5 Jan	A	Lond. Vol. 15 *Ad.* The Revd Father Knox/24 King William Street, *West*/London
		7 Jan	A	Lond. Vol. 15 *Ad.* the same
		9 Jan	A	Lond. Vol. 15
		13 Jan	A	Lond. Vol. 15
		25 Jan	A	Lond. Vol. 15 *Ad.* The Revd F. Knox/24 King William Street/London
		20 Feb	A	Lond. Vol. 15 *Ad.* The Revd F. Knox/24 King William Street, West/London
		22 Feb	A	Lond. Vol. 15 *Ad.* the same
		10 Mar	A	Lond. Vol. 15 *Ad.* the same
		19 Sept	A	Lond. Vol. 9
Lans, John Baptist	1850	25 Dec	A	The Redemptorist Fathers, Clapham
			D	
Lewis, David	1851	19 May	A	Lond. Vol. 15
		21 May	A	Lond. Vol. 15
		30 June	A	Lond. Vol. 15
		6 July	A	Lond. Vol. 15
		25 July	A	Lond. Vol. 15
Lockhart, Martha	1850	5 July	A	St John's Seminary, Camarillo, California
Lumley, Edward	1851	14 Jan	D	
		24 Feb	A	Diocesan Archives, Dublin
Lyon, Barnes and Ellis, Messrs	1851	1 Nov	D	
Marsh, Mrs	1850	11 Sept	H	
Maskell, William	1850	5 July	A	British Museum P. 48682. Add. 37, 824
		15 July	A	British Museum P. 48682. Add. 37, 824

Correspondent	Year	Date	Source	Location, Owner, Address
Maskell, William	1850	4 Aug	A	British Museum P. 48682. Add. 37, 824
		23 Aug	A	British Museum P. 48682. Add. 37, 824
		16 Sept	A	British Museum P. 48682. Add. 37, 824
		19 Sept	A	British Museum P. 48682. Add. 37, 824
		20 Oct	A	British Museum P. 48682. Add. 37, 824
		28 Oct	A	British Museum P. 48682. Add. 37, 824
Memoranda:				
On lending Oratorians for California	1850	6 Sept	A	
Decree releasing the London Oratorians	1850	9 Oct	A	
Coffin's Case	1850	3 Oct	A	
Decree accepting W. G. Penny's resignation	1851	30 Jan	A	(in *Appendix* 2, p. 498)
The passage in *Prepos.* on Dr Achilli	1851	28 July	Pr	(in *Appendix* 3, p. 499)
For Edward Badeley	1851	29 Aug	A	
Alternative version of passage on Dr Achilli	1851	11 Nov	A	
Reasons for a compromise	1851	25 Nov	A	
For Newman's lawyers	1851	towards end of year	A	(in *Appendix* 4, p. 502)
The first stages of the Achilli Trial	1851	22 Dec	A	(in *Appendix* 5, p. 506)
Litany for the Achilli Trial	1851	22 Dec	A	(in *Appendix* 6, p. 509)
Minton, Samuel	1851	13 July	D	
		20 Aug	D	
Monsell, William	1850	9 Dec	A	
		13 Dec	A	
	1851	10 Feb	A	
		1 May	A	
		11 May	A	
		29 July	A	

528

Correspondent	Year	Date	Source	Location, Owner, Address
Monteith, Robert			A	Major J. B. Monteith, Carstairs, Scotland
Montézon, Fortunat de,	1851	10 Mar	A	Archives of the Jesuit Province of France, Chantilly. [The text is taken from a copy authenticated by the archivist.]
Morris, J. B.	1850	29 July	C	
	1851	12 Jan	A	Lond. Vol. 15
Mozley, Mrs John	1850	27 July	A	J. H. Mozley
		28 Sept	A	J. H. Mozley
			H	1874
	1851	2 Aug	A	J. H. Mozley
Munro, Miss	1851	12 Dec	A	
Northcote, J. Spencer	1850	10 Oct	A	Stoke
		4 Dec	A	Stoke
	1851	28 Feb	A	Stoke
		19 Mar	A	Stoke
		25 Mar	A	Stoke
		28 Aug	A	Stoke
Ornsby, Robert	1851	11 Sept	A	
Penny, W. G.	1851	16 Jan	D	
		18 Jan (I)	D	(not sent)
		18 Jan (II)	D	
Phillipps, A. Lisle	1850	8 Nov	C	(de Lisle, 1, p. 318)
Phillipps, the Hon. Mrs A. Lisle	1850	13 Dec	C	(de Lisle, 1, p. 319)
Phillips, Mrs Lucy Agnes	1851	5 June	A	
		9 Sept	A	
Poole, Mary Imelda	1851	25 Nov	C	(Ward 1, p. 286; Trevor 1, pp. 566–7)
Pope, Simeon Lloyd	1851	25 Oct	A	The Duke of Norfolk
Rossi, Carlo	1850	15 Oct	Pr	Giuseppe Bondini, Della Fondazione dell' Oratorio in Inghilterra, Rome 1852, p. 138
Rossi, Gaudentius	1851	20 Jan	A	St Gabriel's College, Blythe Hall, Ormskirk
Russell, Charles	1850	2 Oct	A	S.J. Dublin
		23 Oct	A	S.J. Dublin
		28 Oct	A	S.J. Dublin
		24 Dec	A	S.J. Dublin

Correspondent	Year	Date	Source	Location, Owner, Address
Ryder, George	1850	5 July	A	*Ad.* George D. Ryder Esqr/The Warren,/Grace Dieu/Whitwick/ Ashby de la Zouch. [re-directed] Hambledon Cottage/Hambledon/ *Henley on Thames.* Postmarks: Birmingham, 5 July; Ashby-de-la-Zouch, 6 July; Henley-on-Thames, 8 July
		20 Sept	A	*Ad.* G. D. Ryder Esqr/The Warren,/Grace Dieu/Whitwick/ Ashby de la Zouch. Postmark: Cheadle 20 Sept.
		21 Sept	C	
		6 Oct	A	
		7 Nov	A	
		26 Nov	A	
		2 Dec	A	
		12 Dec	A	
	1851	1 Jan	A	
		21 Mar	A	
		18 May	A	
		15 Oct	A	*Ad.* G. L. Ryder Esqr/The Warren/Grace Dieu/Whitwick/ Ashby de la Zouch
		31 Oct	A	
		5 Dec	A	
		12 Dec	A	
St John, Ambrose	1850	8 July	A	
			H	1875
	1851	3 Oct	A	(*McGrath,* p. 111)
			H	1875
		3 Nov	A	
			H	1875
		4 Nov (I)	A	
			H	1875
		4 Nov (II)	A	
			H	1875
		6 Nov	A	
			H	1875
		21 Nov	A	
			H	1875

Correspondent	Year	Date	Source	Location, Owner, Address
Schroeter, Baron von	1850	28 Nov	D	(Two)
Seeley, R. B.	1851	31 July	Pr	The *Morning Herald* (2 Aug. 1851), p. 5
		5 Aug	Pr	The *Morning Herald* (7 Aug. 1851), p. 5
			D	(Two)
		9 Aug	Pr	The *Morning Herald* (12 Aug. 1851), p. 5
			D	
Shrewsbury, Earl of	1850	19 July	C	
			D	
		2 Sept	A	
		6 Sept	C	
		10 Sept	A	
		13 Sept	C	
		17 Sept	C	
			D	
Stanton, Richard	1850	8 July	A	
		13 Aug	A	
		28 Aug	A	
		6 Sept	A	
		30 Sept	A	
		3 Oct	A	
		10 Oct	A	
		13 Oct	A	
		23 Oct	A	
		9 Nov	A	
		14 Nov	A	
		24 Nov	A	
	1851	8 Jan	A	
		9 Jan	A	
		25 Feb	A	
		6 Mar	A	
		19 Mar	A	
		7 April	A	
		12 April	A	
		3 May	A	

Correspondent	Year	Date	Source	Location, Owner, Address
Stanton, Richard	1851	11 May	A	
		13 May	A	
		23 May	A	
		6 June	A	
		9 June	A	
		14 June	A	
		22 June	A	
		19 July	A	
		17 Sept	A	
		19 Sept	A	
		14 Oct	A	
		15 Oct	A	
		19 Oct	A	
		4 Dec	A	*Ad.* The Revd F. Stanton,/72 Strada Sta Lucia/Valetta/*Malta*
		12 Dec	A	*Ad. Via Marseilles. By French Packet*/Revd R. Stanton, at Mrs Bowden's/ Strada S. Lucia (?) *Valetta*/*Malta.*
Talbot, George	1850	11 Aug	A	English College, Rome
		23 Oct	A	English College, Rome *Ad.* Al Monsignore/M. Giorgio Talbot, Inglese,/Dell' Anti-Camera della Sua Santità, Al Vaticano/Roma/*Italia* Postmarks: Birmingham 24 Oct.; Calais 25 Oct.; Rome, Nov. [Illegible]
		3 Dec	A	English College, Rome
	1851	3 Feb	A	English College, Rome *Ad.* A. Monsignore Talbot,/Palazzo Vaticano/Roma./Italia/
		1 Sept	A	English College, Rome *Ad.* Al Signore/Il Monsignore Talbot/Il Palazzo Vaticano/Roma/ *Italia*
		27 Oct	A	English College, Rome *Ad.* Al Signore/Il Monsignore Talbot,/Palazzo Vaticano/Roma/ Italia Postmarks: Birmingham 27 Oct.; Rome 5 Nov.
	1851	9 Dec	A	English College, Rome *Ad.* Al Signore Revdo e Cold/Il Monsignore *Talbot*/Il Palazzo Vaticano/Roma/*Italia*

532

Correspondent	Year	Date	Source	Location, Owner, Address
Talbot, George	1851	17 Dec	A	English College, Rome. *Ad.* Al Signore/Il Monsignore *Talbot*/Palazzo Vaticano/Roma/ *Italia.*
		20 Dec	A	English College, Rome. *Ad. Via Marseilles*/Al Illmo e Revmo Signore/Il Monsignore *Talbot*/Il Palazzo Vaticano/*Roma*/ *Italia*/
		26 Dec	A	English College, Rome. *Ad. Via Marseilles*/ Al Illmo e Coldo Signore/Il Monsignore Talbot/Palazzo Vaticano/Roma/ *Italia.* Postmark: Rome 5 Jan.
Theiner, Augustine	1850	15 Aug	D	
	1851	20 Sept	C	
Todd, William Gowan	1850	12 Aug	A	
		20 Aug	A	
Ugolini, Tommaso	1850	24 Dec	D	
Ullathorne, Bishop	1850	19 July	A	Diocesan Archives, Birmingham
		6 Aug	A	Diocesan Archives, Birmingham
		17 Sept	A	Diocesan Archives, Birmingham
			D	
		12 Oct	A	Diocesan Archives, Birmingham
		7 Nov	A	Diocesan Archives, Birmingham (*Trevor* I, p. 533)
	1851	18 April	A	Diocesan Archives, Birmingham
		20 April	A	Diocesan Archives, Birmingham
		28 Oct	A	Diocesan Archives, Birmingham
		5 Nov	A	Diocesan Archives, Birmingham
Unknown Correspondents	1850	Beginning of Dec	C	
	1851	9 Mar	A	Catholic University of America, Washington, D.C.
		12 Nov	A	
Walford, Edward	1851	19 Jan	A	St John's Seminary, Camarillo, California
Walter, John	1850	6 Dec	D	Lond. Vol. 12 (*Trevor* I, p. 537)
Ward, Mrs F. R.	1851	14 Feb	A	
Ward, W. G.	1850	14 Aug	A	Mrs F. J. Sheed
	1851	13 Nov	A	Mrs F. J. Sheed

Correspondent	Year	Date	Source	Location, Owner, Address
Ward, W. G.	1851	26 Nov	A	Mrs F. J. Sheed (*Ward* I, pp. 283–284, W. Ward, *The Life and Times of Cardinal Wiseman*, 2nd ed., pp. 40–1)
Waterton, Charles	1850	7 Aug	D	
Wegg-Prosser, Francis Richard	1851	7 Sept	A	
		10 Sept	A	
		18 Sept	A	
		24 Sept	A	
		25 Sept	A	
		27 Sept	A	
		3 Oct	A	
Wells, Frederick Fortescue	1851	10 Dec	A	Lond. Vol. 15
Whateley, Messrs John and George	1851	1 Nov	D	
Wilberforce, Henry	1850	15 Nov	A	Georgetown
			H	1876
		28 Dec	A	Georgetown (*Ward* I, pp. 624–7; *Trevor* I, p. 521)
			H	1876
	1851	11 Mar	H	1876
		23 Mar	A	Georgetown
			H	1876
		10 June	A	Georgetown
			H	1876
		27 Sept	A	Georgetown
		5 Dec	A	Georgetown
		16 Dec	A	Georgetown
		19 Dec	A	Georgetown
			H	1876
		30 Dec	A	Georgetown
			H	1876
Wilberforce, Mrs Henry	1851	11 Sept	A	Georgetown
			H	1876
Wiseman, Cardinal	1850	22 Nov	A	
Wood, Mrs	1850	7 Dec	A	(*Ward* I, p. 257)

Correspondent	Year	Date	Source	Location, Owner, Address
Woodward, Jonathan Henry	1851	13 June	A	The Newman Preparatory School, Boston
Young, John	1851	24 Oct	C	

There is also at the Birmingham Oratory a photostatic copy of a short treatise in Newman's hand on 'Whether *explicit faith* in the Holy Trinity and Christ be now *necessary*, by the nature of the case, for *justification* and *glorification*?' An incomplete copy of this, in the handwriting of William Lockhart, has written at the top, 'Copied from a M.S. letter by J. H. Newman—written probably about 1850,' and at the side, [sent] 'with F. Lockhart's kind regards'

This treatise has nothing of the form or appearance of a letter, and so it will be included among Newman's Theological Papers.

Index of Persons and Places

Index of Persons and Places

The index to Volume XI contains notices of almost all the persons who occur in that volume, and the indexes to subsequent volumes notices of those who occur in them for the first time. These are not repeated, and so, for persons and places already mentioned in those volumes, reference back is here made by an (XI) or (XII) etc. inserted after such names.

References are given, in the case of persons mentioned for the first time in this volume, to *The Dictionary of National Biography* or *The Dictionary of American Biography*, and failing them, to Frederick Boase, *Modern English Biography*, or Joseph Gillow, *Bibliographical Dictionary of the English Catholics*; also occasionally to other printed works. Much of the information is derived from the correspondence and other material in the archives of the Birmingham Oratory, and from various private sources.

Acheson (XIII), Lady Olivia (1816?–52), 12, 32, 77–8, 84, 93, 163–4, 169, 272, 282, 288, 290–1, 298–300, 302, 304, 374–5, 457–8, 482.

Achilli, Giovanni Giacinto, born at Viterbo in 1802, joined the Dominicans in 1819, studied in Rome, was ordained priest in 1825, and in 1827 appointed professor of philosophy at the seminary in Viterbo. For two seductions of women there he was deprived of his professorship and his faculties. Two similar offences occurred at Capua, whither he was sent, 1834–5. In 1840 there was the case of violation in the sacristy of St Peter's Church at Naples, from which city he was twice expelled by the Police, 1840–1. In June 1841 in Rome, he was sentenced by the Inquisition to do penance for three years in the remote Dominican house at Nazzaro. From there he fled almost at once to Corfu, where he opened a Protestant chapel and had an affair with the wife of a tailor, appearing before the Court in July 1843. Next he was at Zante with the wife of a chorus singer. In July 1847 he was appointed professor in the Protestant College at Malta, but was dismissed for preventing an inquiry into the conduct of two other apostate priests there, whose immorality he had encouraged. In 1849 in Rome during the Revolution, he was married to a Miss Heley. The Evangelical Alliance brought him to England in 1850 and he toured the country denouncing the corruptions of Rome, and claiming to have been punished by the Inquisition for heresy. At least four cases of seduction or attempted seduction were laid to his door in London. With the support of the Evangelical Alliance he brought his action against Newman in Nov. 1851. By the conclusion of the trial in 1853, Achilli was quite discredited and fled to America, where he became a Swedenborgian. He sent his wife back to Italy and in Dec. 1859, by which time he had a snow-white beard, was brought before a Justice of the Peace in Jersey City, on a charge of adultery with a Miss Bogue. He deserted her and his eldest son, aged eight, at the Oneida Community, New York, in March 1860, leaving a letter in which he implied that he would commit suicide and said that spirits would carry him off to where he would be allowed to see the Lord, xvi–xviii, 310–11, 318–19, 335–48, 352, 355–64, 391–2, 397–9, 408–70, 474–85, 491–2, 501–510.

Acquerone (XI), Louis, 495–6.

Acton, Sir John Dalberg, first Baron Acton (1834–1902), xvii, 290.

Ainsworth, Mrs, Sophia Hanmer, 98

Alban, see Wells, Frederick Fortescue.

Alcester Street, Birmingham, 40, 63, 126, 243, 299, 432.

Alderson, Sir Edward Hall, 32.

Alemany, Joseph Sadoc (1814–88), was born at Vich in Catalonia, and joined the Dominicans in 1829. After studying in Italy and being ordained priest in 1837 at Viterbo, he went as a missionary to Kentucky and Ohio in 1841. He was consecrated first Bishop of Monterey, at Rome on 30 June 1850. He collected priests in Ireland on his return journey to San Francisco, where the Irish pioneers welcomed him back in Dec. In 1853 he became the first Archbishop of San Francisco, and retired in 1884 to Spain. (*DAB*, I, 161), 54–6, 58–60, 131–2.

Allen (XI), John (1810–86), 120, 124.

Allies (XI), Thomas William (1813–1903), 3, 6, 48, 64–6, 68–9, 75–6, 80, 95–6,